Russian Language Studies
in North America

Russian Language Studies in North America

New Perspectives from Theoretical and Applied Linguistics

Edited by
Veronika Makarova

ANTHEM PRESS
LONDON · NEW YORK · DELHI

Anthem Press
An imprint of Wimbledon Publishing Company
www.anthempress.com

This edition first published in UK and USA 2013
by ANTHEM PRESS
75–76 Blackfriars Road, London SE1 8HA, UK
or PO Box 9779, London SW19 7ZG, UK
and
244 Madison Ave. #116, New York, NY 10016, USA

First published in hardback by Anthem Press in 2012

© 2013 Veronika Makarova editorial matter and selection;
individual chapters © individual contributors

The moral right of the authors has been asserted.

All rights reserved. Without limiting the rights under copyright reserved above,
no part of this publication may be reproduced, stored or introduced into
a retrieval system, or transmitted, in any form or by any means
(electronic, mechanical, photocopying, recording or otherwise),
without the prior written permission of both the copyright
owner and the above publisher of this book.

British Library Cataloguing-in-Publication Data
A catalogue record for this book is available from the British Library.

Library of Congress Cataloging-in-Publication Data
The Library of Congress has cataloged the hardcover edition as follows:
Russian language studies in North America : new perspectives from theoretical and
applied linguistics / edited by Veronika Makarova.
   p. cm.
Includes bibliographical references and index.
ISBN 978-0-85728-784-7 (alk. paper) – ISBN 0-85728-784-2 (alk. paper)
 1. Russian language–Phonology. 2. Russian language–Study and teaching–Canada.
3. Russian language–Study and teaching–United States. 4. Russian language–Spoken
Russian–Canada. 5. Russian language–Spoken Russian–United States. 6. Linguistics–
Research–Canada. 7. Linguistics–Research–United States. I. Makarova, Veronika.
PG2131.R87 2012
491.707'07–dc23
2012004987

ISBN-13: 978 1 78308 046 5 (Pbk)
ISBN-10: 1 78308 046 9 (Pbk)

This title is also available as an ebook.

CONTENTS

List of Tables and Figures vii

Introduction xi
Veronika Makarova

Part One   Language Structures and their Interface

1. Phonetics. Tracing Emotions in Russian Vowels 3
   Veronika Makarova and Valery A. Petrushin

2. Phonology. Vowel–Zero Alternations in Russian Prepositions: Prosodic Constituency and Productivity 43
   Lev Blumenfeld

3. Morphology and Lexicology Interface. Latest Russian Neologisms: The Next Step towards Analytism? 71
   Julia Rochtchina

4. Syntax. Bi-nominative Sentences in Russian 85
   Igor Mel'čuk

5. Psycholinguistics. The Effect of Grammatical Gender in Russian Spoken-Word Recognition 107
   Irina A. Sekerina

Part Two   Applied Linguistic and Sociolinguistic Analysis

6. Communicative Language Teaching and Russian: The Current State of the Field 133
   William J. Comer

7. Low-Proficiency Heritage Speakers of Russian: Their Interlanguage System as a Basis for Fast Language (Re)Building 161
   Alla Smyslova

8. Superior Speakers or "Super" Russian: OPI Guidelines Revisited   193
   Ludmila Isurin

9. Who Am I?: Cultural Identities among Russian-Speaking Immigrants of the Third (and Fourth?) Wave and their Effects on Language Attitudes   215
   David R. Andrews

10. Russian Language History in Canada. Doukhobor Internal and External Migrations: Effects on Language Development and Structure   235
    Gunter Schaarschmidt

Afterword   261
Veronika Makarova

Index   265

LIST OF TABLES AND FIGURES

Tables

Table 1.1	Descriptive statistics for unstressed vowels (mean/std) and p-value for one-way analysis of variance; N = 3891	10
Table 1.2	Descriptive statistics for stressed vowels (mean/std) and p-value for one-way analysis of variance; N = 1393	11
Table 1.3	Descriptive statistics for accented vowels (mean/std) and p-value for one-way analysis of variance; N = 325	12
Table 1.4	Vowel duration across emotional states	26
Table 1.5	Energy across emotional states	28
Table 1.6	F0 across emotive states, in Hz	29
Table 4.1	Properties of the six lexemes of the verb BYT´ 'be'	100
Table 5.1	Experiment 1: The mean proportion of fixations to the target in Regions 1, 2 and 3 (%)	119
Table 5.2	Experiment 2: The mean proportions of fixations to target and competitor in Regions 1, 2 and 3 (%)	125
Table 6.1	Preprogram OPI scores by percentage of students at each level of study	140
Table 6.2	Varieties of input and input comprehension checks	144
Table 6.3	Types and distribution of communicative activities	147
Table 6.4	Types and distributions of language-focused activities	148
Table 8.1	OPI assessment criteria	199

Table 8.2	Analysis of narrative samples	204
Table 8.3	Analysis of descriptive samples	206
Table 8.4	Circumlocution across the groups	209

Figures

Figure 1.1	Waveforms and pitch contours of an exclamatory utterance produced with different emotions by a female speaker	7
Figure 1.2	Average durations of vowels in neutral and emotive speech modes in the unstressed, stressed and accented vowels datasets	13
Figure 1.3	Average energy of vowels in neutral and emotive speech modes in the unstressed, stressed and accented vowels datasets	15
Figure 1.4	Average F0 values of vowels in neutral and emotive speech modes in the unstressed, stressed and accented vowels datasets	17
Figure 1.5	Average F0 derivative values in neutral and emotive speech modes in the unstressed, stressed and accented vowels datasets	19
Figure 1.6	Spectral profiles for vowels extracted from speech portraying the following emotions: anger, fear, happiness, neutral and surprise	23
Figure 1.7	F1 and F2 of the stressed vowels	30
Figure 2.1	Syllable structure of a phrase *s straxom* (with fear)	52
Figure 3.1	A collage representing text samples that reflect the emerging of a new 'double orthography' system in Russian	76
Figure 5.1	The two types of visual display in Experiment 1 (no cohorts)	114
Figure 5.2	Experiment 1: The probability of fixating the target (*red car*) and color competitor (*red squirrel*) over three regions in the same-gender condition, as a function of word order (%)	121

Figure 5.3	The two types of visual display in Experiment 1 (cohorts)	122
Figure 5.4	Experiment 2: The probability of fixating the target (*orange jar*) and competitors (*orange bow/fan*) over three regions as a factor of cohort/no-cohort condition (%)	126
Figure 6.1	Structured input activity	154
Figure 7.1	First classifications of heritage speakers in the USA	163
Figure 7.2	Distribution of contexts for cases across pre-course essays (%)	177
Figure 7.3	Distribution of nouns, modifiers and personal pronouns case by case across pre-course essays (%)	177
Figure 8.1	Cohesion in narration	204
Figure 10.1	Doukhobor settlements near the Moločna River in Tavria, Russia	238
Figure 10.2	Doukhobor settlements in the Caucasus, Russia	240
Figure 10.3	Early Doukhobor settlements in Saskatchewan	243
Figure 10.4	Doukhobor settlements in British Columbia	245

INTRODUCTION

Veronika Makarova
University of Saskatchewan

This book is a unique collection of research papers representing current directions in Russian language studies in Canada and the United States. The book is integrated thematically by its focus on Russian language structure and dynamics, as well as by the regional themes pertinent to the maintenance and acquisition of the Russian language in the US and Canada. Traditionally, Slavic and Russian studies in these countries have involved mostly literature, history, politics and culture. This collection of research papers reflects recent changes in Russian studies with a focus on language structure, language use, pedagogy and teaching methodology. At least four major trends are responsible for these changes.

First, the rapid economic and social changes in Russia that occurred after the collapse of the Soviet Union in combination with the development of information technology have triggered an unprecedented change in the language structure and use, which now attracts the attention of linguists (e.g., Ryazanova-Clarke and Wade 1999). The lexical system of modern Russian is characterized "by an increased instability of the boundaries between the centre and the periphery" (Ryazanova-Clarke and Wade 1999, 75), i.e., some words from the periphery are moving into the center, while some central words are marginalized. Words change their meanings and undergo re-connotation; the morphological word formation system is extremely active; new loan words appear in abundance; and the grammatical system registers changes in preposition use, acquires a larger class of indeclinables and displays a growing tendency towards analyticity (Ryazanova-Clarke and Wade 1999).

Second, the Russian language remains one of the world's top ten languages in terms of its number of speakers, and is gaining new ground in sociolinguistic research. On the one hand, the controversies surrounding the new status of Russian diasporas and of the Russian language in the former republics of the

Soviet Union have attracted the attention of linguists (e.g., Korth 2005; Wylegala 2010). On the other hand, following a dramatic retreat with the collapse of the Soviet Union, there is some evidence of a linguistic revival of Russian in the area. For example, increasingly positive attitudes toward the Russian language were reported in some post-Soviet states, such as Georgia, Moldova and Armenia (Ciscel 2008; Gradirovski and Esipova 2008). The number of secondary school students receiving education in Russian increased in Belarus (Demoscope 2005), and regional authorities were given some freedom in handling Russian language education in the Ukraine (Rezchikov 2010). Russian continues to function as the lingua franca in the region, although this function is being constantly redefined (Pavlenko 2006, 2008).

Third, the presence of linguists and second language acquisition specialists in language tuition particularly at the university level is openly advocated by the Modern Languages Association, since linguistics courses appeal to students and "linguists enrich the foreign language major through their ability to offer courses in second language acquisition, applied linguistics, dialectology, sociolinguistics, history of the language, and discourse analysis" (MLA n.d.). Consequently, in order to attract more students, Russian programs are becoming more interested in supporting research in the Russian language and in Russian teaching methodologies. The new generation of Russian scholars who obtained their PhDs in the US and Canada in the last decade are helping to meet this demand in Russian language studies.

Fourth, on the North American linguistic landscape, there is an increase in the amount of research devoted to Russian sociolinguistics and issues related to the language as it is spoken in Russia and the post-Soviet states, and also to Russian spoken locally in the US and Canada. Russian settlers in Alaska and Doukhobors in Western Canada established the historic roots of the language in North America. Immigration from Russia after the Revolution of 1917–18 and during the Soviet era resulted in the growth of Russian-speaking diasporas, further strengthened during the post-perestroika wave of economic and political immigration from the countries of the former Soviet Union. This recent wave gave a new impetus to the development of Russian as a minority language in North America. In the last decade, the Russian language in the US has become a "social climber," rising to the tenth rank among mother tongues in the US overall, and fifth in New York and Oregon (US English Foundation 2010). In Canada, Russian is one of the top 20 languages by the number of speakers according to the 2001 and 2006 census statistics. Between 2001 and 2006, the Canadian population speaking Russian as the mother tongue increased from 94,555 to 136,235 (roughly 44 percent); and approximately one-half of this increase was due to immigration from the Russian Federation (Statistics Canada 2007).

This inflow of Russian-speaking immigrants in North America has lead to the creation of a new direction in Russian language studies: research of heritage Russian speech and language acquisition by heritage Russian learners. Beginning with the late 1980s, teachers of Russian in Canada and the US were confronted with something they were not prepared for: the appearance in the traditional Russian-as-a-foreign-language university classes of second-generation immigrants from Russia and the countries of the former Soviet Union. Like most other heritage learners, they were an inconvenience for a number of reasons: first, they varied in the level of their competence in Russian, depending on the amount of time spent in a former Russian-speaking environment, the amount of Russian used in the family, the educational background of their parents, and other factors. This made their placement in a particular level of traditional second language (L2) acquisition extremely problematic. Second, their expectations and learning objectives were different from those held by mainstream L2 learners, as they were primarily interested in increasing their written and oral proficiency skills. Some universities resolved the issue in a radical way, by banning heritage learners from Russian language classes. Yet in the situation of dwindling enrolments in language classes, most other language programs were reluctant to simply turn students away. Necessity being the proverbial mother of invention, a new methodology of teaching Russian as a heritage language gradually emerged. One of the landmarks in this development is the special issue on Russian in the *Heritage Language Journal* (2008), as well as the appearance of a number of research papers dedicated to teaching Russian as a heritage language (e.g., Polinsky 2000; Kagan and Friedman 2003; Kagan and Dillon 2006).

In the North American context, due to the change in the role of Russian from a predominantly "foreign" language to one of the languages spoken locally in Canada and the US, new directions of research have emerged dealing with the teaching of Russian as a heritage language, with Russian speech processing, and with Russian-English contact and bilingualism.

All the above factors make the focus on Russian language studies pertinent, timely and significant. The purpose of this book is to provide a comprehensive overview of some of the dimensions of Russian language research in Canada and US, with a focus on elements of structure, as well as on language dynamics and change. This book brings together eleven authors from four universities in Canada, four universities in the United States, one college and one American company. The scholars represent a cross-section of academic generations ranging from young, promising researchers to those who have long established reputations in the field. No single doctrine or school of linguistic analysis is followed in the book. Quite the opposite, we aim to represent a variety of outlooks and perspectives in the area of Russian language studies. All the authors have their unique voices and writing styles which were not in any way restricted.

Perhaps the most important feature of the book is the way it reflects the growing trend in linguistic studies towards higher interdisciplinarity. Even the traditional "structural" branches of theoretical and experimental linguistics are represented in the first part of the book as "reaching out" to other disciplines, whereby a phonetics study is linked with speech processing technologies, a phonological study is informed by language history, syntactical analysis is inseparable from semantics, an issue of neologisms in lexicology is shown to affect the foundations of Russian morphology and syntax, and the grammatical gender is explored with an advanced psycholinguistic technique of eyetracking. The dynamic aspect of modern Russian language studies is further emphasized in the second part of the book, which contains papers in the area of applied linguistics dealing with the teaching of Russian as a foreign language vis-à-vis the new area of teaching Russian as a heritage language, followed by a unique socio-cultural exploration of the intersections of language and identity, and a diachronic description of Doukhobor Russian (a seriously endangered variety of Russian spoken in Canada).

Overview of Contents

The book is divided into two parts. The first part, "Language Structures and Their Interface," includes chapters with more traditional "structural linguistics" content, but they are notable for their emphasis on interdisciplinary connections.

In Chapter 1, Veronika Makarova and Valery Petrushin report the results of an experimental phonetic study that investigates the effect of selected emotive states (neutral (unemotional), surprise, happiness, anger, sadness, and fear) on the acoustic characteristics of Russian vowels. The research data come from the RUSLANA (Russian Language Affective) database, which incorporates samples of speech simulating six emotive (affective) states. The results outline the parameters which are salient for the expression of affect at the segmental level. The study shows that the acoustic expression of emotions in Russian has some unique features as well as some features observed earlier in other languages. The authors suggest that the emotive states fall into natural classes, depending on the proximity/distance of the parametric values. The potential applications of the findings to the synthesis and automatic recognition of emotional speech for Russian are outlined.

Chapter 2 by Lev Blumenfeld investigates the phonology of Russian vocalic alternations known as "*yers*," i.e., vowels that alternate with zero (a vowel deletion) under complex morphological and phonological conditioning.

These vowel alternations are notorious for displaying a puzzling inconsistency in their behavior in prepositions versus verbal prefixes. In an investigation based on the Russian National Corpus data and informed by language history and prosodic structure analysis, the author proves that this variability is largely not random, but relates to the productivity and compositionality of the morphological structure.

Julia Rochtchina in Chapter 3 provides the evidence of an inflow of new words borrowed into Russian mostly from English at the end of the twentieth and the beginning of the twenty-first century. Many of these words have a structure "alien" to Russian morphology. The author identifies their place in Russian grammar as a new morphological category of polyfunctional lexemes with a broad (non-standard) grammatical valency and illustrates their various graphic representations. A thought-provoking discussion is focused on the question of whether the proliferation of such lexemes may mean the morphological deconstruction of Russian and its shift towards higher analytism.

The next chapter by Igor Mel'čuk (Chapter 4) is devoted to the syntactical analysis of Russian bi-nominative sentences. Bi-nominatives in Russian often perplex speakers and researchers of other languages, as these sentences consist of two noun phrases in the nominative case with or without the copula "be" between them. Examples of Russian bi-nominative sentences are compared with those found in other languages (Salishan, Turkish, Latin, etc.). The author addresses the question of the operational criteria that allow one to decide which of the nominative phrases is the syntactic subject, and which is the predicate. While previous research studies include semantic, communicative, word order, instrumental case, and copula agreement criteria, the author proves that the syntactic structure of a sentence is basically determined by its semantic structure. The identification of the syntactic subject depends on the choice made in the process of the lexicalization of the underlying/original semantic structure. The communicative structure is also of crucial importance, but its effects are secondary to the semantic relations.

The concluding chapter in the first section (Chapter 5) by Irina Sekerina reports the results of eyetracking experiments aimed at investigating the effect of grammatical gender and its temporal span in Russian spoken-word recognition. The materials in both experiments consisted of a gender-marked color adjective and a target noun; they were either immediately adjacent to each other (the nonsplit word order) or separated by a verb (the split-constituent word order). The critical manipulation was in the grammatical gender of the two objects of the same color, the target and the color competitor. The gender-marked color adjective either matched in gender with the target or with both target and competitor. The subjects responded to instructions requiring them to move one of the objects. The word recognition (of the target and competitor) was measured via the timing of the eye fixation on the object. The results provide evidence for the grammar-based account of gender effect in Russian spoken-word recognition.

The second part of the book, entitled "Applied Linguistic and Sociolinguistic Analysis," includes contributions in the areas of teaching Russian as foreign and heritage languages, sociolinguistics and language history.

In Chapter 6, William J. Comer surveys the theory and history of communicative language teaching (CLT), and shows how it has been implemented in the teaching of Russian in North America. The chapter analyzes Russian-language teaching materials for the presence of CLT features such as comprehensible input, meaning-based communicative activities, and meaning-based activities to teach language forms. It recommends several new approaches (i.e., information gap activities, structured input, processing instruction and task-based language lessons) that will help learners map language form to meaning during communicative interaction.

Alla Smyslova, in Chapter 7, expands the scope of current research on heritage learners by introducing new data on the language production of Russian heritage speakers of the low-proficiency level in a university classroom environment. Her subject group includes individuals who were born in the US or arrived there at a pre-school age. The author analyzes the subjects' Russian language performance data collected with a diagnostic test that establishes baseline language levels and language characteristics of the subject group as well as assesses the degree of first-language retention. The analysis focuses on the nominal system. The patterns of heritage learner interlanguage production are shown to display evidence of internalized grammatical structures. The strengths of heritage learners in language acquisition are identified, and a suggestion is made about incorporating those strengths into heritage Russian instruction.

Chapter 8 by Ludmila Isurin examines the existing ACTFL (American Council on the Teaching of Foreign Languages) guidelines for the Superior level of oral proficiency. The study looks at narrative/descriptive/circumlocution patterns elicited from three groups of participants: Russian monolinguals, Russian-English bilinguals and speakers of Russian as a foreign language. The results of the qualitative and quantitative analysis show that the foreign language learners outperformed monolinguals in all tasks while their performance did not differ from the "bilinguals." The chapter raises a question regarding the ACTFL's guidelines and calls for revisiting them in order to approximate their requirements to the naturalistic setting.

Chapter 9 by David R. Andrews surveys the history of the major waves of Russian-speaking immigrants in the US and addresses the issue of language maintenance and language identity within the immigrant groups. The author focuses on the Russian-speaking Jewish immigrants in the third and fourth waves of Russian immigration and argues that Jewish ethnicity is a factor in their language attitudes, although not in a simplistic cause-and-effect way. Equally important is the Soviet origin of those in the third and fourth waves, and the interplay of Soviet and Jewish identities. The author demonstrates that the incorporation of Anglicisms into the Russian speech of immigrants works as a linguistic accompaniment to the process of adaptation. By using these lexical innovations, they simultaneously maintain their allegiance to the much-valued Russian speech community, while also signaling that they know the ins and outs of the new society as well as any native-born North American.

The history of the Doukhobor Russian language in Canada is examined in the concluding chapter by Gunter Schaarschmidt. The chapter also outlines some of the specific features of Canadian Doukhobor Russian. In particular, the author illustrates an interplay between the colloquial and ritual functional styles in Doukhobor Russian. The unique features of Doukhobor Russian are explained by its largely oral tradition, relative geographic isolation, deliberate resistance to the influence of Canadian English, and the influence of Ukrainian, dating mainly to the first generation of settlers in the province of Saskatchewan. This study is the first major work introducing the language history and structure of Doukhobor Russian.

Concluding remarks by the editor in the afterword address the future of Russian studies in Canada and the US.

This book will be of interest to linguists, applied linguists, Slavic and Russian linguists, as well as to teachers and advanced learners of Russian in university settings worldwide. The volume will also be of general interest for the Russian-speaking communities in North America. This book could be recommended for graduate and advanced undergraduate courses in Russian and Slavic studies, as well as for graduate and senior undergraduate reading courses in linguistics.

Overall, this book contributes to the development of the area of Russian language studies, linguistics, sociolinguistics, applied linguistics, psycholinguistics, and the teaching of Russian as a foreign and heritage language in North America and globally. We hope that this collection of a variety of interrelated research studies will inspire future research.

Acknowledgments

The editor would like to thank first and foremost all the contributors for their devotion to Russian language studies and their generous efforts spent on making this volume unique. Special thanks go to Richard Julien who volunteered to proofread the whole book and to Laura Champ who assisted in formatting and proofing the manuscript. The University of Saskatchewan should also be acknowledged for providing the editor with a sabbatical leave, without which the book would not have been completed, as well as for the provision of a book publication grant. Special thanks go to Anthem Press for believing in the future of Russian language studies and of this collection, to Brian Stone for final copyediting of the manuscript, and to Ms. Janka Romero for her patience and encouragement.

References

Bilaniuk, L. 2005. *Contested Tongues: Language Politics and Cultural Correction in Ukraine*. Ithaca, NY: Cornell University Press.

Ciscel, M. 2008. "Uneasy Compromise: Language and Education in Moldova." *International Journal of Bilingual Education and Bilingualism* 11: 373–95.

Demoscope. 2005. "V školax rjada stran russkij jazyk po-prežnemu imeet širokoe rasprostranenie," 7–20 February. Online: http://www.demoscope.ru/weekly/2005/0189/barom02.php (accessed 12 December 2011).

Gradirovski, S. and N. Esipova. 2008. "Russian Language Enjoying a Boost in Post-Soviet States." Gallup, 1 August. Online: http://www.gallup.com/poll/109228/Russian-Language-Enjoying-Boost-PostSoviet-States.aspx?version=print (accessed 12 December 2011).

Gribanova, V. 2009a. "Phonological evidence for a distinction between Russian prepositions and prefixes." In G. Zybatow, D. Lenertová, U. Junghanns and P. Biskup (eds), *Studies in Formal Slavic Phonology, Morphology, Syntax, Semantics and Information Structure: Proceedings of FDSL 7, Leipzig 2007*, 383–96. Frankfurt: Peter Lang.

———. 2009b. "The phonology and syntax of sub-words." Paper presented at Generative Linguistics in the Old World, 16 April.

Halle, M. 1959. *The Sound Pattern of Russian*. The Hague: Mouton.

Heritage Language Journal. 2008. Special Issue on Russian as a Heritage Language. *Heritage Language Journal* 6(1). Online: http://www.international.ucla.edu/languages/heritagelanguages/journal/volume6-1.asp (accessed 12 March 2011).

Kagan, O. and K. Dillon. 2006. "Russian Heritage Learners: So What Happens Now?" *Slavic and East European Journal* (50th Anniversary Issue) 50(1): 8.

Kagan, O. and D. Friedman. 2003. "Using the OPI to Place Heritage Speakers of Russian." *Foreign Language Annals* 36: 536–45.

Korth, B. 2005. *Language Attitudes towards Kyrgyz and Russian: Discourse, Education and Policy in Post-Soviet Kyrgyzstan*. Berlin: Peter Lang.

Lightner, T. M. 1972. *Problems in the Theory of Phonology. Vol. 1: Russian Phonology and Turkish Phonology*. Edmonton: Linguistic Research.

Modern Language Association. n.d. "Foreign languages and higher education: New structures for a changed world." Online: http://wwww.mla.org/flreport (accessed 12 December 2011).

Pavlenko, A. 2006. "Russian as a Lingua Franca." *Annual Review of Applied Linguistics* 26: 78–99.

———. 2008. "Multilingualism in Post-Soviet Countries: Language Revival, Language Removal, and Sociolinguistic Theory." *International Journal of Bilingual Education and Bilingualism* 1: 275–314.

Polinsky, M. 2000. "A Composite Linguistic Profile of Speakers of Russian in the U.S." In O. Kagan and B. Rifkin with S. Bauckus (eds), *The Learning and Teaching of Slavic Languages and Cultures*, 437–65. Bloomington, IN: Slavica.

Rezchikov, A. 2010. "Zakonomernoje Reshenie." *Vzgljad*, 25 May. Online: http://www.vz.ru/politics/2010/5/25/405157.html (accessed 12 December 2011).

Ryazanova-Clarke, L. and T. Wade. 1999. *The Russian Language Today*. London and New York: Routledge.

Rubach, J. 1986. "Abstract Vowels in Three-Dimensional Phonology: The Yers." *Linguistic Review* 5: 247–80.

US English Foundation. 2010. "Language rankings." US English Foundation, 12 July. Online: http://www.usefoundation.org/userdata/file/Research/language_rankings.pdf (accessed 12 December 2011).

Wylegala, A. 2001. "Minority Language as Identity Factor: Case Study of Young Russian Speakers in Lviv." *International Journal of the Sociology of Language* 201: 29–51.

Part One

LANGUAGE STRUCTURES AND THEIR INTERFACE

Chapter 1

PHONETICS. TRACING EMOTIONS IN RUSSIAN VOWELS

Veronika Makarova
University of Saskatchewan

Valery A. Petrushin
Opera Solutions, San Diego, California

The advantage of the emotions is that they lead us astray, and the advantage of science is that it is not emotional.

—Oscar Wilde (1891)

I. Introduction

This chapter examines acoustic clues of six emotional states (neutral, surprise, happiness, anger, sadness and fear) in the production of Russian vowels. The findings are presented and discussed for three groups of vowels: unstressed, stressed and pitch accented. The research data come from the RUSLANA (Russian Language Affective) database of Standard Russian.

Emotions "convey the psychological state of a person" (Iliev et al. 2010, 445). They are "conceived to be natural bodily experiences and expressions, older than language, irrational and subjective, unconscious rather than deliberate, genuine rather than artificial, feelings rather than thoughts" (Edwards 1999, 272). Humans can express and identify emotions with a variety of communication forms including vocal (linguistic, verbal art) and non-vocal (facial expressions, shaking, changes in skin coloration, blood pressure, heart rate, sweating, posture, clothing, hairstyle, non-verbal art, gesticulation and behavioral patterns) (Anolli and Ciceri 2001; Iliev et al. 2010).

Expression of emotions in speech currently attracts scholars from a wide range of disciplines, such as literary criticism, neuroscience, anthropology, pragmatics, communication sciences, psychology, physiology, linguistics, applied linguistics, education, engineering, computer science, psychotherapy and psychiatry (Wierzbicka 1997; Johnstone and Scherer 2000; Pavlenko 2005; Imai 2007). All the structural levels and most functional forms of language serve to express emotions. Linguistically, emotions are rendered via phonetic (acoustic), graphic, phonological, morphological, lexical, syntactic, sociolinguistic, discoursal (textual and pragmatic) devices as well as their combinations (Cowie et al. 2001; Bazzanella 2004). Specifically, lexical cues of affect include words perceived to be associated with particular emotions, e.g., 'wrong' and 'damn' are associated with negative emotions (Cowie et al. 2001). Discourse clues of emotions include particular types of verbal responses which were influenced by emotions, such as rejection, repetition, rephrase, ask, start-over, etc. (Edwards 1999). Emotions in discourse are seen as "a way of talking" that can be contrasted and used on occasion, and may include rhetorical opposites and contrasts or sets of conversational templates and scenarios (Edwards 1999, 278). An example of a mixed clue (both visual and acoustic) is the degree of jaw movements correlating with the emotion of irritation (Banse and Scherer 1996). It is often extremely hard to disentangle some of the emotional cues or estimate their exact contribution to perceived emotion, since they are expressed at multiple levels of language as well as by non-linguistic cues and their interactions (Dietrich et al. 2006). Despite all the variability of the expression of emotions in language, human subjects can identify emotions even in very short extracts of speech (such as one vowel) containing only acoustic clues (Toivanen et al. 2006).

The expression of emotion in languages has identifiable common characteristics as well as unique language-specific features (Lutz 1988; Wierzbicka 1997; Goddard and Wierzbicka 2002). It has been claimed in earlier research that Russian has some "specifically Russian" emotional terms as well as unique syntactical ways of expressing emotions (Levontina and Zalizniak 2001). This chapter focuses on the expression of emotion in Russian via the acoustic parameters of Russian speech.

The task of analyzing linguistic portrayals of emotion is made even more challenging due to disagreements among scholars about the definitions and classifications of emotions (Nordstrand et al. 2004; Scherer 2000; Zervas et al. 2007). Dimensional approaches view emotion as a continuum or gradual transition; they often map emotions in two- or three-dimensional space continua (Osgood 1957; Davitz 1964; Plutchik 1980; Nordstrom et al. 2004; Grimm et al. 2007). However, for reasons of simplicity, most phonetic studies (Nordstrom et al. 2004; Waaramaa et al. 2006) follow the discrete or category approach, which identifies a few basic emotions that are considered distinct from each other (Ekman 1979; Iida 2002). In this study, we also follow the discrete approach. From the commonly identified list of basic emotions (Iliev et al. 2010), we have selected five states (fear, joy, sadness, surprise and anger) which are examined against the "neutral" or un-emotive state.

In phonetic studies of emotive and affective speech, most of the attention so far has been given to prosodic correlates of emotion, primarily to pitch parameters, such as the types, magnitudes, duration and steepness of pitch movements and the declination within phrases (Banse and Scherer 1996; Paeschke and Sendlmeier 2000). Some characteristics of the temporal and rhythmical organization of speech as well as intensity have also been shown to be relevant for emotive information (Scherer 1989; Arnfield et al. 1995; Stibbard 2000). Other suprasegmental parameters which have been shown to contribute to the expression of emotion in speech include voice quality, pauses and boundaries (Cowie et al. 2001; Gobl and Chasaide 2003; Min Lee and Narayanan 2005).

It has been observed that some segmental features, such as segmental durations, spectra and formant frequencies are also salient for the expression of emotion (Min Lee and Narayanan 2005, Kienast and Sendlmeier 2000; Cowie et al. 2001; Tickle 2000; Fernandez 2004). The total list of features singled out by researchers as acoustic correlates of emotive states can vary from approximately thirty (McGilloway et al. 2000) to over one hundred (Fernandez 2004).

Acoustic characteristics of vowels have been named among segmental clues of emotion, but there has been some disagreement with respect to what exactly happens to vowel quality under affect. While some studies conclude that vowel quality significantly changes under emotion (Fernandez 2004), some other studies show that emotions do have an impact on vowel quality, though this effect is minimal (Szameitat et al. 2009). Some explanations of the changes of vowel characteristics under affect are found in the speech production studies that show the articulatory changes in emotional states, such as the changes in the lip opening, rising, protrusion and rounding (Caldognetto et al. 2004) and in tongue movements (Fonàgy 1976). Another observed change in emotive vowels is the increase of the values of formants (F3 and F4) under some negative emotions, which is explained by a more tense and shortened vocal tract (Waaramaa et al. 2006). Some recent experiments suggest that the observed impact of some emotions on articulation (such as the vertical and lateral labial distance) may differ by the type of vowel (Nordstrom et al. 2004). All the above-mentioned research studies have been performed on languages other than Russian.

This chapter contributes to the field by investigating emotion-related parameters in the acoustic characteristics of Russian vowels. The materials for the study were retrieved from RUSLANA, a Russian affective speech database which represents the phonemes, major syntactical and intonation contour types in Russian (Makarova and Petrushin 2002). Emotions were simulated by the speakers. This procedure is so commonly employed in other phonetic experiments and emotive databases (Nordstrom et al. 2004; Toivanen et al. 2006) that it has been called "the preferred way of obtaining emotional voice samples in the field" (Scherer 2003, 232). The database and the extracted features are described in the following section.

Our study pursued the following major goals, to:

1. Investigate the effect of emotive-affective state on major acoustic parameters of Russian vowels grouped by accentual type (accented, stressed, unstressed);
2. Investigate the effect of emotive-affective state on major acoustic parameters of individual Russian vowels.

In this study, we investigated the parameters of Russian vowel phonemes which we denote in SAMPA transcription as /a/, /i/, /u/, /e/, /o/, /1/, whereby the symbol /1/ is used in this chapter to represent the high central vowel, as the one found in the Russian word *syr* (cheese).

II. Materials and Methods

II.1. The database

The RUSLANA (Russian Language Affective) database includes the recordings of speakers of Standard (St. Petersburg) Russian portraying the following six emotional states: neutral, anger, fear, happiness, sadness, and surprise. These emotions are typically represented in phonetics and speech processing studies among 'archetypal emotions' (Cowie et al. 2001; Banse and Scherer 1996). The database also represents the major syntactical types of Russian (statements, 'yes-no,' alternative and wh-questions, echo-questions and exclamations) and basic intonation contours that are linked with those sentence types (Bryzgunova 1977). All the phonemes of Russian have been included in the database. RUSLANA includes utterances from 61 subjects (12 male and 49 female). Each speaker recorded ten sentences of different syntactical type and intonation pattern portraying the above-mentioned six emotional states, that is, each speaker produced 60 utterances. Figure 1.1 shows one exclamatory utterance produced with different emotions by a female speaker.

All the data were recorded on a portable digital audio tape recorder, Sony TCD-D8 at 48 kHz sampling rate, via Sennheiser headphone set, in a soundproof recording studio of the Department of Phonetics, St. Petersburg State University, St. Petersburg, Russia. The obtained recordings were converted into monophonic Windows PCM format at 32 kHz sampling frequency and 16-bit resolution.

Figure 1.1. Waveforms and pitch contours of an exclamatory utterance produced with different emotions by a female speaker

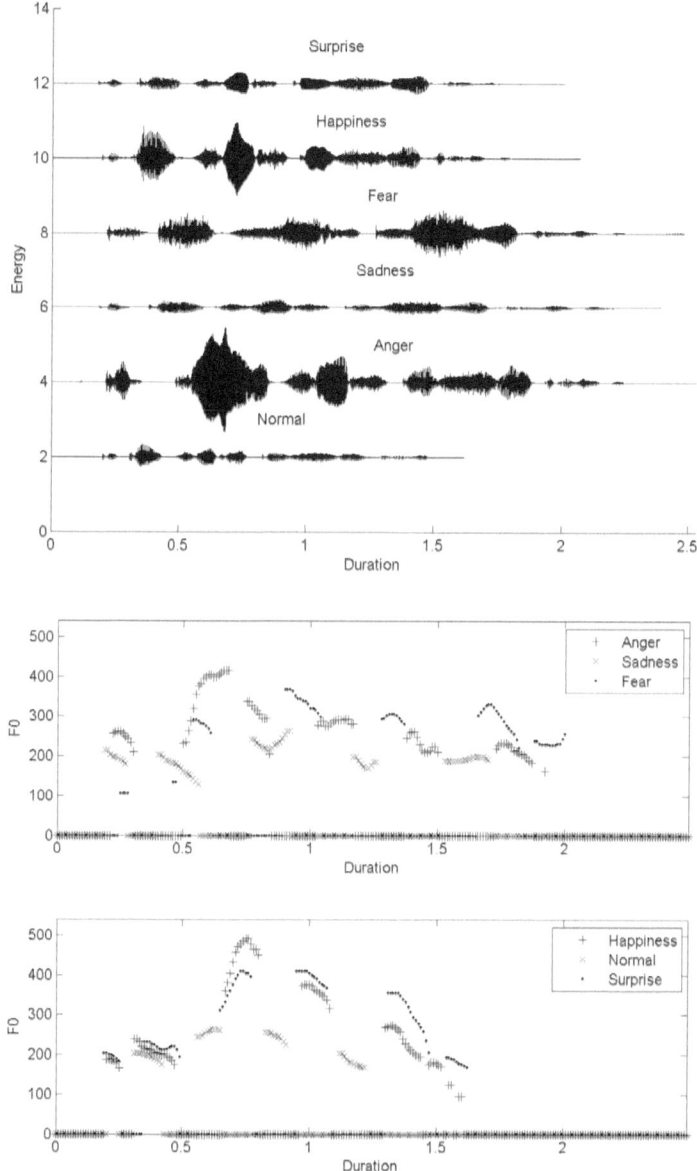

In this study, we used 600 utterances from ten speakers (five male and five female). These ten speakers were selected based on the results of the database evaluation. In the process of evaluation, 30 speakers of Standard Russian (10 males and 20 females) were requested to perform two evaluations of the randomly presented stimuli. In the first evaluation, the listeners were requested to identify the emotion they heard portrayed in each utterance. In the second evaluation, they ranked how well every utterance portrayed a given emotion on a ten-point Lickert scale. The speakers whose utterances ranked the highest in both evaluations were selected for the study to ensure the quality of emotion portrayal.

II.2. Feature extraction

The RUSLANA database provides a number of acoustic features for each utterance with a 10 ms step interval. It also provides phoneme-level labeling for all utterances. We used these data to estimate features for each phoneme in every utterance. The following features have been extracted and analyzed:

- Phoneme duration (Dur);
- Percentage of voiceness;
- Average energy (E);
- Average fundamental frequency value (F0);
- Average F0 derivative (F0deriv);
- Average formant values (F1, F2, F3);
- Average formant bandwidths (BW1, BW2, BW3).

Additionally, the values of average power spectrum on logarithmic scale were estimated for the following 16 sub-bands: 0–500 Hz, 501–1000 Hz, 1001–1500 Hz, 1501–2000 Hz, 2001–2500 Hz, 2501–3000 Hz, 3001–3500 Hz, 3501–4000 Hz, 4001–5000 Hz, 5001–6000 Hz, 6001–7000 Hz, 7001–8000 Hz, 8001–10000 Hz, 10001–12000 Hz, 12001–14000 Hz, 14001–16000 Hz. These power spectrum features are denoted here by letters "Fq" followed by the upper bound of frequency range, for example, the sub-band 2501–3000 Hz is denoted as Fq3000.

In total, the features for about 17,100 occurrences of phonemes have been extracted. The phoneme-level labeling for vowels allows for the distinction between unstressed, stressed, and pitch accented vowels. In our analysis, we used 325 occurrences of pitch accented vowels, 1393 occurrences of stressed vowels and 3,891 occurrences of unstressed vowels.

The extracted features were subjected to Univariate ANOVA analysis to determine the effect of emotion type on variability of every parameter. The analysis was conducted for all the instances of every vowel phoneme in the database, as well as separately for accented, stressed and unstressed vowels. The effects were considered significant at a p-value less than 0.05. Subsequent post-hoc analysis was performed which employed multiple pair-wise comparison tests using Tukey's honestly significant difference criterion. The latter tests were performed for each pair of emotion types, such as anger/sadness, anger/fear, etc., and for all parameter means that showed the significant effect of emotion type in the preceding ANOVA analysis. These procedures allowed us to determine whether every feature significantly varies with the factor of emotion type, and if so, which of the pairs of emotional states show significant differences in the average feature values.

III. Results

III.1. Vowel groups (accented, stressed and unstressed vowels)

This section describes the features which were found to be significantly different across the six emotive-affective states for the three vowel groups: unstressed, stressed and accented.

III.1.1. The effect of emotion type on major vowel parameters

For all the three vowel types, emotions have a statistically significant effect on the variability of all 25 parameters analyzed in the study: vowel duration (Dur), average energy (E), average fundamental frequency (F0), and all the power spectrum features; first, second and third formants (F1, F2, F3), F0 derivative, and formant bandwidths (BW1, BW2, BW3).

Average values for the analyzed parameters by emotive type of the three groups of vowels are represented below in Tables 1.1–1.3.

We will comment briefly on some of the findings represented in the Tables 1.1–1.3.

Vowel durations

Emotion type is a significant factor in the variability of duration in all the three vowel groups (unstressed, stressed and accented). In all the three vowel groups, neutral vowels have the smallest duration, i.e., all emotive states extend vowel durations. Emotive unstressed vowels are on the average 7.7 ms longer than the neutral ones (11 percent of the average duration of an unstressed vowel in the dataset); emotive stressed vowels are on average 12.2 ms longer than neutral vowels (14 percent of the average vowel duration); and the analogous extension for emotive accented vowels is 25.0 ms (22 percent of the average vowel length). Predictably, vowel duration within one emotive set decreases consistently from 'accented' to 'unstressed,' which is a consequence of the vowel length extension with the increased degree of prominence.

In all the three groups, there are significant differences in the durations of sad/neutral, and afraid/neutral vowels. In the accented vowels group,

Table 1.1. Descriptive statistics for unstressed vowels (mean/std) and p-value for one-way analysis of variance; N = 3891

Feature	Neutral	Sad	Afraid	Angry	Happy	Surprised	p-value
Duration(ms)	63.5/31.9	70.8/33.8	72.0/34.7	76.3/38.4	68.9/33.4	68.1/33.3	**0.00000**
Energy (rms)	0.027/0.031	0.032/0.023	0.039/0.033	0.075/0.056	0.063/0.043	0.044/0.031	**0.00000**
F0 (Hz)	194.3/97.2	200.1/93.7	225.5/92.8	224.2/78.3	247.0/89.8	225.1/87.3	**0.00000**
F0 der (Hz/s)	−144.3/344	−130.1/305	−159.3/369	−190.7/448	−167.5/515	−161.2/526.5	0.17068
F1 (Hz)	393.4/150.2	395.1/146.8	378.6/140.8	458.4/123.3	445.8/125.9	425.4/115.4	0.15021
F2 (Hz)	888.0/387	899.2/369	959.6/378	1040.6/311	1014.3/312	961.8/295	**0.00000**
F3 (Hz)	1643.6/20.5	1676.8/20.1	1734.0/20.0	1788.4/19.7	1802.1/20.25	1774.1/20.4	**0.00000**
F1BW (Hz)	175.9/5.3	178.5/5.2	176.0/5.2	163.3/5.1	173.2/5.2	183.1/5.3	0.15021
F2 BW (Hz)	543.1/14.6	526.0/14.4	482.3/14.3	615.0/14.1	583.0/14.4	555.4/14.6	**0.00000**
F3 BW (Hz)	284.8/10.4	285.8/10.2	300.0/10.2	326.7/10.3	317.4/10.3	318.9/10.3	**0.00901**
Fq500 (dB)	−61.8/6.5	−60.7/7.6	−59.4/8.3	−54.1/6.2	−54.8/5.9	−57.1/5.8	**0.00000**
Fq1000 (dB)	−71.1/10.4	−69.7/11.0	−70.5/11.9	−60.3/10.0	−62.2/9.5	−66.1/9.6	**0.00000**
Fq5000 (dB)	−92.9/10.2	−90.9/10.7	−87.4/9.8	−80.8/10.3	−82.2/10.8	−87.3/9.70	**0.00000**
Fq10000 (dB)	−104.1/8.3	−102.1/8.1	−96.9/9.2	−93.6/7.5	−94.3/7.4	−98.7/7.4	**0.00000**

Table 1.2. Descriptive statistics for stressed vowels (mean/std) and p-value for one-way analysis of variance; N = 1393

Feature	Neutral	Sad	Afraid	Angry	Happy	Surprised	p-value
Duration(ms)	74.6/24.0	86.8/28.0	85.4/29.6	88.1/27.7	89.6/32.2	84.3/26.9	**0.000000**
Energy (rms)	0.028/0.016	0.032/0.022	0.050/0.040	0.069/0.034	0.077/0.050	0.051/0.026	**0.000000**
F0 (Hz)	146.8/50.6	157.8/52.6	210.1/62.2	196.5/65.4	218.0/57.6	188.9/46.3	**0.000000**
F0 der (Hz/s)	−42.8/209.5	−17.7/178.2	−74.3/270.5	−31.0/328.2	−6.4/392.1	32.7/352.8	**0.00414**
F1 (Hz)	401.3/89.6	405.3/85.0	402.2/86.6	428.3/106.7	438.8/92.8	416.7/83.5	**0.000000**
F2 (Hz)	1050.9/337	1048.5/297	1050.5/257	1107.1/297	1118.2/285	1066.8/286	**0.02574**
F3 (Hz)	1837.9/24.0	1858.5/25.1	1883.9/25.1	1864.4/26.3	1847.4/24.3	1854.6/24.1	0.84641
F1 BW (Hz)	139.9/6.7	157.7/7.0	165.4/7.0	137.1/7.4	152.3/6.8	146.4/6.8	**0.04199**
F2 BW (Hz)	668.3/25.0	638.4/26.2	578.5/26.1	668.6/27.3	672.2/25.3	681.0/25.1	0.05351
F3 BW (Hz)	336.1/18.4	351.9/19.2	360.5/19.2	338.1/20.1	387.1/18.6	358.1/18.5	0.43640
Fq500 (dB)	−59.9/4.8	−59.3/5.7	−56.2/6.7	−53.0/4.3	−52.6/5.3	−55.0/4.5	**0.000000**
Fq1000 (dB)	−71.8/8.8	−71.5/10.0	−68.0/11.3	−62.1/9.0	−60.9/9.7	−66.2/9.5	**0.000000**
Fq5000 (dB)	−94.2/9.2	−92.4/10.6	−86.0/9.1	−81.6/9.3	−82.1/9.1	−86.9/9.0	**0.000000**
Fq10000 (dB)	−105.3/8.3	−102.9/8.8	−97.0/9.1	−94.1/8.0	−93.8/7.0	−97.8/7.2	**0.000000**

Table 1.3. Descriptive statistics for accented vowels (mean/std) and p-value for one-way analysis of variance; N = 325

Feature	Neutral	Sad	Afraid	Angry	Happy	Surprised	p-value
Duration(ms)	92.2/29.6	132.5/46.3	117.4/38.9	112.4/34.5	106.1/34.7	117.9/38.8	**0.00000**
Energy (rms)	0.024/0.012	0.028/0.014	0.039/0.028	0.085/0.056	0.063/0.035	0.039/0.020	**0.00000**
F0 (Hz)	241.3/64.2	258.3/64.8	294.2/78.8	289.2/92.2	300.6/89.8	280.4/77.0	**0.00047**
F0 der (Hz/s)	163.4/482.3	24.0/236.1	−76.8/493.9	−90.6/650.1	−139.9/672	141.6/679.2	**0.01936**
F1 (Hz)	457.0/ 98.2	456.1/110.0	415.1/93.8	499.4/124.7	463.0/108.6	447.6/118.0	**0.00399**
F2 (Hz)	931.0/245.2	920.9/165.4	926.9/225.3	1025.5/172	967.7/194.4	878.8/199.9	**0.00889**
F3 (Hz)	1846.1/58.2	1877.6/54.5	1827.6/53.1	1860.8/55.5	1921.4/53.1	1818.0/62.8	0.80446
F1 BW (Hz)	204.8/16.3	181.9/15.3	173.4/14.9	152.1/15.5	162.8/14.9	200.4/17.6	0.14677
F2 BW (Hz)	488.6/38.5	573.2/36.0	422.4/35.1	511.2/36.7	465.9/35.1	427.6/41.5	**0.03944**
F3 BW (Hz)	390.6/35	367.0/33	364.3/32.1	353.8/33.5	356.6/32.1	413.2/37.9	0.84101
Fq500 (dB)	−62.6/4.5	−61.9/3.9	−58.8/6.0	−54.7/4.7	−55.1/5.4	−58.6/4.5	**0.00000**
Fq1000 (dB)	−68.8/7.7	−68.3/9.3	−67.9/10.5	−58.7/9.9	−61.9/9.2	−64.0/7.9	**0.00000**
Fq5000 (dB)	−91.1/9.2	−85.5/8.5	−82.6/8.1	−73.5/10.6	−78.1/8.4	−83.6/11.0	**0.00000**
Fq10000 (dB)	−101.5/6.6	−99.8/6.2	−93.8/7.0	−92.3/5.2	−93.3/6.6	−96.3/8.9	**0.00000**

maximal vowel duration is found in the production of the simulated 'sad' emotive state (132.5 ms average), followed by 'surprised' and 'afraid' (117.9 and 117.4 ms), with the shortest emotive vowels belonging to the 'happy' state (106.1 ms). These differences in duration across emotive states are statistically significant for 'sad/happy,' 'sad/neutral,' 'afraid/neutral' and 'neutral/surprised' states.

A different distribution of duration across emotive states is found in the stressed vowel group, where the 'happy' state has the longest duration (88.1 ms), closely followed by the 'angry' (88.1 ms), 'sad' (86.8 ms), 'afraid' (85.4 ms) and 'surprised' (84.3 ms) emotive states. Statistically significant are the differences in duration between neutral vowels, on the one hand, and all the emotive vowels, on the other. There are no statistically significant differences across any pairs of emotive stressed vowels.

Yet another picture emerges from the durational distributions in the group of unstressed vowels, in which the longest vowel duration is found in the 'angry' state (76.3 ms), followed by 'afraid' (72.0 ms), 'sad' (70.8 ms), 'happy' (68.9 ms) and 'surprised' (68.1 ms). The unstressed group of vowels has significant differences in duration between 'sad/neutral,' 'afraid/neutral,' 'angry/sad,' 'angry/happy,' 'angry/neutral' and 'angry/surprised' states. Figure 1.2 below represents the average duration values for accented and unstressed vowels.

Figure 1.2. Average durations of vowels in neutral and emotive speech modes in the unstressed, stressed and accented vowels datasets

Panel a. Duration of unstressed vowels across emotive states

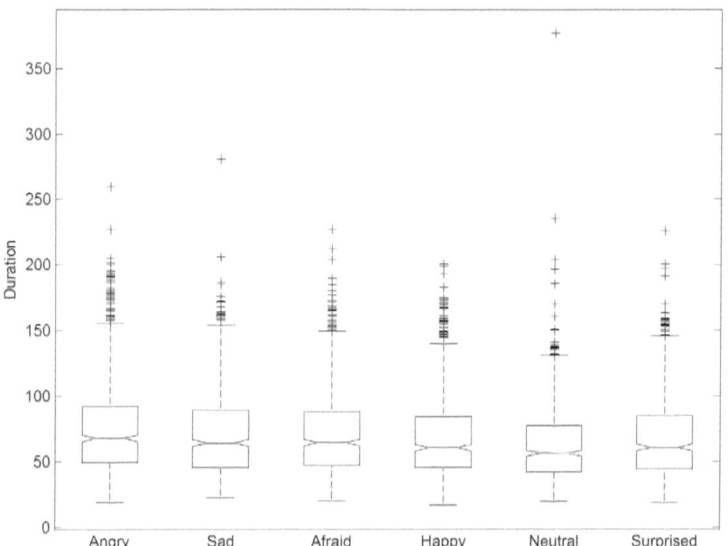

Figure 1.2. Continued

Panel b. Duration of stressed vowels across emotive states

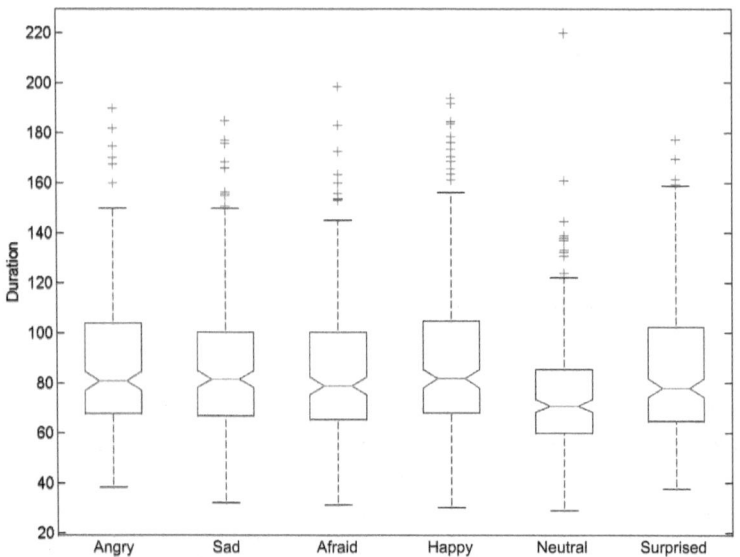

Panel c. Duration of accented vowels across emotive states

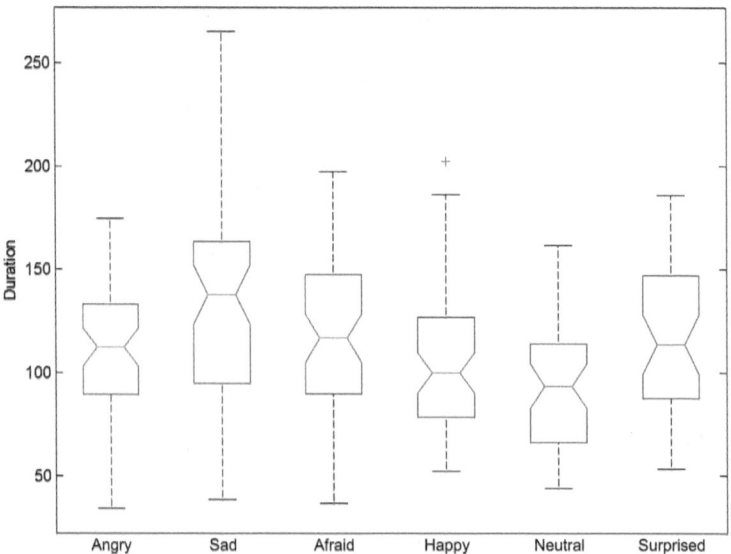

III.1.2. Energy

In all the three vowel datasets, vowels in neutral utterances have the lowest energy (0.027, 0.028 and 0.024 rms in the unstressed, stressed and accented datasets, respectively), closely followed by vowels in the 'sad' emotive state (0.032, 0.032 and 0.028 rms, respectively). The emotive states displaying the highest vowel energy in all the datasets are 'angry' (0.075, 0.069 and 0.063 rms in the unstressed, stressed and accented datasets) and 'happy' (0.063, 0.077 and 0.063 rms). 'Surprised' and 'afraid' vowels have very close values in the medium energy range varying between 0.039 and 0.051 rms. Figure 1.3 below shows the energy distribution of accented, stressed and unstressed vowels by emotive state.

Post-hoc analysis revealed the existence of a statistically significant difference in energy values across all the pairs of emotions with the exception of 'sad/neutral' and 'afraid/surprised' in all the accentual subsets. In addition, no significant differences were found in energy between 'angry/happy' vowels in the stressed set group, and the pairs 'sad/afraid,' 'sad/surprised' and 'afraid/neutral' yielded no significant differences in the accented vowels subset.

Figure 1.3. Average energy of vowels in neutral and emotive speech modes in the unstressed, stressed and accented vowels datasets

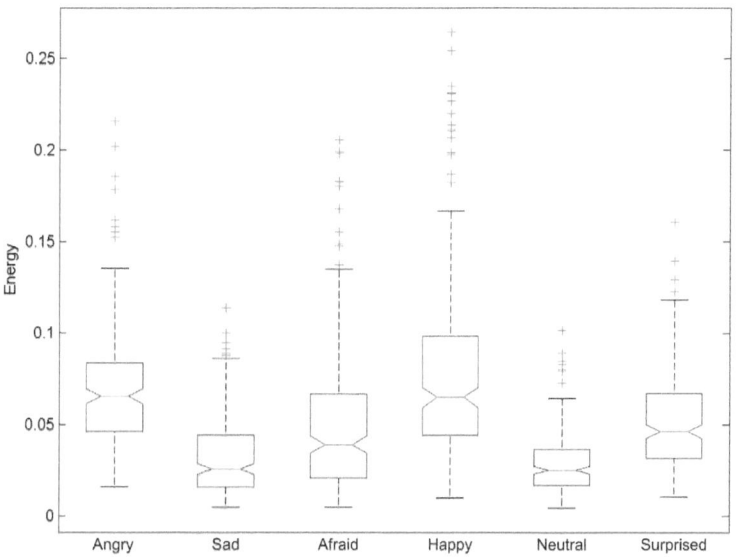

Panel a. Energy of unstressed vowels across emotive states

Figure 1.3. Continued

Panel b. Energy of unstressed vowels across emotive states

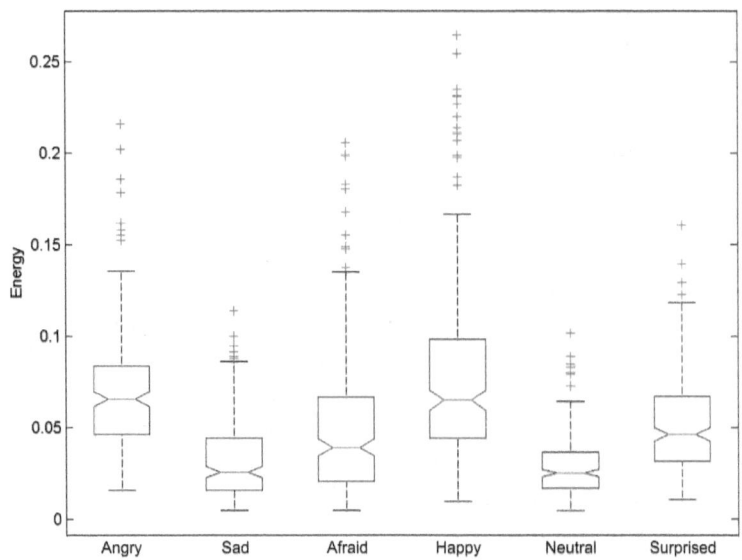

Panel c. Energy of accented vowels across emotive states

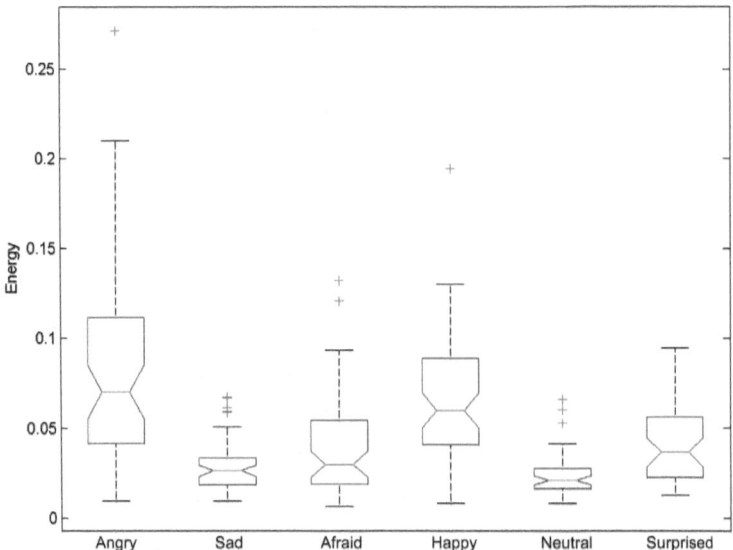

III.1.3. F0

Emotive states have a significant impact on the F0 values in all the three accentual datasets. In all the three vowel groups, neutral vowels have the lowest F0 values (194.3, 146.8 and 241.3 Hz for the unstressed, stressed and accented datasets) closely followed by 'sad' vowels (200.1, 157.8 and 258.3 Hz). Vowels articulated with the emotion of happiness have the highest F0 values (247.0, 218.0 and 300.6 Hz), followed by vowels with the emotion of fear (225.5, 210.1 and 294.2 Hz). Somewhat lower close values of F0 are observed for vowels with 'angry' (224.2, 196.5 and 289.2 Hz) and 'surprised' emotive states (225.1, 188.9 and 280.4 Hz).

On average, neutral vowels are lower than 'emotive' vowels by 30 Hz in the unstressed set, 47.5 Hz in the stressed set and 43.2 Hz in the accented set; that is, the maximum difference in values between the neutral and emotive vowels is found in the stressed vowels dataset. It is interesting to observe that all the three vowel sets exhibit close similarities in terms of parametric differences across emotive states. In other words, F0 is a significant factor in emotive state differentiation not only for accented vowels, but for stressed and unstressed vowels as well. Figure 1.4 below represents the average F0 values for accented, stressed and unstressed vowels.

Figure 1.4. Average F0 values of vowels in neutral and emotive speech modes in the unstressed, stressed and accented vowels datasets

Panel a. F0 of unstressed vowels across emotive states

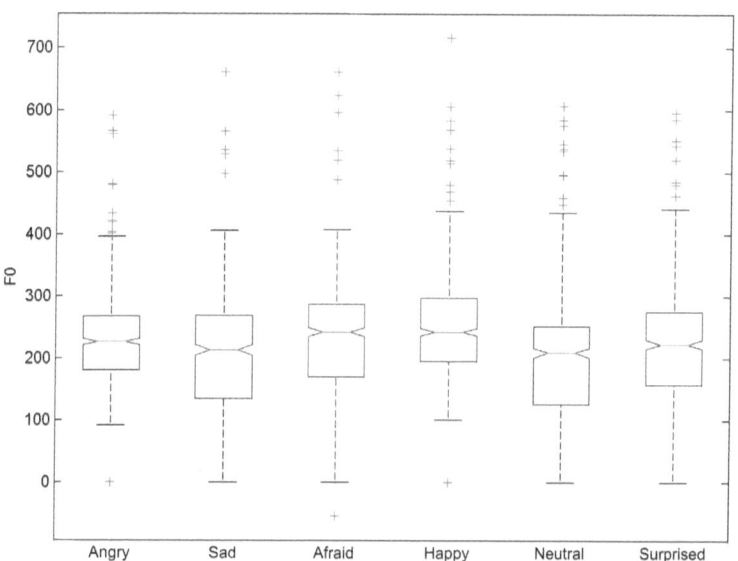

Figure 1.4. Continued

Panel b. F0 of stressed vowels across emotive states

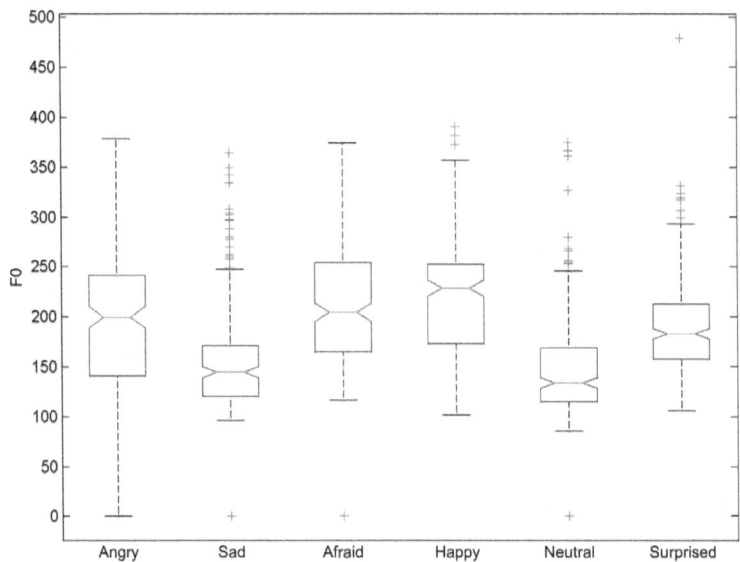

Panel c. F0 of accented vowels across emotive states

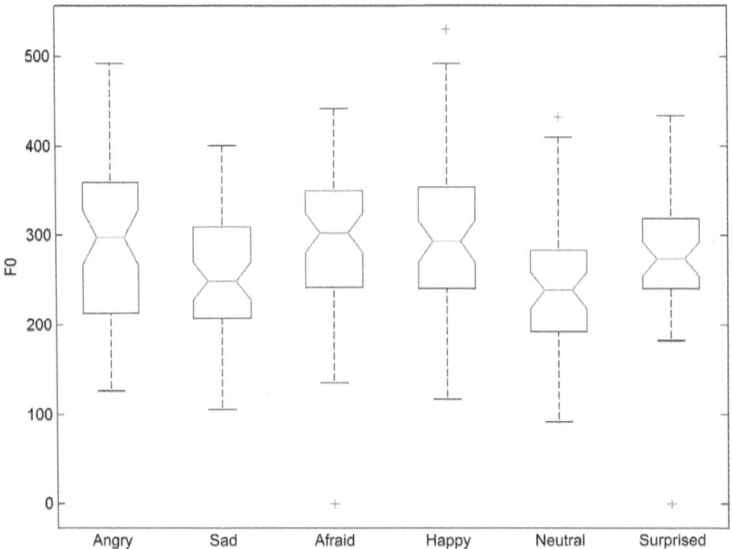

Post-hoc analysis shows that in the unstressed set, the differences across F0 values are significant for all the pairs of emotive states except 'angry/afraid,' 'angry/surprised,' 'sad/neutral' and 'afraid/surprised.' In the stressed dataset, there are no significant differences only for the following pairs of emotive states: 'angry/afraid,' 'angry/surprised,' 'sad/neutral' and 'afraid/happy.' In the accented vowels dataset, significant differences were observed for F0 values in the following four pairs of emotive states: 'angry/neutral,' 'sad/happy,' 'afraid/neutral' and 'happy/neutral.'

III.1.4. F0 derivative

F0 derivate (a change in F0 value per second) is informative of the direction and magnitude of pitch movements in a phrase. A positive value of F0 derivative indicates a rising tone, whereas a negative value indicates a falling tone. The absolute value (modulus) of F0 derivative stands for the magnitude of pitch change. Figure 1.5 below shows that in the group of accented vowels, 'neutral' and 'surprised' emotive states display higher (positive) values of F0 derivative, which means that they are associated mostly with rising pitch movements, whereas the 'sad' state has a positive low modulus value, which suggests a mostly flat contour with

Figure 1.5. Average F0 derivative values in neutral and emotive speech modes in the unstressed, stressed and accented vowels datasets

Panel a. F0 derivative of unstressed vowels across emotive states

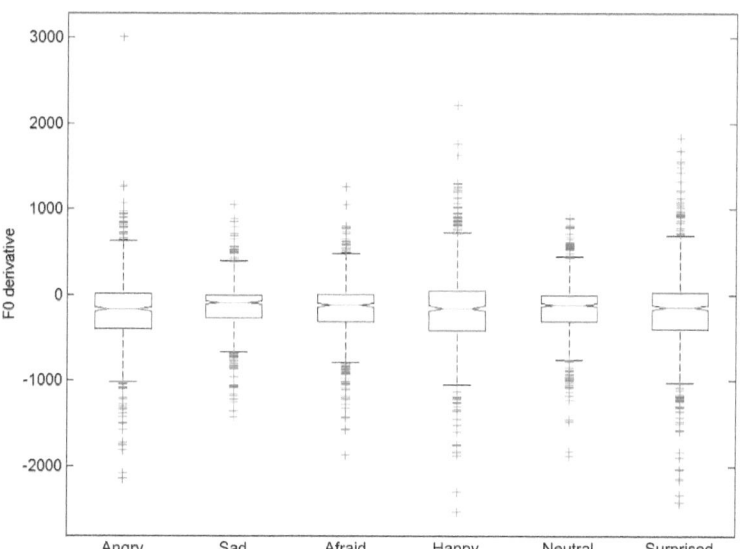

Figure 1.5. Continued

Panel b. F0 derivative of stressed vowels across emotive states

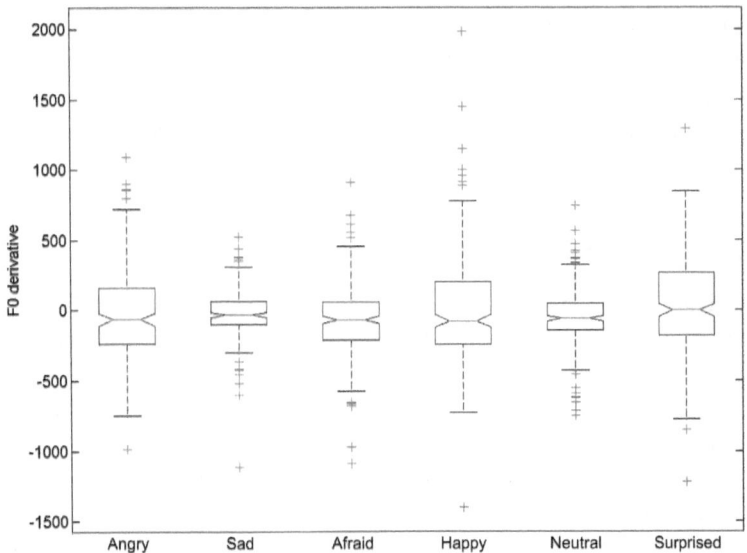

Panel c. F0 derivative of accented vowels across emotive states

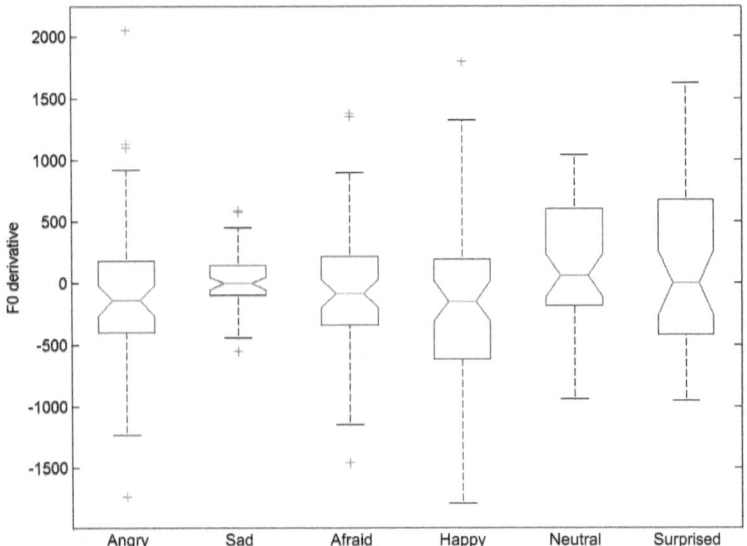

rising movements of small magnitude. 'Happy,' 'angry' and 'afraid' states have negative F0 derivative values, i.e., these emotions are associated with falling pitch movements. The stressed vowel group has negative values of F0 derivative (i.e., stressed vowels have mostly falling pitch movements), with the exception of the 'surprised' state with positive F0 derivative values indicative of the predominance of rising tones. Unstressed vowels display only high negative values of F0 derivatives, which suggests the predominance of falling tone boundaries in unstressed syllables.

Post-hoc analysis shows significant differences in F0 derivative values for the following pairs of emotive states in the accented set: 'angry/neutral,' 'sad/happy,' 'afraid/neutral' and 'happy/neutral.' In the stressed set, there are significant differences only in the pair of emotive states 'afraid/surprised.' There are no significant differences in F0 derivative values across any emotive states in the unstressed vowel dataset.

III.1.5. Formants

F1 and F2

Emotion has a significant effect on F1 and F2 values in all the three vowel groups. 'Angry' and 'happy' emotive states yield the highest F1 and F2 values in all the three vowel datasets (see Table 1.1). Higher formant values may be connected to a lowering and fronting of articulators (jaw and tongue positions) during the expression of these emotive states. On the other hand, 'sad,' 'afraid' and 'neutral' have lower values of F1 and F2, which could be connected to more constricted (raised and centered) articulators during the production of these emotions.

In the accented vowels dataset, statistically significant differences were found only between 'angry/afraid' states for F1 and 'angry/surprised' for F2. In the set of stressed vowels, the differences in F2 values are not significant for any emotion pairs, whereas F1 values are significant for 'angry/afraid,' 'angry/ neutral,' 'sad/happy,' 'afraid/happy' and 'happy/ neutral.'

In the group of unstressed vowels, the differences in F1 values are significant for all the pairs of emotions except for 'angry/happy,' 'sad/afraid,' 'sad/ neutral,' 'afraid/neutral' and 'happy/surprised.' In the same group, F2 value differences are significant for all the pairs of emotive states except for 'angry/ happy,' 'sad/neutral,' 'afraid/surprised' and 'happy/surprised.'

F3

Emotion was found to have a significant effect on F3 variability only in the group of unstressed vowels (presumably because the unstressed vowels sample is the largest). Post-hoc analysis shows that significant differences in F3 values exist for the following pairs of emotions: 'angry/sad,' 'angry/neutral,' 'sad/happy,' 'sad/surprised,' 'afraid/neutral,' 'happy/neutral' and 'neutral/surprised.'

III.1.6. Formant bandwidths

F1 BW is significantly influenced by emotion type only in the 'stressed' vowel group, but post-hoc analysis does not reveal significant differences across any pairs of emotive states. The highest F1 BW values are found in the 'afraid' state (165 Hz), followed by 'sad' (157 Hz) and 'happy' (152 Hz); the lowest F1 BW values are in 'neutral' (139) and 'angry' emotive states.

F2 BW is significantly affected by emotion in the 'unstressed' and 'accented' vowel groups. In all the three vowel groups, F2 BW has the smallest values for 'afraid' emotive state. The pair-wise comparison shows significant differences in F2 BW values between 'sad/afraid' in the accented vowel group. In the unstressed vowel dataset, F2 BW significantly differs across 'angry/sad,' 'angry/afraid,' 'angry/neutral,' 'angry/surprised,' 'afraid/happy,' 'afraid/neutral' and 'afraid/surprised' states.

F3 BW values vary significantly with emotion only in the unstressed vowel group, where the emotive pair with significant differences is 'angry/neutral.' The distribution of F3 BW values is group-specific.

The contrast between the high F1 BW values and low F2 BW values in vowels articulated with the 'afraid' emotive state is rather interesting to observe, but hard to explain. Formant bandwidths are known to have little effect on the identification of vowels, but vowels with a narrower bandwidth are marginally easier to identify (Cheveigne 1999), whereas wider BW or more 'smeared' formants may relate to lesser muscular control during the vowel articulations. The 'afraid' state therefore seems to exhibit less articulation precision along the vowel height (F1) dimension, but more precision along the frontness/backness (F2) dimension.

III.1.7. Vowel spectra

All the spectral bands are informative of the portrayed emotion. Similarly to overall energy, in all the spectral sub-bands, the emotive state with the highest energy is 'angry,' closely followed by 'happy,' whereas the emotive state with the lowest energy is 'neutral,' closely followed by 'sad', and the values for 'afraid' and 'surprised' are in the middle. Vowel spectra for the three vowel datasets are represented below in Figure 1.6. The spectral area with the maximum parametric differences across emotive states is between 5000 and 1000 Hz. The emotions with the maximum number of statistically significant differences

Figure 1.6. Spectral profiles for vowels extracted from speech portraying the following emotions: anger – solid line and upward-pointing triangle markers; sadness – dashed line and cross markers; fear – dotted line and circle markers; happiness – dashed line and downward-pointing triangle markers; neutral – solid line and square markers; and surprise – dashed-dotted line and diamond markers

Panel a. Unstressed vowels dataset

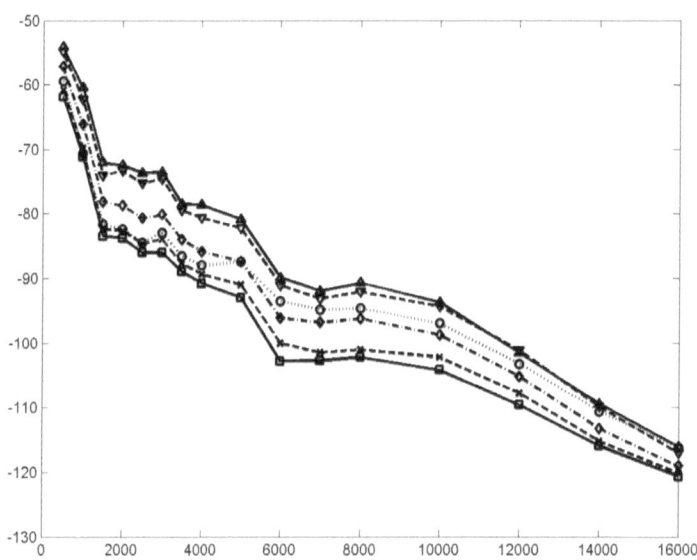

Panel b. Stressed vowels dataset

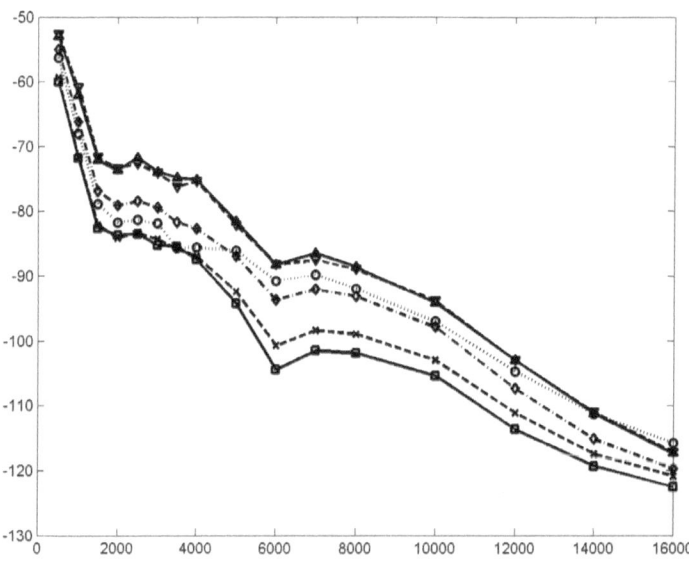

Figure 1.6. Continued

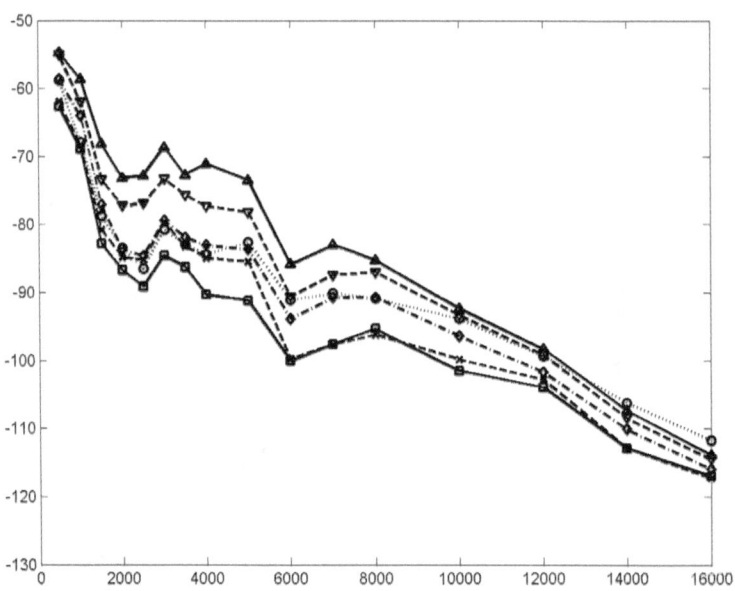

Panel c. Accented vowels dataset

revealed in post-hoc pair comparison is between 'angry/sad,' 'angry/neutral,' 'happy/sad,' 'happy/neutral,' 'angry/afraid' and 'angry/surprised.' The minimal differences are between 'sad/neutral,' 'afraid/surprised' and 'happy/angry.'

III.1.8. Emotional states and associated parameters

Emotional states are associated with specific vowel characteristics. It is impossible to identify the exact list of parameters responsible for the expression of every emotion within the framework of the current analysis, since a combination of parameters in conjunction with the vowel articulatory and accentual type is in play. However, we can still outline a few vowel parameters which are consistently linked with certain emotions, as shown below.

- *Neutral:* low duration, low energy, low F0 values and low energy across the whole spectrum, medium formant (F1, F2, F3) and BW2 values, positive F0 derivative, high BW1, BW3 values.
- *Sadness:* high duration, low energy, low values of F0 and low energy across the whole spectrum, low positive values of F0 derivative, medium values of F1 and BW1, low F1, high F2, BW2, F3, medium BW3 values.

- *Fear:* medium vowel duration, energy and all Fq-features from 500 Hz to 8000 Hz and high energy in the spectrum area from 10000 Hz to 16000 Hz.
- *Anger:* medium vowel duration, high energy, high values of spectral energy, medium F0 values, low negative F0 derivative, high F1, F2, low BW1, high BW2, medium F3, and low BW3 value.
- *Surprise:* high vowel duration, medium energy, medium energy across the spectrum, medium height F0 values and high positive values of F0 derivative.
- *Happiness:* low vowel duration, high energy, high spectral energy values under 12000 Hz, medium spectral energy values at 14000 Hz and 16000 Hz, high F0, low negative F0 derivative, high F1, F2, F3, low BW1 and BW2 and medium BW3.

Post-hoc pair-wise comparisons have shown that parametric distances across pairs of emotive sates are unequal: acoustic parameters of some emotive states are closer than others. The pairs of emotional states with maximum parametric differences and minimum overlapping parameters are: anger/neutral, happiness/neutral, anger/sadness, sadness/happiness and anger/surprise. Emotional states with the minimal parametric differences are sadness/neutral, anger/happiness and fear/surprise.

III.2. Individual vowels

In contrast to the previous section that reported the parameters of the vowels grouped by accentual type, this section describes some major acoustic parameters of individual vowels in neutral and emotional speech.

Variation of vowel durations under emotive states

Duration of the six vowels is represented in Table 1.4 below.

The analysis shows that in the 'neutral' state, there is a significant increase in duration from unstressed to stressed and from stressed to accented vowels. In the unstressed group, the relative vowel lengths can be represented as i < 1 < u < a < e, which reflects the general universal trend for close vowels to have shorter durations than open vowels (except for the vowel /e/). Vowel /o/ is not found in Standard Russian in the unstressed position, which is represented by 'N/A' in the table. In the stressed and accented positions, the distribution of vocalic duration is different: i < u < o < e < a < 1. In these datasets, /i/ is still the shortest vowel, however, the longest vowel is /1/.

Statistically significant differences in vowel durations across emotional states were obtained in these data only for unstressed and stressed /a/, /i/,

Table 1.4. Vowel duration across emotional states

Vowels	i			i			e		
	unstr	str	acc	unstr	str	acc	unstr	str	acc
N	154	30	8	963	288	50	339	289	68
Sig	X	X	X	0.000	0.0142	X	X	X	0.0163
angry	59.57	79.1	65.33	60.77	71.54	84.2	99.85	88.3	117.9
sad	59.1	87.4	96.92	57.02	70.9	108	88.29	86.5	136.8
afraid	55.97	87.1	116,9	57.3	67.2	95.4	90.57	83.5	134.4
happy	50.16	79.9	74.86	54.03	73.24	96.7	92.05	86.5	104.2
neutral	60.87	109	112.97	48.99	61.4	69.3	75.3	83.28	92.39
surprised	49.43	87.6	67.51	53.82	66.47	125	86.50	80.8	119.2

Vowels	a			u			o		
	unstr	str	acc	unstr	str	acc	unstr	str	acc
N	1844	337	80	335	85	27	N/A	364	92
Sig	0.0042	0.0017	X	X	X	X	N/A	0.03	0.0101
angry	75.89	99.68	131.1	85.2	92.9	82.1	N/A	92	120.5
sad	71.8	95.51	139.9	70.3	83.7	91.9	N/A	92	151.8
afraid	74.13	98.36	121.1	72.8	81.5	106.3	N/A	91	117.4
happy	70.57	105.1	121.3	71.3	86.6	81.9	N/A	92	113.3
neutral	65.62	82.94	107.5	63.2	66.6	88.5	N/A	77	89.13
surprised	70.72	98.6	131.2	67.9	82.3	83.8	N/A	88	115.3

accented /e/, stressed and accented /o/, which may reflect differences in sample size across the vowels. Further research is necessary to find out whether these results are explained by the differences in vowel samples (numbers of different vowels per three accentual categories), or whether there could be individual use of vowel length across the emotional states. Similar to our findings for vowel groups, the neutral state in all the individual vowels tends to have shorter vowel duration than emotional states.

III.2.2. Energy

Energy of the five Russian vowels is represented in Table 1.5 below.

The three accentual groups did not demonstrate consistent increases in energy with the increase of vowel prominence. In the unstressed vowel group, the energy distribution can be represented as u < i < 1 < e < a; in the stressed group the distribution is u < 1 < i < o < e < a. In the accented group, energy distribution is u < o < i < e < a < 1. While /i/ is the shortest vowel, /u/ has the lowest energy, whereas /e/ and /a/ have the highest duration and energy in the sample. While unstressed /1/ has relatively low energy and duration, stressed /1/ has low energy, but the highest duration, and accented /1/ is the longest vowel with the highest energy in the sample. This unusual behavior of stressed and accented /1/ may reflect the intrinsic quality of this vowel in Russian. It is often suggested by teachers of Russian as a foreign language that /1/ has higher muscular tension, which may require additional length. This assumption, however, needs to be supported by further evidence and a sample more balanced by individual vowel frequencies.

We observed significant differences in energy across emotive states for all the individual vowels (except for the stressed /1/ vowel which has very low frequency in the sample). Similar to the results for all the vowels described in the previous section, 'happy' and 'angry' states are associated with highest energies, 'neutral' and 'sad' with the lowest energies and 'surprised' and 'afraid' with medium energies.

III.2.3. F0

Average F0 values in individual vowels across the emotive states are represented below in Table 1.6. Within the neutral emotive states, F0 values are the highest for the accented vowels, lower in the unstressed vowels and the lowest in the unstressed vowels group. Unstressed vowels do not show differences in pitch depending on the features front/back, open/close. In the group of stressed vowels, lower vowels (/a/, /o/) have lower pitch than high vowels (/1/, /i/, /u/), which may be a reflection of the intrinsic vowel qualities. In the group

Table 1.5. Energy across emotional states

Energy	l			e			i		
unstr	unstr	str	acc	unstr	str	acc	unstr	str	acc
N	154	30	8	339	289	68	963	288	50
Sig	0.00955	0.02923	X	0	0	0.00025	0	0	0.03863
angry	0.052	0.0557	0.11243	0.0711	0.0679	0.0785	0.0631	0.0516	0.0702
sad	0.0349	0.0255	0.01394	0.0325	0.0336	0.0277	0.0283	0.0206	0.0268
afraid	0.0383	0.0508	0.02085	0.0351	0.0492	0.0379	0.0375	0.0357	0.0259
happy	0.0712	0.0812	0.0706	0.0575	0.072	0.058	0.055	0.053	0.0584
neutral	0.0242	0.0189	0.0439	0.0259	0.032	0.0263	0.0226	0.0214	0.0219
surprised	0.0367	0.0473	0.07455	0.0477	0.0514	0.0401	0.0392	0.0363	0.0312

Energy	a			u			o		
unstr	unstr	str	acc	unstr	str	acc	unstr	str	acc
N	1844	337	80	335	85	27	364	92
Sig	0.000	0.000	0.000	0.000	0.001	X	N/A	0	0
angry	0.0797	0.0914	0.1198	0.0582	0.0398	0.0573	N/A	0.0745	0.0735
sad	0.0335	0.0399	0.0367	0.0239	0.0250	0.0180	N/A	0.0376	0.0277
afraid	0.0407	0.0564	0.0483	0.0342	0.0475	0.0269	N/A	0.0606	0.0427
happy	0.0676	0.1016	0.068	0.0504	0.0420	0.0497	N/A	0.0866	0.0717
neutral	0.0304	0.0344	0.0264	0.0204	0.0178	0.0139	N/A	0.0296	0.0214
surprised	0.0462	0.0634	0.05	0.0331	0.0316	0.0235	N/A	0.057	0.0356

PHONETICS. TRACING EMOTIONS IN RUSSIAN VOWELS   29

Table 1.6. F0 across emotive states, in Hz

F0	ɨ			e			i		
	unstr	str	acc	unstr	str	acc	unstr	str	acc
N	154	30	8	339	289	68	963	288	50
Sig	0.002	X	X	0.018	0	X	0	0	X
angry	**228.9**	**254.9**	**315.8**	**229.8**	**198.6**	290.1	**236.3**	**199.2**	301.4
sad	**202**	**192.6**	**278.7**	**224.4**	**159.3**	252.5	**193.2**	**166.9**	248.3
afraid	**245.6**	**258.9**	**315.8**	**230**	**220.1**	309.3	**227**	**211.9**	230.5
happy	**275.6**	**243.8**	**354.5**	**263.5**	**217.3**	281.7	**251.6**	**238.6**	315.6
neutral	**198.4**	**170.2**	**262.3**	**209.1**	**156.2**	233.1	**185.9**	**159**	276.7
surprised	**231.5**	**207.7**	**291.5**	**255.4**	**192.2**	289.6	**233.6**	**206.6**	253.2

F0	a			u			o		
	unstr	str	acc	unstr	str	acc	unstr	str	acc
N	**1844**	337	80	335	85	27	N/A	364	92
Sig	**0.000**	0.000	X	0.02	X	X	N/A	**0.000**	X
angry	**209.7**	**193**	274.8	**224.0**	**188.1**	279.4	N/A	**191.4**	297.9
sad	**191.8**	**149**	254.9	**192.0**	**135.3**	258.6	N/A	**160.7**	270.3
afraid	**218.3**	**201.8**	296.3	**215.1**	**197.6**	278.6	N/A	**205.8**	314.2
happy	**233.3**	**206.5**	275.3	**234.8**	**192.8**	297.7	N/A	**217.6**	319.7
neutral	**188.4**	**138.1**	228.4	**190.2**	**125.7**	218.8	N/A	**141.8**	242.6
surprised	**212.9**	**181.2**	282.5	**205.6**	**172.4**	301.7	N/A	**182.4**	278.8

of accented vowels, the vowels with the highest F0 are /i/ and /1/ followed by /o/, whereas /a/ and /e/ have medium pitch heights, and /u/ has the lowest F0 value.

In terms of F0 variation under the effect of emotive state, statistically significant differences were observed across F0 values of all the individual vowels (unstressed and stressed variants), but not for any of the accented variants. The latter could be caused either by a small sample of accented vowels or by the strong influence of the tonal types (rising, falling, rising-falling) on the pitch values of accented vowels. The 'happy' state is associated with high F0 values for all the vowels. 'Neutral' and 'sad' have the lowest F0 values. 'Angry,' 'surprised' and 'afraid' are characterized by medium F0 values.

III.2.4. Formants F1 and F2

The values for the F1 and F2 in the stressed vowel neutral dataset are represented graphically below (Fig. 1.7).

The distribution of formant 1 and 2 values correlates with the articulatory descriptions of Russian vowels. The vowel /1/ appears to be half-close rather than close. This suggests that both articulatory and acoustic characteristics of /1/ require further investigation. It should be mentioned that the obtained formant values in this experiment and represented in Figure 1.1 are more 'central' than the usually reported formant values, since in this experiment the values were pooled together for five male and five female subjects and the features including formants were extracted from the whole durations of the vowels (including formant transitions).

F1 and F2 values are significantly affected by emotional states, whereby the effect of F1 appears to be stronger than for F2. 'Angry' and 'happy' states have higher values of F1 and F2, while 'sad,' 'neutral,' 'afraid' have lower ones.

Figure 1.7. F1 and F2 of the stressed vowels

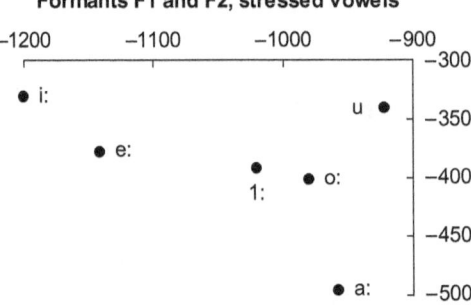

IV. Discussion

It has been argued that emotions play an essential role in rational decision making, perception, learning and a variety of other cognitive tasks (Picard 1997; Hyun et al. 2010). They further contribute to "actions, reactions, dispositions, motives and other psychological characteristics" that can serve as explanations of human conduct (Edwards 1999, 288). In this way, a better understanding of human emotions and their expressions provides us with insight into human behavior and its motivation.

The identification of human emotions is done by interpreting many clues, including facial feature recognition and recognition of acoustic features (Zervas et al. 2007). Our study points to the importance of the acoustic characteristics of vowels as a subset of emotive clues embedded in human speech. Our findings are of particular significance for automatic man–machine dialog systems that, on an increasing scale, are required to include the ability to identify and reproduce the emotive-affective domain of human speech (Petrushin 2002), since emotional interaction is believed to be a prerequisite of intelligent behavior (Hyun et al. 2010). Failure to account for the emotive-affective domain of human speech can decrease the efficiency of an automatic dialog system and can cause communication breakdown and increase costs (Batliner et al. 2000). Yet, due to its high variability, emotional speech presents a challenge for speech recognition. Recognizers that were trained only on neutral speech can drop their performance reliability by about 30 to 60 percent when they are exposed to affective speech (Min Lee and Narayana 2005). The high quality recognition and synthesis of human emotion depends on the extraction of acoustic parameters responsible for the perceived emotive effect in real speech.

Emotions present a considerable difficulty for identification and classification not only for automated recognizers, but for human listeners as well (Cowie et al. 2001). This is caused in part by the huge variability of parameters of emotive speech and partly by the lack of clear emotive labels. It is also difficult to disentangle the effect of various parameters on emotion portrayal. Even in experiments involving human perception of highly controllable synthesized speech stimuli (Gobl and Chasaide 2003), there was no one-to-one mapping between the acoustic parameter under investigation and the emotion type.

Another difficulty is connected with culture- and language-specific features in the expression of emotion. Some parameters of emotion expression (mostly connected with the primary physiological states) are believed to be universal and language-independent (Pell et al. 2009; Makarova and Petrushin 2009). However, some other features (related to the expression of affect controlled by the speaker) can be language-dependent (Pell et al. 2009). It is therefore necessary to consider language-specific features in emotion recognition and synthesis and involve a wide range of languages in speech research.

To the best of our knowledge, our study is the first corpus-based study of the segmental features contributing to the expression of affect in Russian. Our study shows that all the examined acoustic parameters (vowel duration, energy, F0, F1, F2, F3 and their bandwidths as well as all the spectral energy bandwidths within 0–16000 Hz) are significantly affected by emotion type. In this way, our study confirms earlier findings which find that the acoustic expression of emotions is highly complex and involves multiple parameters (Moziconnacci 2001).

IV.1. Durations

Some earlier findings have shown that certain emotions such as anger are associated with syllable and vowel lengthening (Mozziconacci 2001). Russian was previously shown to display a significant increase in vowel duration in the accented syllable under the emotion of surprise (Fischer and Batliner 2000; Makarova 2000). Our study demonstrates that the role of vowel duration in the expression of affect in Russian is not only highly significant, but is also applicable to a wider range of emotions.

Predictably, accented vowels in our data are longer than the stressed ones and the stressed vowels are longer than the unstressed ones. While it is well known that Russian vowels lengthen with prominence (Beloshapkova 1999, 79) and that vowels in many world languages lengthen with tonal accents (Ladd 2008), our experiment demonstrates that not only stressed and accented, but unaccented vowels as well lengthen with all the analyzed emotions. We also find an interaction of the accentual type of the vowels with the emotive type in the distribution of vowel durations.

One of the unexpected findings in our analysis of stressed and accented vowels is the high duration of /1/ in these datasets as compared to other vowels. This result may reflect the intrinsic quality of this vowel in Russian. This assumption, however, needs to be supported by further experimental evidence due to low frequency of /1/ in the datasets.

IV.2. Total energy

Vowel energy is known to be a highly salient factor in the production of emotions (Ververidis and Kotropoulos 2006), which is confirmed in our experiment. In the described dataset, neutral vowels have the lowest energy, closely followed by the 'sad' subset, which agrees with previous data showing that when people are sad or calm, they speak quietly (Hyun et al. 2010, 55).

'Sad' in earlier research, however, tends to have lower energy than neutral vowels (Ververidis and Kotropoulos 2006; Iida 2002), which is not the case in our study of Russian vowels. On the other hand, in accordance with previous research that demonstrates an increased amount of energy in the states of arousal (Hyun et al. 2010), the emotive states yielding the highest vowel energy in our data are 'happy' and 'angry.' In earlier experiments with other languages, 'anger' was also found to yield the highest energy (Ververidis and Kotropoulos 2006; Iida 2002).

IV.3. F0

Similar to earlier research (Ververidis and Kotropoulos 2006; Pell et al. 2009), F0 values in our study are highly significant for the expression of emotions. The innovative result in our experiment is that emotions impact the F0 values not only of accented vowels, but also of stressed and unstressed vowels. This points to the significance of pitch heights in the overall contour and not just in the accented syllables. This can be interpreted as a fact in favor of the contour approach to tone, which is predominant in Russian intonation analysis (Svetozarova 1998), over autosegmental approaches (Igarashi 2006).

Our analysis shows that F0 of vowels in the neutral dataset is the lowest (closely followed by the 'sad' dataset), whereas the highest F0 values are found in vowels portraying the emotive state of happiness. An earlier study of emotion expression in Farsi also shows that emotive vowels have higher average vowel pitches than neutral vowels, but the highest pitch is found in 'angry' utterances (Gharavian et al. 2010).

F0 differences across the three accentual vowels groups could be explained by pitch lowering in the stressed vowels, since pitch participates in Russian in the realization of stress and falling pitch in stressed syllables with high pre-accented syllables are common (Bryzgunova 1977). The highest pitch values are found in the accented vowels, which reflect the commonality of rising and rising-falling pre-nuclear and nuclear tones in Russian (Makarova 2000).

IV.4. F0 derivative

F0 derivative is used in the descriptions of acoustic characteristics of affect (Bitouk et al. 2010), but not very frequently. Yet, as our study shows, this is a parameter informative of the predominant direction and magnitude of the pitch movements not only in the vowels in accented syllables, but in the whole contour (stressed and unstressed vowels). Moreover, F0 derivative is significant in the expression of emotions. While an analysis of 'pitch slope' in vowels in

Farsi (Gharavian et al. 2010) shows that falling pitch movements prevail in all the analyzed emotional types (neutral, angry, happy, surprised), our analysis of F0 derivative values reveals positive values for 'sad,' 'neutral' and 'surprised' vowels in the accented group and for 'surprised' vowels in the stressed group. These positive values are indicative of the predominance of rising pitch movements in these emotive states.

IV.5. Formants (F1, F2, F3)

Formants are known to undergo changes in emotion and serve as an emotive clue (Iliev et al. 2010). In our study, F1 and F2 are significantly affected by emotional states. 'Angry' and 'happy' have higher formant values, while 'sad,' 'afraid' and 'neutral' states yield lower formant values. Earlier research makes the connection of anger with hyperarticulation (Mozziconacci 2001), which may induce the formant shift.

F3 values have relatively little effect on the perception of neutral vowels in Russian (Chistovich, et al. 1979). Some experiments with other languages demonstrate that F3 may slightly contribute to the expression of emotion, which is explained by increased tension associated with some emotions and the resulting rising of the larynx and shortening of the vocal tract (Waaramaa et al. 2006). Our study shows that F3 values can be informative of the emotive type in Russian, although the effect was only observed for the group of unstressed vowels.

The F1 and F2 formant values for Russian vowels in our study are similar, but somewhat lower than earlier reported (Kouznetsov 2002). This can be explained by averaging the values from ten speakers, whereas the above research presented the values only for one speaker. An interesting finding in our experiment is higher F2 values of the vowel /1/ than earlier reported (Chistovich and Kozhevnikov 1965), which may indicate lower articulation of this vowel and needs further investigation.

IV.6. Formant bandwidths

Formant bandwidths are known to have little effect on the identification of vowels in neutral speech, but narrower bandwidth vowels are marginally easier to identify (Cheveigne 1999). Earlier experiments conducted with other languages have shown that certain emotive states (such as stress or depression) result with slackened articulation which manifests acoustically as wider formant bandwidths (France et al. 2000; Ververidis and Kotropoulis 2006). More 'smeared' (wider BW) formants should therefore be indicative of lesser muscular control during the vowel articulations. Paradoxically, in our study, the 'afraid' state displays the highest F1 BW values and the lowest F2 BW values, i.e., lessened muscular control in the vertical dimension, but not in the horizontal dimension.

IV.7. Spectra

Identifying the "best frequency band of the power spectrum in order to classify emotions" is believed to be one of the most contradictory and elusive areas in acoustic studies of emotions (Ververidis and Kotropoulos 2006, 1170). Our study shows that in Russian, the whole spectral band is highly significant of emotions, whereas the most 'emotion-sensitive' area of the spectrum is between 5000 and 10000 Hz. This confirms earlier findings which determine that spectra of voiced and unvoiced segments can be employed as a cue for emotion recognition (Paeschke and Sendlmeier 2000).

IV.8. Emotion clusters

It has been suggested that emotional states can be divided into categories or groups (Cowie et al. 2001). Speech processing research indicates that some acoustic parameters can be similar across certain emotional states (Murray and Arnott 1996), whereas speech perception studies show that some emotions are misconstrued for one another by human listeners (Scherer et al. 2001). Our study demonstrates the proximity of the acoustic characteristics of anger and happiness (higher intensity, slower speaking rate, higher voicing, greater magnitude of pitch movements). This goes contrary to some other studies which show that anger has very distinctive parameters and is therefore easier to identify than other emotions (Grimm et al. 2007), or to the studies that demonstrate distinct characteristics of 'happiness' on the one hand and an overlap in parameters between 'sadness' and 'anger' on the other hand (Nordstrand et al. 2004).

We also observed that anger and happiness have some features similar to the ones found in 'surprise' (higher F0 maxima, higher F0 SDs). Fear and sadness have respectively lower values for the above features and also display flattened contours with smaller magnitudes of pitch movements and fewer accents. As in some other studies (Grimm et al. 2007; Nordstrand et al. 2004), we similarly observed the proximity of some parameters of neutral and sad utterances. These results suggest that a classification of emotions is possible for Russian based on the proximity/distance of their acoustic expression and on their correct/incorrect identification by human listeners, and that this classification will have some language-specific features as well as features shared with other languages.

IV.9. Specific emotions and their acoustic correlates in comparison to available data from other languages

A comparison to some earlier studies of the acoustic features of affect in other languages shows that Russian has a common feature in the expression of affect, as well as some language-specific features.

Fear

Similar to the expression of fear in English, German, Hindi and Arabic (Pell et al. 2009), Russian 'fear' has high F0 values. While 'fear' in English, Hindi and Arabic has increased speech rate, Russian behaves similarly to German without an increase in speech rate. While fear in English and Finnish (as well as in vocalization by macaques) was connected with high intensity (Leinonen et al. 2003), in Russian, fear has low intensity.

Sadness

In many languages 'sadness' is characterized by low tempo or high vowel duration, low energy, low values of F0 and low energy across the whole spectrum (Pell et al. 2009). Very similar results were also observed in our study. An interesting difference in Russian is low positive values of F0 derivative (indicative of flat slightly rising pitch movements), medium values of F1 and BW1, but low F2 and high F2BW values.

Anger

The acoustic parameters for 'anger' seem to strongly vary across languages (Juslin and Laukka 2003; Pell et al. 2009). Similar to Hindi, Russian has high F0 average values for anger, which is in contrast with moderate height of F0 averages in English and German and low height in Arabic (Pell et al. 2009). Contrary to the tendency for anger to have a faster speech rate (Murray and Arnott 1993), in Russian, anger has medium vowel durations. High intensity of anger in Russian is in common not only with other languages (Finnish and English), but also with vocalization by macaques (Leinonen et al. 2003).

Surprise

Experiments with other languages show that 'surprise' has the highest average F0 (Pell et al. 2009). This is not the case in Russian, where average F0 values in the utterances expressing surprise are higher than in neutral utterances, but lower than F0 values in utterances portraying happiness and anger.

Happiness

As in other languages (Pell et al. 2009; Gharavian et al. 2010), 'happiness' in Russian has a similarly high energy, but in contrast to some other languages, the vowel duration is relatively low.

IV.10. Limitations of the study

The results of the study have to be treated with caution because of a few limitations. First, the vowel group samples differed in size, since due to the accentual type of Russian, the recorded speech data had significantly more stressed vowels than accented, and more unstressed vowels than stressed. Second, as determined by the limitations of the analysis mechanisms and resources, our study did not include some acoustic parameters such as voice quality, that are known to be employed at least to some extent in the portrayal of emotional states (Gobl and Chisaide 2003).

V. Conclusion

Our study shows that vowel quality does contribute to the expression of emotive characteristics in Russian. All the examined acoustic parameters of vowels (duration, energy, F0, F0 derivative, power spectrum, formants and their bandwidths) contribute to the expression of affect. In the expression of affect in Russian, we find some similarities with other languages and even with primate communication, but we also observe some language-specific features.

The formant values obtained for stressed Russian vowels confirm the articulatory and acoustic descriptions of Russian vowels (Chistovich and Kozhevnikov 1965), however, the formant characteristics of /1/ suggest that it may be a half-close vowel.

Our research finds practical implications in speech synthesis and recognition. Our database RUSLANA is the only source of emotive speech database collections listed for Russian in a survey of emotional speech recognition by Ververidis and Kotropoulos (2006).

The results are limited by the number of subjects and segments employed. Further investigations of emotive characteristics of Russian speech conducted with a more diverse speech sample are necessary. Future research should also address the effect of acoustic parameters employed in this study on the perception of emotion by Russian listeners.

References

Anolli, L. and R. Ciceri. 2001. "The Voice of Emotions: Steps to a Semiosis of the Vocal Non-vocal Communication of Emotion." In C. Cavé, I. Guaïtella and S. Santi (eds), *Oralité et gestualité: Interactions et comportements multimodaux dans la communication*, 175–8. Paris: L'Harmattan.

Arnfield, S., P. Roach, J. Setter, P. Greasley and D. Horton. 1995. "Emotional Stress and Speech Tempo Variation." *Proceedings of the ESCA-NATO Tutorial and Research Workshop on Speech under Stress*, 13–15. Lisbon, Portugal.

Banse, R. and K. Scherer. 1996. "Acoustic Profiles in Vocal Emotion Expression." *Journal Personality Social Psychology* 70 (3): 614–36.

Batliner, A., K. Fischer, R. Huber, J. Spilker and E. Nöth. 2000. "Desperately Seeking Emotions Or: Actors, Wizards, and Human Beings." *Proceedings of the ISCA Workshop on Speech and Emotion: A Conceptual Framework for Research*, 195–200. Belfast, Northern Ireland.

Bazzanella, C. 2004. "Emotions, Language and Context." In E. Weigand (ed.), *Emotion in Dialogic Interaction: Advances in the Complex*, 55–72. Amsterdam: John Benjamins.

Beloshapkova, V. A. 1999. *Sovremennyj Russkij Jazyk*. Moscow: Azbukovnik.

Bitouk, D., R. Verma and A. Nenkova. 2010. "Class-Level Spectral Features for Emotion Recognition." *Speech Communication* 52: 613–25.

Bryzgunova, E. A. 1977. *Zvuki i intonacija russkoj rechi*. Moscow.

Caldognetto, E. M., P. Cosi, C. Drioli, G. Tisato and F. Cavicchio. 2004. "Modifications of Phonetic Labial Targets in Emotive Speech: Effects of the Co-production of Speech Emotions." *Speech Communication* 44 (1–4): 173–85.

Chistovich, L. A. and V. A. Kozhevnikov (eds). 1965. *Speech: Articulation and Perception* [In Russian]. Moscow: Nauka.

Chistovich, L. A., R. L. Sheikin and V. V. Lublinskaja. 1979. "'Centres of Gravity' and Spectral Peaks as the Determinants of Vowel Quality." In B. Lindblom and S. Öhman (eds), *Frontiers of Speech Communication Research*, 143–57. New York: Academic Press.

de Cheveigne, A. 1999. "Formant Bandwidth Affects the Identification of Competing Vowels." *Proceedings of the 14th International Congress of Phonetic Sciences*, 2093–6. San Francisco.

Cowie, R., E. Douglas-Cowie, G. Tsapatsoulis, G. Votsis, S. Kollias, W. Fellenz and J. Taylor. 2001. "Emotion Recognition in Human-Computer Interaction." *IEEE Signal Processing Magazine* 18 (1): 32–80.

Davitz, J. R. 1964. "Auditory Correlates of Vocal Expression of Emotional Meaning." In J. R. Davitz (ed.), *The Communication of Emotional Meaning*, 101–2. New York: McGraw-Hill.

Dietrich, S., H. Ackermann, D. P. Szameitat and K. Alter. 2006. "Psychoacoustic Studies on the Processing of Vocal Interjections: How to Disentangle Lexical and Prosodic Information?" *Progress in Brain Research* 156: 295–302.

Edwards, D. 1999. "Emotion Discourse." *Culture and Psychology* 5: 271–91.

Ekman, P. 1979. "About Brows: Emotional and Conversational Signals." In M. von Cranach, K. Foppa, W. Lepenies and D. Ploog (eds), *Human Ethology: Claims and Limits of a New Discipline: Contributions to the Colloquium*, 169–248. New York: Cambridge University Press.

Fernandez, R. 2004. "A Computational Model for the Automatic Recognition of Affect in Speech." PhD thesis, Massachusetts Institute of Technology, Cambridge, MA.

Fischer, K. and A. Batliner. 2000. "What Makes Speakers Angry in Human-Computer Conversation?" *Proceedings of the 3rd Workshop on Human-Computer Conversation*, 3–5. Bellagio, Italy.

Fonàgy, I. 1976. "La mimique buccale." *Phonetica* 33: 31–44.
France, D. J., R. G. Shiavi, S. Silverman, M. Silverman and M. Wilkes. 2000. "Acoustical Properties of Speech as Indicators of Depression and Suicidal Risk." *IEEE Transactions on Biomedical Engineering* 7: 829–37.
Gharavian, D., M. Sheikhan and M. Janipour. 2010. "Pitch in Emotional Speech and Emotional Speech Recognition using Pitch Frequency." *Majlesi Journal of Electrical Engineering* 4: 19–24.
Gobl, C. and A. N. Chasaide. 2003. "The Role of Voice Quality in Communicating Emotion, Mood and Attitude." *Speech Communication* 40: 189–212.
Cliff, G. and A. Wierzbicka (eds). 2002. *Meaning and Universal Grammar: Theory and Empirical Findings*, 2 vols. Amsterdam: John Benjamins.
Grimm, M., K. Kroschel, E. Mower and S. Narayanan. 2007. "Primitives-Based Evaluation and Estimation of Emotions in Speech." *Speech Communication* 49: 787–800.
Hyun, K. H., E. Kim and Y. K. Kwak. 2010. "Emotional Feature Extraction Method based on the Concentration of Phoneme Influence for Human-Robot Interaction." *Advanced Robotics* 24: 47–67.
Igarashi, Y. 2006. "Intonational Patterns in Russian Interrogatives." In Y. Kawaguchi, I. Fonágy and T. Moriguchi (eds), *Prosody and Syntax*, 175–96. Amsterdam: John Benjamins.
Iida, A. 2002. "A study on corpus-based speech synthesis with emotion." PhD thesis, Graduate School of Media and Governance, Keio University, Japan.
Iliev, A. I., M. S. Scordilis, J. P. Papa and A. X. Falcão. 2010. "Spoken Emotion Recognition through Optimum-Path Forest Classification Using Glottal Features." *Computer Speech and Language* 24: 445–60.
Imai, Y. 2007. "Collaborative learning for an EFL classroom: Emotions, language and communication." PhD thesis, University of Toronto.
Johnstone, T. and K. R. Scherer. 2000. "Vocal Communication of Emotion." In M. Lewis and J. M. Haviland-Jones (eds), *Handbook of Emotions*, 220–335. New York: Guildford.
Juslin, P. N. and P. Laukka. 2003. "Communication of Emotions in Vocal Expression and Music Performance: Different Channels, Same Code?" *Psychological Bulletin* 129: 770–814.
Kienast, M. and W. F. Sendlmeier. 2000. "Acoustical Analysis of Spectral and Temporal Changes in Emotional Speech." *Proceedings of the ISCA Workshop on Speech and Emotion: A Conceptual Framework for Research*, 92–7. Belfast, Northern Ireland.
Kouznetsov, V. B. 2002. "Spectral Dynamics and Classification of Russian Vowels." *Acoustical Physics* 48: 752–5.
Ladd, D. R. 2008. *Intonational Phonology*. 2nd ed. Cambridge: Cambridge University Press.
Leinonen, L., M.-L. Laakso, S. Carlson and I. Linnankoski. 2003. "Shared Means and Meanings in Vocal Expression of Man and Macaque." *Logoped Phoniatr Vocol* 28: 53–61.
Levontina, I. B. and A. A. Zalizniak. 2001. "Human Emotions Viewed through the Russian Language." In J. Harkins and A. Wierzbicka (eds), *Emotions in Crosslinguistic Perspective*, 291–336. Berlin: Mouton de Gruyter.
Lillard, A. 1998. "Ethnopsychologies: Cultural Variations in Theories of Mind." *Psychological Bulletin* 123 (1): 3–32.
Lutz, C. 1988. *Unnatural Emotions: Everyday Sentiments on a Micronesian Atoll and Their Challenge to Western Theory*. Chicago: University of Chicago Press.
Russell, J. A. 1991. "Culture and the Categorization of Emotions." *Psychological Bulletin* 110 (3): 426–50.

Makarova, V. 2000. "Acoustic Cues of Surprise in Russian Questions." *Journal of the Acoustical Society of Japan* [in English] 21 (5): 243–50.
Makarova, V. and V. A. Petrushin. 2002. "Ruslana: A Database of Russian Emotional Utterances." *Proceedings of the 7th International Conference on Spoken Language Processing*, 2041–4. Denver, CO.
——. 2009. "Tracing Emotions in Russian Vowels." *Proceedings of the 2009 Annual Conference of the Canadian Linguistic Association*, 15. Fredricton, New Brunswick.
McGilloway, S., R. Cowie, E. Douglas-Cowie, S. Gielen, M. Westerdijk and S. Strove. 2000. "Approaching Automatic Recognition of Emotion from Voice: A Rough Benchmark." *Proceedings of the ISCA Workshop on Speech and Emotion: A Conceptual Framework for Research*, 207–12. Belfast, Northern Ireland.
Min Lee, C. and S. S. Narayanan. 2005. "Toward Detecting Emotions in Spoken Dialogs." *IEEE Transactions on Speech and Audio Processing* 13 (2): 293–303.
Mozziconacci, S. 2001. "Emotion and Attitude Conveyed in Speech by Means of Prosody." *Proceedings of the 2nd Workshop on Attitude, Personality and Emotions in User-Adapted Interaction*, 1–10. Sonthofen, Germany.
Murray, I. and J. Arnott. 1993. "Toward the Simulation of Emotion in Synthetic Speech: A Review of the Literature on Human Vocal Emotion." *Journal of the Acoustic Society of America* 93: 1097–108.
——. 1996. "Synthesizing Emotions in Speech: Is it Time to get Excited?" *Proceedings of the 4th International Conference of Spoken Language Processing*, 1816–19. Philadelphia, PA.
Nordstrand, M., G. Svanfeldt, B. Granstrom and D. House. 2004. "Measurements of Articulatory Variation in Expressive Speech for a Set of Swedish Vowels." *Speech Communication* 44: 187–96.
Osgood, C. E., G. J. Suci and P. H. Tannenbaum. 1957. *The Measurement of Meaning*. Urbana: University of Illinois Press.
Paeschke, A. and W. F. Sendlmeier. 2000. "Prosodic Characteristics of Emotional Speech: Measurements of Fundamental Frequency Movements." *Proceedings of the ISCA Workshop on Speech and Emotion: A Conceptual Framework for Research*, 75–80. Belfast, Northern Ireland.
Pavlenko, A. 2005. *Emotions and Multilingualism*. Cambridge: Cambridge University Press.
Pell, M. D., S. Paulmann, C. Dara, A. Alasseri and S. A. Kotz. 2009. "Factors in the Recognition of Vocally Expressed Emotions: A Comparison of Four Languages." *Journal of Phonetics* 37: 417–35.
Petrushin, V. 2002. "Creating Emotion Recognition Agents for Speech Signal." In K. Dautenhahn, A. H. Bond, L. Canamero and B. Edmonds (eds), *Socially Intelligent Agents. Creating Relationships with Computers and Robots*, 77–84. New York: Kluwer Academic Publishers.
Picard, R. 1997. *Affective Computing*. Cambridge, MA: MIT Press.
Plutchik, R. 1980. *Emotion: A Psychoevolutionary Synthesis*. New York: Harper and Row.
Scherer, K. R. 1989. "Vocal Measurement of Emotion." In R. Plutchik and H. Kellerman (eds), *Emotion: Theory, Research and Experience*, vol. 4, 233–59. San Diego: Academic Press.
——. 2000. "Psychological Models of Emotion." In J. C. Borod (ed.), *The Neuropsychology of Emotion*, 137–62. Oxford: Oxford University Press.
——. 2003. "Vocal Communication of Emotions: A Review of Research Paradigms." *Speech Communication* 40: 227–56.
Scherer, K. R., R. Banse and H. G. Wallbott. 2001. "Emotion Inferences from Vocal Expression Correlate across Languages and Cultures." *Journal of Cross-Cultural Psychology* 32 (1): 76–92.

Stibbard, R. 2000. "Automated Extraction of ToBI Annotation Data from the Reasing/Leeds Emotional Speech Corpus." In R. Cowie, E. Douglas-Cowie and M. Schroder (eds), *Proceedings of the ISCA Worshop on Speech and Emotion: A Conceptual Framework for Research*, 60–5. Belfast: Queen's Univeristy.

Svetozarova, N. D. 1998. "Intonation in Russian." In D. Hirst and A. Di Cristo (eds), *Intonational Systems*, 261–74. Cambridge: Cambridge University Press.

Szameitat, D. P., K. Alter, A. J. Szameitat, D. Wildgruber, A. Sterr and C. J. Darwin. 2009. "Acoustic Profiles of Distinct Emotional Expressions in Laughter." *Journal of the Acoustical Society of America* 126 (1): 354–66.

Toivanen, J., T. Waaramaa, P. Alku, A.-M. Laukkanen, T. Seppanen, E. Vayrynen and M. Airas. 2006. "Emotion in [a]: A Perceptual and Acoustic Study." *Logopedics Phoniatrics Vocology* 31: 43–8.

Ververidis, D. and C. Kotropoulos. 2006. "Emotional Speech Recognition: Resources, Features and Methods." *Speech Communication* 48: 1162–81.

Waaramaa, T., P. Alku and A.-M. Laukkanen. 2006. "The Role of F3 in the Vocal Expression of Emotions." *Logopedics Phoniatrics Vocology* 31: 153–6.

Wierzbicka, A. 1997. *Understanding Cultures through Their Key Words: English, Russian, Polish, German and Japanese*. Oxford: Oxford University Press.

Wilde, O. 1891. *The Picture of Dorian Gray*. Retrieved from Project Gutenberg. Online: http://www.gutenberg.org/etext/174 (accessed 19 January 2012).

Zervas, P., I. Mporas, N. Fakotakis and G. Kokkinakis. 2007. "Evaluation Intonational Features for Emotion Recognition in Speech." *International Journal on Artificial Intelligence Tools* 16: 1001–14.

Chapter 2

PHONOLOGY. VOWEL–ZERO ALTERNATIONS IN RUSSIAN PREPOSITIONS: PROSODIC CONSTITUENCY AND PRODUCTIVITY

Lev Blumenfeld
Carleton University

I. Introduction

Many Russian prepositions have two realizations, with and without the final vowel. For example, *s* 'with,' *k* 'to' and *iz* 'from' sometimes appear as *so*, *ko*, and *izo*, respectively. Sometimes only the consonant-final variant is possible, such as *v(*o) dome* 'in the house,' *s(*o) drugom* 'with a friend,' etc. Sometimes, both versions are acceptable: *v(o) sne* 'in sleep/dream,' *s(o) množestvom* 'with many.' In some cases, the variant with the final vowel predominates, such as *ko mne* 'to me,' *so mnoj* 'with me.'

In this chapter, I investigate the conditions determining the choice between the variants with and without the vowel *-o* (which surfaces as either [a] or [ə], and is called a "*yer*," as explained below), and relate those conditions to syntactic and semantic factors, as well as to other aspects of Russian phonology, most notably the behavior of stress.

The discussion below is couched in standard generative phonology (Halle 1959; Chomsky and Halle 1968; Lightner 1972). In this framework, underlying (phonemic) forms are related to surface forms via a series of transformations, also known as rules or processes, which affect the features and segments of the representations. The standard Chomsky-Halle framework is enriched by the theory of prosodic hierarchy (Selkirk 1984; Hayes 1989). The sequence of segments is understood to form a hierarchy of constituents of progressively increasing size – syllable, stress foot, prosodic word, and phrase. In this chapter, only syllables and prosodic words will be relevant.

The choice of the theoretical framework is made for expository convenience. The facts discussed below can be easily accommodated in another theory, although the details of their interpretations might be different. With these theoretical preliminaries in place, let me turn to a more detailed description of the problem presented by Russian prepositions.

Before turning to the choice between the prepositions with and without vowels, it is necessary to establish the prosodic structure of preposition-noun sequences, and sequences of prefixes and verbs, which behave similarly. Evidence for these structures is contradictory (Matushansky 2001; Steriopolo 2007; Gribanova 2009, 2010). Some processes that apply across the boundary between a preposition or prefix and the following word diagnose it as a word boundary, while other processes diagnose no prosodic boundary at that location. This contradiction can be called the "Cliticization Paradox," explained in detail in Section I.1 below.

Secondly, there is evidence both for and against the notion that prepositions and verbal prefixes – which are largely homophonous and have a common historical source – have identical prosodic structure and phonological behavior. I will refer to this problem as the "Unity Paradox." In particular, vowel reduction, devoicing and palatalization apply in the same way across a preposition-noun boundary as they do across a prefix-verb boundary (Matushansky 2001). On the other hand, the vowel–zero alternation known as *yer* realization appears to distinguish the two categories (Gribanova 2009).

The key to solving the paradoxes is that the empirical complexity of the *yer* facts have been underappreciated in the literature. Here I take a closer look at the data on *yer* realization with prepositions, using both the Russian National Corpus (RNS) and Google.[1] Once the facts are sorted out, and once the intricate phonotactic, syntactic and lexical factors that affect *yer* realization are brought to light, it is possible to resolve the two paradoxes by inferring the correct prosodic representation of the structures involving prefixes and prepositions.

As I show, all of these conditions point to the existence of two types of preposition-noun and prefix-verb groups whose prosodic structure is shown in (1)a and (1)b. The choice between them depends on syntactic and lexical grounds, and the phonological behavior of *yer* realization and other processes

---

[1] Data and statistics from the RNS were collected using manual searches of the entire corpus. Google was used to approximate the statistical distribution of variants (see below); the numbers in the tables in this chapter represent Google's reported number of occurrences using manual searches of the entire Internet. Individual examples reported in this chapter were selected from the top results of the searches in the RNS or Google.

follow from prosodic structure. As I will argue below, establishing the correct prosodic structure will lead to a resolution of the Unity Paradox.

(1)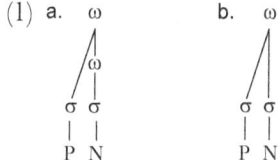

The starting point of the discussion in Section I is the claim by Matushansky (2001) that verbal prefixes and prepositions share many phonological characteristics and the contrary claim by Gribanova (2009) that they are distinguished by the behavior of the *yers*. In the remainder of this section I lay out the arguments showing the phonological unity of the two categories, and show that both prefixes and prepositions form a prosodic unit with the following word. In Section 2 I turn to *yer* realization, which has been claimed to distinguish prefixes from prepositions phonologically. I show the difference between lexical and phonotactic versions of that process and argue that it applies only in a lexically restricted set of cases. The key proposal of the chapter is found at the end of Section II, where I sketch out the analysis of *yer* realization in prepositions. Section III summarizes the facts of the so-called rule of stress retraction, whose behavior parallels that of *yers* in relevant ways. In Section IV, I argue that the behavior of *yers* and of stress retraction in verbal prefixes, while superficially dissimilar to that of prepositions, shows the same characteristics, and must be analyzed in the same way, vindicating the phonological unity of prefixes and prepositions.

Before proceeding, a word is in order on the nature of the data. While the focus of the investigation is the standard Moscow dialect, as described in prescriptive manuals such as Avanesov (1968), and used by native speakers, certain practical idealizations have been made. These idealizations are standard in generative linguistics, and do not generally undermine the soundness of the conclusions. First, no distinction is assumed between 'spoken' and 'written' versions of the language as far as the factors under investigations are concerned. This is, of course, a simplification, but a necessary one, given that all of the data comes from corpora that comprise both written language and transcriptions of speech. Secondly, the speech community of the corpus is assumed to be dialectally homogeneous. That this is an idealization will become especially clear below once the variable nature of the data comes to light, but one that is not damning, given the size of the corpus and the clarity of the tendencies that are discussed in this chapter.

I.1. Diagnostics of phonological wordhood: Prepositions and prefixes

There are a number of diagnostics of phonological wordhood that suggest that both verbal prefixes and prepositions are cliticized to the following words and that the two categories, even though they are distinct syntactically, behave in a phonologically identical way (Matushansky 2001).

I will start with prefixes. Most basically, the prefix-stem complex is assigned a single stress. Final devoicing does not apply to the prefix-final Cs (2)a but does devoice word-final consonants in the identical environment in (2)b (here and below, consonants and vowels are denoted as C and V, respectively).

(2) a. /pod-igratʲ/ → podygratʲ 'play into someone's hands'
    b. /rod # igry/ → rot ygry 'type of play'

Vowel reduction also treats the prefix-verb complex as a single word. In Standard Russian, unstressed /o/ and /a/ surface as [a] either when word-initial or when a stressed syllable follows in the same phonological word, and surface as [ə] elsewhere (Avanesov 1968). The boundary between the prefix and the stem is not treated as a word boundary by this rule, because prefix vowels which precede a stressed syllable (pretonic vowels) come out as [a] (3)a, in contrast to pretonic vowels in the preceding phonological word, which are [ə] (3)b.

(3) a. /pod-lézʲtʲ/ → padlézʲtʲ 'climb up to'
    b. /górəd # ómsk/ → górəd # ómsk 'the city of Omsk'

Likewise, the stem-initial vowel in a prefixed verb does not count as word-initial for the purposes of reduction and its vowel surfaces as [ə], not [a], as the following illustrates.

(4) a. /ostorožničatʲ/ → astaróžničatʲ 'behave carefully.$_{IMPF}$'
    b. /s-ostorožničatʲ/ → səstaróžničatʲ 'behave carefully.$_{PF}$'

The final diagnostic for wordhood is the behavior of the second-position clitic *že*, which normally attaches after the first phonological word of the phrase. Clearly, *že* is never inserted after a prefix in the middle of a prefixed verb, which once again confirms that prefixes are not words.

The diagnostics mentioned above behave identically for the unit formed by a preposition and the following word. Only one stress is assigned to the sequence. Final devoicing does not apply to the preposition (5)a. The reduction rule treats the preposition as part of the following phonological word, because its vowel, when pretonic, is realized as [a] (5)b. The word-initial vowel, which normally surfaces as [a] when unstressed, is not treated as word-initial when preceded by a preposition (5)c. Finally, the second-position clitic *že* cannot be inserted between a preposition and the following noun (5)d.

(5) a. /iz okon/ → iz ókon 'from windows' (final devoicing)
b. /pod óknami/ → pad óknəmi 'under windows' (pretonic reduction)
c. /oguréc/ → aguréc 'cucumber' (word-initial reduction)
 /s ogurcóm/ → s əgurcóm 'with a cucumber'
d. na léto že 'but for the summer' *na že léto (2nd position clitic)

In sum, the diagnostics suggest that both prefixes and prepositions form part of the phonological word with the following material and that the two categories behave alike. Following Gribanova (2009), I will refer to this unified phonological category as "P."

However, there are at least two processes which diagnose the boundary between a prefix or preposition and the following word as a full word boundary. The behavior of underlying /Ci/ sequences is sensitive to the type of boundary separating the consonant *C* and the following vowel *i*. Within words, the outcome depends on whether the consonant in question is a velar and on the identity of the suffix to which the vowel belongs. For velars, the outcome of word-internal /Ki/ (where /K/ is any velar) is different from what happens across words. Before suffixes the velar is palatalized, resulting in [kʲi], while between words the vowel is backed, resulting in [ky].

For verbal prefixes, the behavior of the boundary cannot be ascertained because there are no prefixes ending in a velar. Prefixes which end in other consonants condition backing of the following vowel, not palatalization of the final consonant of the prefix, as evident from the example in (2)a above.

The one velar-final preposition *k*, however, unambiguously behaves like a separate word because it conditions backing of the following vowel.

(6) a. /k ide/ → k yde 'to Ida'
b. /k igre/ → k ygre 'to a game'

The second diagnostic that suggests a word boundary between a prefix or preposition and the following word is hiatus resolution, i.e., what happens when two vowels become adjacent to each other. Word-internally, hiatus is resolved by deleting the first vowel (7)a, but it is tolerated across word boundaries (7)b. Both prefixes and prepositions fail to lose their vowel when attached to vowel-initial words (7)c.

(7) a. /palʲto-iško/ → palʲtʲiško 'coat.$_{DIM}$'
b. /palʲto iry/ → palʲto Iry 'Ira's coat'

c. /po-igratʲ/ → poigratʲ 'play for some time'
d. /na obed/ → na obed 'for dinner'

The evidence from backing and hiatus resolution is consistent with the phonological unity of P, but appears to contradict the conclusion that P and following hosts form a single prosodic word. This paradox can be solved by appealing to other phonological pressures that prevent palatalization and hiatus resolution from applying across the P-stem boundary.

For palatalization, the simplest solution is to assume that all the consonants at the ends of prepositions are [+back] in their underlying form, and this feature protects the consonant from palatalizing. Some have objected that it is an accident that all prepositions seem to have such a feature – a richness of the base problem (Gouskova 2012). Such an objection carries little weight, however, because the *only* preposition that requires such underlying specification of [+back] is the velar *k*.

As for hiatus-resolving vowel deletion, it is plausible that the rule does not in fact exist at all (Gouskova 2010). Not only does it fail to apply within words, but the examples commonly cited in support of the hiatus resolution like (7)a have an alternative analysis: the final -*o* might be treated as a morpheme, not part of the stem.

Finally, it is important that the phonological unity of P and the host is supported by the most productive phonological rules of Russian, such as final devoicing and vowel reduction.

A supporting piece of evidence for the treatment of P as phonologically unified with the following item is that the class of prepositions which behaves as described above is defined prosodically, not syntactically. There are stressed prepositions which behave like separate phonological words, e.g. *ókolo* 'near,' *méždu* 'between,' *vokrúg* 'around.' They bear their own stress, in addition to the stress of their complement; they undergo final devoicing (8)a; they behave as a separate domain for vowel reduction, in that their final vowel surfaces as [ə] even when pretonic and the initial vowel of the following word counts as word-initial (8)b; finally, a second-position clitic can be inserted between a stressed preposition and the following word (8)c.

(8) a. /vokrúg dóma/ → vakruk dóma 'around the house' (final devoicing)
b. /ókolo dóma/ → ókələ dóma 'near the house' (pretonic reduction)
/vokrúg ogurcóv/ → vakrúk agurcóv 'around cucumbers' (word-initial reduction)
c. vokrúg že ogurcóv 'but around cucumbers' (2nd position clitic)

Another behavior that distinguishes stressed from unstressed prepositions is the inability of the latter to stand on their own, without a following word (9)a, in contrast to stressed prepositions (9)b.

(9) a. *v ili iz   'in or out'
    b. ókolo ili méždu   'near or between'

All these behaviors point to the phonological unity of P, and to the prosodification of P with the following word.

II. *Yer* Realization

II.1. Introduction

Gribanova (2009) argues that despite the apparent unity of P, the process of *yer* realization (YR) distinguishes prefixes from prepositions phonologically.

YR involves vowel–Ø alternations that have their origin in the fall of the Common Slavic short vowels *ŭ* and *ĭ*, called *yers*. By a sound change known as Havlík's Law, a *yer* lowers to *o* or *e* if the following syllable contains a *yer*, iteratively right-to-left. All *yers* unaffected by lowering get deleted (see e.g., Borkovsky and Kuznetsov 1965; V. Kiparsky 1979). Havlík's Law deposited vowel–Ø alternations in the synchronic grammar of Russian, as illustrated in the following examples. The *yer* may be in the root (10)a, or it may be the final sound of a prefix or a preposition (10)b.

		OLD RUSSIAN	RUSSIAN	
(10) a.	Root alternations	rŭt-ŭ	rot	'mouth.$_{\text{NOM/ACC}}$'
		rŭt-a	rt-a	'mouth.$_{\text{GEN}}$'
b.	Prepositions	vŭ rŭt-ŭ	v rot	'into mouth.$_{\text{ACC}}$'
		vŭ rŭt-u	vo rtu	'in mouth.$_{\text{LOC}}$'
c.	Prefixes	podŭ-žĭg-l-ŭ	pod-žog	'kindled.$_{\text{MASC.PST}}$'
		podŭ-žĭg-l-a	podo-žg-l-a	'kindled.$_{\text{FEM.PST}}$'

Based on Havlík's Law, it is expected that a P-final *yer* should be realized whenever the P attaches to a root containing a *yer* which is itself not realized. In other words, YR in P is conditional upon attaching to the zero alternant of a morpheme with a V–Ø alternation.[2]

---

[2] The analysis of YR as a synchronic rule has a long tradition in generative phonology. See Halle (1959); Lightner (1972); Matushansky (2001).

This expectation is generally borne out for prefix-verb sequences, but not for preposition-noun ones. The data below show that YR applies before some nouns (11)a, but not before others of similar structure (11)b.

(11) a. son   'sleep.$_{NOM}$'   vo sne   'in sleep.$_{LOC}$'
     denʲ   'day.$_{NOM}$'   ko dnʲu   'to day.$_{DAT}$'
     vesʲ   'all.$_{NOM}$'   so vsem   'with all.$_{INSTR}$'
     rot   'mouth.$_{NOM}$'   izo rta   'from mouth.$_{GEN}$'
  b. penʲ   'tree.stump.$_{NOM}$'   s pnʲa   'from tree.stump.$_{GEN}$'
     pʲos   'dog.$_{NOM}$'   k psu   'to dog.$_{DAT}$'
     lʲon   'flax.$_{NOM}$'   iz lʲna   'from flax.$_{GEN}$'

In addition to nearly exceptionless failure of YR on the preposition in examples such as *s pnʲa*, there is much inter- and intra-speaker variability (Steriopolo 2007; Gribanova 2009; see also Eskova 2000). Such failure of YR and variability are absent at the prefix-verb juncture, which leads Gribanova (2009) to conclude that prefixes and prepositions are phonologically different, and attach in different levels in Gribanova's serial framework.

In what follows I will explore the underpinnings of the variability and exceptions to YR in prepositions and show that the distribution of variants with and without YR is systematic. The facts, together with their analysis in terms of the prosodic structure of the P-noun complex, support the claim that prefixes and prepositions are phonologically unified.

II.2. Phonotactic and lexical YR

One of the difficulties with synchronic YR in prepositions is that phonotactics influences it, but does not completely determine the outcome. The core phonotactic generalization is that sequences *ss*, *vv* and *sv* are avoided word-initially when a consonant follows. If the preposition *s* or *v* is attached to a word beginning with a *sC* or *vC* cluster, YR applies to break up the cluster (Matushansky 2001, Steriopolo 2007). This happens even when there is no V–Ø alternation in the stem, as in the following examples.

(12) *#ssC   *#vvC   *#svC
      so sredstvom 'with means'   vo vrede 'in harm'   so vredom
                                                                    'with harm'
      so starikom 'with an old man'   vo vpadine 'in hole'   so vpadinoj
                                                                    'with hole'

In addition, YR may occur before clusters where sonority increases toward the nucleus, against the Sonority Sequencing Principle (the SSP; Clements 1990), such as the ones consisting of a liquid and an obstruent.

In order to verify these claims, I gathered data from the Google corpus, i.e., the corpus that comprises the Russian portion of the Internet (searches performed in November 2010).[3] The following table contains the frequency of YR across the phonotactic contexts and in three monoconsonantal prepositions. Each cell of the table corresponds to the cluster type at the beginning of the noun to which the preposition attaches. The first consonant of that cluster is indicated by the row and the second consonant by the column. I selected two or three words of each type for the search. For example, in the *labial fricative-stop* cell, I searched for prepositional phrases containing *vdova* 'widow,' *vpadina* 'crevasse' and *vdox* 'inhalation.' The full list of words searched is shown in this chapter's appendix. The three numbers in each cell show the averaged frequency of YR for all the words of that type with the monoconsonantal prepositions *s*, *v* and *k*. Thus, for example, the average rate of YR for the three words just cited is 65.4 percent with *s*, 87.8 percent with *v* and 3.17 percent with *k*.

Cells where data are impossible to collect are shaded (for example, there are no words beginning with velar fricatives followed by stops). Some cells are pooled together, such as those where the first consonant is a liquid, because there are not enough words exemplifying individual cluster types.

(13)

	Stop	Coronal fricative	Velar fricative	Labial fricative	Nasal	Liquid	
Stop	0.35	1.63		0.17	0.05	0.15	*s*
	0.97	0.06		1.84	0.02	0.61	*v*
	0.26	0.08		2.37	0.17	0.22	*k*
Cor.fr.	99.2	31.0	97.3	96.8	98.9	96.9	*s*
	0.1	0.07	0.01	0.44	0.09	0.14	*v*
	0.18	0.13	0.02	0.82	0.16	0.07	*k*
Vel.fr.				0.1	3.98	0.16	*s*
				0.08	0.45	0.59	*v*
				0.23	2.42	0.16	*k*
Lab.fr	65.4	93.0		1.19	41.09	1.77	*s*
	87.8	98.5		60.87	96.05	98.11	*v*
	3.17	11.97		2.14	9.81	0.55	*k*
Nasal					0.8	4.1	*s*
					(92.45)	15.42	*v*
					2.69	6.88	*k*
Liquid	32.31						*s*
	16.62						*v*
	6.14						*k*

---

[3] The limitations of using Google as a corpus are too well known to rehearse here. Yet its use here is justified, because for the purpose of getting a rough picture of the statistical tendencies of YR in various contexts, Google's weaknesses are outweighed by its chief strength – its size.

The table generally corroborates the standard claims: that the clusters in (12) condition YR, and that sonority-violating clusters condition optional YR. One exception is the low frequency of YR in *s+ss* sequences (31 percent, compared to nearly obligatory YR in other #*s+sC* clusters). Also, contrary to the standard claims, the clusters beginning with *v* do not cause the preceding *s* to be realized with a *yer* when a liquid or another labial follows.

The abnormally high frequency of YR in *v* + nasal + nasal context, parenthesized in the table, is due to the idiom *sojtis^j vo mnenii* 'agree,' which is so frequent that it drowns out the general pattern of lack of YR in that phonological context.

A plausible analysis of the pattern makes use of syllable structure. Consonants in the syllable margin which violate sonority sequencing are not part of the syllable itself, but are adjoined to it at the level of the foot or the prosodic word (the so-called syllable appendix) (Green 2003; Kiparsky 2003; Steriopolo 2007). In Steriopolo's (2007) analysis, the pattern in (13) results from constraints that prohibit a complex appendix, high-ranked for appendices consisting of two fricatives, and lower-ranked for other appendices.

The following figure illustrates the structure of a phrase such as *s straxom* 'with fear,' where YR applies to yield *so straxom*. Since the *s* of the stem violates sonority sequencing, it is not parsed as part of the initial syllable, but adjoined to it at the higher level. The preposition *s* also must form part of the syllable appendix. The high-ranked constraint against two-fricative appendices forces YR. (O, N and C stand for 'onset,' 'nucleus' and 'coda,' respectively).

The fact that the preposition *iz* does not exhibit YR under the circumstances illustrated in (13) corroborates the analysis: its final consonant can form a coda of the preceding syllable and thus does not render complex the appendix of the following syllable. I refer the reader to Steriopolo (2007), where this analysis is spelled out in more detail.

However, not all instances of YR are phonotactically motivated; in (11)a, for example, *izo rta* and *ko dn^{j}u* are not, in terms of (13). I will call the version of YR that applies in such cases 'lexical.' It applies to prepositions before roots with V–Ø alternations, as would be expected from a synchronic reflex of Havlík's Law. As mentioned above, not all words with the *yer* alternation in the root condition YR in the preposition. In the following table I placed the

Figure 2.1. Syllable structure of a phrase *s straxom* (with fear)

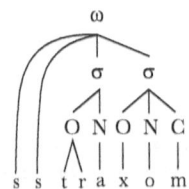

CVC items that could potentially condition YR on the preposition, i.e., those that have V–Ø alternations. They are placed in the cells that correspond to the initial two consonants in the zero alternant, e.g. *pʲos* 'dog' (genitive *psa*) is in the *stop-coronal fricative* cell of the table. The items that in fact undergo YR with significant frequency are shaded.

(14)

	Stop	Coronal fricative	Velar fricative	Labial fricative	Nasal	Liquid
Stop		pʲos			denʲ, penʲ, tʲma	
Cor.fr.				šov	son	
Vel.fr.						zlo
Lab.fr.		vesʲ	vošʲ			
Nasal			mox		1SG *mne, mnoj*	
Liquid	lʲod, lob, rot			lev, rov	lʲon	

This table shows that lexical YR is distinct from phonotactic YR. There are words like *denʲ* and *tʲma* which have a structure that does not cause phonotactic YR, but the prepositions before these nouns are still often realized with a *yer*. The pattern is truly lexical: *denʲ* and *penʲ* have similar stop + nasal clusters, but are at the opposite extremes with respect to YR: the former conditions it frequently, the latter almost never. Another distinction between the two versions of YR is that lexical YR applies not only to the monoconsonantal prepositions *s*, *v* and *k*, but also to *iz* and *ot*, e.g., *izo rta* 'from the mouth' and *oto sna* 'from sleep.'

In this respect, verbs are not different from nouns: they show both phonotactic and lexical YR. The phonotactic factors in verbs are the same and cause obligatory prefixal YR. Verbs like *so-svatatʲ* 'match (for marriage),' *vo-vleč* 'drag into' and *so-vratitʲ* 'lead into temptation' have no V–Ø alternations in the stem and thus provide no motivation for YR in the prefix, but it still applies due to the constraints in (12).

Even though both phonotactic and lexical YR apply in verbal prefixes, they lack the variability characteristic of prepositional YR. In the following sections I show that at least some of this variability is not random, but is due to syntactic restrictions on YR.

II.3. Restrictions on YR

II.3.1. Lexical splits

The clearest set of facts that demonstrate the influence of the lexicon are lexical splits, homophones which behave differently with respect to YR. Gribanova (2009) pointed out the example of *množestvo*, when meaning 'many' the word conditions YR, but when meaning 'mathematical set' it does not. Nearly all of the examples of *v množestve* in the Russian National Corpus (RNC) refer to the mathematical concept.

In some cases, the lexical split is not as clear. One example is the behavior of *vvod*, which can mean 'bringing in troops,' or 'enter(ing)' in the computer context. The following table shows the highly significant difference in YR in *v(o) vvode voisk* 'in bringing in troops,' where it is relatively more likely, compared to *v(o) vvode parolʲa* 'in entering the password,' where it is less likely.

(15) Google data

	voisk	parolʲa
v vvode	3580	2470
vo vvode	8910	1280

$c^2 = 1706.15$; $p < 0.0001$

In both cases, the newer form – *množestvo* 'mathematical set,' *vvod* 'enter' – are less likely to condition YR. This indicates loss of productivity of the process; newly coined items are less likely to undergo it than established items.

Sometimes the forms with YR are parts of fixed idioms, like earlier mentioned *sojtisʲ vo mnenii* 'agree,' which skewed the statistics in (13). The idiomatic nature of this expression can be seen in the following data from the RNC, which shows that YR in that phrase is nearly obligatory, while it is far from being so in the general case.

(16) RNC data

	YR	no YR
v(o) mnenii	390	141
soitisʲ v(o) mnenii	43	1

In other words, these examples can be thought of as (partial) idioms. The phrase with YR is restricted to a special meaning. For a more detailed discussion of lexical aspects of YR in prepositions, see Eskova (2000).

II.3.2. Non-complements

YR does not apply indiscriminately any time a potential trigger follows a potential target but is favored in a narrow set of syntactic environments. Most basically, YR is more likely to occur when the triggering noun is the complement of the target preposition. For example, the forms of the 1SG pronoun require YR on the preceding monoconsonantal preposition (17)a. However, when the same form of the pronoun is the complement of some other word, YR does not apply (17)b. The corpus example in (17)e illustrates the same effect.

(17) a. k*(o) mne   'to me'
     v*(o) mne   'in me'
     s*(o) mnoj   'with me'

   b. k(*o) mne   neizvestnomu   čeloveku
     to I.$_{DAT}$ unknown.$_{DAT}$ person.$_{DAT}$
     'to a person unknown to me'

   c. v(*o) mne   neizvestnom   gorode
     in I.$_{DAT}$ unknown.$_{LOC}$ city.$_{LOC}$
     'in a city unknown to me'

   d. s(*o) mnoj   interesujuščimsja   čelovekom
     with me.$_{INST}$ taking.interest.$_{INST}$ person.$_{INST}$
     'with a person who takes interest in me'

   e. posle "Emblematiki", nesoveršennogo skolka k mne jasnoj teorii
     after   *Emblematics*   imperfect   replica to I.$_{DAT}$ clear.$_{DAT}$ theory.$_{DAT}$
     'after *Emblematics*, an imperfect replica of a theory that was clear to me'
                         (A. Bely, "Why I Became a Symbolist")

This constraint is nearly obligatory for lexical YR. In phonotactic YR the effect is weaker, as in the word *vs^{j}o* 'all,' which is eligible for phonotactic YR with all three monoconsonantal prepositions. The Google corpus contains examples with and without YR, two of which are shown below. In these cases, *vs^{j}o* is not the complement of the preposition, but of the following participle.

(18) a. pros^{j}ba   k   vs^{j}o   znajuščim   i   vs^{j}o   umejuščim
     request   to   all.$_{ACC}$ knowing.$_{DAT}$ and   all.$_{ACC}$ capable.$_{DAT}$
     'a request to those who know everything and are capable of doing everything'

   b. obraščajus^j ko   vs^{j}o   znajuščim
     address.I$_{SG}$ to   all.$_{ACC}$ knowing.$_{DAT}$
     'I address those who know everything'

A special case of this effect is that lexical YR fails to apply in front of quoted material, while phonotactic YR variably applies in such circumstances.

(19) a. videla   ego   v   "vdove blanko"
        see.PST.FEM   him   in   *La viuda de Blanco*
        'I saw him in *La viuda de Blanco*'

   b. v(o) "Sne Nikanora Ivanoviča"
      'in "Nikanor Ivanovič's dream"'

In (19)a, YR fails to apply before a quotation despite the phonotactic conditions that favor it. The example (19)b. refers to a well-known and often mentioned chapter in Bulgakov's novel *The Master and Margarita*. The title of this chapter begins with the word 'dream' and thus the preposition before it is eligible for YR. The following statistics from Google compare the frequency of YR before *sne* 'dream.$_{LOC}$' in general with that before *sne Nikanora* and show that YR is much less frequent when the preposition precedes quoted material.

(20) Google data

	sne	*sne nikanora*
v	41000	72 (0.18%)
vo	3060000	2370 (0.08%)

$c^2 = 48.18; p < 0.0001$

The RNC is too small to carry out the same comparison, but the same effect can be seen by comparing YR frequency in the general case with that the context where *sne* precedes any personal name.

(21) RNC data

	sne	*sne*+name
v	42	15
vo	6076	210

Fisher's exact, $p < 0.0001$

The upshot of this section is that the best circumstances for YR are those where the structure is the most basic: a P followed by its complement N.

II.3.3. Non-transparent prepositional semantics

Not only the structure but also the meaning of sequences undergoing YR is restricted. Prepositions whose spatial or temporal semantics is transparent are more likely to undergo YR than those which are idiosyncratically selected by the verb. Consider the sequence v(o) sne 'in sleep/dream.' If the preposition v has a locative meaning, the *yer* is nearly obligatory. When the same preposition is selected by a verb such as 'need' or 'lose faith,' the *yer* is either problematic or impossible, as the following data illustrate.

(22) a. videtʲ v*(o) sne 'see in a dream'
videtʲ v*(o) tʲme 'see in the darkness'

b. delatʲ čto-l. v*(o) sne 'do something in a dream'
delatʲ čto-l. v*(o) tʲme 'do something in darkness'

c. nuždatʲsʲa v(ʔo) sne 'need sleep/dream'
nuždatʲsʲa v(*o) tʲme 'need darkness'
razuveritʲsʲa v(ʔo) sne 'lose faith in the dream'
preuspvatʲ v(ʔo) sne 'excel at sleeping'
zaklʲučatʲsʲa v(ʔo) sne 'to be the matter of sleep'

The following corpus evidence supports this claim. Generally, the sequence v(o) sne is realized without a *yer* about 0.3 percent of the time. But when it is the object of the verb *need*, that figure rises to 35 percent, a highly significant difference.

(23) Google data

	sne	vidit v(o)sne 'sees in dream'	nuždaetsja v(o) sne 'needs sleep'
v	30,900	2160	12,100
vo	10,400,000	767,000	22,300
%v	0.3%	0.28%	35%

Non-transparent ("quirky") prepositions favor *yer*-less forms

II.3.4. Possession

The next factor influencing YR involves the possessor of the complement noun. Consider the following two examples. The choice of *yer*-ful form of the preposition *vo*, but not the *yer*-less *v*, necessitates the interpretation of its object as possessed by the syntactic binder of the noun, in these cases the subject of the sentence.

(24) a. Petja letaet vo sne
    P   flies in dream
    'Peter flies in (his own) dream'

b. Petja letaet v sne
    P   flies in dream
    'Peter flies in (someone else's) dream'

RNC examples of *v sne* are rare, but support this claim.

(25) a. dit'o   plačet   **v sne**   Dmitrija
    child   cries   in dream   Dmitry.$_{GEN}$
    'a child is crying in Dmitry's dream'
                    (Bakhtin, *Problems of Dostoevsky's Poetics*)

b. Vjačiku xotelos' kak možno dol'še ostavat's'a **v sne** Gul'nary
    Vjačik wanted as-long-as-possible remain in dream Gulnara.$_{GEN}$
    'Vjačik wanted to stay in Gulnara's dream as long as possible'

The effect is also found with the nouns *rot* 'mouth' and *lob* 'forehead.'

(26) a. Pet'a vynul   izo   rta   šarik.
    P   removed from mouth   ball.$_{DIM}$
    'Peter took out a ball from (his own) mouth'

b. Pet'a vynul   iz   rta   šarik.
    'Peter took out a ball from (possibly someone else's) mouth'

(27) a. Pet'a našel   vo   rtu   šarik.
    P   found   in   mouth   ball.$_{DIM}$
    'Peter found a ball in (his own) mouth'

b. ?Pet'a našel   v   rtu   šarik.
    P   found   in   mouth   ball.$_{DIM}$
    'Peter found a ball in (possibly someone else's) mouth'

A consequence of this effect is that *v rtu* 'in mouth,' *iz rta* 'from mouth' and other similar phrases are strongly favored in the context of dead bodies, statues and more generally, individuals other than the subject of the phrase with the preposition. This effect is supported by corpus evidence. In the RNC the sequence *v rtu* refers mostly to dead bodies, as the following examples show.

(28) a. U mʲortvyx naxodili **v rtu** seno
'They found hay in dead people's mouths'

b. trup zaxripel, **iz rta** vypolzla černaja, kak smertʲ, slʲuna
'The dead body wheezed, and saliva, black as death, crept from its mouth'

c. **iz rta** Puruši voznikli žrecy (braxmany), iz ruk – voinskoe soslovie (kšatrii)
'Priests (brahmins) were created from Purusha's mouth; warriors (kshatriyas) from his hands'

d. vypuskanie ognʲa **iz rta** […] vovse ne est nečto, svojstvennoe tolko skazke
'letting out fire from the mouth […] is not something that occurs only in folk tales' (Propp, *Morphology of the Folk Tale*)

e. šnuroček tolʲko čudesnyj, kak makaronina, visit **iz rta** puški
'only a lovely string, like a strand of spaghetti, hangs from the cannon's mouth' (B. Žitkov)

The effect is found only for inalienably possessed Ns ('mouth,' 'dream,' 'forehead') but not alienably possessed ('ditch,' 'day,' 'ice,' 'moss,' 'tree stump'). The syntactic analysis of this effect need not concern us here. What is crucial is that the phrases with YR are restricted in their meaning in a way that phrases without YR are not. Once again, both structurally and semantically, the application of YR is the special case.

II.3.5. *Analysis*

The significance of the foregoing is that it is easier to characterize the set of environments where YR applies than those where it does not. Failure of YR is the general case, while its application is lexically restricted.[4]

---

[4] It is worth emphasizing that the claim of generality is not one of frequency. Failure of YR may, and often is, less frequent than its application. Rather, the set of contexts where YR applies form a more natural class than the set of contexts where YR does not apply.

Before proceeding with the analysis, there should be a comment on the variable nature of the data. As table (13) and other corpus data presented above show, none of the effects are absolute. However, the statistical tendencies displayed by the data are clearly grammatical in nature and can be explained by many standard approaches to variability (e.g., Hayes 2000; Boersma and Hayes 2001; Anttila 2006) which analyze the data using the same mechanisms as categorical grammaticality. In what follows I will abstract away from the variability and treat the tendencies as if they are absolute, but it should be understood that the generalizations are subject to optionality.

Assuming that YR is a rule of the phonology, the distinction between the cases where YR applies and those where it does not can be explained by differences in prosodic structures. As shown in the introductory section, there is ample evidence to prove that the prepositions and prefixes (P) are prosodified together with their host. Assuming that YR, just like the processes discussed in Section 1, also applies within the phonological word, there is a structural paradox. On the one hand, we have cases like *izo rta*, where YR applies, and which clearly constitute a single prosodic word. This can be seen, for example, in the pretonic reduction of the realized *yer* [izartá]. On the other hand, there are cases like *iz rta* where YR fails, but there is no other indication that this sequences does not form a single prosodic word. Final devoicing fails to apply in *i*[z]*rta* just as in the examples from (2). In the cases where a prepositional *yer* fails to be realized despite phonological conditions requiring its realization, diagnostics conflict on the nature of the boundary between P and the host.

This paradox can be resolved by establishing the correct representation of the relevant structures. It is common in prosodic phonology that prosodic constituency can be misaligned with morphosyntactic constituency. Such misalignment can take the shape of resyllabification, bracketing paradoxes or adjunction (e.g., Itô and Mester [1992] 2003, 2006). Adjunction is a violation of strict layering (Selkirk 1984), i.e., the principle that each higher-level category contains only members of the next-lower-level category. It is commonly assumed not to be an inviolable principle but an optimum which is not always attained. Given the possibility that strict layering can be violated, the paradox is resolved. There is a representation that allows us to have the cake and eat it too – one that treats as a prosodic word both the host of P as well as the entire P-host complex. This is shown in (29). The preposition is not just prosodified with the following phonological word, but adjoined to it.

(29)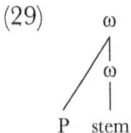

For the analysis in (29), it is necessary to define two types of each prosodic category: a maximal one which is dominated by no other category of the same type and the minimal one which does not dominate any category of the same type (30) (cf. Ito and Mester 2006). In case there is no adjunction, $\text{C{\scriptsize AT}}_{max}$ and $\text{C{\scriptsize AT}}_{min}$ coincide.

(30) a. $\text{C{\scriptsize AT}}_{max}$: not dominated by any other C{\scriptsize AT} of the same type
     b. $\text{C{\scriptsize AT}}_{min}$: not dominating any other C{\scriptsize AT} of the same type

Phonological processes apply within prosodic domains and can be specified to apply within either the maximal prosodic word (ω_{max}), or the minimal prosodic word (ω_{min}). In Russian, stress, reduction and devoicing take ω_{max} as their domain, while YR takes ω_{min}.

The difference between phrases where YR applies and those where it does not are represented in (31). In the general case, the preposition adjoins to a prosodic word as in (29). In a lexically restricted set of cases, the preposition does not adjoin but forms a prosodic word together with its host (31)b. The phonological processes mentioned in Section 1 (devoicing, reduction, etc.) take ω_{max} as their domain and hence apply to both structures. But because lexical YR takes ω_{min} as its domain, it applies only to the inner word in (31)a, as well as to the entire structure of (31)b. It does not apply to the maximal word in (31)a This expresses the fact that in the default case, a sequence of a preposition with the following word does not undergo YR.

(31)

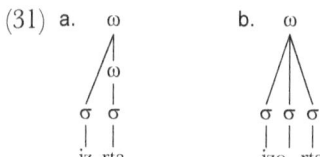

Phonotactic YR is different from lexical YR in that it also applies (optionally) within ω_{max}.

This picture represents a familiar pattern where lexicalized phrases undergo univerbation. Idiosyncrasy in meaning entails formal reduction, in this case, reduction from a structure like (31)a to (31)b.

Before taking up Gribanova's (2009) claim that the prepositions and verbal prefixes differ phonologically in their level of attachment, i.e., the Unity Paradox, it is necessary to investigate stress retraction, another phonological process that variably applies to prepositional phrases.

III. Stress Retraction

The nature of the prepositional *yer* behavior can be made clearer with a parallel to another idiosyncratic aspect of their phonology: the so-called stress retraction rule (SR). The conditions under which the two processes take place and restrictions on them are similar.

III.1. Lexical SR

In Common Slavic and Old Russian, each morpheme was either lexically accented on one of the syllables or unaccented. By the Basic Accentuation Principle (BAP), the leftmost accent surfaces; if all morphemes are unaccented, the leftmost syllable is accented (e.g., Kiparsky and Halle 1977). Prepositions are part of the phonological word and unaccented. Thus, when combined with unaccented nouns (in the so-called "mobile accentual paradigm") they bear stress. This has the appearance of "retraction" of stress onto the preposition. While SR was obligatory in Old Russian, it gradually lost its productivity in the twelfth to sixteenth centuries as documented by Zalizniak (1989). The synchronic situation, investigated by Ukiah (1998) is the result of that loss of regularity.

SR has a status in the phonology of Russian similar to that of YR, but in a sense the situation with SR is simpler than with YR. There is no complicating factor of phonotactics and the lexical effects similar to those observed in the preceding section are more apparent. In the following sections, I briefly describe those lexical effects and show the formal connection between SR and YR.

III.2. Conditions under which lexical SR does not apply

III.2.1. Lexical splits

Just as with YR, there are a large number of idioms that require SR, while identical strings in their non-idiomatic use are produced without SR. For example, *za gorod* 'for the city' has the idiomatic meaning 'to the countryside' with SR (*zá gorod*) and the literal meaning without SR (*za górod*). This can be seen, for example, in that the complement noun cannot be modified: *zá gorod Moskvu 'for the city of Moscow' is impossible with SR. These and other similar examples are shown below. In each case, the expression without SR has the literal meaning and the expression with SR the idiomatic one.

(32) WITHOUT SR   WITH SR
    za górod   'for a city'   zá gorod   'to the countryside'
    za górodom   'behind the city'   zá gorodom   'in the countryside'
    pod góru   'under the hill'   pód goru   'downhill'
    do smérti   'until death'   dó smerti   'extremely'

In some cases, the forms with SR only occur as part of larger idioms, e.g., *podnʲatʲ ná smex* 'make fun of' (lit. 'lift on laughter'); *vzʲatʲ grex ná dušu* 'take responsibility for' (lit. 'take the sin on one's soul'); *zub ná zub ne popadaet* 'extremely cold' (lit. 'one tooth doesn't hit the other'). Just as with YR, the failure of the application of the rule is the general case, while forms with SR are restricted to a few special cases.

III.2.2. Non-complements

Syntactic restrictions parallel to those seen in YR are found with SR as well. Most basically, the noun must be the object of the preposition in order to be eligible for retraction. The relevant examples are difficult to construct due to awkward word order, but there is a clear contrast between the sentences with SR (33)a and those without (33)b. The example (33)a is ungrammatical. Lack of SR greatly improves the phrase (33)b (this is the reading where *gólovu* is the object of *mojuščix*; an alternative irrelevant reading 'on the head of the people who wash,' where *gólovu* is the object of the preposition, is also available).

(33) a. *ná golovu mojuščix lʲudej
       on head washing people
      'on people washing the head'

    b. ?na gólovu mojuščih lʲudej

    c. *ná zimu žduščix kanadcev
       on winter waiting Canadians
      'on Canadians waiting for winter'

    d. na zímu žduščix kanadcev

III.2.3. Non-transparent prepositional semantics

Just as YR, SR is subject not only to formal restrictions but also to semantic ones. The dispreference for SR in constructions with non-transparent prepositional semantics is illustrated below. It parallels the similar effect observed with YR.

(34) a. nadejatʲsʲa 'have one's hope set in' *ná spinu 'back', *ná golovu 'head'
    b. vystupatʲ 'voice support of' *zá gorod 'city'
    c. zastupitʲsʲa 'defend' *zá gorod 'city'
    d. borotʲsʲa 'fight for' *zá golovu 'head'
    e. serditʲsʲa 'be angry at' *ná zimu 'winter'

III.2.4. Possession

As observed by Ukiah (1998), SR displays a possession effect similar to the one found with YR. In phrases with retraction, if the noun is inalienably possessed, its possessor must be its binder.

(35) a. íz domu   'from (necessarily one's own) house'
    iz dóma   'from (possibly someone else's) house'
   b. ná spinu   'on (one's own) the back'
    na spínu   'on (possibly someone else's) back'
   c. dó smerti   'until (resulting in one's own) death'
    do smérti   'until (possibly someone else's) death'
   d. ná bok   'onto (its own) side'
    na bók   'onto the side (of possibly something else)'

A consequence, also observed by Ukiah (1998), is that SR is disfavored when the possessor of the complement of the preposition is overtly expressed.

(36) a. ná golovu   'on the head'
    ná spinu   'on the back'
    ná nogu   'on the leg'

   b. na gólovu Petra Ivanoviča   'on the head of Petr Ivanovič'
    na spínu Petra Ivanoviča   'on the back of Petr Ivanovič'
    na nógu Petra Ivanoviča   'on the leg of Petr Ivanovič'

The accentual subcorpus of the RNC supports this proposition with examples like the following.

(37)   i   vot   narvals'a   **na nógu**   Krisa   [...] Keržakov
    and   there   struck   on leg   Kris.$_{\text{GEN}}$ Keržakov
    'and Keržakov [...] stuck Kris's leg'

III.2.5. Conclusion

The pattern of SR further supports the picture in (31). If the stress rule (the BAP) takes ω_{min} as its domain, then retracting sequences can be represented as having a preposition univerbated with its host as in (31)b, while non-retracting ones have an adjoined preposition as in (31)a. Once again, the lexically restricted and idiosyncratic uses involve a structure that is phonologically more reduced.

The consequence of the preceding two sections is that there are two types of prepositions, prosodically speaking. In the general case, prepositions attach as in (31)a. In a few lexically restricted cases, they form the structure as in (31)b, which manifests itself through the application of YR and SR. I will refer to the two prosodic types of prepositions as "inner P" and "outer P." It warrants emphasizing that the distinction is made here only on prosodic grounds; I make no commitments about the syntactic differences between them.

In the following section I turn to verbal prefixes, where YR and SR also apply, and argue that the same prosodic division between inner and outer P is also relevant.

IV. YR and SR in Verbs

The starting point of the discussion of verbal prefixes is the standard distinction between the so-called lexical and superlexical prefixes made on morphosyntactic grounds (Svenonius 2004). Lexical prefixes are distinguished by semantic idiosyncrasy and an ability to modify the aspectual and argument structure of the verb. Lexical prefixes have the hallmarks of being in some strict syntactic sense 'closer' to the stem of the verb than superlexical prefixes. For a formal implementation of what this closeness means, see Svenonius (2004) and Gribanova (2010).

The distinction between the two types of prefixes has not been previously claimed to have direct phonological consequences. As I show here, it does.

First, consider SR. It applies in verbs as well as nouns where it leads to stressing the initial syllable, potentially including the prefix, if all morphemes are lexically unaccented. Whether the prefix counts as 'initial' for the purposes of the stress rule is just as idiosyncratic as whether the preposition counts as initial for SR in the nominal context. The pattern of lexicalization of verbal SR was investigated by Ostrogorskaia-Jakšič (1987).

Based on her data, it appears that there is a previously unnoticed generalization: only lexical prefixes may receive stress according to SR. Examples of typical prefixes undergoing SR are in (38)a; all are lexical by the standard criteria. Most telling is the semantic idiosyncrasy of the derived form, whose meaning cannot be fully predicted either from the meaning of the stem or the prefix. Another example that supports the argument that the prefixes in (38)a are lexical is that they attach to perfective stems (see Svenonius 2004 and Gribanova 2010 for discussion of this criterion). As the data show, SR treats the lexical prefix as part of the stress domain.

If a verb has both a superlexical and a lexical prefix, the superlexical one will appear outside of the lexical one. Further, because lexical prefixes cannot stack, in any verb with two or more prefixes all but the innermost one must be superlexical. In (38)b, the same items are shown with second prefixes which must be superlexical. Here, SR never treats the outer prefix as part of the stress domain.

(38) a. pó-zvannyj   'called'   (past passive participles)
        íz-brannyj   'chosen'
        ná-nʲatyj   'hired'
        pró-dannyj   'sold'
        pére-dannyj   'transferred'
        dó-pityj   'drunk up'

    b. pod-ná-nʲatyj   'hired in addition to'
        ras-pró-dannyj   'sold out'
        za-pró-dannyj   'sold in advance'
        ne-dó-pityj   'not drunk up'
        pere-pró-dannyj   'sold a second time'

In other words, the syntactic closeness of the lexical prefixes and the stem is reflected in their phonological closeness in that they form the domain in which SR applies.

The next question is whether YR also patterns differently in lexical and superlexical prefixes. Unfortunately, here the facts are somewhat murky but suggestive in the same direction: YR appears more likely with lexical prefixes. The limiting factor is that there are only two C-final superlexical prefixes, the completive *ot*- and the exhaustive *iz*+RFL, neither of which is fully productive. Further, superlexical prefixes attach to imperfective stems which are realized with a *yer* due to an independent lengthening rule. Thus no *yer* in the prefix is expected to surface anyway, at least not due to lexical YR.

However, in some marginal cases the superlexical prefixes do attach to stems whose structure makes YR phonologically possible. The data suggest that the YR in superlexical prefixes is *variable*. The following examples are from Google.

(39) a. ja svoi tri s polovinoj žizni uže **ot-spal**
        'I have already slept my three and a half lives'

        deti uže pol dnevnogo sna **ot-spali**
        'the children slept half of their daily measure of sleep'

        ja uže vesʲ **iz-ždalsʲa**
        'I am sick and tired of waiting'

b. na prirode v palatke uže svoe **oto-spal**
'I've slept my share in the tent out in nature'

ja v armii uže svoe **oto-spal**
'I've already slept my share in the army'

teb‌ʲa ja **izo-ždalsʲa** v pux i prax!
'I am completely sick and tired of waiting for you!'

The distinction between lexical and superlexical prefixes appears to have phonological consequence in both SR and YR. SR is possible in lexical prefixes and ruled out in superlexical ones; YR is necessary in lexical prefixes and possible in superlexical ones. This parallels the division between inner and outer prepositions and can be represented prosodically by the two structures in (31).

The basic consequence of this discussion is that the phonological behavior of prepositions and prefixes is unified. Gribanova's (2009) conclusion to the contrary is due to comparison of inner prefixes and outer prepositions, which are starkly different with respect to both YR and SR. An added difficulty that clouds the comparison is that prepositions are much more productive than even superlexical prefixes – in fact, the prepositions are fully productive. For these reasons, the lexically restricted type that results in (31)b. is easier to spot in the case of prefixes. Once the right categories are compared, however, Matushansky's (2001) generalization about the phonological unity of P is vindicated.

The findings of the paper can be summarized in the following table, which shows the phonological domains which the various processes take.

(40)

ω_{min}	ω_{max}
lexical YR SR	phonotactic YR vowel reduction devoicing

Let me now highlight the conclusions of this study. The distribution of the prepositional variants with and without the final vowel was found to depend on a large number of factors: lexical, syntactic, semantic and phonological. In a nutshell, the variants with the vowel (where YR applies) occur in a narrower set of contexts than the general variants without YR, even if in particular circumstances the YR cases might be more frequent. Those narrower contexts are limited to particular idioms, to narrow syntactic contexts where the noun that follows the preposition is its syntactic object, and to contexts where the object is possessed by the referent of the higher syntactic constituent, typically the subject of the phrase. The key finding is that these restrictions are not unique to YR, but they also determine whether an unrelated rule of stress retraction applies to the preposition-noun sequence. The upshot is that there must be some representational difference between sequences that undergo YR and SR, and the ones that do not. In the theoretical context of this chapter, the representational difference is expressed in terms of the structures in (1) and (31): the processes apply whenever the preposition forms a single prosodic word with the following item.

Appendix. Words used in the Google searches in (13)

	Stop	Coronal fricative	Velar fricative	Labial fricative	Nasal	Liquid
Stop	ptitsa ptenec tkač	psar^j psix kseroks		gvozd^j kvas dver^j	kniga knopka tmin	trʲapka plač kren
Cor.fr.	stul spor skorost^j	ssora ssuda ssadina	sxema sxodka	svet sv^{j}az^j svinʲja	sneg smena smex	srub sryv sladkoe
Vel.fr.				xvat xvost	xmyr^j xna	xrap xlopok xram
Lab.fr	vdova vpadina vdox	vzʲatka vzor vzdox		vvod vvedenie vvoz	vnušenie vmestilišče vnimanie	vlast^j vranʲjo vlaga
Nasal					mnenie mnitelʲnost^j	nrav mraz^j
Liquid	rtut^j; rvotnoe; lʲdina; lʲvica; lʲvenok					

References

Anttila, Arto. 2006. "Variation and opacity." *Natural Language and Linguistic Theory* 24 (4): 893–944.

Avanesov, Ruben I. 1968. *Russoe literaturnoe proiznošenie*. Moscow: Prosveschenie.

Boersma, Paul and Bruce Hayes. 2001. "Empirical Tests of the Gradual Learning Algorithm." *Linguistic Inquiry* 32: 45–86.

Borkovsky, V. I. and P. S. Kuznetsov. 1965. *Istoričeskaja grammatika russkogo jazyka*. Moscow: Nauka.

Chomsky, Noam and Morris Halle. 1968. *The Sound Pattern of English*. New York: Harper and Row.

Clements, G. N. 1990. "The Role of the Sonority Cycle in Core Syllabification. In John Kingston and Mary E. Beckman (eds), *Papers in Laboratory Phonology I: Between the Grammar and Physics of Speech*, 283–325. Cambridge: Cambridge University Press.

Gouskova, Maria. 2010. "The phonology of boundaries and secondary stress in Russian compound" *The Linguistic Review* 27 (4): 387–448.

_____. 2012. "Unexceptional segments." Forthcoming, to appear in *Natural Language and Linguistic Theory*. Pre-press version of article available online: https://files.nyu.edu/mg152/public/downloads/gouskova_unexceptional_segments_nllt.pdf (accessed 19 January 2012).

Green, Anthony. 2003. "Extrasyllabic Consonants and Onset Well-formedness." In C. Fery and R. van de Vijver (eds), 238–53. *The Syllable in Optimality Theory*. Cambridge: Cambridge University Press.

Gribanova, Vera. 2009. "Phonological evidence for a distinction between Russian prepositions and prefixes." In G. Zybatow, D. Lenertová, U. Junghanns, and P. Biskup (eds), *Studies in Formal Slavic Phonology, Morphology, Syntax, Semantics and Information Structure: Proceedings of FDSL 7, Leipzig 2007*, 383–96. Frankfurt: Peter Lang.

_____. 2010. "Composition and locality: The morphosyntax and phonology of the Russian verbal complex." PhD thesis, University of California Santa Cruz.

Halle, Morris. 1959. *The Sound Pattern of Russian*. The Hague: Mouton.

Hayes, Bruce. 1989. "The Prosodic Hierarchy in Meter." In Paul Kiparsky and Gilbert Youmans (eds), *Phonetics and Phonology I: Rhythm and Meter*, 201–60. San Diego: Academic Press.

Hayes, Bruce. 2000. "Gradient Well-formedness in Optimality Theory." In Joost Dekkers et al. (eds), *Optimality Theory: Phonology, Syntax, and Acquisition*, 88–120. Oxford: Oxford University Press.

Itô, Junko and Armin Mester. [1992] 2003. "Weak Layering and Word Binarity." In Takeru Honma et al. (eds), *A New Century of Phonology and Phonological Theory: A Festschrift for Professor Shosuke Haraguchi on the Occasion of His Sixtieth Birthday*, 25–65. Tokyo: Kaitakusha.

_____. 2006. "Prosodic Adjunction in Japanese Compounds." In *Proceedings of FAJL 4*, Osaka, Japan. MIT Working Papers in Linguistics.

Kiparsky, Paul. 2003. "Syllables and Moras in Arabic." In C. Fery and R. van de Vijver (eds), *The Syllable in Optimality Theory*, 147–82. Cambridge: Cambridge University Press.

Kiparsky, Paul and Morris Halle. 1977. "Towards a Reconstruction of the Indo-European Accent." In Larry M. Hyman (ed.), *Studies in Stress and Accent*, 209–38. Southern California Occasional Papers in Linguistics No. 4. Los Angeles: Department of Linguistics, University of Southern California.

Kiparsky, Valentin. 1979. *Russian Historical Grammar: The Development of the Sound System*. Ann Arbor: Ardis.

Lightner, Theodore. M. 1972. *Problems in the Theory of Phonology. Vol. 1: Russian Phonology and Turkish Phonology*. Edmonton: Linguistic Research.

Matushansky, Ora. 2001. "On Formal Identity of Russian Prefixes and Prepositions." *MIT Working papers in Linguistics* 42:217–53.

Russian National Corpus. http://www.ruscorpora.ru/ (accessed November 2010).

Selkirk, Elisabeth. 1984. *Phonology and Syntax: The Relation between Sound and Structure*. Cambridge, MA: MIT Press.

Steriopolo, Olga. 2007. "Yer Vowels in Russian Prepositions." In *Proceedings of Formal Approaches to Slavic Linguistics 15: The Toronto Meeting*. 365–85. Ann Arbor: Michigan Slavic Publications.

Svenonius, Peter. 2004. "Slavic Prefixes Inside and Outside VP." *Nordlyd* 32:205–53.

Ukiah, Nick. 1998. "Stress Retraction in Phrases of the Type *ná den'*, *zá sorok*, *né byl* in Modern Russian." *Russian Linguistics* 22:287–319.

Zalizniak, A. A. 1989. "Perenos udareniia na proklitiki v starovelikorusskom." In R. V. Bulatova and V. A. Dybo (eds), *Istoricheskaia aktsentologiia i sravnitelno-istoricheskii metod*, 116–34. Moscow: Nauka.

Chapter 3

MORPHOLOGY AND LEXICOLOGY INTERFACE. LATEST RUSSIAN NEOLOGISMS: THE NEXT STEP TOWARDS ANALYTISM?

Julia Rochtchina
University of Victoria

I. Introduction

This chapter examines Russian neologisms (new words) related to modern technology, the Internet and other forms of media, looks at their orthographic representations and discusses their effect on the Russian morphology, morphosyntax and the tendency towards increased analytism. The sample of Russian neologisms is taken from two major sources: neologism dictionaries and Internet texts. The dictionary entries in the study come from neologism dictionaries published at the end of the twentieth and the beginning of the twenty-first centuries (Zaxarenko, Komarova and Nečajeva 2003; Efremova 2000; Lopatin 2002; Skljarevskaja 1998). These dictionaries serve as a valuable source of information on vocabulary borrowed during the first decade of computerization and popularization of the Internet in Russia. The second source of data in the study is Russian-media texts taken from the Internet: popular blogs, online newspapers and other sites. Internet sites provide us with the most recent borrowings and with illustrations of the use of neologisms found in neologism dictionaries. The Internet data were analyzed with a text parsing program created specifically for this study. The program searched Russian language Internet sites for text contexts and various orthographic representations of new loan words.

The study excluded emails and informal chat rooms so as to restrict the analysis to the most common loan words and discard occasionalisms. The study analyzes the structure of neologisms borrowed into Russian from English and other languages and discusses their impact on the morphological and orthographic structures of contemporary Russian.

II. Analytical Tendencies in Russian

Russian morphosyntax shows a balance between the synthetic and analytic ways of expressing grammatical meanings. Declinable nouns, adjectives, numerals and verbs represent the stronghold of synthetism in Russian morphosyntax, whereas adverbs, conjunctions, interjections, modals and onomatopoeic words appear as islands of analyticity (or analytism), as they are indeclinable and express their grammatical meaning in context by means of syntax.

The tendency of most Indo-European languages towards analytism was discussed in the nineteenth and early twentieth centuries in major works of such scholars as J. Baudouin de Courtenay (1917), V. Vinogradov (1938) and others. Russian displays some analytic features found in common gender nouns (*плакса, сирота*), indeclinable nouns (*пальто, метро*), indeclinable adjectives (*бордо, хакки*) and indeclinable abbreviations (*РОНО, РФ*). However, Russian is a predominantly synthetic (inflected) language: the absolute majority of Russian nouns, verbs and adjectives encode basic grammatical relations by means of inflection.

In the 1960s, a hypothesis about the strengthening of analytic elements in Russian grammar was suggested and verified in the research conducted by a Russian philologist and sociolinguist, M. V. Panov (Panov 1968, 1999). In his studies, Panov analyzed words like *авиа* (avia), *микро* (micro), and defined them as analytical (or indeclinable) adjectives. The appearance of such words in the late twentieth century, which was due to borrowings from English and other languages, was only the beginning of the trend towards analytism. Panov predicted that this tendency would grow, and that the Russian language would gradually move towards further strengthening of analytic features in its morphosyntax (Panov 1968). Today, more than 40 years later, it appears that he was right. As this chapter will show, with the influx of a recent wave of loan words (mostly from English), analytic features have fortified their position in Russian morphology.

A very important observation made by Panov was that the trend towards analytism extends into the parts of speech that traditionally use inflection to express their grammatical meanings (such as nouns and adjectives). Indeclinable nouns like *беж* (beige) first appeared in Russian in the eighteenth century (mostly borrowed from French) and by the twentieth century, the grammatical category of indeclinable adjectives was established (Panov 1968).

The growth of the tendency towards analytism in modern times was observed by Graudina (1998) and Ryazanova-Clarke and Wade (1999). It appears that the trend towards analytism in the Russian language is accelerating with the influx of loan words, which accounted for 7 percent of new vocabulary in the 1990s (Ryazanova-Clarke and Wade 1999). Contemporary

Russian teems with loan words like *мокко* (caffe mocha), *эспрессо* (espresso), *суши* (sushi), *тирамису* (tiramisu), *фондю* (fondue), *барбекю* (barbeque), *патио* (patio) and many others, which form the class of indeclinable nouns (Ryazanova-Clarke and Wade, 1999). The category of indeclinable adjectives, such as *беж* (beige), *бордо* (Bordeaux color) and *хакки* (khaki), described by Panov in the mid-twentieth century (Panov 1968) is no longer perceived as a strange and exotic element of Russian morphology. In the twenty-first century, another grammatical class of analytic lexemes is being formed – the class of polyfunctional words. This class constitutes loan words predominantly borrowed from English that function as nouns and also as analytical modifiers of nouns, adjectives, adverbs and verbs. Examples of this class include words like *онлайн* (online), *Интернет* (Internet) and *шоу* (show). This new category will be discussed in detail below.

Through heavy borrowing from English and other languages, Russian is changing not only its vocabulary, but also its syntactic and morphological structure. In the next section, we will explore this phenomenon.

III. The Age of the Internet as Another Stage of Language Modification

The Russian language has experienced several dramatic changes throughout its history. A contemporary Russian linguist V. Elistratov marks out five stages of "global barbarization"[1] of the Russian language (Elistratov 2000):

1. Petrine (during Peter the Great's reforms);
2. Karamzin-Pushkin (beginning of the nineteenth century);
3. Raznochinetz (mid-nineteenth century);
4. After the October Revolution of 1917 (Soviet period);
5. Perestroika–post-perestroika period (end of the twentieth century).

Radical changes in the lifestyle of a people or in society cause rapid linguistic change (Elistratov 2000). All the periods in Russia listed above were marked by economic, political and social reforms; new concepts and objects appeared, and these changes triggered language modification.

In contemporary times, the global use of English as a language of international communication and the influx of English loan words has caused and continues to cause a significant impact not only on Russian, but on other

---

[1] The term "barbarization" (варваризация) used by Elistratov is perhaps unfortunate, but it does not have any negative connotations in his study.

world languages as well (e.g., the abundance of loan words from English in Japanese is discussed in Daulton 1999).

Mass media and the Internet are perhaps the most influential sources in the introduction of new vocabulary in contemporary Russian. Russia's interlingual and intercultural communication with other countries is noticeably reflected in the process of language evolution. According to the Moscow-based Public Opinion Foundation report (IT 2008), some 32.7 million users in Russia had continuous access to the Internet in the year of 2008, which accounted for almost a third of the country's population. Information technology allows ordinary people to communicate broadly and express their opinions and ideas publicly in writing. Russians today feel comfortable not only to express themselves, but also to play with language structures, words and orthography in Internet chat rooms, blogs and emails.

The age of the Internet clearly marks the next stage in the evolution of the Russian language as well as many other languages worldwide. New vocabulary related to the Internet has become the subject of recent research by Russian linguists. They have tried to explain the meaning of such words as *рунет* (Ru-net), *онлайн* (online) and *портал* (portal) for the Russian audience (e.g., Trofimova 2000, 2001).

This chapter focuses on how new technology and media-related words trigger the acceleration of analytism in Russian morphosyntax. Russians are getting more used to loan words from English as a part of their everyday vocabulary. While at the end of the 1990s these words were foreign to most Russian people, nowadays they no longer are. Many people are becoming accustomed not only to words like *Интернет* (Internet) and *онлайн* (online), but also to the combinations and structures with indeclinable modifiers like *интернет-газета* (Internet newspaper), *онлайн-новости* (online news), *SMS-сообщения* (SMS messages) and *мультимедиа техника* (multimedia technology). Such structures are very unusual for traditional Russian grammar, as Russian modifiers normally change for gender, number and case to agree with the noun they modify.

IV. How Russian Borrows Words from English

Having analyzed the collected data (over 300 items), we were able to single out three patterns of current lexical borrowings from English into Russian.

First, words can simply be calqued, i.e., translated to reflect a new phenomenon or object. In this case, old words are used with the new meaning, as in, for example: *сотовый телефон* – 'cell phone.' Here the English word cell is translated as 'beehive cells': *пчелиные соты*.

Calquing, however, is not a very frequent source of neologisms in contemporary Russian.

Another way of borrowing words is transliteration: English words are written with Cyrillic letters – *компьютер* (computer), *Интернет* (Internet), *плейер/плеер* (player), *пейджер* (pager), *диск* (disc), *онлайн* (online), *ноутбук* (notebook), *смартфон* (smartphone).

Finally, the Russian language has also been adapting English words in their original English orthography: *CD, DVD, IBM, IT, Laptop, Windows*. Borrowings of this type are used in both spoken and written Russian; moreover, they are listed in dictionaries of modern Russian.

As our analysis shows, transliteration and adaptation are the most common mechanisms of borrowings: they are easy to use since, unlike translations (calques), they do not require lexical analysis of the borrowed item.

V. Loan Words and their Orthographic Representation in Russian

In newspapers and magazines, the following words may appear in different orthographic forms: *web* and *веб*, *e-mail* and *имейл, и-мейл, е-мейл*. Most of these words are IT related, but loan words related to other areas may have different orthographic forms as well. For example, *VIP* and *ВИП, вип; PR* and *пиар* are very common in contemporary Russian. Their structure has been earlier addressed in some works on Russian orthography (e.g., Naumenko 2003).

The spread of such loan words leads to some conflict between real word usage and the prescriptive norm. Some Russian linguists are so worried about this new trend that they have referred to such loan words in an emotional rather than analytical manner talking about "hybrid-words, monsters, the internal structures of which are unclear and strange for those who do not know English," about "destruction of the basic principles of Cyrillic orthography," and "barbarization of the language through Latinism" (Ponomarëva 2001, 75–7). It should be noted that these terms that are perhaps not very appropriate in an academic discussion are quoted here not as an endorsement, but as an illustration of the negative attitudes of some Russian prescriptivists towards these neologisms.

The spread of English word use in Russian speech has given rise to a new fashion in today's Russian mass media – the unlimited play on words using elements of both Russian and English words and morphemes. English lexemes written in their Roman characters are often inserted between Russian words, as in show titles "*News блок weekly*" and "*News блок daily*." In some cases, a loan word from English might be rendered partly with Roman and partly

Figure 3.1. A collage representing text samples that reflect the emerging of a new 'double orthography' system in Russian

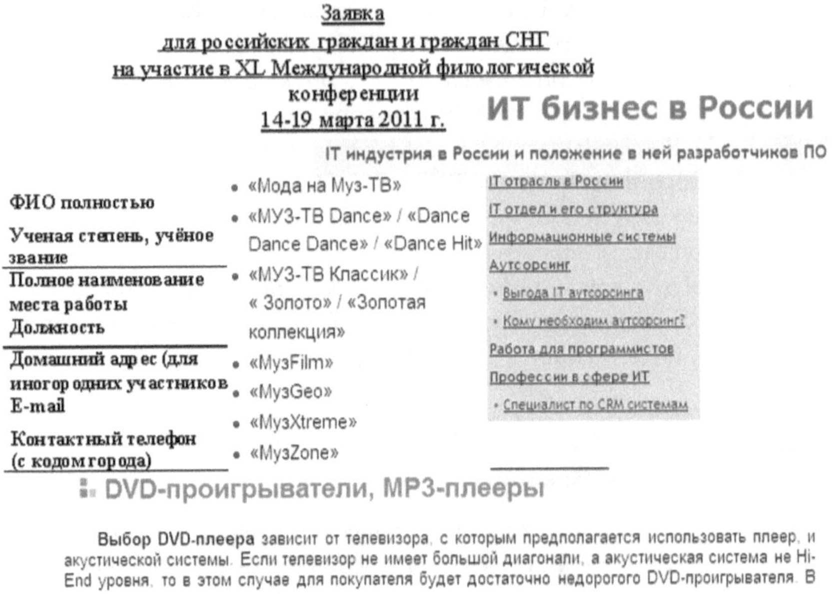

with Cyrillic letters, as in a show title "*Shэйker*." Russian media use blends consisting of a Russian morpheme, or a stem or its part, and an English one, whereby the English part is orthographically rendered with the letters of the Roman alphabet. Examples include: "*наши Finaлисты*" (from a poster in city center of Moscow), "*Deadушки*" (a band playing electronic music), "*Pro-новости*," "*МузXtreme*" and "*МузFilm*" (i.e., television shows titles). Figure 3.1 presents a screen shot from a TV program that has a number of such orthographic blends.

The use of new loan words is widely spread in commercials. Popular newspaper Gazeta.ru[2] offers, for example "*видео-онлайн* трансляцию" (video online broadcasting) and "стандартное *брендирование*" (standard branding). Cell phone commercials provide us with more examples: "Ресурс PreCentral, опубликовал *роадмап* компании HP с её планами по выпуску *портативных гаджетов*" (PreCentral resource published the *roadmap* of HP company with its plans of producing *portable gadgets*).[3]

---

[2] www.gazeta.ru/adbook (accessed 20 July 2011).

[3] www.trubka.ua (accessed 23 July 2011).

Names of famous Western and American brands, words for recreation items, food, new technology and electronics and, of course, words related to the world of the Internet are seen and heard virtually everywhere. *Блендер* (blender), *драйв* (drive), *сайт* (website), *блог* (blog), *блогер* (blogger), *инсайдер* (insider), *аутсайдер* (outsider), *креатив* (creative something), *лузер* (loser), *сноуборд* (snowboard), *фаст фуд* (fast food), *подкаст* (podcast), *смартфон* (smartphone), *гаджет* (gadget), *дизайн* (design), *редизайн* (redesign), *бренд* (brand), *брендинг* (branding) and even *ребрендинг* (rebranding) – these are just some of the examples of English words that the Russian language is currently in the process of assimilating. We provide below illustrations of the contexts in which these loan words are used:

"Новый *креатив* Tuborg Green продолжает тему музыкальных *вечеGREENок*, чей неиссякаемый *драйв* заряжает весь город" (series of television commercials in October 2006: "new *creation* by Tuborg Green continues the theme of musical *Green*venings, that charge the whole city with its inexhaustible *drive*"). Other examples include: "в 2005 на сайте появился первый роман-*подкаст*" (the first *podcast* novel appeared on site in 2005); "проект комплексного *брендинга* для сыродельной компании" (a project of complex *branding* for a cheesemaking company); "провел *ребрендинг* БТА Банка" (executed a *rebranding* of the BTA Bank); "Зубным пастам Splat сделали *редизайн*" (Splat toothpaste underwent *redesign*).[4]

Despite the abundance of new loan words and the increasing occurrence of Russo-English blends, the data show that they do not lead to the complete destruction of Russian synthetic morphology. Many of these neologisms are not really core vocabulary words; they are 'proper nouns,' i.e., names of shows, bands, newspapers and products, and they belong to the periphery of language. Although they are widely used, and therefore cannot be considered occasionalisms, they come in and go out of fashion following the short lifespan of their denotata. These neologisms disappear without entering the core vocabulary, and therefore have little effect on the morphological system. However, the issue of their impact on the orthographical system needs further examination.

As shown in the examples above, when modern English words related to IT, media and pop culture are absorbed into Russian, they can be rendered via Cyrillic graphemes, Roman graphemes or a mixture of both. There are also many instances when the use of Cyrillic orthography for new lexemes is impossible or highly problematic, as in cases of words like *CD, DVD, IT, IP* and *SMS*. They have entered the everyday Russian language through computer slang, where the concision and exactness of transferring information is a

---

4 http://www.adme.ru/pack/zubnym-pastam-splat-sdelali-redizajn-132455/ (accessed 19 February 2011).

priority, and abbreviations are therefore very common. The nature of English abbreviations makes it hard to transliterate them into the Cyrillic writing system. Most attempts to transliterate abbreviations (acronyms, initalisms and alphabetisms) using Cyrillic letters have not been successful because of obvious differences between the Cyrillic and Roman letters and their pronunciations. Moreover, the connection between the component words of the original English abbreviation is lost in Russian transliterations, and English abbreviations written in Cyrillic look rather nonsensical: *сиди, диви́ди, АйТи, АйПи, ЭсЭмЭс*. Some even become a joke, like *PC*, which cannot be transliterated into Russian *ПиСи* because of wrong connotations (in Russian, the word is a homophone with 'pee'). Since the Russian orthography cannot capture these words, they are mostly written in Russian texts with Roman letters. However, using a foreign language character is a violation of the Russian orthographic norm. As Panov mentioned in the late 1960s, such a conflict can be resolved "if the name conflicting the norm is replaced with a different one […] or if the name is gradually included in the norm" (Panov 1968, 30).

In the case of most English loan words in Russian, this conflict appears to be resolved according to Panov's latter scenario (i.e., the 'alien' form gradually infiltrates the norm). Unusual a decade ago, English abbreviations are becoming perceived as the norm. New words and their meanings are recorded in dictionaries, which strengthens their position in modern written and spoken Russian. They also take their place as morphemes and stems in the derivational morphology and participate in the formation of new words, as in Anglo-Russian compounds *IBM-совместимый* (IBM-compatible), *DVD-фильмы* (DVD films), *SMS-сообщения* (SMS messages), *IP-телефония* (IP telephone services), *IT-проект* (IT project), *VIP-зал* (VIP waiting room), etc.

As unusual as it may seem, many neologisms are becoming common and stylistically neutral in their original English orthography, as in the words *операционная система Windows* (Windows Operating System), *MP3-, CD- и DVD-плеер* (MP3, CD and DVD player), *IT-специалист* (IT specialist) and *отправить по e-mail'у* (send by email). At the same time, their Russified versions take their special places among stylistically colored and expressive vocabulary: *виндуза, сидюк, дивидюк, айтишник, мыло / емеля* (Russian slang for 'email,' *мыло*, means 'soap'; *емеля* is a homophone of a Russian name *Emelya*).

In personnel recruitment notes, *IT-специалисты* are wanted, but not *айтишники*; commercials and advertisement columns are offering to install *систему Windows* (not *виндузу*), to sell not *сидюки* and *дивидюки*, but *CD- and DVD-плееры, CD-* and *DVD-диски*. On business cards, people have their *emails* (rarely *электронный адрес* – too long for a business card), but never *мыло* or *емеля* (see examples of Russian business cards in Figure 3.1).

As discussed above, most foreign abbreviations are written in their original English orthography (*CD, IBM, DVD, SMS, IP, IT, PC,* etc.). Examples of abbreviations in Cyrillic include: *Ай-би-эм / ИБМ* (IBM), *ДОС* (DOS), *СД* (CD), *МП3* (MP3), *Би-би-си* (BBC) and *Би-би-эс* (BBS). However, most of these do not survive long in their Cyrillic forms but rather revert to their Roman alphabetic forms. Such abbreviations remain indeclinable in any orthographic representation.

There are some rare examples of when it is possible to write a borrowed abbreviation in Cyrillic, e.g., *ПК – персональный компьютер* (PC – personal computer). However, the clear tendency to keep the English orthography in abbreviations related to information technology cannot be denied.

There are words that are written in Cyrillic and Roman letters, while keeping their original (English) pronunciation: *ИТ* or *IT – информационные технологии* (IT – information technology). Most people who know what the abbreviation stands for would pronounce it as [aitee], even if the word appears in Cyrillic as *ИТ*. In order to verify how this word is used by professionals in the respective arena, I conducted an informal survey among twenty Russians working in the field of information technology. Seventeen participants responded that they pronounce the word *IT* as *«айти»* [aitee], while three preferred not to use the foreign abbreviation at all, but said instead *информационные технологии* (information technology). Nevertheless, even the participants from the latter group mentioned that *«айти»* "does not hurt their ears." None of the participants would pronounce the abbreviation following its Russian spelling *ИТ* as *«ит»* [eet]. Another reason for the preference of the anglicized pronunciation might be the slang word *айтишник* (for an IT specialist), which is currently a widespread Russian word.

Another example of an abbreviation commonly written in both Cyrillic and Roman letters is *СМС* (SMS – short message service). The meaning in Russian is *короткое письменное сообщение*, and *КПС* would be the Russian abbreviation, but it is not used. Those Russians who do not speak English do not know what the abbreviation *SMS* stands for. This fact, however, does not stop them from using the word. *СМС-сообщения* or *эсмэски* is a very popular communication service. Combinations such as *SMS-вирус* (SMS virus), *SMS-вредительство* (SMS damage), *СМС-голосование* (SMS voting), *SMS-оповещение* (SMS notification), *SMS-услуги* (SMS services) and *SMS-чат* (SMS chat) are very common in today's written and spoken Russian.

The above examples suggest the emergence of a new 'double orthography' system that somewhat resembles Japanese script, where foreign loan words are written in the special alphabet katakana (to differentiate them from native Japanese and Chinese loan words written with Chinese characters and the hiragana alphabet). See Figure 3.1 for Russian text samples reflecting this 'double orthography' tendency.

Besides the potential change of the orthographic norm, another important question is whether these innovations might influence the basic tendencies of morphological and syntactic evolution in Russian.

Under the influence of English words and phrases like *CD-записи* (CD records), *DVD-фильмы* (DVD films), *SMS-сообщения* (SMS messages), *IP-телефония* (IP telephoning), *IT-специалист* (IT specialist) and *ИТ-компания* (IT company), Russian has created a number of compounds consisting of an abbreviation and a stem: *РИА-Новости, БТК банк, ТВ-программа*. These examples show how Russian morphosyntax is adopting an English structure. Very often, new abbreviations (both loan words from English and original Russian ones) are used as polyfunctional lexemes. Such lexemes and their impact on Russian morphosyntax will be discussed in the next section.

VI. Polyfunctional Words and their Impact on Russian Morphosyntax

Many neologisms make up a new grammatical category – the category of polyfunctional words. In Russian morphosyntax, the category of polyfunctional words includes lexemes with a broad (non-standard) grammatical valency. These lexemes form a special class of words that do not belong to a particular part of speech. They may function as a noun, an adjective or an adverb depending on the context. They acquire grammatical meaning within the sentence. Some examples of polyfunctional words are provided below.

Экстра can be used as a noun: *читать "Экстру"* (read the "Extra"); an adjective: **экстра**-*специалист* (extra-class specialist); or an adverb: **экстра**-*авангардный* (extra-vanguard). The word **шоу** can be used as a noun: *предвыборные* **шоу** (pre-election show) or an adjective: **шоу**-*индустрия* (show business industry). Similarly, the word **караоке** can also be used as a noun: *народное* **караоке** (people's karaoke) or an adjective: **караоке** *соревнование* (karaoke contest). In analytic languages like English, words are polyfunctional, i.e. one can "see a nice *show*" (the word "show" is a noun), or "*show* a movie" (the word "show" is a verb). An examination of some common loan words in Russian shows that they are polyfunctional. More illustrations of this phenomenon are given below.

The word **онлайн** (which comes from English *online*, or *on line*) can be used in the role of three different parts of speech in Russian.

(1)a. "Мелкий и средний бизнес идет в *онлайн*" (Small and medium-size business goes *online*);[5] (1)b. "шоу в *онлайне*" (show *online*).[6] In these contexts the word *онлайн* functions as a declinable noun.

(2) "Посетители вашего сайта смогут проверить написание и произношение слова сразу в девяти *онлайн*-словарях" (Visitors to your site can check word spelling and pronunciation in ten *online* dictionaries at once).[7] In this latter example the word "*онлайн*" is used as an adjective (attribute), or in Panov's terminology, an analytical adjective.

(3) "Почему ТВЦ может себе позволить транслировать дебаты '*онлайн*'" (Why TVC can afford broadcasting debates "*online*");[8] "Правительство должно быть '*онлайн*'" (The government has to be "*online*"). In these sentences, *онлайн* functions as an adverb.

The opposite of *онлайн* – *офлайн* – is used in a similar polyfunctional way. The word can be used as a noun: "[...] выплеснулось из Интернета в *офлайн*" (it poured offline from the Internet).[9] More often the word is used as an analytical adjective: "участник *оффлайн* опроса" (participant of the *offline* poll).[10] This word is also used as an adverb: "Он сегодня *офлайн*" (He is *offline* today).[11] As can be seen in above examples, the spelling of the word varies in different sources: *офлайн, оффлайн, off-line* or *offline*. This is despite the fact that the word can be found in recently published dictionaries, where the spelling reflected is **офлайн** (Zaxarenko, Komarova and Nečajeva 2003).

The word **медиа** is extremely popular in today's Russian newspapers, which is not surprising. It can be used as a noun: "Произведение, выполненное с использованием современных *медиа*" (A work created with the use of modern *media*).[12] It can also be used as an analytical adjective: "Журналистика – это особый образ жизни. Это такая *медиа*-профессия" (Journalism is a particular way of life. It is a *media* profession).

The word **Интернет** fits the paradigm of Russian masculine nouns and declines just like all regular masculine nouns: "В русском *Интернете* – при всей его молодости – свои традиции" (The Russian *Internet* – despite

---

5 http://www.ng.ru/internet/2003-05-23/10_business.html (accessed 14 May 2010).
6 http://www.cnews.ru/news/top/index.shtml?2003/05/23/144517 (accessed 14 May 2010).
7 http://www.gramota.ru/slovari/forma/ (accessed 20 May 2010).
8 http://www.ng.ru/politics/2003-11-05/2_er.html (accessed 20 May 2010).
9 http://www.pravda.ru/author/1-8491/ (accessed 20 May 2010).
10 http://www.sostav.ru/news/2008/10/29/issl3/ (accessed 22 May 2010).
11 http://gazeta.aif.ru/_/online/moskva/523/08_01 (accessed 22 May 2010).
12 http://www.ng.ru/culture/2003-04-23/8_mars.html (accessed 22 May 2010).

being young – has its own traditions);[13] "отправка SMS из *Интернета*" (sending SMS from the *Internet*).[14]

Along with the word **Интернет**, the Russian language has borrowed and created many unusual (from a morphological point of view) combinations, some of which include: *интернет-сайт* (Internet site), *интернет-связь* (Internet connection), *интернет-технологии* (Internet technology), *интернет-публикации* (Internet publications), *интернет-услуги* (Internet services) and *интернет-магазины* (Internet shops). An example from a Russian paper: "С интернет-связью особых проблем не возникало" (there have been no problems with *Internet* connections) (*МК-воскресенье*, 16 June 2002). Such combinations are often written with a hyphen as compound words; however, the form with two words separated with a space is also quite common: *интернет студия "Муза"* (Internet studio "Muse"). A presenter at a linguistics conference wrote the word combination *интернет дискурс* without a hyphen in her publication: "Интернет дискурс отражает творческие потенции русского языка [...]" (Internet discourse reflects the creative potential of the Russian language) (Galjašina 2004, 469). Obviously, the word **Интернет** is used here as an indeclinable modifier of a noun: *компьютерный (какой?) дискурс* and *интернет (какой?) дискурс*.

In English, the status of the noun-plus-noun (NN) constructions like "karaoke contest" is questionable; they can be treated as compound words (a product of morphological derivation yielding a new lexeme) or as phrases (the product of syntax) (e.g., Payne and Huddleston 2002; Selkirk 1982; Liberman and Sproat 1992). These differences in interpretation are due to the polyfunctionality of English words. In synthetic Russian morphology, inflectional paradigms and inflectional suffixes keep a word 'pinned' to its lexical class, e.g., *показ* is a noun, whereas *показать* is a verb. Even in traditional Russian NN compounds, both parts are declinable: e.g., *царевна-лягушка* (frog princess, nominative case); *царевны-лягушки* (frog princess, genitive case). The new compounds, with words borrowed from English and other languages like **караоке соревнование** (karaoke contest), include an indeclinable borrowed component which can also be found on its own as a free root morpheme. This is somewhat similar to a different traditional Russian compounding pattern of an indeclinable adverb stem plus adjective, like *вечнозелёный* (evergreen), which was not very productive. In this way, the loan words from English erase the boundary between a phrase and a compound and trigger the evolution of polyfunctionality of words in Russian.

Our analysis of new Russian loan words shows that many of them are polyfunctional in their grammatical nature. Some loan words do receive

---

13 http://www.ng.ru/ideas/2001-04-11/8_findmachine.html (accessed 22 May 2010).

14 A promotional page on http://www.velcom.by/ru/private/services/web-sms (accessed 22 May 2010).

traditional Russian orthographic appearance when used as nouns (*дизайн, интернет, онлайн, веб,* etc.). At the same time, they remain indeclinable when used as noun modifiers (in other words as "analytical adjectives" which, as mentioned above, is a relatively new category in Russian grammar) or as verb modifiers (adverbs): *дизайн студия, онлайн-олимпиада, веб-индустрия, работать онлайн*.

In contemporary life, the Internet with its strong connections to other forms of media can be seen as a pathway through which new objects and phenomena and new words denoting them are penetrating the Russian language. Various forms of modern mass media also broaden the boundaries of use of the newest polyfunctional words in contemporary Russian, which, in turn, drives the language structure towards analytism.

VII. Conclusion

Borrowed English loan words in Russian can be seen as a tribute to everything Western and fashionable. Many of these words will very likely disappear and be replaced by new ones. On the other hand, if they persist in their Roman alphabetic forms, this might lead to the creation of a second orthographic system in Russian (the Roman one). On the whole, borrowed words and structures like those analyzed in this chapter affect the Russian grammatical system, pushing it towards analytism and reducing the boundaries between compounds and phrases.

In conclusion, it should be stated that these new elements do not make the Russian language analytic, nor do they cause a morphological destruction of the language. Contemporary Russian remains a synthetic (inflected) language with growing islands of analytism.

Acknowledgments

I would like to express my gratitude to Michael Skrigitil for creating the text parser program for this study, and also to Dr. Evgeny V. Klobukov, Dr. Veronika Makarova and Dr. Sonya Bird for reading this chapter and providing me with helpful feedback.

References

Baudouin de Courtenay, J. 1917. *Vvedenije v jazykovedenije*. Petrograd.
Daulton, Frank E. 1999. "English Loanwords in Japanese: The Built-In Lexicon." *The Internet TESL Journal* 5 (1). Online: http://iteslj.org/Articles/Daulton-Loanwords.html (accessed 20 April 2010).
Efremova, T. F. 2000. *Novyj slovar' russkogo jazyka: Tolkovo-slovoobrazovatel'nyj*. Moscow: Russkij jazyk.

Elistratov, V. S. 2000. "Varvarizacija jazyka, eë sut' I zakonomernosti." Gramota.ru. Online: www.gramota.ru/biblio/magazines/gramota/norma (accessed 14 April 2010).

Galjašina, E. I. 2004. "Kommerčeskoje imja kak rezul'tat individual'nogo slovesnogo tvorčestva v aspekte lingvističeskoy èkspertizy." *Russkij jazyk: istoričeskije sud'by I sovremennost'*, 469. Moscow: Moscow University Press.

Golanova E. I. 1998. "O 'mnimyx složnyx slovax' (razvitije klassa analitičeskix prilagatel'nyx v sovremennom russkom jazyke)." *Liki jazyka. K 45-letiju naučnoj dejatel'nosti E. A. Zemskoj.* Moscow: Nasledije.

Graudina, L. K. 1998. "'S Moskva-tur na Krashoje more!' (Čto-to noven'koje v grammatike?)." *Russkaja reč* 3:45–53. Moscow: Nauka.

Liberman, M. and R. Sproat. 1992. "The Stress and Structure of Modified Noun Phrases in English." In I. A. Sag and A. Scabolcsi (eds), *Lexical Matters*, 131–81. Stanford: Stanford University Press.

Lopatin, V. V., ed. 2002. *Russkij orfografičeskij slovar' Rossijskoj akademii nauk.* Electronic version. Online: http://gramota.ru/slovari (accessed 15 March 2003).

Naumenko, S. V. 2003. "Kirillica & latinica (strukturnyje tipy varvarizmov v sovremennoj orfografičeskoj praktike)." *Rossijskij lingvističeskij ježegodnik* 4–5: 166–9.

PMR. 2008. "33m internet users in Russia." Online: www.ictrussia.com/63175/33m_internet_users_in_Russia.shtml (accessed 30 July 2008).

Panov, M. V., ed. 1968. *Russkij jazyk i sovetskoje obščestvo.* Moscow: Nauka.

———. 1999. *Pozicionnaja morfologija russkogo jazyka.* Moscow: Nauka.

Payne, J. and R. Huddleston. 2002. "Nouns and Noun Phrases." In R. Huddleston and G. K. Pullum (eds), *The Cambridge Grammar of the English language*, 323–524. Cambridge: Cambridge University Press.

Ponomarëva, Z. N. 2001. "Grafičeskij obraz inojazyčnogo slova v sovremennyx russkix tekstax." *Mir russkogo slova* 2: 75.

Ryazanova-Clarke, L. and T. Wade. 1999. *The Russian Language Today.* London and New York: Routledge.

Selkirk, E. O. 1982. *The Syntax of Words.* Cambridge, MA and London: MIT Press.

Skljarevskaja, G. N. 1998. *Tolkovyj slovar' russkogo jazyka XX veka. Jazykovyje izmenenija.* Rossijskaja akademija nauk, Institut lingvističeskix issledovanij. St. Petersburg: Folio-Press.

Trofimova, G. N. 2000. "O čëm poka molčit runet?" Online: http://www.gramota.ru/biblio/magazines/gramota/net/28_11 (accessed 14 November 2000).

———. 2000. "Kto takoj setevoj onlajn?" Online: http://www.gramota.ru/biblio/magazines/gramota/28_34 (accessed 15 December 2000).

———. 2001. "Zaxodite v naš portal!" Online: http://www.gramota.ru/biblio/magazines/gramota/28_60 (accessed 16 February 2001).

Vinogradov, V. V. 1938. *Sovremennyj russkij jazyk (Grammatičeskoje učenije o slove).* Moscow: Nauka.

Zaxarenko, E. N., L. N. Komarova and I. V. Nečajeva. 2003. *Novyj slovar' inostrannyx slov.* Moscow: Azbukovnik.

Zemskaja E. A., ed. 1996. *Russkij jazuk konca XX stoletija (1985–1995).* Moscow: Jazyki russkoj kul'tury.

Chapter 4

SYNTAX.
BI-NOMINATIVE SENTENCES IN RUSSIAN

Igor Mel'čuk
Observatoire de linguistique Sens-Texte
University of Montreal

Krasota – èto istina, a istina – èto krasota
'Beauty is truth, truth beauty'

—John Keats, "Ode on a Grecian Urn"

Russian has a very frequent type of sentence, known as **bi-nominative**: *Rim – stolica Italii* lit. 'Rome capital Italy's.' In this connection, the following well-known problem emerges: What is the syntactic subject and what is the syntactic predicate in such a sentence? The answer to this question, apparently simple, but in fact very tricky, lies in a semantic analysis of bi-nominative sentences.

I. Bi-nominative Sentences in Russian

A Russian bi-nominative sentence has a "kernel" consisting of two Noun Phrases in the nominative [= NP_{NOM}], with or without an explicit form of the verb BYT' 'be' between them. In other words, both the syntactic subject and the syntactic predicative[1] of a bi-nominative sentence are NP_{NOM}s:

(1) a. *Moj syn*$_{NOM}$ *inžener*$_{NOM}$ lit. 'My son engineer' [= 'My son **is** an engineer'].
 b. *Svoistvo*$_{NOM}$ *5 – sledstvie*$_{NOM}$ *sledujuščego fakta* lit. 'Property 5 corollary following fact's' [= 'Property 5 **is** a corollary of the following fact'].

---

1 The predicative is the nominal part of a syntactic predicate formed by the verb BE (or a similar one) and a noun/an adjective/an infinitive.

c. *Rim*$_{NOM}$ – *stolica*$_{NOM}$ *Italii* lit. 'Rome capital Italy's' [= 'Rome **is** Italy's capital'].

d. *Èti ljudi*$_{NOM}$ – *naši druz'ja*$_{NOM}$ lit. 'These people our friends' [= 'These people **are** our friends'].

Such sentences, when they do not have an overt copula, are also known as "nominal sentences" (Rus. *imennye predloženija*).

The present discussion is based on the following crucial fact:

In Russian, a bi-nominative sentence [= BS] necessarily contains a finite form of the verb BYT′: in cases where there is no overt verb form, a BS includes a zero wordform of BYT′, this zero expressing the present indicative of 'be'.

Thus, the Surface-Syntactic Structures [= SSyntSs] of sentences in (1) all contain the verb BYT′ as their top node; for instance, (1a) has the SSyntS shown in (2):

(2)
$$\text{BYT′}_{\text{IND, PRES}}$$
subjectival — copular
MOJ ← modificative — SYN$_{SG}$ INŽENER$_{SG}$

In the present tense of the indicative, BYT′ has the zero wordform $\emptyset^{\text{BYT′}}_{\text{IND, PRES}}$; in all other moods and tenses or under an emphatic stress this verb has overt forms:

(3) *Moj syn **byl** inžener/inženerom* 'My son was an engineer$_{NOM/INSTR}$.' ~
*Moj syn **budet** inženerom* 'My son will be an engineer.' ~
*Moj syn **byl by** inženerom* 'My son would be an engineer.' ~
***Bud′** inženerom!* 'Be an engineer!' ~
*Moj syn i **est′** inžener* ≈ 'My son **is** the engineer.'

For zero wordforms and other linguistic zeros, see Mel'čuk (1974b; 1979; 2002; 2006, 469ff.).

However, this does not mean that I claim the presence of a zero copula form in any BS of any language. Far from it:

- Some languages do not have a copula verb (= 'be') at all; in these languages, BSs are simply without a main verb. One such language is, for instance, Lushootseed (Salishan, British Columbia, Canada).

- Other languages have a copula, but also feature special predicative forms of nouns (and adjectives), which – under particular conditions – are used instead of the copula; as a result, many sentences do not have the main verb. Such are, for instance, Turkic languages; e.g., Turkish says *Demir metal+dIr* lit. 'Iron metal.**is**' (here and below, a dot between English glosses indicates that they correspond to one foreign word or one meaning).
- Still some other languages have a copula, but at the same time allow for BSs without copula, semantically opposed to sentences with one: copula-less sentences, i.e., BSs, express general truths, while those with a copula state particular facts, as in Latin *Omnia praeclara rara* lit. 'All excellent.things rare' vs. *Haec preclara **sunt** rara* 'These excellent.things **are** rare' (Benveniste 1950). This situation is typical of Classical languages – Latin, Ancient Greek, and Sanskrit.

I am saying only that Russian BSs always contain the verb BYT´ 'be,' represented in the present of the indicative by a zero wordform. As a result, the general scheme of Russian BSs is

$$NP_{1\text{-NOM}} + \text{BYT}´ + NP_{2\text{-NOM}}$$

II. The Problem Stated: Preliminary Formulation

The syntactic structure of Russian BSs is the object of a series of interesting papers (Padučeva 1979a, 1979b, 1987; Padučeva and Uspenskij 1979, 1997). The authors examined BSs such as in (4):

(4) a. (i) *Stolica Gollandii – Amsterdam* 'The capital city of Holland is Amsterdam'.
    (ii) *Kratkost´ – sestra talanta* 'Brevity is a sister of talent'.
    (iii) *Moj načal´nik – Maša* 'My boss is Masha'.
    (iv) *Moja zarplata – 70 000 dollarov* 'My salary is $70,000'.
  b. (i) *Èto životnoe – mlekopitajuščee* 'This animal is a mammal'.
    (ii) *Kity – mlekopitajuščie* 'Whales are mammals'.
  c. (i) *Ètot čelovek – Maša* 'This person is Masha'.
    (ii) *Èto Maša* 'This is Masha'.
  d. (i) *Fizkul´tura – èto dolgoletie* 'Physical.exercise is longevity'.
    (ii) *Xleb – èto svoboda* 'Bread is liberty'.
  e.   *Kindza – èto koriandr* 'Kindza is coriander'.

It is not obvious which NP_{NOM} in such a sentence is the syntactic subject and which is the nominal part of the syntactic predicate, i.e., the "predicative." Padučeva and Uspenskij formulate the problem as follows:

> What are the operational criteria that could ensure a univocal and rigorous distinction between the subject and the predicative NP_{NOM}s in Russian BSs?

They convincingly show that the five criteria traditionally used to establish this distinction are not valid in certain cases and thus are not sufficient.

- Semantic criterion: The syntactic predicate normally denotes a semantic predicate 'P' predicated of the subject; in a BS, one NP_{NOM} – the subject – must then be an argument of the other NP_{NOM} (which means 'P'). But in many BSs none of the two NP_{NOM}s is semantically predicated about the other: e.g., (4c–e).
- Communicative criterion: The syntactic predicate expresses the Rheme of the sentence, and the syntactic subject – its Theme. It is well known that in Russian the syntactic and communicative roles are logically independent: almost any element of the sentence may appear in almost any communicative role. Thus, in both sentences *Ivan – moja edinstvennaja nadežda* 'Ivan is my only hope' and *Moja edinstvennaja nadežda – Ivan* 'My only hope is Ivan' the subject is *Ivan*,[2] although in the first sentence the noun *Ivan* is the Theme and in the second, the Rheme.
- Word order criterion: The preceding NP_{NOM} is the subject. But in (4a, iii) it is difficult to consider *moj načal'nik* as the subject: first, it is predicated about Masha; second, in the past or the future this NP appears in the instrumental (see below): *Mo+**im** načal'nik+**om**$_{INSTR}$ byla/budet Maša*. In the sentences *Moj brat – strannyj čelovek* and *Strannyj čelovek moj brat!* (both meaning 'My brother is a strange person'), *moj brat* is obviously the syntactic subject, independently of its position.
- Instrumental case criterion (Peškovskij 1934, 215ff.): The predicative is the NP_{NOM} that gets the instrumental case when the BS is transferred into the past or the future tense.[3] But in several cases – for instance in (4a, iv), (4c, ii) and (4d–e.) – none of the two NP_{NOM}s can appear in the instrumental.

---

2 This can be immediately seen if the sentences are put into the past tense: *Ivan byl$_{MASC}$ moej edinstvennoj nadeždoj* and *Moej edinstvennoj nadeždoj byl$_{MASC}$ Ivan* (the subject remains in the nominative, while the predicative phrase receives the instrumental).

3 The verb BYT' requires that the predicative NP (= its DSynt-actant **II**) be in the nominative if BYT' is in the present indicative; otherwise, the predicative NP may or must be in the instrumental.

(Note, however, that the NP$_{NOM}$ that can alternate with the NP$_{INSTR}$ is necessarily the predicative.)

- Copula agreement criterion: The subject is the NP$_{NOM}$ with which the copula agrees. But in (4c, ii) the copula agrees with *Maša*; is *èto* the predicative? As shown in Padučeva (1987) and Padučeva and Uspenskij (1997), in Russian the main verb never agrees with the subject pronouns ÈTO,[4] KTO and ČTO (***Èto** byl+a*$_{FEM}$ *Maša* / ***Èto** byl+Ø*$_{MASC}$ *Ivan* 'This was Masha/Ivan'; ***Kto** byl+a Maša?* / ***Kto** byl+Ø Ivan?* 'Who was Masha/Ivan?'). If the subject is an NP$_{NOM}$ used autonymously, the copula invariably takes the singular form of the neuter gender (*Motja*$_{FEM}$ *byl+o*$_{NEU}$ *ego prozviščem*$_{NEU}$ / *ego kličkoj*$_{FEM}$ ~ **Motja*$_{FEM}$ *byl+a*$_{FEM}$ *ego prozviščem*$_{NEU}$ / *ego kličkoj*$_{FEM}$ 'Motya was his nickname'; in *Motja*$_{FEM}$ *byl+o*$_{NEU}$ *ego ljubimoe prozvišče*$_{NEU}$ ~ *Motja*$_{FEM}$ *byl+a*$_{FEM}$ *ego ljubimaja klička*$_{FEM}$ 'Motya was his preferred nickname', the nouns PROZVIŠČE and KLIČKA, both meaning 'nickname', are subjects).

Already in 1924, Jespersen ([1924] 1965) analyzed similar BSs in several European languages and put forward the idea of using in difficult cases considerations of "greater specificity or definiteness": the subject is supposed to be more specific or more definite than the predicative. Building upon this idea, Padučeva and Uspenskij propose – instead of the above-mentioned insufficient criteria – that the *referential status* of both NP$_{NOM}$s serve as the criterion for their syntactic roles (for the referential status of nominal phrases, see Padučeva (1979)). Namely, Padučeva and Uspenskij (1997) claim the following:

In a Russian BS,

1. if one of the two NP$_{NOM}$s is more referential than the other one, this NP$_{NOM}$ is the subject;
2. if the referentiality of the two NP$_{NOM}$s is equal, then the subject is the less informative one;

---

[4] This ÈTO ≈ 'it/this' (ÈTO¹I) is of course different from the particle ÈTO (= ÈTO²I), which is used with the copula: *Opasnosti – **èto** byla*$_{FEM}$ *ego stixija*$_{FEM}$ lit. 'Dangers – this was his element'. (Russian has two more lexemes ÈTO: the demonstrative pronoun ÈTO¹II, seen in [–*What is all this racket?*] – *Èto Ivan tam mebel' dvigaet* lit. 'This Ivan is moving furniture there' = 'This is Ivan who is moving furniture there'; and the particle ÈTO²II, used as rheme focalization marker: [–*Did you break the window?*] – *Net, èto Ivan razbil okno* 'It is Ivan who broke the window'.) See Kimmelman (2009). The particle VOT, which is sometimes considered on a par with ÈTO²I, should not be examined in connection with the zero form of BYT': VOT does not combine with any overt form of this verb as a subject (**Vot bylo moë želanie* 'Here was my wish'). VOT is a predicative particle, similar to the French quasi-verbs VOICI et VOILÀ 'here is/are': *Vot Ivan/kniga* 'Here is Ivan/the book'. (A different VOT is seen in *vot ètot* 'exactly this'.)

3. if the two NP$_{NOM}$s do not show a clear-cut difference of referentiality/ informativeness, there is no point of establishing the Syntactic Structure for this BS: the difference between the NP$_{NOM}$s is not parallel to the differences between "normal" syntactic subjects and predicates in all other sentences.

Padučeva's and Padučeva and Uspenskij's description of BSs in Russian is precise and elegant; yet over the years I have been feeling a certain degree of discomfort with their results for two reasons.

- First, why should one bother at all to determine what is the subject and what is the predicative in a "ready" sentence? The analytic, or interpretational, approach always has been suspicious to me. I prefer descriptions carried out with an eye to how to *produce* such BSs. This means that first of all we have to establish their semantic structures.
- Second, if Padučeva and Uspenskij rightly reject communicative considerations as a means for determining the syntactic subject in a Russian BS, then why should we admit the referential status of NPs as such a means? The referential status is as perpendicular to the syntactic roles as is the communicative structure.

These two doubts have led me on a search of a different solution.

III. The Problem Stated: Final Formulation

The solution to be proposed is stated within the Meaning-Text approach, whose main principles and conventions are taken to be known to the reader (see, e.g., Mel'čuk 1974a; 1988, 43–91; 2009). The Syntactic Structure [= SyntS] of a sentence S is only an intermediate representation between its Semantic Structure [= SemS] and its Deep-Morphological (linear) Structure [= DMorphS]. Therefore, in order to decide on the syntactic status of nominative phrases in a BS S we have to consider the transition from S's SemS to its DMorphS. As a result, the problem of the description of Russian BSs is formulated as follows:

> How should the SemS of a Russian BS look, and what semantic rules are needed in order to allow for S's correct construction, in particular, for a correct assignment of the syntactic roles of subject and predicate to both NP$_{NOM}$s?

According to the Meaning-Text approach, no full-fledged Russian sentence can be without a syntactic subject and a predicate (I leave aside all "minor type sentences," including so-called *naming sentences*, Rus. *nazyvnye predloženija*). Consequently, I cannot have recourse, as Padučeva and Uspenskij (1997) do in some cases, to the notion of syntactic indeterminacy; compare as well Yokoyama's (1986, 227–8) proposal that sentences of the type *Èto moj syn* lit. 'This my son' have no subject. I cannot simply say that a BS – any type of BS – shows no distinction between the subject and the predicative.

To answer the above question, I have to indicate the SemS for each type of Russian BS and sketch the semantic rules that will be applied to these SemSs to produce the corresponding Deep-Syntactic Structures (the transition DSyntS ⇔ SSyntS is straightforward from the viewpoint of our topic: the SSynt-subject always stems from DSynt-actant **I**).

IV. The Solution

Based on the data in Padučeva's (1987) and Padučeva and Uspenskij's (1997) papers, I propose a description of Russian BSs relying on a very simple key point:

> There must be a particular semanteme or the absence of a semanteme in the SemS for each type of Russian BSs.

The SemSs and the Sem-rules illustrated below are written in accordance with the general framework of the Meaning-Text theory; the shading in the rules specifies the context – elements that are necessary for the rule to apply, but are themselves not affected by it.

The following six major types of Russian BSs can be semantically distinguished.

1. One of the two NP_{NOM}s is semantically a predicate or a quasi-predicate (boldfaced below) and the other NP_{NOM} is its first argument: **Pričina** *ego gibeli – neponimanie situacii* 'The cause of his death is a misunderstanding of the situation', where we have 'be.the.cause.of(misunderstanding$_1$; death$_2$)' [the subscripts specify the arguments of the predicate].
2. One of the two NP_{NOM}s is the name of a class (boldfaced) and the BS states the inclusion of the denotation of the other NP_{NOM} into this class – as an element or as a subclass; in the SemS, the corresponding meanings are linked by the semanteme 'X is.included.in Y' (Kit_X – **mlekopitajuščee**$_Y$ 'The whale is a mammal' or $Kity_X$ – **mlekopitajuščie**$_Y$ 'Whales are mammals').
3. The two NP_{NOM}s are linked by the semanteme 'X identifies Y for the Addressee': $Èto_Y$ $Maša_X$ 'This is Masha.'

4. The two NP$_{NOM}$s are linked by the semanteme 'X entails Y': *Direktorstvo*$_X$ – *èto odni neprijatnosti*$_Y$ lit. 'Directorship [is] only troubles.'
5. The two NP$_{NOM}$s are linked by the semanteme 'X is.similar.to Y': *Ženščina*$_X$ – *ognennyj napitok*$_Y$ lit. 'Woman [is] fire potion' [V. Brjusov].
6. The two NP$_{NOM}$s are linked by the semanteme 'X means [the same as] Y' (*Koriandr*$_X$ – *èto kindza*$_Y$ 'Coriander is kindza').[5]

These six types of BSs correspond to six different senses – and accordingly, to six different lexemes – of the Russian verb BYT´ 'be'; let us consider those lexemes in turn. For each lexeme it is shown how to represent it in the SemS of the corresponding BS and what Lexicalization/Arborization rules are necessary for the transition "SemS ⇔ DSyntS." (Lexicalization and Arborization are two major complex operations performed during the above-mentioned transition. Lexicalization ensures the selection of the appropriate lexical units for the given meaning, while Arborization organizes these units into an arborescent structure – i.e., the syntactic structure of the sentence-to-be.)

1. BYT´**I.1** in the BS does not correspond to any semanteme in the starting SemS. This means that BYT´**I.1** is semantically empty. It is a genuine copula: it is used not to express a meaning, but – in conformity with the rules of Russian syntax – to "verbalize" a non-verbal item which is semantically a (quasi-)predicate and thus supply the top node of the clause. Actually, BYT´**I.1** is an element of the value of a support verb lexical function **Oper**$_i$ or **Func**$_i$, depending on the type of the (quasi-) predicate under consideration.[6]

In (4a, i), STOLICA 'capital city' expresses a binary quasi-predicate: '**X1** is.the.capital.city.of **Y2**' (of type 1); the SemS of (4a, i) is given in (5):

(5)

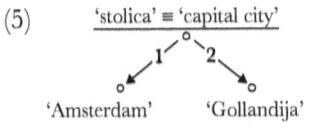

---

[5] The first two of the Russian BS types correspond to the Predicational type in Mikkelsen (2005, 48ff.), while the third one – to her Specificational, Equative and Identificational types.

[6] On lexical functions, see Wanner 1996 and Mel'čuk 2007. Two lexical functions mentioned here are as follows:
- **Oper**$_1$(L) links Deep-Synt-actant A$_I$ of L to L such that A$_I$(L) is the A$_I$(**Oper**$_1$(L)) and L itself is A$_{II}$(**Oper**$_1$(L));
- **Func**$_2$(L) links L to Deep-Synt-actant A$_{II}$ of L such that L itself is A$_I$(**Func**$_2$(L)) and A$_{II}$(L) is A$_{II}$(**Func**$_2$(L)).

This SemS undergoes Arborization by means of two SemS-to-DSyntS rules, one for Sem-dependency **1** and the other, for Sem-dependency **2**; only the first rule is presented in (6).

(6)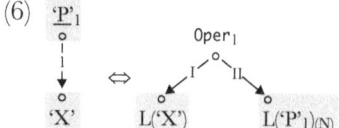

'P' stands for any predicative semanteme of type 1, and 'X,' for any semanteme; L('P') and L('X') mean "lexical expressions of 'P' and 'X'"; the underscoring indicates the communicatively dominant node.

The BS obtained in this way has AMSTERDAM as the subject. The linear arrangement of words is irrelevant in this respect: in *Amsterdam – stolica Gollandii* as well as in *Stolica Gollandii – Amsterdam* it is the noun AMSTERDAM that is the SSynt-subject. The word order expresses here the communicative organization: the first NP_{NOM} is the Theme of the sentence, and the second one, its Rheme. $Oper_1(stolica)$ = BYT´**I.1**, *javljat´sja*, so that we obtain:

For STOLICA ⊆ Synt-Theme

Stolica Gollandii – Amsterdam. ≡ *Stolicej Gollandii javljaetsja Amsterdam.*

For AMSTERDAM ⊆ Synt-Theme

Amsterdam – stolica Gollandii. ≡ *Amsterdam javljaetsja stolicej Gollandii.*

The same description applies to sentences (4a, ii) and (4a, iii), with the quasi-predicates SESTRA and NAČAL´NIK. But sentence (4a, iv) is slightly different. Its SemS appears as (7):

(7)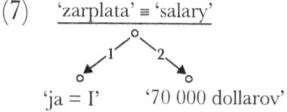

The necessary Arborization rule for Sem-dependency **2** is also different:

(8)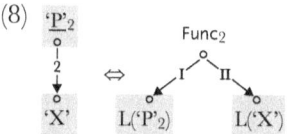

Here, *zarplata* [= L('P')], a quasi-predicate of type 2, is the SSynt-subject, and *70 000 dollarov*, the predicative part of the SSynt-predicate. $Func_2(zarplata)$ = BYT´**I.1**, *sostavljat´*, which gives (in the past tense) *Moja zarplata byla ⟨sostavljala⟩ 70 000 dollarov.*

2. BYT´**I.2** corresponds to the semanteme 'be.included'. BSs (4b, i) and (4b, ii) state the inclusion of the denotation of one NP$_{NOM}$ into the class denoted by the other, the first as an element, and the second, as a subclass.

(9) a. 'byt´.vključen' ≡ 'be.included'

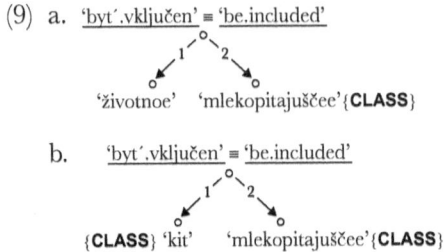

'životnoe'   'mlekopitajuščee'{**CLASS**}

  b. 'byt´.vključen' ≡ 'be.included'

{**CLASS**} 'kit'   'mlekopitajuščee'{**CLASS**}

The relevant Lexicalization and Arborization rules are shown in (10):

(10) a. 'byt´.vključen' ⇔ BYT´I.2

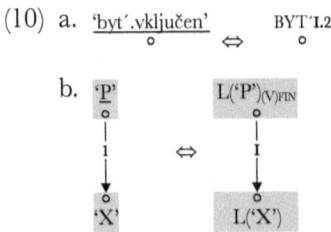

  b. 'P'   L('P')$_{(V)FIN}$
     | |
     1   ⇔   I
     | |
     'X'   L('X')

Arborization rule (10b) states that Sem-actant **1** of any 'P' is implemented by DSynt-actant **I** of L('P'), if the the result of the Lexicalization of 'P' — that is, L('P') — is a finite verb.

In accordance with the proposal in Padučeva (1979a and 1985), the semantic representation of a sentence includes the Referential Structure, where the referential status of each semanteme or configuration of semantemes is explicitly specified. Therefore, the SemSs in (9) are supplied with the indication that here 'mlekopitajuščee' = 'mammal' refers to a class.

3. BYT´**I.3** expresses the semanteme 'X identifies Y for the Addressee or himself'. It is common to speak of "identification" relation and "identity sentences"; in this case, both NP$_{NOM}$s denote the same individual entity or fact. Following a respectable tradition (starting in Russian linguistics, probably, with Arutjunova (1976) and developed by Weiss (1978), Padučeva and Uspenskij (1979, 1997) and Padučeva (1987)), I postulate a special semanteme: 'X identificiruet Y dlja Adresata ili dlja sebja ≡ X identifies Y for the Addressee/ for himself'; the SemS of (4c, i) can then be sketched as follows:

(11) 'identificirovat´' ≡ 'identify'

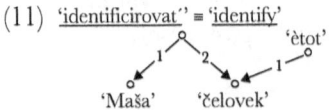

'Maša'   'čelovek'

The Sem-actant X of the semanteme 'X identifies Y' corresponds to the more informative element, that is, to the element that brings more information to the Addressee. Crucially, the BSs of this type have two important properties (Weiss 1978): 1) 'X' and 'Y' in this case must be coreferential; 2) according to the Speaker, 'X' is better known to the Addressee than 'Y.'[7]

This semanteme is expressed in Russian by the verb BYT´**I.3**, and the corresponding Lexicalization rule is (12):

(12)   'identificirovat''   BYT´**I.3**
            o   ⇔   o

The Arborization rule to be used here and in the next case is (10b).

As in other cases, both NP_{NOM}s of this BS can exchange their communicative roles:

(13) a. *Maša*$_{SSynt-T}$ – ⟨*i est*'⟩ *ètot čelovek* 'Masha is this person'.

   b. *Ètot čelovek*$_{SSynt-T}$ – ⟨*i est*'⟩ *Maša* 'This person is Masha'.

But in both of these BSs the subject is *Maša*: the verb BYT´**I.3** agrees only with *Maša* (in the feminine gender), and only the phrase *ètot čelovek* can be put into the instrumental:

(14) a. *Maša*$_{SSynt-T}$ *i byl+a*$_{FEM}$ *èt+im čelovek+om* 'Masha was this person'.

   b. *Èt+im čelovek+om*$_{SSynt-T}$ *i byl+a*$_{FEM}$ *Maša* 'This person is Masha'.

   c. **Maš+ej*$_{SSynt-T}$ *i byl+Ø*$_{MASC}$ *èt+im čelovek+om* 'Masha was this person'.

   d. **Ètot čelovek*$_{SSynt-T}$ *i byl+Ø*$_{MASC}$ *Maš+ej* 'This person is Masha'.

4. NP_{NOM}s are linked by the relation '<u>X entails Y</u>'. The SemS of (4d, i) is straightforward:

(15)   'vleč'' ≡ 'entail'
              o
            1↙ ↘2
             o   o
        'fizkul´tura' 'dolgoletie'

The corresponding Lexicalization rule is (16):

(16) 'vleč''   BYT´**I.4**IND, PRES
       o   ⇔   o

---

7 A recent paper by Goddard and Wierzbicka (2008) proposes 'specificational BE' as a new semantic primitive. To the extent that I am able to judge, their specificational BE corresponds to the Russian BE**I.3**, introduced here.

5. NP$_{NOM}$s are linked by the relation 'X is.similar.to Y'. The SemS of *Žizn' – kopejka* 'Life is a cent' [an adage] is straightforward:

(17)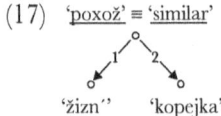

The corresponding Lexicalization rule is (18):

(18) 'poxož' ⇔ BYT´**I.5**$_{IND, PRES}$

6. NP$_{NOM}$s are linked by the metalinguistic relation 'X means Y' ≡ 'X is.a.synonym of Y'. The SemS of (4e) is shown in (19):

(19) 'značit'' = 'be.a.synonym.of'
        ╱¹ ²╲
    'kindza' 'koriandr'

The corresponding Lexicalization rule is (20):

(20) 'značit'' ⇔ BYT´**I.6**$_{IND, PRES}$

Since the relation 'X is.a.synonym.of Y' is symmetrical (= 'X and Y are synonyms'), the corresponding BSs are invertible: *Kindza – èto koriandr* ≡ *Koriandr – èto kindza*. The Speaker chooses the version according to his ideas about the Addressee's knowledge.

V. The Russian Verb BYT´

The verb BYT´ was lexicographically described in much detail in Apresjan (1995, 2009). The author distinguishes 15 senses of this verb, that is, introduces 15 lexemes in the vocable BYT´. Our study, however, requires an addition of the following six lexemes of BYT´ (which partially coincide with Apresjan's BYT´**I.1** and BYT´**I.2**). To make clearer the differences between these lexemes, I will indicate some of their formal properties, without trying to be exhaustive or very consistent: only those properties are listed that help see the differences between the BYT´ lexemes. These are the following six properties:

1. Having or not a full paradigm
2. Having or not the form *est'* in the present indicative
3. Possible parts of speech of X and Y
4. Possible cases of N$_Y$

5. Possibility of using the particles ÈTO ≈ 'this$_N$,' and I [emphasis]
6. Possible synonymous expressions

Examples are given only for BSs. In all the cases considered, N_X is the syntactic subject of the verb.

The six lexemes BYT´, which appear in BSs, are united inside the vocable BYT´ under the rubric I, since all of them are semantically based on the BYT´-copula, i.e., on BYT´**I.1**, which constitutes the semantic bridge between them. The further lexemes of BYT´ are, in accordance with Apresjan's description, grouped as BYT´**II** 'exist,' BYT´**III** 'be located,' etc.

The present description covers neither the BS with numerals (*Dva plus dva – četyre* 'Two plus two is four') nor the syntactic phrasemes of the type *Žena est´ žena* lit. 'Wife is wife.' All illustrative sentences must be conceived as pronounced with the most neutral prosody.

> BYT´**I.1** '*X* is**I.1** *Y*': 1) if Y is a predicate, then BYT´**I.1** is a semantically empty copula, or a purely structural word; 2) if Y is not a predicate, then BYT´**I.1** means 'be.identical.with.'

Formal properties

> 1. BYT´**I.1** can be in any form
> 2. BYT´**I.1** has the form *est´* in the present indicative – but only either in a formal definition (and only if X and Y are both expressed by nouns) or with the particle I
> 3. X can be expressed by a noun, an infinitive and a subordinate clause; Y can be practically anything: a nominal, an adjectival, a prepositional phrase, an appropriate adverb, etc.
> 4. If BYT´**I.1** is not in the present indicative and Y = N, this N_Y is preferably in the instrumental (N_Y in the nominative sounds obsolescent or is colloquial)
> 5. The particles ÈTO and I can be used with BYT´**I.1**,[8] but only if the subject NP precedes
> 6. If X and Y both are nouns, the most current synonyms of BYT´**I.1** are JAVLJAT´SJA and OKAZYVAT´SJA

Amsterdam$_X$ – (èto) stolica Gollandii. | *Maša$_X$ – moj načal´nik / Moj načal´nik – Maša$_X$.* | *Ego ljubov´$_X$ – prostaja prixot´* 'His love is a simple whim'. | *Osen´$_X$ – moë ljubimoe vremja goda* 'Fall is my favorite season'.

> BYT´**I.2** '*X* is**I.1** an element/a subclass of class Y' = 'X is included into the class of Ys'

---

8 The particle I is used only with the overt form *est´*; this indication is part of I's syntactics.

Formal properties

1. BYT′**I.2** can be in any form
2. BYT′**I.2** has the form *est′* in the present indicative – but rather in a formal definition
3. X and Y can be expressed only by nouns
4. If BYT′**I.2** is not in the present indicative and Y = N, this N_Y must be in the instrumental
5. The particle ÈTO can, but the particle I cannot, be used with BYT′**I.2**
6. The most current synonym is JAVLJAT′SJA

Maša$_X$ – *staraja ženščina* 'Masha is an old woman'. | *Akuly*$_X$ – *(èto) ryby, a ne mlekopitajuščie* 'Sharks are fish and not mammals'. | *Kanada*$_X$ – *bol′šaja strana* 'Canada is a big country'.

BYT′**I.3** 'X's referent is **I.1** the same as that of Y, but X is better known to the Addressee than Y' = 'X identifies Y for the Addressee'

BSs with BYT′**I.3** are notorious identity sentences (Padučeva 1987).

Formal properties

1. BYT′**I.3** can be in any form
2. BYT′**I.3** has the form *est′* in the present indicative – but only for the emphasis on X
3. X and Y can be expressed only by nouns
4. If BYT′**I.3** is not in the present indicative, N_Y may be in the instrumental
5. The particles ÈTO and I both can be used with BYT′**I.3**
6. The most current synonyms are BYT′**I.1** NE ČTO INOE, KAK ⟨NE KTO INOJ, KAK⟩, JAVLJAT′SJA and PREDSTAVLJAT′ SOBOJ

Èto (byla) Maša$_X$ 'This was Masha'. | *Maša*$_X$ *i est′ naš gost′* 'Masha is our guest'. | *Marazm*$_X$ – *naš marksizm* 'Marasm is our marxism'/*Marazm*$_X$ *byl naš marksizm* ⟨*našim marksizmom*⟩ 'Marasm was our marxism$_{NOM/INSTR}$'. | *Moë ljubimoe vremja goda – osen′*$_X$ 'My favorite season is fall'. | *Ego povedenie*$_X$ – *obyčnaja bor′ba velikodušija i tščeslavija* 'His behavior is trivial struggle between generosity and vanity'. | *Slava*$_X$ – *jarkaja zaplata na vetxom rubišče pevca* 'Glory is but a bright patch on the worn-our clothing of a poet'. | *Utrennjaja zvezda*$_X$ – *èto Venera* 'The morning star is Venus'.

BYT′**I.4** 'X is **I.1** a sufficient condition for Y' = 'X entails Y'

Formal properties

1. BYT′**I.4** can be in any form
2. BYT′**I.4** has the form *est′* in the present indicative

3. X and Y can be expressed only by nouns
4. If BYT´**I.4** is not in the present indicative, N_Y may be in the instrumental
5. The particle ÈTO is obligatory with BYT´**I.4** in the present (except for some set expressions); the particle I cannot be used
6. The most current synonyms are ZNAČIT´**II** and OZNAČAT´

Kukuruza$_X$ segodnja – èto kolbasa zavtra [N. Xruščëv] 'Corn today is sausage tomorrow.' | *Fizkul´tura est´ dolgoletie* 'Physical exercise is longevity.'

BYT´**I.5** 'X is**I.1** similar to Y'

Formal properties

1. BYT´**I.5** can be only in the present indicative
2. BYT´**I.5** has no form *est´* in the present indicative
3. X and Y can be expressed only by nouns
4. The nominative only
5. The particle ÈTO is possible with BYT´**I.5** in the present (except for some set expressions)
6. ———

Slova$_X$ – serebro, a molčan´e$_X$ – zoloto 'Words are silver, but silence is gold.'

BYT´**I.6** 'X is**I.1** a synonym of Y' = 'X means Y'

Formal properties

1. BYT´**I.6** can be only in the present indicative
2. BYT´**I.6** has the form *est´* in the present indicative – but rather in a formal definition
3. X and Y must be of the same part of speech
4. The nominative only
5. The particle ÈTO is obligatory with BYT´**I.6** (except for some set expressions); the particle I cannot be used
6. Synonymous expressions: ZNAČIT´; ÈTO TO ŽE SAMOE, ČTO…; ÈTO DRUGOE NAZVANIE DLJA…

Suffiks$_X$ – èto affiks, kotoryj sleduet za kornem 'A suffix is an affix that follows the root'. | *Tarxun$_X$ – èto èstragon* 'Tarkhun is estragon'.

For better surveyability, the properties of the different lexemes of the Russian copula BYT´ can be presented in the following table:

Table 4.1. Properties of the six lexemes of the verb BYT' 'be'

	Paradigm	est'-form	Part of speech of X/Y	Case of NY	ÈTO/I	Synonyms
BYT'1.1	full	{+}	X: N, V$_{INF}$, CLAUSE Y: anything	{NOM/INSTR}	{ÈTO, I}	JAVLJAT'SJA, OKAZAT'SJA
BYT'1.2	full	{+}	X: N, Y: N	INSTR	ÈTO	JAVLJAT'SJA
BYT'1.3	full	{+}	X: N, Y: N	INSTR	ÈTO, I	BYT' NE ČTO INOE, KAK
BYT'1.4	full	+	X: N, Y: N	INSTR	ÈTO!	ZNAČIT', OZNAČAT'
BYT'1.5	present only	–	X: N, Y: N	NOM	ÈTO	—
BYT'1.6	present only	{+}	PoS(X) = PoS(Y)	NOM	ÈTO!	ZNAČIT', ÈTO TO ŽE SAMOE, ČTO

Note: The curly brackets {...} mean 'possible under specific conditions'; the symbol ! means 'obligatory'.

The inventory of different BYT´ found in BSs does not claim exclusivity: there can be other senses not covered by it.[9] This, however, will not affect the solution proposed: we will simply have to add another lexeme.

Ambiguity between different BYT´ is of course possible: two different BSs can physically coincide, i.e., have identical signifiers. Thus, sentence (21) can express two different SemSs:

(21) *Ivan – ubijca* lit. 'Ivan murderer'

means either 'Ivan is **a** murderer' (BYT´ is here BYT´**I.1**, since the quasi-predicate 'murderer' has 'Ivan' as its SemA X_1), or 'Ivan is **the** murderer' (BYT´ is here BYT´**I.3**: the name *Ivan* identifies to the Addressee the murderer known to him). In both readings, *Ivan* is the syntactic subject, but only in the second case we can use *i est´*: *Ivan i est´ ubijca* means only 'Ivan is the murderer'. (See Weiss (1978) on the manifestation of this difference in a language with articles.)

Another example (from Padučeva 1979b, 46): the BS in (22)

(22) *Zavedujuščij laboratoriej – fizik* lit. 'The head of the laboratory physicist'

corresponds to four different SemSs:

a. Sentence (22) contains BYT´**I.1**, *zavedujuščij* is a quasi-predicate whose argument is *fizik*: 'A/The physicist is the head of the laboratory'; *fizik* is the subject, and in the past tense, we have *Zavedujušč+im*$_{INSTR}$ *laboratoriej byl fizik*; the intonation contour is ↘.
b. Sentence (22) contains BYT´**I.2**, *zavedujuščij* is used as a referential NP, *fizik* denotes a class: 'Our head of the laboratory is a physicist'; *zavedujuščij* is the subject; in the past tense: *Naš zavedujuščij laboratoriej byl fizik+∅*$_{NOM}$/ *fizik+om*$_{INSTR}$; the intonation contour is ↗ ↘.
c. Sentence (22) contains BYT´**I.3**, *zavedujuščij* and *fizik* both are referential NPs. Then the sentence is an identity statement and expresses one of the two SemSs (both sentences are better in this sense with (*i*) *est´* as the main verb):

   (i) 'It is our head of the laboratory who is this physicist [of whom we are talking]': *zavedujuščij* is the subject; in the past tense: *Naš zavedujuščij*

---

9 The inventory proposed may lack another sense of BYT´: 'X is.called Y,' as in *Zdravstvujte, ja Boris. A Vas kak zovut?* 'Hello, I am Boris; what is your name?' In English, where this way of introducing oneself is more current, BE has such a sense beyond any doubt. See two books on copulas in languages of the world, where the properties and the possible senses of different copulas are presented and discussed, with a rich bibliography: Pustet (2003) and Mikkelsen (2005).

laboratoriej i byl ètot samyj fizik+Ø$_{\text{NOM}}$ */ ètim samym fizik+**om***$_{\text{INSTR}}$ 'It was our head of the laboratory who was this physicist'.

(ii) 'It is this physicist who is our head of the laboratory': *fizik* is the subject; in the past tense we have *Našim zavedujuščim laboratoriej i byl ètot samyj fizik+Ø*$_{\text{NOM}}$ 'It was this physicist who was our head of the laboratory'.

To conclude this section, I would like to consider the case illustrated in the motto:

(23) a. *Krasota – èto istina* 'Beauty is truth'.

This sentence means that something [= 'α'] which is beautiful is also true; therefore, its SemS appears as (23b):

b.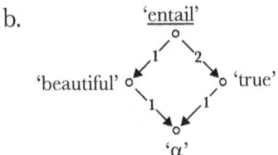

We see here a case of BYT´**1.3** 'X entails Y': one can say *Krasota dlja menja i byla istinoj* 'For me, beauty was truth' or *Krasota dlja menja označala istinu* 'For me, beauty signified truth'.

VI. Some English Equivalents of Russian Bi-nominative Sentences

The main difference between Russian and English bi-nominative sentences is imposed by the different nature of the syntactic structure in both languages. While in Russian the SyntS of a sentence is independent of its Comm(unicative) S, in English, on the contrary, the SyntS is affected by the CommS: the NP corresponding to the Theme tends to be the syntactic subject. Let us compare a pair of English sentences in (24) and their Russian equivalents in (25), with the subject phrases boldfaced:

(24) a. **My only resource** *is my education, experience and the Internet.*
b. **My education, experience and the Internet** *are my only resource.*

(25) a. *Moj edinstvennyj resurs –* **moë obrazovanie, opyt i Internet***.*
b. **Moë obrazovanie, opyt i Internet** *– moj edinstvennyj resurs.*

In (25), we have of course BYT´**1.1** – the empty copula, since RESURS is a quasi-predicate ('X is Y's resource for doing Z').

SYNTAX. BI-NOMINATIVE SENTENCES IN RUSSIAN

In English, the phrase that is the Theme becomes the subject; as a result, the sentences of (24) have different subjects. Not so in Russian: in both sentences of (25) the subject is the same.

To cover such cases, the following Arborization rules are needed in English – (26a) for (24a) and (26b) for (24b). These rules clearly show the main difference with Russian: being the Theme is a crucial factor in the choice of the DSynt-actant **I**, i.e. of the subject.

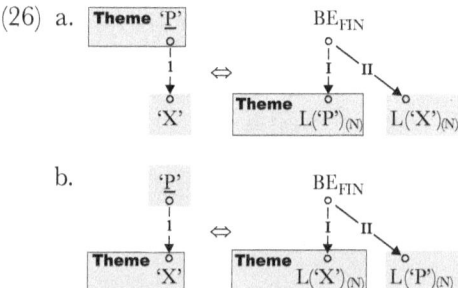

Another example of the same type is (27):

(27) *My only solution **is** pigs.* ~ *Pigs **are** my only solution.*

The agreement of the copula clearly identifies the subject.

VII. Conclusions

The claim of this chapter is straightforward:

> The syntactic structure of a (Russian) sentence is basically determined by its semantic structure.

What lexical expression L is the syntactic subject depends on the choice made in the process of Lexicalization of the starting semantic structure. If the meaning 'L' is lexicalized as L being Deep-Synt-actant **I** of the main verb of the sentence, L ends up as the subject. Whether this is done or not depends in the first place on the semantemes in the SemS and the lexical units available in the language. The communicative structure is also of crucial importance, but its effects are secondary with respect to the semantic relations.

What about Padučeva's (1987) and Padučeva and Uspenskij's (1979) denotational criterion for subjecthood? Their observation that the subjects strongly tend to be more referential than the predicatives is absolutely correct.

However, as I think, this is an important property of subjects rather than a criterion allowing us to decide whether a particular NP$_{NOM}$ is a subject or not.

To close the discussion, I would propose an example of how the results of this chapter can be used in practice, in particular, when teaching Russian. Let us consider a Russian sentence:

(28) a. *Čistoe nakazan'e ètot Pet'ka!* lit. 'Sheer punishment this Pete!'

Which NP is the subject here? The first step is to consider the meaning: sentence (28) means 'Pete is a punishment' – that is, it ascribes to Pete a particular (unpleasant) property; 'punishment' is a predicate. Therefore, we conclude that the sentence contains BYT´**I.1** as a copula, with X = 'Pete' (the subject) and Y = 'punishment' (the nominal part of the predicate). The marked word order expresses focalized rheme ('sheer punishment'). Checking the properties of the verb BYT´**I.1**, we see that all of them are satisfied:

b. *Čistoe nakazan'e byla èta Maška!* lit. 'Sheer punishment was this Mary!'
c. *Čistym nakazan'em okazalas'dlja menja èta Maška!*
 lit. 'Sheer punishment$_{INSTR}$ turned.out.to.be for me this Mary!'

Acknowledgments

The first sketches of the chapter were read, reread and criticized – as always – by L. Iordanskaja; the subsequent versions have profited from criticisms and suggestions by Ju Apresjan, J. Milićević, E. Padučeva and D. Weiss. I thank them all from the depth of my heart.

References

Apresjan, Ju. 1995. *Izbrannye trudy. Tom II. Integral'noe opisanie jazyka i sistemnaja leksikografija.* Moscow: Škola Jazyki russkoj kul´tury.

———. 2009. *Issledovanija po semantike i leksikografii. Tom I. Paradigmatika.* Moscow: Jazyki slavjanskix kul´tur.

Arutjunova, N. 1976. *Predloženie i ego smysl.* Moscow: Nauka.

Benveniste, É. 1950. "La phrase nominale". *Bulletin de la Société de linguistique de Paris* 46 (1). [Reprinted in É. Benveniste. 1966. *Problèmes de linguistique générale.* Paris: Gallimard, 151–67.]

Goddard, C. and A. Wierzbicka. 2008. "New Semantic Primes and New Syntactic Frames: 'Specificational BE' and 'abstract THIS/IT.'" In C. Goddard (ed.), *Cross-Linguistic Semantics,* 35–57. Amsterdam and Philadelphia: Benjamins.

Jespersen, O. 1965/1924. *The Philosophy of Grammar.* New York and London: W. Norton.

Kimmelman, V. 2009. "On the interpretation of *èto* in so-called *èto*-clefts." In G. Zybatow, U. Junghans, D. Lenertová and P. Biskup (eds), *Studies in Formal Slavic Phonology, Morphology, Syntax, Semantics and Information Structure,* 319–27. Frankfurt am Main: P. Lang.

Mel'čuk, I. 1974a. *Opyt teorii lingvističeskix modelej «Smysl ⇔ Tekst»*. Moscow: Nauka [1995²].
———. 1974b. "O sintaksičeskom nule". In A. Xolodovič (ed.), *Tipologija passivnyx konstrukcij. Diatezy i zalogi*, 343–61. Leningrad: Nauka.
———. 1979. "Syntactic, or Lexical, Zero in Natural Language." *Proceedings of the 5th Annual Meeting of the Berkeley Linguistics Society*. Berkeley: University of California–Berkeley.
———. 1988. *Dependency Syntax: Theory and Practice*. Albany, NY: SUNY Press.
———. 2001. *Communicative Organization in Natural Language. The Semantic-Communicative Structure of Sentences*. Amsterdam and Philadelphia: Benjamins.
———. 2002. "Towards a Formal Concept 'Zero Linguistic Sign': Applications in Typology." In S. Bendjaballah, W. Dressler, O. Pfeiffer and M. Voeikova (eds), *Morphology 2000: Selected Papers from the 9th Morphology Meeting, Vienna, 24–28 February 2000*, 241–58. Amsterdam and Philadelphia: Benjamins.
———. 2006. *Aspects of the Theory of Morphology*. Berlin: Mouton de Gruyter.
———. 2007. "Lexical Functions." In H. Burger, D. Dobrovol'skij, P. Kühn and N. Norrick (eds), *Phraseology. An International Handbook of Contemporary Research*, 119–31. Berlin and New York: W. de Gruyter.
———. 2009. "Dependency in Natural Language." In A. Polguère and I. Mel'čuk (eds), *Dependency in Linguistic Description*, 1–110. Amsterdam and Philadelphia: Benjamins.
Mikkelsen, L. 2005. *Copular Clauses: Specification, Predication and Equation*. Amsterdam and Philadelphia: Benjamins.
Padučeva, E. 1979a. "Denotativnyj status imennoj gruppy i ego otraženie v semantičeskom predstavlenii predloženija". *Naučno-texničeskaja informacija* 2 (9): 25–31.
———. 1979b. "Topic and Focus in Russian Bi-nominative Sentences". *Statistical Methods in Linguistics* [SMIL] 3–4: 29–47.
———. 1985. *Vyskazyvanie i ego sootnesennost' s dejstvitel'nost'ju*. Moscow: Nauka.
———. 1987. "Predloženija toždestva: semantika i kommunikativnaja struktura". In V. Petrov (ed.), *Jazyk i logičeskaja teorija*, 152–63. Moscow: AN SSSR.
———. 2009. *Stat'i raznyx let*. Moscow: Jazyki slavjanskix kul'tur.
Padučeva, E. and Uspenskij, V. 1979. "Podležaščee ili skazuemoe?" *Izvestija AN SSSR, serija lit-ry i jazyka* 38 (4): 349–60. [Reprinted in Padučeva 2009, 119–33.]
———. 1997. "Binominativnoe predloženie: problema soglasovanija svjazki". In L. Krysin (ed.), *Oblik slova. Sbornik statej pamjati D.N. Šmelëva*, 170–82. Moscow: Institut Rus. Jazyka RAN, Indrik. [Reprinted in Padučeva 2009, 134–44.]
Peškovskij, A. 1934. *Russkij sintaksis v naučnom osveščenii*. Moscow: Gosučpedgiz.
Pustet, R. 2003. *Copulas: Universals in the Categorization of the Lexicon*. Oxford: Oxford University Press.
Wanner, L., ed. 1996. *Lexical Functions in Lexicography and Natural Language Processing*. Amsterdam and Philadelphia: Benjamins.
Weiss, D. 1978. "Identitätsaussagen im Russischen: ein Versuch ihrer Abgrenzung gegenüber anderen Satztypen". In W. Girke and H. Jachnow (eds), *Slawistische Linguistik 1977. Referate des III. Konstanzer Slawistischen Arbeitstreffen Bochum 27.9.77–29.9.77*, 224–59. Munich: O. Sagner.

Chapter 5

PSYCHOLINGUISTICS. THE EFFECT OF GRAMMATICAL GENDER IN RUSSIAN SPOKEN-WORD RECOGNITION

Irina A. Sekerina
College of Staten Island and the Graduate Center of the City University of New York

I. Introduction

Linguistics is experiencing a fundamental shift in the way it studies language as its object of investigation. While traditional linguistics relied on the introspection of researchers and used a top-down approach that led from theory to empirical facts, modern linguistics is rapidly shifting to an empirical, data-driven investigation of language phenomena (Featherston and Winkler 2009). As experimental data become more and more critical for linguistic theories, this change in paradigm puts psycholinguistics, a branch of linguistics that studies the psychological mechanisms underlying language performance, at the forefront of language science.

Main themes in psycholinguistics closely match the traditional subfields of theoretical linguistics, but the crucial difference between the two is methodology: Psycholinguistics is based on experimental techniques which supply participants' judgments of language stimuli and offer an insight into immediate, moment-to-moment language. Psycholinguistic data often become the critical evidence for distinguishing between competing linguistic theories, as is exemplified by a debate between the head-driven phrase structure grammar (Pollard and Sag 1994) and the government-binding generative grammar (Chomsky 1986) about the nature and typology of empty categories in syntax (Fodor 1993). In addition, psycholinguistic data can provide a powerful impetus for new developments in influential theoretical models, as is the case with the cohort model of spoken-word recognition by Marslen-Wilson (Marslen-Wilson and Welsh 1978).

Slavic psycholinguistics is no exception; for the past ten years, the main forum for theoretical Slavic linguistics in the US, the annual Workshop on Formal Approaches to Slavic Linguistics (FASL), has included psycholinguistic talks that illuminate the contribution of experimental studies of Russian, Serbian, Croatian, Bulgarian and Polish to a variety of topics in linguistic theory ranging from verbal morphology to discourse (Sekerina 2006). But it is especially exciting when a Slavic-specific linguistic phenomenon combined with an innovative experimental technique delivers a decisive argument in a long-debated issue. Such an issue – the role of grammatical gender in spoken-word recognition – is the focus of the present chapter.

In Russian, a language with a robust inflectional morphology and substantial freedom of word order, gender is a particularly strong morphosyntactic feature. It manifests itself in (a) the assignment of nouns to gender categories, and (b) gender agreement of nouns (and pronouns) with corresponding adjectives, participles and verbs. In addition to gender, Russian nouns are morphologically marked for case and number. Adjectives agree with the head noun in gender, case and number, and this agreement is encoded on adjectives in the form of a morphological ending: *krasn-yj/-aja/-oe* 'red $_{\text{MASC/FEM/NEUT-NOM-SG}}$.' Because adjectives do not have to be immediately adjacent to the nouns they modify, these grammatical features including gender are an important grammatical device that establishes global coherence in sentences.

It comes as no surprise that gender effect is robust at the morphosyntactic and semantic levels of sentence processing. The question we address in this chapter is to what extent grammatical gender on the adjective can influence processing of the head noun at the earlier level of analysis, i.e., word recognition, and what its temporal characteristics are. Our results regarding the effectiveness of gender as a constraint on selection of lexical competitors replicate the findings by Dahan, Swingley, Tanenhaus and Magnuson (2000) for spoken-word recognition in French and extend them to a different language (i.e., Russian) and different materials (adjective-noun phrases). Moreover, when used in the syntactic construction with split constituents constrained by appropriate pragmatics, gender information on the adjective can facilitate recognition of the noun, and it happens much earlier in Russian than in French, i.e., *prior* to the noun's appearance in the speech stream.

Early influence of gender information has important consequences for discourse-related interpretative processes, such as the mapping of referential expressions. In addition, the fact that gender information on the nonadjacent adjective can constrain recognition of the head noun constitutes evidence against the form-based account of gender effect in French spoken-word recognition (Dahan et al. 2000). Instead, gender effect in Russian word recognition must originate at the grammatical level of processing as suggested by Weber and Paris (2004). They, however, relied on cross-linguistic materials and demonstrated that the French gender accessed implicitly by bilingual French-German listeners can affect spoken-word recognition of German nouns. This restriction to the cross-linguistic materials was inevitable because they claimed that "within one language, these two accounts (the form- versus grammar-based) are difficult to tease apart" (6). The results of our Russian experiments provide the missing evidence for the grammar-based gender effect from within one language.

1.1. Gender and spoken-word recognition: The gender-matching/ mismatching paradigm

Marslen-Wilson and colleagues (Marslen-Wilson and Welsh 1978) laid the foundation for early research in spoken-word recognition in English. They proposed the influential cohort model, according to which spoken-word recognition starts with identification of the very first phoneme of the word. Because not all the perceptual information is yet available, more than one representation will be activated. Thus, a spoken target noun (e.g., *candy*) will be activated together with competitor nouns that begin with the identical phonetic material (e.g., *candle*), because more than one representation will fit the first part of the perceptual output form (*can-*). All activated lexical candidates will then compete in a recognition race. Subsequent studies that investigated spoken-word recognition of words presented in isolation, i.e., in the absence of context, revealed that listeners' speed of recognition was affected by the size of the neighborhood for the target word and its frequency (Norris, McQueen and Cutler 1995), and possibly, by the size of the vocabulary.

Words, however, are rarely uttered in isolation; typically, spoken-word recognition takes place in the context of surrounding words that can form a phrase with the target words. The phonological, morphosyntactic, semantic and discourse contexts of the target word can influence its subsequent recognition (see McQueen and Cutler 2001, and other articles in the special issue of *Language and Cognitive Processes* 2001, for a comprehensive review). Effects of morphosyntactic information are most robust in languages with rich morphology, and grammatical gender often plays the central role in this process. The main theoretical question of interest is the mechanism of how gender agreement encoded as a grammatical marker on the preceding word affects recognition of the following target word and its temporal characteristics.

Early cross-linguistic studies of grammatical gender effects on spoken-word recognition in French (Grosjean, Dommergues, Cornu, Guillelmon and Besson 1994), Russian (Akhutina, Kurgansky, Polinsky and Bates 1999) and Dutch, German, Italian and Hebrew (see *Journal of Psycholinguistic*

Research 1999) employed the gender-matching/mismatching paradigm in which a prenominal adjective marked for gender was presented before the target noun in a phrase, and it was either congruent in gender with the noun (e.g., *bol'šaja sobaka* 'a big$_{FEM}$ dog$_{FEM}$') or incongruent (e.g. **bol'šoj sobaka* 'a big$_{MASC}$ dog$_{FEM}$'). Participants performed a metalinguistic task with the target (e.g., lexical decision, picture naming or cued shadowing) that was based on elicited production; for example, in the cued shadowing task, they had to repeat each word as soon as they heard it. Gender-incongruent adjectives significantly slowed a participant's repetition (i.e., recognition) of the target noun, demonstrating strong inhibition effects in most studied languages (Friederici and Jacobsen 1999). In contrast, the gender facilitation effect, i.e., faster recognition of the target noun when preceded by a gender-congruent word, was weak and often inconsistent, varying from language to language (Bates, Devescovi, Pizzamiglio, D'Amico and Hernandez 1995; Bordag and Pechmann 2008; Taraban and Kempe 1999) and task to task (Akhutina et al. 1999).

1.2. Gender and spoken-word recognition: Eyetracking

Dahan, Swingley, Tanenhaus and Magnuson (2000) pointed out that difficulty with finding reliable facilitation effect of gender in the gender-matching/mismatching experiments described above could stem from methodological problems. These early experiments relied on metalinguistic production tasks, such as naming decision, picture naming and cue-shadowing, that were performed long after the target noun recognition was completed, and that might have masked an early gender effect. They suggested that the visual world paradigm (Trueswell and Tanenhaus 2004) was better suited for studying effects of contextual constraints on spoken-word recognition because this technique has fine temporal resolution, is independent of metalinguistic production tasks, and does not rely on ungrammatical phrases.

In the past ten years, starting with the seminal paper by Allopenna and colleagues (Allopenna, Magnuson and Tanenhaus 1998), eyetracking in the visual world paradigm has been established as the main method to investigate spoken-word recognition. It lends itself well to test the effect of gender agreement on the preceding word on the target noun recognition. Dahan and colleagues (Dahan et al. 2000) coupled the cohort model and the visual world paradigm to find out whether gender information encoded on the definite article constrained activation of lexical candidates, i.e., nouns, in spoken-word recognition in French. French listeners were presented with four pictures on a computer screen (two of them were buttons and bottles) and were asked to click on the target noun presented with the definite article. In Experiment 1, the definite article was in plural and not marked for grammatical gender (e.g., *Cliquez sur les boutons* 'Click on the buttons'). The participants looked more often at the cohort competitor, namely, the picture that shared initial sounds with the target (*les bouteilles* 'the bottles') than at the two phonologically unrelated distractors (*les chiens* 'the dogs' and *les salières* 'the salt shakers'). This brief activation of the cohort competitor took place approximately 300 ms after the onset of the target, e.g., upon hearing the fragment *les bou-* that the two nouns shared. Remarkably, in Experiment 2, when the plural article was replaced with a singular gender-marked article *le*, the initial set of lexical candidates was constrained: only *le bouton* 'the button$_{MASC}$' was activated, but not the cohort competitor of the different gender, *la bouteille* 'the bottle$_{FEM}$,' eliminating the cohort effect. Critically, the mere presence of grammatical gender information on the article did not result in faster recognition of the target noun (*le zèbre* 'the zebra$_{MASC}$') in the presence of the phonologically unrelated distractor of the same gender (*le balai* 'the broom$_{MASC}$').

To describe the mechanism of this influence of gender information on the article on the target noun recognition, Dahan et al. proposed two explanations, form-based and grammar-based. According to the form-based account, the parser keeps track of the distributional regularities between the preceding article and the target noun, e.g., the probability that *le* will be followed by *bouton* 'button$_{MASC}$.' In contrast, the grammar-based account predicts that all of the present nouns of the same gender should be activated; however, because no such activation of the distractors of the same gender was found, Dahan and colleagues argued that their data supported the form-based origin of the gender effect in French spoken-word recognition.

Weber and Paris (2004) challenged the form-based account of Dahan et al. (2000) when they examined gender effect on spoken-word recognition, using cross-linguistic materials. They presented German article-noun phrases to native French–L2 German bilingual speakers. The German target nouns (e.g., *die Perle* 'the$_{FEM}$ pearl') were selected in such a way that their onsets were phonologically very similar to those of French cohort competitors (*la perle* 'the$_{FEM}$ pearl'); however, French was never mentioned during the experiment. The explicit German target always matched in gender with the implicit French target. In the same-gender condition, the explicit (present in the display) German cohort competitor, *die Perücke* 'the$_{FEM}$ wig,' and the implicit French cohort competitor, *la perruque* 'the$_{FEM}$ wig,' were of the same gender. In the different-gender condition, the gender of each was different (e.g., *die Kanone* 'the$_{FEM}$ canon' in German versus *le canon* 'the$_{MASC}$ canon' in French). Weber and Paris replicated the monolingual cohort effect for nonnative listening in German in the same-gender condition with cross-linguistic materials. French listeners briefly activated the implicit French cohort competitor of the same gender as the German target noun, starting around 200 ms after target onset. In the different-gender condition, the cohort effect was eliminated: French listeners rapidly used gender information on the implicit French cohort competitor, *canon* 'canon$_{MASC}$,' to constrain the initial set of lexical candidates in German, the language of the experiment. The fact that gender information on the article of the implicitly present native French target noun affected the explicitly present L2 German target noun constitutes a compelling argument against the form-based account of such effects (Dahan et al. 2000). The observed cross-linguistic gender effect cannot be form-based because the explicit article was in German while the implicit target noun was in French, and such co-occurrences of two forms from different languages cannot be subject to the same distributional regularities as in one language; therefore, it must be grammar-based.

Similarly, the gender-marked definite article facilitates noun recognition in Spanish. In the looking-while-listening experiment with adults and 2- to 3-year-old children, Lew-Williams and Fernald (2007) showed that both groups were faster (70–100 ms on average) in launching eye movements to the picture of the target noun when it was preceded by the gender-marked article (*la pelota* 'the$_{FEM}$ ball') and paired with the picture of the distractor noun in different gender (*el zapato* 'the$_{MASC}$ shoe') than paired with the distractor of the same gender (*la galleta* 'the$_{FEM}$ cookie'). The gender effect was robust even in the absence of cohort competition.

II. Gender and Spoken-Word Recognition in Russian

The present chapter reports the results of two eyetracking experiments with monolingual Russian adults that tested the effect of grammatical gender on spoken-word recognition. The materials chosen for these experiments consisted of color adjective-noun pairs because Russian does not have articles. We restricted nouns to two of the three-gender Russian system, masculine and feminine, because they dominate the Russian lexicon, 40 percent and 39 percent, respectively (Rice 2004; cf. Akhutina et al. 1999). Neuter nouns were not included in the current experiments not only because of their relative infrequency in the language but also because of a limited number of concrete tokens that could be easily rendered in pictures.

Russian offers a rare opportunity to test the form- versus grammar-based effect of grammatical gender on spoken-word recognition within the same language because it allows other words to intervene between the gender-marked adjective and the head noun it modifies. In the generative grammar, this phenomenon is known as *Split Scrambling*, or the *split-constituent construction*, e.g., *Krasnuju položite mašinku v Poziciju 4* 'Red put car in Position 4' (*Russkaja Grammatika* 1982, 199–214; see Pereltsvaig 2008 for syntactic analysis; Sekerina 1997). It is a grammatically marked option of word order variation in Russian that encodes contrastiveness by separating the adjective from the head noun and moving it to the sentence-initial position. In addition, one of the split-constituent components, either the adjective or the noun, must carry a contrastive pitch accent. The split-constituent construction is undoubtedly a marked option compared to canonical and regular nonsplit scrambled word orders but it is quite frequent in spoken Russian, poetry and folk literature. The split-constituent construction in the Russian experiments described below was created by insertion of a verb *položite* 'put$_{IMPER}$' between the gender-marked adjective and the noun it modified. This increased the distance between the two words to 460 ms on average and allowed us to observe the grammatical gender effect in the form of anticipatory eye movements to the target, i.e., before the noun appeared in speech. If gender agreement information on the adjective can constrain the initial set of lexical candidates, it is predicted to have its effect earlier in Russian than in French (Dahan et al. 2000) and German (Weber and Paris 2004) article-noun pairs where it was detected on average 200–300 ms *after* the onset of the target noun.

Experiment 1 employed no-cohort materials (all the nouns were phonologically unrelated) and was conducted with Russian-dominant bilinguals in the United States. Experiment 2 was based on the findings of Dahan et al. (2000) and relied on the cohort effect established for bilingual Russian adults (Marian and Spivey 2003) and monolingual Russian adults and children (Sekerina and Brooks 2007) in the previous eyetracking studies. Marian and Spivey tested 14 bilingual Russian-English participants in Russian. In the cohort condition, the target object, *spicy* 'knitting needles,' was contrasted with the cohort competitor, *spički* 'matches' in the presence of two distractors. Bilingual participants operating in Russian-only mode looked at the cohort competitor significantly more (18 percent of the time) than at the phonologically unrelated distractor in the same position on the table (5 percent). In our eyetracking experiments (Sekerina and Brooks 2007), we confirmed the robustness of the cohort effect in monolingual adults and 5- to 6-year-old children that manifested itself as interference from the cohort competitor and also established its fine-grained time course: the presence of the lexical competitor slowed down recognition of the target noun by 200 ms on average. Our results demonstrate that nonadjacent gender-marked adjectives can eliminate the cohort effect and provide novel evidence for the grammar-based account of early gender effect within one language, Russian.

III. Eyetracking Studies of Gender Effect on Spoken-Word Recognition in Russian

III.1. Experiment 1: No cohorts

III.1.2. Method

Participants

Sixteen Rutgers University graduate students took part in Experiment 1. They were native speakers of Russian who had lived in Russia all their lives. They came to the United States as a part of the Edmund S. Muskie/Freedom Support Act Graduate Fellowship Exchange Program administered by the American Councils for International Education. All participants were in the US on a J-1 visa and for less than one year at the time of testing, and were required to return to Russia after completion of the program. They were all relatively proficient in English (intermediate level), but were clearly Russian-dominant speakers (graduated from Russian high schools and universities). The participants had normal or corrected-to-normal vision and normal hearing. They were paid small honoraria to participate in the experiment, which took 40 minutes to complete.

Materials

Russian participants were presented with a vertical plastic board that consisted of a central fixation (cross placed over digit 5, Figure 5.1) and four flat colored objects. The objects were made of thin plywood and colored with spray paint. The participants acted out spoken instructions by

Figure 5.1. The two types of visual display in Experiment 1 (no cohorts)

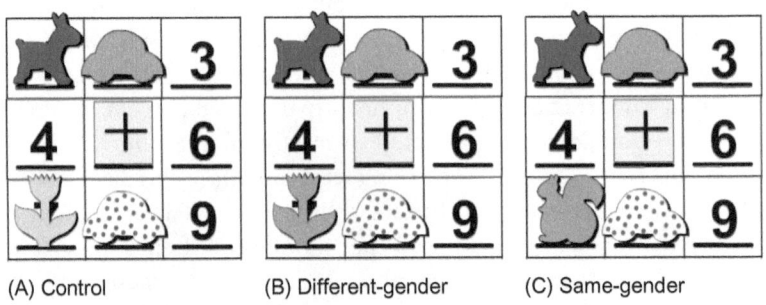

(A) Control   (B) Different-gender   (C) Same-gender

Note: (A) The control scene, consisting of the target (*red car*$_{FEM}$, Position 2), the target's contrast object (*silver car*, Position 8), and two distractors (*green horse*, Position 1; *yellow flower*, Position 7). (B) In the different-gender scene, the yellow flower is replaced with a color competitor of different gender (*red flower*$_{MASC}$). (C) In the same-gender scene, the color competitor of different gender (*red flower*$_{MASC}$) is replaced with a color competitor of same gender (*red squirrel*$_{FEM}$).

physically picking and moving the objects on the board. The objects were (a) the target, *krasnuju mašinku* 'red$_{FEM-ACC}$ car$_{FEM-ACC}$'; (b) the different-gender color competitor, *krasnyj cvetok* 'red$_{MASC}$ flower$_{MASC}$' (Fig. 5.1B), or the same-gender color competitor, *krasnuju belku* 'red$_{FEM-ACC}$ squirrel$_{FEM-ACC}$' (Fig. 5.1C); (c) the target's contrast object (a silver car); and (d) an unrelated distractor (a green horse).

As is typical in the eyetracking paradigm, the selection of objects was constrained by nouns that referred to concrete objects and by how well objects could be recognized by contours alone. Thus, the nouns were common and highly frequent Russian words, and no special efforts were taken to match them in frequency of occurrence. Twenty-four unique target-competitor pairs, with 12 feminine and 12 masculine target nouns, both animate and inanimate, were included in the experiment. Each target in the experimental conditions (e.g., *krasnaja mašina* 'red car$_{FEM}$') was paired with a phonologically unrelated competitors (the competitor in different gender *krasnyj cvetok* 'red flower$_{MASC}$', the competitor in the same gender *krasnaja belka* 'red squirrel$_{FEM}$') and distractors; thus, there were no cohorts among the four objects on the display.

Spoken instructions were commands, e.g., the verb *položite* 'put,' followed by the adjective-noun phrase to put the target object into one of the free positions on the board, and were presented along with the objects in four different positions. Eight different color adjectives were used repeatedly (red, blue, yellow, green, black, orange, purple and silver). All adjectives had grammatical gender unambiguously encoded by their endings: *-yj* (inanimate masculine), *-ogo* (animate masculine), and *-uju* (animate and inanimate feminine). Phonologically, these endings are quite distinct (cf. Akhutina et al. 1999), providing listeners with a strong cue with respect to the gender of the upcoming noun. The instructions were recorded in a soundproof booth, by a female native speaker of Russian, in a mono mode sampling at 22050 Hz. The durations of the three critical regions – the adjective, the noun and the verb – were measured. The mean duration of the adjective was 600 ms, the noun 530 ms, and the verb *položite* 'put' 460 ms.

There were 48 items, 24 experimental and 24 control items. In the experimental items, there were always two objects of the same color but in the control ones, all the objects were of different colors. Two factors were manipulated in the factorial 2 × 2 design, the gender of the target/competitor (different- vs. same-gender) in the visual scene and the word order (nonsplit-constituent vs. split-constituent construction). In the different-gender condition, the target *red car* was in feminine and the color competitor *red flower* was in masculine (Fig. 5.1B). In the same-gender condition, both the target and the color competitor were of the same gender, *red car*$_{FEM}$ versus *red squirrel*$_{FEM}$

(Fig. 5.1C). In the control items (Fig. 5.1A), the target was the only red object in the display. The initial locations of the target and the color competitor as well as their destination locations were randomized across the trials. For the word order manipulation, listeners were given spoken instructions in one of the two word orders, the nonsplit adjective-noun-verb construction (1a) or the split-constituent adjective-verb-noun construction (1b):

(1) a. *Krasnuju*   *mašinku*   *položite*   v *Poziciju* 6
     Red$_{FEM-ACC}$ car$_{FEM-ACC}$ put   in Position 6
   b. *KRASnuju*   *položite*   *mašinku*   v *Poziciju* 6
     RED$_{FEM-ACC}$ put   car$_{FEM-ACC}$ in Position 6
     'Put the red car in Position 6.'

In the nonsplit word order condition (1a), the instruction started with the color adjective-noun pair as the direct object (in the accusative case) of the verb *položite* 'put' in the sentence-initial position. Crucially, the adjective and the noun were immediately adjacent and were moved to the sentence-initial position as a unit. In contrast, example (1b) illustrates the split-constituent condition, with the adjective moved to the sentence-initial position and the noun in its original position. The contrastive accent was always on the adjective which was felicitous in the visual display because of the presence of the color contrast set for two cars, the red and silver one.

Procedure

Participants were seated at an arm's length from the vertical board. Their eye movements were recorded by the ISCAN ETL-500 head-mounted eyetracking system. Eye movements were sampled at a rate of 30 frames per second, and were recorded on a digital SONY DSR-30 videotape recorder. Auditory stimuli were played to the participant through the speakers on the scene monitor which was connected to a separate speech-controlling computer and were superimposed on eye movements. Prior to the experiment, each participant underwent a calibration procedure.

Before each trial the experimenter would position the four flat objects in their designated positions on the board, using photographs of the board as a script. During this preparation time, participants were free to scan the display. Each trial consisted of three instructions; all three were recorded as one sound file, with natural pauses of approximately 400 ms between the instructions. First, participants were instructed to look at the cross that was positioned over number 5 on the board (2a). The second experimental instruction asked the participants to move the target object (2b) followed by a third filler instruction to move another object (2c).

(2) a. *Posmotrite   na krest.*
       Look   at the cross.
    b. *Krasnuju   položite   mašinku   v Poziciju 6.*
       Red$_{FEM}$ put   car$_{FEM}$ in Position 6.
    c. *Teper'   položite   serebrjanuju mašinku v Poziciju 4.*
       Now   put   silver   car in Position 4.
   'Look at the cross.
   Put the red car in Position 6.
   Now put the silver car in Position 4.'

Participants were asked to listen to the instructions and perform the required action as quickly as possible. Their accuracy was almost perfect, with two errors in the entire experiment.

Data treatment

Eye movements were analyzed from the videotape records using the digital SONY DSR-30 VCR with frame-by-frame control and synchronized video and audio input. They were coded manually for each trial in 33 ms time resolution from the onset of the word *cross* in the fixation instruction (2a) until the participant touched the object to be moved in the experimental instruction (2b). The onsets of the four words were noted: the cross, the adjective, the noun and the verb *put*. Eight fixation categories were coded: the cross; the target, *red car*; the different-gender color competitor, *red flower*; the same-gender color competitor, *red squirrel*; the shape competitor, *silver car*; the other distractor; the looks in between objects and the track loss. The looks at the cross, the shape competitor, the other distractor, the looks in between objects, and the track loss combined accounted for 22.5 percent of the eye movement data, and were not analyzed.

In order to compare the proportions of fixations to the three objects of interest – the target and the different-and same-gender competitors – three temporal regions of interest were defined. Region 1 was the adjective region and corresponded to the mean duration of the eight adjectives used in the experiment, 600 ms. This region included the average 100 ms duration of the adjective ending, *-yj/ -ogo*$_{MASC}$*/ -uju*$_{FEM}$, which provided the crucial gender information. Region 2 encompassed the first 300 ms of the noun (in the nonsplit conditions) or the verb (in the split conditions) extending from 601 ms to 900 ms. The programming of eye movement is usually estimated to take place at approximately 200 ms before it is launched. Because it was the morphological ending of the adjective that pointed to the gender of the yet-to-come target noun, anticipatory eye movements to the target were expected to occur in Region 2. Finally, Region 3 was the remaining part of the noun or the verb that extended on average from 901 to 1,500 ms.

For investigation of the gender effect, we restricted our analyses to Regions 2 and 3. We computed the probabilities of fixating each of the three objects of interest (the target and the different- and same-gender competitors) for each condition over time and represented them in graphs. These probabilities indicate the proportion of fixations to each object averaged across all the participants and all the trials, for each 33 ms video frame. Because the fixations to the other objects were not included in the analysis, the fixations to the target and competitor were in complementary distribution, i.e., increased looks to the competitor mean decreased looks to the target, and vice versa.

Two types of data were analyzed for each of the three regions of interest: coarse-grain and fine-grained eye movements. The coarse-grain analysis of fixations allows us to assess general effects of gender information encoded on the adjective upon recognition of the target noun whereas the fine-grained eye movement patterns reveal temporal characteristics of this process. We predicted that we would find a gender effect as soon as the gender agreement information on the adjective becomes available, i.e., in Region 2. If Russian listeners are able to use gender marking on the adjective to restrict their attention to the target noun that matched in gender, there should be more fixations to the target than to the color competitor in the different-gender conditions. And if the gender effect is early, then target recognition the split-constituent conditions should take place in Region 2, *prior* to its appearance in speech. In contrast, in the same-gender conditions, competition between the target and the color competitor should last longer, resulting in fewer fixations to the target noun in Region 2, and target recognition happening later, only after it appears in speech, i.e., in Region 3.

Results and discussion

For the control items, where the target, *red car*, was the only red object in the scene (see Fig. 5.1A), the results were as expected. The listeners used the color adjective *red* early on, starting in Region 1, to identify the target, *car*. The proportion of fixations on the target continued to grow steadily, from 19.0 percent in Region 1 to 66.4 percent in Region 2 to 86.9 percent in Region 3. The looks to the distractors combined accounted for only 3.2 percent, 6.7 percent and 3.1 percent of fixations in Regions 1, 2 and 3, respectively.

A different picture emerged for the fixation analysis of the target noun in the experimental items. Table 5.1 summarizes the proportion of fixations to the target in the three regions of interest, as a factor of the gender of target/competitor (different- vs. same-gender) and word order (nonsplit- vs. split-constituent order).

Table 5.1. Experiment 1: The mean proportion of fixations to the target in Regions 1, 2 and 3 (%)

	Region 1: Adjective 0–600 ms		Region 2: Beginning of noun/verb 601–900 ms		Region 3: End of verb/noun 901–1,600 ms	
	Gender		Gender		Gender	
Word order	Different	Same	Different	Same	Different	Same
Nonsplit	17.6	16.9	60.7	38.7	82.2	69.5
Split	20.8	33.2*	62.3	37.1	82.6	51.4*

The Region 1 adjective (0–600 ms) was not expected to be informative with respect to the gender effect because gender information comes at the end of it making it impossible to identify the target noun by just the beginning of *krasn-* in *krasnuju* 'red.' Indeed, there were no main effects of either gender ($F1[1,15] = 3.99$, $p = 0.0672$) or word order ($F1[2,10] = 1.51$, n.s.) but there was a significant interaction of the two factors ($F1[1,15] = 6.29$, $p = 0.0262$; $F2[2,10] = 6.12$, $p = 0.268$). The listeners looked significantly more to the target noun in the same-gender condition when it was the split-constituent construction (33.2 percent). The proportions of fixations to the target noun did not differ from each other in the other three conditions.

How did the participants manage to identify the target noun in the same-gender, split-constituent construction condition so early, with two red objects of the same gender in the scene? Evidently, they capitalized on another sort of information that was held constant in the split-constituent conditions, i.e., the early contrastive stress on the color adjective. Recall that the constraints on the use of split-constituent construction in Russian require an appropriate pragmatic situation and a contrastive stress on one of the components of the split adjective-noun phrase. The pragmatic interpretation of the same-gender scene (see Fig. 5.1C) requires taking notice that the target *red car* is contrasted with two other objects, *silver car* and *red squirrel*; however, the red squirrel does not have a color contrast of its own, only the red car does. The participants in the experiment were sensitive to this pragmatic nuance of the visual scene and realized that the contrastive stress on the adjective *red* would be appropriate only to distinguish the red car from the silver one (Sekerina and Trueswell 2011).

Region 2 (601–900 ms), which constitutes the first part of the noun in the nonsplit conditions or the verb in the split-constituent conditions, is the crucial time window to evaluate the gender effect in Russian. This is the earliest point in the utterance where the grammatical gender information encoded on the adjective ending could be utilized by the listeners, and they took full advantage of it.

There was a significant main effect of gender, $F1[1,15] = 12.54$, $p = 0.0036$; $F2[2, 10] = 8.6$, $p = 0.0109$. As predicted, the participants were able to resolve competition between the target noun and the color competitor by restricting their attention to the object that matched in gender with the adjective, irrespective of word order. Their fixations to the target were reliably higher in the different-gender than in the same-gender conditions, 61.5 percent versus 37.9 percent. The gender mismatch between the feminine adjective *krasnuju* 'red$_{FEM}$' and the masculine color competitor *cvetok* 'flower$_{MASC}$' effectively precluded the participants from considering the color competitor and directed their attention to the feminine target noun *mašinku* 'car$_{FEM}$.' There was no main effect of word order (all $Fs < 1$). As predicted, in the split-constituent conditions, grammatical gender information alone was sufficient for recognition of the target noun, and it happened before its lexical identity was revealed in Region 3. The significant interaction between gender and word order found in Region 1 became nonsignificant (all $Fs < 1$). The immediate effect of the contrastive stress turned out to be short-lived and completely disappeared in Region 2.

Finally, in Region 3 (901–1,500 ms), the significant main effect of gender found in Region 2 became even stronger, $F1[1,15] = 39.21$, $p < 0.001$; $F2[2, 10] = 12.17$, $p = 0.0036$. As predicted, it interacted with word order, $F1[1,15] = 5.67$, $p < 0.033$; $F2[2, 10] = 4.53$, $p = 0.051$, because in the same-gender conditions, the lexical identity of the target noun in the nonsplit word order (69.5 percent) made it possible for the participants to recognize the target faster than in the split-constituent word order in which the noun was still unfolding in speech (51.4 percent).

A moment-by-moment analysis of eye movements allows us to see clearly the time course of the gender effect. Figure 5.2 displays the probability of fixations to the target and the color competitor in the same-gender condition over first 1,500 ms of the spoken instructions.

First, fine-grained eye movements confirmed the findings from the coarse-grain analysis of fixations in demonstrating the early target noun advantage (dark squares) in the same-gender, split-constituent condition in Region 1. Second, looks to the competitor that start to arise during Region 1 reflect competition between the target noun and the color competitor, but the dynamics differs in the nonsplit and split-constituent conditions. For the nonsplit condition (circles), when the target noun immediately follows the adjective and its lexical identity is revealed in Region 2, the looks to the target noun and the color competitor start to reliably diverge earlier, by the end of Region 2. In contrast, this competition lasts longer in the split-constituent condition (squares), and it does not get resolved until well into Region 3 because the listeners have to wait for the target noun to appear in speech. Thus, the listeners were able to direct their eye movements to the target noun based on

Figure 5.2. Experiment 1: The probability of fixating the target (*red car*) and color competitor (*red squirrel*) over three regions in the same-gender condition, as a function of word order (%)

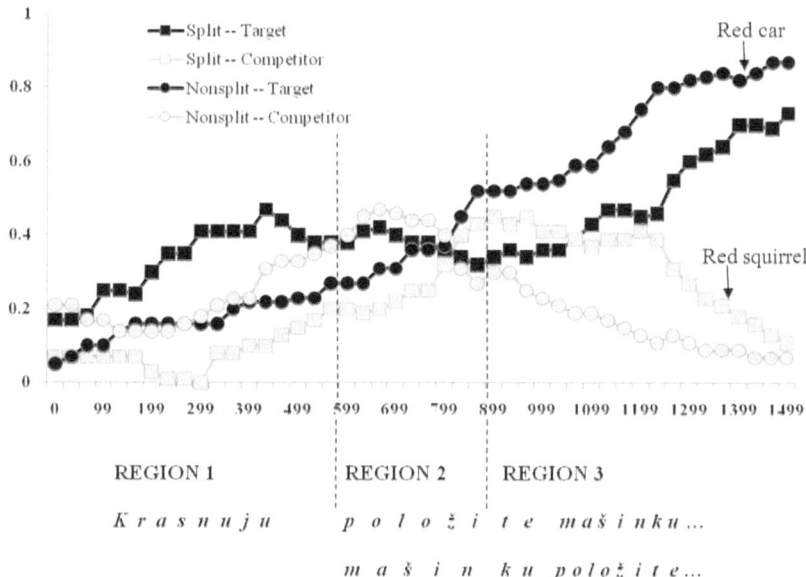

the gender agreement information on the adjective in the same-gender, split-constituent condition before they heard the noun in speech. The effect was early and robust and took place dynamically, as the speech unfolded.

III.2. Experiment 2: Cohorts

Experiment 1 provided evidence for the grammar-based account of the gender effect in Russian spoken-word recognition and showed that the gender information on the color adjective was an effective and early cue in directing the participants' attention to the gender-matching target noun (facilitation effect). Experiment 2 was designed to replicate the inhibitory effect of the gender information on the adjective, i.e., suppression of activation of a gender-mismatching cohort competitor, found by Dahan et al. (2000) for the article-noun phrases in French.

III.2.1. Method

Participants

Twenty-eight undergraduate students from the St. Petersburg State University took part in Experiment 2. They were native Russian speakers who had lived in Russia all their lives and who had normal or corrected-to-normal vision and hearing. They were paid to participate in the experiment, which took about forty minutes to complete.

Materials and procedure

The physical set-up of Experiment 2 was identical to that of Experiment 1. However, because the materials were designed to test the interaction of the cohort effect with gender in Russian, it was not possible to create the objects with phonologically similar names in such a way that they could be recognized by their contours alone. Thus, the objects from Experiment 1 made of thin plywood were replaced with pictures from the Cycowicz, Friedman, Rothstein and Snodgrass (1997) picture set, also used in the French and German experiments (Dahan et al. 2000; Weber and Paris 2004). All pictures were black-and-white line drawings that were colored using image-editing software. The pictures were scaled to fit a 2.5 × 2.5 in. (6.4 × 6.4 cm) square cut out, and laminated. To the best of our knowledge, there are no naming norms for Russian using this picture set. To establish tentative naming norms for this experiment, we asked 12 native Russian speakers to name the target and competitors' pictures. The agreement between the participants' responses and the intended names was 85 percent. Three items (*gorilla*, *peas* and *cake*) created the most discrepancy; when they were taken out, the agreement rate increased to 92 percent. We nevertheless kept these three items in the analysis of the eyetracking data because the discrepancy arose from the fact that the participants in the naming study used a basic category name for the intended picture, and not the more specific one (e.g., referring to the gorilla as *monkey*). They had no problems recognizing the objects. None of the participants from the naming study took part in the eyetracking experiment.

Figure 5.3. The two types of visual display in Experiment 1 (cohorts)

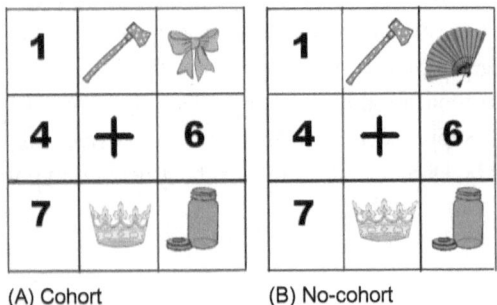

(A) Cohort   (B) No-cohort

Note: (A) The cohort condition, consisting of the target *banku* (orange jar$_{FEM}$, Position 9), the cohort competitor *bant* (orange bow$_{MASC}$, Position 3), and two distractors (purple axe, Position 2; blue crown, Position 8). (B). In the no-cohort condition, the orange bow is replaced with a phonologically unrelated competitor *veer* (orange fan$_{MASC}$).

The participants acted out spoken instructions by physically picking and moving the pictures on the board. The cohort condition included the target, *oranževuju banku* 'orange$_{FEM}$ jar$_{FEM}$'; the different-gender cohort competitor of the same color, *oranževyj bant* 'orange$_{MASC}$ bow$_{MASC}$' (Fig. 5.3A); and two phonologically unrelated distractors, *koronu* 'crown$_{FEM}$' and *topor* 'axe$_{MASC}$.' Note that the initial syllable *ban-* is shared by both referents. In the no-cohort condition, the different-gender cohort competitor, orange bow, was replaced with a phonologically unrelated competitor, e.g., *oranževyj veer* 'orange$_{MASC}$ fan$_{MASC}$' (Fig. 5.3B). Example (3) illustrates an experimental trial paired with the cohort display, with the *orange jar* as the target:

(3) a. *Posmotrite   na krest.*
       Look   at the cross.
    b. *Oranzhevuju   položite   banku   v Poziciju 7.*
       Orange$_{FEM}$ put   jar$_{FEM}$ in Position 7.
    c. *Teper'   položite   lilovyj topor   nad bankoj.*
       Now   put   purple axe   above the jar.
    'Look at the cross.
    Put the orange jar in Position 7.
    Now put the purple axe above the jar.'

The phonological overlap between the selected target and cohort competitor was carefully controlled: the mean number of overlapping phonemes at onset was three, and both nouns had the same stress pattern. The last control is important because stress patterns in Russian cause unstressed vowel reduction that can substantially change the quality of the vowels in the two syllables adjacent to the stressed one. For example, in the target–cohort competitor pair *sovu* 'owl$_{FEM}$' versus *sovok* 'dust pan$_{MASC}$,' the stress falls on the second syllable, changing the vowel quality in the first syllable *sov-* from the underlying /o/ to schwa (cf. Marian and Spivey's (2003) materials that were not controlled in this way). When possible, the number of syllables was also matched. Lexical frequencies for the target-competitor pairs were taken from the online Russian National Corpus, which has 100 million lexical items (Nacional'nyj korpus russkogo jazyka 2003; cf. Marian and Spivey 2003), who used the 1977 and 1993 frequency dictionaries of Russian). To control for lexical frequency in cohort competition, we manipulated assignment of each member of the pair to be target. In one list, the jar was the target and the bow was the competitor, and in the other, the bow was the target and the jar the competitor.

In contrast to Experiment 1, there was no word order manipulation: the experimental instruction was always presented in the split-constituent construction. The only experimental manipulation was presence or absence of the cohort competitor of the same color but of different gender from that of the target. Sixteen experimental trials were constructed, with eight cohort pairs and eight no-cohort pairs. In addition to the eight cohort pairs, eight filler trials and two practice items were included, with a total of 26 trials in the experiment. Filler trials did not contain cohort pairs. The cohort factor together with alternation for target assignment resulted in four presentation lists, with seven participants randomly assigned to each of the lists.

The procedure was identical to the one in Experiment 1. Six fixation categories were coded: the cross; the target *orange jar*; the different-gender color competitors, *orange bow* (cohort) or *orange fan* (no-cohort); the two distractors; the looks in between objects, and the track loss. Besides the looks at the cross, the combined numbers for the two distractors (10.3 percent), the looks in between objects (4.4 percent), and the track loss (5.3 percent) accounted for 20 percent of the fixation data, and were not analyzed. We defined the three regions of interest similar to the ones in Experiment 1: Region 1 for the adjective (0–600 ms), Region 2 for the verb (601–1,100 ms), and Region 3 for the noun (1,101–1,500 ms). Both coarse-grain averaged fixations and fine-grained eye movements to the target and competitor were analyzed for Regions 2 and 3. Note that in contrast to Dahan et al. (2000) and Weber and Paris (2004), who compared proportions of fixations to the competitor with the two unrelated distractors, we will be comparing proportions of fixations to the color competitor in the cohort condition with proportions of fixations to the color competitor in the no-cohort condition. This is necessary because the French and German materials consisted of the gender-marked definite article-noun phrases describing the black-and-white line drawings of the objects. Thus, the definite article could equally well introduce a distractor of the compatible gender not restricted by color. In the Russian experiment, the materials consisted of the color adjective-noun pairs that restricted competition to the pictures of the same color. The distractors' colors were different from the color of target and competitor, and this color incompatibility excluded them from the competitor set as soon as the adjective appeared in speech.

From the previous cohort eyetracking experiments with bilingual Russian-English participants (Marian and Spivey 2003, Experiment 2) and monolingual Russian adults and children (Sekerina and Brooks 2007), we know that cohort competitors in Russian receive more fixations than phonologically unrelated distractors. For our Experiment 2, we predicted that gender information carried by the ending of an adjective would prevent the activation of the cohort competitor that differed in gender from the target, and this would be reflected in coarse-grain fixation analysis. Thus, we expected to replicate an elimination of a cohort effect for the phonologically related competitor of different gender found for the article-noun phrases in French and German. The fine-grained fixation analysis assessed how early gender information would eliminate the cohort effect. If this effect can be demonstrated in the split-constituent construction, as was found in Experiment 1, it should occur early, during Region 2 and prior to noun appearance in speech.

Results and discussion

Table 2 shows the mean proportions of fixations to the target and competitor, both in the role of the cohort competitor and the distractor. We present the analyses based on the competitor because it is fixations to the competitor that are critical in estimation of the cohort effect. Prior to the point where gender information on the adjective could affect recognition of the target noun, there was no difference in fixation proportions to the competitor in the cohort and no-cohort conditions. The overall small proportion of fixations to either the target or the competitor in Region 1 (0–600 ms) is explained by the fact that the participants tended to continue fixating the cross throughout the beginning of the experimental instructions. Region 1 in general is not informative with respect to the gender effect, and ANOVAs revealed no significant difference in fixations between the cohort and no-cohort competitors ($Fs < 1$).

Region 2 (601–1,100 ms) is the critical time window when listeners could use the gender information encoded on the adjective ending to constrain a set of lexical competitors. ANOVAs conducted on the fixations to the color competitor in the cohort and no-cohort conditions revealed that 3.1 percent difference in favor of the cohort competitor was not significant ($Fs < 1$). This indicates that the phonologically similar cohort competitor *bant* 'bow$_{MASC}$' was not activated any more than the phonologically unrelated competitor, *veer* 'fan$_{MASC}$' (see Fig. 5.3). This finding demonstrates elimination of the cohort effect when the target was preceded by a gender-marked adjective. The same pattern of fixations continued in Region 3 (1,101–1,500 ms), with no significant differences in fixations to the competitor in the two conditions ($Fs < 1$).

Table 5.2. Experiment 2: The mean proportions of fixations to target and competitor in Regions 1, 2 and 3 (%)

	Region 1: Adjective 0–600 ms		Region 2: Verb 601–1,100 ms		Region 3: Noun 1,101–1,500 ms	
	Target	Competitor	Target	Competitor	Target	Competitor
Cohort	6.0	4.4	28.0	20.2	56.8	15.0
No-cohort	4.5	4.7	26.3	17.1	59.9	11.9

Figure 5.4. Experiment 2: The probability of fixating the target (*orange jar*) and competitors (*orange bow/fan*) over three regions as a factor of cohort/no-cohort condition (%)

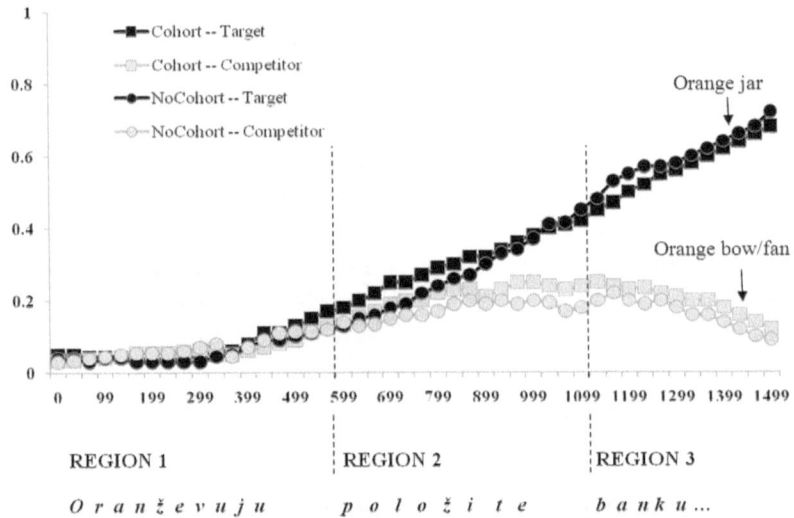

Finally, the fine-grained analysis of time course of the gender effect on cohort activation is represented in Figure 5.4.

Similar to Experiment 1, fine-grained eye movements demonstrate close competition between the target (squares) and the competitor (circles) in both cohort and no-cohort conditions, until the second half of Region 2. The looks to the target started to diverge from the looks to the competitor at approximately 300 ms after the verb onset in Region 2. Once again, as was found in Experiment 1, the listeners were able to resolve competition between the target and the competitor prior to the target appearance in speech. The looks to the cohort and no-cohort competitors reached their peak at the borders of the two regions and started to subside after the target noun onset in Region 3. Crucially, the dynamics of eye movements to the cohort and no-cohort competitor do not differ from each other, showing that the cohort competitor in the gender-mismatching gender was eliminated as a potential lexical candidate in the process of spoken-word recognition in Russian.

IV. General Discussion and Conclusion

The two experiments explored the effect of grammatical gender agreement on spoken-word recognition in Russian and its temporal characteristics. The materials in both experiments consisted of a gender-marked color adjective and a target noun; they were either immediately adjacent to each other (the nonsplit word order) or separated by a verb (the split-constituent word order). The critical manipulation was the grammatical gender of the two objects of the same color, the target and the color competitor. The gender-marked color adjective either matched in gender with the target or with both target and competitor. In Experiment 1, no cohorts, the names of the target and color competitors did not phonologically overlap whereas in Experiment 2, cohorts, the target and the color competitor shared the first three phonemes. When viewing the two objects of the same color while listening to the gender-marked color adjective whose gender was consistent only with the target, Russian listeners fixated the target more and earlier than the color competitor of different gender even in the split-constituent word order. This happened with both no-cohort (Experiment 1) and cohort materials (Experiment 2), i.e., grammatical gender on the adjective successfully eliminated the cohort effect in Russian (Marian and Spivey 2003). These results replicate the ones previously reported in the monolingual French experiment (Dahan et al. 2000) and in the between-language (French-German) experiment (Weber and Paris 2004). In contrast to French and German, the grammatical gender encoded on the modifying adjective influences the noun recognition in Russian much earlier, before the noun's lexical identity is revealed in speech as in the split-constituent construction.

Our results provide new evidence for the ongoing discussion of the nature of spoken-word recognition, what factors constrain it, and temporal characteristics of this process in different languages. Cross-linguistic research is valuable in developing our understanding of spoken-word recognition, by showing which aspects of speech processing are universal and which reflect language-specific adaptations. New data obtained from a wide variety of languages can help us choose a better theoretical account of the data in cross-linguistic spoken-word recognition. The results of the two Russian experiments reported in this chapter contribute to the existing accounts of the gender effect on spoken-word recognition by (a) extending it to a different language, (b) demonstrating its early and robust character and (c) providing empirical evidence for its grammar-based origin. First, our findings extend the previously found elimination of the cohort effect as a factor of grammatical gender in French and German to a different language (Russian) and different materials, the adjective-noun phrases. Second, the Russian split-constituent construction allowed us to demonstrate that gender information can have its effect much earlier than has been possible to test in English or French. Combination of the visual context with contrast sets and the split-constituent construction – whose unique function is to grammatically represent contrastiveness in Russian – facilitates recognition of the noun on average 300 ms *before* the noun is encountered, whereas the gender effect in French and German-French occurred during the first 300–400 ms *after* the onset of the noun.

Finally, using Russian allowed us to overcome limitations imposed by the French article-noun materials of Dahan et al. (2000) and bilingual setting of Weber and Paris (2004). In order to explain the lack of gender effect in the no-cohort condition, Dahan and colleagues argued that because article-noun co-occurrence in French is high, French listeners rely on distributional regularities between the definite article (*le* or *la*) and the form of the following noun during spoken-word recognition. Weber and Paris (2004) rejected this form-based account of the gender effect by showing that competitor activation in the nonnative German was suppressed by gender information from the native French. Their evidence crucially depended on the bilingual setting: They argued that it is unlikely that bilingual speakers compute distributional regularities between the gender-marked article in one language and the noun in the other. However, the problem with Weber and Paris' French-German materials is that they are confounded by the presence of cognates. Elimination of the explicit German competitor, *die Perücke* 'the$_{FEM}$ wig' could be due not to the between-language gender effect but to the fact that it is a cognate of the implicit French competitor, *la perruque* 'the$_{FEM}$ wig.' This cognate facilitation effect is a well-established phenomenon in bilingual word recognition (Lemhöfer and Dijkstra 2004, among others).

The present Russian experiments allowed us to eliminate this confound. The critical evidence to distinguish between the form- and grammar-based accounts of the gender effect in spoken-word recognition comes from unique word order properties of Russian. The split-constituent construction created a natural context in which the gender-marked adjective not only preceded the noun but was also separated from it by an intervening verb. The referential and pragmatic properties of this construction productive in colloquial Russian impose no restrictions on the types of adjectives and nouns that can be used; moreover, even the reverse order, i.e., noun-verb-adjective, is possible. Thus, co-occurrence of a particular color adjective and a noun must be very low, because it is difficult to calculate distributional regularities for split constituents. We can conclude that the gender effect in Russian spoken-word recognition is unlikely to be caused by form-based regularities of this language and must instead originate from the grammatical level of language processing. Thus, the choice of the Russian language has proven invaluable in assessment of the contribution of grammatical and pragmatic constraints that dynamically constrain spoken-language recognition in a moment-by-moment fashion.

Acknowledgments

This research was supported by the National Science Foundation under ADVANCE Grant no. 0137851. Any opinions, findings, conclusions, or recommendations expressed in this article are those of the author and do not necessarily reflect the views of the National Science Foundation. I thank Marina Gagarina for her help with the figure preparation and Dr. Olga Fedorova for conducting the naming pilot study for Experiment 2. I also wish to acknowledge the help of Dr. Anna Maslennikova, Ksenija Terexina and Anna Stol' as well all the undergraduate students at the English Department of the St. Petersburg State University and its Vyborg branch who enthusiastically participated in Experiment 2.

References

Akhutina, T., A. Kurgansky, M. Polinsky and E. Bates. 1999. "Processing of Grammatical Gender in a Three-Gender System: Experimental Evidence from Russian." *Journal of Psycholinguistic Research* 28 (6): 695–713, doi: 10.1023/A:1023225129058.

Allopenna, P. D., J. S. Magnuson and M. K. Tanenhaus. 1998. "Tracking the Time Course of Spoken Word Recognition Using Eye Movements: Evidence for Continuous Mapping Models." *Journal of Memory and Language* 38: 419–39, doi: 10.1006/jmla.1997.2558.

Bates, E., A. Devescovi, L. Pizzamiglio, S. D'Amico and A. Hernandez. 1995. "Gender and Lexical Access in Italian." *Perception and Psychophysics* 57: 847–62.

Bordag, D. and T. Pechmann. 2008. "Grammatical Gender in Speech Production: Evidence from Czech." *Journal of Psycholinguistic Research* 37: 69–85, doi: 10.1007/s10936-007-90600.

Chomsky, N. 1986. *Barriers*. Linguistic Inquiry Monograph 13. Cambridge, MA: MIT Press.

Cycowicz, Y., D. Friedman, M. Rothstein and J. Snodgrass. 1997. "Picture Naming by Young Children: Norms for Name Agreement, Familiarity, and Visual Complexity." *Journal of Experimental Child Psychology* 65: 171–237, doi: 10.1006/jecp.1996.2356.

Dahan, D., D. Swingley, M. K. Tanenhaus and J. S. Magnuson. 2000. "Linguistic Gender and Spoken-Word Recognition in French." *Journal of Memory and Language* 42: 465–80, doi: 10.1006/jmla.1999.2688.

Dijkstra, T., H. J. Schriefers, M. Hasper and B. Schulpen. 2003. "Recognition of Interlingual Homophones in Bilingual Auditory Word Recognition." *Journal of Experimental Psychology: Human Perception and Performance* 29 (6): 1155–79, doi: 10.1037/0096-1523.29.6.1155.

Featherston, S. and S. Winkler, eds. 2009. *The Fruits of Empirical Linguistics. Vols 1 and 2*. The Hague: Mouton de Gruyter.

Fodor, J. D. 1993. "Processing Empty Categories: A Question of Visibility." In G. T. M. Altmann and R. Shillcock (eds). *Cognitive Models of Speech Processing. The Second Sperlonga Meeting*, 351–400. Mahwah, NJ: Lawrence Erlbaum Associates Publishers.

Friederici, A. and T. Jacobsen. 1999. "Processing Grammatical Gender During Language Comprehension." Special Issue: Processing Grammatical Gender, Part I, *Journal of Psycholinguistic Research* 28 (5): 467–84, doi: 1999-03897-002.

Grosjean, F., J.-Y. Dommergues, E. Cornu, D. Guillelmon and M. Besson. 1994. "The Gender Marking Effect in Spoken Word Recognition." *Perception and Psychophysics* 56: 590–8.

Journal of Psycholinguistic Research. 1999. 28 (5). Special Issue: Processing of Grammatical Gender, Part I.

Lemhöfer, K. and T. Dijkstra. 2004. "Recognizing Cognates and Interlingual Homographs: Effects of Code Similarity in Language-Specific and Generalized Lexical Decision." *Memory and Cognition* 32 (4): 533–50.

Lew-Williams, C. and A. Fernald. 2007. "Young Children Learning Spanish Make Rapid Use of Grammatical Gender in Spoken Word Recognition." *Psychological Science* 18 (3): 193–8, doi: 10.1111/j.1467-9280.2007.01871.x.

Marian, V. and M. J. Spivey. 2003. "Competing Activation in Bilingual Language Processing: Within- and Between-Language Competition." *Bilingualism: Language and Cognition* 6 (2): 97–116, doi: 10.1017/S1366728903001068.

Marslen-Wilson, W. D. and A. Welsh. 1978. "Processing Interactions and Lexical Access during Word Recognition in Continuous Speech." *Cognitive Psychology* 10: 29–63.

McQueen, J. M. and A. Cutler. 2001. "Spoken Word Access Processes: An Introduction." *Language and Cognitive Processes* 16 (5/6): 469–90, doi: 10.1080/01690960143000209.

Norris, D., J. McQueen and A. Cutler. 1995. "Competition and Segmentation in Spoken-word Recognition." *Journal of Experimental Psychology: Learning, Memory, and Cognition* 21: 1209–28, doi: 10.1037/0278-7393.21.5.1209.

Nacional'nyj korpus russkogo jazyka [Russian National Corpus]. 2003. Online: http://www.ruscorpora.ru/corpora-intro.html (accessed March 2004).

Pollard, C. and I. A. Sag. 1994. *Head-Driven Phrase Structure Grammar*. Chicago: University of Chicago Press.

Rice, C. 2004. "Optimizing Russian Gender." Talk presented at the 13th Annual Workshop on Formal Approaches to Slavic Linguistics. University of South Carolina, Columbia, SC.

Russkaja grammatika [Russian Grammar]. 1982. Academy of Sciences of the USSR. Vol. 2. *Sintaksis* [Syntax]. Moscow: Nauka.

Sekerina, I. A. 1999. "The Scrambling Complexity Hypothesis and Processing of Split Scrambling Constructions in Russian." *Journal of Slavic Linguistics* 7 (2): 218–65.

⸺. 2006. "Building Bridges: Slavic Linguistics Going Cognitive." In S. Franks, E. Andrews, R. Feldstein and G. Fowler (eds), *Slavic Linguistics 2000: The Future of Slavic Linguistics in America. Glossos 8.* Online: http://www.seelrc.org/glossos/issues/8/sekerina.pdf (accessed 16 November 2011).

Sekerina, I. A. and P. J. Brooks. 2007. "Eye Movements During Spoken-Word Recognition in Russian Children." *Journal of Experimental Child Psychology* 98: 20–45, doi: 10.1016/j.jecp.2007.04.005.

Sekerina, I. A. and J. C. Trueswell. 2011. "Processing of contrastiveness by heritage Russian bilinguals." *Bilingualism: Language and Cognition* 14 (3): 280–300, doi: 10.1017/S1266728910000337.

Spivey, M. J. and V. Marian. 1999. "Cross Talk between Native and Second Languages: Partial Activation of an Irrelevant Lexicon." *Psychological Science* 10 (3): 281–5, doi: 10.1111/1467-9280.00151.

Taraban, R. and V. Kempe. 1999. "Gender Processing in Native and Nonnative Russian Speakers." *Applied Psycholinguistics* 20: 119–48, doi: 10.1017/S0142716499001046.

Trueswell, J. C. and M. K. Tanenhaus, eds. 2004. *Approaches to Studying Word-Situated Language Use*. Cambridge, MA: MIT Press.

Weber, A. and A. Cutler. 2004. "Lexical Competition in Non-native Spoken-Word Recognition." *Journal of Memory and Language* 50: 1–25, doi: 10.1016/S0749-596X(03)00105-0.

Weber, A. and G. Paris. 2004. "The Origin of the Linguistic Gender Effect in Spoken-Word Recognition: Evidence from Non-native Listening." In *Proceedings of the 26th Annual Meeting of the Cognitive Science Society*. Chicago, IL. Online: http://www.coli.uni-sb.de/~aweber/publications.html (accessed October 2004).

Part Two

APPLIED LINGUISTIC AND SOCIOLINGUISTIC ANALYSIS

Chapter 6

COMMUNICATIVE LANGUAGE TEACHING AND RUSSIAN: THE CURRENT STATE OF THE FIELD

William J. Comer
University of Kansas

I. Communicative Language Teaching: An Overview

Communicative language teaching (CLT) as a systematic approach to organizing language instruction has been around for over thirty years. Since its beginnings, it has developed in a number of new directions and spawned several new movements.[1] The purpose of this chapter is to survey the development of CLT, particularly in its relationship to Russian-language instruction in North America and to outline new trends in its development that can be productively applied to teaching Russian.

From a theoretical perspective, CLT rests on the notion that language learning can happen while learners are engaged in exchanging meaningful communication in the target language. Once learners are put into a context where they need to exchange information to accomplish some specific goal (e.g., tell something about themselves, order a meal in a restaurant, buy a train ticket), they will use the language resources that they have available to them and interact with speakers of the target language. If/when they encounter

---

1 In addition to CLT, a number of terms cluster around the notion of teaching a foreign language as a means of communicating. In the 1970s, references to "teaching communicative competence" are frequent. Krashen and Terrell (1983) labeled their methodological ideas about communicative language teaching as "the natural approach." From the 1980s one can see references to "teaching languages for proficiency" and "proficiency-oriented language teaching" in which the goal of instruction is to teach learners to become proficient in communicating in the foreign language (often in relationship to the hierarchical skill set laid out in the ACTFL Proficiency Guidelines).

incomprehensible utterances from non-native learners, target language speakers will engage in a natural negotiation of meaning to ascertain the non-native learners' communicative purpose. "Good" CLT places learners in "real world" communicative contexts, provides learners with language input (models of how to accomplish communicative tasks) and then allows learners to perform communicative tasks, negotiating meaning when communication breaks down. From this negotiation of meaning, non-native learners receive feedback which can help them adjust their expression to match the norms of the target language more closely (Allwright1979; Richards and Rodgers 1986; Lee and VanPatten 1995).

In the most robust implementation of CLT, programs can be characterized as having only a "focus on meaning." Explicit instruction on language form is seen as unnecessary since providing authentic language input, and opportunities for communication and negotiation of meaning, is sufficient for the non-native speakers to attain native-like proficiency in the target language. This model of CLT was theoretically supported by Krashen's (1982) hypotheses about second language acquisition, especially his notion of "comprehensible input" and his distinction between learned and acquired language. In Krashen's model, what language learners absolutely need to acquire in the target language is lots of language input that will be comprehensible to them, but just beyond the limits of their current language abilities. From this comprehensible input they will, as they did in their first language, learn to communicate in the second language and acquire its features (Krashen 1982, 20–2). Krashen limits the role that instruction can play in language acquisition by postulating that consciously learned language cannot be turned into acquired language (i.e., the subconscious language system that can be used for communicating meaning). Learned language can only be used by a language learner's "monitor," which acts as an "editor" checking and repairing the accuracy of the learner's output after it has been "produced" by the learner's acquired language system (Krashen 1982, 15).

From the 1970s onward, CLT with a primary focus on meaning attracted many proponents, especially in the English as a Second Language (ESL) teaching community. Many bilingual programs in Canadian schools also adopted this model for their English and French core and immersion programs (Ullman 1987). However, after years of data collection from Canadian immersion programs, it became clear that, while non-natives could learn to communicate in the second language, their production never developed native-like expression, suggesting that comprehensible input was necessary but not sufficient for second language acquisition to occur (Harley and Swain 1984; Allen, Swain, Harley and Cummins 1990).

Swain (1985) proposed that in addition to comprehensible input, learners needed opportunities to produce output in order to develop native-like accuracy. Others have made the case that language-focused instruction within the framework of the communicative classroom can assist non-natives in improving the accuracy of specific features in their interlanguage (Swain 1991; Doughty 1991; Pica 1994).

With some exceptions (Musumeci 1996; Rogers 2006), most foreign language instruction programs in North American secondary and higher educational institutions did not implement a strong "focus on meaning" version of CLT. Instead, in many foreign language instructional materials in the 1970s and 1980s CLT was instantiated by inserting opportunities for communication into existing instruction, which was often organized around language forms and structures. In textbooks of this period and for the more commonly taught languages, communicative activities were often grafted onto the existing grammatical syllabi (Ruiz 1987; Shelly 1995). In the North American context of foreign language teaching in higher education, CLT has been criticized for having too much focus on language forms to the detriment of meaning (Byrnes 2000).

Faced with the questionable efficacy of a "focus on meaning" and disenchanted with the decontextualized language practice that he termed "focus on forms," Michael Long (1991) suggested a reconciliation in which one could attend to language form within the framework of communication in the target language. This kind of language instruction could be thought of as "focus on form." The research base and the pedagogical implementations for this new direction in CLT began in the late 1980s and were described in the volume *Focus on Form in Classroom Second Language Acquisition* (Doughty and Williams 1998a). This highly important set of papers crystallized a theoretical model for focus on form (FonF) and presented empirical data on its success in implementation. In their introduction Doughty and Williams (1998a) carve out the place for FonF by contrasting it with focus on meaning and focus on forms:

> We would like to stress that focus on forms and focus on form are *not* polar opposites in the way that *form and meaning* have often been considered to be. Rather, focus on form *entails* a focus on formal elements of language, whereas focus on formS is *limited* to such a focus, and focus on meaning *excludes* it. (4, italics of the original)

Since the early 1990s, mainstream work in CLT has explored multiple approaches to implementing classroom FonF, including processing instruction (VanPatten 1996, 2004), structured input (Farley 2004), input enhancement

(Wong 2005), and task-based instruction (Nunan 2004; Pica 2005; Samuda 2001) and others (Doughty and Williams 1998b).

II. Teaching Russian as a Foreign Language and CLT in the Soviet Union

It is interesting to look at how the teaching of Russian as a foreign language developed in the Soviet Union, since Soviet teachers and scholars struggled with some of the same methodological trends and problems that faced second language professionals in North America and Western Europe. Nevertheless, the methodologies that dominated in the Soviet approach to teaching Russian to foreigners differed from those in the West. While the audio-lingual method (ALM), drawing its theoretical and practical tenets from Behaviorism, was truly *the* method for teaching foreign languages for the 1960s in North America (Liskin-Gasparro 1984, 20–1), Soviet methodologists never embraced ALM with anything like the fervor found in the US and Canada. In the struggles between extremely traditional grammar-translation methods and newer "direct" methods (e.g., audio-visual, audio-lingual and others), the main Soviet center for teaching Russian as a second language at Moscow State University split the theoretical and methodological differences creating the *комбинированный метод* or 'combined method' (Kapitonova and Shchukin 1987, 52). In the 1960s, this eclectic combining of techniques would grow into the widely accepted *сознательно-практический метод*, 'the conscious-practical method,' that established as its main goals teaching learners: (1) to communicate in Russian in all modalities; (2) to develop a systematic understanding of the language's structure and usage; and (3) to learn about the Soviet Union and Soviet culture (Kapitonova and Shchukin 1987, 58–70). The "conscious-practical" method shaped the textbook *Russkii iazyk dlia vsekh* (Stepanova, Ievleva, Trushina and Kostomarov 1971), which was published in multiple editions and was adapted into various national editions, including two for North America (Stepanova, Kostomarov and Baker 1984; Ervin 1984).

A more narrowly focused communicative method very similar to the North American conceptions of CLT did develop in Russia in the 1970s, largely promoted by E. I. Passov (1977, 1985). In addition to the communicative focus, the approach valued personalizing language expression and focusing on the learner and the needs, feelings and opinions he/she wants/needs to communicate (Kapitolova and Shchukin 1987, 145). The method found expression in several textbooks, including the widely used *Temp* (Rassudova and Stepanova 1979). It is telling that in their evaluation of this approach, Kapitolova and Shchukin (1987) note its applicability for short-term intensive immersion settings or for the introductory phase of a longer course of study (152).

Although they never state so explicitly, one can speculate that they were skeptical about the limited service role that grammar plays in this model and about the applicability of such a model to other instructional contexts.

Another interesting aspect of the Soviet understanding of the communicative method comes in the ambivalence that its proponents show in relationship to traditional instructional practices. In describing the exercise types to be used in the communicative method, Passov (1977) strongly criticizes языковые упражнения or "language exercises," by which he means various types of mechanical drills (i.e., sentence transformation, substitution drills, fill-ins) because, among other defects, they do not contribute to developing communicative skills. Yet he ends his criticism with the concession that they can be used, especially for homework assignments, when accompanied by *речевые задачи* or 'speech tasks' (58–63).

In the perestroika period, A. A. Leont'ev (1991), a major figure in Soviet psycholinguistics and language teaching, wrote of a rapprochement between the different methods used in the Soviet Union and North America, since they were all united by the common idea that instruction should focus on the second language as a means of communication. While placing communication at the core of language teaching, and optimistically calling for international cooperation in the development of FL teaching methodology, Leont'ev still tried to square the circle by tying this communication core to conscious language learning in the manner of the conscious-practical method (1991, 6). Thus, throughout the Soviet period we can observe a tendency towards methods that allowed the eclectic combining of teaching techniques. This coupled with the absence of a firm tradition of empirical inquiry into second language learning perhaps explains why Russian-language textbooks for beginners developed in Russia, even after the fall of the Soviet Union, have remained methodologically traditional.[2]

---

2 To give three examples: *Russkii iazyk po-novomu* (Aksenova 1999) promises to "обеспечить прочную грамматическиую базу как основу коммуникации," although the book's detailed grammar explanations and grammar drills are never followed by communicative activities. The introduction to *Poekhali: russkii iazyk dlia vzroslykh, nachal'nyi kurs* (Chernyshov 2001) contains no discussion of its methodological approach, but the text is a collection of graded convergent structural drills and texts, with a rare communicative activity. *Zhili-byli* claims to have a communicative orientation, but states that it relies on the conscious-practical method with very slight modifications (Miller, Politova and Rybakova 2009, 4). However, only one activity in each of the 28 lessons asks learners to personalize the modeled language and express their own meanings, while the other exercises are solely mechanical. The methodological traditionalism in the newer Russian textbooks stands in contrast to the provocatively innovative *Hurra po polsku!* series produced in Poland (Małolepsza and Szymkiewicz 2006).

III. Russian-Language Teaching in North America before CLT

In North America, while many teachers of Russian became disenchanted with the audio-lingual method of language teaching by the 1970s, the field of teaching Russian as a foreign language in the US never adopted CLT in its pure "focus on meaning" variant (or at least I have not found such an approach in published textbooks). There was some effort in the profession to advocate for the inclusion of "communicative competence" activities into existing instruction in the 1970s (Dunatov 1976). In a major collection of articles about Russian teaching and learning in the mid-80s, Jarvis (1984), while a proponent of integrating some communicative activities into the classroom, warns against "zealous excesses in communicative competence methodology" (33). In the same volume Nakhimovsky (1984), in proposing classroom activities to teach communicative competence, offers models of meaningful and communicative drills as an innovation for Russian.[3]

Beginning Russian-language textbooks commonly used in North American up to 1994 were primarily grammatically driven; material was arranged by grammatical complexity and reinforced in exercises (typically pattern transformations, fill-ins, cued responses, English to Russian translations) that practiced decontextualized language forms. Authentic language input and communicative tasks were extremely rare (Patten 1984; Rifkin 1992).

Three developments in the 1980s led to a fundamental change in Russian-language teaching materials that were published in the mid-1990s. First was the significant increase in Russian language enrollments that came along with the Gorbachev years.[4] With a larger student base it made sense for commercial publishers to consider new texts for elementary Russian. Second, the downfall of the Soviet Union meant that all existing Russian-language textbooks were out of date in terms of cultural realia, and so a publisher with a new textbook could potentially claim a large share of this unexpectedly opened market.

The third development, and the most significant one in terms of textbook design, was the publication of the ACTFL Proficiency Guidelines for Speaking, Reading, Listening and Writing (1982, 1986). The guidelines spell out a hierarchy of performance criteria that allow for a global rating of second language learners' abilities in each of the language skills. The publication of the guidelines, coupled with significant US federal funding,

---

3 By 1984 such techniques had been circulating for at least a dozen years (Paulston 1972).

4 MLA surveys of US language enrollments document that in 1980 there were 23,987 students of Russian in US higher education; in 1986 there were 33,961; in 1990 the number had grown to 44,626; by 1995 the total had declined to 24,729 – just slightly higher than the 1980 figure (Furman, Goldberg and Lusin 2007).

led to a proliferation of teacher training workshops on testing, tester training and the use and implications of the guidelines for curriculum development and classroom practice (Liskin-Gasparro 2003, 488–9). Indeed the ACTFL guidelines precipitated a "proficiency revolution" which had greater effect on classroom practices, language teaching methodology and textbooks than they have ever had on the theory of second language acquisition since the guidelines themselves "have been heavily criticized as a theoretical construct in second language acquisition" (Liskin-Gasparro 2003, 489).

That the "proficiency revolution" was really out to change the goals and techniques of language teaching, rather than offer a new theoretical understanding of language learning, can be seen from the introduction to one of the widely used "proficiency" methods textbooks. In her *Teaching Languages in Context* Omaggio (1986) writes:

> This book is not designed to raise new dust. It does not propose yet another revolutionary theory of language acquisition or promote new methodologies. Rather, it seeks to extract from our rich heritage of resources and practices those elements that seem most sound and to suggest a way to organize that knowledge and expertise so we can maximize opportunities for the development of proficiency among our students. (xi–xii)

Indeed, the strength of Omaggio's text lies in its detailed exposition of how to link recommended instructional practices to the hierarchy of speaking, reading, listening and writing skills presented in the proficiency guidelines. She has only minimal recommendations for how to link CLT with the teaching of language forms and structure, advocating the use of contextualized practice and meaningful drills (Omaggio 1986, 95–6).

IV. Russian and the Proficiency Guidelines

While the publication of the proficiency guidelines provoked discussions of how to teach Russian, their more immediate impact can be seen in the development of standardized tests to measure learners' abilities. Beginning in spring 1984, the American Council of Teachers of Russian (ACTR) administered ACTFL Oral Proficiency Interviews (OPI) to all students participating in their semester study abroad program in the Soviet Union. Their data from the 658 students participating in these programs through spring 1990 give us the best snapshot of the kind of oral skills that learners developed in North American classrooms in the 1980s (Ginsberg 1992). Table 6.1 presents the results of this OPI testing, giving the percentage of students at each proficiency level matched with their length of college-level study of Russian.

Table 6.1. Preprogram OPI scores by percentage of students at each level of study

OPI ratings	2 Years of study	3 Years	4 Years	5 Years	Total
2 or higher	14.4	10	12.8	24.6	13.2
1+	18.3	15.9	27.7	27.7	20.4
1	54.9	65.9	54.7	43.1	58.3
0+ or lower	12.4	8.15	4.73	4.62	8.02
Total %	100%	100%	100%	100%	100%
Total # of students	153	270	148	65	636

Source: Ginsberg (1992, 30).

The data show that the majority of motivated US students after two, three, four, or even five years of language study performed only at the ACTFL Intermediate level of proficiency.[5] At five or more years of Russian at the college level, over a quarter of students had reached the Intermediate High level but fewer than 25 percent of college students had reached Advanced level proficiency.

The data from ACTR's preprogram Oral Proficiency Interviews are very similar to the student outcomes on the Educational Testing Service (ETS) Advanced Russian Proficiency Test in Listening, and only slightly different from the outcomes on the analogous ETS test in reading. These two tests, developed between 1984 and 1986 in a collaborative project between Russian-language teachers and representatives from ACTFL and the Department of Defense, were based entirely on authentic listening and reading selections and designed to assess learners' skills from the ACTFL Intermediate to Superior levels.[6]

---

5 This population can be considered representative of the US undergraduate population at the time, since ACTR's study abroad programs accepted students from a broad range of North American educational institutions, with different levels of preparation, and different educational backgrounds. There is one significant caveat, however. Students whose data are represented in the pool had already been accepted in the ACTR program and had chosen to participate in it. Thus as a whole they were likely to be more motivated than the general student population. Second, they had been screened for a past history of academic success, since scores on the application grammar and reading test, general college GPA and letters of recommendation all play a part in ACTR's selection criteria for study abroad. Thus, these data likely reflect the outcomes of the better, more motivated students studying Russian at the time.

6 The members of the test development team were Irene Thompson (chair), Tom Beyer, Masha Lekić, Kevin McKenna, and Anelya Rugaleva; the consultants were C. Edward Scebold (ACTFL) and James R. Child (US DoD).

In 1986, approximately five hundred students of Russian (of whom only 12 were heritage speakers) at 48 different US institutions took both ETS tests. In listening, the most frequent rating was Intermediate Mid or Lower. This score was attained by 88 percent of students who had completed three years of Russian, 63 percent of students who had studied the language for four years, and 41 percent of students who had studied the language for five years. Advanced or higher levels of listening proficiency were achieved by only 10 percent of all test takers (ETS 1991, 37).

The reading test scores were much more broadly distributed across proficiency levels. Overall, 31 percent of all test takers scored Intermediate Mid or Lower, 40 percent scored Intermediate High, 18 percent scored Advanced or Advanced High and 12 percent scored Superior or Higher. The testing showed a significant difference between reading abilities of students who had studied Russian for four years, only 50 percent of whom reached at least the Advanced level, and those who had studied the language for five years at the time of testing, 74 percent of whom read at least at the Advanced level. Among students with four years of Russian, 23 percent were reading at the Superior or Higher level, while among students with five years of Russian, 48 percent tested at this level (ETS 1991, 37).[7]

To summarize the overall trend of this testing data we can point out that the mode on the speaking and listening assessments is the Intermediate level and Intermediate High on the reading test. It is interesting to note how uneven skill development can be, even within a single student cohort: while almost half of the students studying the language for five years had developed Superior level reading skills, two-thirds of that same group had listening skills only at the Intermediate level.

By themselves, the data from these three assessments do not allow us to tease out any of the reasons for these outcomes – perhaps the learners just never had enough time on task to achieve a high level of proficiency in Russian (Rifkin 2005). Or perhaps the materials and/or the classroom activities widely used at the time were not effective in preparing learners for the tasks encountered on the tests, particularly in speaking and listening.[8] The better outcomes in reading are not unexpected since the majority of language input that students would have received

---

7 The complete scoring information from the norming sessions is available in the *Advanced Russian Listening and Reading Proficiency Test. Final Project Report–Year 2*. Online: http://www.eric.ed.gov/ERICWebPortal/detail?accno=ED355774 (last accessed 23 November 2011).
8 Anecdotally, I can confirm this disconnection between instruction and testing procedures on the basis of my own language learning history. I had my first OPI in spring 1983 when I had completed three years of Russian language study plus a semester of study abroad. While I felt prepared to talk about myself and to narrate and describe,

from the widely used grammar translation textbooks of the time came in the form of written texts. Students whose learning strategies could not accommodate that kind of focus on grammar and reading most likely discontinued their study of the language long before their third year of instruction. Furthermore, demographic data in the ETS test administration manual suggest that the student cohort who had studied Russian for five or more years were graduate students in Slavic departments or Soviet area studies programs where program success depended on the ability to read sophisticated texts well (ETS 1991, 41). It is hard not to conclude that one reason for the poor listening outcomes among this same population was the lack of access to authentic listening input. In 1986 satellite news broadcasts from the USSR were not easily available; VCRs were expensive, and Russian films (with or without subtitles) were not easy to find.

In a perfect world, teaching should drive testing. In the context of Russian in the 1980s, the ACTFL Proficiency Guidelines and related tests created washback effects in the opposite direction. The guidelines articulated performance standards and the tests gathered samples of student performance, which was poor in relationship to the external performance standards; the poor results motivated discussions of teaching methods and approaches, which finally in the 1990s resulted in publishers producing materials that featured "proficiency-oriented" or "communicatively oriented" tasks.

V. CLT and Beginning Russian Textbooks of the 1990s

In the period 1994–6, large US publishers put out four new beginning level textbooks of Russian that all proclaimed a focus on teaching students to communicate in the target language: *Golosa* (Robin, Henry and Robin 1994), *Nachalo: When in Russia* (Lubensky, Ervin and Jarvis 1996), *Troika* (Nummikooski 1996) and *Russian Stage One: Live from Moscow* (Davidson, Lekić and Gor 1996).[9]

I was completely stumped by the role-play situation, which, in hindsight, the tester clearly selected as an advanced probe. At the time I remember that I felt annoyed since I was being testing with an activity format that I had never encountered in the classroom. Furthermore, in this particular role-play I was tasked to return a pair of shoes to the store and get a refund, but that scenario did not at all match my cultural experience of the Soviet Union. I remember wondering if one could actually do such a thing, never mind what linguistically accurate forms were needed to carry out such a task.

9   An analysis of all levels of Russian textbooks that have appeared since 1990 exceeds the limits of the current study and would be redundant since the new texts have been reviewed in professional journals like *Slavic and East European Journal*. Martin, Robin and Jarvis (1991) and Thompson and Urevich (1991) deserve special note since these innovative and influential books provided models for bringing proficiency-test tasks into the classroom.

While the prefaces to *Golosa* and *Live from Moscow* describe learner outcomes specifically in terms of the ACTFL Proficiency Guidelines, the prefaces to *Nachalo* and *Troika* also mention having a proficiency orientation and teaching communicative language skills. Rifkin (1997) included three of these four in a broad review article, so my goal here is narrower. I consider how the four texts operationalized key components of CLT by analyzing:

1. what kind(s) of language input is featured in the texts;[10]
2. what kind(s) of activities check learner comprehension of the language input;
3. what kind(s) of communicative activities (e.g., expression of personal meaning; role-play situations; information gap activities; verbal games; problem-solving tasks) are included; and
4. what kind(s) of activities are used to focus on language form.

I deliberately focus on the 1990s editions since they are crucial for understanding how the main aspects of CLT have taken form for our profession. The most significant changes made in newer editions will be noted later, although updated editions tend not alter a texts' fundamental approach to language teaching. I have chosen to examine textbooks since classroom activities are most likely to be drawn from them rather than workbooks and other supplements.

V.1. Questions 1 and 2: Input and input comprehension

Although a quantitative answer to Question 1 might be interesting, it would be impossible to measure the exact amount of language input in the texts, since I am using an expansive definition of that term, and the language input is spread among different delivery formats (visual vs. audio vs. video vs. text). Instead I will restrict myself to a qualitative listing of the varieties of language input as well as of input comprehension activities based on an overall perusal of the textbooks.

From Table 6.2, it becomes clear that the new generation of beginning Russian-language textbooks provide significant "comprehensible input" and the input comes in a broad variety of forms and modalities (listening, reading and viewing). Comprehension activities tend to be globally based, where techniques of skimming, scanning, gisting, information extraction and contextual guessing are both encouraged and sufficient to allow the learner

---

10 I am using the word *input* here in its broadest possible sense – what kinds of Russian (vocabulary, dialogs, language usage, prose) do the books provide learners.

Table 6.2. Varieties of input and input comprehension checks

	Main forms of input	Modality	Comprehension checks
Golosa (1994)	Thematic vocabulary with pictures	Visual/reading	Sorting, classifying, making personalized lists, etc.
	Conversations (Razgovory)	Listening	Answer questions in English
	Dialogs	Listening/reading	Matching L1 speech acts to lines in the dialogs
	Authentic texts/realia	Reading/listening	Answer questions in English to extract information
Troika (1996)	Thematic vocabulary with pictures	Visual/reading	none
	Microdialogs (2–6 line exchanges)	Reading	Dialog transformations (cued responses)
	Textbook narratives	Reading	Answer questions (L1/L2)
	Authentic texts/realia*	Reading	Answer questions
Nachalo (1996)	Vocabulary via pictures*	Visual/reading	none
	Video drama of Lena Silina and Jim	Listening/viewing/reading	Comprehension questions (in separate workbook/video guide)
	Microdialogs (4 line exchanges)	Reading	Dialog transformations
	Authentic texts/realia*	Reading	Answer questions

Live from Moscow (1996)		Listening/viewing	Previewing; various viewing activities (multiple choice comprehension; fill-ins; speaker identification; cultural reflection; L1/L2)
	Video drama of Tanya and Dennis		
	Microdialogs (2-4 line exchanges)	Reading	Dialog transformations (cued responses)
	Textbook narratives	Reading	L1 comprehension exercises to extract information
	Authentic texts/realia*	Reading	Answer questions

*Feature does not appear in every chapter.

to complete the assignments. These techniques are very helpful since learners often need the opportunity to apply these strategies to a new language.

These comprehension activities rarely go so far as to make learners process the language input beyond the level of gisting and global comprehension. As will be discussed below, in FonF approaches to CLT, special emphasis is placed on having learners process the input (or at least parts of it) deeply for meaning so that they have an opportunity to map forms encountered in the input with their precise meanings. In the theory of CLT, such activities help learners notice the formal properties of the L2, and they would be a welcomed addition to future editions of these textbooks.

V.2. Questions 3 and 4: Activity types in the new textbooks

It is possible and useful to answer Questions 3 and 4 with both qualitative and quantitative data, since type, nature, distribution and frequency of activities all relate directly to the communicative nature of the textbooks. For this reason, I chose a single chapter from the midpoint of each text (chapter 10 of *Golosa*, book 1; chapter 8 of *Nachalo*, book 1; chapter 9 of *Troika*; and chapter 8 of *Live from Moscow*, volume 1) for detailed analysis. Since chapter structures are stable within a textbook, a detailed view of one chapter gives a reasonable impression of the book's standard practices.

The designation "communicative" is applied to activities which have a focus on meaning and in which students share information and/or opinions verbally in the target language. These activities can include personalized questions as well as role-plays and various kinds of verbal games where learners use the target language to solve a problem. Activities categorized as "Interview classmate" differ from paired Q&A on personalized material since the former usually are open-ended discussions of a topic, while the latter usually have a specific set of questions to be asked/answered. Table 6.3 presents the kinds of communicative activities included in all four texts and their frequency.

As can be seen from the data in Table 6.3, communicative activities have found a place in all the new generation textbooks, with roughly the same number of communicative activities included in each book's chapter. The role-play situation is the most widespread exercise type, and in this the textbooks reflect CLT's priority of having learners use the language to perform speech tasks. One weakness with some of the surveyed role-play situations is that their directions lack clear expectations for how much and what kind of language learners should produce. CLT's emphasis on learners' self-expression is reflected in the frequent inclusion of activities with personalized questions, often multiple times per chapter in all the texts. While personalized questions can lead to a very motivating and engaging classroom discussion, they can sometimes be problematic. If the teacher cannot tell whether the student is expressing an actual personal meaning or is simply

Table 6.3. Types and distribution of communicative activities

	Golosa (1994, bk. 1, ch. 10)	*Troika* (1996, ch. 9)	*Nachalo* (1996, bk. 1, ch. 8)	*Live from Moscow* (1996, vol. 1, ch. 7)
Answer personalized questions		3	5	
Brainstorming				1
Game – 20 questions	1			
Interview classmate	5	2	1	
Interview teacher		1		
Monolog about self	3			1
Monolog/presentation (topic other than self)	1		1	
Paired Q&A on personalized material		2	2	3
Role-play	3	3	4	7
Survey class			1	
Total	**13**	**11**	**14**	**12**

recycling another student's reply, then we cannot conclude that there has been real communication during the teacher-student Q&A. Furthermore, while one student produces a personal answer, nothing (other than politeness) requires other students to attend to that answer. Thus, answers offered in teacher-fronted Q&A exercises are unlikely to become language input for other students if they have no necessity to attend to their classmates' answers. Task-based classroom activities (about which more will be said below) can address these two shortcomings in using personalized questions in the language classroom.

In seeking to quantify and qualify the exercises that focus on language form, I have listed the whole range of activities from all four books in the first column of Table 6.4. Some activity types are listed multiple times because the exact nature of their implementation differs from textbook to textbook. To get a more nuanced idea of the nature of language use the exercises required, I coded each activity according to five parameters:

1. Are student answers at the *sentence* (coded as *S*) or *discourse* level (coded as *D*)?
2. Are learners meant to *personalize* responses (coded as *P*)?
3. Is *meaning* essential for the learner to get the correct answer (coded as *M*)?
4. Can a mostly *mechanical* approach to form lead learners to the correct answer (coded as *MCH*)?

Table 6.4. Types and distributions of language-focused activities

Activity type (nature)	Golosa (1994, bk. 1, ch. 10)	Troika (1996, ch. 9)	Nachalo (1996, bk. 1, ch. 8)	Live from Moscow (1996, bk. 1, ch. 7)
Answer questions (S, P)	2			
Answer questions with cues (S, MCH)			1	
Answer questions with illustrated cues (S, MCH)		1		
Columns exercise (S, M)	2			
Columns exercise (S, MCH)		1	1	3
Columns exercise (S, P)		1		
Columns exercise (S, P, MCH)	2			
Cued responses (S, M)	3			
Fill-in (S, MCH)			2	8
Fill-in (S/D, M)			2	
Fill-in (S/D, MCH)		2		
Fill-in (D, MCH)	2			
Formality judgment (S, M)	1			
Identify aspect (S/D, M)	5			
Make sentences with cues (S, MCH)				2
Make sentences with cues (S, P)				2
Match sentence start with conclusion (S, M)			1	
Match sentences (D, M)				3
Match synonyms (D, MCH)				1
Multiple choice (D, M)			1	
Multiple choice (S, MCH)	1			
Paired Q&A (D, M)		6		
Paired Q&A with cues (D, MCH)			3	24
Read aloud (S, MCH)	1		1	6
Sentence completion (S, P)		1	2	

(Continued)

Table 6.4. Continued

Activity type (nature)	Golosa (1994, bk. 1, ch. 10)	Troika (1996, ch. 9)	Nachalo (1996, bk. 1, ch. 8)	Live from Moscow (1996, bk. 1, ch. 7)
Sentence completion (S, P, MCH)	1			
Slash sentences (S, MCH)		3		
Substitution drill (D, MCH)		1		3
Transformation (S, MCH)		7	2	
Transformation (S/D, MCH)				5
Translation (D, M)	1		4	1
Translation (S, M)	4	5		
Total – Meaning	**16**	**11**	**8**	**4**
Total – Mechanical	**7**	**15**	**10**	**52**
Grand Total	**25**	**28**	**19**	**58**

Coding key: Q&A = question and answer; S = answer at the sentence level; D = answers require two or more sentences connected as dialog or narrative; P = answers reflect personal choices; M = attention to meaning is essential for correct answer; MCH = answers require manipulations of language forms, but attention to meaning is not *required*.

This coding procedure allows one to capture how CLT notions of contextualization and meaningfulness are reflected in work on language forms. To be rated as "meaning essential," an exercise had to be structured so that the student had to attend to meaning to get a correct and verifiable answer. For example, in one "meaning essential" exercise students were asked to form sentences telling the location of one city relative to another. They had a map, a list of cities to compare and the sentence pattern, "X находится на ___ от У." Although this is close to a mechanical pattern drill, it is *not* since students do have to attend to referential meaning in selecting cities and the directional word *(севере/юге/востоке/западе)* for the blank.

Some may object to my definition of mechanical exercises, noting that the language in these exercises is meaningful and that, while students manipulate forms, they *can* simultaneously be thinking about that meaning. I completely agree that the sentences and paragraphs in language-focused exercises in the new generation of textbooks are almost universally meaningful. We have progressed from the textbooks where exercises were lists of unconnected sentences containing virtually random words. However, I would argue that while the sentences are meaningful in these activities, the exercises themselves do not require that students attend to those meanings while they complete them. Students *may* attend to meaning, but they can just as easily answer correctly without thinking about it. For this reason, exercises where attention to meaning is not essential and that involve manipulation of language forms are coded as mechanical.

The data in Table 6.4 show the great variety of exercise types (over 30) that are now in use in language textbooks. All four textbooks reflect CLT's priority of contextualizing language use in that they contain a large number of exercises rooted in super-sentential discourse. Many exercises are framed in the form of paired question-answer dialogs, sometimes with follow-up questions. Personalized content plays a role in language-focused activities in addition to being a feature of communicative activities. Language exercises where attention to meaning is *required* occupy some place in all the texts, but mechanical exercises outnumber them in almost all of the books.[11] The significant presence of mechanical exercises in textbooks is problematic. Since these exercises do not require students' attention to meaning, we cannot be certain that the student will make form-meaning connections while doing them. Reliance on exercises that do not require a focus on meaning or that do not make learners connect form and meaning is a significant inefficiency and lost opportunity in existing textbooks.

A decade and a half after their first publication, all four textbooks are now in new editions with changes ranging from the cosmetic to the broad-sweeping. Retitled as *Live from Russia* (Lekić, Davidson and Gor 2009), the new addition has updated video, pictures and realia, but the communicative and language-focused activities in the sample chapter analyzed are virtually unchanged. *Golosa* (Robin, Evans-Romaine, Shatalina and Robin 2007) has reached a fourth edition with some notable changes. In terms of input, comprehension questions have been added to the dialogs, semi-authentic topical readings framed as an ongoing email exchange and related exercises have been added to every chapter, and short videos with comprehension activities have been added to the textbook's website. In terms of communicative and language-focused activities, much less has been updated. In the sample chapter analyzed, two communicative activities (one interview and the presentation) have been removed and replaced by another role-play and a classroom survey. The language-focused exercises are all of the same type as in the first edition, although some have been added and/or lengthened. *Nachalo* (Ervin, McLellan,

---

11 The number of meaning-based activities in *Golosa* in Table 6.4 may be slightly skewed because the chapter analyzed covered verbal aspect, and the exercises targeting this grammatical category made learners attend to the distinctions in meaning that aspect choice conveys.

Lubensky and Jarvis 2002) has had the biggest reorganization, expanding the language input with realia-based readings in each chapter and incorporating several new exercise formats. After each reading from the soap opera plot, an activity asks learners to focus on some point of language use that occurs in the text (e.g., find cognates; translate specific words; identify tense of verbs, etc.), thus requiring learners to make explicit form-meaning connections in the language input. Many form-focused fill-in exercises at the sentence level have been replaced or complemented by fill-ins in connected discourse (usually at the paragraph level), often with some element of meaning to be determined by the students as they complete the activity (e.g., which tense of the verb belongs in the blank; which verb from the vocabulary bank belongs in the blank and in which tense). More meaning-based activities have been added, and the analyzed chapter now includes an information gap activity, specifically formatted to maintain the "information gap" when students complete the activity in class in pairs. The second edition of *Troika*, released in July 2011, was too late to be considered here.

VI. Communicative Textbooks and Grammar

When we look at the "new generation" of textbooks, we can see that the Russian field in North America has been conceptualizing CLT since the mid-90s as focused on dialogic speech related to functional abilities and personalized language needs (i.e., the learner can talk about himself and carry out typical transactions in a foreign language – ask for something in a store; arrange a hotel room, etc.). For personalization and transactional language to occur, the texts have incorporated a much broader set of thematic vocabulary than earlier textbooks. Focus on carrying out everyday transactions and interactions, a criterion for ACTFL Intermediate level proficiency, has lead to the inclusion of much realia in the new textbooks (e.g., reproductions of menus, shopping receipts, ads for apartments and goods, personal letters and post cards). Personalized questions and role-play activities allow for learners to express themselves in different contexts and about different subjects. It depends entirely on the teacher, however, if these exchanges include the negotiation of meaning when student partners experience miscomprehension. These were all significant advances for the field.

For all the communicatively oriented features of the new textbooks, the treatment of grammatical material and language structure remains very traditional, although one should note that the authors do a good job matching grammatical topics to themes and communicative tasks in each chapter. Nevertheless, when it comes to dealing with Russian's morphology, the texts (with some exception for *Nachalo*'s second edition) consistently resort to the mechanical, form-focused exercises of earlier teaching methods. While never consciously intending to, the texts since the 1990s in many ways reflect the split approach to language teaching inherent in the Soviet conscious-practical method. Some parts of the text practice communication; other parts practice grammar. In their handling of grammar the texts seem to accept without question the notion that form-focused mechanical practice is necessary for the development of accurate language use that can later be deployed in communicative tasks.

This assumption is problematic for a number of reasons. First, it induces learners to think that grammar is only about formal surface accuracy, which obscures the fact that grammatical form contributes to meaning, sometimes being the only element to clarify meaning (e.g., *охотника убил медведь / охотник убил медведя; она за меня / она за мной*). Second, that assumption has been called into question by much SLA research in FonF. VanPatten (1996, 2004), Wong and VanPatten (2003), Wong (2005), Farley (2005), Pica (2005) and Lee and Benati (2007a, 2007b) have all suggested different meaning-focused techniques to teach grammatical features of European and Asian languages. The negative response that Wong and VanPatten's article (2003) evoked from Russianists, many of whom are textbook authors, suggests that the field may still not be ready to leave mechanical practice behind (Leaver, Rifkin, Shekhtman et al. 2004).

VII. New Directions

What can we do to increase the integration of form and meaning during language-focused exercises so that we can reduce the place that mechanical form-focused practice has in the classroom? There are a number of approaches that can help minimize mechanical exercises as a staple of classroom practice. In these approaches where learners have to make form-meaning connections, there are increased chances for vocabulary learning, noticing of grammatical form, and better and deeper comprehension of textual input. All three of these effects can potentially lead to learners getting more language uptake from the input. *Information gap activities*, if properly formatted, allow for targeted form practice as students exchange verifiable information. *Structured input activities* allow for learners to read/listen to target language sentences and make decisions about them (e.g., sorting, ordering, making judgments) while presenting a specific grammatical form. For example, in *Nachalo* (Ervin et al. 2002) students come to know the personalities of the main characters in the soap opera story of Lena Silina and Jim. Knowledge of these personalities can be harnessed when teaching the accusative case of inanimate nouns by providing a structured input activity like the one below. As students read and process the sentences for meaning, they have to suggest a likely character who would be reading the print material in question. The activity is formatted below as the students would have it.

After completing the activity, students read their answers aloud to each other to see if they agree or disagree (thus getting practice pronouncing the new grammatical forms while attending to their partner). At the end of the activity, the teacher can find out what diversity of opinion exists, and see if some answers correspond better than others. In the oral discussion of these sentences the teacher will necessarily vary the word order (e.g., *Газету «Русский спорт» наверно читает Сергей Петрович*) which allows the learners to notice the flexibility of Russian word order (although this exposure certainly will not be enough for them to reproduce it). This activity is only one of several where students work with the accusative case forms in a meaning-based approach, before they have to use this form in meaning-based output activities.

Comer and deBenedette (2010) have described several kinds of *processing instruction (PI) activities* for teaching Russian grammar points in a meaning-focused way. While their quasi-experiment showed no statistical advantage for either PI or traditional mechanical drills, their PI treatments allow for much more of the classroom interaction to be focused on meaning and its connections to language forms. *Task-based language teaching* is another direction in CLT in which significant classroom time can be focused on meaning and language forms, while simultaneously engaging students in learning about cultural differences (Comer 2007). It should be noted that all four of the above activity types can work with either explicit or implicit rule presentation and grammar explanation.

An essential component of task-based activities is the requirement that the task produces a verifiable outcome. Using this notion, it is not difficult to generate a task from current textbooks' frequent paired Q&A activities in which students exchange personal information. To illustrate this transformation, imagine that students are required to record in a table the personal answers from their Q&A exchanges, and that each student has to talk to multiple students. When the information exchange is complete, each student has to look over the recorded answers and use that information to answer some question or draw some kind of conclusion (i.e., the task's outcome). For example, a first-year class has been exposed to the expressions for time and daily activities (e.g., *я обычно ложусь спать в одиннадцать тридцать и встаю в полвосьмого*). For their information exchange task, each student has to talk to five other students in the group, recording their names, bedtimes and rising times. At the conclusion of the information exchange, the teacher asks "Кто в нашей группе спит дольше всех?" To answer this question the students have to analyze the information they gathered and offer an answer that the teacher or other students can verify (by going back to the recorded statements or the original speaker). As student groups report, it may take more than one group to find the answer to the question. In completing this activity there will be multiple opportunities to negotiate and verify meaning, since the numbers *два/девять/десять/двенадцать* are bound to occur, and when there is doubt about a verbal report, the teacher can write on the chalkboard the number that she has heard to see if the number spoken is the number intended. Turning paired Q&A into this kind of learning task means that students have to attend to the information that they learn from their classmates, and it gives their information exchange a non-linguistic purpose. Student use of a table for recording information helps with classroom management since the teacher can monitor students' progress in gathering information visually.

Figure 6.1. Structured input activity

Imagine that it's a Saturday afternoon and all the characters from the *Nachalo* textbook have some time to catch up on their reading. Look at the sentences below and decide who is most likely to be reading what. Compare your ideas about our characters' reading habits with your classmates' guesses, since some sentences may have multiple logical answers.

Саша Круглов	Бабушка Круглова	Дедушка Круглов	
Наталья Ивановна	Сергей Петрович	Лена Силина	Вова Силин
Профессор Петровский		Джим Ричардсон	

1. _____ читает новый роман «Гарри Поттер».

2. _____ читает русскую классику.

3. _____ читает американский учебник «Начало».

4. _____ читает газету «Русский спорт».

5. _____ читает журнал «Мода» (fashion).

6. _____ читает новую книгу «Наполеон и Россия».

7. _____ читает старую книгу «Русская кухня».

8. _____ читает новую биографию «Чайковский и русская музыка».

A fundamental point in these new FonF approaches is that students need to have adequate work on comprehension of forms and matching them to meaning *before* they have to produce them. This contrasts with the current approach where students encounter a few examples of a grammatical form in the input, then receive an explicit grammar explanation with a chart of new endings and then do mechanical exercises where they produce the new form without attention to its meaning. The shortcoming of the current approach is that it deprives learners of the opportunity to notice how the new form works in the language based on a larger set of language input and how the particular forms express a certain syntactic meaning.

Making deep comprehension of language input an initial priority for learners and a regular part of classroom work can inculcate better skills for dealing with textual input, and this would arguably have significant payoffs for the development of reading skills. Robin (2000) sees a proficiency paradox in the fact that we have updated teaching materials and instructional techniques to get students to the ACTFL Intermediate level in speaking after a basic two-year course sequence. Paradoxically, the metaphorical goal posts have changed, and students will need even greater proficiency in the language if they want to work professionally with Russian. Robin's solution is for students to have more contact with Russian, specifically in the form of Foreign Language Across the Curriculum (FLAC) course programming, so that students can continue to work on their language skills while taking courses for their non-Russian majors. FLAC, as well as other content-based approaches to language learning, can be a valuable institutional strategy to contribute to students' language learning, and they can also be a useful idea for curricular planning even inside the language department (Byrnes 2000). However, it is a strategy that relies on students having reading skills other than the skimming, scanning and gisting techniques that are usually applied when working with readers and texts at the ACTFL Intermediate level. To learn to read memoirs, textbook passages and excerpts from other nonfictional books, Russian students will need to have the additional skill of reading Russian intensively, if they are to get anything more than the gist of the text. Students will need to associate key words to grammatical forms and meanings if they are to get even the gist, let alone a more elaborate meaning. If we inculcate those skills from the beginning by making form-meaning connections not only a part of input comprehension activities, but a central part of our classroom grammar work, then we may get students to the reading level needed for FLAC. This is certainly not a call to abandon CLT practices that help students to learn to speak Russian. Rather, it is a call to take the next step in CLT and embark on a path to enhance learners' comprehension of language texts, to foster their abilities to connect form with meaning and to increase their ability to understand texts *and* to talk about them in an intelligent fashion.

The past two decades have seen remarkable growth in the quality and variety of materials available to teach Russian in North America. Learning to communicate in Russian is now a firmly established goal of the curriculum. In the next decade we should search out and test new ways to link communicative language teaching with the teaching of language form. Because of Russian's complex morphology, syntax and vocabulary, our classrooms, despite low enrollment numbers, offer many interesting opportunities for testing FonF techniques and measuring both their qualitative and quantitative results. Expanding this research base is the best hope for innovation in the next generation of Russian textbooks.

References

Aksenova, M. P. 1999. *Russkii iazyk po-novomu*. St. Petersburg: Zlatoust.
Allen, P., M. Swain, B. Harley and J. Cummins. 1990. "Aspects of Classroom Treatment: Toward a More Comprehensive View of Second Language Education." In B. Harley, P. Allen, J. Cummins and M. Swain (eds), *The Development of Second Language Proficiency*, 57–81. New York: Cambridge University Press.
Allwright, R. 1979. "Language Learning through Communication Practice." In C. J. Brumfit and K. Johnson (eds), *The Communicative Approach to Language Teaching*, 167–82. Oxford: Oxford University Press.
American Council on the Teaching of Foreign Languages. 1982. *ACTFL Provisional Proficiency Guidelines*. Yonkers, NY: ACTFL.
———. 1986. *ACTFL Proficiency Guidelines*. Yonkers, NY: ACTFL.
Byrnes, H. 2000. "Meaning and Form in Classroom-Based SLA Research: Reflections from a College Foreign Language Perspective." In J. F. Lee and A. Waldman (eds), *Form and Meaning: Multiple Perspectives*, 125–79. Boston, MA: Heinle and Heinle.
Chernyshov, S. 2001. *Poekhali: russkii iazyk dlia vzroslykh, nachal'nyi kurs*. St. Petersburg: Liden and Denz/Zlatoust.
Comer, W. J. 2007. "Implementing Task-Based Teaching from the Ground Up: Considerations for Lesson Planning and Classroom Practice." *Russian Language Journal* 57:181–203.
Comer, W. J. and L. deBenedette. 2010. "Processing Instruction and Russian: Issues, Materials, and Preliminary Experimental Results." *Slavic and East European Journal* 54 (1): 118–46.
Davidson, D. E., K. S. Gor and M. D. Lekić. 1996. *Russian Stage 1: Live from Moscow. Vol. 1. Textbook*. Dubuque, Iowa: Kendall/Hunt Publishing.
Doughty, C. 1991. "Second Language Instruction Does Make a Difference: Evidence from an Empirical Study of SL Relativization." *Studies in Second Language Acquisition* 13 (4): 431–69.
Doughty, C. and J. Williams, eds. 1998a. *Focus on Form in Classroom Second Language Acquisition*. New York: Cambridge University Press.
———. 1998b. "Pedagogical Choices in Focus on Form." In C. Doughty and J. Williams (eds), *Focus on Form in Classroom Second Language Acquisition*, 197–261. New York: Cambridge University Press.
Dunatov, R., ed. 1976. *Strategies for Teaching and Testing Communicative Competence in Russian*. Urbana, IL: Russian and East European Center, University of Illinois.
Educational Testing Service. 1991. *Advanced Russian Proficiency Test Listening/Reading: Test Manual*. Princeton, NJ.

Ervin, G. L. 1984. *Russian for Everybody: A Supplement.* OSU Slavic papers, nos. 39–40. Columbus, OH: Center for Slavic and East European Studies, Ohio State University.

Ervin, G. L., L. McLellan, S. Lubensky and D. Jarvis. 2002. *Nachalo Book 2.* 2nd ed. Boston, MA: McGraw-Hill.

Farley, A. 2004. *Structured Input: Grammar Instruction for the Acquisition-Oriented Classroom.* New York: McGraw-Hill.

Furman, N., D. Goldberg and N. Lusin. 2007. *Enrollments in Languages other than English in United States Institutions of Higher Education, Fall 2006.* New York: Modern Language Association.

Ginsberg, R. B. 1992. *Language Gains during Study Abroad: An Analysis of the ACTR Data.* Washington, DC: National Foreign Language Center.

Harley, B. and M. Swain. 1984. "The Interlanguage of Immersion Students and its Implications for Second Language Teaching." In A. Davies, C. Cripter and A. P. R. Howatt (eds), *Interlanguage,* 291–311. Edinburgh: Edinburgh University Press.

Jarvis, D. K. 1984. "Communicative Competence: An Overview of the Research and Some Practical Suggestions for the Classroom." In S. Lubensky and D. K. Jarvis (eds), *Teaching, Learning, Acquiring Russian,* 33–44. Columbus, OH: Slavica.

Kapitonova, T. I. and A. N. Shchukin. 1987. *Sovremennye metody obucheniia russkomu iazyku inostrantsev.* 2nd ed. Moscow: Russkii iazyk.

Krashen, S. D. 1982. *Principles and Practice in Second Language Acquisition.* Oxford: Pergamon Press.

Krashen, S. D. and T. D. Terrell. 1983. *The Natural Approach: Language Acquisition in the Classroom.* New York: Oxford University Press.

Leaver, B. L., B. Rifkin, B. Shekhtman et al. 2004. "Apples and Oranges are Both Fruit, But They Don't Taste the Same: A Response to Wynne Wong and Bill VanPatten." *Foreign Language Annals* 37 (1): 125–32.

Lee, J. F., and A. Benati. 2007a. *Delivering Processing Instruction in Classrooms and in Virtual Contexts: Research and Practice.* London: Equinox.

———. 2007b. *Second Language Processing: An Analysis of Theory, Problems, and Possible Solutions.* London: Continuum.

Lee, J. F. and B. VanPatten. 1995. *Making Communicative Language Teaching Happen.* New York: McGraw-Hill.

Lekić, M. D., D. E. Davidson and K. S. Gor. 2009. *Russian Stage One: Live from Russia. Vol. 2. Textbook.* 2nd ed. Washington, DC: ACTR-Kendall Hunt Professional.

Leont'ev, A. A. 1991. "Osnovnye linii razvitiia metodiki prepodavaniia inostrannykh iazykov v SSSR (40-80-e gg.)." In A. A. Leont'ev (ed.), *Obshchaia metodika obucheniia inostrannym iazykam: khrestomatiia,* 4–8. Moscow: Russkii iazyk.

Lightbown, P. and N. Spada. 1990. "Focus-on-Form and Corrective Feedback in Communicative Language Teaching: Effects on Second Language Learning." *Studies in Second Language Acquisition* 12: 429–48.

Liskin-Gasparro, J. E. 1984. "The ACTFL Proficiency Guidelines: A Historical Perspective." In T. V. Higgs (ed.), *Teaching for Proficiency, the Organizing Principle,* 11–42. Lincolnwood, IL: National Textbook Company.

———. 2003. "The ACTFL Proficiency Guidelines and the Oral Proficiency Interview: A Brief History and Analysis of their Survival." *Foreign Language Annals* 36 (4): 438–90.

Long, M. 1991. "Focus on Form: A Design Feature in Language Teaching Methodology." In K. De Bot, R. B. Ginsberg and C. Kramsch (eds), *Foreign Language Research in Cross-Cultural Perspective,* 39–52. Philadelphia, PA: Benjamins.

Lubensky, S., G. E. Ervin and D. Jarvis. 1996. *Nachalo: When in Russia. Book 1.* 1st ed. Boston, MA: McGraw-Hill.

Małolepsza, M. and A. Szymkiewicz. 2006. *Hurra po polsku I: podręcznik studenta.* Krakow: Prolog.

Martin, C., J. Robin and D. Jarvis. 1991. *The Russian Desk: A Listening and Conversation Course.* Columbus, OH: Slavica.

Miller, L. V., L. V. Politova and I. Ia. Rybakova. 2009. *Zhili-byli: 28 urokov russkogo iazyka dlia nachinaiushchikh.* Warsaw: Rossiiskii dom/Zlatoiust.

Musumeci, D. 1996. "Teacher-Learner Negotiation in Content-Based Instruction: Communication at Cross-purposes?" *Applied Linguistics* 17: 286–325.

Nakhimovsky, A. D. 1984. "Principles for a Beginning Russian Course." In S. Lubensky and D. K. Jarvis (eds), *Teaching, Learning, Acquiring Russian,* 45–53. Columbus, OH: Slavica.

Nunan, D. 2004. *Task-Based Language Teaching: A Comprehensively Revised Edition of Designing Tasks for the Communicative Classroom.* New York: Cambridge University Press.

Nummikoski, M. 1996. *Troika: A Communicative Approach to Russian Language, Life and Culture.* New York: John Wiley and Sons.

Omaggio, A. C. 1986. *Teaching Language in Context: Proficiency-Oriented Instruction.* Boston, MA: Heinle and Heinle.

Passov, E. I. 1977. *Osnovy metodiki obucheniia inostrannym iazykam.* Moscow: Russkii iazyk.

———. 1985. *Kommunikativnyi metod obucheniia inoiazychnomu govoreniiu: posobie dlia uchitelei inostrannykh iazykov.* Moscow: Prosveshchenie.

Patton, F. R. 1984. "Russian Language Textbooks for Americans, 1975–82." In S. Lubensky, and D. K. Jarvis (eds), *Teaching, Learning, Acquiring Russian,* 347–59. Columbus, OH: Slavica.

Paulston, C. B. 1972. "Structural Pattern Drills: A Classification." In H. Allen, and R. N. Campbell (eds), *Teaching English as a Second Language,* 129–38. New York: McGraw-Hill.

Pica, T. 1994. "Questions from the Language Classroom: Research Perspectives." *TESOL Quarterly* 28 (1): 49–79.

———. 2005. "Classroom Learning, Teaching, and Research: A Task-Based Perspective." *Modern Language Journal* 89 (3): 339–52.

Rassudova, O. P. and L. V. Stepanova. 1979. *Temp: Intensivnyi kurs russkogo iazyka: Kn. dlia uchashchikhsia.* Moscow: Russkii iazyk.

Richards, J. C. and T. S. Rodgers. 1986. *Approaches and Methods in Language Teaching: A Description and Analysis.* London: Cambridge University Press.

Rifkin, B. 1992. "The Communicative Orientation of Russian-Language Textbooks." *Slavic and East European Journal* 36 (4): 463–88.

———. 1997. "Second Language Acquisition Theory and the New Generation of Russian Language Textbooks." *Slavic and East European Journal* 41 (2): 330–40.

———. 2005. "A Ceiling Effect in Traditional Classroom Foreign Language Instruction: The Data from Russian." *Modern Language Journal* 89 (1): 3–18.

Robin, R., K. Henry and J. Robin. 1994. *Golosa: A Basic Course in Russian. Book 1.* 1st ed. Englewood Cliffs, NJ: Prentice Hall.

Robin, R., K. Evans-Romaine, G. Shatalina and J. Robin. 2007. *Golosa: A Basic Course in Russian. Book 1.* 4th ed. Upper Saddle River, NJ: Pearson.

Rodgers, D. M. 2006. "Developing Content and Form: Encouraging Evidence from Italian Content-Based Instruction." *Modern Language Journal* 90 (3): 373–86.

Ruiz, H. 1987. "The Impregnability of Textbooks: The Example of American Foreign Language Education." In S. J. Savignon and M. S. Berns (eds), *Initiatives in Communicative Language Teaching II: A Book of Readings,* 33–53. Reading, MA: Addison-Wesley.

Samuda, V. 2001. "Guiding Relationships between Form and Meaning during Task Performance: The Role of the Teacher." In M. Bygate, P. Skehan and M. Swain (eds), *Researching Pedagogic Tasks: Second Language Learning, Teaching and Testing*, 119–40. New York: Longman.

Shelly, S. L. 1995. "Reinventing 'Grammar' for Foreign Language Textbooks." In M.A. Haggstrom et al. (eds), *The Foreign Language Classroom: Bridging Theory and Practice*, 199–208. New York: Garland.

Stepanova, E. M., Z. N. Ievleva, L. B. Trushina and V. G. Kostomarov. 1971. *Russkii iazyk dlia vsekh*. Moscow: Progress.

Stepanova, E. M., V. G. Kostomarov and R. L. Baker. 1984. *Russian for Everybody*. Moscow: Russkii iazyk.

Swain, M. 1985. "Communicative Competence: Some Roles of Comprehensible Input and Comprehensible Output." In S. Gass and C. Madden (eds), *Input and Second Language Acquisition*, 235–53. Cambridge, MA: Newbury House.

———. 1991. "Manipulating and Complementing Content Teaching to Maximise Second Language Learning." In R. Phillipson and E. Kellerman (eds), *Foreign/Second Language Pedagogy Research: A Commemorative Volume for Claus Faerch*, 234–50. Clevedon: Multilingual Matters.

———. 1998. "Focus on Form Through Conscious Reflection." In C. Doughty and J. Williams (eds), *Focus on Form in Classroom Second Language Acquisition*, 64–81. New York: Cambridge University Press.

Thompson, I. and E. Urevich. 1991. *Reading Real Russian*. 2 vols. Englewood Cliffs, NJ: Prentice Hall.

Ullman, R. 1987. "The Ontario Experience: A Modular Approach to Second Language Teaching and Learning." In S. J. Savignon and M. S. Berns (eds), *Initiatives in Communicative Language Teaching II: A Book of Readings*, 57–81. Reading, MA: Addison-Wesley.

VanPatten, B. 1996. *Input Processing and Grammar Instruction in Second Language Acquisition*. Norwood, NJ: Ablex Pub.

———. ed. 2004. *Processing Instruction: Theory, Research, and Commentary*. Mahwah, NJ: L. Erlbaum Associates.

Wong, W. 2005. *Input Enhancement: From Theory and Research to the Classroom*. New York: McGraw-Hill.

Wong, W. and B. VanPatten. 2003. "The Evidence is In: Drills are Out." *Foreign Language Annals* 36 (3): 403–23.

Chapter 7

LOW-PROFICIENCY HERITAGE SPEAKERS OF RUSSIAN: THEIR INTERLANGUAGE SYSTEM AS A BASIS FOR FAST LANGUAGE (RE)BUILDING

Alla Smyslova
Columbia University

I. Introduction

The focus on heritage learners in second language acquisition studies is a relatively recent development (e.g., Brinton, Kagan and Bauckus 2008). There is a significant distinction between heritage and foreign language acquisition – the former beginning at home, while the latter takes place in a classroom (UCLA Steering Committee 2000, 339). The establishment of heritage language education as a valid and distinct research field at the turn of the twenty-first century was a landmark event in second language acquisition and foreign language education (Valdés 1995; Peyton et al. 2001; Kagan and Dillon 2001; Lynch 2003). Heritage language studies provide a crucial link between second language acquisition and bilingual education by focusing research attention on the nature of language acquisition by both children and adults; on the revival of the mother tongue; on the unique characteristics of heritage speakers; and the challenges their bilingualism poses for language instruction (Krashen 1998; Andrews 1999; Campbell and Rosenthal 2000; Valdés 2001, 2006; Douglas 2005; Hornberger and Wang 2008; Brinton 2008). Today, heritage Russian speakers constitute a diverse growing population in American and European language classes, which makes Russian an important part of heritage language studies (Brecht and Ingold 1998; Andrews 2000; Zemskaya 2001; Polinsky 2000, 2004, 2006; Polinsky and Kagan 2007; Kagan 2008; Davidson 2010).

The term *heritage speaker* or *heritage learner*, though relatively recent, is becoming more widely used since its first appearance in the Standards for

Foreign Language Learning (ACTFL 1996). Alternately, this group is referred to as *native*, *quasi-native*, or *bilingual* learners speaking their *home* language in the Spanish teaching profession, as *home background* learners speaking *immigrant* or *aboriginal* languages in Australia, or *languages of origin* in France, and as *heritage language* speakers in Canada (Valdés 1995, 2000; Duff 2008).

Various definitions of heritage language learners have been put forth. Some of them are fairly broad, for example: "in the US context, heritage language learners are individuals who have familial or ancestral ties to a particular language that is not English and who exert their agency in determining whether or not they are heritage language learners of that heritage language and heritage culture" (Hornberger and Wang 2008, 27). Some others aim for more specifics defining a heritage learner as "a student of a target language who has been raised in a home where that non-English target language is spoken, who may speak or merely understand the target language, and who is to some degree bilingual[1] in English and the heritage (target) language" (Valdés 2006, 193). The latter definition includes both children of immigrants who are born in the dominant language's environment and learn the heritage language from their parents and also immigrant children who arrive in the dominant language's country at a preschool age. The two groups share dominance of the language learned later, and insufficient or restricted input in their L1 or heritage language (Polinsky 2010).

Figure 7.1 presents my summary of the changes introduced to the classification of US heritage speakers since they have come to the attention of second language researchers and educators. The classifications are based on the age of arrival and the number of schooling years in the country of origin.

From the outset, heritage language scholarship has considered age at the time of arrival in the host country a critical factor in heritage language development, the assumption being that individuals who arrive at an older age maintain their academic language skills better than those arriving at a younger age (Cummins 1993). Recent studies of heritage language speakers in the US affirm that while age at arrival in the US is a strong factor affecting the level

---

1 Interpreting bilingual abilities "as falling along a continuum," Valdés sees bilingualism as "a dynamic condition that essentially involves *more than one* competence, however small that competence might be" (Valdés 2000, 384, 385, emphasis in original). It is necessary to mention here that, as pointed out by Fishman, ascertaining the degree of bilingualism is a very old and complex question approached by investigators from different disciplines with their own specific concerns. Linguists measure the distance between phonetic, lexical, grammatical, semantic and stylistic proficiency, and intactness. Educators approach bilingualism in terms of performance in different contexts. Psychologists are concerned with speed, automaticity and habit strength, while sociologists rely upon relative frequency of use in different settings (Fishman 1964, 34). Fishman called for a combination of interrelated measures of bilingualism. Polinsky considers sequential rather than simultaneous bilingualism to be a common property of heritage speakers (Polinsky 2010).

Figure 7.1. First classifications of heritage speakers in the USA

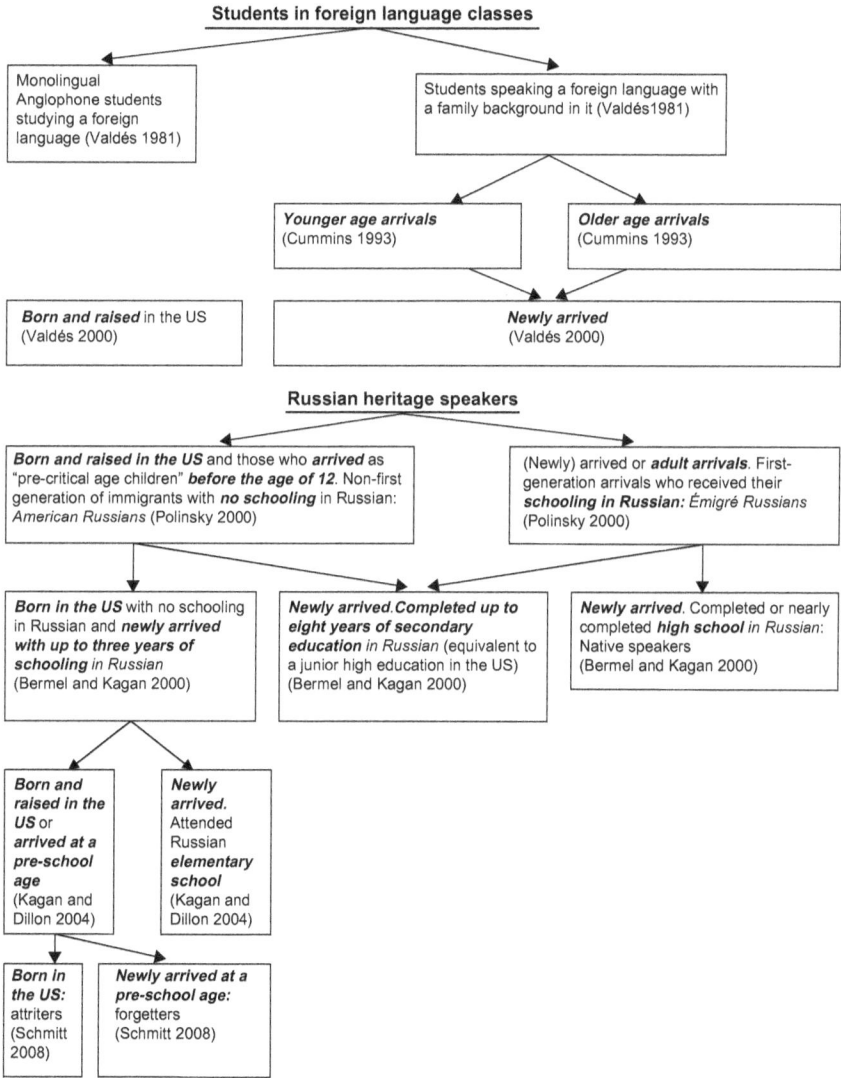

of heritage language competence, there are also other sociolinguistic factors in play that correlate with the level of heritage language proficiency in heritage speakers (e.g., Zemskaya 2000; Valdés 2000). They include, for example, the amount of daily exposure to L1 (i.e., the language spoken in the family) and the level of L1 literacy of the family of the heritage speaker (Zemskaya 2000; Valdés 2000; Isurin and Ivanova-Sallivan 2008; Schmitt 2008).

Previous research addressing Russian heritage learners in the US educational context analyzes oral and written speech production and comprehension by heritage learners, and describes the distinctive patterns of their language and their internalized grammatical systems. Heritage language is seen as a relatively systematic pattern of target language production that reflects various degrees of incomplete acquisition, language attrition and structural loss arising as a result of the learner's interrupted access to formal education in the mother tongue and his or her shift over time to the use of the dominant language as the primary language of communication (Fishman 1991; Garcia and Diaz 1992; Krashen 1998; Polinsky 1997; Campbell and Christian 2005; Gor 2010). Previous studies also examine the significant pedagogical challenges encountered by teachers and instructors of all heritage languages in the US due to the rather large range of individual differences in heritage language skills and proficiency levels (Valdés 1995; McQuillan 1996; Kondo-Brown 2003; Kagan and Dillon 2003; Beaudrie and Ducar 2005; Jensen and Llosa 2007).

It is now common knowledge in the field of foreign language teaching that listening and speaking skills are far better developed among heritage speakers than are reading and writing skills (Fishman 1984; Brisk 2000; Kagan and Bremel 2000; Chevalier 2004; Kagan 2005). Successful heritage curricula have been shown to make extensive use of primary source reading (McQuillan 1996). Many foreign language educators seem to agree that the linguistic skills of heritage language learners are potentially stronger, more intuitive and more native-like than those developed among non-native learners in traditional foreign language programs. Educators also agree that heritage learners relearn or revive their heritage language skills faster than foreign learners acquire similar skills in a foreign language *de nova* (Valdés 2006a; Brinton et al. 2008). However, so far there is a very limited number of studies (Smyslova 2009a) that provide an empirical basis to support these claims scientifically. The need for further research is evident when one considers that if the instructional pathways and methods of teaching this unique and growing population of students are to improve, a more complete understanding of the linguistic system of incomplete acquisition and/or language attrition of heritage students of Russian must be established.

The present study seeks to expand current research on heritage learners by introducing new data on language production of Russian heritage speakers of the low-proficiency level, i.e., those who were born in the US or arrived at a pre-school age, in a university classroom environment.

Performance-based data were collected by means of a special diagnostic test developed by the researcher in a classroom setting. The diagnostic test establishes baseline language levels and language characteristics of the subject group at the intake level and assesses existing measurable levels of first language retention.

This study describes and examines the patterns of heritage learner interlanguage production as evidence of internalized grammatical systems, focusing mainly on heritage learners' levels of control of the sentence-level syntax and nominal system as reflected in the data.[2]

The findings of the study offer insights into the nature of adult language acquisition and the revival of a mother tongue, focusing on Russian heritage learners with a low proficiency level who are maximally removed from native acquirement, and assessing how their strengths can be utilized for more effective language instruction.

The research questions of this study, therefore, may be summarized as follows:

1. Are there common linguistic characteristics of low-level proficiency heritage speakers of Russian that distinguish them from their non-heritage counterparts at the same levels of study?
2. Do low-proficiency heritage speakers show evidence of latent or partially retained interlanguage grammatical structures or underlying linguistic competencies that might serve as the foundation for the design of a dedicated "bridge course" to accelerate or streamline their acquisition (or reacquisition) of Russian?
3. Is there a correlation between language retention and the age at the time of arrival in the US (i.e., born in the US or arrived there at a pre-school age) in this group of heritage learners?
4. What other factors, most particularly related to family background, may have an impact on the fast building or rebuilding of the language proficiency and skills of low-proficiency heritage learners?

Although the study provides a valid empirical analysis of the internalized grammatical system as reflected in a controlled production, the conclusions regarding this relatively small data sample need future confirmation in large-scale studies.

II. Participants

Participants in this study included 19 American students, who at the time of the study were enrolled in heritage Russian language classes at Columbia University in the city of New York. All the participants are children of

---

2 For analysis of verbal morphology see Pereltsvaig (2005, 2008); Romanova (2008); Isurin and Ivanova- Sullivan (2008); Friedman and Kagan (2008); Laleko (2009); Gor (2010).

first-generation immigrants, i.e., they belong to the third and fourth waves of Russian-speaking immigrants to the US. The countries of origin in their families are Ukraine (8), Russia (5), Belarus (2), Latvia (1), Lithuania (1) and Moldova (1).[3] The families of the participants have been living in the US from 14 to 29 years (mean = 20.2; SD = 5.8).

The participants included three males and sixteen females between 18 and 21 years of age at the time of the study (mean = 19.5; SD = 1.0). Thirty three percent of the participants were born in the United States, and the rest arrived in the country between the ages of 1 and 7 (mean = 4.1; SD =1.9). The average age of arrival is 2.9 years of age (SD = 2.6). According to the information solicited from both participants and their parents and grandparents, Russian was the first language of all participants. From the point of view of prevalence of usage, Russian became a secondary language for all of them.

None of the participants in this study had any schooling in a Russian-speaking country prior to their education in the US. In this sense, all of them can be viewed as belonging to the group of lowest-proficiency speakers referred to by Polinsky and Kagan as basilect heritage speakers, i.e., individuals "who are maximally removed from native attainment and who show many deviations from the baseline", and whose proficiency is mostly restricted to home language and who, the authors admit, may not be a homogeneous group (Polinsky and Kagan 2007, 371).

Two students did not know the Cyrillic alphabet and could neither read nor write in Russian. Six students knew how to write in cursive, and the rest could write in block letters only. At best, reading skill of these participants was limited to non-existent. All had significant problems with lexical access and retrieval, and their oral speech was inaccurate with frequent breakdowns.

III. Data Collection Environment, Materials and Procedures

All data were collected in the relatively controlled environment of a classroom setting of the course "Russian for Heritage Speakers" offered at Columbia University. "Russian for Heritage Speakers" is a two-semester course that was designed by the author of this study in 2003 specifically for heritage speakers at the lowest language proficiency level to meet a two-year foreign language requirement. This course is intended for students who were either born in the US of Russian-speaking parents or arrived from a Russian-speaking country at a very early age, who speak and/or listen to Russian at home and who have

---

[3] No information regarding country of origin is available for one of the students who participated in the study.

limited to no reading and writing skills in Russian. The course meets twice a week for seventy-five minutes and is conducted entirely in Russian. The textbook used for the course is *Russian for Russians* by Kagan, Akishina and Robin (2002). The material offered in the textbook is heavily supplemented by readings. All readings are accompanied by audio recordings to facilitate the process of reading skills development by providing both aural and visual input of the same texts.

On the opening day of the semester, the heritage students were required to take a diagnostic test[4] to generate baseline data for assessment of entering levels of Russian proficiency in the heritage group. One of the assignments was to respond in writing – writing in Russian any way they can – to ten questions pertaining to them personally, their families and their interest in the Russian language. Because 2 of the 19 students did not know the Cyrillic alphabet at the time the test was administered, they did not produce essays. One of the 19 students did not take the test at all. In total, 16 essays were elicited for analysis of the language of heritage speakers of this group.

The elicited data are described and translated into numeric frequency scores for ease of assessment and comparison of results. This, in turn, enables the identification of existing patterns in the interlanguage system of the target group and provides the evidence necessary to interpret it.

IV. Heritage Speakers' Language upon Entrance to the Program

This part provides a description and analysis of the structural characteristics of the language of heritage speakers as reflected in the sixteen essays elicited on the first day of classes. The current analysis of the responses constructed by heritage students focuses on three basic structural categories: the level of mastery of the orthographic system; assessment of sentence length and syntactic complexity, and examination of the nominal and pronominal case system.

IV.1. Spelling, capitalization, punctuation

IV.1.1. Spelling

In 1964, Fishman observed that the degree of maintenance in the written, read and spoken language of heritage learners tends to vary significantly.

---

4 For detailed description of the participants, their tests and essays see Smyslova (2009a).

According to his findings, if literacy in the first language is attained prior to interaction with another language, reading and writing skills in the first language may resist shift to the other tongue longer than speaking skills. If, on the other hand, literacy is attained subsequent to such interaction, the reverse may hold true, i.e., reading and writing shift to the other tongue more readily (1964, 35–6). Since all heritage participants in this study were literate in English and their reading and writing had shifted to English, their reading and writing skills in Russian were limited to nonexistent.

An interesting characteristic of the language of low proficiency heritage speakers, which sets them apart from other groups of heritage speakers and non-heritage learners of the language, is the vast superiority of their "*audio* image" of the language (internalized oral and aural grammar) over their "*visual* image" (internalized grammar of the written language). The essays examined here *sound* much more grammatically accurate to a *listener* who *hears* them read aloud than to a *reader* who *sees* them in their written form:

Born in US	*в Филаделфие*
	v filadelfie
	in Philadelphia$_{PREP-PH}$[5]
Arrived at 2	*с радитильими*
	s raditil'imi
	with parents$_{INST-PH}$
	с врзозлами
	s vrzozlami
	with adults$_{INST-PH}$
Arrived at 2	*слушат музку*
	slušat muzku
	(to) listen to music$_{ACC-FEM}$
Arrived at 3	*познакомилась с амирикасьм*
	poznakomilas' s amirikasym
	met an American$_{INST-PH}$
Arrived at 4	*пишю маслиноми краскомы*
	pišiu maslinomi kraskomy
	paint in oil$_{INST-PL-PH}$ paints$_{INST-PL-PH}$

---

5   Some abbreviations: PH – spelled phonetically, ACC – accusative, PREP – prepositional, INST – instrumental, FEM – feminine, INC – incorrect.

> в девиносто-первым году
> v devinosto- pervym godu
> in ninety first_{PREP-PH}

Arrived at 5.5 я не люблю войни
ia ne liubliu vojnu
I do not like war_{ACC-FEM-PH}

This is easily explained by the fact that in many cases heritage speakers pronounce Russian case endings of nouns and modifiers without a corresponding mastery of spelling due to a confusion of letters (English versus Cyrillic, block versus cursive) and the absence of a regular correspondence between graphemes and phonemes in their minds (Bermel and Kagan 2000). Their spelling is essentially phonetic: they write in Russian the way they hear it.

Loewen (2008) found a strong similarity between the types of mistakes made by heritage learners and native speakers since both reflect a spelling based on aural cues. He grouped these mistakes into three broad categories: *vowel reduction*, *consonant* voicing/devoicing, and *transfers* from colloquial speech. All the three are represented in the sample below:[6]

> (1)(Arrived at 5)
> У МЕНЯ НЕТО МНОГА РОТСТВИНИКИХ С КАТОРИМИ Я МАГЮ ГАВАРИТ
> u menia neto   mnoga rotsvinikix   s katorimi   ia magiu gavarit
> I_{GEN}. do not have many relatives_{PL-INC} with whom_{INST-PL-PH} I can speak
>
> ПО РУССКИ, И Я ТОЛКА ОДИН РАС ВИРНУЛАСЬ В РАССИЮ ПОСЛИ ТОВО
> po russki, i ia tolka odin ras virnulas' v rassiu posli tovo
> in Russian, and I only one time went back_{P-PERF} to Russia_{ACC-FEM} after
>
> КАК Я ЮЙХАЛА ОТ ТУДА… Я СТРАШНА ЛЮБЛЮ ФРАНЦУСКИ ИЗИК.
> kak ia iujxala ot tuda… ia strašna liubliu francuski izik
> I went away from there… I terribly like   (the) French language

Not a single occurrence of a word with the hard sign is observed in any of the essays. The soft sign, on the other hand, is there but it is frequently misplaced. Sometimes it is present where it should not be (*сейчасъ* and *папа шутитъ*), in other cases, it is conspicuously absent (*я радилас_*).

---

6 Original script, whether Cyrillic or mixed, has been retained in the examples provided here. All essays written in block letters. In the above examples bold indicates incorrect spelling. For complete texts of essays see Smyslova (2009a).

A jumbled use of ы and и, as in жьвьот for живёт, is also apparent. Additionally, the letter ы appears with its two graphic elements in reverse order (латьнски езьк, учобь, амириканцьм). Additional evidence of the heritage speakers' phonological/orthographic confusion is observed in the following groups or pairs of Cyrillic letters:

- у, о and ю (as in ню or ну in place of но)
- у and ю (as in играйу, лублу, умеу, выючит and кюшац)
- я and е or у (as in езьк, узек)
- й and ё (as in второё год)
- о and ё (as in фсо, рибонак)
- э and е (as in етат, ета)
- ч and ш (as in хашу)
- ш and щ (as in пащьла)
- т and ц (as in радицелй)
- л and р (as in ладитеры)
- в and г (у каво, после тово)

Based on the instances of confusion listed above, it is clear that in addition to vowels in unstressed positions, heritage speakers exhibit limited understanding and control of the grapheme to phoneme correlation of the vowels я, е, ё, э, ю and the consonant й. Heritage learners also demonstrate confusion regarding hushers[7] ш, щ, ж, ч and ц.

Another consistent spelling error observed in the essays is the omission of the double consonants dictated by Russian spelling rules: клас, имигриріьволе, граматика, медлино. Interestingly, the same student might double the consonant in some usages, but not in others. Consider, for example, в русскй школе and по русски, as opposed to мама руская. Only the essays, which were written by students who arrived in the US at the age of 6 and 7, demonstrate systematic and correct adherence to the double consonant spelling rule: граммматика, Одесса, рассказы, в особенности, русский, Россия.

In addition to the orthographic characteristics previously mentioned, the excerpt reproduced below demonstrates another feature observed by Zemskaya (2001, 162) – the systematical transcribing of the Russian vowels у and ю, using the English letters о, оо and ou as well as transcribing Russian consonants with English letters:

---

7 *Hushers* is a convenient descriptive term used in Russian-language textbooks for the sounds spelled by the letters ш, щ, ж *and* ч.

> (2) (Arrived at 4)
> МИНА ЗАВООТ ... МНЕ 18 ЛИТ. Я РАДИЛАС В KIEVE И Я ПАЩЬЛА В
> mina   zavut ...   mne 18 lit.   ia radilas   v kieve   i ia pašč'la v
> My name is ...   I_DAT am 18 years old. I was born in Kiev_PREP and I went to
>
> ЩЬOLO   В АМЕРIКЕ.   МНЕ BELE 3 ГОДА КАГД Я
> šč'olo   v amerike.   mne bele 3 goda kagd
> school_ACC-FEM-PH in America_PREP. I_DAT was 3 years_GEN-SG old when I
>
> ПРЕЯ(НА)LA В AMERIKO.
> ia preia(xa)la   v ameriko.
> arrived in America_ACC-PH.
>
> OU МЕНЯ NET ВРATES И СОСТЕS.   Я ГАVАРОU ПА РУССКУ С МУЕ МАМА
> u menia net brates i sostes.   ia gavaru   pa russku s mue   mama
> I_GEN do not have brothers and sisters. I speak Russian with my_PH mother_NOM-INC
>
> И С МУЕМЕ ДРОUГЕМЕ РОТСVЕНИКАМЁ. Я LOUBLOU ЧЕТАТ И ПЕСАТ И
> i s mueme drugeme   rotsvenikamë.   ia lublu   chetat i pesat i
> and with my_INSTR-PL-PH other_INSTR-PL-PH relatives_INSTR-PL-PH. I love to read
> and write and
>
> OUVLИКАOUS ТИАТРАМ.
> uvlikaus   tiatram.
> (am) interested in theater_INSTR-PH.

Other than the confusion of English and Cyrillic letters and the misplacement of the soft sign, most of the consistent errors discussed above – the misspelling of unstressed vowels and the use of voiceless consonants in place of voiced ones in clusters and in final positions – are common among native speakers of Russian. Such mistakes, however, are not typical of L2 learners of Russian.

IV.1.2. Capitalization

Using upper and lower case letters properly is an important aspect of writing Russian correctly. It is difficult to draw any definitive conclusions about capitalization in the orthographic system of the target group, as fifteen out of nineteen students wrote their essays in block letters. However, based on the data extracted from the essays that were written in cursive, it is possible to outline a few tendencies. On the one hand, the names of languages are capitalized in agreement with the rules of English capitalization, but contrary to the established norms of Russian orthography, for example: *по Русски* and *Русскую льтуратуру*. On the other hand, university names (*в колумбие*) and cities (*филаделфие*) are not capitalized in some essays, which is in violation of both Russian and English capitalization rules. Capitalization is almost totally ignored in one essay, which is written in cursive.

Despite the appearance of what Bermel and Kagan (2000, 420) call "alphabet soup," i.e., the mixed spelling exemplified herein, it is important not to lose sight of the level of language control exhibited by the language forms correctly produced by these learners. This control includes a good number of correct grammatical endings together with correctly used nouns and verbs. This phenomenon certainly supports the conclusion drawn by Polinsky that "an L1 speaker whose acquisition was interrupted at or after the age of 5 already possesses the knowledge of word class (lexical categories) distinctions" (2004, 420). If by interruption of acquisition Polinsky is referring to the age of arrival in the US, then according to the current data, it is reasonable to conclude that those who arrived at an age even younger than 5 and, in some cases, those born to Russian-speaking parents in the US might also possess the knowledge of word class distinctions.

Since the focus of the current study is on what the heritage speakers in the target group have retained from the Russian grammatical system rather than on what is lacking, it is expedient generally to ignore misspellings, as they tend to distract from the larger issues under investigation. Therefore, in what follows, all examples from the essays will be cited with correct spelling, using the notation (ph) to indicate when a word is spelled phonetically (for the original spelling in all pre-program essays see Smyslova 2009a, Appendix A).

IV.1.3. Punctuation

Heritage speakers generally adhere to English rules of punctuation, according to which only non-restrictive relative clauses are set off by commas, whereas Russian sets off all relative clauses with commas. They always use a comma to separate an introductory phrase (which is usually one or more prepositional phrases) thus violating Russian punctuation rules.

IV.2. Sentence length and syntactic complexity

IV.2.1. Essay length

The average length of the essays produced by students is 11.4 sentences, the shortest consisting of 6 sentences and the longest of 18. This amounts to an average of 85.7 words per essay within a range of 43 to 171 words. The mean sentence length for the set of essays under study is thus 7.1 words with 4.4 words per sentence at the lower end of the spectrum and 11.4 words per sentence at the higher end.

VI.2.2. Syntactic complexity

Thirty-one percent of the sentences in the essays under analysis were either compound (10.3 percent) or complex (21.0 percent). Furthermore, all essays contained either compound or complex sentences. In contrast to data from previous studies of heritage speakers (Isurin and Sullivan 2008), which demonstrated a preference for compound or coordinate sentences over complex or subordinate clauses, compound sentences occur less frequently than complex sentences. The only conjunctions occurring in these compound sentences are *и* and *но*. Examples are provided below:

Born in US	(3)	Я хочу стать адвокатом, **но я** только в втором курсе ia xoču stat' advokatom, no ia tol'ko v vtorom kurse I want to become a lawyer, **but** I am only a sophomore
Arrived at 5	(4)	мне 19 лет, **и я** родилась в Москве. mne 19 let, i ia rodilas' v moskve. I am 19 years old **and** I was born in Moscow.

The conjunction *a*, which is the third most frequently used conjunction in Russian compound sentences, does not occur at all in the essays under examination here. Instead, the heritage learners substituted the conjunction *и* where the Russian language requires the use of *a*. We hypothesize that this is due to an overgeneralization of the meaning of the conjunction *и* and to possible interference from English binary conjunctions (and/but) – a contrast to the tripartite system of the Russian language:[8]

Arrived at 4	(5)	Я родилась в Киеве **и я** пошла в школу в Америке. ia rodilas' v kieve i ia pošla v školu v amerike I was born in Kiev, **and** I went to school in America.

This type of mistake is typical for English-speaking learners of Russian, too.

In contrast to the compound sentences discussed above, complex sentences with subordinate clauses occur much more frequently in the heritage speakers' essays. Ninety-four percent of the students used complex sentences, and 92.8 percent of all observed complex sentences are written correctly.[9] This is

---

[8] For detailed analysis of these conjunctions in HS production see Dengub (2010).
[9] Hudson (1994), who studied sociolinguistics perspectives on language registers, concluded that greater use of clause embedding is characteristic of the more sophisticated language typical of university lectures and academic writing.

true not only in the case of sentences that are very similar in structure to their English counterparts, but also of sentences that present a greater challenge to English learners of Russian because of the discrepancies between the basic sentence structure of Russian and English.

With the exception of one essay, which was written by a student who was born in the US, compound sentences occur in all essays. The range of compound sentences per essay is one to six with an average of 2.3 compound sentences per essay. The essays containing only one compound sentence were written by students who arrived in the US at ages 2, 5 ½ and 7. The essay which contains the highest number of compound sentences was submitted by a student who arrived in the US at age 7.

The sentence connectors registered in the essays are (from the most frequently used to the least frequently used): *когда* (age mean = 4.2; SD = 2.7), *чтобы* (age mean = 2.5; SD = 2.5), *потому что* (age mean = 3.3; SD = 3.3), *который* (age mean = 3.0; SD = 2.2), *что* (age mean = 3.3; SD = 3.3), *как*, *поэтому* (age mean for both = 3.3; SD = 3.3), *после того как* (used by a HS who arrived in the US at the age of 7).

While little is known about the ways in which the language system of incomplete learners stores various word classes – such as content and function words – or how the differences between them are realized in incomplete grammars (Polinsky 2004, 421), analysis of the essays reveals that heritage learners at even the lowest proficiency level have a good command of at least one group of function words, i.e., sentence connectors.

Born in US (6) Я беру этот курс ***потому что*** я хочу научиться писать....
ia beru ėtot kurs ***potomu chto*** ia xoču naučit'cia pisat'...
I am taking this course because I want to learn to write...

Born in US (7) Я беру этот класс ***чтобы*** знать ***как*** читать ...
ia beru ėtot klass ***čtoby*** znat' kak čitat'...
I am taking this course to know how to read...

Arrived at 4 (8) Мне было 3 года ***когда*** я приехала в Америку.
mne bylo 3 goda ***kogda*** ia priexala v ameriku.
I was 3 years old when I arrived in America.

According to the current data, the most frequent connectors are *когда* and *чтобы*. Although *когда* is one of the first sentence connectors acquired by non-heritage learners of Russian, *чтобы* is generally quite difficult for English speakers to acquire, especially when it is followed by a noun and a past tense verb. The explanation for its high frequency in heritage Russian may lie in the fact that the sentence connectors *когда* and *чтобы* are acquired at a very early age among native speakers of Russian – between the ages of 2 and 4 (Gvozdev 1961, 365–6).

The relative pronoun *который* appears in L1 of a Russian-speaking child at the age of 3, it is fully acquired only between the ages of 5 and 6 (Gvozdev 1961, 315). The scarcity of this type of relative clause in combination with the errors associated with the use of *который* is viewed as positive evidence of a decline in relativization structures among heritage speakers of Russian (Polinsky 2000, 2008a; Isurin and Ivanova-Sullivan 2008; Friedman and Kagan 2008).

While this connector presents much trouble for non-heritage learners of Russian, it occurs frequently in the heritage speakers' essays under study and is used not only in the nominative case, but also in oblique cases (Examples 1, 9):

Born in US
(9) Я имею брат **которому***(ph)* двадцать лет и сестричку **кому** семь
    ia imeiu brat **kotoromu**   dvadcat' let i   sestričku komu sem'
I have a brother who$_{\text{DAT-PH}}$ is twenty years and a sister$_{\text{ACC-FEM}}$ who$_{\text{INC}}$ is seven

---

It is interesting to note that the connector *который* is not used in the correct form in reference to feminine nouns in any essay. Even the student who used it correctly in reference to a masculine noun substituted the required feminine form with an interrogative pronoun in the same clause (Example 9). The substitution of the interrogative pronouns *кто/что* for the standard relative pronoun, however, is acceptable in colloquial Russian.

The connector *поэтому* that appears with some delay in the language of non-heritage learners, and in the case of English-speaking learners of Russian is often substituted by *так*. No cases of substitution of this kind were registered in the essays by heritage learners.

Summarizing the syntactic analysis of the heritage language data, it is quite apparent that sentence length and complexity vary significantly in the essays of the heritage learners under study. Contrary to the earlier findings (Isurin and Ivanova-Sullivan 2008), a preference for complex over compound sentences has been observed among heritage subjects. Of the three conjunctions most widely used in the Russian language to connect compound sentences, only two of them – *и* and *но* – were observed with any frequency among the heritage speakers. The third conjunction, *а*, was not registered in the essays. The types of mistakes made in the use of these conjunctions are similar to the mistakes made by English-speaking learners of Russian. Heritage learners tend to use them correctly when the usage is identical in the two languages and incorrectly when the usages in the two languages do not overlap. These findings testify to the considerable influence of the dominant language – English – on the structure of compound sentences.

The heritage learners of the current study, who represent the lowest proficiency level, exhibited a variety of complex sentence connectors in their essays, some of which are very difficult for non-heritage learners and appear in their language system only at higher levels of functional proficiency.

In future research, it would be worthwhile to compare the sentence length of heritage learners at low proficiency level to the development of sentence length and sentence complexity among native Russian speakers and non-heritage learners at various levels of language development.

IV.3. Cases

Previous studies of heritage Russian (Polinsky 1997, 2000, 2008b) claim that one of the most characteristic features of heritage Russian (referred to as American Russian in Polinsky's study) that distinguishes it from other varieties of Russian is the reduction of the case system. According to Polinsky, the loss of oblique cases leads to a systematic restructuring of the case system in heritage Russian. In simplest terms, this leads to the replacement of dative with accusative and of accusative with nominative. As a result of this case shift, Polinsky argues, American Russians develop a two-case system limited to the nominative and accusative cases (Polinsky 1997, 375–81; 2008b, 153).

This "restructuring of cases" phenomenon did not emerge in other studies (Isurin and Ivanova-Sullivan 2008), nor is it supported by the current data. On the contrary, all six cases are represented in the language of heritage speakers as reflected in the essays. Figure 7.2 shows contexts registered for each case in the diagnostic essays. Accusative has by far the largest number of contexts at 38.2 percent,[10] almost twice as many as for prepositional and instrumental (17.4 percent each) and genitive (16.4 percent). There are significantly fewer contexts for dative case (10.6 percent). Correct case forms are actually used in 88 percent of all instances.

As shown in Figure 7.3, the ratio between nouns, modifiers[11] and personal pronouns varies significantly from case to case.

---

10 Both Gvozdev (1961, 379) and Vakhterov (1913, 433) found that in the speech of child L1, the accusative case falls in second place after nominative in terms of frequency of usage (*частота употребления*), leaving all the other cases far behind.

11 Borrowing the terminology used by Timberlake (2004, 207), adjectives, demonstrative and possessive pronouns are referred to as modifiers.

Figure 7.2. Distribution of contexts for cases across pre-course essays (%)

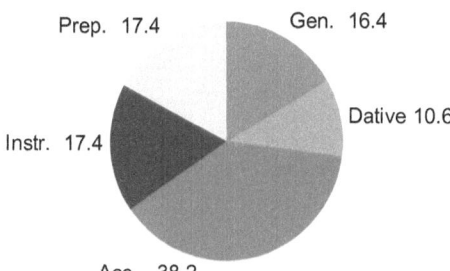

Figure 7.3. Distribution of nouns, modifiers and personal pronouns case by case across pre-course essays (%)

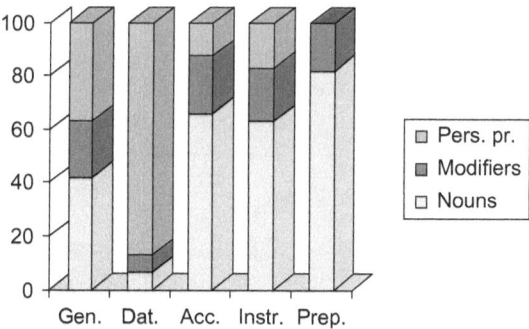

Overall, the collected data demonstrate that the case system in the language of heritage speakers is better preserved in nouns than in modifiers or personal pronouns. This serves to support the conclusion drawn by Polinsky (2004, 425) that incomplete learners do not treat word classes equally. Rather, they have selective control of nouns and adjectives, and they favor nouns over adjectives. The inferior performance on the part of incomplete learners in adjectival cases has been explained in the literature by the learners' limited experience with them and compared with late development of adjectives in Russian and Hebrew-speaking children's L1 (Gvozdev 1961; Berman 1988). It is important to emphasize here that beginning non-heritage learners of Russian also avoid using modifiers in general and adjectives in particular in their production.

The following section presents some additional analysis of distribution data of cases in the speech of heritage Russian learners.

IV.3.1. Accusative case

As mentioned, the overall number of contexts for the accusative case and the correct use of the accusative rank highest among all case forms in the heritage language data. The essays clearly demonstrate that the heritage speakers used the accusative case correctly with inanimate masculine nouns, neuter nouns, both singular and plural nouns, as well as with modifiers of these nouns.

The absence of a distinct accusative form for masculine and neuter inanimates and their coincidence with nominative form might indeed be a plausible explanation for the frequency and accuracy of the accusative form in the heritage essays were it not for the frequency of correct feminine forms ending in -y that account for at least half of the accusative usages in the essays:

Born in US	(10) буду читать **русскую**(ph) **литературу**(ph) budu čitat' russkuiu literaturu (I) will read Russian$_{ACC-FEM-PH}$ literature$_{ACC-FEM-PH}$
Arrived at 4	(11) сестра плохо помает **русскую реч** sestra ploxo pomaet russkuiu reč sister badly understands$_{INC}$ Russian$_{ACC-FEM}$ speech

For these feminine nouns, the accusative case form does not coincide with the nominative case form. Hence, we must reject the nominative-accusative morphological syncretism argument as a plausible explanation for the high percentage of correctly used accusative case forms. Nor does the age at arrival appear to be a factor here, as the singular feminine form ending in −y occurs in the essays of subjects who arrived at various ages including those who were born in the US.

Gvozdev (1961, 380) concluded that evidence of differentiation between subjects and objects – including feminine nouns ending in −y in the accusative – is abundant in the speech of children speaking Russian as L1 beginning with the age of 2. It is our contention that this fact explains the frequency and accuracy of the accusative form in the speech of the heritage speakers in this study. The accusative form errors registered in the essays under study here are made by heritage learners of different age at arrival.

Animate noun forms in the accusative case exhibit syncretism between accusative and genitive forms. The correct genitive form for animate objects in syntactic contexts requiring the accusative appears in children's L1 much later than the singular feminine accusative form −y (Gvozdev 1961, 380). While the latter appears before the age of 2, the former appears only two years later. Up to that point, children continue to use the same form as in accusative inanimate nouns, i.e., the nominative form. The difficulty of these forms for heritage speakers can be explained by the developmental order of their acquisition in child language. The inconsistency of a heritage speaker who uses the correct accusative −*y* form for a feminine object while using the nominative form instead of the required genitive for the animate masculine object in the same construction (Example 12) might serve as an evidence of it.

Born in US	(12) я имею **брат** и **сестричку**
	ia imeiu brat i sestričku
	I have a brother_NOM-INC and a sister_ACC-FEM

However, the correct form of such nouns is manifested occasionally, and its occurrence seems to have no correlation with age at arrival in the US in the present data:

Born in US	(13) **моего** (ph) **брата** зовут Джереми
	moego brata zovut džeremi
	my_ACC-MASC-ANIM brother's_ACC-MASC-ANIM (name) is Jeremy
Arrived at 5.5	(14) я читала **Пушкина**
	ia čitala puškina
	I read Pushkin_ACC-MASC-ANIM
Arrived at 7	(15) читать **Достоевского**
	čitat' dostoevskogo
	(to) read Dostoevsky_ACC-MASC-ANIM

Personal pronouns are represented with only one form in the data – first person singular *меня*. Again, this is consistent with the developmental order of pronouns in child L1, where *меня* appears between the ages of 2 and 3 (Gvozdev 1961, 215). Interestingly, at this age *меня* occurs exclusively in the context of *меня зовут*. Its use is likewise limited in the heritage essays. Only in one essay written by a student who arrived in the US at age 7 it occurs in the phrase *меня научили*.

As evidenced by the use of *-y* forms for feminine objects in the accusative and the accusative forms of animate masculine nouns in the data analyzed here, the heritage speakers in the study clearly differentiated both subject and object usages and forms.

IV.3.2. Prepositional case

The prepositional case, together with the instrumental case, was required in 17.4 percent contexts and was second only to the accusative case in terms of the number of correct case forms. In child L1, the acquisition of prepositions denoting location and the prepositional form of singular nouns is complete by the age of 3, far earlier than the acquisition of its other two functions – instrument and time (Gvozdev 1961, 246). In the present dataset, the prepositional case was used mostly to denote location (66 percent) with a one hundred percent accuracy that can be viewed as an example of the token frequency effect (Romanova 2008). In far fewer cases, it was used in contexts of instrument and time (29.8 percent and 4.2 percent accordingly):

Arrived at 5	(16) кататься **на лошади** katat'sia na lošadi (to) ride a horse$_{PREP}$
Arrived at 4	(17) в девиносто первом(ph) **году** v devinosto-pervym godu in ninety first$_{PREP-PH}$

In the prepositional case, modifiers are limited to two words: *русский*, as in разговаривать *на русском языке*, учиться в *русской* (ph) *школе* and *мой*, as in в *моей* (ph) *семье* (ph). There are no personal pronouns in the prepositional case registered in the data.

The current data yielded yet another interesting fact, namely that heritage speakers do not confuse accusative and prepositional case forms when distinguishing destination and location – a common error among non-heritage learners of Russian. In contexts where the accusative case is required to express destination, both of the required prepositions – *в* and *на* – are used correctly, however, *на* is registered only in the essay, written by a student who arrived in the US at the age of 7. These findings are analogous to child language acquisition data where both prepositions *в* and *на* appear simultaneously, but the preposition *на* occurs with far lower frequency (Gvozdev 1961, 382).

IV.3.3. Instrumental case

Instrumental case ranks third among the cases in terms of frequency of use in the essays (15.6 percent) after the accusative (39.3 percent) and prepositional (19 percent). In 90 percent of occurrences, instrumental forms are governed by the preposition *с*. This particular usage of the instrumental case appears in child L1 at the age of 2 ½ (Gvozdev 1961, 391). This developmental reality may account for the fact that in 75 percent of contexts requiring the instrumental case, correct forms were used in the essays including the subjects who were born in the US. Examples of these forms have been already given earlier in the chapter.

In contrast to accusative and prepositional cases, in the essays of heritage learners, the instrumental case has a good representation of plural noun forms (*с друзьями, с родителями, с родственниками, с взрослыми*). At the same time, it is noteworthy that the writer of one essay, who was born in the US, uses correct plural forms but misses instrumental markers in the singular forms (*с бабушка, с дедушка*).

Modifiers are used in the instrumental case almost three times less frequently than nouns (20 percent and 63 percent accordingly). These modifiers are overwhelmingly limited to the first person singular possessive pronoun *мой*. There are very few other occurrences of modifiers in the instrumental (see Examples 18, 20 and 21), and those who used them arrived in the US between the ages of 3 and 5.

Arrived at 4	(18) **с моими** (ph) **другими** (ph) **родственниками** (ph)
	s moimi drugimi rodctvennikami
	with my$_{INSTR\text{-}PL\text{-}PH}$ other$_{INSTR\text{-}PL\text{-}PH}$ relatives$_{INSTR\text{-}PL\text{-}PH}$

The heritage subjects exhibit limited control of instrumental forms in much the same way non-heritage learners at the intermediate level mix correct and incorrect forms – depending on relative levels of attention to form at the moment of speech: *с моими родители* (born in US), *с мои подругама* (arrived at 4).

Personal pronouns in the instrumental case are limited to the use of third person forms as follows: masculine *с ним* and feminine *с ней* (both were observed in the essays of those born in US, as well as of those who arrived between the age of 1 and 7), and plural *с ними* (born in US). While these particular forms present a significant challenge to non-heritage learners of Russian and require a long time to develop accuracy and automaticity in their use, the heritage learners' essays demonstrate correct use irrespective of the subjects' age at arrival and place of birth. At first glance, the correct use of these forms supports the general tendency in different languages under attrition according to which pronominal paradigms are retained longer than their nominal counterparts (Polinsky 1997). The current data yield similar results, though only with respect to very limited numbers of pronominal forms. Their retention is therefore attributed to their high frequency token count in speech at home. The fact that in one essay, where all noun and modifier forms are used incorrectly, the pronominal form *с ним* is correctly expressed suggests this may indeed be the case.

Previous studies have found that other functions of the instrumental case are essentially missing in heritage language, noting specifically the absence of the predicative function in general and after the verb *стать* in particular. In the current data, in addition to the contexts where instrumental is governed by the preposition *с* discussed above, there are several examples of its use when governed by a verb – one of which is *стать* (see Example 19) – were observed as follows:

Born in US	(19) я хочу стать **адвокатом** ia xoču stat' advokatom I want to become a lawyer$_{INSTR}$
Arrived at 3	(20) занимаюсь **французским** (ph) **языком**(ph) zanimaius' francuzskim iazykom (I) study the French$_{INSTR\text{-}PH}$ language$_{INSTR}$
Arrived at 4	(21) я пишю **маслиноми краскомы** ia pišiu maslinomi kraskomy (I) paint in oil$_{INST\text{-}PL\text{-}PH}$ paints$_{INST\text{-}PL\text{-}PH}$

Although the form and functions of the instrumental case are not completely acquired by heritage learners of low proficiency, the instrumental case is nevertheless well represented in their language system and indicative of a solid foundation for future full acquisition of the case.

IVII.3.4. Genitive case

The genitive case ranks fourth among the cases in terms of frequency of use (14.8 percent). The genitive is the first case in our sample in which the frequency of use of personal pronouns (37 percent) exceeds that of modifiers (21 percent). This, however, is a matter of multiple tokens of one word form: *у меня*. Given the high frequency of this particular form in speech, this can only be viewed as yet another example of the token frequency effect.

Genitive case is governed by both verbs and prepositions. It is also used with explicit quantifiers and to denote a possessor. Lastly, it is required in the genitive of negation. In 82 percent of occurrences in the essays under review, genitive forms are governed by prepositions with the preposition *у* overshadowing the remaining genitive prepositions – *из-за* (*из-за сплошного интереса*), *из* (*из их детства*) and *для* (*для моего персонального развлекания*), which occur only once or twice each.

The preponderance of preposition-governed forms of genitive can be readily explained by the fact that the preposition-governed function is the first among genitive functions to appears in child L1 – generally between two and a half and three years old (Gvozdev 1961, 229, 245). Among prepositions requiring genitive, *у* appears earliest, followed shortly thereafter by *из, без* and *для*.

There are two essays where prepositions that require genitive are consistently followed by nominal forms in the nominative case. Since the only other genitive form occurring in these essays is the pronominal *у меня* – the previously mentioned form of very high frequency – it is more likely that these two students, both US-born, lack the genitive in their heritage language system.

Other genitive case functions occur far less frequently in the essays than the preposition-governed genitive. Genitive following quantifiers occurs in only 10 percent of all genitive contexts (*пару страниц, несколько раз*). Genitive contexts denoting possessors are registered at four percent (*стихи Маршака, книги Александра Дюма, поэму Пушкина*). Likewise, four percent of genitive contexts belong to the genitive of negation (see Examples 22 and 23). Verb-governed genitive is not registered.

Arrived at 5 (22) у меня нето мнoга ротствиниких
u menia neto mnoga rotsvinikix,
I_{GEN-SG} do not have many relatives_{GEN-PL-ADJ-INC}

Arrived at 5 (23) у меня нет братов и систров
u menia net bratov i sistrov
I_{GEN-SG} do not have brothers_{REG-GEN-PL-INC} and sisters_{REG-GEN-PL-INC}

Genitive forms denoting possessors are used correctly in the singular irrespective of whether a heritage speaker arrived in the US at the age of 2 or 7. The plural forms, however, are far less stable. The genitive plural ending *-ов* that begins to appear in child L1 at the age of 3 and stabilizes closer to 4 (Gvozdev 1961, 278, 286) is the only genitive plural noun ending rendered in the essays (Example 23). Aside from *-ов*, heritage learners use the genitive plural adjectival ending for a noun (Example 22) and even the English *-es* plural ending (Example 1). The overgeneralization of *-ов* in place of other genitive plural endings, i.e., *-ев* [*братов] and *-ей*, also follows the developmental pattern of child L1, where *-ов* is first to appear, followed by *-ей* and then *-ев* between ages 5 and 6 (Gvozdev 1961, 289, 316). It is also important to mention the overgeneralization of *-ов* as a plural ending in contexts where the genitive case is not required at all (*у меня разные интересов*). The zero ending (*страниц, раз*) is most likely the result of the frequency of use of these particular words.

Thus, the data suggest that the genitive form is not established in the heritage language system of low-proficiency learners. The genitive plural endings are far from fully developed among the heritage learners in the study and, as such, require special attention and intentional instruction.

IV.3.5. Dative case

Dative is the least frequent case in the essays under analysis, accounting for only 11.3 percent of examples. In 87 percent of these examples, dative forms are used in the context of an individual's age. Additional occurrences of the dative include the ones with an agent and the verb *нравиться* and following the preposition *по*, which appears only at the age of 7 in child L1 (Gvozdev 1961, 331):

Arrived at 3	(23) очень **по мне** скучает očen' po mne skučaet a lot me$_{DAT}$ misses

Dative is the only case where 26 out of 31 forms are pronominal. The overwhelming majority, though, are the instances of the first person singular *мне*. Far fewer are third person singular masculine *ему*, and one – third person singular feminine form *ей*. All three pronominal forms appear in child L1 between the ages of 2 ½ and 3 (Gvozdev 1961, 229, 245, 270), the first being *мне* and the last, *ей*. Beyond these three forms of personal pronouns, other pronouns are used incorrectly even in the context of one's age:

Born in US	(24) **у кого** (ph) будет двадцать два года u kogo budet dvadcat' dva goda who$_{GEN-INC}$ will be twenty-two years old

Nouns without modifiers (Example 25) are used in the correct form. When a noun is accompanied by a modifier, however (Example 26), both the noun and its modifier appear in the nominative form rather than in the required dative.

Born in US	(25)	**Карине** (ph) 16, **Джерему** 12
		karine 16 džeremu 12
		Karina_DAT-FEM (is) 16 Jeremy_DAT-MASC (is) 12
Arrived at 2	(26)	*моя сестра* двадцать лет
		moia sestra dvadcat' let
		my_NOM-INC sister_NOM-INC (is) twenty years old

Another important observation here is that when writing about age (in a total of 31 examples), the heritage speakers made the correct choice of case forms after numbers as follows: *один год*; *полтора, два, четыре, двадцать два года*; and *лет* – irrespective of age at arrival. This observation is true of heritage subjects born in the US as well. Only two examples of incorrect case forms were observed in this context, both occurring after the number *двадцать один*, and both heritage learners used the word *лет* instead of the required *год*. One of these students arrived in the US at the age of 1 and the other at the age of 7. Interestingly, the student who arrived at the age of 1 used the correct form after the number *один*.

It is very likely that the frequency of use of these forms accounts for their accuracy. In her discussion of genitive forms, Polinsky (1997, 379) found that even among the weakest speakers, contexts in which case forms are governed by numbers were very well preserved. Her conclusion was that this might be explained by their highly specialized function as count forms, although according to her data, the same combinations failed in spontaneous speech. Regardless of what accounts for its maintenance, it is clear that the correct usage of forms governed by numbers gives heritage speakers a significant advantage over non-heritage learners of Russian, who often confuse the forms *год*, *года*, and *лет* when they are used in combination with numbers.

The current analysis of the heritage speaker's essays revealed that despite undeniable problems with the Russian case system, this system is nevertheless well represented in the language of the heritage speakers and reflects the developmental pattern and order of acquisition of child L1, though in a slower fashion. While heritage learners at this level of proficiency might struggle to represent case endings orthographically, they are clearly well aware of their presence.

The data extracted from the essays and highlighted herein do not support hypotheses (Polinsky 2000; Zemskaya 2001) about the simplification of the nominal declension system by heritage Russians. It is clear from the examples enumerated above that the heritage speakers in this study have neither abandoned the oblique cases governed by verbs or prepositions nor replaced them with the nominative case. We did not observe a reanalysis of the accusative as the case of the indirect object. Correct case forms were used in 87 percent of all syntactic contexts in the essays under study. In the remaining contexts, heritage speakers most often substituted oblique case forms with the nominative; however, we also registered instances where one oblique case form was used in place of another.

Across all oblique cases, the number of forms marked correctly is considerably higher than those registered as incorrect in all three analyzed categories – nouns, modifiers and personal pronouns. Overall, the data demonstrate that the case system is better preserved in nouns than in modifiers and personal pronouns, and in modifiers than in personal pronouns. The use of personal pronouns in the data is overwhelmingly limited not only to first person singular forms, but also to a very small number of syntactic contexts. At the same time, heritage speakers demonstrate the use of correct forms in instrumental case third person forms, as well as include the required consonant linking н that presents such a challenge to non-heritage learners of Russian. All of the above is most likely evidence of the token frequency effect.

V. Conclusions

While the present analysis is limited to a relatively small sample of low-proficiency heritage learners of Russian, it raises questions about the issue of age at arrival in the US as a significant predictor of ultimate attainment in Russian for heritage learners. The data analysis led to the conclusion that language retention or loss in this group of heritage learners – those who are maximally removed from native attainment – does not in any way correlate with whether they were born in the US or arrived here at a pre-school age.

The evidence strongly suggests that in this particular group, age at arrival does not necessarily mean simultaneous interruption of exposure to the mother tongue. In most cases, actual interruption did not occur until the child started school at the age of 6. Prior to starting school, they stayed with grandparents who had limited to nonexistent knowledge of English. The study demonstrates that it is exposure to the Russian language in the family before beginning school in English and not the age at arrival that affects their Russian language skills most significantly and facilitates the fast (re)building of language skills and proficiency.

Whether they were born in the US or arrived here at a pre-school age, the low-proficiency heritage learners in the study demonstrated acquisition of the specified grammatical and syntactic frame of Russian. The restructuring of the case system in their production did not emerge in this study. Although heritage learners may not always be certain how to represent case endings orthographically, their interlanguage demonstrates an awareness of their presence in the system of cases. Moreover, case representation in heritage learner production follows the developmental pattern, i.e., order of acquisition, of child L1, though in a slower fashion: the frequency and accuracy of forms that emerge earlier in L1 are higher in the heritage language than of those forms that emerge later.

A special course designed for the lowest-proficiency heritage learners should take into consideration the unique characteristic of this group – namely that their aural/oral grammatical system is much more highly developed than their control of written forms of the language – and should capitalize on the transferability of this knowledge by creating an abundance of opportunities for them to see and hear texts simultaneously. In this way their language proficiency can be (re)built over a considerably shorter period of time than is necessary for non-heritage learners of Russian to reach similar language proficiency levels. A different study by the author (Smyslova 2009b) showed that after only one semester of instructional intervention based on the abundant reading and simultaneous presentation of texts in aural and written forms, the heritage speakers under study performed better than non-heritage learners after four semesters of Russian when tested on listening, reading and writing skills. Likewise, upon completion of the two-semester course of studies, heritage speakers' performance in these three skills was superior to that of the non-heritage learners of Russian with six semesters of Russian instruction.

Although the current study provides a valid empirical analysis of the language of low-proficiency heritage learners of Russian entering a college-level Russian course specifically designed for heritage learners, the conclusions regarding this relatively small data sample need future confirmation by larger-scale studies. Nevertheless, this study offers valuable insights about the interlanguage system of the lowest-proficiency level heritage speakers of Russian. By gathering and examining data on the subject groups' language performance to assess existing measurable levels of language retention, the current research contributes to the existing body of research literature on adult second language acquisition and successful pedagogical approaches to teaching this unique group of language learners.

References

American Council on the Teaching of Foreign Languages. 1996. *Standards for Foreign Language Learning: Preparing for the 21st Century*. Yonkers, NY: National Standards in Education Project.

Andrews, David. 1999. *Sociocultural Perspectives on Language Change in Diaspora: Soviet Immigrants in the United States (Impact: Studies in Language and Society)*. Amsterdam and Philadelphia: Benjamins.

Beaudrie, Sara, and Cynthia Ducar. 2005. "Beginning Level University Heritage Programs: Creating a Space for All Heritage Language Learners." *Heritage Language Journal* 3 (1).

Berman, R. 1988. "Word Class Distinctions in Developing Grammars." In Y. Levy, I. M. Schlesinger and M. D. S. Brainer (eds), *Categories and Processes in Language Acquisition*, 47–72. Hillsdale, NJ: Lawrence Erlbaum Associates.

Bermel, Neil and Olga Kagan. 2000. "The Maintenance of Written Russian in Heritage Speakers." In Olga Kagan and Benjamin Rifkin (eds), *The Learning and Teaching of Slavic Languages and Cultures*, 405–36. Bloomington, IN: Slavica.

Brecht, Richard D. and C. W. Ingold. 1998. "Tapping a National Resource: Heritage Learners in the United States." ERIC Digest. Washington DC: ERIC Clearinghouse on Languages and Linguistics. Online: http://www.cal.org/resources/digest/0202brecht.html (accessed 30 November 2011).

Brinton, Donna M., Olga Kagan and Susan Bauckus, eds. 2008. *Heritage Language Education: A New Field Emerging*. New York and London: Routledge.

Brisk, M. 2000. *Literacy and Bilingualism: A Handbook for All Teachers*. Mahwah, NJ: Lawrence Erlbaum Associates.

Campbell, Russell N. and J. W. Rosenthal. 2000. "Heritage Languages." In J.W. Rosenthal (ed.), *Handbook of Undergraduate Second Language Acquisition*, 165–84. Mahwah, NJ: Lawrence Erlbaum Associates.

Campbell, Russell N. and Donna Christian. 2005. "Directions in Research Intergenerational Transmission of Heritage Languages." *Heritage Language Journal* 3 (1).

Chevalier, Joan F. 2004. "Heritage Language Literacy: Theory and Practice." *Heritage Language Journal* 2 (1).

Cummins, Jim. 1993. "Bilingualism and Second-Language Learning." *Annual Review of Applied Linguistics* 13:51–70.

Davidson, Dan. 2010. "Federal Investment in the Academic and Educational Sector: Producing the Expertise, Teachers and Programs for World Languages." Testimony before the US Senate Committee on Homeland Security and Governmental Affairs Subcommittee on Oversight of Government Management, the Federal Workforce, and the District of Columbia on "Closing the Language Gap: Improving the Federal Government's Foreign Language Capabilities," July 29.

Dengub, Evgeny. 2010. "The Conjunctions I, A, and NO: A Comparison of Usage by Heritage and Traditional Students of Russian." *Slavic and East European Journal* 54 (1): 147–64.

Douglas, Masako O. 2005. "Pedagogical Theories and Approaches to Teach Young Learners of Japanese as a Heritage Language." *Heritage Language Journal* 3 (1).

Duff, Patricia. 2008. "Heritage Language Education in Canada." In Donna M. Brinton, Olga Kagan and Susan Bauckus (eds), *Heritage Language Education: A New Field Emerging*, 149–64. New York and London: Routledge.

Fishman, Joshua A. 1964. "Language Maintenance and Language Shift as a Field of Inquiry: A Definition of the Field and Suggestions to Its Further Development." *Linguistics* 9: 32–70.

———. 1991. *Reversing Language Shift: Theoretical and Empirical Foundations of Assistance to Threatened Languages*. Clevedon: Multilingual Matters.

Friedman, Debra and Olga Kagan. 2008. "Heritage Language Narratives." In Donna M. Brinton, Olga Kagan and Susan Bauckus (eds), *Heritage Language Education: A New Field Emerging*, 149–64. New York and London: Routledge.

Garcia, R. and C. Diaz. 1992. "The Status and Use of Spanish and English among Hispanic Youth in Dade County (Miami) Florida: A Sociological Study." *Language and Education* 6: 13–32.
Gor, Kira. 2010. "Nonnative Processing of Verbal Morphology: In Search of Regularity." *Language Learning* 60 (1): 88–126.
Gvozdev, A. N. 1961. *Voprosy izuchenija detskoj rechi*. Moscow: Izdatel'stvo Akademii Pedagogicheskikh Nauk RSFSR.
Hornberger, Nancy H. and Shuhan C. Wang. 2008. "Who Are Our Heritage Language Learners? Identity and Biliteracy in Heritage Language Education in the United States." In Donna M. Brinton, Olga Kagan and Susan Bauckus (eds), *Heritage Language Education: A New Field Emerging*, 3–35. New York and London: Routledge.
Hudson, Alan. 1994. "Diglossia as a Special Case of Register Variation." In Douglas Biber and Edward Finegan (eds), *Sociolinguistics Perspectives on Register*, 294–314. New York: Oxford University Press.
Isurin, L. and T. Ivanova-Sullivan. 2008. "Lost in Between: The Case of Russian Heritage Speakers." *Heritage Language Journal* 6 (1).
Jensen, Linda and Lerena Llosa. 2007. "Heritage Language Reading in the University: A Survey of Students' Experiences, Strategies, and Preferences." *Heritage Language Journal* 5 (10).
Kagan, Olga. 2003. "Heritage Speakers' Potential for High Level Language Proficiency." In Heidi Byrnes and Hiram Maxim (eds), *Advanced Foreign Language Learning: A Challenge to College Programs*, 99–112. Boston, MA: Heinle and Heinle.
———. 2005. "In Support of Proficiency-Based Definition of Heritage Learners: The Case of Russian." *International Journal of Bilingual Education and Bilingualism* 8: 213–21.
———. 2007. "Continua of identity and language competence: A case study of heritage learners of Russian." Presentation, UCLA, AAAL, April. Online: http://www.cal.org/heritage/involved/aaal2007/kagan.pdf (accessed 9 September 2008).
Kagan, Olga, Tatiana Akishina and Richard Robin. 2002. *Russian for Russians*. Bloomington, IN: Slavica.
Kagan, Olga and Kathleen Dillon. 2001. "A New Perspective on Teaching Russian: Focus on the Heritage Learner." *Slavic and East European Journal* 45 (3): 507–18.
Kondo-Brown, Kimi. 2003. "Heritage Language Instruction for Post-secondary Students from Immigrant Backgrounds." *Heritage Language Journal* 1 (1).
Krashen, Stephen D. 1998. "Heritage Language Development: Some Practical Arguments." In Stephen D. Krashen, Lucy Tse and Jeff McQuillan (eds), *Heritage Language Development*, 3–13. Culver City, CA: Language Education Associates.
Laleko, Oksana. 2009. "On Predicates of Variable Telicity and Aspect in Heritage Russian." Paper prepared for the 83rd Annual Meeting of the Linguistics Society of America (LSA 2009), San Francisco, 8–11 January.
Loewen, Donald. 2008. "Overcoming Aural Proficiency: Pitfalls for Heritage Learners In Russian Cyberspace." *Heritage Language Journal* 6 (1).
Lynch, Andrew. 2003. "The Relationship between Second and Heritage Language Acquisition: Notes on Research and Theory Building." *Heritage Language Journal* 1 (1).
McQuillan, J. 1996. "How Should Heritage Languages Be Taught? The Effects of a Free Voluntary Reading Program." *Foreign Language Annals* 29: 56–72.
Pereltsvaig, Asya. 2005. "Aspect Lost, Aspect Regained: Restructuring of Aspectual Marking in American Russian." In P. Kempchinsky and R. Slabakova (eds), *Aspectual Inquiries*, 369–95. Dordrecht: Kluwer.

———. 2008. "Aspect in Russian as Grammatical rather than Lexical Notion: Evidence from Heritage Russian." *Russian Linguistics* 32 (1): 27–42.

Peyton, Joy Kreeft, Donald A. Ranard and Scott McGinnis, eds. 2001. *Heritage Languages in America: Preserving a National Resource*. Washington, DC: Center for Applied Linguistics and Delta Systems.

Polinsky, Maria. 1997. "American Russian: Language Loss Meets Language Acquisition." In Wayles Browne, Ewa Dornisch, Natasha Kondrashova and Draga Zec (eds), *Formal Approaches to Slavic Linguistics: The Cornell Meeting 1995*, 370–406. Ann Arbor, MI: Slavica.

———. 2000. "A Composite Linguistic Profile of a Speaker of Russian in the U.S." In Olga Kagan and Benjamin Rifkin (eds), *The Learning and Teaching of Slavic Languages and Cultures*, 437–65. Bloomington, IN: Slavica.

———. 2004. "Word Class Distinctions in an Incomplete Grammar." In Dorid Diskin Ravid and Hava bat-Zeev Shyldkrot (eds), *Perspectives on Language and Language Development: Essays in Honor of A. Berman*, 419–34. Tel Aviv: Kluwer Academic Publishers.

———. 2006. "Incomplete Acquisition: American Russian." *Journal of Slavic Linguistics* 14 (2): 191–262.

———. 2007. "American Russian: Language Loss Meets Language Acquisition." In Wayles Browne, Ewa Dornisch, Natasha Kondrashova and Draga Zec (eds), *Formal Approaches to Slavic Linguistics: The Cornell Meeting* 1995, 370–406. Ann Arbor, MI: Slavica.

———. 2008a. "Relative clauses in Heritage Russian: Fossilization or Divergent Grammar?" Paper delivered at the 16th Formal Approaches to Slavic Linguistics (FASL).

———. 2008b. "Heritage Language Narratives." In Donna M. Brinton, Olga Kagan and Susan Bauckus (eds), *Heritage Language Education: A New Field Emerging*, 149–64. New York and London: Routledge.

———. 2010. "Reanalysis in Adult Heritage Language: A Case for Attrition." *Studies in Second Language Acquisition*. Special Issue on the Linguistic Competence of Heritage Speakers, June.

Polinsky, Maria and Olga Kagan. 2007. "Heritage Languages: In the 'Wild' and in the Classroom." *Language and Linguistic Compass* 1.

Romanova, Natalia. 2008. "Mechanisms of Verbal Morphology Processing in Heritage Speakers of Russian." *Heritage Language Journal* 6 (1).

Schmitt, Elena. 2008. "Early Bilinguals: Incomplete Acquirers or Language Forgetter?" *Issues of Multiculturalism and Multilingualism in Modern Education System*. Studia Humaniora Et Paedagogica Collegii Narovensis 3 (2): 311–30.

Smyslova, Alla. 2009a. "Developing four-skill literacy among adult heritage learners: Effects of linguistic and non-linguistic variables on the attainment of low-proficiency heritage students of Russian within a dedicated college-level bridge course." Dissertation, Bryn Mawr College, PA.

Smyslova, Alla. 2009b. "Low-Proficiency Heritage Speakers of Russian: Comparing Effects of Instructional Intervention on Language Skills Development in Heritage and Non-Heritage Learners of Russian." In Richard D. Brecht, Ljudmila A. Verbitskaja, Maria D. Lekic and William P. Rivers (eds), *Mnemosynon. Studies on Language and Culture in the Russophone World: Presented to Dan E. Davidson by his Students and Colleagues*, 211–27. Moscow: Azbukovnik /Institut russkogo jazyka.

Vakhterov, V. P. 2007/1913. *Osnovy novoy pedagogiki*. Arzamas: Arzamassky gosudarstvenny pedagogichesky institute.

Valdés, Guadalupe. 1995. "The Teaching of Minority Languages as 'Foreign' Languages: Pedagogical and Theoretical Challenges." *Modern Language Journal* 79 (2): 299–328.

———. 2000. "The Teaching of Heritage Languages: An Introduction for Slavic-Teaching Professionals." In Olga Kagan and Benjamin Rifkin (eds), *The Learning and Teaching of Slavic Languages and Cultures*, 375–403. Bloomington, IN: Slavica.

———. 2001. "Heritage Language Students: Profiles and Possibilities." In Joy K. Peyton, Donald A. Ranard and Scott McGinnis (eds), *Heritage Languages in America: Preserving a National Resource*, 37–77. McHenry, IL: CAL.

———. 2006a. "Making Connections: Second Language Acquisition Research and Heritage Language Teaching." In R. Salaberry and B. A. Lafford (eds), *The Art of Teaching Spanish: Second Language Acquisition from Research to Praxis*, 193–212. Washington, DC: Georgetown University Press.

———. 2006b. "Toward an Ecological Vision of Languages for All: The Case of Heritage Languages." In Audrey Heining-Boyton (ed.), *2005–2015: Realizing Our Vision of Languages for All*. 135–151. Upper Saddle River, NJ: Pearson/Prentice Hall World Languages.

Valdés, Guadalupe, Sonia V. Gonzalez, Dania L. Garcia and Patricio Urzua. 2008. "Heritage Learners and Ideologies of Language: Unexamined Challenges." In Donna M. Brinton, Olga Kagan and Susan Bauckas (eds), *Heritage Language Education: A New Field Emerging*, 107–31. New York and London: Routledge.

UCLA Steering Committee. 2000. "Heritage Language Research Priorities Conference Report." *Bilingual Research Journal* 24: 333–46.

Zemskaya, Elena Andreevna, ed. 2001. *Iazyk Russkogo Zarubež'ia: Obščie Processy i Rečcevye Portrety*. Moscow and Vienna: Wiener Slawisticher Almanach.

Chapter 8

SUPERIOR SPEAKERS OR "SUPER" RUSSIAN: OPI GUIDELINES REVISITED

Ludmila Isurin
The Ohio State University

The purpose of the study is to examine the existing guidelines set by the American Council on the Teaching of Foreign Languages (ACTFL) for the Superior level of oral proficiency in the light of naturalistic data. The study looks at narrative/descriptive/circumlocution patterns elicited from three groups of participants: Russian monolinguals (N = 23), Russian-English bilinguals (N = 10), and speakers of Russian as a foreign language (N = 8). The data on bilinguals and monolinguals were collected through interviews on selected topics and the data for the foreign language group were gathered through the OPIs (Oral Proficiency Interviews). The results of the qualitative and quantitative analysis showed that the foreign language learners outperformed monolinguals in all tasks while their performance did not differ from the bilinguals'. The chapter questions the ACTFL's guidelines and calls for revisiting them in order to approximate their requirements to the naturalistic setting.

Preface

As a well-educated native speaker of Russian, I still felt a bit uneasy about the OPI procedure. According to the ACTFL guidelines, one needs to be certified as a Superior speaker of the language to become an OPI tester in that language. What if I am not "superior enough" in speaking my native language? I carefully monitored my speech and performed exactly how the OPI guidelines prescribed during my interview. A few weeks later I proudly put my "superiority" certificate on the wall in my office.

I. Introduction

The ACTFL provisional proficiency guidelines and the Oral Proficiency Interview (OPI) derived from them have been one of the major frameworks adopted by American higher education in teaching and assessing oral skills in foreign language (FL) learners for the last two decades. The OPI test remains the only nationally recognized test to measure oral skills in a foreign language across all languages taught in the US as a second language (L2). The OPIs have been serving numerous practical purposes in helping the governmental agencies, business companies, and educational institutions evaluate the speakers' linguistic performance and estimate their ability to use those skills in real life. The importance and widespread use of the test is evident from the following number: ACTFL conducts 8,000–10,000 interviews annually (Swender 2003) in addition to semi-formal interviews run by certified testers for the internal use of the institutions with which they are affiliated. An undeniable importance of the testing procedure is evident from numerous publications in the last two decades (see Liskin-Gasparo 2003 for further references) and a special issue on OPI in *Foreign Language Annals* (2003). The contributors to the publication address different aspects of the OPI procedure, its usefulness and limitations, as well as its implications for pedagogical practice. The test and the guidelines that it entails influence the design of the curriculum where oral skills in a foreign language become a focal point of a communicative approach adopted by most language departments. The latter implies that, in a classroom, students are engaged in different communicative activities targeting a certain proficiency level and that they are eventually getting prepared for passing the test if they need to land a job or got academically/professionally promoted (Rifkin 2003). Therefore some scholars and educators dealing with the ACTFL guidelines work on improving the curricula that would better incorporate the existing requirements for the oral proficiency levels established by the ACTFL (Rifkin 2003; Norris and Pfeifer 2003; Hertzog 2003). Others look at the tests' outcomes in order to see how different learning backgrounds are reflected in the test results (Rubio 2003), or how to use the existing guidelines to test a specific population of language learners, e.g., heritage speakers (Kagan and Friedman 2003).

Along with studies showing a success in applying the ACTFL guidelines to measuring the speaking skills (Surface and Dierdorff 2003), a number of publications express a growing concern with the reliability of the existing guidelines (Malone 2003; Luecht 2003; Chalhoub-Deville and Fulcher 2003), especially when those guidelines are applied to the least commonly taught languages (Watanabe 2003). Liskin-Gasparo (2003) summarizes the major categories of criticism that the OPI has faced over the years and gives reasons for its undeniable success in American academia. One of the categories of discontent with the test concerns its validity and weak empirical basis. However even those scholars who call for further comprehensive research with a broad investigation of empirical data seem to restrict the area of research to studying the content and procedure of the OPIs themselves (Chalhoub-Deville and Fulcher 2003). Conversely, the data elicited through the OPIs undergo scrutiny in the absence of any naturalistic data that could give a different reference point and shed an additional light on the test limitations.

Another line of thinking concerns the monolingual bias and the almost unattainable goal of "nativeness" that is present in the field of second language acquisition (SLA). Cook (2002) called for a new perspective on L2 learners who are often wrongly viewed as two monolinguals or speakers of two different languages embodied in one person. According to him, multi-competence is not "the imperfect cloning of mono-competence" (Cook 2002, 7) and the SLA research should acknowledge the fundamental differences between L2 speakers and monolinguals. "While the question of what ultimate attainment in a second language is not resolved, there is no intrinsic reason why it should be the same as that of a monolingual native speaker" (Cook 2002, 6).

The latter became a focal point of the plenary address delivered by Lourdes Ortega at the annual AAAL conference (2010) where she stressed the need for the bilingual turn and move away from the monolingual bias in the SLA research.

If according to Cook, the mind and performance of the L2 speaker differ from those of monolinguals, and if a new approach to L2 learners is highly encouraged according to Ortega (2010), we had better take a different angle in approaching our target population.

The present study attempts to pull the OPI agenda from a conventionally accepted area of testing methodology and look at it from a different angle. The research question that I pursue in this chapter is the following: do native speakers perform the same way as the Advanced High and Superior speakers of a foreign language if the OPI procedural restrictions are removed but the tasks used in the discourse remain the same? In my research, I take a different perspective on the OPI by comparing the empirical data obtained from the OPIs with the naturalistic data collected from native speakers, both monolingual and bilingual.

II. Study

II.1. Participants

The study looks at the narrative/descriptive data obtained from two groups of native speakers, i.e., Russian monolinguals (N = 23) and Russian-English bilinguals (N = 10), and compares that with the corresponding performance of advanced learners of Russian as a foreign language (N = 8). The pool of

Russian monolinguals was recruited in St. Petersburg, Russia. There were 23 participants (F = 13, M = 10) and the age varied from 32 to 60. Ten female graduate students who teach Russian as a foreign language in an American university represented the group of Russian-English bilinguals. The age in this group varied from 25 to 47 and the participants had resided in the US for up to 14 years by the time of the study. The Russian-English bilingual participants were professionally involved in teaching Russian and had a high level of first language maintenance. Finally, a group of advanced learners of Russian as a foreign language consisted of eight speakers of different linguistic backgrounds, i.e., Bulgarian (N = 2), Serbo-Croatian (N = 2), Slovak (N = 1), Hindi (N = 1) and English (N = 2). According to the OPI results, this group rated as Superior (N = 5), Advanced High (N = 2), and Advanced Mid (N = 1) in Russian as a foreign language.

The content of the OPI test does not consider possible linguistic variations in the target language performance that might have been the result of different first language backgrounds. Conversely, speakers of five different languages rather than a homogeneous group of English speakers provided the OPI data. Participants in all three groups were college educated. For the sake of brevity, the above three groups will be referred to as Russian monolinguals (ML), Russian-English bilinguals (BL) and foreign language learners (FL) later in the chapter. The inclusion of a Russian-English bilingual group into the experimental design was done for a few reasons. First, their daily involvement in teaching Russian in the US could guarantee a high maintenance of the native language. Second, a task aimed at circumlocution about linguistically unfamiliar topics was offered to that group. The findings on the latter will be compared with the similar task used in the ML and FL groups of participants. Third, this group was well aware of the ACTFL guidelines that they were supposed to implement in their daily teaching. In other words, I was interested to see whether their performance in L1 may have become influenced by their conscious adherence to those requirements in their professional life. Finally, bilinguals may provide a better reference point than monolinguals when we compare their performance with that of Advanced and Superior L2 speakers, provided that both groups speak the same two languages in question. This suggestion fits well into the latest line of thinking in the field of SLA and bilingualism that was discussed earlier in this chapter. The present study looks at L2 performance of L2 learners of Russian and compares it with L1 performance of Russian-English bilinguals as well as Russian monolinguals. I believe that this perspective not only enriches the analysis but also contributes to the ongoing debate of where bilinguals and monolinguals stand in the ever-changing linguistic environment and who should serve as a reference point of the "standard" L1 speaker.

II.2. Materials

ML and BL participants were interviewed on a few selected autobiographical topics aimed at eliciting narration and description, e.g., birthday celebration, New Year's/Christmas celebration, vacation and house/apartment description. In addition, 3 ML, 10 BL and 6 FL participants were asked to explain how to log in to the Internet and retrieve email. Those topics were further probing into the speakers' ability to narrate on linguistically unfamiliar concepts. The FL group underwent the OPI testing and was double rated to confirm the reliability of the results. Topics for narration/description in this group included the narration on a visit to a new country/city, last vacation, process of applying for a job/graduate program, describing a campus/town/country, etc. Samples of narration, description, and circumlocution were identified in the OPIs and selected for the analysis.

II.3. Procedure

ML participants were interviewed via telephone. The researcher individually interviewed the BL participants in her office. All interviews were tape-recorded and later transcribed. The group of FL participants was selected from a bank of the interviews that the researcher conducted in the process of her OPI certification. All participants in this group were interviewed in person. The interviews were double rated and the certified trainer responsible for her certification process confirmed ratings. Only speakers of the Superior and Advanced level were chosen for the analysis. The standard OPI at this level of proficiency lasts for about thirty minutes. However, the present study looked only at the learners' ability to describe and narrate in compliance with the ACTFL guidelines as well as their ability to circumlocute on a specialized topic. The discourse samples pertaining to the above topics were identified and transcribed for the analysis. There was a difference in how the three groups were interviewed in this study and in the role of an interlocutor in each case, i.e., an interviewer for the ML and BL participants and an OPI tester for the FL group. In case of the ML and BL participants, the interviewer would ask a question in order to elicit an autobiographical narrative and did not prompt or encourage any continuation of the discourse if the speaker did not show an intention to do so. In other words, the discourse would go until the topic is exhausted by the speaker and the interviewer would move on to the next one. In contrast, in case of the OPI procedure, at the very beginning of the interview, the participants were asked to produce as much speech as possible to make the sample ratable and the tester would constantly go for more details to elicit enough speech for subsequent rating. As a result, the OPI samples carry traces of the tester's interruptions and additional questions while the FL and ML groups would freely narrate on the topic until they felt that it was exhausted. That was a fundamental difference in the procedure that will be considered in the discussion part of the chapter.

The chapter is structured as follows. After a brief discussion of the ACTFL guidelines regarding narration, description and circumlocution, the predictions are formulated. Then the chapter reports on the findings from the present study. The result section will open with a qualitative and quantitative analyses of the narrative task followed by similar analyses of the descriptive task. Then a separate analysis of discourse characteristics on specialized topics that require circumlocution is given. The discussion section follows the results and the chapter concludes with a section on study limitations and implications for future research.

III. ACTFL Standards

I should specify that by introducing a group of native speakers and comparing their performance with FL learners who underwent the OPI procedure I go against the ACTFL guidelines that describe OPI as a "testing method that measures how well a person speaks a language by comparing that individual's performance of specific language tasks, not with some other person's performance, but with the criteria for each of the nine proficiency levels described in the ACTFL Proficiency Guidelines" (1999). Yet the comparison of educated L1 speakers' performance with that of a highly proficient L2 learner is crucial for this study. Assuming that the developed criteria were originally based on a hypothetical level of language proficiency of educated native speakers, I find the comparison of OPI results with a naturalistic data legitimate. As mentioned earlier, only superior and advanced level L2 speakers were chosen for analysis. This section will look at the guidelines defining those two levels and it will focus only on a few tasks that were under scrutiny in the reported study. The ACTFL assessment criteria for speaking break down into four major requirements, i.e., global tasks and functions, context/content, accuracy and text type (see Table 8.1).

Each higher level of proficiency assumes that the speaker has passed all the requirements of the preceding levels. In other words, a Superior speaker will be able to narrate and describe in all major time frames even if it is not specified for that level of proficiency as a required global task. At the same rate, the speaker of each high sublevel of the lower level of proficiency (e.g., Advanced High) is expected to demonstrate certain skills required by the higher level (e.g., Superior). To illustrate this, we should

Table 8.1. OPI assessment criteria

Proficiency level	Global tasks and functions	Context/ content	Accuracy	Text type
Superior	Discuss topic extensively, support opinion and hypothesize. Deal with linguistically unfamiliar situation	Most formal and informal settings	No patterned errors in basic structures	Extended discourse
Advanced	Narrate and describe in major time frames and deal effectively with an anticipated complication	Most informal and some formal settings	Understood without difficulty by speakers unaccustomed to dealing with non-native speakers	Paragraphs

expect a Superior and Advanced L2 speaker to narrate and describe in an extended discourse or paragraph length, respectively. In narration, the tester needs to elicit a cohesive paragraph-length or extended discourse with a complete story being told from beginning to end. In description, the same type of a cohesive paragraph length or extended discourse with lots of details is required. The Superior speakers are also expected to demonstrate an ability to deal with a linguistically unfamiliar situation. An Advanced High speaker may also be asked to circumlocute on a linguistically unfamiliar topic. The latter is tested in two different ways. The tester acts as a naïve monolingual and can ask the interviewee to explain any of the complex concepts that the speaker chose to name in his/her L1, or he can offer a role-play at the end of the OPI. Role-plays are usually based on an interviewee reading a task from a card chosen by the tester. The role-play cards are developed by the ACFTL as part of the OPI procedure. Each level has a different set of cards aimed at eliciting required skills. An example of the cards used for the Superior level is the one that targets the knowledge of innovative terminology in the field of computers and Internet use. Since this particular role-play was used in the present study, I will quote its content here. The task reads as follows: "Explain to a classmate/ co-worker how to 'log on' to the school/office email account in order to send and retrieve e-mail messages." After an interviewee reads out the instruction in English, he/she is supposed to explain a course of action without using any words in a non-target language. If an English word appears in the discourse, a tester needs to ask the person to circumlocute in order to demonstrate his/her ability to explain complex linguistic concepts in the target language. This illustrates the difference between a naturalistic setting where the discourse does not necessarily reflect all those techniques and the OPI setting where the latter techniques are considered necessary tools to measure the speaker's language proficiency.

IV. Predictions

I suggest that in the absence of elicitation techniques that are usually used by an OPI tester, the naturalistic discourse produced by the native speakers will be different in the following ways:

1. The length of the produced samples on a given topic will be smaller than required by the OPI guidelines. In other words, native speakers will not necessarily produce an extended discourse in their narratives. This can be demonstrated by a word and clause count.
2. Native speakers will not necessarily use as many cohesive devices that are conventionally considered as an indication of a paragraph-length or extended discourse.
3. Their descriptive narratives will not have as many details as expected by the ACTFL guidelines. This can be found by counting the number of modifiers.
4. Finally, they will use borrowings to narrate on innovative topics that are known as 'linguistically unfamiliar topics' in the ACTFL guidelines.

If the above hypotheses are supported by the findings of the study we may suggest two things: either native speakers of Russian who are college educated and who are presumably highly proficient speakers of Russian do not fall into the category of Superior speakers according to the prescribed ACTFL guidelines, or the OPI guidelines and the framework that defines language training in US higher education are unrealistic.

V. Results

It should be acknowledged that all three groups had a varying number of narrative/descriptive samples elicited from each participant and the group in general. I also analyzed linguistic features such as words, clauses, cohesive devices and modifiers in terms of mean numbers per participant that considered a number of samples that was elicited in each individual case.

V.1. Narration

The analysis of the narratives was based on the interview samples elicited from all three groups of participants. Altogether, 125 samples for the monolingual group, 33 samples for the bilingual group and 16 samples for the OPI group were selected for the analysis. I should repeat that elicitation technique like additional questions asked by the tester could contribute to longer narratives for the FL group. The tester's utterances were removed from the discourse samples when the calculations of words, clauses, and cohesive devices were made. The following are the examples of the typical narratives produced by both groups:

ML speaker:
- INTERVIEWER: Расскажите, как вы справляли Новый год?
- PARTICIPANT: Новый год мы справляли дома, всей семьей, мы собрали стол, смотрели телевизор, слушали позднее поздравления Путина, потом праздновали Новый год, смотрели телевизор, у нас во дворе было много фейерверков – мы смотрели, а потом легли спать.

[INTERVIEWER: Tell me how you celebrated New Year.
PARTICIPANT: We celebrated New Year at home, all the family, we put the table together, watched the TV, later we listened to Putin's congratulations, then we celebrated New Year, watched the TV. There were lots of fireworks outside – we watched and then went to sleep.]

BL speaker:
- INTERVIEWER: Расскажите, как вы справляли свой последний день рождения?
- PARTICIPANT: Как раз он у меня был недавно. Я почти забыла. Я проснулась утром, не помнила, что у меня день рождения. Boyfriend напомнил. Он мне подарил цветы, сводил меня в ресторан. Да, и еще он мне подарил день в spa. Но это на следующий день было, потому что день рождения у меня был в пятницу, а день в spa был в субботу. [Что вы там делали?] А что же я там сделала? Массаж, маникюр и педикюр. Хотели facial сделать, но я отказалась. Потому что он купил такой package и в принципе я могла выбирать любые услуги. Это было в Palaris-e, потому что он студент, денег у него мало, поэтому он купил, где смог. Я бы не сказала, что это самая хорошая spa, которую можно найти в Коломбусе.

[INTERVIEWER: Tell me how you celebrated your last birthday.
PARTICIPANT: Actually it just happened. I almost forgot. I woke up in the morning, did not remember that it was my birthday. My boyfriend reminded me. He gave me flowers, took me out to a restaurant. Also he gave me a day in a spa. But it was the next day, because my birthday is on Friday and the spa day was on Saturday. (What did you do there? – interviewer) Well, what did I do there? A massage, manicure and pedicure. They wanted to do a facial but I refused. Because he bought a package where I could pick any service. It was at Polaris, because he is a student, he does not have much money, so he bought it where he could. I would not say that it is the best spa in Columbus.]

FL speaker at the OPI:

INTERVIEWER: Как попал в Москву?
PARTICIPANT: Мой папа в 89-ом он работал Я забыл как фирму зовут, она большая туристическая фирма, и они офис в Москве открывали, и послали его, чтоб он работал в Москве, и он там был два года, и потом мы приехали где-то в 95-ом.
INTERVIEWER: И вы каждое лето ездили домой в Югославию?
PARTICIPANT: Или в Югославию чуть-чуть, или на Кипр. Но мы ездили в Югославию каждой зимой, каждой весной, где-то четыре раза в год ездили.
INTERVIEWER: У вас там семья есть?
PARTICIPANT: Все бабушки, дедушки, все в Югославии

[INTERVIEWER: How did you get to Moscow?
PARTICIPANT: My dad, he worked in the 89th. I forgot the name of the firm, it's a big tourist company and they opened an office in Moscow, and they sent him to work there, and he was there for two years, and then we came around 95.
INTERVIEWER: Did you go to Yugoslavia every summer?
PARTICIPANT: Either to Yugoslavia for a bit or to Cyprus. But we went to Yugoslavia every winter, every spring; we went there about four times a year.
INTERVIEWER: Do you have a family there?
PARTICIPANT: All grandmothers, grandfathers, all are in Yugoslavia.]

The samples were analyzed for the number of words and clauses, and then a separate analysis of cohesive devices was done. In this study, a clause is defined as any minimal unit discourse, which has a verb in its structure. I should acknowledge that this definition might render some problems. First, not all-structural elements will have a verb, yet they have a meaning of a sentence. Second, in oral discourse the speaker tends to drop both subjects and predicates from the grammatical surface of the utterance. However, for the simplicity of the analysis, I decided to follow the Broersma and de Bot (2006) and Broersma, Isurin and de Bot (2009) definition of a clause as a production unit, i.e., an utterance that contains maximally (but not minimally) one main verb. An example of a clause from the present corpus is given below (a slash marks the end of the basic clause):

Basic clauses (N = 4):
Я родилась в Индии/ я получила свое образование там в Индии/ то есть закончила школу/, потом университет/.

[I was born in India/ I got my education there, in India/ that is, I graduated from school/, then university/.]

Since the definition of clause and subsequent analysis may cause some problems and confound the data, no further analysis will be done against this category. This also allowed the inclusion of intra-clausal as well as inter-clausal conjunctions. Both categories are considered essential for discourse cohesion. Cohesion and coherence of a discourse is considered a crucial guideline for the Advanced and Superior level of speakers. Following the earlier study by Watanabe (2003), the present research looked only at cohesion and the latter was further narrowed down to a category of so-called lexical cohesion, i.e., conjunctions. The following four categories of conjunctions were singled out in the narrative data:

1. Additive: *и, также, кроме того* 'and, also, besides';
2. Adversative: *но/а, наоборот, однако* 'but, on the contrary, nevertheless';
3. Causal: *потому что, поэтому* 'because, thus/so';
4. Temporal: *потом, после* 'then, after.'

The results of the analysis are summarized in Table 8.2.

One-way ANOVA followed by the Tukey post-hoc was performed to analyze the data. The dependent variables of words, clauses and cohesion were tested between the three groups. The results showed that FL speakers produced more words per sample than the ML group, $F (2, 38) = 33.5$, $p < 0.01$; and more clauses per sample than ML group, $F (2, 38) = 44.2$, $p < 0.01$. Moreover, FL speakers produced more cohesive devices per sample than ML: $F (2, 38) = 28.6$, $p < 0.01$. No significance was reached between FL and BL groups across all variables. The separate analysis of different cohesive categories is illustrated in Figure 8.1. FL speakers outperformed monolinguals in all categories of cohesive devices.

Table 8.2. Analysis of narrative samples

Criteria/group	ML: 125 samples	BL: 33 samples	FL: 16 samples
Number of words in a narrative (total/mean)	5560/46	2427/73.5	2111/132
Number of clauses in a narrative (total/mean)	683/5.5	573/17.4	345/21.6
Total number of cohesive devices in a narrative (total/mean)	311/2.5	205/6.2	147/9.2

Figure 8.1. Cohesion in narration

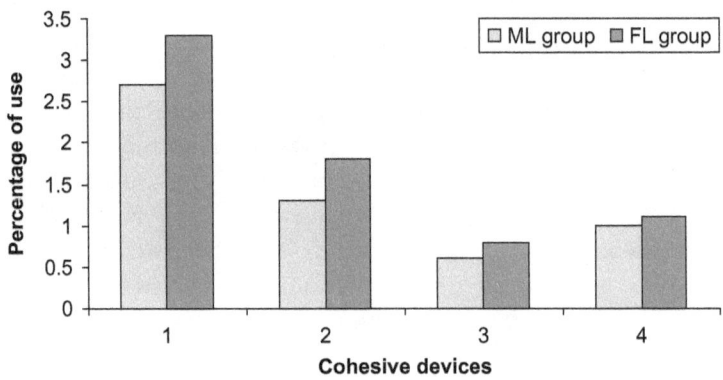

1 – Additive conjunctions
2 – Adversative conjunctions
3 – Causal conjunctions
4 – Temporal

V.2. Description

The analysis of description was based on 23 samples elicited from the ML group, 10 samples from the bilingual group, and 16 samples elicited from the FL group. Below are typical examples of the descriptive discourse from both groups.

ML speaker:
    INTERVIEWER: Опишите, пожалуйста, свою квартиру.
    PARTICIPANT: Двухкомнатная квартира на пятом этаже пятиэтажного дома. Комнаты небольшие: одна 20 метров, другая 9 или 11 – не помню.

Маленькая кухня около 6 метров, небольшой коридор. Ну, для среднестатистического русского это нормально.

[INTERVIEWER: Would you please describe your apartment.
PARTICIPANT: Two-room apartment on the fifth floor of a five-story building. The rooms are not big: one is 20 meters, another 9 or 11 – do not remember. A small kitchen around 6 meters, small hall. Well, for an average Russian it is OK.]

BL speaker:
INTERVIEWER: Опишите, пожалуйста. свою квартиру.
PARTICIPANT: Duplex…на приятной такой очень тихой и зеленой улочке. Огромные деревья, которые цветут весной. У нас потолок скошенный, cathedral ceiling, loft. Очень светлое помещение.

[INTERVIEWER: Would you please describe your apartment
PARTICIPANT: A duplex… on a very nice, quiet and green street. Huge trees that blossom in the spring. We have a tilted ceiling…a cathedral ceiling, a loft. The place is very light…]

FL speaker at the OPI:
INTERVIEWER: Это была первая страна, в котрую вы приехали до сих пор?
PARTICIPANT: Я посетила много стран.Три года я жила в Норвегии.
INTERVIEWER: Интересно.Что вы там делали?
PARTICIPANT: Я училась в университете и мне там очень понравилось.
INTERVIEWER: А что вам понравилось?
PARTICIPANT: У них страна очень красивая, люди тоже очень хорошие. Но страна мне так понравилась, это как бы парадиз. Просто там природа такая красивая: горы, снег, море, мне очень понравились. И, кажется, что там ритм жизни умеренный, не как в Америке, например, не как в моей стране, а люди там живут очень здорово, очень медленно. Они не волнуются, там просто мне казалось, что я там как бы..мне там быо 23, 24, 25 лет, и мне казалось что мне 20, 18 лет.
INTERVIEWER: Интересно, почему?
PARTICIPANT: Ну потому что, как я сказала, там люди занимаются спортом и жизнь очень медленная. Там такие вещи, например, как работа, или карьера, политика не важны. Что для них очень важно, это их семья и просто гармония с миром.
INTERVIEWER: Это очень хорошее чувство

[INTERVIEWER: Was it the first country that you came to?
PARTICIPANT: I have been to many countries, I lived in Norway for three years.

INTERVIEWER: Interesting, what were you doing there?
PARTICIPANT: I studied at the university, I liked it very much there.
INTERVIEWER: What did you like there?
PARTICIPANT: They have a beautiful country and people are very nice too. I like the country a lot, it's like a paradise. The nature is very beautiful there: mountains, snow, sea, I liked it. And it seems that their life pace is steady, not like in America or in my country, and people live there very healthy, very slowly. They do not worry. It felt like I was …I was 23, 24, 25 there but it felt like I was 20, 18.
INTERVIEWER: Interesting, why?
PARTICIPANT: Well, as I said, people do sports there and life is very slow. Things like work and career, politics are not important there. What is important for them is their family and simply a sense of harmony with the world.
INTERVIEWER: This is a very good feeling.]

First, descriptive narratives were analyzed for a number of words and clauses and then an analysis of modifiers and conjunctions was made. The modifiers were defined as adjectival forms that described nouns. Next, the conjunctions *где* [where], *куда* [to where], and *который* [which] and its inflected forms were singled out as cohesive devices used to introduce relative clauses. The latter are considered the most characteristic subordinate clauses used in description.

Table 8.3 illustrates the results of the analysis.

Same one-way ANOVA followed by the Tukey post-hoc was used to analyze the data from the descriptive task. The results showed that FL speakers

Table 8.3. Analysis of descriptive samples

Group/criteria	ML group: 23 samples	BL group: 10 samples	FL group: 16 samples
Number of words in a narrative (total/mean)	1347/59	1094/109.4	2550/159.4
Number of clauses in a narrative (total/mean)	107/4.7	205/20.5	331/20.7
Number of cohesive devices in a narrative (total/mean)	17/0.7	10/1	18/1.1
Number of modifiers (total/mean)	120/5.2	80/8	139/8.7

produced more words per sample than ML group, $F (2, 38) = 15.06$, $p < 0.01$ and more clauses per sample than ML group, $F (2, 38) = 21.2$, $p < 0.01$. Also FL speakers produced more modifiers per sample than ML, $F (2, 38) = 4.97$, $p < 0.01$. There was no significant difference in the use of cohesive devices between the two groups, BL and FL. Again, no significance was reached between FL and BL groups across all variables.

V.3. Circumlocution

One of the requirements prescribed by the ACTFL guidelines for the Superior level of oral proficiency is to demonstrate the speaker's ability to handle a linguistically unfamiliar issue, this is also known as ability to circumlocute. Participants in all three groups were selectively offered the same task, i.e., the interviewer/tester would ask them to explain how to log on to the Internet in order to retrieve an email.

Below are the excerpts from the speech samples produced by the three groups:

ML speaker:

> Подхожу к компьютеру, включаю процессор, потому что он всегда в полувыключенном состоянии, в режиме ожидания. Потом включаю почтовую программу... потом связываюсь с другой системой интернетовской, вхожу на интернет через provider-а и потом я ставлю мышку – стрелочку синенькую – на получение почты. Нажимаю стрелочку, тут же появляется табло, окошечко.

[I go to the computer, turn the processor on, because it is always in a sleeping mode. Then I turn the mail program on. Then I get connected to another Internet program. I get there through a provider. Then I draw a mouse – a blue arrow – to mail reception. Then I click the arrow, and immediately an icon, a window comes up.]

BL speaker:

> Вначале надо залогиниться, потом ввести password.... У меня Outlook, поэтому мне вообще возиться не надо, он весь preset, все by default. Так что я включаю компьютер, кликаю мышкой на иконку Outlook-а. И сразу он ретривит мой почтовый ящик.

[First you have to log in, and then enter a password... I have Outlook, so I do not have to deal with that, it's all preset, all by default. So I turn the computer on, click the icon with the mouse. And it retrieves my mailbox.]

FL speaker at the OPI:

INTERVIEWER: Я не знаю, как проверить свою электронную почту. Вы можете мне помочь?
PARTICIPANT: Все, что нужно сделать – открывайте Интернет-Эксплоре*р*.
INTERVIEWER: А как его открыть? Руками?
PARTICIPANT: Нет, не руками. Мышкой наводите на Интернет-Эксплорер, просто навести на Интернет-Эксплорер, нажать два раза на левую кнопку, и окрывается Интернет-Эксплорер. После этого нужно подсоединиться на Web-страницу школы или офиса, какой имейл вы бедете проверять. И нужно написать ваше имя и ваш пароль и нажать на кнопку sign-in.
INTERVIEWER: А что это?
PARTICIPANT: Ну это кнопка, которую вы нажимаете, и когда вы ее нажмете, вы войдете в новое окно, окно откроется и там будут ваши новые послания.

[INTERVIEWER: I do not know how to check my e-mail. Can you help me?
PARTICIPANT: All what you need to do is to open Internet Explorer.
INTERVIEWER: How should I open it, with my hands?
PARTICIPANT: No, not with hands. Get your mouse to the Internet Explorer, simply get to Internet Explorer, click left button twice and it will open. Then you have to get connected with the Web-page of your school or office, whatever e-mail you are going to check. Then you have to write your name and a password and click on 'sign-in' button.
INTERVIEWER: What is this?
PARTICIPANT: Well, this is a button that you click on, and when you do a new window will open and your new mail is going to be there.]

The analysis of circumlocution was based on three samples produced by the ML group, 10 samples produced by the BL group, and 6 excerpts from the FL performance on the same task. After the total number of words produced by each group on this task was counted, the samples were analyzed for English borrowings used by the participants. The results are summarized in Table 8.4.

The FL participants produced fewer English words per sample than monolinguals and bilinguals. I should mention that in all instances when an English word was produced, the tester would go for clarification and the speaker had to demonstrate his/her ability to explain the term in Russian. A separate analysis on borrowings was done in order to see which non-target words entered the speakers' lexicon. The examples are summarized in Table 8.5.

Note that both BL and FL speakers used the word "icon" in its Russian variant of *иконка* that means a religious icon, while the ML participants referred to it as *окошко* (window). Also, the word "click" was borrowed in its English form by six BL speakers and one FL speaker, while the ML participants referred to it by using Russian equivalents *щелкнуть, нажать* (click, press). The above results show that the FL participants discuss a linguistically unfamiliar topic in a 'purer' Russian than both groups of native speakers. No statistical analysis could be performed on this task due to a relatively small number of borrowings in two groups of participants.

Table 8.4. Circumlocution across the groups

Criteria/group	ML (3 samples)	BL (10 samples)	FL (6 samples)
Number of words (total/mean)	537/179	775/77	869/145
Use of English borrowings (total/mean)	6/2	16/1.6	6/1

Table 8.5. Lexical borrowings

ML group	BL group	FL group
Processor	Password	Sign-in
Inbox	User name	Account
Provider	Inbox	Server
Server	Log-in	Cursor
File	Icon	Icon
Email	Go	Click
	Mailbox	
	Website	
	Dial-up	
	Account	
	Email	
	Desktop	
	Preset	
	Default	
	Retrieve	
	Click	

VI. Discussion and Concluding Remarks

The results of the present research provided support for all predictions made at the onset of the study. Monolingual speakers produced shorter speech samples than the FL speakers both on narration and description tasks. This was found in the number of words and clauses per sample produced by each group in narration and description tasks. Monolingual speakers used fewer cohesive devices that are conventionally considered as an indicator of a paragraph-length or extended discourse. That was evident from findings on the narration task. Moreover, monolinguals used fewer modifiers than FL speakers in their descriptive samples. Finally, the two groups of native speakers used more English borrowings to narrate on innovative topics than the FL group. From the beginning I specified reasons why the bilingual group was included in the analyses (see section II.1). One of the reasons was to see whether this group could serve as a better reference point for the FL group. The results of the statistical analysis showed no significant difference between the BL and FL groups while both reached significance across most variables when compared with monolinguals.

This raises a question: whom should we consider as a reference point in the OPI procedure? If monolinguals are taken as a reference point, then we could question the necessity of having highly demanding goals in the OPI guidelines that are not met by highly educated native speakers of that language. If bilinguals are used as a reference point then we can argue that both groups of L2 learners may serve as a better match in comparing their performance and setting the guidelines for oral proficiency. The finding on the bilingual group needs further investigation. The only speculation that I would offer is that BL speakers in this study were foreign language teachers in a US university. Their pedagogical training and subsequent active teaching required their familiarity with the ACTFL guidelines for oral proficiency that they supposedly followed in their everyday teaching. This may have shaped their own performance in Russian in such a way that they would better fit in the ACTFL guidelines for Superior speakers than their monolingual counterparts (more information on the bilingual group and their performance can be found in Isurin 2007). If the comparison between the FL and BL groups does not sound like a plausible or legitimate alternative, then we should look into revisiting the ACTFL guidelines in order to make them more reflective of native-like linguistic performance.

The results of the present study showed that the second language learners going through the OPI procedure may indeed demonstrate a higher linguistic performance than college educated native speakers. The question is: who is a Superior speaker? There is no doubt that the FL participants in this study got certified as Advanced and Superior speakers and demonstrated an excellent performance on all tasks prescribed by the ACTFL guidelines. At the same time, I have no reason to doubt that the monolingual speakers participating in the study are Superior level speakers and would be qualified as such had they been offered an official OPI. My argument is that monolingual speakers in the L1 environment would not interact the way the ACFTL guidelines prescribe unless the interlocutor uses specific elicitation techniques. Thus, the entire issue of having those highly demanding guidelines and adopting the FL curriculum to meet those guidelines seems to be artificial and not reflective of the linguistic reality. The present study showed that the FL speakers could indeed be more verbal and produce more words, clauses, cohesive devices and modifiers than native speakers in their narratives. It also revealed that FL speakers have a better ability to express complex innovative concepts without using English borrowings. However, I question the necessity of such outstanding performance. The current situation with a linguistic norm-breaking and norm-regulation in Russia results in an enormous influx of new words entering the language, e.g., six to seven foreign words enter the Russian language every day (see Lunder and Roesen 2006 for further references) which inevitably leads to new foreign words becoming part of the speaker's lexical system. In this situation, adherence to 'pure' language in the area that was mostly affected by the current wave of borrowings seems inadequate. In other words, instead of adopting the ACTFL guidelines to the classroom curriculum and raising generations of speakers who know *what* they have to do and *how* they should perform in order to pass the test for a desired level of oral proficiency, we should reconsider those guidelines and make them more adaptable to the changing reality.

Our goal should be to educate the students and teach them the language that is closely approximated to what they find in the naturalistic setting. However, an unquestionable compliance with the ACTFL guidelines produces armies of FL speakers who join the ranks of government and business employees as Superior speakers of the second language. Where does it leave the native speaker? Are they less Superior than the ACTFL certified Superior speakers? Or should we admit that by applying the ACTFL guidelines to measuring the oral proficiency level the FL Superior speakers may become more Superior than we ever need them to be? Those are the questions that call for further research by scholars working on assessment and curriculum design.

VI.1. Study limitations

In conclusion, I would like to acknowledge possible limitations of the present study. The major limitation comes from the methodological approach used in the study. Three groups of the participants performed on similar tasks through different elicitation techniques. Two groups of native speakers were interviewed while the foreign language learners were administered an OPI. The interlocutor's participation in those tasks is different and might have resulted in different outcomes. Ideally, all three groups should have been both interviewed and given an OPI. Another limitation is in the elicitation procedure. Monolingual participants were interviewed via a telephone, while the BL and FL participants had face-to-face interview. That might have affected the length of the produced samples by the monolingual speakers. I call for further research to see whether the linguistic performance of the FL speakers changes if the OPI elicitation techniques are removed and the situation is approximated to the naturalistic setting. The present study made a first step in this direction.

Acknowledgments

I appreciate valuable comments made by Professor Kees de Bot (University of Groningen, the Netherlands) on an early version of this chapter. Thanks to his feedback my discussion of the bilingual's participation in this study was reinforced.

References

ACTFL. 1999. *Oral Proficiency Interview Tester Training Manual*, ed. E. Swender. Yonkers, NY: ACTFL.
Broersma, M., L. Isurin, K. de Bot and S. Butlena. 2009. "Triggered Code-Switching: Evidence from Dutch-English and Russian-English Data." In L. Isurin, D. Winford and K. de Bot (eds), *Multidisciplinary Approaches to Code Switching*, 103–29. Amsterdam: Benjamins.
Broersma M. and K. de Bot. 2006. "Triggered Codeswitching: A Corpus-Based Evaluation of the Original Hypothesis and a New Alternative." *Bilingualism: Language and Cognition* 9 (1): 1–13.
Chalhoub-Deville, M. and G. Fulcher. 2003. "The Oral Proficiency Interview: A Research Agenda." *Foreign Language Annals* 36 (4): 498–506.
Cook. V. 2002. "Background to the L2 User." In V. Cook (ed.), *Portraits of the L2 Users*, 1–28. Clevedon: Multilingual Matters.
Foreign Language Annals. 2003. Special Issue on OPI. *Foreign Language Annals* 36 (4).
Herzog, M. 2003. "Impact of the Proficiency Scale and the Oral Proficiency Interview on the Foreign Language Program at the Defense Language Institute Foreign Language Center." *Foreign Language Annals* 36 (4): 566–71.
Isurin, L. 2007. "Teachers' Language: The Effects of L1 Attrition." *Modern Language Journal* 91 (3): 357–72.
Kagan, O. and D. Friedman. 2003. "Using OPI to Place Heritage Speakers of Russian." *Foreign Language Annals* 36 (4): 536–44.

Liskin-Gasparro, J. 2000. "The Proficiency Movement: Current Trends and a View to the Future." In O. Kagan and B. Rifkin (eds), *The Learning and Teaching of Slavic Languages and Cultures*, 9–28. Bloomington, IN: Slavica.

———. 2003. "The ACTFL Proficiency Guidelines and the Oral Proficiency Interview: A Brief History and Analysis of Their Survival." *Foreign Language Annals* 36 (4): 483–90.

Luecht, R. 2003. "Multistage Complexity in Language Proficiency Assessment: A Framework for Aligning Theoretical Perspectives, Test Development, and Psychometrics." *Foreign Language Annals* 36 (4): 527–35.

Lunde, I. and T. Roesen, eds. 2006. *Landslide of the Norm. Language Culture in Post-Soviet Russia*. Bergen, Norway: University of Bergen.

Malone, M. 2003. "Research on the Oral Proficiency Interview: Analysis, Synthesis, and Future Directions." *Foreign Language Annals* 36 (4): 491–7.

Norris, J. and P. Pfeifer. 2003. "Exploring the Uses and Usefulness of ACTFL Oral Proficiency Ratings and Standards in College Foreign Language Departments." *Foreign Language Annals* 36 (4): 572–80.

Ortega, L. 2010. "The bilingual turn in SLA." Plenary delivered at the Annual Conference of the American Association for Applied Linguistics. Atlanta, GA, 6–9 March.

Rifkin, B. 2003. "Oral Proficiency Learning Outcomes and Curricular Design." *Foreign Language Annals* 36 (4): 582–8.

Rubio, F. 2003. "Structure and Complexity of Oral Narratives in Advanced-Level Spanish: A Comparison of Three Learning Backgrounds." *Foreign Language Annals* 36 (4): 546–54.

Surface, E. and E. Dierdoff. 2003. "Reliability and the ACTFL Oral Proficiency Interview: Reporting Indices of Interrater Consistency and Agreement for 19 Languages." *Foreign Language Annals* 36 (4): 507–19.

Swender, E. 2003. "Oral Proficiency Testing in the Real World: Answers to Frequently Asked Questions." *Foreign Language Annals* 36 (4): 520–7.

Watanabe, S. 2003. "Cohesion and Coherence Strategies in Paragraph-Length and Extended Discourse in Japanese Oral Proficiency Interviews." *Foreign Language Annals* 36 (4): 555–65.

Chapter 9

WHO AM I?: CULTURAL IDENTITIES AMONG RUSSIAN-SPEAKING IMMIGRANTS OF THE THIRD (AND FOURTH?) WAVE AND THEIR EFFECTS ON LANGUAGE ATTITUDES

David R. Andrews
Georgetown University

I. Prologue

In the fall of 1985, when I was a graduate exchange student in Moscow, I had the most remarkable conversation with my best Russian friend, Maksim Kagan (a pseudonym to maintain confidentiality). It was Gorbachev's first year as secretary general of the Communist Party, but before he had formally introduced the policy of glasnost that ushered in the vast changes of the last twenty plus years. I was with Maksim, a 22-year-old in his final year at the university, on one of our weekend excursions about the city. I cannot recall what attraction we were visiting, but I do remember the topic of conversation: we had begun talking about Moses and Passover. However, it was not Maksim, the Russian Jew, explaining the basic history of Passover to me, but rather I, an American non-Jew, relating it to him. I was completely surprised that Maksim knew nothing about Passover except the word itself ("*Pasxa*," which also means Easter and must therefore be preceded by the adjective "Jewish") and the name of Moses (Moisej). Unlike some Soviet Jews at the time, he and his family had never concealed or denied their Jewishness in an attempt to assimilate; indeed, with their recognizably Jewish surname, it would have been impossible to do so. While fully acculturated into Soviet-Russian life and nonobservant religiously, they were proud of their heritage, felt group solidarity with other Jews, and were committed to combating expressions of anti-Semitism in the Soviet Union. For his part, Maksim was amazed that I, a non-Jew, should know anything about Passover at all. He was even more astonished when I told him that in the Western world, the Passover story was common knowledge, at least among educated people.

Almost four years later Maksim and his parents resettled in California, joining a population of Russian speakers in North America that now numbers around a million. These predominantly Jewish former Soviets constitute a unique speech community whose language has been the focus of my scholarly work for almost thirty years.[1] I provide the personal anecdote about Maksim to help frame the major focus of this chapter: an analysis of the complex mix of Russian, Soviet, Jewish and, later, North American cultural identities that has shaped this group of immigrants and its effect on their language attitudes and linguistic behavior. Maksim's specific example also illustrates a different, albeit related, problem: how exactly to classify the various migrations of Russian-speakers from the motherland during the twentieth century, the discussion of which I begin below.

II. The Three (or Four) Waves: Preliminary Remarks

The three (or four) successive groups of emigrants from the Soviet Union and/or its successor states are popularly known as the three "waves" ("*volny*" in Russian).[2] The First Wave was precipitated by the Russian Revolution of 1917, as those opposed to the new regime fled the country and formed a diaspora of approximately a million people across many different countries. The original locus of emigration was Paris, but there were also sizable contingents in Germany before the rise of Nazism in the 1930s, in the Baltic republics before their annexation by the Soviet Union in 1940, elsewhere in Eastern Europe until the Second World War, and in Manchuria before the rise

---

[1] Exact figures for both the overall population and the percentage of Jews are hard to come by, both because of classifications by the receiving countries (refugees vs. immigrants) and the common phenomenon of "mixed marriages" in the post–World War II period. Remennick (2007, 18) writes that of the approximately 250,000 who left the Soviet Union during the détente era, "about 130,000 moved to the West, mostly to the US." As for the post-Soviet migration, she cites 700,000 individuals in the US and 80,000 in Canada (2007, 365). Chiswick (1997, 233) and Remennick (2007, 176) estimate the percentage of Jews in the US cohort at 80 percent, while Remennick (2007, 375) offers 50 percent for Canada.

[2] Note that as a linguist interested in manifestations of the Russian language abroad, I refer here specifically to the three waves of Russian speakers. Later in the chapter, where I address the problematic usage of the term "wave," I will treat its other major application, i.e., its designation of successive Jewish emigrations.

of Chinese communism in 1949. The communities in North America were originally quite small but grew gradually throughout the 1920s and 1930s.[3] Many members of the First Wave came from the upper classes; indeed, Gold (2002, vii) specifically calls it the "emigration of the aristocracy." However, as Raeff (1990, 5) and Huntington (1933, 24–8) assert, many other social classes were represented, including artists, scientists, scholars and government officials not of the nobility; artisans and craftspeople; and Cossack peasants. Still, the fact that a significant portion of the First Wave was composed of the pre-Revolutionary elite – Huntington (1933, 25) uses the apt phrase "an aristocracy of intellect" – played a large role in its overall sociocultural mindset, as we shall see.

The Second Wave was the migration after World War II. As Pierce (1999, 2) and Kouzmin (1988, 53) maintain, writing from a Canadian and Australian perspective respectively (although the characterization also applies to this population in the US), the term "Second Wave" actually includes two sociologically distinct groups. The first were members of the First Wave and their descendants who had originally settled elsewhere, as described above, and who subsequently emigrated from there. The second, and larger, part was made up of Soviet citizens who had been uprooted during the Second World War and later emigrated to the West, often via the displaced persons' camps of Europe. The first subgroup, of course, had more in common with the First Wave, but it helped shape the language attitudes of the whole in emigration.

The Third Wave dates from the early 1970s, when the Brezhnev regime eased emigration restrictions for Soviet Jews. According to official policy, the destination of all these emigrants was Israel. Under Soviet law Jews were considered a separate ethnic group or nationality regardless of their native language, and Jewish applicants for exit visas would now be allowed to claim Israel as their national homeland. In other words, for the Soviet government this was not emigration, but repatriation. Because the Soviets had severed diplomatic relations with Israel after the 1967 Arab–Israeli War, arrangements were made through the Dutch embassy, which represented Israeli interests in Moscow. Emigrants then left for a transit point in Vienna, from where their entry into Israel was to be processed. Many emigrants of the détente era did, in fact, go to Israel; Remennick (2007, 18) cites 130,000 out of an estimated 250,000. The almost fifty percent that insisted on other destinations, usually the US, went from Vienna to Rome, where by the

---

3 See Huntington (1933, 299) for a report from the secretary general of the League of Nations on the estimated population of Russian émigrés in various countries, released in August, 1930. No figures are given for the US or Canada, although Huntington suggests a population of several thousand in the US at that time. Raeff (2000, 55) puts the Russian population in the US at approximately 40,000 by the early 1930s.

mid-1970s representatives of the Hebrew Immigrant Aid Society (HIAS) were there to assist them.

The problem of further nomenclature originated in the 1980s. After peaking at more than 50,000 in 1979, emigration dropped by more than half in 1980 and by that number again the following year. By 1982 it had virtually ground to a halt, where it remained for the next five to six years. Only in 1989 did it once again reach the level of the late 1970s, and by 1990 the yearly exodus was at least twice as large as any of the 1970s.[4] Most commentators (e.g., Gitelman 1997; Remennick 2007) attribute the hiatus in the middle 1980s to Cold War tensions over the Soviet invasion of Afghanistan, although others (e.g., Ro'i 1997; Salitan 1997) insist that internal political and economic considerations had more of an impact on Soviet emigration policy. In any case, does this new migration constitute a separate Fourth Wave, as it is commonly called in Israel and Europe (e.g., Trier 1996; Pfandl 1994), or is it more accurate to consider it a continuation of the Soviet-era Third Wave? For instance, my friend Maksim and his parents joined his older brother and wife, as well as other members of their extended family, who had emigrated in the late 1970s. Are they, then, truly members of a separate emigration cohort? We will return to this question later in the chapter. Until then, I will refer to the emigration that began in the 1970s as the Third/Fourth Wave.

As mentioned in footnote 1, this wave is predominantly Jewish, but not exclusively so. During the détente era non-Jews were allowed to accompany their Jewish spouses, and such marriages were common by the 1970s. Furthermore, Soviet citizens of only partly Jewish heritage routinely received exit visas, and by the late 1970s, these included some ethnic Russians with only the most tenuous claims to Jewish ancestry. Sometimes cultural luminaries, both Jewish and non-Jewish, were also allowed or even forced to emigrate, and others defected while abroad. Finally, after the collapse of Soviet socialism in the early 1990s and the almost total relaxation of emigration restrictions, people of any ethnicity could leave freely. The Russian-speaking community of North America is therefore not a cultural monolith, but rather a complex web of interacting subgroups. Remennick's (2007, 8–9) description of it, shortened here, is particularly apt:

> The American and Canadian landscapes of Russian-speaking minorities include [...] Jewish refugees [...] mingl[ing] with former Soviets of any ethnic background who came to work on job visas [...] independent Russian-speaking immigrants who arrived directly from the F[ormer] S[oviet] U[nion] [and] those who re-migrated from Israel [...] winners of the Green Card (Diversity) Lottery,

---

4 See the charts in Ro'i (1997, 53) and Dominitz (1997, 119).

members of persecuted religious minorities (Pentecostals and Baptists), Armenian refugees, and former Soviet spouses and parents of American and Canadian citizens – to name just the main groups comprising the "Russian mosaic."

Still, however, the Jewish component of the population is sufficiently large to determine much of the intergroup dynamics and therefore to have the greatest impact on overall language attitudes. This tripartite cultural identity – Russian, Jewish and former Soviet – plays a formative role in shaping the community.

III. Language Maintenance, Language Contact and the Russian Waves

Every immigrant group has confronted the problem of language maintenance versus language shift. Perhaps the classic work on this topic is the 1966 *Language Loyalty in the United States* by Fishman et al. Fishman and his co-authors cite several reasons for the rapid de-ethnization of immigrant groups in the United States (applicable to Canada as well), including widespread industrialization and urbanization, opportunities for upward mobility contingent upon acculturation into the mainstream, a highly mobile population which leads to the dissolution of ethnic enclaves, the appeal of the new mass culture, and often the immigrants' own desire to discard old ideas and start life anew. Equally important are purely pragmatic considerations; mastery of English is traditionally a precursor to economic survival and success. Immigrant languages are also central to the study of language contact, a subfield of linguistics formulated by Uriel Weinreich ([1953] 1979) and Einar Haugen ([1953] 1969). Both scholars describe the many innovations, ranging from simple lexical borrowing to complex changes in morphology and syntax, that routinely take place among bilingual populations the world over. It is in this context that I have studied and written about (most notably, D. Andrews 1999, 2006, 2008) the Russian language in the US for many years.

Fishman also notes that de-ethnization was faster for immigrant groups that arrived before World War II because of their low level of literacy and less developed sense of national consciousness. For their part, Weinreich and Haugen consider immigrant languages a special subgroup in contact situations because of their unequal power relationship with the language of the host society; immigrants usually regard their mother tongue as less prestigious. In both respects, of course, the Russian First Wave stands out as a conspicuous exception. As Raeff asserts throughout his appropriately named monograph *Russia Abroad* (1990), the highly educated First Wave saw itself as the last bastion of genuine Russian culture. Their mission was to nurture and preserve it in exile, as well as to transmit it to the next generation. In the very early years there was still hope that the new Soviet regime would be defeated and that the First Wave could return home, Russian high culture intact. Even when such hopes faded, the First Wave remained vigilant. Language played a special, virtually sacred, role in their society; in Raeff's (1990, 109) words, it "provided the essential ingredient of consciousness and identity of Russia Abroad." As such, the First Wave was especially insistent on linguistic purity. Its leaders were equally critical of the new acronyms and jargonisms of Soviet Russian and the intrusion of foreign elements into Russian from the languages of the various host countries. The two issues were inextricably linked in the popular perception, and articles about these threats to proper usage regularly appeared in the First Wave press.[5]

Despite the professed devotion to unsullied Russian, there was nevertheless a certain amount of direct borrowing and other types of language interference (semantic extension and even neologisms) in the speech of the First Wave. Golubeva-Monatkina (1993a, 1993b, 1994b) and Granovskaja (1995) note and discuss these developments in the language of the European diaspora, as do Wells (1932) and Benson (1957, 1960) – the latter writing both about the First and Second Wave – among émigrés in the United States. Fedorova (2012) also points out that Anglicisms of the First Wave play an important role in the travelogues of several prominent Soviet writers who visited the US in the 1920s and 1930s, both as an object of the writers' derision and as a stylistic device to underscore the "otherness" of American culture. Still, however, the puristic ethos was the recognized ideal and recommended mode of linguistic behavior. These attitudes continued with the Second Wave. First, as we have noted above, some members of the so-called Second Wave were actually First Wavers and their descendants who had originally settled in Europe and Manchuria and migrated anew from there. This part of the population already shared the linguistic values of the First Wave. As for the displaced persons, Raeff asserts (1990, 6–7) that they had little interest in joining the First Wave's Russia Abroad; rather, he says, they were seeking only peace and security after the terrors they had experienced under Stalin and during the war. The reality is a bit more complicated. Anyone of the Second Wave interested in Russian-language maintenance in North America, or even in interacting with the established Russian community there for purely pragmatic reasons,

---

5 For a detailed analysis of the language of the émigré press between 1919 and 1939, as well as its importance as a social "glue" holding together this far-flung diaspora, see Zelenin (2007). For more on the negative reactions of the First Wave to so-called impure Russian, see Golubeva-Monatkina (1994a) and Granovskaja (1995).

was dependent on the network of private institutions (schools, religious and cultural organizations, etc.) founded by the First Wave. In this way earlier language attitudes were perpetuated.

The situation is different among the Third/Fourth Wave, as is apparent to anyone who knows the language and has spent even a little time in one of the Russian-speaking enclaves of many North American cities. Russian is spoken everywhere, but it is full of English borrowings and other English-inspired lexical innovations that far exceed any such developments in contemporary mainstream Russian. To be sure, there is a significant degree of individual variation and no shortage of purists among the Third/Fourth Wave as well, but the overall speech community is much more tolerant of the phenomenon than the previous Russian waves. Indeed, there is often a deliberate playfulness to it, especially in advertisements and signs in shop windows that would leave a proper First Waver aghast. Furthermore, I submit that these developments are not at all a sign of disrespect for the Russian language, as the purists charge, and also that there are specific sociocultural factors that have encouraged them.

It is sometimes alleged that the Third/Fourth Wave is less puristic because it is less emotionally invested in the language altogether, a result of its being predominately Jewish rather than ethnic Russian. Throughout years of fieldwork I have heard this opinion numerous times, not only from members of the previous migrations but also from a few Third/Fourth Wavers themselves, regardless of background. Upon analysis, however, this argument seems spurious. By the 1970s the vast majority of Soviet Jews had been fully acculturated into the secular Russian tradition; as Birman (1979, 49) insists, they had long since "embraced Russian culture, literature and even history as their own." The deep respect for erudition and intellectual achievement in the Russian context, reinforced by high levels of education, is emphasized in the literature time and again. To wit, Chiswick (1997, 242–3) notes that in the 1990 census, male Soviet-Jewish immigrants in the US reported an average of 14.8 years of formal education, greater than that of other foreign-born men (11.7 years), native-born men (13.1 years) and Asian-born men (14.3 years). Gold (1997, 262) puts the figure at 13.5 years for the entire Soviet-Jewish immigrant community and notes that this is a year longer than the average among the broader US population. Considering that the traditional Soviet school year, six days a week and ten months a year, was substantially longer than in the US, these figures are indeed striking. Ritterband (1997, 326–7) treats these high levels of education among Soviet Jews from a more sociocultural perspective. Although the education was Russian, not Jewish, in content, it allowed them to honor Jewish ideals of learning and scholarship while simultaneously identifying with the Russian intelligentsia and Russian high culture. Remennick (2007, 32–3) lists a number of Jews who made it to the very pinnacle of Russian high and popular culture and later (203–4) mentions Jewish intellectuals for whom Russian high culture "was at the core of their self-concept and self-esteem." She also documents (233–4; 305–6) how Soviet-Jewish immigrants in both the US and Canada are forging ties with the former Soviet Union (FSU) and helping to build a transnational network of Russian-language communication via modern media, including satellite television and the Internet.

What, then, to make of the 1988 article by Kouzmin in the influential *International Journal of the Sociology of Language*? Based on a series of interviews she had conducted in second and third wave communities in Australia, Kouzmin concludes that the Jewish ethnicity of her third wave informants supersedes their loyalty to the Russian language and impacts most directly, and negatively, on their prospects for language maintenance. In my 1999 monograph I devote several pages to this study and question its assertions for many reasons (44–7). I will not repeat that discussion here, except to say I based my objections on the specific questions Kouzmin asked, her subsequent refinement of these questions during the interview process, the difference in her familiarity with the informants of the two respective groups, and the two groups' own unequal statuses as established immigrants versus newcomers.[6] In any case, while Kouzmin's conclusions are certainly overstated, the Third/Fourth Wave does indeed seem less militant about the preservation of some mythically pure Russian than the previous two groups, as I mention above. I contend that Jewish ethnicity is a factor in their language attitudes, although not in the simplistic cause-and-effect way that it is usually presented, and that I attempt to refute here. Equally important are the Third/Fourth Wave's Soviet origin and the interplay of Soviet and Jewish identities.

IV. The Origins of Third/Fourth Wave Language Attitudes, Pre- and Post-emigration

There are many components to the Third/Fourth Wave's more relaxed attitude toward the incorporation of borrowings and other foreign elements into their Russian. First, in contrast to the First Wave, émigrés of the 1970s and later never regarded themselves as the last hope for the preservation of Russian culture. To be sure, many were hostile toward the Soviet regime until it collapsed, but even the most disaffected former dissidents and intellectuals

---

[6] I hasten to add that I am in no way suggesting malice on Kouzmin's part; I simply disagree with her methodology and analysis.

knew intuitively that the culture itself was not at stake; after all, the Soviet Union had produced *them*. In the post-Soviet period it would be even more unlikely for émigrés to regard themselves as the sole protectors of the culture, even if they might be ambivalent about the current course of Russia and the other FSU states.

While a full discussion is impossible here, another factor is the greater degree of borrowing from English into Russian during the Soviet period. Especially after World War II English became the foreign language of choice among the intelligentsia, and by the 1970s there were many more English borrowings in the contemporary standard language than in the speech of the First Wave. Even purists among the Third/Fourth Wave in the US and Canada surely use "legitimate" Anglicisms that the First Wave would have considered immigrant barbarisms. Furthermore, these pre-existing Anglicisms facilitate the adoption of additional borrowings in immigration, when the speakers become immersed in the English language. The collapse of European socialism ushered in another great influx of borrowings, as the post-Communist space assimilated previously unfamiliar economic, political and social concepts as well as new material items.[7] Soviet immigrants of the post-Soviet period were even more used to the practice of using English borrowings to denote new realia.

Even more important was the immigrants' relationship to English after arrival. As is well known, immigrant groups in North America have long been subject to intense assimilation pressures. By the 1970s there had perhaps emerged a more enlightened attitude toward our multicultural heritage, at least in more liberal circles. However, anti-immigrant backlash is alive and well and, by all indications, it has only intensified in the United States over the last ten to twenty years. While mainly directed at Latin Americans, these sentiments also extend to other immigrant groups. In any case, the English language is still very much a prerequisite for economic advancement – in fact, all the more so in this era of "global English" – and the Third/Fourth Wave is well aware of this fact. Levkov (1984, 123) reports that although 90 percent of respondents in a sampling project were pleased about their decision to emigrate, most felt that their socioeconomic status in the United States was lower than it had been in the Soviet Union. A better command of English was seen as a primary way of raising it. In other sampling projects, Feinstein (1981, 50) found that an overwhelming majority acknowledged that mastery of English was essential to economic well-being, and Gilison (1981, 50) reports that learning English was rated the single greatest concern of recent immigrants. Chiswick (1997, 236) also emphasizes the "intensive investments in acquiring English language skills" among the Third/Fourth Wave. Overall,

---

7 For a full exploration, see the collection edited by E. Andrews (2008).

his detailed demographic analysis reveals an indisputable correlation between knowledge of English and upward mobility.

The situation in Canada is perhaps even more fraught. On the one hand, Canada is often regarded as the "kinder, gentler" partner in North American culture. Anti-immigrant expressions there are generally less intense, and respect for multiculturalism seems more pervasive. After all, Canada has had to grapple with its own bilingual and bicultural traditions in the still ongoing efforts to ensure its continuation as a unified nation. On the other hand, as Remennick (2007, 279–311) details in her chapter on former Soviet Jews in Toronto, professional licensing requirements are even more stringent than in the US. Most immigrants there face extensive re-training and re-licensing, all via English, if they wish to work in their former professions, especially in such fields as accounting, education, engineering, law, medicine and psychology. For them, the acquisition of English is even more urgent than for their American counterparts, who nevertheless face similar challenges. Undoubtedly the obsession with learning English has contributed to a general receptivity among many Third/Fourth Wavers in both countries to the incorporation of English borrowings into their Russian speech.

These concerns were only intensified by the Third/Fourth Wave's Soviet background. These immigrants were the product of an ideology that glorified the concept of labor and provided virtually full employment. Until the end of the Soviet period and even beyond, stories about unemployment and the dog-eat-dog capitalism of the West were a staple in the press. Even if they dismissed these accounts as propaganda, many immigrants still harbored a fear in the back of their mind that they could wind up homeless and sleeping on a street grate. As Shasha and Shron (2002, xi) write in the preface to their book containing thirty different personal accounts by Soviet immigrants, "the United States was the country of the enemy, the country of capitalism."[8] Third/Fourth Wavers therefore attached particular importance to their professional identities as an indicator of their potential success, or even survival, in immigration. Rothchild (1985, 192), who conducted dozens of personal interviews with Soviet-Jewish immigrants, writes that many believed "they would be lost forever" if they could not master English well enough to work in their previous professions and spoke "as if they had no identity beyond that conferred by their certificates and diplomas." Chiswick (1997, 236–7), Gold (1997, 275) and Remennick (2007, 25–6) also note this strong affinity between professional identity and self-esteem. Remennick traces it directly to

---

8 The first account is actually by a descendant of the First Wave. All the rest are Soviet immigrants of the 1970s or later.

these immigrants' prior lives as Soviet Jews and their culture of success and achievement despite institutionalized anti-Semitism at all levels of society.

In fact, it is not uncommon for Soviet immigrants to describe their new environment as not just another country, but a different planet. Arkadin (1983, 44) writes of landing in the "spaceship USSR-USA," and two of Shasha and Shron's (2002, 68, 182) interviewees make explicit comparisons to Mars and Martians. Others speak of having to undergo a total transformation; for instance, Remennick (2007, 204) cites one woman who declared that she needed to discard her previous convictions "and become [a] new, functional, and rational person, an American." Throughout my work on the Russian of the Third/Fourth Wave, I have argued that Anglicisms often serve as a symbol of adaptation to and mastery of this bewildering culture, this polar opposite of Soviet socialism. Such borrowing can easily take place below the level of consciousness in situations of extreme culture shock, like those above. Remennick (2007, 206–7; 224) also mentions a related phenomenon: the tendency of some Soviet immigrants to rank others by how well they have adapted to the new country, including their knowledge of English. She asserts that when immigrants build new personal and professional networks, they try to associate with others at their own perceived social level or higher, based both upon pre-immigration and current status. The use of English borrowings might also be a useful tool in such interactions, both for those doing the judging and those being judged.

Adding to these feelings of disorientation is a lack of understanding on the part of the North American mainstream. First, consider the very designation "Russian," and why it is a source of confusion even to Third/Fourth Wavers themselves. In the Soviet Union, as mentioned above, Jews by definition were not Russian, a term reserved only for members of that particular East Slavic ethnic group. This distinction was reinforced by the fact that a Soviet citizen's nationality was recorded on the internal passport, which served as a basic identification card, and on many other official documents. Therefore Soviet Jews, even the most acculturated, almost never called themselves Russian before emigration. That situation changed almost immediately on this side of the Atlantic. Before the collapse of socialism, North Americans often used "Russia" and "Russian" as colloquial shorthand for the entire Soviet Union and all its peoples. Moreover, while many North Americans realize that the Third/Fourth Wave is predominantly Jewish, most are unaware that Soviet Jews were officially a separate nationality in that country. What else would most Americans and Canadians call Russian-speaking immigrants from the Soviet Union/FSU other than Russians?

Moreover, Russian was usually the native language of Jews even in the non-Russian republics of the Soviet Union. Large numbers of Third/Fourth Wavers have come from Ukraine, Belarus and the Baltic states, almost all speakers of Russian. These people would have found it doubly strange to call themselves Russian while still in the Soviet Union/FSU. Ultimately, some Third/Fourth Wave immigrants do begin to call themselves Russian, both to reflect their linguistic and cultural reality and to simplify explanations for the majority population. Many others, however, do not and never will. The issue is far from trivial. As Ripp (1981, 163–4) points out, labels do matter when a group is trying to make sense of its identity and especially to construct a new one. Ripp relates an encounter he had with a group of Soviet-Jewish adolescents in Brooklyn, in which he asked if they called themselves Russians. No, they said, and not just Jews either. They then debated a number of possible designations – Russian-American Jew, Soviet-emigrant Jew, Soviet-American who was forced to emigrate – but seemed satisfied with none of these.

Various commentators cite the conflict with the established American and Canadian Jews who had helped the Third/Fourth Wave to emigrate and who were half anticipating the *shtetl* Jews of their grandparents' generation rather than educated, urbanized bearers of Russian culture. Ritterband (1997, 339) puts it the most pithily:

> Perhaps American Jews expect Tevye the Milkman [from the musical *Fiddler on the Roof*] to step out of the airplane and instead they greet Vladimir the nuclear engineer.

Remennick (2007, 190–1) also makes explicit reference to *Fiddler on the Roof* as having shaped the expectations of Western Jewry. As Gold (1997), Ritterband (1997) and Remennick (1997) all detail, Soviet-Jewish immigrants have quite different notions about what it means to be Jewish. Consistent with their Soviet backgrounds, they tend to view it in ethnic rather than religious terms. North American Jews have been disappointed by Soviet-Jewish immigrants' lack of religious knowledge and practice and their unfamiliarity with Jewish history. On the other hand, immigrants resent not being accepted on their own terms. One of Remennick's (2007) Canadian informants complained that she was "not Jewish enough" for Canadian Jews, but that "being Jewish mean[t] something else" to her. This "something else" is also thoroughly explored in the literature. Both Gold (1997) and Ritterband (1997) note that on many measures, Soviet-Jewish immigrants rate as even more Jewish than their North American counterparts. They are more likely to live in predominantly Jewish neighborhoods and to want to keep living among other Jews, to have only Jews among their closest friends, to have thoughts of emigrating to Israel and to have friends and relatives there, and to believe that Jews can only depend on other Jews in times of crisis. Gold (2007, 268) mentions the not unusual phenomenon of younger immigrants, even those who came as small children, speak English natively and attend American colleges and universities, to socialize almost exclusively within their own peer group. Remennick (2007, 245) opens her chapter on sexuality with a quote from an interviewee, who states that immigrant women prefer to date and marry Russian Jewish men rather than commitment-phobic Americans. As Gitelman (1997, 35–6) sums it up, Soviet-Jewish immigrants strongly identify as Jews, even if they are weakly affiliated in the ways that North American Jews define it. This characterization certainly applies to my friend Maksim. He might not have known the Passover story, but he would certainly have been shocked if someone had called him a not-so-good Jew because of it.

This mutual misunderstanding spills over into other areas. Leighton (1979, 288), Gold (1997, 264, 279) and Remennick (2007, 197–202) all note the political conservatism of most Soviet-Jewish immigrants and their alienation from the liberal left, which includes most North American Jews. Meanwhile, disaffected American Jews are quick to point out that many immigrants received various forms of public assistance after first arriving in the US and that older immigrants rely on it still. Remennick underscores this contradiction by the subheading she assigns to her section on American politics: "Living on Welfare, but Voting Republican." Remennick also cites a particular conundrum in Canada. There, immigrants are accepted under the point system for the work skills and qualifications they possess, but re-licensing requirements often make it impossible for them to practice their previous professions and thereby nullify the reason they were admitted in the first place. This paradox is a source of great frustration for the affected immigrants.

Disillusionment on both sides can lead to mutual stereotyping of personal behavior and intellect. Remennick (2007, 294) writes of immigrants in Toronto who complain of being unable to befriend native-born Canadians because of the latter's "cold and uninterested demeanor [...] and arrogance." In several places (204–5, 369, 374) she also notes the perception among many Soviet immigrants that both high culture and the educational system in the old country were unequivocally superior to anything that might be found in North America. One of her interviewees complained that the only things he could talk about with American acquaintances were sports and television. Here the previously mentioned allusions to *Fiddler on the Roof* take on an added dimension: stereotypes of ill-informed North Americans who get their information about the world from popular entertainment rather than traditional avenues of learning. Even more extreme, one of Ripp's (1984, 125) interviewees insisted that any Soviet schoolchild knew more about the United States than any professional American Sovietologist knew about Russia. On the other side of the equation, Simon (1977, 78) writes of American Jews who consider Soviet immigrants "pushy, aggressive, and obnoxious" and of American specialists who cavalierly dismiss the immigrants' cherished academic and professional qualifications. Sometimes the rhetoric can become ludicrously shrill, as in the assertion by an American rabbi to Ripp (1984,155) that Soviet-Jewish immigrants "lack the basic concepts of humanity, let alone of Judaism." Conflict exists inside the Russian-speaking community as well. An immigrant of the détente era, Glazov (1975) tells of encounters with members of the previous waves who were disdainful of his Sovietized language and mannerisms. Ripp (1984, 25–6) quotes a Second Waver who declares that the very worst attribute of the Third Wave is its language.

How does this alienation from the North American mainstream affect language attitudes? At first glance it is tempting to conclude that the conditions I describe in the last few paragraphs would make the Third/Fourth Wave less receptive to the incorporation of Anglicisms into their Russian speech. The effect, however, is quite the opposite, and I submit that the reason lies in the Third/Fourth Wave's origin not only as Soviets, but also specifically as Soviet Jews. In her overview of Soviet Jewry at the time of emigration, Remennick (2007, 13–52) describes a "persecuted elite" with a "built-in fighter spirit and [...] drive to overcome barriers." She writes of the mantra that Soviet-Jewish parents have always passed on to their children: that they must be ten times better than any Russian, and then no one will be able to deny them their rightful place and just rewards. It was this determination and adaptability under adverse conditions that the Third/Fourth Wave brought with it to North America. These immigrants understand intuitively that they have to strive hard in order to thrive in this new culture that in many ways is the polar opposite of their old one. The incorporation of Anglicisms into their Russian speech, whether conscious or unconscious, is a linguistic accompaniment to the process of adaptation. By using these lexical innovations, they simultaneously maintain their allegiance to the much-valued Russian speech community while also signaling that they know the ins and outs of the new society as well as any native-born North American, and maybe even ten times better.

V. Three or Four Waves?

Let us now address the question of numbering the waves and its broader social implications. On this there is much variation in the literature. In all the articles that I cite from Lewin-Epstein, Ro'i and Ritterband's 1997 *Russian Jews on Three Continents*, the term "Fourth Wave" is never used, although the great bulk of the glasnost-era and post-Soviet emigration had taken place by then. Gitelman (1997, 25) refers specifically to "the emigration of the 1970s–90s" and Gold (1997, 261) speaks of a single Soviet-Jewish community in the United States from the mid-1970s on. Later, in his foreword to Shasha and Shron's book, Gold (2002, vii) writes of a Third Wave that began in the 1970s and "extends through today." For their part, Shasha and Shron use the words "last wave of Russian immigrants" in their very subtitle; as mentioned in footnote 8, the book is a compilation of the life stories of immigrants from the 1970s through the 1990s. Chiswick (1997, 242), while he does contrast the adaptation of earlier and later immigrants, speaks of Soviet immigrants from 1965 to 1990 as a single cohort. Ritterband also surveys different time periods ranging from 1979 to 1991 but treats the Soviet-Jewish community in the US as a whole. Clearly, then, for these commentators the Third and Fourth Waves are a unified group.

In contrast, Remennick (2007, 169–77) does differentiate four distinct groups of immigrants and uses the term Fourth Wave for the emigration that took place primarily in the 1990s. However, she is numbering not waves of Russian speakers, but rather waves of Jews. In her count, the first wave was the "great migration" of Jews from the Russian Empire in the last two decades of the nineteenth and first two decades of the twentieth centuries, the second was composed of Holocaust survivors, and the third is the détente-era emigration. Jacobs and Paul (1981, 1–7) arrive at the term "Third Wave" in the same way, by numbering the migrations of Jews; their book predates the post-glasnost emigration, so of course there is no mention of a fourth wave. It is coincidence, then, that the term "Third Wave" can apply to the détente-era group both as Russian speakers, the way that I and others (e.g., Ripp) treat it, and as a Jewish migration. However, even when numbering Russian-speaking waves, the issue is not so clear-cut. While the first migration of Jews was primarily Yiddish-speaking and is therefore usually excluded from the Russian count, there were undoubtedly people among them for whom Russian was the primary language. Moreover, as Raymond and Jones (2000, 52–8) point out, there were already Russians in both the US and Canada, most often from the peasantry, before the arrival of what is traditionally called the First Wave, or the post-1917 emigration. Raymond and Jones emphasize the difficult relations between these earlier migrants and the aristocratic newcomers, whom the authors specifically refer to (untraditionally) as a "second wave."[9]

There seems to be more justification for separating the last migration(s) into two distinct waves for Israel, however. As Gitelman (1997, 28–9) notes, the détente-era emigration actually contained two subgroups: one, compelled by Zionist ideology, that went to Israel mostly between 1971 and 1974; the other, non-Zionists who went primarily to the United States starting around 1975. While the latter also certainly wanted to escape the institutionalized anti-Semitism

---

9 The two books by Vil'čur (1914, 1918) also testify to a vibrant Russian-speaking community in the US, whether ethnic Russian or Jewish, before the arrival of the First Wave.

of the Soviet Union, they were motivated more by economic and pragmatic concerns than by religion. Gitelman (1997, 30), Paltiel, Sabatello and Tal (1997, 285) and Remennick (2007, 5) all emphasize the importance of a 1989 change in US immigration policy, after which Soviet Jews were no longer granted refugee status. Thousands who would presumably have gone to the US were now being diverted to Israel. The new emigrants to Israel therefore had more in common with their 1970s counterparts who had chosen the United States. In a section under the heading "Third Wave versus Fourth Wave," Trier (1996, 40–1) insists that the two groups in Israel "contrast sharply," based on their dissimilar life experiences in the Soviet Union/FSU and the above-mentioned motivations for emigrating. While they do not use the term "Fourth Wave," Paltiel, Sabatello and Tal (1997) also clearly differentiate this immigration cohort from the détente-era migrants, both demographically and socioculturally. Remennick (53–168; 365) offers another reason to consider the Fourth Wave a separate group in Israel. Its sheer size there (one million people, constituting 20 percent of the present-day Jewish population) has permanently altered the fundamental make-up and dynamics of Israeli society in a way that the smaller Third Wave did not. As for the US and Canada, both migration streams constitute only a minute fraction of the overall population.

In the United States the 1989 change in immigration policy led to granting preference to those who already had first-tier relatives there, precisely the case of my friend Maksim and his parents. Much of the 1990s influx was therefore for purposes of family reunification, strengthening the case for considering the post-glasnost migration simply the numerically larger part of a single wave that began in the 1970s. From a sociocultural perspective, this is one group, including the operation of the language attitudes that I have discussed throughout this chapter. For Canada, with its point system and admission by economic criteria, the détente-era and post-glasnost migrations are also socioculturally similar. Remennick (2007, 279–311) does stress the difference between direct migrants from the FSU and those who re-migrated from Israel in the 1990s cohort; the former arrived with little or no experience of Western and/or Jewish culture, while the latter gained exposure to both from their time in Israel. This is indisputably true, but the latter's remigration from Israel is also an indicator that many would have gone directly to North America in the first place, if they had had that option. Therefore, we can consider the migration from the 1970s onward a unified whole, although not as unequivocally as for the United States.

VI. Future Prospects

Before we treat the prospects for long-term language maintenance, it is necessary to make an important distinction. The English-inspired lexical innovations that I write about here are usually thought to be the precursor of language shift, but the two are actually very different phenomena. The Last Wave, to borrow Shasha and Shron's term, collectively understands this fact on a subconscious level in a way that the First and Second Wave could never grasp. Haugen (1969, 70–2) puts it most eloquently. He observes that interference resulting from language contact is simply the speakers' way of adjusting the old language to the new culture. Immigrants who disdain the old tongue have the option of simply dropping it in favor of English. Maintaining the language, albeit in a form different from the standard, is actually a sign of allegiance and respect.

What I describe above are general trends and tendencies. It was never my intention to suggest that the Soviet-Jewish immigration is a sociocultural monolith. As might be expected, there has been a great variety of chosen paths, from attempts at complete assimilation into mainstream North American culture to the rigorous preservation of all things Russian. Some have remained as secular as they had been in the Soviet Union, while others have embraced their identity as Jews. Of the latter group, a small percentage have rejected their Russian identity, seeing the two as incompatible. Most, however, have integrated not only their Jewish and Russian selves, but also their new identity as North Americans. We are now seeing the children of this latter wave in our universities, and many are trying to maintain and/or rediscover their heritage by taking courses in the Russian language and culture and then by studying or working in the FSU. Those who take advantage of such opportunities are achieving a level of bilingual and bicultural competence that the descendants of the first two waves could only envy. Perhaps most exciting, some of them are enriching Slavic studies with new explorations of the history and role of Jewish culture in Russia, topics that are much more pursuable now in the post-Soviet era.

In her final discussion of the "Russian street" in North America – the transnational lifestyle of some contemporary Soviet-Jewish immigrants who divide their time between the West and the FSU, partake of the global Russian media and found institutions like Russian-speaking kindergartens and clubs for their children – Remennick (2007, 379) suggests that we check again on widespread language maintenance in about fifty years. Alas, I think that is overly optimistic, given the assimilation pressures inherent in North American culture as well as the ever-increasing role of English as a global lingua franca. Remennick (2007, 221–3) does cite a survey conducted between 1998 and 2000 among 18- to 32-year-olds in New York, including those born in the US, revealing that 53 percent continued to use Russian with family and friends at least some of the time. Like Gold, she also emphasizes the tendency even among younger, fully acculturated immigrants to socialize mainly within their own peer group. More indicative, however, is her discussion of the

79ers' Association in San Francisco, a social group for the children of the détente-era emigration. On the homepage of their website, they try to attract other members of what they call Generation-R, or those of "Russian-Jewish-American hybrid culture." Tellingly, this appeal, in which potential participants' "rusty Russian" is mentioned, is in English. Still and all, the "Russian street" will result in greater transmission of Russian to the third generation than the First and Second Waves were able to achieve.

And what about my friend Maksim? In 1992 I attended his wedding to a Soviet-Jewish woman originally from Kiev. They rented out a Russian restaurant for the evening, and for a minute I thought that I had stepped back into Moscow of 1985. I quickly learned differently, however. The language and food were Russian, but the wedding ceremony was performed by a rabbi. Maksim broke the glass under his foot, we sang Mazel Tov a dozen times and then danced the Hava Nagila. These were rituals that Maksim and his family had certainly picked up only after arrival on the new "planet." For the rest of the evening the band played mostly American pop music, with a few Russian songs thrown in. It was an eclectic mix of cultures and traditions. To this day the language of Maksim's household is Russian, albeit with the usual admixtures of Anglicisms. This distinctively immigrant language prevails even at gatherings of the extended family, which includes an older generation with very limited English proficiency. In fact, the elderly use this type of language, too. It is not ostentatious or forced, but simply their natural and spontaneous mode of communication. Maksim's two daughters, now teenagers, are both typical California girls and Russian-American Jews. They certainly know Russian well enough to pass it on to their children, if they so choose. In sum, Maksim and his family are an excellent example of a culture and language that are unquestionably hybridized, but also living and vibrant.

References

Andrews, David R. 1999. *Sociocultural Perspectives on Language Change in Diaspora: Soviet Immigrants in the United States*. Amsterdam and Philadelphia: John Benjamins.

―――. 2006. "The Role of Émigré Russian in Redefining the 'Standard.'" *Journal of Slavic Linguistics* 14(2): 169–89.

―――, ed. 2008. *Heritage Language Journal* 6 (1). Special Issue on Russian as a Heritage Language, comprised of six articles and an introduction by D. Andrews as guest editor.

Andrews, Ernest, ed. 2008. *Linguistic Changes in Post-Communist Eastern Europe and Eurasia*. Boulder, CO: East European Monographs.

Arkadin, L. 1986. "Brajton Bič glazami amerikanskogo sociologa." *Novyj amerikanec* 10–11: 43–4.

Benson, Morton. 1957. "American Influence on the Immigrant Russian Press." *American Speech* 32 (4): 257–63.

―――. 1960. "American-Russian Speech." *American Speech* 35 (3): 163–74.

Birman, Igor. 1979. "Jewish Emigration from the USSR: Some Observations." *Soviet Jewish Affairs* 9 (2): 46–63.
Chiswick, Barry R. 1997. "Soviet Jews in the United States: Language and Labour Market Adjustments Revisited." In Noah Lewin-Epstein, Yaacov Ro'i and Paul Ritterband (eds), *Russian Jews on Three Continents: Migration and Resettlement*, 233–60. London: Frank Cass.
Dominitz, Yehuda. 1997. "Israel's Immigration Policy and the Dropout Phenomenon." In Noah Lewin-Epstein, Yaacov Ro'i and Paul Ritterband (eds), *Russian Jews on Three Continents: Migration and Resettlement*, 113–27. London: Frank Cass.
Fedorova, Lioudmila. 2012. "Yankees in Petrograd, Bolsheviks in New York: America and Americans in Russian literary perception." Unpublished book manuscript.
Feinstein, Stephen C. 1981. "Soviet-Jewish Immigrants in Minneapolis and St. Paul: Attitudes and Reactions to Life in America." In Dan N. Jacobs and Ellen Frankel Paul (eds), *Studies of the Third Wave: Recent Migrations of the Soviet Jews to the United States*, 57–75. Boulder, CO: Westview Press.
Fishman, Joshua A. et al. 1966. *Language Loyalty in the United States: The Maintenance and Perpetuation of Non-English Mother Tongues by American Ethnic and Religious Groups*. The Hague: Mouton.
Gilison, Jerome M. 1981. "The Resettlement of Soviet Jewish Emigrés: Results of a Survey in Baltimore." In Dan N. Jacobs and Ellen Frankel Paul (eds), *Studies of the Third Wave: Recent Migrations of the Soviet Jews to the United States*, 29–56. Boulder, CO: Westview Press.
Gitelman, Zvi. 1997. "'From a Northern Country': Russian and Soviet Jewish Immigration to America and Israel in Historical Perspective." In Noah Lewin-Epstein, Yaacov Ro'i and Paul Ritterband (eds), *Russian Jews on Three Continents: Migration and Resettlement*, 21–41. London: Frank Cass.
Glazov, Yuriy. 1975. "The passing of a year… The Russian world viewed from America." *Studies in Soviet Thought* 15 (4): 273–90.
Gold, Steven J. 1997. "Community Formation among Jews from the Former Soviet Union in the United States." In Noah Lewin-Epstein, Yaacov Ro'i and Paul Ritterband (eds), *Russian Jews on Three Continents: Migration and Resettlement*, 261–83. London: Frank Cass.
———. 2002. "Foreword." In Dennis Shasha and Marina Shron (eds), *Red Blues: Voices from the Last Wave of Russian Immigrants*, vii–ix. New York and London: Holmes & Meier.
Golubeva-Monatkina, N. I. 1993a. "Ob osobennostjax russkoj reči potomkov pervoj èmigracii vo Francii." *Russkij jazyk za rubežom* 2: 100–5.
———. 1993b. "Zametki o russkix rečevyx tradicijax vo Francii." *Russkaja slovesnost'* 4: 75–9.
———. 1994a. "Russkaja èmigracija o russkom jazyke." *Russkaja slovesnost'* 3: 73–7.
———. 1994b. "Grammatičeskie osobennosti russkoj reči potomkov èmigrantov 'pervoj volny' vo Francii." *Filologičeskie nauki* 4: 104–11.
———. 1995. *Russkij jazyk v "rassejanii": Očerki po jazyku russkoj èmigracii pervoj volny*. Mosow: Rossijskaja akademija nauk.
Haugen, Einar. [1953] 1969. *The Norwegian Language in America: A Study in Bilingual Behavior*. Bloomington, IN: Indiana University Press.
Huntington, W. Chapin. 1933. *The Homesick Million: Russia-out-of-Russia*. Boston, MA: The Stratford Company.
Jacobs, Dan N. and Ellen Frankel Paul, eds. 1981. *Studies of the Third Wave: Recent Migration of Soviet Jews to the United States*. Boulder, CO: Westview Press.
Kouzmin, Liudmila. 1988. "Language Use and Language Maintenance in two Russian Communities in Australia." *International Journal of the Sociology of Language* 72: 51–65.
Leighton, Lauren G. 1979. "The Third Emigration and the West." *Studies in Soviet Thought* 19 (4): 286–94.

Levkov, Ilya. 1984. "Adaptation and Acculturation of Soviet Jews in the United States: A Preliminary Analysis." In Robert O. Freedman (ed.), *Soviet Jewry in the Decisive Decade, 1971–1980*, 109–43. Durham, NC: Duke University Press.
Lewin-Epstein, Noah, Ro'i, Yaacov and Ritterband, Paul, eds. 1997. *Russian Jews on Three Continents: Migration and Resettlement*. London: Frank Cass.
Pfandl, Heinrich [Pfandl', Xajnrix]. 1994. "Russkojazyčnyj èmigrant tret'ej i četvertoj volny: Neskol'ko razmyšlenij." *Russkij jazyk za rubežom* 5–6: 101–8.
Paltiel, Ari M., Ethan F. Sabatello and Dorith Tal. 1997. "Immigrants from the Former USSR in Israel in the 1990s: Demographic Characteristics and Socio-economic Absorption." In Noah Lewin-Epstein, Yaacov Ro'i and Paul Ritterband (eds), *Russian Jews on Three Continents: Migration and Resettlement*, 284–321. London: Frank Cass.
Pierce, Richard A. 1999. "Russians." In *Encyclopedia of Canada's Peoples*. Multicultural Canada. Online: http://www.multiculturalcanada.ca/Encyclopedia/A-Z/r3/ (accessed 29 November 2011). [Print version in Paul Robert Magosci (ed.), *Encyclopedia of Canada's Peoples*. Toronto and Buffalo: University of Toronto Press.]
Raeff, Marc. 1990. *Russia Abroad: A Cultural History of the Russian Emigration, 1919–1939*. New York and Oxford: Oxford University Press.
Raymond, Boris and David R. Jones. 2000. *The Russian Diaspora, 1917–1941*. Lanham, MD and London: Scarecrow Press.
Remennick, Larissa. 2007. *Russian Jews on Three Continents: Identity, Integration, and Conflict*. New Brunswick and London: Transaction Publishers.
Ripp, Victor. 1984. *From Moscow to Main Street: Among the Russian Emigrés*. Boston and Toronto: Little, Brown and Co.
Ritterband, Paul. 1997. "Jewish Identity among Russian Immigrants in the US." In Noah Lewin-Epstein, Yaacov Ro'i and Paul Ritterband (eds), *Russian Jews on Three Continents: Migration and Resettlement*, 325–43. London: Frank Cass.
Ro'i, Yaacov. 1997. "Soviet Policy towards Jewish Emigration: An Overview." In Noah Lewin-Epstein, Yaacov Ro'i and Paul Ritterband (eds), *Russian Jews on Three Continents: Migration and Resettlement*, 45–67. London: Frank Cass.
Rothchild, Sylvia. 1985. *A Special Legacy: An Oral History of Soviet Jewish Emigrés in the United States*. New York: Simon and Schuster.
Salitan, Laurie P. 1997. "Ethnic and Related Factors in Soviet Emigration Policy, 1968–1989." In Noah Lewin-Epstein, Yaacov Ro'i and Paul Ritterband (eds), *Russian Jews on Three Continents: Migration and Resettlement*, 68–86. London: Frank Cass.
Shasha, Dennis and Marina Shron. 2002. *Red Blues: Voices from the Last Wave of Russian Immigrants*. New York and London: Holmes & Meier.
Simon, Rita J. 1997. *In the Golden Land: A Century of Russian and Soviet Jewish Immigration in America*. Westport, CT and London: Praeger.
Trier, Tom. 1996. "Reversed Diaspora: Russian Jewry, the Transition in Russia and the Migration to Israel." *Anthropology of East Europe Review* 14 (1): 34–43.
Vil'čur, M. 1914. *V amerikanskom gornile: Iz zapisok immigranta*. New York.
———. 1918. *Russkie v Amerike*. New York: Pervoe russkoe izdatel'stvo v Amerike.
Weinreich, Uriel. [1953] 1979. *Languages in Contact: Findings and Problems*. The Hague: Mouton.
Wells, H. B. 1932. "The Russian Language in the United States." *The American Mercury*, April: 448–51.
Zelenin, Aleksandr. 2007. *Jazyk russkoj èmigrantskoj pressy (1919–1939)*. Tampere: Tampere University Press.

Chapter 10

RUSSIAN LANGUAGE HISTORY IN CANADA. DOUKHOBOR INTERNAL AND EXTERNAL MIGRATIONS: EFFECTS ON LANGUAGE DEVELOPMENT AND STRUCTURE

Gunter Schaarschmidt
University of Victoria

I. Introduction

At present, there are about 30,000 Doukhobors in Canada (a higher estimate, i.e., 40,000, is given in Tarasoff 2002, ix): 12,300 in British Columbia; 8,000 in Saskatchewan; 3,000 in Alberta and the rest in other provinces (Popoff 1983, 117). Language maintenance among the Doukhobor population is estimated at about 60 percent, although this figure contains a large number of semi-speakers, especially among the younger generation (see Schaarschmidt 1998). The present linguistic analysis will concentrate on the effects the internal and external migrations of the Doukhobor community have had on the structure and development of the language beginning with the settlement in Milky Waters in 1802.[1] We shall present four synchronic slices in the development of Doukhobor Russian: (1) the formation stage of a compromise language in Milky Waters (Section III); (2) the leveling process in the Transcaucasian stage

---

[1] This chapter may at times use the terms "language," "style" and "dialect" interchangeably. Doukhobor Russian is a language with four functional styles while the Doukhobor "dialect" should be more adequately called "colloquial style" (see, in this respect, Schaarschmidt 2005). A general discussion on the interrelation between migration and linguistic analysis is beyond the scope of this chapter. An interesting case study can be found in King (1992).

(Section IV); (3) the development of three functional styles in the early years in Canada (Sections V and VI); and (4) the slow but inevitable erosion of these functional styles especially since the 1940s (Section VI).[2]

Even before the Doukhobors' mass emigration to Canada in 1899, their language was distinct from both Standard Russian and Russian dialects, first as a result of the resettlement from all parts of the Russian Empire to the Crimea, and later, the forced resettlement of the group from the Crimea to Transcaucasia, i.e., to an area with non-Slavic populations. These and other factors – including the interplay between the colloquial and ritual functional styles – set Doukhobor Russian in Canada apart not only from Doukhobor Russian in the Republic of Georgia but also from other types of émigré Russian in North America.

It must be said at the outset that in the diachronic description of an oral tradition, the investigator faces some special challenges (see, in this respect, Bouquiaux and Thomas 1992). The lack of a supradialectal written or literary language prevented the reallocation of norms well into the twentieth century. Thus, the oral form of literature (psalms, hymns, prayers, etc.) was often used in the colloquial language, and vice versa, elements of the colloquial language found their way into the ritual language.

The general diachronic outline of this chapter is based on Schaarschmidt (1995) but the data have been supplemented by what we know today about the formal properties of language variation and change as presented, for example, in Siegel (1985); Trudgill (1998); Trudgill et al. (2000) and Kerswill (2002).

II. The Doukhobors

The term *duxoborcy* seems to have been coined in 1786 by Nikifor, Archbishop of Slovenia (Inikova 2000, 2). Apparently, the term was initially used in a pejorative sense: Archbishop Ambrosius of the Russian Orthodox Church implied by the term that a group of dissident Russian peasants fought against the Spirit of God (Russian *dux* 'spirit,' *borec* 'wrestler'). The Doukhobors eventually adopted the term (also in a newer variant *duxobor*, with the feminine form *duxoborka*, and two alternate plural forms, viz., *duxobory* and *duxoborcy*), but understood it in the meaning "wrestling with and for the Spirit of God" (Popoff 1983, 113).

---

[2] The term "functional style" has its origin in the Prague school of linguistics (see Chloupek and Nekvapil 1987); however, the definition of "functional style" seems to be somewhat narrower than the terms "special language" or "scientific style/language" in the sense that its usage is often restricted to the written language, e.g., in Simeon (1969, 381).

The Doukhobors are not a religious sect; perhaps it would be more appropriate to label Doukhoborism as a "social movement" (Ewashen and Tarasoff 1994, 34). More importantly, however, Doukhoborism is a philosophy – the movement "inherited the spiritual tradition of Russian philosophical thought" (Momonova 1995, 6). The essence of the Doukhobor belief system has been summarized aptly by Vladimir Tchertkoff (1854–1936), co-founder with Leo Tolstoy and others of the publishing house *Posrednik* (The Intermediary) and Free Age Press. Tchertkoff was exiled to England in 1897 because of his publicizing of the Doukhobors' plight in the Caucasus. As there are many misconceptions about the Doukhobor belief system, it may be worth quoting an excerpt from Tchertkoff's summary (1900 [1993], 2):

> The foundation of the Doukhobors' teaching consists in the belief that the Spirit of God is present in the soul of man, and directs him by its word within him [...] Worshipping God in the spirit, the Doukhobors affirm that the outward Church and all that is performed in it and concerns it has no importance for them. The Church is where two or three are gathered together, i.e. united, in the name of Christ. They pray inwardly at all times [...] they assemble for prayer-meetings, at which they read prayers and sing hymns, or psalms as they call them [...] The teaching of the Doukhobors is founded on tradition. This tradition is called among them the "Book of Life," because it lives in their memory and hearts. It consists of psalms, partly formed out of the contents of the Old and New Testaments, partly composed independently [...] they hold all people equal, brethren. They extend this idea of equality also to the Government authorities; obedience to whom they do not consider binding upon them in those cases, rather than involving competing lexical items from different languages, when the demands of these authorities are in conflict with their conscience [...] They consider murder, violence, and in general all relations to living beings not based on love, as opposed to their conscience, and to the will of God. The Doukhobors are industrious and abstemious in their lives, and always truthful in their speech, accounting all lying a great sin.

III. The Formation of a Compromise Language

When Tsar Alexander decided to create a concentrated settlement of the Doukhobors in the area near the Moločna River (whence the English term "Milky Waters"), he also created the foundation for the rise of Doukhobor Russian, originally as a mixture of dialects, a sort of koine, later as a language with distinct functional styles.

Figure 10.1. Doukhobor settlements near the Moločna River in Tavria, Russia

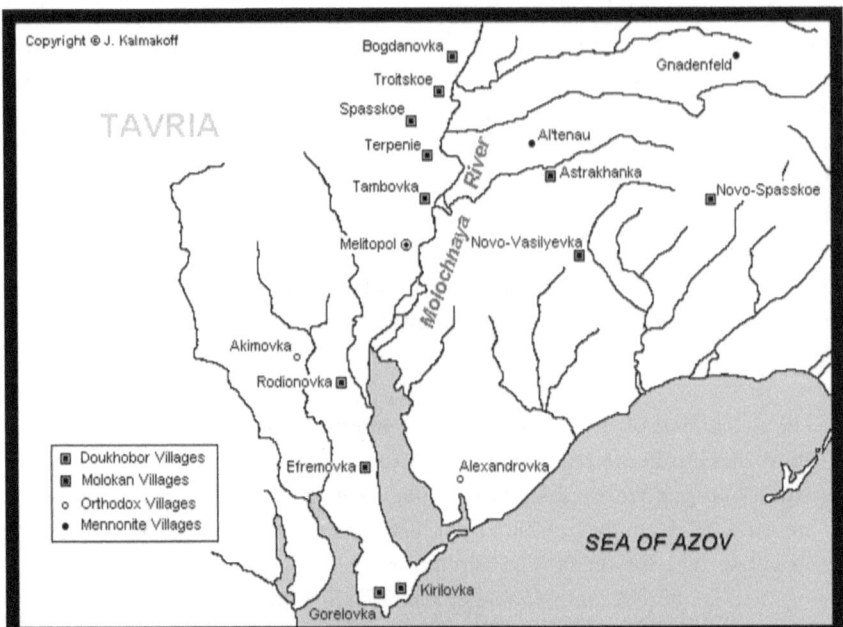

MOLOCHNAYA DOUKHOBOR SETTLEMENT
Melitpol district, Tavria province, Russia 1802–1845

This figure is reproduced by permission from the Doukhobor Genealogy Website (www.doukhobor.org). Copyright Jonathan J. Kalmakoff. All rights reserved.

According to Trudgill, new-dialect formation proceeds generally in three stages (quoted here from Kerswill 2002, 679):

Stage	Speakers involved	Linguistic characteristics
I	Adult migrants	Rudimentary leveling
II	First native-born speakers	Extreme variability and further leveling
III	Subsequent generations	Focusing, leveling and reallocation

There is a great deal of variability in the time-depth of koineization, with focusing possible already by Stage II, and the absence of focusing sometimes persisting over several generations of Stage III. In this section, we deal with Stage I, what Siegel calls the "pre-koine." This is the unstabilized stage at the beginning of koineization. A continuum exists in which various forms of the varieties in contact are used concurrently and inconsistently. Leveling and some mixing has begun to occur, and there may be various degrees of reduction, but few forms have emerged as the accepted compromise (Siegel 1985, 373).

Thus, after the resettlement from all areas of the Russian Empire, the Doukhobors found themselves in a concentrated settlement with various dialects being used side by side for daily communication purposes. The only uniting feature at this point was the ritual functional style (hereafter "ritual language" or "ritual style"). As we have no direct evidence of the Doukhobor colloquial functional style (hereafter "dialect" or "colloquial style") of this period or for a good one hundred years before the Canadian period, many of the features enumerated in the subsequent sections of this chapter are based on: (1) the evidence gleaned from interviews with second and third generation speakers in the 1950s and 1960s; (2) interference phenomena in the ritual language and (3) the experience gained in the internal reconstruction of other languages.[3] We can thus only assert for the Milky Waters period that rudimentary leveling was in process and that, because of the interruptions in this process caused by the migrations to Transcaucasia and Canada, the leveling process took longer than it normally takes for a non-migrant community of speakers.

IV. Resettlement to Transcaucasia

Tsar Alexander's benevolent attitude towards the Doukhobors was replaced by his successors: Tsar Nicholas's decision to force them into submission. A contemporary writer and eyewitness from Estonia, who had received a grant from the Governor of the Caucasus to travel in the area and was thus quite biased, describes the situation (Petzholdt 1867, 104–5; my translation):

> But, as I already indicated, various excesses on their part forced the government that was otherwise very tolerant in religious matters to take severe measures against these sects. As a consequence of these measures all Doukhobors and a large part of the Molokans were exiled to Transcaucasia in the years 1841 and 1842. Only those who saw their wrong ways and became converted to the correct faith by entering into the bosom of the Orthodox Church were allowed to remain in their old settlements and in the possession of their estates.

---

3 In recent years, several eyewitness travelogues in German describing the Doukhobor settlements in Tavria (Schlatter 1836) and Transcaucasia (von Paucker 1865; Petzholdt 1867) have been discovered and translated into English. With the possible exception of von Paucker, none of the three had any comments on the linguistic structure of Doukhobor Russian. Von Paucker made a few sociolinguistic comments by presenting Doukhobors' forms of address in German translation – he was an established Russian linguist and spoke Russian fluently (von Paucker 1885, 49–51).

The deserted villages were resettled with crown estate peasants from other areas (Ukraine, Central Russia) while the exiled were assigned land in various areas of Transcaucasia for the construction of new villages. Since they had been sent to the Caucasus as a punishment, it goes without saying that they were not assigned the most fertile lands; on the contrary, they received in part very inhospitable areas and were forced to adjust to the conditions as well as they could.

We may assume that this period marked the continuation of Stage I, i.e., the rudimentary leveling process, but also the beginning of Stage II with the first

Figure 10.2. Doukhobor settlements in the Caucasus, Russia

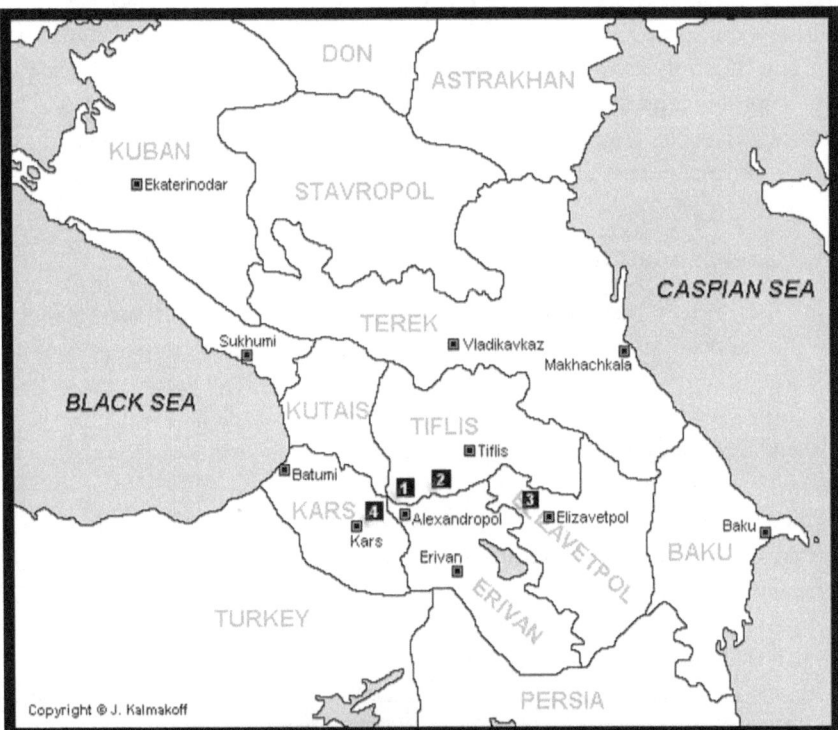

DOUKHOBOR SETTLEMENTS IN THE CAUCASUS, RUSSIA, 1841–1899

1. Akhalkalaki district, Tiflis province (modern Georgia)
2. Borchalin district, Tiflis province (modern Georgia)
3. Kedabek district, Elizavetpol province (modern Azerbaijan)
4. Zarushat/Shuragel districts, Kars province (modern Turkey)

This figure is reproduced by permission from the Doukhobor Genealogy Website (www.doukhobor.org). Copyright Jonathan J. Kalmakoff. All rights reserved.

native-born speakers showing extreme variability and further leveling. By the time adult speakers migrated to Canada in 1899, both the variability and the leveling were part of their dialect and were, to some extent, reflected in the ritual style. The features enumerated below are based on interviews with speakers in their 60s and 70s, i.e., those who migrated from Transcaucasia to Canada (see also Harshenin 1961).

IV.1. Loans from non-Slavic languages

Many such loans are contained in Tarasoff (1963) although it is not always clear whether they are actually general loans in Russian, as exemplified by the apparent Doukhobor loan from Turkic *džiranka* 'deer', for which there exist the Standard Russian variants *džejran*, *dzeren* and *zeren/zerenka*, referring, however, to a kind of antelope (see Fasmer 1964–73, I: 510–11; II: 95). The Doukhobor language in present-day Georgia also contains many loans from the adjacent or co-territorial non-Slavic languages (Beženceva 2007, 123–6), but here again many assumed Doukhobor loans may in fact also be loans in Standard Russian or internationalisms, as exemplified by *mazun* 'matzoon/madzoon' (a type of yoghurt), cf. Standard Russian *maconi*, borrowed from Armenian.

IV.2. Phonemic variability

This refers first and foremost to the lack of palatalization as in Belarusian or Ukrainian, e.g.:[4] *redko* 'rarely': [retka]/[r'edka]; *kisa* 'pussy-cat': [kysa]/[kisa]/[k'isa]; *krest* 'cross' [krest]/[kr'est]/[xrest]/[xr'est]; the lowering of *i > y*, see *kisa*; the vacillation between *g* and *h* (or voiced γ), e.g.: *gora* 'mountain': [gora]/[gara]/[hara]/[hora]/[γara]/[γora]; the alternation in the phonetic representation of unstressed *e* and *o*, e.g.: *nesu* 'I am carrying': [n'esu]/[n'isu]/[n'asu]/[nesu] and the foregoing example *gora*; the variation *f/xv*, e.g.: *sapfirnyj* 'sapphire' [saxvirnyj]/[saxvernyj]/[safirnyj]/[samfirnyj].

IV.3. Morphological variability

Examples here include the loss of the desinence of the third person singular of verbs as well as the generalization of the desinence *-ov* in the genitive

---

[4] The forms in italics are graphemic representations while the forms in square brackets are broad phonetic representations. Where only graphemic representations are given, it is understood that the phonetic representations are irrelevant to the argument.

plural for all genders, e.g.: *xodit/ xodit'/ xodi;*[5] *lamp/ lampov; okon/ oknov* (the latter has also been observed in the speech of Russian migrants elsewhere; see, e.g., Zemskaja 2001, 90).[6]

IV.4. Lexical variability

We may cite here the triple variation *bystro/ šibko/ švidko* 'quickly,' but in most cases, rather than involving competing lexical items from different languages, there is typically a lexical preference for colloquial terms, such as *puzo* for *život* 'belly, stomach,' *snoska* for *jajco* 'egg,' *skrost'* for *vezde* 'everywhere,' *dosel'* for *očen' davno* 'a long time ago,' or *kabyt'* for *kažetsja* 'it seems.'

IV.5. Syntactic variability

We note here the loss of the use of oblique cases with numeral expressions, e.g.: *okolo dvux časov/ okolo dva časa* 'around two o'clock,' and the replacement of the plural imperative with the second person plural indicative: *vzyjdite/ vzojdëte* 'enter!/ you will enter'; *stan'te/ stanete* 'get up!/ you will get up' (see also VI.5.4. below).

An apparent Doukhobor Russian innovation is the replacement of the neuter gender by the feminine gender in the first generation (and its parents) and the second generation (Inikova 1995, 156). The loss of the neuter gender may have been caused by the coalescence of unstressed *o, a, e* in post-tonic desinences and that coalescence was then extended to stressed endings and modifiers, i.e., correctly *èta žába* 'this toad': (phonetically) *èta sála* 'this lard,' therefore *mojá žába* 'my toad': **mojá sála* 'my lard.' This coalescence can be seen widely in the Anglicization of place-names, such as *Ootischenia*, a locality in Castlegar, BC, referred to in a modern spelling *Ooteshenie* in Tarasoff (2002, 470), cf. Russian *utešenie* 'consolation.'

IV.6. Sociolinguistic variability

The politeness pronoun *vy*, which seems to have been modeled on French in Standard Russian, was rejected by the Doukhobors who "believed on religious

---

5 The omission of the third person present tense suffix is found in the Russian dialects of the Nikolaevsk region (see, in this respect, Barannik and Miževskaja 1986, 122). Perhaps, then, the influence of Ukrainian merely reinforced a latent tendency.

6 The generalization of the ending *-ov* in the genitive plural has also been observed in Russian dialects (see, for example, Barannik and Miževskaja 1986, 52–3). This is thus a latent tendency in order to simplify the morphology of the genitive plural which is the most complex of Russian cases with five possible ending suffixes, i.e., *-ov, -ev, -ëv, -ej, -Ø*.

grounds that all men should be treated equally linguistically and socially" (Vanek and Darnell 1971, 272). Thus, *vy* for them was always plural, never singular; they would accept *ty est' xorošij xlopčik/vy est' xorošie xlopčiki* 'thou art a fine fellow/you are fine fellows' but not **vy est' xorošij xlopčik* 'you are a fine fellow.'

V. Emigration to Canada

The year 1895 marked an important milestone in the roughly 165-year-old history of the Doukhobor movement: a symbolic burning of firearms in the village of Orlovka in Transcaucasia, an area to which the Doukhobors had been exiled from the Crimea by Tsar Nicholas I. This pacifist challenge to

Figure 10.3. Early Doukhobor settlements in Saskatchewan

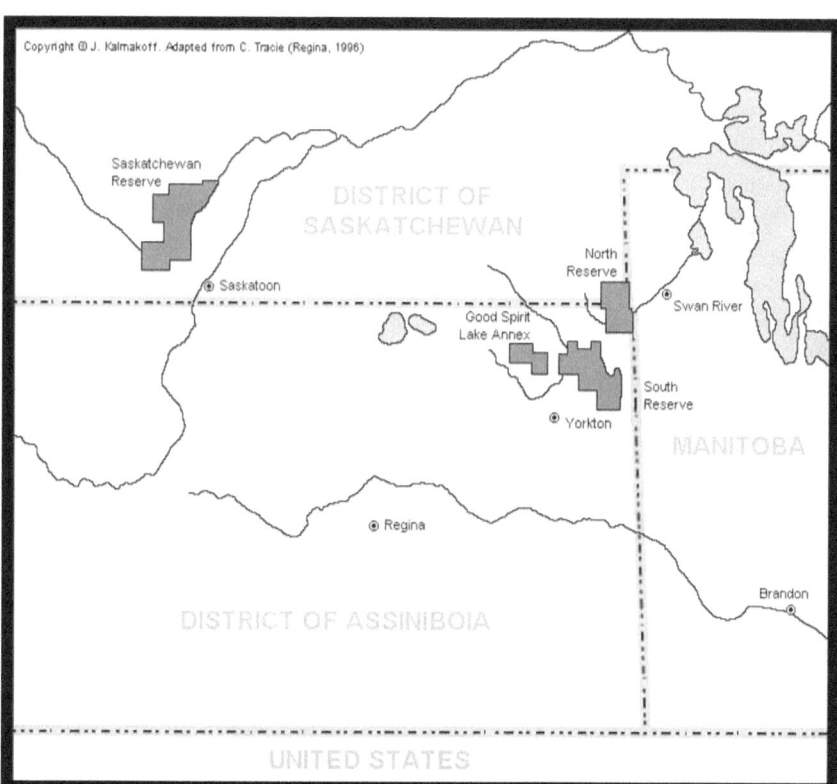

DOUKHOBOR RESERVES SASKATCHEWAN, 1899

This figure is reproduced by permission from the Doukhobor Genealogy Website (www.doukhobor.org). Copyright Jonathan J. Kalmakoff. All rights reserved.

the authorities a few years after the introduction of general conscription in Transcaucasia, constituted the proverbial glove thrown at Tsar Nicholas II. The latter promptly responded by launching a massive persecution campaign against the Doukhobors with the avowed goal of their extermination. This campaign would no doubt have succeeded if not for the intervention by Leo Tolstoy and Quaker friends in England who came up with the funds to organize a mass emigration of 7,500 Doukhobors (approximately one third of the total Doukhobor population in Russia at the time) to Canada in 1899. In Canada, the Doukhobors established 61 villages in what was later to become the province of Saskatchewan (Ewashen and Tarasoff 1994, 17–18).

V.1. Reinforcement of Ukrainian features

This migrant period saw the conclusion of Stage II as well as the beginning of Stage III. Focusing, i.e., the selection of one of the competing forms, was considerably impeded by the influence of the language of the "Galicians," i.e., of Ukrainian.[7] In terms of the process of reallocation, this period also saw the refunctionalization of social and linguistic forms of language to establish initially three and eventually four norms of Doukhobor Russian (see, in more detail, Section VI below).

The reinforcement of the Ukrainian language influence is seen in particular in the re-establishment of Ukrainian features such as the ones listed in Section IV above. An interesting example in this respect is the intrusion of such features in the ritual functional style, for example in the psalm entitled "Against Appendicitis" recorded in Veregin, Saskatchewan, in 1970 (Mealing 1972, 299–300). This psalm contains the line: *Na gore na okejane na vysokom vikijane...* 'on the mountain, on the ocean, on the high?' The form *vikijane* has puzzled translators who left it untranslated or marked it with a question mark (Mealing 1972, 299). It does look like a hypercorrect Ukrainian version of *okean* with prosthetic *v* and *o* > *i* in a closed syllable, like in correct Ukrainian *vikno* 'window,' cf. Russian *okno*. It must be remembered here that hymnody was passed on orally from generation to generation, and to facilitate memorization, psalms resorted to well-known rhetorical devices, such as repetition and alliteration. Meaning in this case was generally sacrificed in favor of sound (see, in particular, Schaarschmidt 2008a, 116–17). Ukrainian influence can also be seen in the spelling of certain place-names, personal names and the names of holidays or festivities. Perhaps most noteworthy in this respect is the place-name *Veregin* in Saskatchewan. This name is of course based on *Verigin*

---

[7] Young (1931, 35) reports cases of intermarriage between Doukhobors and Ukrainians.

with *e* showing the Ukrainian lowering of original *i*. For the same reason, the term for 'commemorative feasts' is often spelled *pomenki* instead of *pominki*.

V.2. English influence

In this migrant period the influence of Canadian English was generally restricted to the area of loan words in the work domain and in the interchange with Canadian authorities (see, in this respect, Tchertkoff 1900; Harshenin 1964, 1967).

Figure 10.4. Doukhobor settlements in British Columbia

DOUKHOBOR SETTLEMENT AREAS IN BRITISH COLUMBIA, 1908–1938

This figure is reproduced by permission from the Doukhobor Genealogy Website (www.doukhobor.org). Copyright Jonathan J. Kalmakoff. All rights reserved.

VI. Move to British Columbia

In 1907 the Canadian government insisted on the individual filing of homesteads (anathema to the Doukhobors' communal life) and on an oath of allegiance to the king (in conflict with their conscience concerning authorities). As a result, 5,000 Doukhobors moved to British Columbia between the years 1908–13 where they purchased land from private owners, an act that did not require an oath of allegiance.

The move to a relatively secluded area in British Columbia free from Ukrainian interference, allowed the Doukhobor community to conclude Stage III, i.e., the focusing, leveling and reallocation of linguistic features resulting in the demarcation of three functional styles: the colloquial language, the ritual language, the written language and eventually Canadian English.

VI.1. Colloquial style

This in essence refers to the South Russian dialect koine that the Doukhobors maintained well into our days as the primary means of communication at home and generally in the private sphere (see, especially, Schaarschmidt 1995). There is no doubt that the past 40 years have considerably reduced the maintenance rate of the dialect due to what is known in sociolinguistics as "language planning." Compulsory schooling and, ironically, the inclusion of Russian, viz. Standard Russian in the curriculum have resulted in some form of language planning. This process is generally deemed necessary in modern society in spite of the fact that there is no proof that a speech community that is not "modern" must by necessity lack linguistic maturity and a rich language differentiation (a paraphrase of Jernudd 1972, 56). Canadian educational authorities did their best to impress upon the Doukhobors that "with the absence of a formalized, *written* body of literature, their way of life was void of cultural content" (Friesen 1995, 143, emphasis in original). Of course, the Doukhobors were not alone in this process of cultural discrimination on the part of school authorities. The First Nations people in British Columbia shared the same fate, and the result of this denigration of their oral tradition was a concomitant decline in language maintenance.

The Doukhobor dialect is considered by many of the frequent visitors from Russia to be archaic and somewhat "contrived" and "incomplete" (Golubeva-Monatkina 1997, 35). This heterostereotype downgrading amplified the Doukhobor speakers' autostereotype perception of their dialect as not being genuine Russian, but a form of Ukrainian. Concerning the assumed Ukrainian influence on Doukhobor Russian, one must carefully distinguish between South Russian dialectal features that are shared with Ukrainian dialects and genuine Ukrainianisms not found in South Russian dialects. Thus, the assumed Ukrainian origin for the Doukhobor pronunciation of Standard Russian *g* as *h* (Vanek and Darnell 1971, 289) can be rejected on the basis of a detailed phonological description of the dialect which actually shows either *h* or γ in free variation.

VI.2. Ritual style

The notion "ritual style" refers to the entire set of psalms, hymns and prayers including the "constitution" of the Doukhobors as laid down in the "Book of Life." Although hymnody was not free from influences of the colloquial style as well as from both non-Russian and non-Slavic interference, the ritual style has been the constant in the various migrations (see, especially, Schaarschmidt 2008a). It was also the uniting feature of the Saskatchewan Doukhobors, i.e., those who did not join the move to British Columbia, and the British Columbia Doukhobors.

Singing is very important for the Doukhobor community. In essence, the psalms and prayers contain the main elements of a tradition that is not otherwise fixed in a written form. These oral works are composed in a very ancient Russian Church Slavonic form of language that is often no longer comprehensible even to educated members of the community. In the last 40 years, since the inception of compulsory schooling, many of the psalms and prayers have been recorded in written form and have been translated into English. Until that time, most of them were learnt by heart and enriched with regional elements (for the most part, Ukrainianisms). As Sulerzhitsky (1982, 99) puts it:

> The Sunday reciting of psalms, besides having an instructive, prayerful significance, is at the same time an ongoing corrective process. If someone reciting a psalm makes an error, not only of a word, but even in the order of words having no significance, he will be sure to be corrected by one or sometimes more voices. In the main, the base of the Doukhobor dogma – their view of the world – is stated in the psalms.

The psalms embody a large part of the Doukhobor belief system, somewhat like a basic religious "constitution" (Mealing 1975, 51), as in the set of ten psalms entitled "From the Common Views of the Christian Community of Universal Brotherhood," one of which (no. 5) is given below with an interlinear and a free translation (some of the words have been corrected; it is not clear whether these words were typing errors in Mealing's work, or whether they were handed down orally in this way and lost some of their grammar).

Mir	*sostoit*	*iz*	*dviženija;*	*vsë*	*stremitsja*	*k*
World	consists	from	movement;	all	strives	to

soveršenstvu	*i*	*čerez*	*ètot*	*process*	*staraetsja*
perfection	and	through	this	process	it strives

soedinit'sja	*so*	*svoim*	*načalom,*	*kak*	*by*
to unite	with	its	beginning	as	if

vozvratit'	*sozrevšij*	*plod*	*semeni.*
to return	having ripened	fruit	to seed

'The world is based upon going forward; all things strive for perfection, and through this process seek to rejoin their source, as ripe fruit yields seeds [probably incorrectly in Mealing 1975, 53: "as seeds yield ripe fruit"].'

The psalms also reveal a great deal about the linguistic evolution of Doukhobor Russian; the Doukhobors' oral tradition was composed primarily in a form of Russian Church Slavonic (not Old Church Slavonic, as suggested by Mealing 1972, 16–17, or stylized Russian as claimed at least for recitative psalms, by Harshenin 1964, 39n3). Even though they are composed in Russian Church Slavonic, they have picked up elements of colloquial Doukhobor Russian in their long oral tradition. Thus, a linguistic analysis can aid a great deal in elucidating many of the "obscure" passages or words that have defied translation or analysis. The following excerpt from the psalm "The Trumpets Speak with Thunder" will serve to illustrate this point (Mealing 1972, 216–7).

Ot	*Ioanna*	*Bogoslova;*	*ot*	*gromova*	*syna...*
From	John	God's word	from	thunder	son.

Evangelie	*evangel'skoe.*	*Prijdëmte*	*vo*	*blaga,*
Gospel	Evangelist	Let us come	into	goods

saxvernogo (?)	*vosxvalim.*
sapphire one	we sing praise

'From [the time of] John the speaker-of-God, from [the time of] the Son of Thunder...the Evangelist's Gospel [my translation; Mealing has "Evangelist of the Gospel"]. Let us come [Mealing has "we come"] into riches [Mealing has, quite incorrectly, "we faithful ones"], to the Sapphire one we sing praise.'

The phrase *saxvernogo vosxvalim* has puzzled the analysts because of the *xv* in *saxvernogo* (for discussion, see Mealing 1972, 217, fn. 3); as surmised by Bonč-Bruevič (1909 [1954]: 239), the correct form of this word in Russian would be *safirnogo/ sapfirnogo*, an adjective based on the noun *sa(p)fir* 'Sapphire' (Fasmer 1964–73, III:566). The *xv* in the form found in the psalm is easily explained: the phoneme *f* in Doukhobor Russian alternates freely with *xv* (see also Harshenin 1961, 64).

VI.3. Written style

Although almost synonymous with the Standard Russian literary language, the written style as it slowly evolved among the Doukhobors in the 1930s shows many features of the colloquial style (see, in this respect, Golubeva-Monatkina 1995; 2004, 359–76). As late as the 1940s, those few Doukhobors that were able to read and write fulfilled the function of scribes for the rest of the population (see, for example, Malov 1948, 207). Illiteracy in Russia was high – at the rate of 80 percent as late as 1897 (Rašin 1951), so it is not surprising that very few Doukhobors learned how to read and write. As Petr N. Malov writes: "with very few exceptions, the Doukhobors did not write books, nor did they keep systematic records of their history. They preferred to make history and let others write about it" (1948, 6; my translation).

VI.4. Canadian English

During the first decade of the Doukhobors' stay in Canada, Canadian English had a low functionality. Massive borrowings from English are of a relatively recent date – after all, the Doukhobors had come to Canada "to preserve the cultural identity of which their language is an intimate part" (Harshenin 1964, 39).[8] Thus, they borrowed from English what was absolutely essential to their work environment, i.e., terms relating to the railroad, sawmills, gadgets, units of measure and money (see the list compiled by Harshenin 1967, 216–30). The situation changed radically with the passing of the Community Regulation Act in British Columbia in 1914. The Act, among other things, mandated "regular attendance at school of all children between the ages of seven and fourteen" (Tarasoff 2002, 32). Since the schooling of the children in English also involved the parents who were at that time largely monolingual, the functionality of this style began to cut into the domain of the colloquial style. This in turn led to the beginnings of code switching, i.e.,

---

8 The Doukhobor migrants shared this emphasis on language maintenance with other forms of émigré Russian, such as the first wave of Russian émigrés after the Bolshevik Revolution of 1917 (see, in this respect, Polinsky and Pereltsvaig 2003, 4).

the switching in mid-sentence from one language to the other. To be sure, this was a gradual and very slow development since the emphasis on using Russian was still prevalent and reinforced by Russian-language instruction at home, in special schools and eventually as part of the Russian-language curriculum in elementary and high schools as well as at the kindergarten level.

The Doukhobors did not emigrate to Canada in order to learn English. Quite the contrary: they expected to continue to use Russian in Canada, educate their children in Russian and, for the large majority of them, maintain their dialect as well as their ritual language. When their spiritual leader Peter Verigin stated in a letter to Leo Tolstoy, "teaching literacy to the children, including the girls, must be considered a priority right at the start," he had in mind literacy in Russian, not in English (Donskov 1995, 43). However, as early as 1900, there arose a need for a grammar of English for Russian speakers to satisfy needs beyond workplace and trading contacts with Anglophone Canadians. The author of this grammar, Anna Tchertkoff, wife of Vladimir Tchertkoff (see Section II, above) subtitled this grammar as being aimed at the "Russian settlers in America" (Anna Tchertkoff 1900, ii). In her preface, she writes that she wrote the grammar in response to demands by the Doukhobors having settled in Canada.

A Canadian writer was able to make fun in her generally somewhat biased diary of the heavily accented English spoken by the Doukhobors in the late 1930s (O'Neail 1962, 104). The passage she quotes shows typical Russian interference phenomena, such as palatalization before front vowels (*monya* 'money,' *gyet* 'get,' *Nyelson* 'Nelson'); rendering short vowels in a stressed syllable as long vowels (*mawnt'* 'month,' *t'eengs* 'things,' *mawder* 'mother'); *t'* (aspirated *t*) for voiceless *th* (*mawnt'*, *t'eengs*), and *d* for voiced *th* (*dot* 'that,' *mawder*); and the postpositioning of the possessive, an archaism in Russian but typical of Doukhobor speech (*mawder-my* 'my mother') (see also Schaarschmidt 2010, 35–6). When Hazel O'Neail returned to the area in 1962, i.e., 24 years later, she was able to note that "the old accent lingers in some cases, though not nearly as pronounced, and in many I caught not a trace at all. Further, the offensive 'and' which used to preface every remark [...] seems to have disappeared altogether" (O'Neail 1962, 141). Today, more than one generation later, only Doukhobors in their eighties and nineties show traces of an accent in English. All others speak a Canadian English of the Western variety, and for most of them English is becoming their first language.

VI.5. Russian retreats

VI.5.1. Marginalization of the colloquial style

During the first years in Canada, children learned Russian at home, and exposure to English was minimal. After mandatory schooling in English was introduced, Russian instruction began to be taught in special classes after school and in the evenings using the so-called *bukvari* 'primers' from the old country (Tarasoff 2002, 32). By the early 1980s, government-funded Russian language programs both in kindergarten and schools up to grade 12 became established in British Columbia (Tarasoff 2000, 60). The University of Victoria in British Columbia organized workshops at Selkirk College in Castlegar, where Russian language and folklore were taught to aid in the training of Russian-language teachers.

While the continuing ritual-style practices and organized instruction in Russian clearly staved off the decline of Russian-language competence, they also furthered the marginalization of the colloquial style. The Doukhobor colloquial style is not yet extinct since there is still at least one generation around that practiced it as the language at home until as late as the 1940s and beyond. Revitalizing this style will face the enormous challenge of competition with the Standard Russian (Moscow) colloquial language, and Doukhobor Russian will thus probably wither away quietly with the passing of third-generation speakers.

VI.5.2. Translations of ritual texts into English

The ritual language continues to flourish if only because of the various festivals, prayer meetings, funerals and other traditional events. However, translations of ritual texts are often used these days instead of the oral Russian versions at these events. The reasons for this are to be sought in part in the linguistic complexity of ritual texts, in part in audience-specific considerations, i.e., if the audience is mainly English (tourist groups, etc.), the English translations are most likely to be presented. Nonetheless, at the festivals and *pominki* (commemorative feasts) that the author of the present contribution attended in Castlegar in the last five or six years, many attendees were singing the texts by heart, while others were using text sheets in Russian as an aid (see also Inikova 1995, 158). The many local choirs as well as choirs formed in cities such as Vancouver and Victoria quite often present mixed Russian-English programs and in singing the Russian psalms, they are often unclear about the precise meaning of certain words or passages (the trained Slavic linguistics specialist is then often consulted and is able to help in identifying the precise meaning).

VI.5.3. Standardization of ritual texts

Because of the above-mentioned obscure passages in ritual texts, the latter are nowadays often presented in standardized versions where "standardized" here means "brought in line with the Standard Russian literary language." Such standardized versions are published regularly in the monthly *Iskra*. These efforts reinforce the knowledge of Russian among present-day Doukhobors but they do not appeal to the large number of members that have, in effect, become monolingual in English (knowing a few Russian words and expressions here and there). For the latter, only English translations or possibly, code-switched variants will do the job.

VI.5.4. Code switching in ritual style

VI.5.4.1. "Psalm No. 166"

A free translation of the entire psalm can be found in Mealing (1989, 126–7) where he also provides the following introductory remarks:

> This beautiful psalm (whose imagery recalls the Baltic exile, self-imposed, of many *skopcy* and *xlysty* [radical sectarians]) symbolizes the experience of suffering believers as a journey, against hard odds set by the Lord, to a mystical Jerusalem. Three speakers appear: a narrator, who sets the stage and records actions; the young men, witnessing believers; and the Lord. Tribulations are symbolized both by the human and anti-Christian opposition of the Antiochus figure, and by threatening natural objects and forces. The youths have two duties: to press against opposition and to wait in patience. The "ship of Noah" appears in the NT as a type of salvation through both righteous acts and faithful witness (I Peter 3, 20–22).

Most of the obscure passages and Russian words or expressions in ritual texts are due to four factors:

1. the basic Russian Church Slavonic structure of Doukhobor hymnody;
2. the mnemonic devices typical of an oral tradition that in order to be handed on from generation to generation required the extensive use of repetitions and alliterations;
3. the non-Russian and non-Slavic incursions due either to the neighboring communities that the Doukhobors encountered in their migration history or to biblical references;
4. the apparent incursions of the colloquial style.

It will be sufficient here to show the workings of all four of the above factors in an excerpt from "Psalm No. 166" which we will present in what seems to be an original version with a free translation taken from Mealing (1995, ii). An interlinear translation of the excerpt can be found in Schaarschmidt (2008a, 46–7). The numbers in parentheses in the text refer to one or more of the four factors listed above and detailed in Section VI.5.4.2.

Mladye (1, 4) moi junoši, vy projdëte lesy tëmnye, vzyjdite (1, 4) na gory krutye, pristupite (4) k morju černomu, stan'te (4) že vy na Noev korabl' (3). Bujny (1) vetry sbuševalis' (2), čërno (1) more vskolyxalos' (2). Slëzno vosplakalis' (2) mladye (1) junoši pered Gospodom: Gospodi! Gospodi! Počto dopustil bujnye vetry buševat' (2), morskie volny volnovat (2), čërno (1) more kolyxat' (2), čto nel'zja projti v Tvoj Erusalim-grad (1, 3) posmotret' tam velik (1) stolb ognennyj. On že vozsijaet ot zemli i (4) do neba.

[My young men, you will go on through shadowy forests, you will go up into lofty mountains, you will come to the gloomy sea, you will embark in Noah's ship. The wild winds were uproarious, the dark sea was stirred up. The young men wept bitter tears before the Lord: Lord, Lord! Why allow the wild winds to rage, the waves of the sea to billow up, the dark sea to heave? It is impossible for us to come to your Jerusalem-town, there to look at the great fiery pillar, it shines from earth to heaven.]

VI.5.4.2. Analysis

The numbers in parentheses in the following analysis follow the four factors listed above and refer to those in the text above.

(1) *Mladye* 'young': this appears to be a Church Slavonicism as Russian colloquial style has *molodye*; the other possibility is that it is a reduced form of *molodye* with the first of the two unstressed vowels eliding; this theory would receive some support if another example can be shown to be due to vowel reduction (see (4) below).
vzyjdite 'you will rise': a Church Slavonic form for Russian *vzojdëte*; the suffix *-ite* would point to an imperative plural form, however, one might assume that the stress was on the root as in Russian *vyjdete* with resulting vowel reduction *e > i* (see (4) below).
bujny vetry 'wild winds,' *čërno more* 'black sea,' *velik stolb* 'great pillar': short-form adjectives are not used in an attributive position in Russian but were used in this way in Church Slavonic.
Erusalim-grad 'Jerusalem-town': *grad* is the Church Slavonic form of Russian *gorod*.
(2) The alternation of the perfective reflexives *sbuševalis'* 'were raging'; *vskolyxalos'* 'was heaving,' *vosplakalis'* 'were crying out' with the imperfective infinitives *buševat'* 'to rage,' *volnovat'* 'to become ruffled,' *kolyxat'* 'to heave' is a good example of the kinds of mnemonic devices employed in folk poetry and in the psalms with their parallelisms and alliterations. The symmetry is not perfect, as shown by the contrast *vosplakalis'* vs. *volnovat'*, with meaning sacrificed to the alliteration *volny volnovat'* 'to ripple waves.'

(3) Bits of biblical onomastics are thrown in to add to the volume of heaving water (*Noev korabl'* 'Noah's ark') or to emphasize the desired place of destination (*Erusalim-grad* 'the city of Jerusalem').
(4) The apparent mixing of second-person plural and imperative plural suffixes (*projdëte* 'you will pass,' *pristupite* 'you will step to' vs. *vzyjdite* 'you will rise,' *stan'te* 'you will board') may reflect the colloquial style unless the latter two can be explained in terms of vowel reduction. The conjunction *i* in the phrase *ot zemli i do neba*, lit. 'from the earth and to the sky' might convey the meaning 'even,' i.e., emphasis, but it could also be a reflection of the repetitive conjoining of clauses in the colloquial style as transferred into the Doukhobors' still incomplete English in the 1930s as noted by O'Neail (1961, 141).

VI.5.4.3. Code switching

We have attempted to demonstrate elsewhere the irrecoverable losses involved in the translation into English of psalms like "Psalm No. 166" (see Schaarschmidt 2008a, 47–9). It is also true, of course, that imperatives and irregular verb conjugations can place a heavy burden on a young generation of language learners. But what if one were to allow code switching, i.e., the shifting in mid-sentence from one language to another, in ritual style in the same way that it occurs in the colloquial style of Russian-English bilinguals? Such a code-switched version retaining most if not all of the mnemonic devices and cultural-content onomastics of "Psalm No. 166" might look as follows (repeated here from Schaarschmidt 2008a, 115):

> *Mladye moi junoši*, you will go on through *lesy tëmnye*, you will go up into *gory krutye*, you will come to *morju čërnomu*, you will embark in *Noev korabl'*.
> *Bujny vetry sbuševalis', čërno more vskolyxalos'. Mladye junoši vosplakalis'* before the Lord: Lord, Lord! Why allow *bujnye vetry buševat', morskie volny volnovat', čërno more kolyxat'*? It is impossible for us to come to your *Erusalim-grad*, there to look at the *velik stolb ognennyj*, it shines from earth to heaven.

We thus rest our case here trying to provide an alternative to the full-scale translating of Doukhobor psalmistry. Perhaps this alternative, rather than the either-or question of Russian vs. English, will also "contribute to new ways for Doukhobor identity to be figured, perhaps enabling Doukhoborism to survive into the second century dating from its arrival in Canada" (Rak 2004, 54). Another question we might have to look into one of these days is whether, given complete free translations of the psalms into English, such as the one given above for "Psalm No. 166", these are in fact memorizable in the same way that the Church Slavonic psalms have been handed down orally for hundreds of years.

VII. Conclusion and Outlook

The present chapter has concentrated on the effects of the various migrations of the Doukhobor community on language structure and development. The effect of these migrations alone set Doukhobor Russian apart from other forms of émigré Russian in North America. There is neither time nor space here to enter into the details of the similarities and divergences of Doukhobor Russian but in addition to external and internal migrations we may enumerate the following: (1) the largely oral tradition; (2) its relative geographic isolation and thus cohesiveness; (3) the deliberate resistance to the influence of Canadian English; and (4) the reinforcement of Ukrainian features in the language during the first generation of settlement in Saskatchewan. Each one of these features deserves a more thorough investigation and comparison with other heritage languages.

We have argued elsewhere, for example, that the oral tradition or the ritual style have been instrumental in aiding the preservation of the colloquial language (Schaarschmidt 2008a). This seems to be at variance with reports that an insistence on carrying out ritual functions exclusively in Russian has had the effect of lowering language maintenance (Gerber 1985, 100–8). In the Doukhobor community, too, there are views that one can "find something deeply present in such potent texts, even through the mask of translation" (Mealing 1995, 41). An even stronger view seems to be prevalent among the younger generation of Doukhobors, i.e., 29 years or younger, who do not see a causal relation between the use of Russian and the maintenance of the Doukhobors' culture and belief systems (Friesen and Verigin 1996, 147). Similarly, the cohesiveness and geographic isolation of a heritage language community may not be as important a factor as is commonly thought (see, for example, the case of an Estonian community in the US in Walko 1989, 140–7).

Perhaps, as in many studies of empirical phenomena that are not scientifically testable in terms, for example, of crucial experiments, the truth is a gray area rather than a question of black and white. For Doukhobor Russian for example, ritual functions could be carried out in a code-switched variety of hymnody (see also Schaarschmidt 2008b), and cohesion and geographic isolation vs. dispersion may not be as important factors in the age of the Internet.[9]

Views such as the ones referred to above regarding the value of ritual texts in translation and the downplaying of Russian in the maintenance of

---

9 See, in this respect, the website of the Union of Spiritual Communities of Christ (USCC) (http://www.usccdoukhobors.org), the Spirit Wrestlers website hosted by Koozma J. Tarasoff (http://www.spirit-wrestlers.com), the website of the monthly *Iskra (Voice of the Doukhobors)* with a respectable song collection (http://www.iskra.ca), and the Doukhobor Genealogy Website run by Jonathan J. Kalmakoff (http://www.doukhobor.org [all four last accessed 22 November 2011]).

cultural and ritual activities do not seem to bode well for the future of the Doukhobor Russian language. However, it seems there are at least an equal number of persons who seek to maintain the ritual language in Russian and perhaps even to revitalize the colloquial language even though the latter may be closer to the Standard Russian variety. The important thing is that "supporting a minority group's efforts to hang on for one or two more generations might prove central to future revitalization efforts" (Dorian 1994, 801). Like in the case of many other heritage languages or of First Nations languages, this means to support the "incomplete acquisition" of such languages resulting in one or two generations of "semi-speakers" of Doukhobor Russian (see, for the notion "incomplete acquisition," Polinsky 2006; for the notion "semi-speaker," Dorian 1977 and, more recently, FPHLCC 2010, 14). Approaches in the teaching of heritage languages that stress complete acquisition and fluency and are opposed, for example, to code switching as an interim stage seem in most cases to have had a negative effect on the motivation of the learners.

Finally, a question that needs to be addressed is why it should be so important to maintain and revitalize at least some Russian language functions in the Doukhobor community. This question has been answered by no one better than an Australian language specialist who points out that the loss of languages can be compared to the decimation and eventual extinction of animal and plant species. For language, changes in environment would mean that, to quote Wurm (1991, 3),

> the cultural and social settings in which a given language had been functioning, usually for a very long time, have been replaced by new and quite different ones as a result of irresistible culture contact and clash, with the traditional language unsuited for readily functioning as a vehicle of expression of the new culture.

To continue with Wurm (1991, 17): "With the death of a language [...] an irreplaceable unit in our knowledge and understanding of human thought and world-view has been lost forever." The loss of the dialect reflects the general leveling of dialectal differences in the world's languages and is therefore as common a process as the loss of lesser used languages. Revival of dialects does occur, but in the case of Doukhobor Russian it would be made more difficult due to the competition of the dialect with Standard Russian. The loss of a special language like Doukhobor ritual language can only be compared to the loss of other special languages in the world, such as the loss of Latin in Christian churches, the loss of scientific language in the smaller languages (and even some of the major languages; see, in this respect, Schaarschmidt 1997) of the world, or perhaps the loss of writing systems such as cuneiform, Egyptian hieroglyphics and Mayan.

For both the Doukhobor colloquial style and, even more so, for the ritual style there is an indication that revitalization efforts will be successful, but postponement for another generation might prove to be fatal. In this case, the fault will not be internal or external migrations, since the Doukhobors in British Columbia have lived there for more than 100 years now, but must be sought in sociopolitical and economic factors similar to those affecting other heritage language groups as well as the First People's languages.

References

Barannik, L. F. and G. M. Miževskaja. 1986. *Russkaja dialektologija. Sbornik upražnenij*. Kiev and Odessa: Vyšča škola.
Beženceva, Alla. 2007. *Strana Duxoborija*. Tbilisi: Russkij klub.
Bonč-Bruevič, Vladimir. 1909 [1954]. *Životnaja kniga duxoborcev*. St. Petersburg: B.M. Wol'f. (*Materialy k istorii i izučeniju russkogo sektantstva i raskola, 2*.) [Reprinted Winnipeg, Manitoba: Regehr's Printing.]
Bouquiaux, Luc and Jacqueline M. C. Thomas. 1992. *Studying and Describing Unwritten Languages*. Trans. James Roberts. Dallas, TX: Summer Institute of Linguistics.
Chloupek, Jan and Jiří Nekvapil. 1987. *Studies in Functional Stylistics. Linguistic and Literary Studies in Eastern Europe*, 36. Amsterdam: John Benjamins.
Donskov, Andrew, ed. 1995. *Leo Tolstoy – Peter Verigin: Correspondence*. New York, Ottawa and Toronto: Legas.
Dorian, Nancy C. 1977. "The Problem of the Semi-speakers in Language Death." *International Journal of the Sociology of Language* 12: 23–32.
――――. 1994. Review of *Endangered Languages*, by R. H. Roberts and E. M. Uhlenbeck (eds), *Language* 70: 797–802.
Ewashen, Larry A. and Koozma J. Tarasoff. 1994. *In Search of Utopia. The Doukhobors*. Castlegar, BC: Spirit Wrestlers Associates.
Fasmer, Maks [Vasmer, Max]. 1964–73. *Ètimologičeskij slovar' russkogo jazyka*. 4 vols. Trans. and supplemented by O. N. Trubachëv. Moscow: Progress.
FPHLCC. 2010. *Report on the Status of B.C. First Nation Languages 2010*. Brentwood, BC: The First Peoples' Heritage, Language and Culture Council. Online: http://www.fphlcc.ca (accessed 10 January 2011).
Friesen, John W. 1995. "Schooling and the Doukhobor Experience." In K. J. Tarasoff and R. B. Klymasz (eds), *Spirit Wrestlers. Centennial Papers in Honour of Canada's Doukhobor Heritage*, 137–45. Hull, QC: Canadian Museum of Civilization.
Friesen, John W. and Michael M. Verigin.1996. *The Community Doukhobors: A People in Transition*. Ottawa: The Borealis Press.
Gerber, Stanford Neil.1985. *Russkoya Celo. The Ethnography of a Russian-American Community. Immigrant Communities and Ethnic Minorities in the United States and Canada* 11. New York: AMS Press.
Golubeva-Monatkina, N. I. 1995. "O sovremennoj russkoj reči kanadskix duxoborov." In T. Lønngren (ed.), *Istorija i geografija russkix staroobrjadčeskix govorov*, 19–26. Moscow: Akademija Nauk/Tromsø Norway: University of Tromsø.
――――. 1997. "O russkoj reči 'russkix kanadcev' (èmigracija 1899–1960 gg.)." In *Sociopragmatika i prepodavanie inostrannyx jazykov. Sbornik nauchnyx trudov*, 30–5. Moscow: Moskovskij gosudarstvennyj institut meždunarodnyx otnošenij.

———. 2004. *Russkaja èmigrantskaja reč' v Kanade konca XX veka. Teksty i kommentarii*. Moscow: Editorial.
Harshenin, Alex P. 1961. "The Phonemes of the Doukhobor Dialect." *Canadian Slavonic Papers* 5: 62–71.
———. 1964. "English Loanwords in the Doukhobor Dialect, 1." *Canadian Slavonic Papers* 6: 38–43.
———. 1967. "English Loanwords in the Doukhobor Dialect, 2." *Canadian Slavonic Papers* 9 (2): 16–30.
Inikova, Svetlana A. 1995. "Problema soxranenija russkogo jazyka v inoètničeskoj srede na primere kanadskix duxoborcev." In T. S. Šentalinskaja (ed.), *Russkij fol'klor v inokul'turnom okruženii*, 152–61. Soxranenie i vozroždenie fol'klornyx tradicij. Sbornik naučnyx trudov 68 (6). Moscow: Gosudarstvennyj respublikanskij centr russkogo fol'klora.
———. 2000. "Spiritual Origins and the Beginnings of Doukhobor History." In A. Donskov, J. Woodsworth and C. Gaffield (eds), *The Doukhobor Centenary in Canada*, 1–21. Ottawa: University of Ottawa.
Jernudd, Björn H. 1972. "Language Planning as a Type of Language Treatment." In *Linguistic Communications* 6: 41–6. Working Papers of the Linguistic Society of Australia. Clayton, Victoria: Monash University.
Kerswill, Paul 2002. "Koineization and Accommodation." In J. K. Chambers, Peter Trudgill and Natalie Schilling-Estes (eds), *The Handbook of Language Variation*, 669–702. Oxford: Blackwell.
King, Robert D. 1992. "Migration and Linguistics as Illustrated by Yiddish." In Edgar C. Polomé and Werner Winter (eds), *Reconstructing Languages and Cultures*, 119–39. Berlin: Mouton de Gruyter.
Malov, Petr N. 1948. *Duxoborcy, ix istorija, žizn' i bor'ba*. Thrums, BC: Peter N. Maloff.
Mealing, Mark F. 1972. Our people's way. A study in Doukhobor hymnody and folklore. PhD diss., University of Pennsylvania. Ann Arbor, Michigan: University Microfilms.
———. 1975. *Doukhobor Life. A Survey of Doukhobor Religion, History, and Folklife*. Castlegar, BC: Cotinneh Books.
———. 1989 "On Doukhobor Psalms." *Canadian Literature* 120: 117–32. Online: http://cinema2.arts.ubc.ca/units/canlit/pdfs/articles/canlit120-Doukhobor%28Mealing%29.pdf (accessed 10 January 2011).
———. 1995. "Doukhobor Psalms: Adornment to the Soul." In K. J. Tarasoff and R. B. Klymasz (eds), *Spirit Wrestlers. Centennial Papers in Honour of Canada's Doukhobor Heritage*, 39–50. Hull, QC: Canadian Museum of Civilization.
Momonova, Maria 1995. "The Doukhobor Movement in Contemporary Culture." In K. J. Tarasoff and R. B. Klymasz (eds), *Spirit Wrestlers. Centennial Papers in Honour of Canada's Doukhobor Heritage*, 3–8. Hull, QC: Canadian Museum of Civilization.
O'Neail, Hazel. 1962. *Doukhobor Daze*. Sidney, BC: Gray's Publishing.
Paucker, Johann Heinrich von [Johann Heinrich von K].1865. "Die Duchoborzen in Transkaukasien." *Baltische Monatsschriften* 11 (March): 240–50. [Originally published using the pseudonym "von K"; reprinted under the author's real name in *Deutsche Rundschau für Geographie und Statistik* 4, October–November 1881, 18–21, 66–9.] Online: http://www.doukhobor.org/VonK.htm (accessed 15 January 2011).
———. 1885. *Die Familie Paucker in Ehstland* [Estland] *und Rusland* [Russland] *1757–1885*. Reval: Reval Observer. Online: http://books.google.ca/books?id=BEkWAAAAYA

AJ&pg=PA51&dq=%22Deutsche+Rundschau+f%C3%BCr+Geographie+und+S
tatistik%22+1881&hl=en&ei=Jk66TID_L8ugnQed3o3mDQ&sa=X&oi=book_re
sult&ct=result&resnum=10&ved=0CE0Q6AEwCTgU#v=onepage&q=%22Deuts
che%20Rundschau%20f%C3%BCr%20Geographie%20und%20Statistik%22%20
1881&f=false (accessed 10 January 2011).
Petzholdt, Alexander. 1867. *Der Kaukasus*. Vol. 2. Leipzig: Hermann Fries. Online: http://books.google.ca/books?id=cijXAAAAMAAJ&source=gbs_slider_thumb (accessed 10 January 2011).
Polinsky, Maria. 2006. "Incomplete Acquisition: American Russian." *Journal of Slavic Linguistics* 14 (2): 191–261.
Polinsky, Maria and Asya Pereltsvaig. 2003. Review of *Jazyk russkogo zarubežja. Obščie processy i rečevye portrety* by E. A. Zemskaja. *Heritage Language Journal* 1. Online: http://www.international.ucla.edu/languages/article.asp?parentid=3727 (accessed 10 January 2011).
Popoff, Eli A. 1983. "The Doukhobors." In C. P. Anderson, T. Bose and J. I. Richardson (eds), *Circle of Voices. A History of the Religious Communities of British Columbia*, 113–19. Lantzville, BC: Oolichan Books.
Rak, Julie. 2004. *Negotiated Memory: Doukhobor Autobiographical Discourse*. Vancouver and Toronto: University of British Columbia Press.
Rašin, A. G. 1951. "'Gramotnost'' i narodnoe obrazovanie v Rossii v XIX i načale XX v." *Istoričeskie zapiski* 37: 28–80.
Schaarschmidt, Gunter. 1995. "Aspects of the History of Doukhobor Russian." *Canadian Ethnic Studies* 27 (3): 197–204.
———. 1997. "Tagalog and the Level of LSP." In M. I. Kaplun (ed.), *IV Meždunarodnaja konferencija po jazykam dal'nego vostoka, jugovostočnoj Azii i zapadnoj Afriki*, 138–46. Moscow: MSU.
———. 1998. "Language in British Columbia." In John Edwards (ed.), *Language in Canada*. 461–68. Cambridge: Cambridge University Press.
———. 2005. "Four norms – one culture: Doukhobor Russian in Canada." In Rudolf Muhr (ed.), *Standardvariationen und Sprachideologien in verschiedenen Sprachkulturen der Welt. Standard Variations and Language Ideologies in different Language Cultures around the World*, 137–50. Vienna et al.: Peter Lang Verlag. Also published in TRANS: Internet-Zeitschrift für Kulturwissenschaften (Internet Journal for Cultural Sciences) 15/2003. Online: http://www.inst.at/trans/15Nr/06_1/schaarschmidt.htm (accessed 1 December 2009).
———. 2008a. "The Ritual Language of the British Columbia Doukhobors as an Endangered Functional Style: Issues of Interference and Translatability." *Canadian Slavonic Papers* 50 (1–2): 102–22.
———. 2008b. "Code-switching im Sorbischen und im Duchobor-Russischen als eine mögliche Zwischenstufe in der Erhaltung und Revitalisierung von Minderheitensprachen in der EU und in Kanada." *Lětopis* 55 (2): 109–25.
———. 2010. "English for Doukhobors: 110 Years of Russian-English Contact in Canada." In Nadezhda L. Grejdina (ed.), *Aktual'nye problemy kommunikacii i kul'tury* 10. *Sbornik naučnyx trudov rossijskix i zarubežnyx učenyx* 30–43. Moscow and Pyatigorsk: Pyatigorsk State Linguistic University. Online: http://www.doukhobor.org/Schaarschmidt-Russian-English.htm (accessed 10 January 2011).
Schlatter, Daniel. 1836. *Bruchstücke aus einigen Reisen nach dem südlichen Russland in den Jahren 1822–1828. Mit besonderer Rücksicht auf die Nogayen-Tataren am Asowschen Meere*. St. Gallen and Bern: Huber. Online: http://www.doukhobor.org/Schlatter.htm (accessed 3 September 2010).

Siegel, J. 1985. "Koines and koineization." *Language in Society* 14: 357–78.
Simeon, Rikard. 1969. *Enciklopedijski rječnik lingvističkih naziva* 1. Zagreb: Matica Hrvatska.
Sulerzhitsky, L. A. 1982. *To America with the Doukhobors*. Regina, SK: Canadian Plains Research Centre. [Translation of *V Ameriku s duxoborcami*. In *Iskra* (Grand Forks, BC), 1960.]
Tarasoff, Koozma J. 1963. "Cultural interchange between the non-Slavic peoples of the Soviet Union and the people of Russian background in the greater Vancouver area." Term paper, Slavonic Studies, University of British Columbia, Vancouver.
———. 2002. *Spirit Wrestlers: Doukhobor Pioneers' Strategies for Living*. Brooklyn, NY: Legas/Ottawa: Spirit Wrestlers Publishing.
Tarasoff, Koozma J. and Robert B. Klymasz, eds. 1995. *Spirit Wrestlers. Centennial Papers in Honour of Canada's Doukhobor Heritage*. Hull, QC: Canadian Museum of Civilization.
Tchertkoff [Čertkoff], Anna. 1900. *Praktičeskij učebnik anglijskogo jazyka. Russian-English Handbook*. London: A. Tchertkoff, Free Age Press.
Tchertkoff, Vladimir. 1900 [1993]. *Christian Martyrdom in Russia. Persecution of the Doukhobors*. London: A. Tchertkoff, Free Age Press. [Reprinted, preface by Koozma J. Tarasoff and Larry A. Ewashen. Castlegar, BC: Spirit Wrestlers Association, 1993.]
Trudgill, P. J. 1998. "The Chaos before Order: New Zealand English and the Second Stage of New-dialect Formation." In E. H. Jahr (ed.), *Advances in Historical Sociolinguistics*, 1–11. Berlin: Mouton de Gruyter.
Trudgill, P. J., E. Gordon, G. Lewis and M. Maclagan. 2000. Determination in New-dialect Formation and the Genesis of New Zealand English." *Journal of Linguistics* 36: 299–318.
Vanek, Anthony L. and Regna Darnell. 1971. "Canadian Doukhobor Russian in Grand Forks, B.C.: Some Social Aspects." In R. Darnell (ed.), *Linguistic Diversity in Canadian Society*, 267–90. Edmonton, AB and Champaign, IL: Linguistic Research.
Walko, M. Ann. 1989. *Rejecting the Second Generation Hypothesis: Maintaining Estonian Ethnicity in Lakewood, New Jersey. Immigrant Communities and Ethnic Minorities in the United States and Canada* 44. New York: AMS Press.
Wurm, Stephen A. 1991. "Language Death and Disappearance: Causes and Circumstances." In Robert H. Robins and Eugenius M. Uhlenbeck (eds), *Endangered Languages*, 1–17. Oxford and New York: Berg.
Young, Charles H. 1931. *Ukrainian Canadians*. Toronto: Nelson.
Zemskaja, Elena A., ed. 2001. *Jazyk russkogo zarubež'ja. Obščie processy i rečevye portrety. Wiener slawistischer Almanach*, 53. Vienna: Institut für Slavische Philologie.

AFTERWORD

Veronika Makarova

The development of linguistics, applied linguistics and the language teaching in the last fifty years has been dominated by the studies investigating the English language. This situation is beginning to change as "the success of modernism in integrating all the communities into the global whole has created greater visibility for the local" (Canagarajah 2005). The globalization of the use of English as the language of international communication encounters its opposite trend in the growing interest towards local languages "to resist the colonizing thrust of English" (Canagarajah 2006, 586). Linguistic research becomes increasingly more enriched by explorations of languages other than English coming into the forefront of academic discussions. As pointed out – quite paradoxically in a collection of papers on English-language teaching – "among the darkness of the 'English only' movement and the destruction resulting from the hegemony of English, there is a faint ray of hope" (Hall and Eggington 2000, xiii). Among these signs of hope in North America is the first national conference on heritage languages in America held in 1999 (Hall and Eggington 2000), and the establishment of the *Heritage Language Journal* in 2003.

Largely due to the growth of Russian-speaking communities around the world in the last few decades, Russian in particular is getting more involved in the advanced linguistic, neurolinguistic, psycholinguistic and sociolinguistic research and related studies (e.g., Baerman 2011; Goddard 2011; Xiang et al. 2011). We can see increased interest in the issues of Russian language, identity and culture intertwined with languages, identities and cultures of other ethnic groups (e.g., Shneer 2011; Elias 2011; Angermeyer 2010). A significant body of extant research has been done with the speech of Russian-speaking immigrants and Russian-English bilinguals (e.g., Geyer et al. 2010; Pavlenko and Malt 2011). The maintenance of Russian as a minority language is also being examined (e.g., Kopelovich 2011). It is predictable that this growing interest in Russian language studies will remain sustained, and that this volume will enhance further research in this sphere.

As one of the world's major languages, Russian shares the dichotomy of the global and local. This hybridity is represented in our book's structure. In Part One, the linguistic studies of the Russian language have the validity for the description of the Russian language spoken in many areas of the world. In particular, chapter three continues the discussions of the post-perestroika changes in the Russian language initiated in the Russian studies in the 1990s (Ryazanova-Clarke and Wade 1999). We are witnessing the final stages of transition in Russia towards a new social structure. Since language change is strongly determined by sociological factors (Comrie, Stone and Polinsky 1996), this period offers unique opportunities to a linguist "to see abrupt changes evolve into continuous tendencies" (ibid., 2). It is therefore pertinent to develop the direction of contemporary Russian language studies to protocol the state of language structure and to trace the direction of language change.

By contrast, applied linguistic studies in Part Two reinterpret Russian language use, teaching and acquisition refracted through the prism of the local North American context where Russian is spoken as a minority heritage language. Collectively, these research studies demonstrate that Russian has firmly established itself in applied linguistic research in Canada and the US. In addition, there is a tremendous potential for new research developments in this geographical region, particularly in the spheres of Russian studies related to psycholinguistics, bilingualism, language maintenance, heritage language studies and language pedagogy.

This book will potentially contribute to the fields of linguistics, applied linguistics and Russian language studies, coupled with developing "a pluralistic mode of thinking where we celebrate different cultures and identities" (Canagarajah 2005, 20).

References

Angermeyer, P. S. 2010. "Interpreter-mediated Interaction as Bilingual Speech: Bridging Macro- and Micro-sociolinguistics in Codeswitching Research." *International Journal of Bilingualism* 14: 466–89.

Baerman, M. 2011. "Defectiveness and Homophony Avoidance." *Journal of Linguistics* 47: 1–29.

Brutt-Griffler, J. 2002. *World English: A Study of its Development*. Clevedon: Multilingual Matters.

Canagarajah, A. S. 2005. "Reconstructing Local Knowledge, Reconfiguring Language Studies." In A. S. Canagarajah (ed.), *Reclaiming the Local in Language Policy and Practice*, 3–24. Mahwah, NJ: Lawrence Erlbaum.

———. 2006. "The Place of World Englishes in Composition: Pluralization Continued." *CCC* 57 (4): 586–619.

Comrie, B., G. Stone and M. Polinsky. 1996. *The Russian Language in the Twentieth Century*. 2nd ed. Oxford: Clarendon Press.

Elias, N. 2011. "Russian-speaking Immigrants and their Media: Still Together?" *Israel Affairs* 17: 72–88.
Geyer, A., P. J. Holcomb, K. J. Midgley and J. Grainger. 2011. "Processing Words in Two Languages: An Event-related Brain Potential Study of Proficient Bilinguals." *Journal of Neurolinguistics* 24: 338–51.
Goddard, C. 2011. "The Lexical Semantics of Language (with Specific Reference to Words). *Language Sciences* 33: 40–57.
Hall, J. K. and W. G. Eggington. 2000. *The Sociopolitics of English Language Teaching*. Clevedon, UK: Multilingual Matters.
Kopelovich, S. 2011. "How Long is 'the Russian Street' in Israel? Prospects of Maintaining the Russian Language." *Israel Affairs* 17: 108–24.
Pavlenko, A. and B. C. Malt. 2011. "Kitchen Russian: Cross-linguistic Differences and First Language Object Naming by Russian-English Bilinguals." *Bilingualism: Language and Cognition* 14: 19–45.
Ryazanova-Clarke, L. and T. Wade. 1999. *The Russian Language Today*. London and New York: Routledge.
Shneer, D. 2011. "The Third Way: German-Russian-European Jewish Identity in a Global Jewish World." *European Review of History* 18: 111–21.
Xiang, M., B. Harizanov, M. Polinsky and E. Kravtchenko. 2011. "Processing Morphological Ambiguity: An Experimental Investigation of Russian Numerical Phrases." *Lingua* 121: 548–60.

INDEX

abbreviation 72, 78–80
accentuation 6, 15, 17, 24–5, 27, 32–3, 37, 62, 64
   Basic Accentuation Principle 62
acronym 78, 220
accuracy 117, 134–5, 152, 178, 180–1, 185, 187, 198–9
activity 137, 142, 146–9, 151–4
   communicative 136–8
   language-focused 135, 148–50, 152
   task-based xvi, 136, 147, 153
adjective xv, 72–3, 80–3, 85, 87, 108, 110, 112–3, 115–21, 124–8, 176–7, 215, 249, 253
Advanced Russian Proficiency Test 140
adverb 72–3, 80–3, 97
affect xiv, 3–6, 9, 22, 30–4, 36–7
agreement xv, 89, 103, 108–10, 113, 118, 121–2, 126, 171
alternation (phonological) xiv–xv, 44, 49–50, 52–3, 241, 253
   root alternation 49
American Council on the Teaching of Foreign Languages (ACTFL) xvi, 133, 138–40, 142–3, 151, 155, 162, 193–4, 196–8, 200, 207, 210–11
American Council of Teachers of Russian (ACTR) 139–40
analytism xv, 71–2, 74, 83
Anglicism xvii, 220, 223, 225, 228, 232
anglicization 242
anti-Semitism 216, 225, 229
arborization 92–5, 103
article (grammatical) 101, 110–13, 121, 124, 128
assessment 141, 167, 198–9, 211
   criteria 198–9
audio-lingual method 136, 138

bilingual xvi, 109, 111, 113, 124, 128, 134, 161–2, 193, 195–6, 201, 204, 208, 210, 219, 224, 231, 254, 261
bilingualism xiii, 161–2, 196, 262
bi-nominative sentence (= BS) xv, 85–105
borrowing xv, 71–5, 79, 82–3, 200, 208–11, 219–20, 221–5, 241, 249
boundary 44, 46–8, 60, 82
   word 44, 46–7
   prosodic 44

capitalization 171–2
case xv, 74, 77, 82, 88–9, 100, 108, 116, 152–3, 167–9, 174–8, 180–7, 242
   accusative 116, 152–3, 168, 176, 178–81, 186
   dative 176–7, 184–6
   genitive 53, 82, 176, 178–9, 182–5, 241–2
   instrumental xv, 88, 95, 97–9, 168, 176, 180–2, 186
   nominative xv, 82, 88n2, 90, 97, 99, 175–6, 178–9, 183–4, 186
   oblique 175–6, 186, 242
   prepositional 168, 176, 180–1 (*see also* preposition)
circumlocution xvi, 193, 196–200, 207–9
clause 92, 97, 100, 172–3, 175, 200–4, 206–7, 210, 211, 254
   subordinate 97, 173, 206
clitic 46–8
Cliticization Paradox 44, 46–9
coalescence 242
code switching 249, 252, 254, 256
Cold War 218
colloquial style xvii, 235, 239, 246–7, 249–54, 257
Common Slavic 49, 62

communicative language teaching (CLT) xvi, 133–59
competitor (lexical) xv–xvi, 108, 109, 111–18, 120–8
complement 48, 54–7, 62, 64; *see also* non-complement
compromise language 235, 237–9
conjunction 24, 72, 173, 175, 203–4, 206, 254
connector 174–6
consonant 43, 46–8, 50–3, 55, 169–71, 186
  voicing 169
  devoicing 44, 46–8, 169
constraint 52–5, 108, 110, 119, 128
contextual guessing 143
copula xv, 86–7, 89, 92, 97, 99, 101–4
  copula agreement xv, 89
  zero copula 86
core programs 134
corpus xv, 32, 44–5, 51, 54–5, 57, 59–60, 123, 203
Cyrillic alphabet 75–9, 166–7, 169–71

database xiv, 3, 5–8, 37
desinence 241–2
devoicing 44, 46–8, 60–1, 67, 169
diagnostic test xvi, 164, 167
dialect 45, 235–9, 241–2, 246–7, 250, 256
  dialect formation 238
dialectal leveling 235, 238–41, 245–6, 256
dictionary 71, 75, 78, 81, 123
discourse xii, 4, 108–9, 147, 150–1, 195, 197–204, 210
distractor (lexical) 111–15, 117–18, 122–5
Doukhobor xii, xiv, xvii, 235–52, 254–7
  beliefs 237, 255
  language xi–xviii, 235–7, 239, 241, 244, 246–7, 249–51, 254–7, 261–2
  migrations 235, 239, 247, 255, 257
DSynt-actant 88, 91, 94, 103

Educational Testing Service (ETS) 140–2
emigrant 216–7, 226, 230
emigration 216–18, 222, 225, 228–9, 232, 236, 243–4
  wave 216, 218, 222, 229–31
emotion xiv, 3–37

acoustic clues of 3–4
acoustic feature 8, 31, 36
clusters 35
expression xiv, 4–5, 21, 24, 31–7
recognition xiv–xvi, 31–2, 35, 37
essay 167–86
  length 172
  syntactic complexity 167, 172–3
eye movement 112–13, 116–18, 120, 124, 126
eyetracking xiv–xv, 110–16, 122, 124

F0 derivative 8–9, 19–21, 24–5, 33–4, 36–7
"focus on meaning" 134–5, 138, 146, 150
"focus on form" (FonF) 135, 146, 152, 155–6
formant 5, 8–9, 21–2, 24, 30, 34, 37–8
  F1 8–9, 21–2, 24–5, 30, 32, 34–6
  F2 8–12, 21–2, 24–5, 30, 32, 34–6
  F3 5, 8–12, 21–2, 24–5, 32, 34
formant bandwidth 8–9, 22, 34
fundamental frequency (F0) 8–12, 17–21, 24–5, 27, 29–30, 32–7; *see also* F0 derivative

gender xiv–xvi, 72, 74, 89, 95, 107–29, 242
  feminine 95, 112, 115, 120, 175, 178–9, 181, 184, 242
  masculine 81, 112, 115, 120, 175, 178–9, 181
  neuter 89, 112, 178, 242
  gender agreement 108–10, 113, 118, 121, 126
  gender-matching 109–10, 121
  gender-mismatching 109–10, 120–1, 126
gisting 143, 146, 155

Havlík's Law 49, 52
Hebrew Immigrant Aid Society (HIAS) 218
heritage language (Russian) xiii–xiv, xvi–xvii, 161–5, 175, 178, 182–4, 187, 261–2
  curricula 164
  education 161, 163–6, 168–70
  instruction xvi, 184, 187
  speaker xvi, 141, 161–70, 172–73, 175–80, 183, 185–7, 194
  teaching xiii–xiv, xvi–xvii, 162, 164, 187

heritage language (non-Russian) 255–6, 261
heritage learner xiii, xvi, 161–5, 167–70, 173–8, 180–7
hiatus 47–8

identity sentence 94, 98
idiom 52, 54, 62–3, 67
immersion programs 134
information extraction 143
interjection 72
interlanguage system 165, 167, 187
Internet 51, 71, 73–5, 77, 81–3, 197, 199, 207–8, 222, 255
input xvi, 134–5, 138, 141–7, 143n10, 150–2, 154–5, 162, 167
IT 75, 77–80

jargonism 220
Jews
    Russian 215–18, 216n1, 221–2, 224–32
    culture/identity 215–18, 230–2
    heritage 216, 218, 223, 231
    refugee 216n1, 218–19, 230
juncture 50

koine 237–8, 246
koineization 238

language contact 219–22, 231
language maintenance 196, 219–22, 230–1, 235, 246, 255, 262
"language planning" 246
layering 60
    strict layering 60
lexeme xv, 73, 75, 77, 80, 82, 89n4, 92, 96–7, 99–101
lexical split 53–4, 62–3
lexicalization xv, 65, 92, 94–6, 103
listening 7, 31, 35, 37, 109–12, 115–20, 125–8, 138–45, 152, 164, 166, 168, 187
loan word xi, 71–80, 82–3, 241, 245

Meaning-Text approach 90
media 71, 74–7, 81, 83, 222, 231
mistake 169, 171, 173, 175
modal 72

modality 136, 143–4
modifier 73–4, 82–3, 112, 127, 169, 176–8, 180–2, 184, 186, 200, 206–7, 210–11, 242
mono-competence 195
monolingual xvi, 111–13, 124, 127, 163, 193, 195–6, 199, 201, 203, 208, 210–12, 249, 252
mood 86
    indicative mood 86–7, 88n3, 96–9, 242
morpheme 48–9, 62, 65, 75–6, 78, 82
morphology xiv–xv, 71–3, 77–8, 82, 108–9, 151, 156, 165n2, 219
morphosyntax 71–2, 74, 80
Moses 215

"naming sentence" 90
narrative xvi, 144–5, 149, 193, 195, 197–8, 200–1, 203–4, 206, 211
    autobiographical 197
"nominal sentence" 86
nominal system xvi, 165
non-complement 54, 63
norm 74–5, 78, 80, 122, 134, 141n7, 171, 211, 236, 244
noun xv, 44, 47, 50–1, 53, 57–8, 62–5, 67–8, 72–4, 77, 80–3, 85, 87–8, 93, 97–9, 108–13, 115–21, 123–8, 152, 169, 172, 174–84, 186, 206, 249

Old Russian 49, 62
onomatopoeic word 72
Oral Proficiency Interviews (OPI) 139–40, 193–213
orthography 70, 74–80, 83, 167, 170–1, 185, 187
output 109, 134–5, 153

palatalization 44, 47–8, 241, 250
participle 55, 66, 108
Passover 215–16, 227
pause 5, 116
phonetics xiv, 1–41, 241–2
phonology xiv, 43–70
phonological word 46–8, 60, 62
phonotactics 44–5, 50–3, 55–6, 61–2, 67

phrase xv, 5, 19, 43, 46, 51–2, 54, 58–9, 61, 63–4, 67, 80, 82–3, 85, 88–90, 95, 97, 102–3, 107–11, 115, 119, 121, 124–5, 127, 172, 179, 217, 249, 254
   noun phrase xv, 85, 108, 111, 115, 119, 121, 124–5, 127
polyfunctional word 73, 80–3
possession 57–9, 64, 67, 181–3, 239, 250
predicate xv, 85, 88, 90–3, 97, 101–2, 104, 203
   semantic predicate 88
   syntactic predicate 85n1, 88
predicative 85, 87–91, 93, 103, 182
prefix xv, 44–7, 49–50, 53, 60–1 65–7
   verbal prefix xv, 44–7, 53, 61, 65
preposition xi, xv, 43–68, 97, 172, 176, 181–4, 186
pretonic 46–8, 60
proficiency xiii, xvi, 114, 133–4, 133n1, 138–43, 151, 155, 162–8, 174, 176, 182, 184–7, 193–4, 197– 200, 207, 210–11, 232
proficiency guidelines 133n1, 138–9, 142–3, 194, 198
pronoun 54–5, 89, 108, 175–82, 184, 186, 242
prosodic xv, 5, 43–5, 48, 50, 52, 60–1, 65, 67–8
prosody 97
psycholinguistics xvii, 107–30, 137, 261–2
   Slavic 108
punctuation 172

quasi-predicate 91–3, 101

reading 138–45, 150–1, 153–5, 164, 166–8, 187, 199
recording 6, 37, 78, 115–17, 153–54, 167, 197
referential status 89–90, 94
referential structure 94
rheme 88–9, 93, 104
ritual language 236, 239, 246, 250–1, 256; *see also* ritual style
ritual style 239, 241, 247, 251–2, 254–5, 257
Russian Church Slavonic 247–8, 252

scanning 143, 155
semanteme 91–5, 103
semantic rule 90–1
semantics xiv–xv, 43, 57, 63, 65, 67, 85, 88, 90–2, 94, 97, 103, 108–9, 220
   prepositional semantics 57, 63
      non-transparent prepositional semantics 57, 63
sentence xv, 6, 58, 80, 85–90, 92–4, 101–4, 108, 113, 116, 137, 147–9, 151, 165, 167, 172, 174–6, 203, 250, 254
   length 167, 172, 175–6
   complexity 44, 138, 173, 175–6
   compound sentence 173–6
   type 5–6, 85, 90–3, 95, 103
skimming 143, 155
specificity 89
spelling 79, 81, 167–70, 172, 242, 244
standardized test 139
stress 3, 6, 8–9, 11, 13–5, 17–1, 23, 25, 27, 30, 32–4, 37, 43, 45–6, 48–9, 61–2, 64–7, 86, 119–20, 123, 242, 250, 253
   retraction 45, 61–8
   emphatic stress 86
structure xi, xiii, xv–xvii, 1, 44–5, 50, 52–3, 56–7, 60–1, 64–8, 71, 73–5, 80, 83–4, 87, 90–2, 102–3, 107, 135–6, 139, 165, 174–6, 199, 202, 235, 252, 255
   communicative structure xv, 90, 103
   semantic structure xv, 90–6, 101–3
   syntactic structure xv, 86–7, 90–2, 102
subject xv, 58–9, 67, 85, 88–91, 93, 95, 97, 101–4, 179, 187, 203

target xv–xvi, 54, 109–27, 208
   target group 167, 171–2
   target language 133–5, 142, 146, 152, 162, 164, 196, 208
task (in language teaching) xvi, 110, 136–8, 141–3, 146–7, 151–4, 196, 198–9, 206–12
task-based instruction xvi, 136, 153
tense 86, 88, 93, 101–2, 151, 174, 242n5
   present tense 86, 242n5
   past tense 88n2, 93, 101–2, 174
   future tense 88

test xvi, 8, 112–14, 139–42, 164, 167, 187, 193–201, 203, 207–8, 211
textbook 135–9, 142–7, 149–50, 152–6, 167, 170
  design 138
theme 88, 93, 102–3
Tolstoy, Leo 237, 244, 250
"transfers" 169
translation 75, 136, 138, 142, 149, 247–8, 251–2, 254–5
transliteration 75, 78

valency xv, 80
variability xv, 4, 8–9, 21, 31, 50, 53, 60, 238, 241–2
  lexical 242
  morphological 241
voice quality 5, 37
vowel xiv–xv, 3–41, 43–69, 123, 169–70, 250, 253–4
  accented 3, 6–9, 12–22, 24–5, 27, 30, 32–4, 37
  alternation (phonological) 44, 49–50, 52–3, 241, 253
  deletion xiv, 48
  duration 8–14, 24–7, 32, 36–7
  energy 8–12, 15, 22, 24–5, 27–8, 32–3, 36–7
  formant: *see* formant

formant bandwidth: *see* formant bandwidth
intensity 5, 35–6
  and phonemic variability 241
  reduction 44, 46–8, 60–1, 67, 123, 169, 253–4
  spectra 22–3, 25, 32, 35
  stressed 3, 6, 8–9, 11, 13–15, 17–22, 25, 27, 30, 32–4, 37, 46, 48–9, 123
  and syntactic factors 43–4, 53–67
  "Unity Paradox" 44–5, 61
  unstressed 3, 6, 8–10, 13, 15–17, 19, 21–2, 25, 27, 30, 32–4, 37, 46–7, 49, 123, 170–1, 242, 253
verb xv, 44, 46, 50, 57, 65–8, 72–3, 80, 82–3, 85–9, 92, 94–104, 108, 113, 115–9, 124–8, 151, 174, 182–4, 202–3, 241, 254
viewing 127, 143–5

word class 172, 174, 177
word recognition xv, 108–10, 127–8
  spoken-word recognition xv–xvi, 107–28
writing xiv, 74, 78, 139, 164, 167–8, 171, 173, 185, 187, 217, 220, 256
yer xiv, 43–5, 49, 52–3, 57, 60, 62, 66
  deletion xiv, 48

www.ingramcontent.com/pod-product-compliance
Lightning Source LLC
Chambersburg PA
CBHW021821300426
44114CB00009BA/262

Michael Kidd

STAGES OF DESIRE

*The Mythological Tradition
in
Classical and Contemporary Spanish Theater*

The Pennsylvania State University Press
University Park, Pennsylvania

Publication of this book has been aided by a grant from The Program for Cultural Cooperation Between Spain's Ministry of Culture and United States' Universities.

Library of Congress Cataloging-in-Publication Data

Kidd, Michael, 1968–
   Stages of desire : the mythological tradition in classical and contemporary Spanish theater / Michael Kidd.
      p.   cm. — (Penn State studies in Romance literatures)
   Includes bibliographical references and index.
   ISBN 0-271-01912-3 (cloth : alk. paper)
   1. Spanish drama—Classical period, 1500–1700—History and criticism.   2. Spanish drama—20th century—History and criticism.   3. Desire in literature.   4. Mythology, Greek, in literature.   5. Mythology, Roman, in literature.   I. Title.   II. Series.
PQ6102.K53   1999
862.009'353—dc21   98-43337
                                                                 CIP

Copyright © 1999 The Pennsylvania State University
All rights reserved
Printed in the United States of America
Published by The Pennsylvania State University Press,
University Park, PA 16802-1003

It is the policy of The Pennsylvania State University Press to use acid-free paper for the first printing of all clothbound books. Publications on uncoated stock satisfy the minimum requirements of American National Standard for Information Sciences—Permanence of Paper for Printed Library Materials, ANSI Z39.48-1992.

para Adriana—
Escrito está en mi alma vuestro gesto . . .

Ὁ φιλόμυθος φιλόσοφος πώς ἐστιν ὁ γὰρ μῦθος σύγκειται ἐκ θαυμασίων.
—Aristotle, *Metaphysics*

Rapiebant me spectacula theatrica plena imaginibus miseriarum mearum et fomitibus ignis mei.
—Augustine, *Confessions*

No hay en el mundo fuerza como la del deseo.
—García Lorca, *Yerma*

Contents

	Preface	ix
1	Myth, Theater, and Desire	1
2	Three Authors in Search of a Story: The Emplotment of Desire in the Sixteenth-Century Theater	19
3	The Rules of Desire: The Rise of the *Comedia Nueva*, c. 1600–1636	63
4	For Art's Sake: From Conventional to Radical Desire in the Early Twentieth-Century Theater	125
5	Postwar, Postmodern, and Beyond: Liberating Desire in the Theater of Dictatorship and Democracy	181
	Epilogue: Future Desires	225
	Appendix 1: Summary of Principal Plays Studied	227
	Appendix 2: Spanish and English Equivalents of Mythological Figures	229
	References	233
	Index	257

Preface

The study that follows organizes my response to an issue that has captivated and perplexed my imagination for some time: the persistence of Greco-Roman mythology in the Spanish theatrical tradition. Although I have found the question of desire to be at the heart of the issue and have accordingly ordered my readings around this critical concept as outlined in Chapter 1, each of the individual analyses is also intended to function discretely in order to provide a fuller picture of the adaptation of myth in the Spanish theater. Where space has permitted, I have made an effort to present secondary material relevant to the plays' mythological context, but not necessarily to the question of desire.

The organization of the study is chronological, and the chapters correspond to generally recognized historicoliterary periods located on either side of the conceptual break spanning the eighteenth and nineteenth centuries. On the far side of that break, in Chapter 2 I cover the pre-Lopean playwrights of the sixteenth century, and in Chapter 3 I examine myth during the apogee of the *comedia nueva*, or roughly the first third of the seventeenth century. On the nearer side, in Chapter 4 I survey the twentieth century before the Spanish Civil War, while in Chapter 5 I focus on the postwar twentieth century through the 1980s. Although I make passing references to numerous plays, my principal aim is literary and analytical rather than archaeological or philological. While I consistently seek to contextualize the plays I discuss within the sociopolitical milieu and the theatrical tradition of the periods in which they were written, I do not aim to provide a history of myth in the peninsular theater. Instead, in each chapter I concentrate on a limited number of mythological works (two or three) that I consider representative of the period in question. In the interest of arriving at broad conclusions within this limited scope of inquiry, the works chosen for analysis embody the widest possible cross section of authors, dates of composition, and source myths. In all cases except one (to be discussed in Chapter 2), the mythological referent is readily apparent either in the title of the play or in the development of plot and characters. In Appendix 1 I provide a summary of the principal works studied.

The names of mythological personages mentioned throughout the analysis are given in the version used by the Spanish playwrights when reference is to the character in the adaptation; the standard Latin form is used to refer to the mythological prototype. English equivalents are provided in Appendix 2 for those unfamiliar with the Spanish spellings. Geographical names are referred to in English.

The format used for citations is as follows. For classics of literature and criticism, unless the work is a play or a poem with individually numbered lines, page numbers of the edition cited are given first, followed by a location using the internal divisions of the text; thus "39; 2.1" could mean, for example, page 39, act 2, scene 1 of a play or, alternatively, page 39, part 2, chapter 1 of a work of prose. In the case of Plato and Aristotle, the internal divisions cited are the widely used page and column notations (as in "559b–560c") that correspond to the first standard modern editions of those authors. If the work cited is a play or a poem with individually numbered lines, the reference is to line numbers within the larger units of the text, as in "*Iliad* 16.430–61." When poems or plays do not have individually numbered lines or contain sections in prose, page numbers will be used, indicated by the notation "pp." where confusion could arise. Italics in quoted material are reproduced from the original unless otherwise indicated, and capitalization is modified, where necessary, to conform to sentence syntax. In addition, suspension points present in the original are reproduced without intervening spaces (...), whereas spaced ellipses (. . .) indicate the omission of quoted material.

Quotations of ancient Roman authors are provided both in the original Latin and in English translation; those of Greek writers are normally cited in translation only, except where it has proved useful to cite directly from the Greek. In those cases, the text is reproduced in English transliteration according to the following guidelines: breathing marks and accents are eliminated; iota subscript is written as an adscript; eta and omega are identified with a macron to distinguish them from epsilon and omicron. Translations from the classical Latin are my own; translations from the Greek are those of the Loeb Classical Library, although I have occasionally seen fit to elaborate on certain words or phrases. Out of considerations of space, I have left quotations from the modern Romance languages untranslated and have supplied my own renderings of secondary German sources without reproducing the original passages.

In the completion of this project I owe a heavy debt of gratitude to a truly extraordinary mentor, John W. Kronik, whose untiring commitment to my work and consistently constructive criticism will loom large as an ideal, if impossible, model for me throughout my career. Frederick Ahl, Walter Cohen, Antonio Monegal, and María Antonia Garcés also contributed invaluably to improving the study. Additionally, I benefited from the kindness and generosity of Michael McGaha, who encouraged me throughout the project and provided me with numerous bibliographical materials and advice during its research and composition. Likewise, Alfred Rodríguez offered me a sympathetic and perceptive reading of the completed manuscript. To all these friends and colleagues I extend my most heartfelt thanks and appreciation.

I would also like to acknowledge the generous support of the Mellon Foundation, whose fellowship allowed me to devote myself fully to my project and complete it in a timely fashion. Cornell University awarded me an additional year of invaluable support. Furthermore, I wish to extend my appreciation to the unsung heroes of Interlibrary Services at Cornell's Olin Library, whose hard work and dedication gained me access to scores of otherwise inaccessible materials and whose courtesy and professionalism, together with the attentiveness of the entire Olin staff, always made my time in the library an enjoyable experience.

Several portions of this book have been previously published or are currently in press. "Myth, Desire and the Play of Inversion: The Fourteenth Eclogue of Juan del Encina" appeared in *Hispanic Review* 65 (1997): 217–36. "Libidinal Expression and Artistic Repression: Juan Timoneda's *Tragicomedia llamada Filomena*" was read at the Fifteenth Golden Age Theatre Symposium at the University of Texas at El Paso (March 8–11, 1995) and subsequently appeared in *Texto y Espectáculo: Selected Proceedings of the Fifteenth International Golden Age Theatre Symposium (March 8–11, 1995) at the University of Texas, El Paso*, ed. José Luis Suárez García (York, South Carolina: Spanish Literature Publications, 1996), 74–85. "Triangular Desire and Sensory Deception in Francisco de la Cueva y Silva's *Trajedia de Narciso*" appeared in *MLN* 110 (1995): 271–83 (© Johns Hopkins University Press, 1995). "The Performance of Desire: Acting and Being in Lope de Vega's *El laberinto de Creta*" was published in *Bulletin of the Comediantes* 47 (1995): 21–36. "Playing with Fire: The Conflict of Truth and

Desire in Benito Pérez Galdós's *Electra*" appeared in *Anales Galdosianos* 29–30 (1994/95): 105–20; lamentably, it contained several factual errors regarding the possible relationship between the characters Máximo and Electra. A corrected version, translated into Spanish from the discussion that appears in Chapter 4 of this book (pp. 130–45), was read at the IX Coloquio Internacional de Filología Griega at the Universidad Nacional de Educación a Distancia in Madrid (March 4–7, 1998) and is scheduled to appear in the conference proceedings (ed. Juan Antonio López Férez). Likewise, a Spanish version of the essay on Jacinto Grau was read at the same symposium the previous year (VIII Coloquio Internacional de Filología Griega, March 5–8, 1997) and will also be appearing in the proceedings (ed. López Férez). I am grateful to all these venues for their support of my work.

Because *Stages of Desire* was close to publication in Cambridge University Press's "Studies in Latin American and Iberian Literature" before the abrupt cancellation of that series, I would like to express my thanks to the series editor, Aníbal González, for all his advice and encouragement, as well as to the two anonymous referees whose meticulous, erudite, and generous readings of the manuscript immeasurably improved its final version. Whatever flaws remain in it are undoubtedly my own. Finally, my deepest gratitude goes to Fred de Armas, who rescued the project from editorial limbo and argued for its inclusion in the series in which it now appears.

1

Myth, Theater, and Desire

The Lure of Myth

Horrific, uncanny, seductive: the tales of classical mythology have captured the imagination of Spanish playwrights throughout the history of the peninsular theater. Dramatists of the early modern period and of the twentieth century have been particularly susceptible to the spell of the ancient stories.[1] In the sixteenth and seventeenth centuries, plays that recreate the Greco-Roman myths can count among their authors such historically significant figures as Juan del Encina, Lope de Vega, Guillén de Castro, Tirso de Molina (Gabriel Téllez), Calderón de la Barca, and Juana Inés de la Cruz (Juana Ramírez y Asbaje), as well as lesser-known drama-

---

1. I prefer the term *early modern* for the period corresponding roughly to the sixteenth and seventeenth centuries, traditionally known in Hispanism as "the Golden Age." I avoid the latter designation on the grounds that it is a quirky, uncritical term complicitous with the hierarchical structures of canon formation that are endemic to the period it presumes to name. Its usage unnecessarily isolates Hispanic criticism from that of other European literatures of the same period, in which the term *early modern* is standard.

tists such as Cristóbal de Virués, Gabriel Lobo Lasso de la Vega, and Francisco de la Cueva y Silva, to name only a representative few.

The eighteenth and nineteenth centuries witness a marked decline in the production of mythological plays. Most works that could fit into the category are not true re-creations but rather loose translations of a Greek or Roman play, as is the case with Vicente García de la Huerta's *Agamenón vengado* (1778), based on the earlier Spanish version by Pérez de Oliva. Similarly, many of the plays of Bretón de los Herreros were Spanish renditions of French translations from the Greek or Latin. As Ivy McClelland observes regarding the eighteenth century, "The humanity, insight, and dramatic force of Euripides at his best, the wild spirituality of Aeschylus, the brooding silences of Sophocles, the imaginative thought, the fire, and the poetry of all of them, passed over the epoch's head" (48), going on to cite the ridicule that Juan Pisón y Vargas, in a parodic work from 1786, directs "not really against 'bad' imitations . . . but against any imitation of the Greeks at all" (51). In the following century, the well-known playwright Martínez de la Rosa's apparent need to justify his *Edipo* (1832) in a lengthy scholarly introduction, together with the surprise produced by the play's success in the theater (Cook 444–48), attests to the apparently meager state of classical drama in Spain at the height of the Romantic movement.

In contrast, the twentieth century has seen a strong revival of myth not only south of the Pyrenees but also in the rest of Europe and America, as Gilbert Highet has documented (chap. 23). In Spain, a long line of distinguished playwrights have tried their hand at reformulating classical models in the dramatic context, including Benito Pérez Galdós, Miguel de Unamuno, Jacinto Grau, Gonzalo Torrente Ballester, and Antonio Buero Vallejo. Other playwrights so inclined include José María Pemán, José Bergamín, María José Ragúe Arias, Concha Romero, and Luis Riaza, among many.

This cursory survey raises several intriguing questions that could form the basis for a common analysis of such plays. First, what analogous thematic and structural features do the myths possess that might offer a clue to their great appeal among the dramatists? Second, what techniques do the dramatists share in adapting myth to a postclassical literary tradition? How do they balance fidelity to the classical model against the need for artistic and ideological innovation, assuming that the play is more than a loose translation?

Despite the widespread presence of myth, there has been little attention paid to it as a category of its own in the Spanish theater, even within period-defined analyses. Consequently, none of the preceding questions has been adequately addressed. In work done on the early modern theater, which claims the largest volume of plays based on classical myth, there is nothing equivalent to José María de Cossío's *Fábulas mitológicas en España*, in which the author analyzes a wide variety of Greco-Roman myths in Renaissance and baroque poetry. Instead, myth in the early modern theater tends to be discussed in relation to individual writers, to isolated myths, or to the influences of certain ancient authors. None of these approaches treats it as a subject worthy of study in its own right.[2]

What is true for the study of the early modern period is doubly true for that of the twentieth century, where Greco-Roman myth is normally discussed only insofar as it is directly relevant to the text at hand. Most studies that treat some aspect of myth in modern Spanish drama deal either with a specific author, in whom myth is relevant in just a few plays, or, occasionally, with a particular myth as it appears among several authors.[3] One exception to this trend is María José Ragué Arias, who has analyzed myth in contemporary peninsular drama on a larger scale than has any other critic. Nevertheless, several methodological parameters prevent her work from representing a truly comprehensive cross section of

2. For example, myth in Calderón has attracted considerable attention from recent critics such as Mooney, Chapman, DiPuccio, O'Connor, ter Horst, and Greer, to name only a few, while McGaha has devoted a series of studies to Lope de Vega's mythological plays. Several excellent analyses have traced the presence of individual myths in the major genres and authors of the early modern period: Barnard (on Apollo and Daphne), Cabañas (Orpheus), Gallego Morell (Phaethon), Glaser and Schrader (Ulysses), Levan (Circe), Lida de Malkiel (Dido), Moya del Baño (Hero and Leander), and J. Turner (Icarus) are representative of this approach. Finally and more generally, Schevill's monograph on Ovid, Palli Bonet's on Homer, and Díaz-Regañón's on the Greek tragedians have considerably advanced the state of knowledge on the subject. A notable exception to these methodologies is the doctoral thesis of Rosa Helena Chinchilla, which traces the evolution of classical myth in the early modern period through an examination of various authors and genres. Although her transgeneric approach allows her to treat myth as a general phenomenon of the period, it does not permit a detailed analysis of the dramatic genre as a means of mythic expression. Similarly, the excellent collection of essays edited by Francisco Ruiz Ramón and César Oliva, *El mito en el teatro clásico español*, lacks a central thesis concerning the nature of myth in the theater.

3. For example, Iglesias Feijoo's study on Buero Vallejo and Finkenthal's on Galdós both include excellent analyses of those authors' plays that are based on classical myth. With regard to specific myths, the figure of Ulysses in particular—whose long journey home after a devastating war has captured the imagination of Spanish playwrights after their own ravaging civil war—has received attention from Ragué Arias, *Lo que fue Troya*, chaps. 1 and 5; Rogers; Lamartina-Lens; Cazorla, "El retorno de Ulises"; and Paulino.

twentieth-century Spanish plays. Her doctoral thesis, although of wide scope in its analysis of Greek myth in twentieth-century Spanish drama, limits itself to the study of female protagonists; similarly, two of her published monographs, *Los personajes* and *Els personatges*, treat broad themes in Greek myth but only within the regional theaters of Galicia and Catalonia, while the third, *Lo que fue Troya*, begins with the year 1939.

The diminished discussion of myth in the contemporary period is partially attributable to the gradual decline through the centuries of the number of playwrights who model their works on specific myths of classical antiquity. The reasons for this decline are difficult to specify. Some have postulated that the "organic" worldview implicit in Greek drama, for example, expired with the rise of rationalist epistemologies in the sixteenth and seventeenth centuries (Steiner). Others have sought to explain what replaced this type of worldview in drama (Abel). Whatever its cause, the effect of the decline is the absence of an obvious pattern or clear-cut trajectory to attract critical attention.

Furthermore, because the lexical range of the term "myth" has broadened considerably in the twentieth century—a phenomenon related to the centrality of mythology in various schools of modern anthropology (Frazer, Malinowski, Lévi-Strauss), psychology (Jung), and literary theory (Frye)—one is more likely to find it used in conjunction with an indigenous Hispanic figure such as Don Juan or Segismundo rather than with any theme or personage from the Greek or Roman tradition. The greater number of works that one might consider mythic in this broad sense, combined with the frequency with which they are studied, has blurred awareness of connections between modern plays clearly based on myths of classical antiquity. Nevertheless, the fact remains that classical myth has continued to be a viable, although perhaps limited, option for many playwrights of the contemporary period.

A study of myth in Spanish theater of the early modern period and of the twentieth century is therefore justified by the abundance of primary sources and the scarcity of secondary ones that treat them as a unit. The smaller number of original mythological plays from the eighteenth and nineteenth centuries suggests that these periods may be legitimately eliminated from such a study.[4] The reduced field of inquiry rendered by this

---

4. Significantly, the collection of essays recently edited by Claude Dumas, which focuses on the nineteenth century, concentrates not on ancient myth but rather on the wider interpretation of the term mentioned above. Furthermore, it extends generically into prose and poetry and geographically into Latin America.

methodological procedure obviously precludes achieving the exhaustive historical detail of a study such as Cossío's. Even so, a thorough analysis of a handful of plays from better-known as well as less-famous authors from the two apogees of Spanish dramatic production can begin to provide answers to some of the basic questions concerning myth as a general phenomenon in Spanish theater.

Myth and Desire: Toward a Working Definition

Aristotle was the first to study systematically the relationship between myth (Lat. *mythos* < Gk. *muthos*) and theater. In chapter 6 of the *Poetics*, he states that *muthos* in the strict sense of an "arrangement of incidents" ([*sunthesin tōn pragmatōn*] 24–25; 1450a) forms the soul ([*psuchē*] 26–27; 1450a) of tragedy because it is an imitation of the action ([*estin de tēs men praxeōs ho muthos hē mimēsis*] 24–25; 1450a). In a later chapter, he uses *muthos* in the looser, but related, sense of "story," "narration," or "formulated speech" that the term had carried since the beginnings of the written Greek language.[5] In speaking of the best types of stories on which to base tragedies, he observes that "at first poets accepted any plots (*muthous*), but to-day the best tragedies are written about a few families— Alcmaeon for instance and Oedipus and Orestes and Meleager and Thyestes and Telephus and all the others whom it befell to suffer or inflict terrible disasters" (46–47; 1453a). This type of myth is deemed "best" for tragedy because it has the capacity to arouse fear (*phoberon*) and pity (*eleeinon*) in the spectator, the characteristics most "peculiar" (*idion*) to the genre (44–45; 1452b–1453a).

Whether myth as used by Aristotle in the second sense still retains today the power to invoke fear and pity, that is, whether it retains its relation to tragedy, is a largely metaphysical question. Any post-Aristotelian definition of tragedy, unless it limits itself to merely formal features that most modern readers would probably not view as essential to the genre, must address the impossible question of what elements combine to produce fear

---

5. E.g., Homer, *Od.* 3.94, 4.324. Originally, the term appears to have made no distinction between true and false content. As philosophical discourse developed and intensified between the eighth and fourth centuries, *muthos* came to be contrasted with *logos* and adopted the meaning of "fiction" as opposed to historic truth (e.g., Plato, *Phaedo* 212–13; 61b and *Protagoras* 128–29; 320c).

and pity in the spectator, since it is these emotional, nonquantifiable responses that continue to be the best measure of the "feel" of tragedy. Such is not the immediate focus of this study, and tragedy will be considered only when strictly relevant to the question of myth or desire in the plays discussed.

The present analysis is directed more toward the sense of myth as an "arrangement of incidents" that can be manipulated to produce works of artistic innovation not only in the theater but in other genres as well, for it is a similar manipulation that begins to set apart the sophisticated use of myth by literary artists from the traditional, oral narrations that originally gave it expression.[6] Paul de Man shows that this literary usage is already present in Homer:

> All literatures, including the literature of Greece, have always designated themselves as existing in the mode of fiction; in the *Iliad*, when we first encounter Helen, it is as the emblem of the narrator weaving the actual war into the tapestry of a fictional object. Her beauty prefigures the beauty of all future narratives as entities that point to their own fictional nature. The self-reflecting mirror-effect by means of which a work of fiction asserts, by its very existence, its separation from empirical reality, its divergence, as a sign, from a meaning that depends for its existence on the constitutive activity of this sign, characterizes the work of literature in its essence. (17)

In addition to Homer, authors who made frequent use of mythology for literary ends include Hesiod, the Greek tragedians, Virgil, Ovid, and Seneca. Although not all of them represented myth in a dramatic format, they all frequently served as inspiration to scores of playwrights of the postclassical tradition.

Aristotle distinguishes *muthos* in the strict sense from character (*ēthē*), which he judges to be second in importance for tragedy (26–27; 1450a–b). Yet character is virtually inextricable from the literary versions of myth

---

6. As Michael Simpson notes, myths "are the product of oral societies, not literate ones, and so it is spoken, not written, language that is the original province of myth" (3). In Greece this point is aptly demonstrated in the figure of the Muses, who must be appealed to for inspiration by Hesiod and Homer and the entire literary tradition that follows. That the Muses are conceived of as the daughters of Memory (Mnemosyne) indicates their symbolic function as vehicles for the preservation of myths in a culture without writing. On the traditional nature of myth, see Burkert, *Structure* 2. For characteristics of the recitation of oral myth, see Vernant 206–7.

narrated or dramatized in the above corpus of authors, and Aristotle himself recognizes that while not essential to drama, character is often developed "for the sake of" (*dia*) the action (24–25; 1450a). Expanding on the basic Aristotelian definition, in the present study I will use the term "myth" in the following sense: an arrangement of incidents and characters as exemplified in the principal authors of classical literature.[7] In addition, "mythology" will refer to a corpus of myths of a given cultural tradition such as the Greco-Roman one.[8]

In Spain, the early modern dramatists tended to take their myths from such Roman sources as Ovid's *Metamorphoses*, Virgil's *Aeneid*, and Seneca's tragedies. Seneca in particular, being a native of what is now Córdoba, exercised a special fascination over Spaniards of the period, most of whose knowledge of Greek sources was filtered through conventional wisdom or Roman literature. By contrast, writers of the twentieth century, perhaps influenced by revisionary works such as Nietzsche's *Birth of Tragedy* and Freud's famous reading of the Oedipus myth (as in *Interpretation* 307–9; chap. 5), have turned with increasing frequency to a wide array of Greek sources, although they often still read them through the lens of Seneca and other Roman writers (see Ahl, *Sophocles' Oedipus* 2).

Because of their divergent sources, each period witnesses a general preference for a different set of mythological figures. In the early modern period, stories surrounding the characters of Orpheus, Narcissus, Pyramus and Thisbe, Dido, Perseus, Venus and Adonis, Apollo and his many loves, Hercules, and Cephalus and Procris are particularly widespread. In contrast to these, twentieth-century playwrights have focused on heroes and heroines such as Oedipus, Phaedra, Electra, Antigone, Thyestes, Agamemnon, Clytemnestra, Medea, and Ulysses. Yet, although sources and preferences differ in the two periods, certain unifying features of the mythological tradition help to explain the appeal of the myths to Spanish playwrights from both time periods.

---

7. It is possible, but problematic, to differentiate myth into further categories such as legend, saga, fable, folklore, fairy tales, and "true" myth (see, for example, Kirk, *Myth* 31–41 and *Nature* 13–37; Burkert, *Structure* 1–34; Thompson; Graves 1:10; Rose 12–14). Such a division in the present context would only amount to splitting hairs unnecessarily, since the Spanish playwrights drew freely and indiscriminately from all these categories.

8. Although Kirk, *Nature* 21–22 suggests eschewing when possible this use of "mythology" and reserving the term for its more etymological meaning of the study of myths, I see nothing to be gained from defying hundreds of years of usage in order to create a distinction that most of the Spanish writers to be studied do not recognize.

Northrop Frye has suggested that "in terms of narrative, myth is the imitation of actions near or at the conceivable limits of desire" (136). Although vague, Frye's observation proves to be surprisingly useful in addressing the content of the myths chosen for adaptation by Spanish playwrights, since many of them narrate, apart from the obvious element of sexual or erotic desire implied in the tales mentioned above, what may tentatively be termed "negative" desires and their manifestations: hatred, jealousy, rejection, rivalry, aggression, and vengeance. The early modern period's well-known obsession with honor makes myths that treat themes of jealousy, rivalry, and vengeance most appealing. In the twentieth century, Freudian psychology has perhaps created greater interest in narcissism and incest, for example, whereas the Spanish Civil War forms a natural backdrop to the dramatization of such themes as rivalry, aggression, and hatred. An elaboration of Frye's suggestive statement with several theories from both the ancient and modern worlds will explain these motifs in terms of three categories of desire that function as primary character impulses in drama. Rather than providing a clinically accurate typology of desire or a full exposition of the many theories on the subject, the outline that follows is fundamentally literary and eclectic insofar as it borrows freely from different philosophic and psychological sources in order to propose a coherent model that can be used to explain desire as a structural and thematic principle for the adaptation of myth in the theater.

As is well known, in his *Republic* Plato proposed banishing from his ideal state poetic imitation as expressed in the theater. While this draconian measure might offend modern democratic and artistic sensibilities, behind it lie important clues to identifying qualities of Greek myth that have continued to exercise a compelling attraction over playwrights. In book 2 of the *Republic*, Plato proposes a censorship (*epistatēteon*) of the stories (*muthoi*) "that Hesiod and Homer and the other poets related to us" (1:176–79; 377c–d), that is, the principal stories of Greek mythology that became the favorite subject of the fifth-century tragedians. Plato's objection to such stories at this stage in the dialogue is that they represent the gods—who in his conception can be a source of nothing but good—in an unfavorable light, subjecting them to the basest passions of mortals (1: 182–87; 379a–d). It is not until book 10 of the *Republic* that Plato returns to the subject and states his principal objection to institutionalized storytelling in the theater:

> I think you know that the very best of us, when we hear Homer or some other of the makers of tragedy imitating one of the heroes who is in grief, and is delivering a long tirade in his lamentations or chanting and beating his breast, feel pleasure, and abandon ourselves and accompany the representation with sympathy and eagerness, and we praise as an excellent poet the one who most strongly affects us in this way. (2:458–59; 605c–d)

> And so in regard to the emotions of sex [*aphrodisiōn*] and anger [*thumou*], and all the appetites [*epithumētikōn*] and pains [*lupērōn*] and pleasures [*hēdeōn*] of the soul which we say accompany all our actions, the effect of poetic imitation is the same. For it waters and fosters these feelings when what we ought to do is to dry them up. (2:462–63; 606d)

The myths dramatized in theater, Plato argues, appeal to that irrational element of the soul that "loves, hungers, thirsts, and feels the flutter and titillation of other desires [*epithumias*], the irrational and appetitive [element]—companion of various repletions and pleasures" (*Republic* 1:396–99; 439d). In order best to control this irrational component of the soul, Plato suggests, the well-governed state should forbid the representation of such myths within its borders.

In this sense, myths for Plato are akin to dreams, as he explains in a remarkable passage from book 9 of the *Republic*, which, despite its length, deserves to be quoted in full:

> "Of our unnecessary pleasures [*hēdonōn*] and appetites [*epithumiōn*] there are some lawless ones [*paranomoi*], I think, which probably are to be found in us all, but which, when controlled by the laws and the better desires [*beltionōn epithumiōn*] in alliance with reason, can in some men be altogether got rid of, or so nearly so that only a few weak ones remain, while in others the remnant is stronger and more numerous." "What desires do you mean?" he said. "Those," said I, "that are awakened in sleep when the rest of the soul, the rational, gentle and dominant part, slumbers, but the beastly and savage part, replete with food and wine, gambols and, repelling sleep, endeavours to sally forth and satisfy its own instincts [*ēthē*]. You are aware that in such case there is nothing it

will not venture to undertake as being released from all sense of shame and all reason. It does not shrink from attempting to lie with a mother in fancy or with anyone else, man, god or brute. It is ready for any foul deed of blood; it abstains from no food, and, in a word, falls short of no extreme of folly and shamelessness." (2:334–37; 571b–d)

Dreams incarnate precisely those desires (*epithumiai*) that, in the form of dramatic *muthoi*, Plato would prefer to banish from his republic. As may be gathered from the above passages, such desires principally include lust, gluttony, and the urge to aggression.[9]

Based on the writings of various ancient authors, including Plato, Jung's concept of libido provides a coherent theory of desire that is readily applicable to the literary texts to be analyzed in this study:

[Libido] denotes a desire or impulse which is unchecked by any kind of authority, moral or otherwise. Libido is appetite in its natural state. From the genetic point of view it is bodily needs like hunger, thirst, sleep, and sex, and emotional states or affects, which constitute the essence of libido. (135–36)

[T]he concept of libido as desire or appetite is an *interpretation* of the process of psychic energy, which we experience precisely in the form of an appetite. We know as little about what underlies it as we know about what the psyche is *per se*. . . . We would be better advised, therefore, when speaking of libido, to understand it as an energy-value which is able to communicate itself to any field of activity whatsoever, be it power, hunger, hatred, sexuality, or religion, without ever being itself a specific instinct. (137)

Whereas libido for Jung was undifferentiated psychic energy, one product of which was sexual desire, Freud insisted on equating libido with the sexual instincts, which he always sought to oppose in hierarchical relation

---

9. Plato considers lust and gluttony, which he calls *epithumiai*, to be lawless desires. Aggression, when it reaches the extreme of murder and other "foul deeds of blood," is also considered lawless. Technically speaking, however, violence is a corrupt product of the spirited *thumoi*, which can, under separate circumstances and in conjunction with reason, act as a brake on the irrational *epithumiai* (*Republic* 1:396–405; 439d–440c).

to some other mental force.[10] What is important for the purposes of this study is that both Freud and Jung identify three distinct types of longing—aggressive, sexual, and nutritive (hunger and thirst)—that confirm the various manifestations of desire or *epithumia* that Plato, on a more intuitive basis, identified at the core of myth. A brief explanation of these three categories will attest to their prominence in classical mythology.

The desire for aggression, most prominently manifested in violence and the will to power, is, according to Freud, "an original, self-subsisting instinctual disposition in man, and . . . constitutes the greatest impediment to civilization" (*Civilization* 77). Walter Burkert explains this predisposition to violence as the residual trace of the roughly 95 to 99 percent of human evolutionary history devoted to the hunting and slaughtering of animals: "From this perspective, then, we can understand man's terrifying violence as deriving from the behavior of the predatory animal, whose characteristics he came to acquire in the course of becoming man" (*Homo Necans* 17). Whatever its cause, aggression is so widespread in Greek and Roman mythology as to be impossible to summarize briefly. Seneca and the Greek tragedians are particularly well known for dramatizing or narrating brutal acts of violence, but the prominence of aggression is perhaps best emphasized by signaling its frequency in Ovid, usually better known as a love poet. Ovid, in fact, seems to delight in narrating the goriest scenes imaginable, as the following passages from the *Metamorphoses* illustrate:

Clamanti cutis est summos direpta per artus,
nec quicquam nisi vulnus erat; cruor undique manat,
detectique patent nervi, trepidaeque sine ulla
pelle micant venae; salientia viscera possis
et perlucentes numerare in pectore fibras. (6.387–91)

[As (Marsyas) screamed, his skin was ripped from the surface of his limbs, leaving nothing but an open wound. Blood flowed

---

10. In his early writings, Freud posited a differentiation between what he called, on the one hand, the ego instincts or instincts of self-preservation such as hunger and thirst, and, on the other, the sexual instincts, which he termed libido (*Three Essays* 83; "Psychogenic Visual Disturbance" 55). In 1914 he elaborated his theory of narcissism, in which he observed a "libidinal complement to the egoism of the instinct of self-preservation" ("On Narcissism" 56), thus undermining the earlier opposition. Finally, in 1920 he developed a new distinction, between the libidinal instincts (eros), which now included hunger, thirst, and sexual desire, and the death instincts (thanatos), manifested in the desire for aggression (*Beyond* 65; *The Ego* 39).

everywhere, the sinews lay bare, and the tremulous veins pulsed
unprotected. You could count the quivering entrails and the exposed
vital organs in his chest.]

Figitur hinc duplici Gryneus in lumina ramo
eruiturque oculos, quorum pars cornibus haeret,
pars fluit in barbam concretaque sanguine pendet. (12.268–70)

[Gryneus was gored in the eyes by the antlers and his eyeballs were
gouged out. One of them stuck to the horns while the other rolled
down his beard and was suspended in a mass of congealed blood.]

Peleus . . . mediam ferit ense sub alvum.
Prosiluit terraque ferox sua viscera traxit
tractaque calcavit calcataque rupit et illis
crura quoque inpediit et inani concidit alvo. (12.388–92)

[Peleus hit (Dorylas) squarely in the belly with his sword. The
centaur lept forward and dragged his entrails along the ground wildly,
trampling and rupturing them as he went. His own legs became
ensnared in his intestines, and he fell foward with an empty
stomach.]

The reader who, unlike Dorylas, has retained the stomach to continue
will find similar descriptions placed liberally throughout the *Metamorphoses*, arguably the single most influential source of classical mythology
from the Renaissance to the present.

Sexual desire is equally prominent in classical mythology, although as a
motif it is curiously absent from Greek tragedy, with the important exception of Euripides' *Hippolytus*. In contrast, Venus's role as one of the three
main patrons of the Roman state, together with the convenient palindromic relation of Roma-Amor—which Roman poets exploited to the
fullest—ensured the central place of erotic desire in Latin literature. Under this rubric must be included not only explicit sexual desire for the
other but also repressed or veiled ("aim-inhibited") forms of erotic relations such as familial ties and friendships, as Freud explains:

> The nucleus of what we mean by love naturally consists (and this is
> what is commonly called love, and what the poets sing of) in sexual

> love with sexual union as its aim. But we do not separate from this—what in any case has a share in the name "love"—on the one hand, self-love, and on the other, love for parents and children, friendship and love for humanity in general, and also devotion to concrete objects and to abstract ideas. Our justification lies in the fact that psycho-analytic research has taught us that all these tendencies are an expression of the same instinctual impulses; in relations between the sexes these impulses force their way towards sexual union, but in other circumstances they are diverted from this aim or are prevented from reaching it, though always preserving enough of their original nature to keep their identity recognizable (as in such features as the longing for proximity, and self-sacrifice). (*Group Psychology* 22–23)

The salient characteristic of erotic desire that will allow its identification in literary texts is a longing for the union of two objects, whereas aggressive desire seeks the separation or annihilation of one object with respect to another.

There is, as Freud has noted, an intimate structural relation between aggression and sexuality, especially in men: "The sexuality of most male human beings contains an element of aggressiveness—a desire to subjugate; the biological significance of it seems to lie in the need for overcoming the resistance of the sexual object by means other than the process of wooing. Thus sadism would correspond to an aggressive component of the sexual instinct which has become independent and exaggerated and, by displacement, has usurped the leading position" (*Three Essays* 24). This relationship is widely thematized in mythological texts, perhaps most prominently in the acts of rape that so frequently occur in ancient literature. It is also the subject of the theories that René Girard develops in *Deceit, Desire, and the Novel* and elaborates further in *Violence and the Sacred*. According to Girard, violence, often expressed in the form of sacrifice, is frequently the result of a competitive situation that arises when two subjects actively desire the same object. For Girard, this object may represent the fulfillment of any desire, but it routinely presents itself as a sexual object. Desire is deemed mimetic, or mediated, inasmuch as one subject desires precisely *because of* another's similar desire. Girard cites the example of Don Quixote, who desires exactly what his model, Amadís de Gaula, desires and thus invents Dulcinea as the object of his erotic fantasies (*Deceit*, chap. 1). In *Violence and the Sacred*, Girard goes on to show how this configuration of desire forms the basis for many of the conflicts of mythology.

Girard's theories may be read as a transposition of Freudian psychological categories to a sociological or anthropological level. In this sense, he has been extremely helpful to critics who have examined the frequent triangular relationships in seventeenth-century Spanish theater. In *Mimesis conflictiva*, for example, Cesáreo Bandera employs Girardian theory as the basis for studying Calderón's *La vida es sueño* (in addition to the *Quixote*). Similarly, in *Deceit Plus Desire Equals Violence*, Debra Andrist applies a Girardian model to twelve plays by Lope and six by Calderón, concluding that, in both authors, "the interaction of the characters is of a triangular nature, pivoting on the concept of honor" (183). Additionally, the 1991 convention of the Modern Language Association devoted a panel to the topic "Girardian Criticism and the Comedia," with Girard as respondent (see *PMLA* 106 [1991]: 1333). While Bandera and Andrist do not concentrate on mythological texts, Girard proves to be particularly helpful in reading such plays from the early modern period. Narrower in scope than Freudian and Jungian theory, his model is nevertheless compatible with theirs and may be considered as an additional formulation to aid in explaining the expression of erotic and aggressive desires.[11]

The nutritive desires constitute the most elemental of the three categories inasmuch as the subject cannot survive without their satisfaction. Precisely because of their somatically determined nature, they might be more accurately termed a "need" rather than a desire. Again, however, the literary, as opposed to clinical, focus of this study must be emphasized. Freud himself often relied on the great poets in the absence of verifiable medical evidence and, in the matter at hand, cites Schiller to the effect that "we can classify under 'hunger' or under 'love' every active organic instinct of our souls" ("Psychogenic Visual Disturbance" 55). Elsewhere he states that "in every way analogous to *hunger*, libido is the force by means of which the sexual instinct, as, with hunger, the nutritional instinct, achieves expression" ("Twentieth Lecture" 322).

---

11. Walter Burkert's *Homo Necans*, originally published the same year as the French version of *Violence and the Sacred*, arrives at some of the same conclusions reached by Girard, as Burkert himself notes in the preface to the English translation of his book (xiii). Because Burkert's work concentrates exclusively on classical, mainly Greek, texts, it has not gained the widespread currency of Girard's, but his claim that the "most exciting themes in myth come from the realm of sexuality and aggression" (33) validates the present study's approach to mythology. Girard and Burkert are the subject of the collection of essays titled *Violent Origins*, edited by Hamerton-Kelly.

Certain well-known stories from mythology bear out the importance of the nutritive desires, not simply in acts of eating and drinking but in genuine motives that determine characters' actions. Although hunger is a more prominent motif than thirst, both are strongly embodied in the figure of Tantalus, tortured in Hades by the river and by fruit-laden trees that remain forever beyond his reach. Hunger alone figures conspicuously in the myth of the voracious Erysichthon, for example, and eating, the satisfaction of hunger, is an integral, if ghastly, part of the cannibalistic narratives of Procne, Tereus, and Philomela and of Atreus and Thyestes (descendants of Tantalus). It is thus wholly justifiable to include hunger and thirst in the hermeneutical framework of this study even while recognizing that they might fulfill a more limited role than the aggressive and sexual desires.

The importance of the three categories of desire in mythology is apparent not just in their manifestation but also in their prohibition, in the form of taboo, "a primaeval prohibition forcibly imposed (by some authority) from outside, and directed against the most powerful longings to which human beings are subject. The desire to violate it persists in their unconscious; those who obey the taboo have an *ambivalent* attitude toward what the taboo prohibits" (Freud, *Totem* 34–35). Significantly, the three most prominent taboos in classical myth are those that prohibit sexual intercourse (as in the Oedipus myth), murder (again in the story of Oedipus as well as in the *Oresteia*), and various acts of eating and drinking (exemplified in the etiquette of sacrifice as encoded, for example, in the myth of Prometheus related in Hesiod's *Theogony*).

A final demonstration of the centrality of the nutritive, erotic, and aggressive desires in myth is their full expression in the most famous figure of mythology, Hercules. Hercules' prodigious strength, as employed in his famous labors, endows him with a capacity for extreme violence that he does not hesitate to use. Additionally, he is well known for his gluttony, so mercilessly ridiculed in Aristophanes' *Birds*, for example, as well as for his insatiable lust, which resulted in the birth of numerous children. In the Spanish medieval period, in fact, Hercules' infamous lust became the source of a legend that attributed to him much of the Spanish population (Alfonso X, *Estoria de Espanna* 57; chap. 8).

The three categories of desire, whether differentiated from the start, as Freud believed, or the product of a primordial libidinal energy, as in Jung's conception, are undoubtedly closely related and often become confused insofar as "the same object may serve for the satisfaction of several instincts simultaneously" (Freud, "Instincts" 88). In addition to the fact that sexuality is frequently confused with aggression, the sexual act is often associated with eating or the act of consumption, a similarity borne out by numerous semantic parallels in the popular vocabularies of many European languages, both ancient and modern. Finally, eating is routinely linked with violence and the sacrificial act, as Walter Burkert amply demonstrates in *Homo Necans.*

This, then, is the essential model of desire with which the present analysis will be concerned: a model that finds an already solid foundation in the ancient world, in Plato's *Republic,* and that is enriched, but not substantially altered, by the twentieth-century theories of Freud, Jung, Girard, and Burkert. While it would certainly prove interesting to delve further into contemporary psychoanalytic theory as represented in the works of Melanie Klein or Jacques Lacan, for example, doing full justice to these thinkers would necessitate a digression unwarranted in the context of this study given that the model thus far elaborated is sufficient for addressing the texts at hand. Nonetheless, since an occasional isolated reference to the work of Lacan will prove useful, a schematic summary of his thought seems called for.

One of the central tenets of Lacan's thought, and the one that best illustrates its evolution from its Freudian model, is that desire is symbolically articulated to the extent that it is mediated by language. Taking off from the work of the Swiss linguist Ferdinand de Saussure, Lacan emphasizes the importance of the signifier (the written word or acoustic image) over the signified (the idea or concept called forth by the signifier) in analytic practice: "The passion of the signifier now becomes a new dimension of the human condition in that it is not only man who speaks, but that in man and through man *it* speaks (*ça parle*), that his nature is woven by effects in which is to be found the structure of language, of which he becomes the material, and that therefore there resounds in him, beyond what could be conceived of by a psychology of ideas, the relation of speech" (Lacan 284). Since, according to Saussure, the relationship between language and reality is representational and ultimately arbitrary, desire, for Lacan, can never by fully satisfied but instead is constantly frustrated by the adult subject's inability to access the realm of the "Real" and recuperate the illusion of unity that is shattered once he or she is forced, through language, to enter the realm of the "Symbolic": "In any case, man cannot aim at being whole (the 'total personality' is another of the deviant premises of modern psychology), while ever the play of displacement and condensation to which he is doomed in the excercise of his functions marks his relation as a subject to the signifier" (287). As Kaja Silverman has succinctly stated, "One could say of the Lacanian subject that it is almost entirely defined by lack" (151). It is this idea of lack, of the infinite deferral of the realization of desire, that will occasionally prove useful throughout the analysis as a supplement to the tripartite model of desire developed independently of Lacanian theory.[12]

Because of their rich symbolic potential, structural flexibility, and poetic, if not scientific, association, the three categories of desire form a particularly useful axis along which Spanish playwrights model their adaptations. Achieving the balance between artistic innovation and respect for the classical model is not an easy task. On the one hand, changing too much risks severing completely the link with the myth that inspired the adaptation. On the other, too much reverence for the model creates a rigidity that leaves little room for artistic innovation. Simply stated, the thesis of the present study is that playwrights frequently achieve the necessary balance between tradition and innovation through a reorientation of desire in the classical models. The close affiliation of the three desires lends itself well to the creative process involved in adapting myth, a process that often looks to build on thematic analogies and structural similarities. The different categories can be manipulated, combined, or expanded in ways that maintain the general ingredients of the *muthos* while permitting the addition of other elements that reflect the particular concerns of the playwrights and their historical periods. In the following analyses I seek to chart the course of Spanish dramatists as they navigate the challenges and pitfalls of mythological adaptation.

---

12. Marshall 110–12 provides an excellent summary of the voluminous bibliography on Lacan. The interested reader may also wish to pursue the work of Julia Kristeva, whose writings greatly expand on Lacan's view of desire as linguistically mediated. See Marshall 113 for a bibliography.

2

Three Authors in Search of a Story

The Emplotment of Desire in the Sixteenth-Century Theater

A common misconception regarding mythological plays of early modern Spanish literature is that such works begin to appear only in the late sixteenth century. J. P. Wickersham Crawford perhaps inaugurates this idea when he claims that Francisco de la Cueva y Silva's *Trajedia de Narciso* (c. 1580) is "interesting as a unique example of the dramatic use of mythological material which attained such favor in the court plays of the following century" (*Spanish Drama* 174–75). Writing much more recently, José María Díez Borque confirms Crawford's assertion by suggesting that Cueva y Silva "da a la mitología los anchos campos del drama" (*Los géneros* 122).

These statements are simply not supported by the facts. In a recent lecture ("From Mantua to Madrid"), Michael McGaha suggests that the mythological play begins at least as early as Juan Timoneda's *Tragicomedia llamada Filomena* (1564), modeled on the story of Procne and Philomela from book 6 of Ovid's *Metamorphoses*. Moreover, in the same aforementioned studies in which they credit Cueva y Silva with the origin of the mythological play, both Crawford (160) and Díez Borque (113) refer to a work by Juan Cirne from 1536, *Tragedia de los amores de Eneas y de la reyna Dido*, which is clearly based on book 4 of Virgil's *Aeneid*.

In addition, classical models inspire two novels in dialogue form from the first half of the sixteenth century. In 1536 Cristóbal de Villalón based his *Tragedia de Mirrha* on the tale from book 10 of the *Metamorphoses*, and in 1547 Sebastián Fernández published his *Tragedia Policiana*, inspired by Ovid's story of Pyramus and Thisbe (*Met.* 4), among others. While clearly not meant for stage representation, these works further document the use of classical myth in the early dramatic medium.

The presence of these works should be no cause for surprise. The formative period of the Spanish theater coincides with the fruition of the wider European Renaissance, and writers naturally looked to the classical tradition in seeking stories for dramatic adaptation. A study of Greco-Roman myth in the early modern Spanish theater must therefore begin with the sixteenth century, framed at one end by the origins of the genre and at the other by the conceptual break implied in Lope de Vega's *comedia nueva*. Besides the works mentioned above, potential candidates for such a study would include Cristóbal de Virués's *Elisa Dido* (c. 1580), Gabriel Lobo Lasso de la Vega's *Tragedia de la honra de Dido restaurada* (1587), and Juan de la Cueva's *Tragedia de la muerte de Ayax Telamón, sobre las armas de Aquiles* (1588).

One characteristic of the Spanish theater's formative period, in which all these works were written, is the search for a universal formula of plot construction that Lope's *comedia nueva* ultimately supplied. The rapidness with which different schools of drama came and went suggests that they were all searching in vain for this technique. The imperative of "delightful instruction," which can be traced back to Horace (333–34), implicitly guided the search insofar as its fulfillment satisfied two unspoken but crucial objectives of the early playwrights. First, their works had to be capable of engrossing and entertaining the audience, whether the latter consisted of nobility, as in the early part of the century when wealthy aristocrats were the main patrons of theater, or of the working-class theatergoers who became increasingly important after the commercialization of drama around the middle of the century. The simple fact was that if playwrights did not entertain they had little chance of competing for audience demand. Second, in light of the stern contemporary debates over the morality of the theater (see Cotarelo, *Bibliografía*), the ability of the piece to claim that it was edifying the public proved to be a viable defense against powerful opponents.

Besides being faced with Horace's dicta, artists were confronted with the literary imperatives of enormously prestigious contemporary writers such as Erasmus, whose *Ciceronianus* (1528)—a work very popular in Spain, moreover (Bataillon 314)—calls for not only "imitation" but "emulation" of the classics: "Imitation looks toward likeness, but emulation looks toward superiority. And so if you put before you Cicero, entire and alone, . . . you must not merely overtake him but you must outstrip him" (58).[1] Erasmus concludes that "no one was ever so finished an artist that you could not find in his work something which could be done better" (127). Many playwrights were able to address both the Horatian and Erasmian objectives through a remodeling of the architecture of desire in the myths with which they chose to work. An analysis of several relevant plays will reveal the methods that the playwrights employ in rewriting myth as well as how those methods fit into the historical and literary context of the Renaissance.

All of the plays cited above are explicitly based on myths of classical antiquity: both their plots and characters clearly indicate the antecedents from which they are drawn. Such works will normally be the only object of analysis in this study in order both to limit the field of inquiry and to avoid the difficult problem of the recognizability of mythological patterns when they are not specified by the author. However, one initial exception to this general rule will be useful. Although Juan del Encina's *Égloga de Plácida y Vitoriano* (1513) is not overtly based on a classical model, a careful analysis reveals it to be a subtle and original reworking of Ovid's tale of Pyramus and Thisbe. Given Encina's paramount importance in the history of Spanish theater, it is appropriate to begin the present study with the play that is at once the "first great *comedia*" (ter Horst, "Duke and Duchess" 20) as well as the first original Spanish dramatic rewriting of a classical myth. In addition, in this chapter I will consider the plays of Timoneda and Cueva y Silva mentioned above. A reading of their works along with Encina's will reveal the progressive stages in the use of desire in the sixteenth-century theater's rewriting of ancient myths.

While necessarily excluding other mythological plays of the same period, the proposed selection is justified in the first place by the works' common Ovidian source, whereas the other plays cited are culled from such diverse sources as Virgil, Justin, and Livy. Furthermore, as María Rosa Lida de Malkiel has shown, it is probable that writers such as Virués and certainly Lobo Lasso de la Vega, in assuming the role of defending the

---

1. Cf. Quintilian 76–77; 10.2.4. See Pigman for a full discussion of *imitatio* and *emulatio* in the Renaissance.

"honor" of Dido against the artistic Virgilian tradition, conceived of themselves as writing not so much literature as history (106–20), a position that carries their plays beyond the scope of the present analysis. In the second place, the plays of Encina (1468–1529), Timoneda (1520?–1583), and Cueva y Silva (d. 1628) form an ideal unit for comparison because of their timely placement at three crucial junctures in the history of the sixteenth-century secular theater: the beginnings (Encina), the rise of the commercial theater through the influence of Italian theater companies (Timoneda), and the vogue of classical tragedy (Cueva y Silva) immediately preceding the advent of Lope de Vega.

Desire and the Play of Inversion: The Fourteenth Eclogue of Juan del Encina

The *Égloga de Plácida y Vitoriano* is a dramatization of sexual desire manifested in the self's striving for union or communication with the other. The relation between the two lovers is governed by a longing to contemplate, interact with, and possess the beloved. Plácida's very name confirms the hedonistic relationship, as Suplicio's comment to Vitoriano at the beginning of the play suggests: "Plácida, según te plaze . . ." (353).[2] The obsession of both protagonists with the other's physical characteristics further documents the nature of their relationship. Plácida refers to Vitoriano as "lind[o]" (214) and "bello" (216), while his description of her leaves little doubt as to the character of his desire: "En mirar sus perfeciones / se despiden mis enojos, / he por buenas mis passiones. / ¡O, qué rostro y qué faciones, / qué garganta, boca y ojos! / ¡Y qué pechos / tan perfetos, tan bien hechos, / que me ponen mill antojos" (801–8). He longs to possess her and reconstructs her presence within the limits of his own identity: "Dentro en mí contemplo en ella; / siempre con ella me sueño; / no puedo partirme della" (817–18). Encina derives the nature and trajectory of these desires from a manipulation of Ovid's story of Pyramus and Thisbe (*Met.* 4.55–166) in order to give form and structure to his play.

Of the many critics who have discussed Encina's *Égloga de Plácida y Vi-*

---

2. Given this explanation offered within the play itself, it is puzzling to read the following: "Why his [Vitoriano's] beloved should be dubbed 'placid' or 'tranquil' is not obvious and seems ironical" (Sullivan 99).

toriano, only Donald McGrady has noticed an explicit similarity between its structure and that of Ovid's tale of Pyramus and Thisbe.³ Observing that "both in Encina's play and in the story of Ovid's *Metamorphoses* (Book IV), a lover resolves to commit suicide upon finding, next to a spring or stream, the body of his/her beloved, who has just performed self-murder" (139), he does not elaborate on these promising connections but simply adds in a note: "To be sure, the surrounding circumstances in the two stories are quite different, but the correspondences are such to seem beyond the realm of coincidence" (140 n. 3). Although McGrady deserves credit for being the first to recognize fundamental parallels between the Latin myth and the Spanish play, the connections go well beyond his brief remarks. A full understanding of Encina's longest and most complex eclogue requires a detailed analysis both of the explicit similarities between the two works and of the ways in which Encina uses the Ovidian model.

Regarding what one might call iconographic similarities—that is, descriptions of static objects or conditions—the stream cited by McGrady provides an important link to Ovid's *gelidus fons* (*Met.* 4.90). Encina has Vitoriano first spy Plácida's dead body next to a *fuente* (1428–29), which is reconfirmed in line 2254. The importance of the image is underscored by its mention in both the *argumento* and the *introito* that precede the play.⁴

Although it may seem incidental, the *fons* was a key element in the transmission of Ovid's story throughout the medieval and Renaissance periods. In Boccaccio's enormously popular *Elegia di Madonna Fiammetta* (c. 1343), Lady Fiammetta is careful to include the *fons* in her short synopsis of Ovid's story in chapter 8 (153). Boccaccio's *novella* was translated into Spanish in 1497 in Encina's hometown of Salamanca (Schevill 113 n. 84), although the playwright probably could have read it in Italian, given his extensive visits to Italy. In addition to this key source, a large portion of late medieval and early Renaissance iconography dealing with the Pyr-

---

3. Stanislav Zimic remarks that the stories of Hero and Leander and of Pyramus and Thisbe "de seguro inspiraron de modo importante a Encina" (311) but gives no further explanation. Rambaldo (Encina 260n) simply repeats McGrady's assertion. Gimeno (74, 85) notes the significance of Pyramus and Thisbe when they are alluded to in the text but does not view their story as a general outline for Encina's. Testa's study of the Pyramus and Thisbe theme in early modern poetry makes no mention of Encina, nor does either of Hart's studies that purport to trace the myth throughout its European manifestations.

4. Even if Joseph Meredith is correct in suggesting that "we do not need to attribute the prose argument to Encina" (18), the fact that the *fuente* would have been specified by the printers who supplied the *argumento* attests equally to its importance.

amus and Thisbe story consistently included Ovid's *fons* in the form of a stream or fountain (see, for example, Schmitt-Von Mühlenfels: plates 5–7, 14–17).

A second important visual element that links the two stories is their common nocturnal setting. Ovid describes how the two lovers steal outside for their meeting when "lux . . . praecipitatur aquis, et aquis nox exit ab isdem" 'the daylight plunged into the waters and the night arose from the same waters' (4.91–92). In Vitoriano's opening monologue, he addresses Plácida in a surprised apostrophe, "¿Tú dormiendo y yo velando?" (309), suggesting the presence of the night that was to provide cover for the lovers' encounter. Shortly afterward, in his first meeting with Suplicio, Vitoriano must call out to his friend in order to wake him (329), at which the latter replies: "Muchas veces te he rogado / y pedido y suplicado / que de noche no andes fuera" (339–41). The night, like the image of the stream, is a key element in the transmission of the myth of Pyramus and Thisbe, appearing in the same passage of Boccaccio cited above and in at least one of the works of art analyzed by Schmitt-Von Mühlenfels (plate 5, in which the moon is clearly present).[5]

The final iconographic similarity linking the two tales is the curious fact that both of the female characters are in a state of partial or complete undress when they commit suicide. Ovid narrates that Thisbe, on fleeing from the lioness at the spot of her planned rendezvous with Pyramus, "tergo velamina lapsa reliquit" 'left her shawl behind on the ground' (4.101). The same article of clothing is mentioned again as a *tenuis amictus* in line 104 and as a *vestis* in 107. Akin to something like a light, probably revealing, cape or shawl, Thisbe's garment, when subsequently mauled

---

5. Time in *Plácida y Vitoriano* is a rather complicated issue. As in most of early modern literature, in Encina chronology is generally driven not by an objective, external measure of unity but rather by the exigencies of the plot. The same logic also governs space. In a fascinating analysis Ronald Surtz locates the origin of these conventions in the spatiotemporal conception of the liturgy (35–44). Extending into many other dramatic works of the early modern period, they might also be explained by Alexander A. Parker's pithy principle of "the primacy of theme over action, with the consequent irrelevance of realistic verisimilitude" (706–7). Similar principles govern nondramatic works such as the *Quixote* (see Morón Arroyo 246–61). Even so, with the exception of a few inconsistencies such as those noted by Raymond Grismer (127)—which might be attributed, nonetheless, to exaggeration or simplicity, given that they come from the mouths of the comic shepherds—the play appears to take place in the course of one night, beginning with the planned nocturnal encounter of the lovers and ending with the daybreak that marks the discovery of Plácida's body. For more details, see Gimeno (88 n. 7). In any case, whatever chronological inconsistencies may exist in the play should not serve to dismiss the importance of its predominantly nocturnal setting.

by the lioness, most likely leaves her close to naked, and she is represented in this state by many medieval and Renaissance artists. Lady Fiammetta says that Pyramus found not simply one garment but rather her "clothing" [*vestimenti*], and in many of the paintings exhibited by Schmitt-Von Mühlenfels Thisbe appears undressed whereas Pyramus is clothed (see, in particular, plates 7, 17, 24).

This circumstance helps to explain the puzzling statement that Plácida makes before killing herself: "Por menos embaraçarme / en los miembros impedidos, / para más presto matarme, / muy bien será desnudarme / y quitarme los vestidos / que me estorvan" (1288–93). That she actually does undress is confirmed later when, after she has been resurrected by Mercurio, Vitoriano must tell her somewhat awkwardly to put her clothes back on (2466). Ann Wiltrout interprets Plácida's action as an effort to liberate herself of earthly possessions (9); there is no evidence, however, of this line of reasoning in the play. It may be that Plácida's statement simply represents, in the absence of a lioness to destroy her clothing, the rationalization of an element that Encina did not wish to eliminate, given its strong presence in the iconographic trajectory of the myth.

The first example of narrative as opposed to iconographic similarities between the two stories is the prose *argumento* that recounts the circumstances immediately preceding the action of Encina's play. It describes Plácida and Vitoriano as "amándose ygualmente de verdaderos amores" (184). This detail would not be significant if it did not defy the entire tradition of courtly love, whose novelty consists partially in the "elevation of the beloved to a place of superiority above the lover."[6] Given the ubiquitous presence of courtly love in early modern Castilian literature (Green, *Spain* 1:96), any departure from its conventions deserves full attention and explanation.

According to Robert Hathaway, the "neoplatonic conception [of love] starts with equality, true although sometimes hidden" (40). Accordingly, one might argue that the equality of love with which Encina's play begins is due to the influence of Neoplatonism that the author perhaps absorbed while in Italy or even, as Américo Castro suggests, while under the tutelage of the celebrated humanist Antonio de Nebrija at the University of Salamanca ("Lo hispánico" 1942:54). Wiltrout (2) argues for just such an assimilation by Encina, and Gillet (315–16) observes a similar phenome-

---

6. Denomy 20; see also Van Beysterveldt, *La poesía* 61–62; Gillet 345; Green, *Spain* 1:72–78; Hathaway 39–46.

non in his contemporary Bartolomé de Torres Naharro, who spent a significant amount of time in Italy as well.[7] Gimeno, in contrast, cites the concept of *amor complido* in Don Juan Manuel as a model for the "verdadero amor" of Plácida and Vitoriano (62–63). Without discounting any of these possibilities, one can suggest yet another precedent for the equality of Encina's lovers: that reflected in Ovid's statement that Pyramus and Thisbe "ex aequo captis ardebant mentibus ambo" 'burned equally with captive senses' (4.62).

McGrady has already suggested that the planned double suicide of Plácida and Vitoriano betrays an Ovidian influence, but in the circumstances surrounding the event one finds even more compelling similarities at the narrative level between Encina's and Ovid's works. A careful reading of Vitoriano's verbose speech upon discovering Plácida's corpse ("Vigilia de la enamorada muerta," 1547–2186), long scorned by most critics as offensive, tedious, or trivial, discloses some of the most patent connections with the tale of Pyramus and Thisbe.[8]

First of all, Vitoriano puts forward the idea that Plácida deserves a longer life because of her devoutness: "Vitam y misericordiam / mereció su devoción, / que no sentencia de muerte, / ni tormento, ni passión" (2065–68). This passage corresponds closely to Pyramus's complaint that "e quibus illa fuit longa dignissima vita" 'of both of us she was most deserving of a long life' (4.109). Second, Vitoriano recognizes that he is to blame for his lover's death: "Ne recorderis peccata / de Plácida, ques sin culpa, / pues mi culpa la desculpa" (2037–39; see also 2131–34). Pyramus expresses a similar thought in the following way:

> Nostra nocens anima est. Ego te, miseranda, peremi,
> in loca plena metus qui iussi nocte venires
> nec prior huc veni. (4.110–12)

---

7. See also Green, *Spain* 1:127–28 for Neoplatonism in Torres Naharro. Hathaway, however, would probably be skeptical with regard to Neoplatonic theory in Encina, asserting as he does that its "impact on the earliest theatre was minimal" (39).

8. Objections to the *vigilia* are found in Cotarelo y Mori, "Juan del Encina" 177; Menéndez Pelayo, Prólogo lxxxix; Kohler, *Representaciones* 12; Álvarez de la Villa 220; Turk 322; Austin 170; López Morales, *Tradición* 207; Van Beysterveldt, *La poesía* 281; and Sullivan 102. Only Gimeno 83 and ter Horst, "*Ut Pictura Poesis*" 16 seem to have appreciated the importance of the *vigilia* in the play. For an extended discussion of its sources and formal features, see Mancini.

[My conscience is to blame. I have ruined you, wretched girl, for I asked you to come to this dreadful area in the middle of the night without coming first myself.]

Third, Vitoriano prays to the "deus de amor" (1817) for his own death in order to join his beloved: "Confitebor a ti, dios, / secundum la tu justicia, / júntanos a estos dos" (1953–55).[9] He asks to be punished in return for Plácida's absolution from all blame: "Fidelium deus de amor, / de todos presta alegría, / a Plácida da el favor; / y a mí la pena y dolor, / y que muera en este día" (2107–11). Although the idea of sacrificing himself to redeem the sins of his beloved carries clear Christian and possibly Neoplatonic connotations, as Wiltrout observes (9), such associations should not conceal the play's debt to Ovid, which is made manifest in this case by Pyramus's own prayers for death: "Nostrum divellite corpus / et scelerata fero consumite viscera morsu, / o quicumque sub hac habitatis rupe leones!" 'Dismember my body, o whatever lions live ye beneath this cliff, and devour in ferocious gulps my guilt-ridden insides!' (4.112–14).[10] Pyramus concludes that only the timid beg for death (4.115) and decides to take the matter into his own hands by killing himself. Vitoriano reaches the same decision after his prayers to Cupido apparently go unanswered (2139–40).

Finally, Vitoriano's desire to share Plácida's grave with her—"A ti, dios, / suplico que a todos dos / des en muerte una posada" (2136–38)—recalls Thisbe's plea to her absent parents to "quos certus amor, quos hora novissima iunxit, / conponi tumulo non invideatis eodem" 'not begrudge a joint burial to those whom true love and the most recent circumstances have brought together' (4.156–57).

Any one of the features linking Encina's work to Ovid's tale of Pyramus and Thisbe could, by itself, easily be dismissed as coincidental or derivative of different sources. The *fons*, for example, is an important element of the *locus amoenus*, whose minimum ingredients are, according to Ernst Robert Curtius, "a tree (or several trees), a meadow, and a spring or brook" (195). The motif of the common grave, furthermore, recalls Melibea's entreaty to her father in *Celestina* 20 (Rojas 334), and many critics have noted the influence of Rojas's work as well as of other penin-

---

9. See also 1657–61, 1708–9, 1729–30, 1945–46, and 1993–96.
10. Cf. Lucan 2.312 and the discussion in Ahl, *Lucan* 244.

sular sources on *Plácida y Vitoriano*.[11] Others have suggested a perceptible role of Italian sources in the composition of Encina's work.[12] While such arguments may be compelling, they do not preclude Encina's knowledge and use of material from Ovid as well. His debt to the *Remedia Amoris* in the play has already been established.[13] From the cumulative evidence presented above, it seems reasonable to conclude that the influence of book 4 of the *Metamorphoses* was no less important. The mention of Pyramus and Thisbe by Vitoriano himself, within the fictional boundaries of the play (2311) and as the culmination of a long list of allusions to famous couples of antiquity (see 385–97, 1274–76, 1702–4, 2310), serves as a final confirmation of this conclusion.[14]

Given that the *Égloga de Plácida y Vitoriano* is based on the story of Pyramus and Thisbe, the first point to note regarding Encina's use of his model is that the eclogue *begins* with the lovers' planned nocturnal encounter that is the *culmination* of Ovid's story. Plácida's opening monologue makes it clear that she had expected to meet with Vitoriano in the countryside through which she now roams in distress (89–94). The actual process of falling in love, described with care by Ovid (4.59–64), is presupposed in the prose *argumento* of the play. Also presupposed in this brief prologue is a "cierta discordia, como suele acontescer" (184–85) between the two lovers. Since the *discordia* leads to the frustrated encounter and ultimately to Plácida's suicide, it is the sine qua non of the play and an analysis of Encina's adaptation of Ovid must begin with it.[15]

Commentators have often wondered about the reasons for Vitoriano's break with Plácida. Van Beysterveldt explains the protagonist's actions as

---

11. Cotarelo 178; Menéndez Pelayo, Prólogo lxxxvii–lxxxviii; Bonilla 105; Meredith 18; Valbuena [Prat], *Literature* 32; Turk 329; Crawford, *Spanish Drama* 27; Ruiz Ramón, *Historia . . . desde* 47; Hathaway 63; Sullivan 99; López Morales, "*Celestina.*"

12. Mazzei 47–53; Kohler, *Representaciones* 15, *Sieben* 41; Crawford, *Spanish Drama* 27; Austin 168; Hathaway 68–69; Sullivan 99; McKendrick 13; Pérez Priego 75. But see Menéndez Pelayo, Prólogo lxxxvi; Álvarez de la Villa 197; Meredith 21; and Shergold 145, all of whom question the importance of Italian sources.

13. Crawford, *Spanish Drama* 26; Hathaway 63; Gimeno 71–72; Sullivan 99.

14. It is not inconceivable that Encina would have read Ovid in Latin. If that was not the case, he could have become acquainted with the myth of Pyramus and Thisbe in Castilian through the thirteenth-century *General Estoria* of Alfonso el Sabio, in which the tale appears intact (195–201; 2.70–74), or in one of the many vernacular manifestations of the immensely popular story (see Hart).

15. Whether the *argumento* was added by the printers is irrelevant, for the *discordia* is implied throughout the entire play.

an attempt to escape the bonds that love would imply (*La poesía* 278), whereas Hathaway can offer only the *Celestina* as a possible answer to the question (63 n. 18). The overlooked Ovidian connection offers an equally convincing explanation of this "enigmatic" (in Hathaway's words) relationship.

Ovid's narrator states that the lovers' parents strictly opposed their children's union but offers no reasons for the opposition: "Taedae quoque iure coissent, / sed vetuere patres" 'They would have been united in the bonds of matrimony as well, but their parents forbid them' (4.60–61). The conflict between the wishes of the parents and the desires of the children forms an axis of tension in the story that precipitates the violent ending. Derived from this unexplained conflict, the disagreement between the lovers in *Plácida y Vitoriano* is a structural exigency that, in the absence of the parents, allows Encina to reproduce the myth's fundamental antagonism. He converts this antagonism into viable dramatic form by placing the obstacle between the protagonists themselves rather than in some absent, external cause. The play as a whole represents two major movements that trace the tension between the conflicting desires of the lovers and that are followed by a synthesis resolving the opposition.

Several critics have commented on the scenes in the play centering on the two comic shepherds, Gil and Pascual. Crawford suggests that these scenes serve as prototypes for the later *paso* or *entremés* and are introduced for comic relief (*Spanish Drama* 27). López Morales expands on this idea:

> Descontando la última participación de los pastores, que cierra la obra, las otras dos actúan como pautas bien definidas que dividen la acción dramática en tres partes. Cada una de esas partes forma en sí un pequeño núcleo argumental que se caracteriza por un creciente desarrollo emotivo. Adviértase que las escenas propiamente pastoriles no están distribuidas al azar, ni tampoco en términos de equipolencia, sino que, por el contrario, aparecen en los momentos de mayor tensión dramática, precisamente para desvanecerla. A estos descansos emocionales llamamos, en terminología moderna, entreactos. (*Tradición* 207–8)

López Morales's three "nuclei" (1–1192, 1193–2274, and 2275–578, counting the shepherd scenes as part of the unit that they terminate) correspond closely to the *enlace*, *clímax*, and *desenlace* that Rosalie Gimeno perceives in the play (68).[16] Regardless of terminology, the three sections of the play may be read as the result of Encina's reconfiguration of the sexual desires present in Ovid's story.

The first of the three units cited by López Morales, from the beginning of the play to line 1192, dramatizes the consequences of the *discordia* mentioned in the *argumento*. Plácida, "encendida en viva llama," as Gil describes (28), reacts violently when Vitoriano does not appear as planned. Her long opening monologue (89–256) is characterized by an emotional turmoil that oscillates between desperation, hatred, and love. The equality of her relationship with Vitoriano shattered, her actions and vocabulary are now indeed reminiscent of the tradition of courtly love, but with a curious twist: she seems to be playing the role of the (male) lover rather than the (female) beloved. It is she who burns with desire for her lover, and it is her love that goes unrequited.

Plácida describes her relationship to Vitoriano as one of potentially life-threatening bondage and servitude, typical language of the lover in the courtly tradition: "Mi vida, mi cuerpo y alma / en su poder se trasportan, / toda me tiene en su palma" (113–15), and similarly: "mas sólo por le servir / querría, triste, bivir" (123–24). The deification of the beloved by the lover, another trope frequent in courtly love (see Gillet 337–44; Green, *Spain* 1:73), is evident in the following sentence: "Tráyote puesto en retablo / y adórote como a Dios" (161–62). It is unclear whether Plácida is referring in these lines to Vitoriano or to Cupido. The language of the verses that directly precede them, "¡O maldito dios de amor, / que me tratas tanto daño!" would seem to indicate the latter, but there is a later instance in the play in which Vitoriano refers to a human character (Flugencia) as his "dios de amor" (637). The resulting ambiguity, in which Vitoriano and Cupido become indistinguishable for Plácida, intensifies the trope of the deification of the beloved. Bruce Wardropper notes that this type of heresy forms the basis of the tragedy in *La Celestina* ("Metamorphosis" 50), but, coming from the mouth of a woman, Placida's phrase contrasts strikingly with Calisto's in *Celestina* 1, for example (Rojas 93). Plácida even suggests that, like Calisto, she may have considered the services of a go-between but realizes that such measures would be of no avail: "Contra tal apartamiento / no prestan hechizerías / ni aprovecha encantamiento" (169–71).

---

16. Other critics have devised different schemes for dividing the play. See Kohler, *Sieben* 41; Crawford, *Spanish Pastoral* 45; Sullivan 96–97; Mazzei 49.

If Plácida represents the values and vocabulary of the pursuer or *galán*, Vitoriano's responses to her throughout most of the first movement accord with the norms expected of any respectable lady: to dismiss and forget the suitor. Curiously, however, the beginning of his first monologue closely corresponds, lexically speaking, to Plácida's. Addressing himself as "captivo de tal señora," he wonders how he can escape her power. His answer carries the same tinges of desperation as do Plácida's laments: "Nunca espero libertarme / de tan dichosa prisión, / ni de aquesta fe apartarme; / es ya impossible mudarme / que allá queda el coraçón" (263–69). Despite the play's somewhat inconsistent conception of time (see n. 5, this chap.), at this point one may safely assume that Vitoriano has already decided to break with Plácida, for, when he subsequently meets with Suplicio, his friend states, "Yo pensava / que tu fe ya la olvidava" (358–59), to which he replies, "Verdad es que lo quisiera / por averlo prometido" (361–62). Vitoriano's earlier recognition that it is "impossible mudarme" thus demonstrates the same kind of emotional seesawing associated with Plácida, until he finally confirms his resolve to leave her in line 273. From this point on the main movement of the first "nucleus" that López Morales discusses is characterized by the tension between Plácida's desire for Vitoriano and his corresponding rejection of her desire. This apparent inversion of courtly roles is the first in a long series of inversions that comes to characterize the play.

The figure of Suplicio reinforces the conflict between the lovers. Vitoriano seeks his friend's advice in order to stay firm in his resolution to break with Plácida, and Suplicio assures him that he will offer a way to forget her (364–65). The advice given, that "el amor de una señora / se quita con nuevo amor" (380–81), recalls Ovid in both *Ars Amatoria* 2.358 and *Remedia Amoris* 444.[17] While the influence of Ovid's treatises on love is obvious, Suplicio's character may also be viewed as derived from the tale of Pyramus and Thisbe. In reconfirming Vitoriano's decision to leave Plácida and in offering him advice on how to do so, Suplicio widens the breach between the two lovers and amplifies the primary tension of the play. Significantly, Vitoriano will later refer to himself as being in Supli-

17. Sullivan's statement (accepted by McGrady 139) that "Suplicio's advice . . . closely follows Ovid's *Remedies of Love*, book II" (99) must be understood to refer to the *Ars Amatoria*, for the *Remedia* is not divided into books. The passages following *Remedia* 444 also provide Encina, as Hathaway notes (63), with most of the famous couples of antiquity that he refers to in lines 385–400 of *Plácida y Vitoriano* (the one exception being the example of Jason and Medea: see Gimeno 316n).

cio's hand (836), an image that recalls the way in which he had earlier described Plácida's control over him. In a structural sense Suplicio may be read as a replacement for the parents in Ovid's tale. While Sullivan suggests that Suplicio's name "could stand for 'entreaty' or more likely 'torment,' since this personage agonizever [sic] his friend's erratic and desperate behavior" (99), given his role in breaking up the lovers, it is also possible that Suplicio's name indicates the suffering he inflicts on others.

Indeed, Vitoriano is miserable after his decision to leave Plácida. Following his halfhearted attempt at pursuing Flugencia (537–648), he realizes that he cannot carry out Suplicio's advice because he cannot forget Plácida: "Verdad es que tu servicio / me fuera gran beneficio / no siendo tal mi cuydado; / mas mis males / han cobrado fuerças tales, / que son de fuerça y de grado" (779–84). The three hundred or so lines from this point in the text to the beginning of the first pastoral scene of the shepherds (1075) mark the closing of the first "núcleo argumental": Vitoriano's desire has come full circle while Plácida's, once rejected, has prompted her to vanish. Suplicio, for his part, gives up on advising his friend, declaring angrily, "Estás della tan vencido / que jamás pornás olvido / ni otra nunca bien querrás" (827–29). In the remaining lines Vitoriano discovers that Plácida has disappeared (905–11), regrets having left her, and considers committing suicide (947–76), but is restrained by Suplicio (984–92), who then consults the shepherds about Plácida's whereabouts (999–1074). Vitoriano slips away unseen, setting the stage for the second nucleus of action.

After the shepherds' scene and the *villancico*, Plácida reappears to recite another long monologue, establishing a symmetry with the first part of the play.[18] In this second part, however, the passions of the lovers are inverted. Instead of desiring Vitoriano, Plácida now tries precisely to stop longing after him, lamenting that "mas más fe y más causa veo / para dar fin al desseo / como hize al alegría. / Coraçón, / esfuerça con la passión, / fenezca ya tu porfía" (1250–55). Invoking Cupido (1304), she wanders off, apparently intent on committing suicide. Several critics have compared this speech of Plácida's to one by Dido in the *Aeneid*, although the references are unclear.[19] What does seem reminiscent of Virgil is Plácida's

---

18. Gimeno 78 believes that the *villancico* is to be sung by Plácida, but this possibility seems unlikely, since her name does not appear in the text until *after* the termination of the song.

19. Sullivan notes that "Plácida's words of farewell to life closely resemble those of the abandoned Dido in book II of Virgil's *Aeneid*" (99). He is followed in this observation by

suicide by the sword that Vitoriano unwittingly leaves behind (see Gimeno 370n).

At this point Vitoriano and Suplicio reappear in their search for Plácida. Vitoriano's long "echo" speech that follows (1320–419), traditionally scorned and dismissed by the critics in the same sentence as his "Vigilia de la enamorada muerta," is important for several reasons when read within the context of myth and desire. First, it demonstrates that Vitoriano's sexual desires for Plácida are now firmly reestablished. While no technical tour de force, the lyricism of the echo verses at least serves to convince the spectator of the protagonist's sincerity and underscores the irony that Plácida has just left the scene contemplating suicide because she believed Vitoriano no longer desired her. The speech thus confirms the main movement of the second nucleus as an inversion of the first: Vitoriano, who earlier rejected Plácida's advances, now desperately seeks her, while she, lost in hopeless despair, flees from him and all civilization.

Second, the echo speech calls forth as subtext another famous myth from Ovid's *Metamorphoses*: the story of Narcissus and Echo in book 3 (339–510). Apart from its very form, which imitates Echo's responses to Narcissus and which becomes relatively common in Renaissance poetry (Knoespel 7) and especially in the Spanish pastoral novel (Álvarez de la Villa 217), the first lines of Vitoriano's oration are enough to establish an Ovidian connection: "Aunque yo triste me seco, / eco / retumba por mar y tierra" (1320–22). The sentence recalls the circumstances of Narcissus's death as he, wasted by self-love, "liquitur et tecto paulatim carpitur igni" 'melts and is slowly eaten away by a hidden fire' (3.490), while Echo, with her "resonis vocibus" 'resounding voice' (3.496), returns the sounds of his lamentations. In addition, the subtext of Narcissus and Echo hints at the communication gap between Plácida and Vitoriano that seems to have been the cause of much of their troubles. Rather than serving as an obligatory allusion to the classics so frequent in the Renaissance or, worse, a "pueril é insufrible escena" (Menéndez Pelayo, Prólogo xcv), the echo

---

McGrady 139, who is in turn followed by Rambaldo (Encina 225n). The curious reader will find no such precedent for Plácida's speech in book 2 of the *Aeneid*, in which the queen of Carthage never, in fact, opens her mouth. Perhaps the reference is to one of her soliloquies in book 4 (for example, vv. 534–52, 590–629, 651–62), but these bear little formal or thematic similarities to Plácida's oration other than the fact that both heroines are distressed and contemplating suicide. Plácida does compare herself directly to Dido, and Vitoriano to Aeneas, in line 1276, but these references do not stand out from a list of other classical personages who suffered through similar circumstances.

speech works to heighten the sense of impending disaster in the play.[20] Only eight lines later, Vitoriano and Suplicio discover Plácida's dead body by the spring (1428–29).

The brook, already noted as an important iconographic element in the transmission of the myth of Pyramus and Thisbe, is also fundamental in the story of Narcissus, who falls hopelessly in love with his own image reflected in its waters. The appearance of the spring at this point in the text, just after the echo speech, works as a seam that further integrates the two popular Ovidian tales for a brief moment. After all, Vitoriano's earlier flight from Plácida, which, according to Van Beysterveldt (*La poesía*), obeys his fear of involvement with the Other, is also reminiscent of Narcissus's rejection of Echo in favor of his own ego. The narcissistic subtext recedes ironically, however, when Vitoriano faints from distress and Suplicio, fearing that he has died, splashes a handful of water from the spring in his friend's face to revive him (1469). Unlike its effect on Narcissus, to whom water brings death, water revives Vitoriano from apparent death and, in the tradition of the "fonte frida" (see Wardropper, *Spanish Poetry* 245), renews his desire for the Other. The story of Narcissus now withdraws behind the wider contours of the tale of Pyramus and Thisbe. Suplicio's statement, "Un sepulcro os haré junto, / pues ambos juntos moristes" (1463–64), uttered just before he uses the water to revive Vitoriano, reinforces this movement by recalling the motif of the common grave.

When Vitoriano awakens from his fainting spell and discovers that his own sword was the instrument of Plácida's death, he becomes suicidal himself and launches into his "Vigilia de la enamorada muerta." This oration, followed by another "comic-relief" scene with the shepherds Gil and Pascual (whose aid Suplicio has requested in burying Plácida) closes the second nucleus of action.

Upon careful inspection, the desires that inform the first two movements of the play reveal two poles of the basic opposition of Ovid's tale, which Encina repolarizes in order to structure his play. In the story of Pyramus and Thisbe, the desire between the two lovers is equal and unfailing throughout the entire narrative, while the resistance offered comes from without, in the figure of the parents. Encina begins with the same equality of desire but quickly renders it unequal from within (Vitoriano's

---

20. Gimeno 80, the only critic to have taken the echo speech seriously, arrives at similar conclusions.

rejection of Plácida) in order to make the tension of the classical model dramatically effective. He creates a mirror image of this structure of desire in the second movement (Plácida's flight from Vitoriano). Thus Robert ter Horst, in a highly suggestive reading, claims that Encina works as "a kind of dramaturgical Marcilio Ficino, mediating between the doctrine of desire and the dogmas of non-desire" ("*Ut Pictura Poesis*" 14). As Gimeno explains, "Al ser doble el hilo argumental, la estructura de las tres unidades centrales también se bifurca; es decir, hay dos enlaces, dos momentos climáticos y dos desenlaces (uno en relación con Plácida y otro en relación con Vitoriano)" (69). The result, in this instance, leaves in the spectators the impression that the two lovers have each acted out precisely what the other desires simply with the wrong timing.

The third nucleus begins at line 2283 with Vitoriano's preparations for suicide. Entrusting his soul to Venus, since Cupido "siempre me pone en olvido" (2297), he raises his sword to stab himself, setting the stage for a fulfillment, in reverse order, of Ovid's tale (Pyramus is the first to kill himself, believing Thisbe to have been devoured by the lioness; she then commits suicide on discovering his body). But Encina has more surprises in store. Just as the second movement of the play may be read as an inversion of the first, so here in the third, instead of resolving the tension by following the Ovidian model, Encina inverts that model. Venus appears to detain Vitoriano's hand in its self-destructive cause and tells him that "esto todo / ha sido manera y modo / de tu fe esperimentar" (2320–22). Chastising him for ignoring her power (2331), she summons her brother Mercurio to raise Plácida from the dead, which he promptly accomplishes with cheerful goodwill (2380). The two lovers are reunited, Suplicio returns with Gil and Pascual, and the play ends amid festivities of song and dance.

Many critics have considered the appearance of Venus at the end of Encina's play to be an unanticipated intervention, a *dea ex machina* borrowed from the Italian pastoral tradition in order to effect a miraculous resolution of the conflict.[21] This assertion is not entirely accurate. Although technically speaking the goddess does resolve a situation that seemed destined to end disastrously, Bruce Wardropper is also correct in stating that Venus is "no *dea ex machina* but the goddess who has been presiding over the lover's [*sic*] destinies from the start" ("Metamorphosis" 50 n. 14; see also Gimeno 83). In other words, Venus's role as goddess of

---

21. Crawford, *Spanish Drama* 27; Mazzei 50; Hathaway 68–69; Sullivan 99.

love in some way necessitates her intervention in order to reunite those who had never really stopped loving each other equally.

But Venus's appearance also seems consistent with Encina's constant play of inversion, whose general movements I have sought to trace in the present analysis. If the play inverts the standards of courtly love in having Plácida pursue the skittish Vitoriano in the first nucleus, if it then inverts that pursuit in the juxtaposition of the second nucleus to the first, it seems fitting that the play's tension should be resolved with another inversion, from suffering and disaster to joyous reconciliation. The effect sets a powerful precedent in the peninsular theater, as Francisco Ruiz Ramón observes (*Historia . . . desde* 48–49). Furthermore, if Wardropper is correct in reading *Plácida y Vitoriano* as an "inversion of a religious truth" ("Metamorphosis" 50), then he confirms on an ideological level the structural and generic inversions analyzed above, in addition to the interesting linguistic (from Spanish to Latin) and geographical (from town to country) reversals suggested by ter Horst (*"Ut Pictura Poesis"* 16). But his statement obliges one to confront the troublesome question of whether Encina's text represents a Christian or a pagan worldview, or something between or outside both of these (Neoplatonism or courtly love, for example). Does the desire that informs and structures the text amount to heresy from a Christian perspective, or is it contained by a farcical framework that does not transgress the limits of "what was permitted by the conventional 'medieval taste for humorous blasphemy,'" as Otis Green claims (*Spain* 3:205)?[22]

The question is a formidable one complicated by several factors. In the first place, Christian and pagan elements in the Renaissance had become so fused as to be virtually inseparable. Jean Seznec's remarkable study, *The Survival of the Pagan Gods*, is one long testament to the fusion of forms and ideas that constituted the Renaissance. As he notes with regard to the allegorical tradition: "Neoplatonic exegesis, which had presented [the humanists] with hitherto undreamed-of possibilities of reconciliation between the Bible and mythology, had now so obscured the distinction between the two that Christian dogma no longer seemed acceptable in anything but an allegorical sense" (99). The convergence of Christian and pagan elements in the doctrines of Neoplatonism forms a matrix from which it is impossible to extricate any one element. The omnipresence of the courtly tradition in Spain adds yet another dimension to this matrix

---

22. Mancini's conclusion supports Green's. In contrast to their view see, for example, Valbuena Prat, *Literatura dramática* 32, *Historia del teatro* 31, *Historia de la literatura* 1:365; Bonilla 106; Wardropper, "Metamorphosis" 49; and ter Horst, *"Ut Pictura Poesis"* 16.

and must also be considered as a possible influence on Encina's play, if a negative one.

Furthermore, *Plácida y Vitoriano* was written not in Spain but in Rome, at the height of the Italian Renaissance (1513). Nowhere was the amalgam of form and ideology discussed by Seznec more pronounced than in the Eternal City, the seat of both the pagan and Christian empires. In addition, the audience for which the play was written should not be overlooked. Whereas the piece was performed in the residence of the Cardinal Arborea, probably to commemorate some festive occasion, the crowd in attendance apparently consisted of "piu putane spagnole . . . che homini italiani," as a contemporary testimony of the recital suggests (qtd. in Crawford, *Spanish Pastoral* 44). Because of the circumstances of its composition and performance, then, Encina's play does not fall squarely within the rubric of Green's *Spain and the Western Tradition*.[23]

As both a citizen of Spain and a resident of Rome for a considerable period, Encina was well placed to assimilate elements from many different and conflicting traditions, perhaps without even being aware of their sources himself. This factor, combined with the playful structure of inversion that informs the text, makes it virtually impossible to arrive at the least common denominator among the various layers of signification, as Van Beysterveldt observes (*La poesía* 236). For example, the intervention of Venus and Mercurio at the end of the play, while perhaps representing the triumph of paganism, can at the same time be comfortably read within the Christian allegorical tradition. The fusion of Venus with the Virgin Mary was common in Renaissance iconography (Wind 24). Mercury's role as messenger of the gods, furthermore, closely associates him with the angels, the messengers of the Christian god. Thus Venus's intervention on behalf of Vitoriano through the mediation of Mercurio is not incompatible with the popular medieval tradition in which the Virgin used angels to intervene on behalf of lost souls, as in Gonzalo de Berceo's *Milagros de nuestra señora*.

The metaphor of love as fire is another element whose origin defies the attempt to locate it within any consistent tradition. The passion of Plácida and Vitoriano for each other is frequently expressed, both by them and by other characters of the play, in terms of this ancient topos.[24] Both Gillet

---

23. Perhaps this fact accounts for the uncustomary carelessness of Green's discussion of the play, evident in the error-filled plot summary (*Spain* 3:205) apparently gleaned from Crawford.

24. See, for example, lines 28, 854, 865, 888, 1220–21, 1387–90, and 1405–8. It is difficult to accept Van Beysterveldt's statement that "lo que sorprende en las églogas de Encina es la

(353–55) and Green (*Spain* 1:127–28) identify the symbol of "purifying fire" with Neoplatonic theory, popularized in particular by Pietro Bembo's speech at the end of Castiglione's *Courtier;* Schevill (41, 60), however, identifies the same phraseology with Ovid, and it was indeed a standard topos of Latin literature, as amply demonstrated in book 4 of the *Aeneid* (to be discussed in Chapter 3). The tale of Pyramus and Thisbe is no exception and employs such key words as *ardebant* (62) and *ignis* (59).

The reader who, like so many of the play's commentators, wishes to read Encina's text as a parody that vindicates one tradition over another thus faces a potentially infinite task. The textual signifiers lead from one signified to another and back again in a way that forces any object of parody into constant recession beneath the various layers of meaning. Thus the final scene mentioned above can be read simultaneously as a mocking of the Christian tradition by the pagan gods and as an allegory in which the latter are themselves denigrated by their inherent status as corrupt precursors of Christian deities.

These difficulties come about, however, only when one attempts to read the desires in the text as fixed markers of the playwright's ideology, a move that implicates the reader in a process of ideological valorization probably not unlike the type that led to the play's ban by the Inquisition in 1559. If, by contrast, the opposing desires of the myth of Pyramus and Thisbe are viewed as a mainly structural foundation of the *Égloga de Plácida y Vitoriano*, then the appraisal of their ideological accretions becomes a less urgent and less distracting matter. The length and experimental nature of Encina's last play suggest that he was working on a means for creating an exciting and coherent plot that would transcend the liturgical tradition of his other eclogues. He appears to have turned to the desires encoded in classical myth, without having to accept their implicit ideology, as the most appropriate tools for achieving his goal.

Libidinal Expression and Artistic Repression: Juan Timoneda's *Tragicomedia llamada Filomena*

The *Égloga de Plácida y Vitoriano* is completely lacking in aggressive desires such as hatred, jealousy, and the pursuit of vengeance that characterize

---

ausencia casi absoluta de estos términos referentes al fuego como símbolo de la pasión amorosa" (*La poesía* 47).

so many Greco-Roman myths. Van Beysterveldt suggests that the absence of these elements creates an "anemic" conception of love peculiar to Encina's theater (*La poesía* 48). A half century later, motivated by the growing economic viability of theater and the resulting need to captivate audience attention, Juan Timoneda's *Tragicomedia llamada Filomena* remedied the "anemia" of Encina's piece.[25] Based on the story of Procne, Tereus, and Philomela in *Met.* 6.401–674, Timoneda's play is structured around a complex fusion of the three basic categories of desire, which surface thematically in horrific acts of gluttony, sexuality, and aggression. Whereas Encina's method with respect to the classical model is structural in the sense that he fashions the play out of a reconfiguration (inversion, repetition, juxtaposition) of the architecture of desire in the story of Pyramus and Thisbe, Timoneda's is more thematic or analogical in that he constructs his plot through an associative process that elaborates and expands on the desires present in the Ovidian myth.[26]

The first of these desires belongs to the erotic category to the degree

25. Controversy surrounds the patrimony of the *Tragicomedia llamada Filomena* and the rest of the volume known as the *Turiana* in which the play was published. In his "Advertencia" to the Doménech edition of the play, Menéndez Pelayo states, "En cuanto a los pasos, farsas, comedias y tragicomedias de la *Turiana*, creemos . . . que no pasó de editor, o a lo sumo de refundidor. Ni él dice haberlas compuesto, sino que 'las sacó a luz,' lo cual es muy diverso" (n.p.). Responding to this objection and others, Juliá Martínez argues for "una identidad de técnica [de la *Turiana*] que hace suponer un solo autor, y resulta difícil identificarlo con otro que no sea el propio Timoneda" (Timoneda, *Obras* 3:viii). Elsewhere he finds it unlikely that Timoneda would resort to the "subterfugios vanos" of concealing the names of the real authors of the works contained in the *Turiana* when on other occasions, such as his publication of the works of Alonso de la Vega and Lope de Rueda, he possessed the "honradez y sinceridad de poner al frente de sus obras los nombres de aquellos cuyas eran" ("Originalidad" 94). Juliá Martínez refers to certain allusions in *Filomena* such as the "vinos de La Roda y San Clemente" and the "buenas roscas de Utrera," arguing that they betray Timoneda's authorship "por las lecturas de las obras reunidas en su librería, y las relaciones que mantenía con el resto de España" (96). He concludes that "puede quedar sentado que a este escritor le pertenecen los *Autos* y la *Turiana* en su totalidad, aunque, como todo poeta, se inspirase en fuentes más o menos directas, pero nunca tomadas a la letra" (101). Based on Juliá Martínez's observations and in the absence of a more likely author, in the present analysis I ascribe authorship of *Filomena* to Timoneda as a hypothetical point of departure in order to determine if the claim can be supported by further internal evidence.

26. Unless he was able to read Latin, an ability for which there is no documentary evidence (see n. 31, this chap., however), Timoneda most likely became familiar with the story of Tereus, Procne, and Philomela through the translation of Jorge de Bustamante (Beardsley, item 42), which takes extreme liberties with the text but eliminates nothing essential from the Ovidian myth. This translation may well be the "Ouidio en romance" referred to in the inventory taken of Timoneda's bookshop upon his death in 1583 (see Timoneda, *Obras* 1:xliii). Timoneda probably culled some of the variations he introduces in the play from Bustamante, but the most significant innovations are his own.

that it corresponds to the aim-inhibited sexuality that Freud identifies as the prototype for familial relations (see above, Chapter 1, pages 12–13). Progne opens the play by informing her husband Tereo of the intentions that she has been harboring for some time:

> Sabrá, señor rey Tereo,
> que tengo muy gran passion
> dentro de mi coraçon
> porque ha mucho que no veo
> a mi padre Pandion.
>
> Tambien he sido informada
> como de hermosura llena
> tengo vna hermana oluidada,
> noble honesta y agraciada
> que la llaman Filomena:
> por solo vella padesce
> mi alma pena excessiua. (215)

Joseph Gillet (355–57) notes that the word *passión* in Spanish originally carried the passive meaning of "suffering" but that, at least by the time of Carvajal's *Tragedia Josephina* (1535), the term was already beginning to demonstrate the active sense of passion or sexual desire. Progne's use of the word participates in the semantic widening of *passión* insofar as it betrays decidedly erotic, although aim-inhibited, intentions: she desires the company of not only her sister but also her father even as she feels pain at their absence. Her attitudes toward her family are worth examining, for Ovid's Procne expresses no desire to see her father. Moreover, Timoneda devotes a generous amount of attention to Progne's attempts to convince Tereo of her intentions, whereas Ovid spends barely five lines (440–45) on it.

Progne's relation to her husband is problematic from the beginning. In Ovid's version of the story she does not fall in love with Tereus but serves merely to cement a political alliance between him and her father (6.424–28), and their wedding is full of evil omens:

> Eumenides tenuere faces de funere raptas,
> Eumenides stravere torum, tectoque profanus
> incubuit bubo thalamique in culmine sedit. (430–32)

[The Furies carried torches stolen from a funeral and laid out
the marriage couch, and an impious owl watched over them from the
roof and sat at the top of the wedding chamber.]

While initially retaining the mediatory function of Procne, which he explains in the *introito* (212), Timoneda eliminates the reference to the baleful Furies. Even so, it is clear from the relationship between the spouses that things are not at all well. In another departure from Ovid, Timoneda has Progne complain to Tereo that

> muchas veces h'embiado
> con los pajes de palacio
> a llamalle con cuydado,
> pero jamás le han hallado
> tener vn poco de espacio.
>
> Muy gran tiempo ha que desseo
> declaralle mi intencion,
> y aun que busco algun rodeo
> tan tarde en tarde le veo
> que me causa admiracion. (214)

Tereo's desires are clearly tied up in the governance of the state, in light of which, as José Miguel Regueiro notes, "se evidencia la distancia que separa a los esposos" (244). Progne's "gran passion," to the extent that it conveys suffering, is perhaps due not only to the absence of her father and sister but also to the lack of a viable husband. The passive suffering of *passión* becomes a source of active desire that in sublimated form fixes on her only other close relations. In faintly suggesting her unsatisfied sexual desire at the beginning of the play, Timoneda provides even greater justification for Progne's wish to leave Thrace and visit her family. That she longs to meet her sister without ever having known her—another detail added by Timoneda—heightens the sense of the heroine's desperation.

Tereo is offended at his wife's suggestion and opposes her wishes, warning that, given the tendency of people to gossip, "dirá quien lo supiere / que va de mala manera" (216). His unease at the thought of what others might say is the first hint of the importance of speech and the desire for communication in the play. The compromise that he finally suggests to appease Progne is the same one that Ovid narrates and that, dramatized by Timoneda, leads ultimately to disaster.

Tereo's voyage to Athens to bring back Filomena is significant for several reasons. In the first place, he must abandon the affairs of state and leave them in the hands of his wife. In the process he again denies her wishes—this time to accompany him to Athens—because he fears possible revolts in the land:

> Princesa muy valerosa,
> bien os quisiera lleuar
> pero pienso en otra cosa
> qu'esta tierra es peligrosa
> y se nos podria alçar.
>
> Por tanto es bien que quedeys
> por Reyna y gouernadora
> pues todo lo posseys
> y a vuestro mandar teneys
> estos Reynos, gran señora. (220–21)[27]

Tereo's departure without Progne not only symbolically transfers to her the aggressive component of desire needed to govern and suppress revolts; it also allows him to assume her erotic desire toward her family. In this way the couple undergo a type of role reversal—not unlike that of Plácida and Vitoriano in Encina's work—that establishes the trajectory of desire for the rest of the play.

On arriving in Athens in scene 2, Tereo is stricken by passion for Filomena at first sight. In his monologue at the beginning of the following scene, he addresses Cupido, "Rey soberano," and describes his own condition with all the familiar vocabulary of Ovidian love: *angustia, pena, sanar, remediar, passion,* and so on (234–35). In scene 4, after their arrival in Thrace, Tereo makes a halfhearted attempt at convincing Filomena to give in to him "por que en ser de mi muger / hermana, no haurá sospecha" (240–41). Tereo's effort to seduce his sister-in-law before deciding to rape her is probably taken from the long dialogue between the two characters that Jorge de Bustamante inserts in his "translation" of the tale

---

27. This detail, inasmuch as it is completely lacking from Ovid's account, is perhaps a hint at the fear of revolt or heresy in the contemporary Spanish reign of Philip II, who was already beginning to feel the burden of his far-flung empire (see Elliott 229).

(fols. 93v–95r).[28] In choosing this variation of the myth—an "emulation" of Ovid in the true Erasmian sense of the word—Timoneda dramatizes Tereo's inability to use language to achieve his goals, for the horrified Filomena immediately rejects his advances:

> En verdad, señor Tereo,
> mi verdadero cuñado,
> que no creyera ni creo
> que esse tan bestial desseo
> jamás huuieras pensado:
> desecha de ti, señor,
> tan nefando pensamiento,
> ten de los dioses temor,
> no hagas tal deshonor
> a mí que tanto lo siento. (241)

Filomena's characterization of Tereo's desire as *bestial* and of his thought as *nefando* (a quasi-legal term associated with the *pecado nefando*, or sodomy [see Real Academia]) appropriately signifies his animal-like inner nature and anticipates the impending transformation of his desires from the erotic to the violent and the criminal.

After she rejects him, Tereo decides to resort to force (242). In the act of rape, which the spectators are mercifully spared but which nevertheless looms ominously behind the scenes, the erotic desire that has characterized so much of the play up to this point suddenly becomes infused with unmistakable violence. The aggressive desires that the king apparently applied to suppressing rebellions in Thrace and that he was forced to cede to his wife upon leaving for Athens now resurface with unmitigated brutality.

The rape of Filomena is the manifestation of a transitional state of Tereo's character, in which there still remain traces of erotic desire mixed in with the violence. Timoneda tips the scale in favor of violence by dramatizing the king's ultimate act of savagery toward his sister-in-law. After he has raped her, Filomena warns that if he does not kill her she will tell others of his crime (243). To prevent her from doing so Tereo ties her hands behind her back, cuts out her tongue, and imprisons her in a tower

---

28. Although the attempt at seduction seems to have a precedent in antiquity, as Apollodorus's comments suggest (2:101; 3.14.8), it is improbable that Timoneda would have had access to such sources.

in the woods (243–44). While these acts closely follow the version of the story found in the *Metamorphoses*, it is significant that Timoneda omits the gruesome detail that in Ovid represents the culmination of Tereus's desires: "Hoc quoque post facinus (vix ausim credere) fertur / saepe sua lacerum repetisse libidine corpus" 'And still after this crime (horrible even to imagine), it is rumored that he repeatedly satisfied his lust on her mutilated body' (6.561–62). The elimination of this element emphasizes the diminished role that sexuality plays in the king's mind, having been subsumed by his desire for violence.

When the two shepherds Silvestro and Sorato discover Filomena's mutilated body in scene 5, they treat her kindly and take her into their hut, where they give her food (not, however, before making several crude jokes at her expense that recall the antics of Encina's Gil and Pascual). In the following scene Sorato delivers to Progne the quilt into which Filomena, lacking the ability to speak, has embroidered her story. When the queen unravels the quilt and reads of the outrage, she explodes in anger: "O Tereo, marmol duro, / qué te mereció su lengua? / pues por los dioses te juro / que quando estés mas seguro / yo vengaré tan gran mengua" (251). Progne now acts in full accord with her newly acquired powers of ruling Thrace in her husband's absence. Perhaps having had a taste of the violence needed to govern a rebellious land, she does not lack the brazenness and cruelty necessary to plan her macabre revenge on Tereo.

Dressing herself as a villager (a bacchant in Ovid), the queen flees into the woods, finds Filomena, and brings her back secretly to the palace. The two then conspire to avenge Filomena's rape and mutilation and to bring about Tereo's ruin. But the revenge selected by Progne makes the crime pale by comparison: "A Hithis quiero tomar / qu'es su hijo muy amado, / y luego le degollar / y darselo en manjar / quando le tenga guisado: / esto determino hazer, / y será muy brevemente / para me satisfazer" (256). Notably absent from Progne's decision is the emotional wavering that Ovid describes in his heroine: "Sed simul ex nimia mentem pietate labare / sensit" 'Yet at the same time she felt her mind wavering from an excess of kindness' (6.629–30). Timoneda's omission of this speck of humanity from a story that has not lost its shock value even today further accentuates the pitiless extremes to which Progne's violence and desire for revenge have carried her.

The delirium culminates in the final scene, in which the ghastly banquet is prepared and served. An inevitable consequence of the adaptation of the myth from a narrative to a dialogic setting is that, in the absence of stage directions, Filomena's silence dooms her to near erasure from the text, and there is no mention made of her hurling the boy's severed head into Tereo's lap, as she does in Ovid. Yet when Tereo dies on the spot after learning the true contents of his dinner, Filomena's presence is implied in her sister's morbid congratulations: "Agora contenta estó; / hermana, vengada estás. / Su pago le hauemos dado, / huygamos por encubierto" (260).

It is significant that Timoneda eliminates the avian metamorphosis that occurs at this point in Ovid's story as well as in earlier Greek versions of the myth. Although on the one hand this change might stem from a concession to growing concerns for verisimilitude, on the other it offers a way of punishing the protagonists for their violence. This need for a moralizing ending responds to the Horatian imperative and, as Rinaldo Froldi observes (80), will come to characterize the use of mythological material in the seventeenth-century theater.

Since metamorphosis in Ovid often functions as a brake to chaos, as a means of putting a halt to violence or at least of displacing violence into a context in which it is expected and permitted (the animal world), the transformation of Tereo into a hoopoe, as occurs in Ovid, would offer no punishment whatsoever but rather would allow him to continue following his darkest desires with impunity.[29] His death, by contrast, imparts a moral message, clarified in the final *canción* for anyone who might be doubtful: "Quán mal que le succedió / al supremo rey Tereo / su suzio y bestial desseo, / pues la vida le costó" (262). The other alternative to metamorphosis, besides death, is the status quo: humanity. By leaving Progne and Filomena in their miserable human condition, scorned by their peers and subject to the same desires that have propelled them into violence, Timoneda may be punishing them with a fate worse than death. They can certainly expect no sympathy from other humans if the Maestresala, who laments the death of his king and curses the "reyna mal inclinada" (261), serves as any indication.

Intimately connected with the lust and violence so prominent in the play is the motif of hunger, expressed through numerous references to food and eating and dramatized in the figure of Taurino the *simple*. Most critics have viewed Taurino's role in the play as superfluous at best, ob-

---

29. In the specific case of the hoopoe, the baseness of its desires is emblematized in its habit of scavenging from animal waste (Biedermann 176).

structive at worst, for reasons summarized by María del Pilar Aróstegui: "El simple recibe en esta obra la unánime repulsa de la crítica que considera sus intervenciones excesivas, desmesuradas y fuera de lugar, convirtiendo la obra en un monstruo donde el melodrama alterna con la farsa de feria" (215).[30] Valbuena Prat (*Historia de la literatura* 1:782) and Ruiz Ramón (*Historia . . . desde* 108) have been the most measured in their judgments of Taurino's role, considering him an important step in the evolution of the figure of the *gracioso* of the later *comedia*. But his role goes beyond purely historical import, and, when viewed within the context of myth and desire, his appearances in the play acquire a unique significance.

Most of the "intrusions" that have gained Taurino the label of "impertinent" are connected with his constant desire for keeping his stomach full. One such case occurs near the end of scene 2, just before Tereo sees Filomena for the first time. The *simple* becomes so overwhelmed by hunger that he takes to stealing food from the chicken coop:

> Que como se descuydauan [los criados]
> y el vientre se me solsia
> fuy al corral adonde estauan
> las gallinas, y le daban
> al puerco grande porfia:
> y como reñir las vi
> arremetí a la caldera,
> la media les engullí,
> viera picaços en mí
> que de poco me muriera. (231)

This episode cannot be considered meaningless, being so closely followed by Tereo's first sight of Filomena, whom his sexual appetite will soon lead him to "consume." Significantly, scene 2 ends with a banquet in which all participate, and the sating of hunger implied in the meal, although it might appear to center on Taurino, also anticipates Tereo's own violent act of sexual satiation two scenes later.

When viewed in this light, Taurino's incessant references to food create a strong artistic justification for the gory banquet of the last scene. It is grotesquely fitting that Tereo dies in the act of satisfying his hunger (nu-

---

30. Examples of this negative assessment may be found in Mérimée, *L'Art* 181; Crawford, *Spanish Drama* 128; Reynolds 98; and Regueiro 247.

tritive desire) by consuming his own son—the result of his lust (sexual desire) toward his wife—when it was lust that led him to the violence (aggressive desire) committed against Filomena. Taurino's comments after Tereo's death have no doubt contributed to the general disgust that critics express for him: "O cena mal derramada / por el suelo, estás perdida! . . . Mejor será que cenemos / agora que está caliente" (261). Yet in an uncanny way Taurino brings attention to an important point easily overlooked: the "cena mal derramada" necessarily includes the body of Tereo now lying dead on the floor. Through his "impertinence" the *simple* underscores the symbolic fusion of desire that has formed the matrix of the play: Hithis, the product of lust and now transformed into food to satisfy his father's hunger, has ended up killing Tereo through the violence of the grisly revelation.

At the same time that Taurino is dominated by hunger, he is associated with violence and sexual appetite by the fate of his name, which, in addition to suggesting both the Spanish *toro* and the Latin *taurinus*, is a reminder of the beastly desires that rule his character.[31] The Spaniards of the early modern period considered the bull an "animal feróz, principalmente irritado," whose violent nature was frequently tested against humans in the popular pastime of bullfighting. Yet its ferocity was understood to be connected to its virility, so that "castrado, y amansado se domestica" (Real Academia). Bullishness was necessarily linked to ferociousness and sexual appetite, and thus Taurino, far from superfluous in the play, may be viewed as a nexus of the different desires that are variously manifested in the protagonists.

Consistent with all of these associations, Taurino is often referred to by words also used for animals: "nescio albardado" (219), "azemilon majadero" (219), "cochino" and "huron" (225), "bellaco espaldas de buey" (228), "animalazo sin ley" (228), and so on. But he is not the only one to whom these epithets might apply. His name, at the same time that it carries bullish connotations, also bears a subtle resemblance to that of the king: TauRinO / TeReO. In this respect it is appropriate that Taurino alone should accompany Tereo on his embassy to Athens, to the amazement of the Mayordomo (223). Similarly, in the second half of the play, when Progne is overcome by madness and the desire for revenge upon learning of Tereo's crime, she requests Taurino's assistance both in find-

---

31. If Timoneda adapted Taurino's name from *taurinus*, which seems possible (*taurino* does not appear in the *Dic. de Aut.*), his assumed ignorance of Latin would have to be rethought.

ing Filomena (252–53) and in setting the table for the grim banquet of scene 7 (258). In both cases, the *simple* functions as a mirror that reflects the most urgent desires of the protagonists.

These desires are densely encoded in one of the central episodes in the plot of the play: Tereo's severing of Filomena's tongue. This incident offers important clues for both interpreting the play and resolving several difficult issues surrounding its composition. Tereo's principal objective in cutting out Filomena's tongue is to silence her and thereby prevent her from spreading word of his crimes. But besides figuring prominently in communication, tongues are used for kissing, an important manifestation of sexual desire, and for eating, an act that satisfies nutritive desire. By cutting out her tongue, Tereo metaphorically deprives Filomena of the means for satisfying several of the most basic human urges.

The king's crimes may take on even greater significance when read within the context of the historical circumstances surrounding the play's production. The *Tragicomedia llamada Filomena* was written, or at least published, in 1564. Ten years before, Charles I had been replaced by his decidedly more insular son Philip II. In 1558 a decree was issued banning the importation of foreign books into Spain. The following year Spaniards were forbidden to study at foreign universities, long an intellectual lifeline to the peninsula. In the same year (1559), the stern Inquisitor Valdés issued his Index of Prohibited Books, greatly amplifying the bans of 1545 and 1551. With the publication of the Index, unprecedented powers, including the right to search public and private libraries, were granted to officials for the purpose of seizing prohibited books. In 1563, the year before the publication of Timoneda's play, the Council of Trent concluded its proceedings, firmly establishing Spain as the principal agent in the Counter-Reformation.

According to J. H. Elliott, "There seems no reason to doubt that the measures of 1558–59 administered a drastic shock to Spanish intellectual life" (223). It is likely that Timoneda would have felt threatened by the rising tide of intolerance under Philip II, if not for ideological reasons stemming from his own popular brand of humanism, then at least for personal and financial reasons. He was, after all, a bookseller *and* a playwright who had profited in the relatively liberal atmosphere of midcentury Valencia as described by Froldi (48). He may have chosen to write a play about the myth of Philomela precisely because its central act of jarring mutilation expressed in sufficiently veiled form a grim commentary on the rapidly deteriorating state of artistic expression in the Spain of the Counter-Reformation, epitomized in the publication of the 1559 Index.

Figuring in the Index was Juan del Encina's fourteenth eclogue. If the reading of *Plácida y Vitoriano* proposed earlier carries any validity, it seems fitting that Timoneda would have chosen a classical myth as a means of protesting a law that banned the first mythological play of the Spanish theater. All these factors further justify placing the disputed authorship of *Filomena* in Timoneda's hands, making him an important forerunner of those playwrights who would later appropriate classical myth for political motives.

Triangular Desire and Sensory Deception: Francisco de la Cueva y Silva's *Trajedia de Narciso*

In a fascinating study of the myth of Narcissus in medieval and Renaissance literature, Kenneth J. Knoespel refers to the unusual power of Ovid's tale (*Met.* 3.339–510) "to elaborate psychological crisis and invite its resolution" (59). He concludes that the myth "posed an invitation for medieval and renaissance poets to invent new visions and narrative strategies that would resolve the confusion portrayed in Narcissus' experience at the fountain" (105). Writing approximately a generation after Timoneda's play, during the vogue of classical tragedy in Spain, Francisco de la Cueva y Silva in *Trajedia de Narciso* responds to the challenge identified by Knoespel by extracting and amplifying the plot of the Theban story and relocating it in a context in which the thematic and structural patterns soon to be codified by the *comedia nueva* can be observed in nascent form. Using both Encina's technique of reorganizing the structure of desire in the classical model and Timoneda's approach of elaborating desires already present in the myth, Cueva y Silva creates a highly original version of the Narcissus tale in this little-known play.[32]

32. Bonilla y San Martín refers to the *Trajedia de Narciso* as "una de las obras más perfectas que ha producido, en lo mitológico, el Teatro español" (144). Despite this encomium, the play has received almost no attention since its modern publication by Crawford in 1909, and Bonilla himself offers nothing to explain or justify his high praise for it. Crawford, too, refrains from literary criticism in the introduction to his edition of the piece and limits himself in a later work to the observation that it "is marked by good taste, and the descrip-

The action of the play is generated by the consequences of what can be described structurally as two triangles of desire. The desires of the first such configuration extend past the beginning of the play but are clearly implied in Júpiter's opening monologue. The spectator learns that Júpiter gave Eco an eloquent tongue so that "á Juno hablando me detenga, / Quando á buscarme con temor se aplica, / Y para que en palabras la entretenga, / Mientras que yo duermo con mi ninfa amada, / Sin que á cortar los dulzes lazos benga" (8–12). Juno becomes so enraged at Eco for this offense that she takes away her voice as punishment. Thus far the account of Eco follows Ovid's (359–69) rather closely. What Cueva y Silva adds is the following variation told by Júpiter:

> Y Eco, mirando el aspero castigo
> Con que de Juno la crueldad crecia,
> Sin speranza ni señal de abrigo,
> Declaróle por señas que diria
> Con que de mí supiese si el azento
> Y la lengua que tuvo, le boluia.
> En esto Juno rreciuio contento,
> Y á trueco d'escuchar todas mis faltas,
> La boz entera le boluio al momento.
> Contole luego las cautelas altas
> Que e tenido con nimphas, ¡o traydora!
> Que por mal tuyo en la lealtad me faltas. (16–27)

On hearing of Júpiter's infidelities, Juno behaves toward him as if she "fuera de marmol" (28). From this moment on Júpiter struggles to win back the marbled heart of his sibling-wife.

The structure of this relationship is clearly triangular but not of the mimetic type described by Girard (see above, Chapter 1, pages 13–14). Instead of two rival subjects converging on a single object, as in Girard's model, the first triangle of desire in the *Trajedia de Narciso* dramatizes the

---

tion of the death of Narcissus is well done" (*Spanish Drama* 174). Although Diego Catalán begins his article on Cueva y Silva by lamenting the lack of attention paid to the playwright, he devotes none himself to the *Trajedia de Narciso*, nor does Díez Borque after briefly mentioning it in the passage cited at the beginning of this chapter. The play goes completely unmentioned in the widely read and cited histories of Spanish theater by Valbuena Prat and Ruiz Ramón as well as in Alfredo Hermenegildo's study of tragedy in the Spanish Renaissance and Louise Vinge's extensive treatment of the myth of Narcissus in western European literature.

sexual libido of the subject, Júpiter, as it bifurcates and is channeled toward two different objects: Juno on the one hand and his "ninfa amada" on the other. Although the structure of the triangle does not correspond to the Girardian model, the result it produces is the same: a spiraling edifice of violence manifested in the form of jealousy, hatred, and vengeance.

The violence is initiated by Juno's silencing of Eco. But when the nymph allies herself with the goddess on the condition that her voice be returned, she incurs Júpiter's wrath for having betrayed him. In typical Olympian fashion, he decides to punish her with a penalty far outweighing the crime. Summoning Cupido along with the Fury Tesifone, he orders the two to work together so that Eco will die "rrebuelta en amorosas tramas" (49). Cupido is to make her feel the pangs of love and Tesifone is to stir up "entre ella y otra alguna, / Un ardiente yra y un furor constante" (66). Having originally served as an accomplice to the amorous desires of Júpiter only to incur the rage of Juno, Eco now becomes a victim of violence as Júpiter seeks to give her a punishment "tal que dure / Mientras durare mi divina alteza" (35–36). As mediator in the triangle of desire implicating Júpiter, Juno, and the unnamed nymph, Eco is quickly converted into a pawn in an Olympian struggle of sex and power.

Through Eco's mediation, the struggle is displaced or refracted from the divine plane to the human one. In order to make Eco's love as agonizing as possible, as Júpiter has commanded, Cupido decides to have her fall in love with Narciso: precisely the character determined resolutely to resist "al brauo fuego / De amor" (282–83), as he tells his page Tindaro. Conveniently, one of Eco's sister nymphs, Niseyda, is also in love with Narciso, and it becomes easy for Tesifone to stir up jealousy and suspicion between the two friends, for, as she explains later, "del puro amor los zelos nazen" (378).

After she confirms her suspicions by coaxing Eco into disclosing her feelings for Narciso, Niseyda fumes with rage: "¡O crudo zelo rrabioso! / ¿Qué corazon animoso / Biue á quien tu ley no asombre? / La firme estrecheza quitas. / Quebrantas la fuerza suya. / O Eco, Dios te destruya, / Que asi á tu muerte me yncitas" (251–57). The two nymphs then accost Narciso as their competition for his favor intensifies. When he asks what they want from him, Eco replies, "Gozar ambas venturosas / Dese dulce paraiso" (296–97), but Niseyda makes it clear that she has no intention of sharing Narciso with her former friend: "Niseyda tan solo puede / Ser parte en esto" (298–99).

Directly following from the consequences of Júpiter's love triangle with Juno and the nymph, another triangle has thus been formed implicating Eco, Niseyda, and Narciso. Whereas the first may be described as having a subject and two objects, the second is more properly mimetic in the Girardian sense, that is, comprising two subjects in active competition for the same object. The two nymphs come to loathe each other in their rivalry, and, as Girard might predict, the mimetic structure ultimately leads to violence when Niseyda murders Eco with a dagger (774–81).

Narciso, meanwhile, is completely oblivious to the nymphs' torment and rivalry over him, displaying a passivity and indifference that confirm his role as their object of desire. He is so unfamiliar with the discourse of love that when Eco writes him a letter warning him not to trust the "finjidos enojos" of Niseyda and assuring him that "no ay amor sino el que en mí consiste" (516–17), he must ask his page Tindaro to explain her language to him (640–42). His reaction demonstrates the incomprehension of one who has been completely free from the tyranny of desire and its complexities: "¿No está donosa / La novedad del caso? ¿Quién pensara / que á tanta fuerza amor llegar pudiera, / Dentro de un pecho casto y encogido, / Que asi de la bergüenza desatara / Con duras manos el estrecho nudo?" (644–49). In so staunchly resisting desire for the other, Narciso becomes unknowingly vulnerable to desire for the self.

Cueva y Silva's treatment of the myth of Narcissus differs substantially but not radically from Ovid's. The Latin poet makes it clear that "multi illum iuvenes, multae cupiere puellae" 'many young boys and many maidens desired him' (353); he simply confines himself to telling one of their stories, that of Echo. Cueva y Silva expands on the clues offered by Ovid and, in a way described by Knoespel, elaborates the story in order to fit it into a new context: the patterns of jealousy, rivalry, and revenge that would frequently come to characterize the *comedia nueva* and that can be explained in terms of Girard's theory of mimetic desire.

Girardian theory also offers a unique way of interpreting the death of Narciso from within the new context that Cueva y Silva gives it. For Girard, the only way that the spiraling cycle of violence fueled by suspicion and vengeance can be halted is through the sacrifice of an innocent victim (*Violence* 18–19, 37, 102). The mythical figure of Oedipus is just such a figure (*Violence* chap. 3). In the *Trajedia de Narciso* it is Narciso who fulfills this function. In the play, as in Ovid's version, Narciso arrives at a cool fountain after exerting himself in hunting. Seeing his own image in its waters, he instantly falls in love and, unable to move from the spot, pines away and dies.³³ With his death the long train of violence that began on Olympus is finally contained. Narciso, on whom the rival nymphs projected their desires, instead of reinitiating those desires by directing them onto another external object, redirects it back upon himself, so that when he dies the contagion of mimetic desire is extinguished with him.

His death, in providing the most economical way out of the crisis of violence that Cueva y Silva has spawned in his departure from Ovid's version of the tale, thus takes on the appearance of a sacrifice. The oracle had already predicted Narciso's death should he ever come to know himself. The injustice of this prophecy converts Narciso into the ideal scapegoat. Cueva y Silva's solution to what Girard calls the "sacrificial crisis" is to use the fulfillment of the oracle to stop the contagious violence. The playwright adds a further touch of his own to his hero's death. Whereas Ovid reports that Narcissus comes upon the fateful fountain "studio venandi lassus et aestu" 'exhausted from the heat and the zeal of hunting' (413), in the Spanish play the object of Narciso's hunt is Eco herself. At the end of act 3 he decides to find out if the voice that is being returned to him is really hers: "Pues ¿quieres dulce Tindaro que bamos / Ambos á dos por medio el ancho bosque / A saber en qué parte está encubierta, / Y entender cierto si la voz es suya?" (1015–18). Eco, whom Narciso had earlier rejected, now becomes both the object of his chase and the cause of his death, for by following her voice he comes upon the fountain that is to be his ruin.

There is an intriguing poetic economy in this turn of events, because Eco, whose mimetic desire led her to her own destruction, now incites a desire in Narciso that leads him to his death, with which the spiral of desire neatly closes in on itself. But when the mothers of Narciso and Niseyda (who dies shortly after Narciso) cry before Júpiter for vengeance (1384), they threaten to reinitiate the cycle of violence. To prevent this, Júpiter calmly reminds Liriope of the oracle that had predicted her son's death, which she chose to ignore. As a consolation to the grieving mothers he offers the following words:

33. Several passages of exceptional lyricism in which Narciso addresses the image appear to have been taken almost directly from Ovid. In particular, verses 1118–61 and 1170–89 correspond closely to *Met.* 3.442–73 and 477–79; 1274–81 are derived from 3.487–90. The similarities lead one to suspect that Cueva y Silva must have known Ovid well, if not in Latin then at least through one of the sixteenth-century translations of the *Metamorphoses* (see Beardsley, items 42, 98, 105, and 112). Depending on when Cueva y Silva actually composed the *Trajedia de Narciso*, a matter still open to speculation, some of the translations may not have been available to him.

> Aora callad, pues tanto os lo encomiendo,
> Que yo dexaré de ellos tal memoria
> Que quantos viuen oy, tengan ynvidia,
> Porque á Niseyda boluerè en estrella,
> Y á Narciso, pues ffue flor de hermosura,
> En flor que á las demas llebe bentaja,
> La qual tendrá tambien el mismo nombre
> De Narciso. (1419–26)

Through the metamorphosis, Júpiter ensures the peace that has been secured by the sacrifice of Narciso.

Although reading Cueva y Silva's Narciso as a sacrificial victim might seem far-fetched, there may actually be a precedent for it in Ovid's text itself. The story of Narcissus occurs in the middle of book 3 of the *Metamorphoses*, which is devoted almost entirely to the history of Thebes. The narrator cites Narcissus as the first case that proves the "fide vocisque ratae" 'reliability and assured utterances' (341) of the seer Tiresias. Curiously absent from this context is Oedipus, the notorious king of Thebes whose tabooed crimes were also divined by Tiresias. If one is prepared to accept the validity of Girard's view of Oedipus as the "prime example of the human scapegoat" (*Violence* 77), then it is not incongruous that Narcissus should appear precisely where the reader, both ancient and modern, would most expect the story of Oedipus. Ovid may have sought to displace such a widely known story, held up as a model by Aristotle and others, with one that is probably his own invention.[34]

The triangular configurations of desire upon which the play is based are informed by two important themes that serve to emphasize the illusory nature of the objects of desire. Knoespel observes with respect to Ovid's tale that two "phenomenological problems presented by the story make it into a privileged narrative both for the investigation of light and sound" (107). Cueva y Silva dramatizes these phenomenological problems in the themes of voice and vision, demonstrating that all objects of desire are potentially illusory insofar as they are inspired by either sound (through the language of seduction) or sight (through the vision of the beloved).

---

34. The sacrificial character of Narcissus, if doubtful in Cueva y Silva, is resoundingly confirmed in Juana Ramírez y Asbajc's (Sor Juana Inés de la Cruz's) *El divino Narciso*, in which the mythical character is portrayed as a historical double of Christ. For the originality of the Narcissus myth in Ovid, see Vinge 11 and Bömer 537–38.

Sound and the sense of hearing manifest themselves first of all through the voice of Eco, which becomes one of the most effective agents of deception in the play. Júpiter explains that he endowed Eco's tongue with "eloquencia rrica" (7) in order to distract Juno from his affairs with the nymphs. But the voice created to ensure the fruition of his lustful desire for the nymph proves to be deceptive and ends up frustrating his desire toward his wife. As a final revenge he decides to convert Eco's voice into an echo:

> La boz que me causó tal descontento
> Quiero que permanezca lamentando
> Perpetuamente su mortal tormento,
> El cuerpo todo en ella y retorna[n]do
> Para que siempre llore y que rrepita
> Lo que otro alguno fuere pronunciando.
> Pero en esto el poder se le limita
> De que solas las silabas postreras
> Profiera y lo rrestante se le quita.
> Estará en balles y en cabernas fieras,
> Porque dentro en las cauas hondas suene
> El azento de Eco. Mas de beras,
> Su boz sin acabar quiero que pene,
> Pues ella me a dañado, descubriendo
> Lo que á mi Juno tan ayrada tiene. (831–45)

But even when deprived of its powers to initiate conversation, Eco's voice does not lose its deceptive force and seeks its own revenge on Narciso by leading him to his destruction at the fountain.

The oracle that first predicted this destruction is another manifestation of the ambiguity of sound. Following Ovid, Cueva y Silva dramatizes the rejection of the oracle but, unlike him, does so explicitly in the figure of Liriope, who responds to the Sabio: "Yo pienso que me engaña quien s'esfuerza / A querer lo futuro declararme" (134–35). Liriope's suspicion is odd, for she had herself requested to know Narciso's future and had promised not to question the oracle's meaning (104–7). In a deft stroke of irony, Cueva y Silva has Liriope disregard precisely the words that might have saved her son's life whereas the latter, in contrast, is driven to his doom by following the empty words of Eco.

The principal cause of Narciso's deception is his own image, a point that emphasizes the second phenomenological problem encoded in the myth: vision. Ovid skillfully alludes to the ambiguity of vision in the language of the oracle: "Vana diu visa est vox auguris" 'For a long time the voice of the seer seemed empty' (3.349). The passive construction *visa est*, although normally translated as "seemed," literally means "was seen." The synaesthetic language of the oracle announces the importance of vision in addition to speech, for just as the sense of hearing is subject to distortion by desire, so too is sight, as Narciso recognizes at the end of act 3: "Ojos son las entradas que rreciben / Los rrayos de amor hasta que tocan / En el zentro del pecho y las entrañas, / Llebandose la vista por su palma" (999–1002). Love is referred to as blind both in this play and elsewhere because vision allows itself to be deceived with respect to the desired object. Like hearing, vision has no monopoly on truth and cannot in itself distinguish the real from the imaginary. Thus Narciso comes to "know himself" by believing in the reality of the insubstantial image in the fountain. Like the hollow voice that led him to the spot, the reflection proves to be deceptive and unattainable and ultimately leads to his death.

Narciso is not the only one deceived by sensory input. Niseyda first appears on the stage carrying a portrait of Narciso that she describes in the following way:

> Una imaxen traigo aqui
> De tu divina ffigura,
> Desdeñosa aunqu'es pintura
> Por ser sacada de ti.
> Myrola y hallola ayrada,
> Tratola y hallola muda,
> Tanto que me tiene en duda
> Si es la viua ó la pintada.
> Mas quiza, pues tu belleza
> En ella se trasladó,
> Tu estampa se fabricó
> Segun tu naturaleza.
> Pero si de tu trasunto
> Tan graue pena rreciuo,
> El dolor que causas vivo,
> ¡Quánto subirá de punto! (166–81)

Niseyda's confusion before the image of Narciso attests already in act 1 of the play to the deceptive power of vision. She is mystified by the portrait's disdain and muteness, qualities that ironically make it a more realistic representation of the introverted Narciso. Just as Eco's hollow speech deceives Narciso, so the latter's own portrait, because of its inability to speak, deceives Niseyda so much that she is unable to tell if the image is real or painted. Mortals thus find themselves in a quandary in which silence proves to be just as deceptive as sound and even becomes anthropomorphized at the end of the play when Júpiter asks the character Silencio to see to it that "aquestos hechos no se digan / En publico" (1437–38).

The combination of sight and sound or their corresponding lack forms a deadly mimesis that becomes a major theme of the play. The topic is fully exploited in act 4, where Cueva y Silva juxtaposes Narciso's deception at the fountain with a dream that Niseyda has while lying on the grass near the water. The sentences with which she begins talking in her sleep, "¿Es sueño aqueste ó deseo? No toco la blanca mano" (1070–71), signal the crucial function of desire in the play by emphasizing one of the similarities between dreams and desires: the fact that both often have illusory or unrealizable objects. The image of the "blanca mano," surely a reference to Narciso's hand, continues to elude Niseyda both in her dreams and in her waking desires. She continues:

> ¡Oxala tan benturosa,
> Sueño el cielo me criara,
> Que aquella mano tocara
> Que triunfa de mi gloriosa!
> Pero traydor, no me afflixas
> Tantas bezes con burlarme,
> Y en esto del engañarme,
> Suplicote te corrixas. (1086–93)

Yet the *engaño* is not something that can be "corrected," since it is endemic to the nature of vision and the senses in general. Niseyda soon recognizes this fact even in her sleep: "Amor, dexame dormir. / Mas no es mylagro que llegues / A qu'el sosiego me niegues, / Pues me niegas el viuir" (1110–13). *Sosiego* can never be gained through love because the objects of love, inasmuch as they are interpreted through the senses, are subject to distortion and infinite deferral. The only ultimate cure for this remarkably Lacanian representation of love is death, as Niseyda finally concludes: "Sin duda que si acabase / De partir de aquesta vida, / Que ymaxino que la herida / Del corazon se templase" (1190–93). The final irony is that after waking and just before dying, she glimpses Narciso's body lying on the ground by the fountain but now believes what she sees to be a fantasy: "¡O Dios, cómo me maltrata / Pensamiento tan estraño! / Ya pareze que le miro / Tendido muerto en el suelo, / Y que yo desago el belo / Del alma dando un suspiro" (1260–65). As happens with so many of the other characters, Niseyda trusts her senses precisely when they deceive her and rejects them the few times that they reflect the truth. In this way sensory ambiguity becomes one of the main causes of the frustration of desire in the play.

The fragments of Niseyda's monologue recited while she dreams both confirm her earlier confusion before the painted image of Narciso and simultaneously parallel the latter's deception by the same image reflected in the water. Cueva y Silva heightens even further Narciso's madness by having him initially believe that the echoes from his own voice, returned by Eco, are emanating from the image in the water: "¿Eres tú quien rrespondio, / Bella ymagen, á mis quexas? / ¿Por qué confuso me dexas? / Dime sí, ó rresponde no" (1202–5). Narciso's deception reaches its maximum in this scene as he ascribes otherness to both a reflection of his own face and an echo of his own voice and believes them both to be emanating from the same source. Although he realizes afterward that he has been deceived by Eco's voice (1251–53), the visual image in the fountain is too powerful for him to break away and he soon suffers from the same fate as Niseyda.

The echo, the oracle, the portrait, and the reflection all confirm the illusory nature of the senses and the instability of the structures of triangular desire. In so clearly juxtaposing the two triangles traced in this analysis, Cueva y Silva emphasizes several points that can serve to explain his use of the myth. First, whereas for the Olympians deception and the instability of desire may lead to frustration, for mortals it can lead to death. Through the direct juxtaposition of the two planes of reality, the play points to the wretchedness and frailty of the human condition even more than does Ovid's narrative. The contrast is confirmed in a last unsettling display of power, as Júpiter calmly kills Hersilia, Eco's servant, so that she will not disclose to Juno anything that has just happened.

Second, the configuration of gender in the second (human) triangle of desire is noteworthy. The traditional active and passive roles of men and women are inverted, given that the aggressive nymphs pursue the decidedly feminine Narcissus. After all, stereotypically male love, according to Freud, is anaclitic, that is, directed onto external objects, whereas feminine desire tends to be narcissistic, or directed onto the subject's own libido ("On Narcissism" 69–70). When Narciso rejects the nymphs only to fall in love with his own image, he confirms the inversion of the traditional gender types. By having Eco compete with Niseyda for his love in a display of "masculine" aggression, Cueva y Silva makes that inversion even more evident.

The manipulation of the myth in this way follows a rationalizing tendency that, according to Knoespel, is one of the principal methods that post-Ovidian poets use to engender their own version of the tale of Narcissus (106). The story of a beautiful youth loved by girls and boys alike but able to fall in love only with his own image was bound to disconcert in the honor-driven, heterosexual, and male-dominated society of sixteenth-century Spain. The general reader would most likely have intuitively anticipated Freudian theory by recognizing in Narcissus a stereotype of feminine behavior and desire. One way to adapt the myth for such readers without completely destroying it would be to saturate the whole tale with such irony that no possible doubt could remain as to the play's ethical perspective. Creating aggressive female characters who rival and kill one another for Narciso is one way of affirming this perspective. The ironization of desire serves to rationalize those elements of the story that would have most unsettled the general public.

In addition, the first triangle of desire functions to counterbalance and contain the second. The story of Narciso, so central in Ovid's myth, is really only a minor incident triggered by the principal triangle of desire. Anchoring the play in the reality of late sixteenth-century Spain while still disguised in the garb of classical antiquity, the ménage à trois involving Júpiter, Juno, and Eco serves as an exemplum that dramatizes the stereotypically male and therefore more perfect structure of desire in which adultery, lying, and cover-ups are not only permitted but rewarded. Júpiter, after all, despite his misbehavior, ends up with everything he wants. After Eco, Niseyda, and Narciso have all died as a result of his desire for vengeance, Júpiter's final order to Silencio to hide everything until he can placate his wife (1437–39) anticipates his eventual reunion with her: the same desire with which the play opens. Male authority coupled with female submission is the hermeneutical lens through which Cueva y Silva reads Ovid's myth of Narcissus and with which he ultimately fixes its meaning in the play.

The *Trajedia de Narciso* dramatizes in mythological form many of the motifs and patterns that were soon to become familiar in the *comedia nueva*: adultery, jealousy, rivalry, vengeance, repression, and, less frequently, murder. The ingredients are nearly identical to those of the infamous "casos de la honra" that Lope de Vega recommends as the best foundation for dramatic plots (*Arte nuevo* 327). As in Lope's own *Castigo sin venganza*, Cueva y Silva's piece results in a punishment—murder—that far outweighs the victim's flaws, a circumstance that most likely underlies the play's announced (in the title) attempt at tragedy.[35] The complex triangles of desire that lead to Narciso's sacrifice upon the altars of mimetism anticipate the familiar structures of the *comedia nueva* that, in a few extreme cases (see below, Chapter 3 n. 16), would require the unjust death of a wife in satisfaction of the rigorous logic of honor. In view of the esteem in which Cueva y Silva was held by such contemporaries as Cervantes and Lope de Vega (Catalán 132), the *Trajedia de Narciso* may have served as an important prototype not only for the mythological play of the seventeenth century but also for the much more widespread *comedia de honor*.

All of the plays analyzed in this chapter were written when the theater in Spain was still being theorized in regard to its form and its role in society. One of the problems that plagued many authors was that of plot fashioning: how to produce plays that would both delight and instruct, the two ancient Horatian imperatives, as well as satisfy the Renaissance demand for originality. Three playwrights from different moments of the sixteenth-century theater all responded to the problem in similar ways. At the beginning of the century, Juan del Encina, perhaps the most interested in the fundamentals of plot construction, was also the least concerned with morality and didacticism. His *Égloga de Plácida y Vitoriano* is an attempt to use the sexual desires of the myth of Pyramus and Thisbe not so much to convey ideological messages as to sustain the dramatic movements and tensions necessary to surpass his own religious model. Later in the century, responding to public taste at the moment when drama was becoming a viable economic venture, Juan Timoneda fashions the plot of his *Tragicomedia llamada Filomena* through an expansion of the various desires present in the myth of Procne, Tereus, and Philomela. Although he ends the play with a decidedly moralizing message, his choice of the myth of Philomela may reflect an implicit criticism of the increasingly restric-

---

35. One of the characteristics ascribed to tragedy during this period is a disastrous ending, as demonstrated in the words of Alonso López Pinciano. In an influential treatise on the subject, he notes that "la tragedia tiene tristes y lamentables fines; la comedia, no" (19). For a discussion of López Pinciano's theories, see Shepard.

tive monarchy of Philip II. Finally, Francisco de la Cueva y Silva, writing during the vogue of classical tragedy just prior to the solidification of the *comedia nueva*, uses the desires in the myth of Narcissus as the point of departure for his *Trajedia de Narciso*. By ironizing desire through the creation of a plot formed from a double triangular structure, he represents the values of contemporary society that would become institutionalized in the *comedia nueva*.

Both temporally and thematically, Encina is the furthest from the *comedia nueva*. The absence of jealousy and of the obsession with honor noted by Van Beysterveldt creates a rarefied atmosphere that is far removed from the passions of seventeenth-century Spanish drama. Timoneda draws closer to those emotions with help from the horrific myth of Philomela and manages to add a distinctly Spanish flavor to his piece with the antics of Taurino and veiled allusions to contemporary circumstances. Still, the loose, seven-scene structure of the play is only a distant relative of the more tightly woven, post-Cervantine productions. Cueva y Silva comes closest to a Lopean or Calderonian sensibility with the baroque structure of the *Trajedia de Narciso*. The economy and precision with which the play's movements unfold and the underlying preoccupations that they reveal (vengeance, justice, masculine authority) give one the distinct impression of being at the threshold of the *comedia nueva*. When read together, the three plays are representative of the tradition that playwrights of the seventeenth century would have at their disposal when they too turned their eyes to the desires of classical mythology.

3

The Rules of Desire

The Rise of the Comedia Nueva, *c. 1600–1636*

The formation of the *comedia nueva* in the 1580s supplied a framework in which the problems of plot construction discussed in the preceding chapter could begin to be worked out. First associated with the dramatic theory and practice of Lope Félix de Vega Carpio, the norms of the *comedia nueva* (henceforth simply *comedia*, a general term independent of specifically comic associations and roughly equivalent to "drama" in modern Spanish and English) quickly influenced the country's dramatic establishment and secured the unity of a national theater. From this point on, playwrights interested in adapting classical mythology were faced with a series of well-known conventions that heavily influenced their manipulation of source material. Thus, despite the claim of traditional criticism that classical mythology in early modern Spanish literature is always "intended" allegorically in the manner of Juan Pérez de Moya's *Philosophía secreta*, the basic concerns of the mythological plays coincide with those of the broader *comedia*.[1]

---

1. For examples of the allegorical approach, see Green, "Fingen los poetas"; and Chapman. The theory owes much of its debt to studies such as those of Seznec and Allen, and, as

At the same time, the desires encoded in the ancient stories, which continued to form a frequent basis for adaptation, did not always fit squarely into the mold of the *comedia*. The seventeenth-century *comedia mitológica* emerged as a hybrid product of this tension between national imperatives and ancient traditions. In struggling to adapt the desires of myth to the *comedia*, playwrights ended up producing works that belonged fully to neither, works as notable for their departure from the precepts of the *comedia* as for their often bizarre reconstructions of mythology. A brief review of the conventions of the *comedia* during its apogee (roughly 1600–1644) will help to provide a more thorough understanding of this process.[2]

One of the principal sources of conflict in the *comedia* is the literary honor code so often deployed in the plays.[3] Lope addresses this theme in his brief, tongue-in-cheek *Arte nuevo de hacer comedias* (1609), which, more than anything else, helped to codify the conventions of the *comedia*. In a frequently cited passage on the material he considered appropriate for stage representation, he declares, "Los casos de la honra son mejores, / porque mueven con fuerza a toda gente" (327–28). Although many critics, following José Montesinos's fundamental article, view the *Arte nuevo* as an ironic text, no one has ever questioned the sincerity of these statements on honor. Honor has the capacity not only to "move with force" the spectators in the audience, as Lope suggests, but also to motivate the actions of the protagonists on the stage, as C. A. Jones argues:

Denise DiPuccio notes with regard to Calderón, it is employed partly as "a defensive reaction against those critics who condemn the pieces as empty visual pageantry" (12). Her premise that both views "are narrow, and fail to account for the thematic complexity and dramatic artistry of Calderón's *comedias*" (2) applies not only to Calderón but to the other authors studied in this chapter as well.

2. The year 1644 suggests itself as a symbolic date for the end of the *comedia*'s prime insofar as it witnessed the forced closure of the public stages in observance of a period of royal mourning. Although the theaters reopened only a few years later, the decadence of a genre with different concerns, such as those noted by Aubrun (*La comedia* 49), was clearly under way.

3. Whether this convention reflected the real life of the times is a largely irrelevant matter. Américo Castro perpetuated the essentially romantic theory of a fundamentally mimetic theater by citing in his classic article on honor ("Algunas observaciones") a gamut of medieval and Renaissance documents purportedly confirming the real-life existence of an honor code similar to the one that governs the theater. For a review of the mimetic theory and its proponents up through the 1920s, see Fichter 47–57. The idea is still widespread in contemporary criticism, as the following judgment of Valbuena Briones illustrates: "Estos dramas [Calderón's honor plays], lo repetimos una vez más, no desenfocan ni exorbitan realidad alguna, sino que se atienen estrictamente a ella" (Prólogo xxxix).

"The justification of the honour theme in the Spanish drama of the Golden Age is to be found where the dramatists themselves found it, in its success as a motive" (209). In order to examine the "puesto privilegiado" of honor as a motive (Ruiz Ramón, *Historia . . . desde* 142) and the utility of mythology in the motivational design, a preliminary distinction must be drawn between two different characteristics of honor.

Ramón Menéndez Pidal explains that "aunque la honra se gana con actos propios, depende de actos ajenos, de la estimación y fama que otorgan los demás" (156). Gustavo Correa enhances this characterization into one that distinguishes between *honra vertical*, normally related to virtue or inner worth, and *honra horizontal*, a product of exterior, social factors and synonymous with fame or reputation (100–101). Américo Castro suggests a semantic differentiation between the two concepts: "El honor *es*, pero la honra pertenece a alguien, actúa y se está moviendo en una vida" (*De la edad* 69). The permanent quality of Castro's *honor*, indicated by the use of the verb *ser* (as opposed to *estar*), links it to Correa's *honra vertical*, whereas the fluctuation of *honra* implies the horizontal dimension of Correa's concept.[4]

Unfortunately, while the two concepts that Castro labels *honor* and *honra* are separable as ideas in the *comedia*, the playwrights themselves are not nearly as precise in their choice of signifiers, as Serrano Martínez, Poesse, and Toro ("Ehrbegriffe") all conclude.[5] Nevertheless, the distinction possesses a practical significance and, though not employed by all critics, will be maintained in the present study where a semantic differentiation between the two concepts is crucial.

Although Alfonso de Toro notes that honor in the sense of fame or opinion dominates in the *comedia*, he emphasizes that there is nevertheless "una buena cantidad de dramas de honor donde honor/honra tiene el sentido de *virtud*" ("Sistema" 184–85). To understand the function of both *honra* and *honor* in the theater, it is useful to consider some of the complex social or "horizontal" characteristics of the former in comparison with the latter. Toro is helpful in this regard in a later article ("Ehrbe-

---

4. See also Van Beysterveldt, *Répercussions* 35 and Valbuena Briones, Prólogo xxiii.

5. Van Beysterveldt objects to such conclusions on modern philological grounds (*Répercussions* 35); writers of the period, however, lacked the chronological distance and methodological tools that would have allowed them to make his fine distinctions. Within the works of single authors, confusion is the rule: see Arco y Garay 441 for the case of Lope; Gillet 192 for Calderón; and La Du 13 for Guillén de Castro. For the historical differences between the terms in extraliterary sources, see Caro Baroja and Gutiérrez Nieto. See also Artiles, "Bibliografía" for a thorough review of the literature on the subject.

griffe" 677), identifying two distinct sets of associations with the binary *honor/honra*: on the one hand, *virtus, dignitas, pudor, virginitas* (that is, inner good or *honor*), and, on the other, *reverencia, dinero, potestad, obsequio, aplauso, esplendor, reputación, ilustre familia* (outer good or *honra*). As seen from the different manifestations of each term, in contrast to the interior and personal nature of *honor, honra* is an abstract, exterior force, larger and more powerful than any one person (except for the king, who dispenses *honra*: see Correa 100). The more *honra* one has, the more respect and influence that person wields. In this sense *honra* is equivalent to *potestad*, in Toro's words, and Alfonso García Valdecasas suggests that it legitimates a participation in public power (120). Because of this characteristic, a society governed by the desire for *honra* necessarily leads to a competitive situation in which the individual seeks social prestige within the group (Ayala 156).

Just as *honra* can be gained, so it can be lost or damaged: "Así es que [la honra] se pierde igualmente por actos ajenos, cuando cualquiera retira su consideración y respeto a otro: una bofetada, un mentís deshonran si no se vengan" (Menéndez Pidal 156). The loss of *honra* for men was most often associated with the *honor* of women, since they were seen as the repositories of male reputation (García Valdecasas 155–56). The loss of a woman's *honor* (virtue, chastity) led to the loss of a man's *honra*, and, consequently, the slightest suspicion of the woman's fidelity, even when groundless, brought immediate dishonor if publicized. The unjustness with which a man's reputation could be so easily damaged by actions over which he had no control (such as the sexual exploits of a woman) has the effect of reducing the characters of the *comedia* to the status of marionettes controlled by the strings of unknown powers. It is not without justification that Louis de Viel-Castel notes a formal similarity between honor and the ancient Greek concept of fate (397).

When *honra* was damaged, the offended person had few options for, as Donald Larson explains, if "anything is clear in Golden Age discussions of honor, it is that a man simply must, no matter what his inner inclination, avenge an insult to his reputation" (13). Honor was usually restored through an act of *venganza*, whose inclusion in the social sphere of *honra* made it closer in kin to justice than to the modern concept of vengeance (Stuart 248; Artiles, "La idea" 21–27). The indisputable violence of the restorative act, which could go as far as the murder of an innocent person, was a means through which the aggressive component of honor was expressed.

Finally, the concept of *celos* is important for understanding the function of *honra* in the Spanish drama. Much more than signifying simple jealousy, as it is often translated, *celos* in classical Spanish is closer to the English "suspicion" or "doubt" as well as to the modern Spanish *recelo*: "Usado siempre en plural, [*zelos*] vale la sospecha, inquietud, y rezelo, de que la persona amada haya mudado, ò mude su cariño, ò aficion, poniendola en otra" (Real Academia). As such, it is integrally related to the grave necessity that compelled men to guard their *honra*: "Los celos de honra son, en primer término, como resultado de una obligación, no como fruto de una pasión. El marido tenía el deber de velar por la integridad de la honra familiar y el de vindicarla si era manchada" (García Valdecasas 170–71).

These observations are sufficient to suggest the great attraction that *honra* must have held as a motive for playwrights. Dramatically speaking, the concept functions as a formulaic superstructure into which the author introduces particular variables that upset the existing balance of power. The desire for either augmenting or restoring *honra* provokes reactions in the characters, *celos* being among the most prominent, that provide a prime motivating force for the plot of the play. In contrast, the internal and personal qualities of *honor* seem to foster its development in the narrative genre, as Menéndez Pidal notes (170). However, when used in the sense of virginity or chastity, *honor* was an extremely effective catalyst that motivated the machinery of *honra*.

The issue becomes a question of the particular variables that the artist uses in order to disrupt the honor code and set the plot in motion. One such variable is erotic desire, employed to such an extent that the conflict between love and honor is rightly viewed as one of the defining features of the *comedia* as a genre (Reichenberger 1970: 164).[6] The stories of classical antiquity, filled as they were with acts of raw sexuality, offered a mine of potential conflicts with the rigid honor code, and playwrights did not hesitate to appropriate the strong desires of myth for this goal. Yet, as will become apparent, the frequently uneasy meshing of the form of the *comedia* with the content of mythology often enabled an ironic treatment of some of the *comedia*'s most cherished conventions, a possibility that authors handled in strikingly different ways.

---

6. Love in the *comedia* is almost always equivalent to erotic desire, as Margaret Wilson 42 and Díez Borque, *Sociología* 44 point out.

Three playwrights supremely concerned with questions of honor were Lope de Vega (1562–1635), Guillén de Castro (1569–1631), and Pedro Calderón de la Barca (1600–1681), and a great deal of contemporary criticism has focused on their use of the theme.[7] Yet these studies consistently ignore the significant contributions of each of the authors to the corpus of mythological plays of the period. A detailed analysis of several such works with occasional references to others will reveal the creation of the curious *comedia mitológica* as both a move to harness the conflicts of classical myth to the *comedia*'s rules of desire and a simultaneous resistance of myth to those rules.

The plays selected for analysis represent not only the wide thematic range of myth to which the dramatists had access but also different stages of development in the first half of the *comedia*, from approximately 1600 to 1636. The works by Lope (*El laberinto de Creta*) and Castro (*Dido y Eneas*) most likely date from the earliest period of the genre, corresponding roughly to the patronage of Philip III (1598–1621). Calderón's *Los tres mayores prodigios* (1636) comes from the same year as *La vida es sueño*, a moment that "parece señalar el apogeo de la comedia española, pero al mismo tiempo anuncia su disgregación" (Aubrun, *La comedia* 78).[8] The year before, in fact, had witnessed the death of Lope de Vega, an event that left Calderón to reign supreme in both palaces and public theaters. The three plays are thus poised at distinct critical moments of the rise and apogee of the *comedia* as an institution. In addition, they are representative of two general stylistic periods of seventeenth-century theater: *El laberinto de Creta* and *Dido y Eneas* come from the Lopean school of dramatists, whereas Calderón's piece obviously belongs to the Calderonian cycle. Registering a diversity in both chronology and technique, the trio forms an ideal sampling in which to study the dramatic handling of myth.

---

7. For recent analyses of honor in Lope, see Larson and Zuckerman-Ingber; for Castro: La Du and W. Wilson, chap. 4; for Calderón: Honig and Lewis.

8. The dates of the plays by Lope and Castro are, as in the case of so many *comedias*, provisional. Although not published until 1621 in Lope's *Decimosexta parte*, *El laberinto de Creta* must have been written before 1618, for, as Menéndez Pelayo notes, "está citada en la segunda lista de *El Peregrino*" (Vega, *Comedias mitológicas* xlvi). Morley and Bruerton 346–47 place it between 1610 and 1615. Mérimée, *L'Art* 547 places the composition of *Dido y Eneas* in 1599, but Bruerton 119 locates it between 1613 and 1616. There is greater consensus regarding the dates of Calderón's plays. Those suggested by Harry W. Hilborn, which still represent the standard critical opinion, are followed in this analysis.

The Domestication of Desire: Union of Form and Content in Guillén de Castro's *Dido y Eneas*

Guillén de Castro is noteworthy for his remarkably smooth reinscriptions of previous material into the *comedia*. John Weiger, for example, suggests that "donde reside la grandeza del valenciano es en su habilidad de tomar situaciones (de la historia, de la épica, del Romancero, de la novela) y adaptarlas a lo que es, a fin de cuentas, el *arte nuevo* de su época, o sea, la 'comedia nueva' de Lope de Vega" (15). A study of Castro's proficient adaptation of classical myth in *Dido y Eneas* will serve as a point of departure for reading the later plays of Lope and Calderón, which bear the traces of a more unruly mixing of myth with the conventions of the *comedia*.

No myth was as politicized in the Spanish classical period as the story of Dido. One of the crucial issues was her fidelity or lack thereof to the memory of her dead husband (and uncle) Sychaeus. The intellectual tradition had been polarized since medieval times by two radically contradictory variants: the famous Virgilian tale in which the queen falls in love with the Trojan refugee Aeneas and commits suicide when he abandons her to found Rome (*Aen.* 1–4); and a lesser-known (to modern readers) version, popularized by the Roman historian Justin (2d or 3d century A.D.), in which Dido never encounters Aeneas but instead kills herself to resist the advances of the Numidian king Iarbas and remain faithful to her deceased husband (Justin 132–37; 18.4–6). The extraordinary popularity of Justin in Spain, related to his status as the only ancient author to give special attention to the country's legendary past (Lida de Malkiel 59), led to the wide diffusion of his account of Dido. It persisted, unlike in the rest of Europe, well into the seventeenth century. In addition, the Spanish ecclesiastical tradition lent moral authority to this version of the story and held up Dido as a model of chastity and widowhood (Lida de Malkiel 76–81).

While Dido's fidelity is a crucial element in the popularity of the Justinian account of her story, there is another important issue that accounts for the polarization of the myth. The historical coloring of Justin's narrative led it to gain favor among those who opposed the deception and immorality of fiction: "El antiguo reproche, puramente intelectual, de que la Dido de la *Eneida* no es la Dido de la historia se teñirá de colorido moral y justificará el receloso ponerse en guardia ante el arte que, con su halago, se sobrepone a la desnuda verdad de los hechos" (Lida de Malkiel 63–64). As the worth of fiction was nowhere more loudly debated than in discussions of drama, the moralistic attitude toward the Dido myth radically shaped its treatment in the Spanish theater.[9]

The first dramatization of the myth, Juan Cirne's *Tragedia de los amores de Eneas y de la reyna Dido* (1536), strictly follows the Virgilian epic. Significantly, the author was not Spanish but Portuguese; furthermore, the play remained long forgotten in the Spanish Renaissance (Mérimée, *L'Art* 576) and is rarely mentioned even in contemporary histories. In contrast, the next two appearances of the story in the theater bow to the politically safe view of the time in their dramatization of the Justinian variant. The austere moralism of Cristóbal de Virués's *Elisa Dido* (c. 1580) displaces the Virgilian narrative in lauding the virtue and chastity of the "eroica i gran muger, única al mundo" (169).[10] Even more remarkable for the apparent zeal of its convictions is Gabriel Lobo Lasso de la Vega's *Tragedia de la honra de Dido restaurada* (1587), written in order to, as the author explains in the *argumento*, "deshazer la común y errada opinión en que están los que ignoran la verdadera historia de la casta Dido, a quien Vergilio, en su *Eneyda*, fabulosamente y con siniestra relación agrauia, contra la opinión de tantos y tan graues autores" (83).

Such was the vehemence of those eager to defend the reputation of Dido. The issue was even debated in the famous Valencian academy of the Nocturnos in the session of October 7, 1592 (Mérimée, *L'Art* 577–78 n. 2). One of the members present was Guillén de Castro, and, although there are no records of what he said during the debate (if he spoke at all), he must have had many ideas on the subject. Although, in the above mentioned note, Mérimée cites instances in which Castro criticizes the Virgilian tradition, these were always isolated cases and never formed the basis of a plot in any of his plays. In fact, Castro may well have intuited that in eliminating the overpowering desire of Dido for Aeneas as Virgil narrates it, Virués and Lobo Lasso de la Vega also eliminated an important structural element of the myth that made it ideal for dramatization.

---

9. In addition, a psychological explanation of Spain's obsession with Dido—one that is more difficult to document, of course—may lie in her portrayal as an African. In light of Spanish medieval history, her union with the European Aeneas is rich in symbolic potential.

10. If there is anything of Virgil's "dux femina facti" 'woman in charge of affairs' (*Aen.* 1.364) in this verse, it is significant that Virués would have developed a trait that exists in Dido before she is "corrupted" by Aeneas.

Significantly, their plays are characterized by a sporadic plot design, and there is no evidence that either ever achieved any popularity.

If Castro recognized this defect, his keener sense of stagecraft probably suggested the Virgilian alternative, as Sandra Craft proposes (9). Still, he may have borrowed from Lasso the idea of foregrounding Dido's *honra*, which he perhaps realized would form an ideal conflict with her love for Eneas. Whether or not Castro actually conceived of the idea for *Dido y Eneas* in this way, his play must be read as part of a dialectical process created by the politically charged background of the myth's long trajectory.[11]

Many commentators of the piece have noted its "fidelity" to the Virgilian model.[12] But Castro was not a slavish imitator. Each incident in the plot of the play is significant insofar as it is carefully chosen from a larger pool of variants that necessarily included the Justinian source, familiar to the lay public by that time (Lida de Malkiel 61).[13] The basis for selection of the incidents is precisely their ability to achieve dramatic unity and sustain interest through the portrayal of the strongly conflicting desires of love and honor.

In an article devoted to *Progne y Filomena*, Edward Friedman observes offhand that in *Dido y Eneas* Castro "finds unity in the parallel struggle between loyalty and love that faces both Dido and Eneas" (213). If loyalty is understood to include honor, then Friedman's formulation represents an accurate description of the structural principle of the play as well as of book 4 of the *Aeneid* itself. But his assumption in the following sentence that Dido "chooses" love and Eneas, loyalty does not do justice to the wide spectrum of desires with which they mutually struggle.

In staging their struggle, Castro goes to great lengths to select and arrange incidents from the *Aeneid* that demonstrate remarkable parallels between the protagonists even before they meet each other in Carthage. In this way the dramatic movements that arise from their desires acquire a strong sense of balance. The first similarity is that both Dido and Eneas

---

11. It is a pity that the play titled *Llegada de Eneas a Cartago*, by Alonso de las Cuevas, has not survived. Cited in Pérez Pastor 16, its title appears to indicate a more Virgilian-based plot that may have served as a precedent for Castro.

12. Mérimée, *L'Art* 577; Craft 12; Lida de Malkiel 20; W. Wilson 32.

13. Castro probably also extracted some secondary material for his play from Spanish ballads. Eliza Pérez 71 maintains, in fact, that the peninsular lyrical tradition was Castro's main source of material for *Dido y Eneas*, but this claim is disputed by Powers 332. More recently, W. Wilson 32-33 has demonstrated convincingly that the ballads play the comparatively minor role of adornment at certain junctures of the Virgilian narrative.

are refugees of violence, the manifestation of aggressive desire. Dido describes to Hiarbas at the beginning of act 1 how her brother Pigmaleón (not the same Pygmalion of Ovidian fame, who will be discussed in detail in Chapter 4 of this study) murdered her beloved husband Siqueo in order to acquire his great wealth. Siqueo's ghost then appears to her "con mortal despecho, / la cara cenicienta y amarilla, / vertiendo sangre, el corazón deshecho, / y una espada con fuerza y con mancilla, / desde la guarnición asida al pecho, / y a la espalda sangrienta la cuchilla" (167) and tells her to flee her home. She crosses the sea and lands in Hiarbas's Libya. The play begins with diplomatic exchanges between Dido and Hiarbas. As Dido tells her story and announces her intention to found Carthage, Hiarbas is stricken with desire for her: "Ese color perdido, / que huyendo fué de su mortal desmayo, / para mi corazón un rayo ha sido / que abrasa dulcemente con ser rayo" (166). Having just fled from the violence of her brother, Dido will soon find herself forced by her loyalty (*honor*) toward Siqueo to flee from the amorous advances of Hiarbas.

Eneas's first appearance in the play occurs also in act 1, amid the chaos and horror of the destruction of Troy. War, as the most violent manifestation of aggressive desire, is the ideal backdrop for establishing a parallel between Eneas and Dido. The Trojan War, moreover, is particularly appropriate because it was started by a man's (Paris's) overpowering desire for a woman (Helen), a scenario that suggests the Girardian pattern of rivalry in love as the cause of violence. Like Dido, Eneas loses his beloved spouse Creusa to the violence, and, like Siqueo, Creusa reappears as a ghost to tell her husband to flee: "Errante y peregrino, / sigue tu estrella, que te irá guiando / hasta el reino latino" (171).[14]

Fleeing similar situations and propelled by similar apparitions, Dido and Eneas come together at Carthage, where they are instantly attracted to each other. For both in different ways, love poses a grave risk and direct conflict with their honor. In Dido's case, honor is initially a personal, interior respect that she feels toward her dead husband. Because of this feeling she has chosen not to profane Siqueo's memory. Whereas her virtue (*honor*) thus preserves Siqueo's reputation (*honra*), she soon exteriorizes her *honor* and objectifies it in the form of a legal code not unlike the code of conduct that governs so many baroque dramas.

At the end of act 1 Dido is confronted by an ambassador who asks for

14. Cf. Virgil's Creusa: "Longa tibi exsilia, et vastum maris aequor arandum; / et terram Hesperiam venies" 'You will endure a lengthy exile and will plow the wide surface of the sea, and you will come to the land of Hesperia' (*Aen.* 2.780–81).

her hand in marriage on the part of Hiarbas. An unexpected incident, of Castro's own invention, interrupts the messenger and provides an answer to his request. The character Celio bursts onto the scene with his sister Celeusia to accuse her of seeing another man after the death of her husband. He tells Dido that he immediately killed the man with a dagger and would have done the same to Celeusia but was detained by her officials (178–79). Dido's judgment is striking for its rigor and cold detachment. When Celeusia confesses to the accusation, the queen replies:

> Pues esenta, pues esenta
> lo que declaran mis leyes
> y pronuncian mis sentencias,
> ¿no has oído? ¿No has sabido,
> que la mujer que no sea
> tan observante y tan casta
> que en su viudez permanezca
> todo el tiempo de su vida,
> y del muerto esposo tenga
> el tálamo no manchado
> con obras ni con sospechas,
> en mi ley nunca violada,
> por mi dignidad suprema,
> mando que la quemen viva
> para que la infamen muerta,
> porque así al esposo mío,
> a quien circuyen estrellas,
> suba la digna alabanza
> de sus memorias eternas? (179)

She finishes by rewarding Celio for the murder.

This episode serves several immediate purposes. First, it sends an unspoken but powerful message to Hiarbas's ambassador. Second, as Rina Walthaus points out (82), Celeusia incarnates the sexual desire of women. Her punishment both symbolizes the burning of sexual desire soon to overtake Dido and recalls the manner of the heroine's suicide in the *Aeneid*. In addition, while being dragged off to execution, Celeusia cries out to the queen: "Ruego a los cielos que tengas / la misma desdicha mía; / podrá ser que entonces veas / si es desculpa el querer bien" (179). Dido's response, that "venga / por mí su mismo castigo, / si caigo en la misma afrenta" (179), sets a trap into which she will be led by her own passion for Eneas.

Most important for this reading, the Celeusia incident is a key to understanding Castro's rewriting of the Virgilian myth. Lida de Malkiel suggests an interesting interpretation of Celeusia's name: "Un nombre como el de Celeusia (es decir, Seleucia), la víctima del rigor de Dido, arrastra el eco de los varios Seleucos cuyos turbulentos reinados llenan buena parte de las *Historias filípicas*" (62). What she does not note is that the metathesis required to produce *Celeusia* from *Seleucia* creates a name that, together with the brother's (*Celio*), subtly suggests the net of *celos* in which the two characters are trapped.[15] The pattern of infidelity, suspicion, and vengeance that the episode reveals suggests an underlying code of conduct strikingly similar to that which governs the so-called wife-murder plays of the *comedia*.[16] In having Dido endorse this behavior, Castro skillfully adapts her Virgilian role as a general lawgiver (see *Aen*. 1.507) to one as a codifier of the specifically Spanish *ley de honor*. Furthermore, it is precisely this role as lawgiver and founder of the social relations of Carthage that preserves her power and reputation as queen, as Celio's amazed response to her judgment implies: "¿Quién no alaba tus grandezas?" (179). The enormous stakes involved in her love toward Eneas become clear: to violate the very code that she has established would imply destroying not only her *honor* but also her *honra*.

Eneas is in a similar situation. The epithet that Castro commonly applies to him, *pío* (also *piadoso*), borrowed from Virgil's *pius*, suggests his special relation to the gods as one who is "devóto, inclinado à la piedád, dado al culto de la Religión, y a las cosas pertenecientes al servicio de Dios y de los Santos" (Real Academia). Eneas's *piedad* is close to the meaning of *honor* insofar as it is a personal, interior quality related to the person's virtue. It also demonstrates the causal relation between *honor* and *honra*, since his fame (*honra*) as a hero directly depends on his piety (*honor*). Disobeying the gods, which his love toward Dido entails (because it keeps him from reaching Italy), implies betraying his goodness and destroying his reputation.

After demonstrating in act 1 the stakes that both Dido and Eneas have

15. Castro's manipulation of names in this way is consistent with Ovidian wordplay as seen throughout the *Metamorphoses*. See Ahl's discussion in *Metaformations*.

16. The most famous examples of these notorious dramatizations of the honor code are Lope's *El castigo sin venganza* and Calderón's *A secreto agravio, secreta venganza*, *El médico de su honra*, and *El pintor de su deshonra*. Although the case of Celeusia in *Dido y Eneas* is distinct in that Celeusia's husband is dead, the consequences are the same as they would be if he were alive. The role of the brother as enforcer of the woman's honor is not unusual and dates back to Torres Naharro's *Comedia Himenea* of 1517.

in maintaining their honor, Castro dramatizes in acts 2 and 3 the conflict between this sentiment and their love. The conflict is played out in three separate stages. In the first, Dido resists her erotic desire precisely to preserve her honor, whereas Eneas's amorous passion makes him ignore his obligation to the gods. In the second, Dido gives in to her love, while Eneas begins to realize the damage that his own feelings are doing to his honor. Finally, the conflict comes to divide the two completely as the Trojan leaves Carthage to follow the will of the gods even though fully aware of the queen's continued love.

Castro's skillful use of asides signals the first stage of Eneas and Dido's relationship. At the beginning of act 2, just after they have met, the following subliminal exchange takes place: "Dido.—(*Aparte.*) ¡Qué agradable cortesía! / ¡Qué amable naturaleza! / ¡Qué valor! ¡Que policía![17] / Eneas.—(*Aparte.*) Su respeto y su belleza / suspenden el alma mía" (180); and later, after Eneas has begun telling his story: "Eneas.—(*Aparte.*) ¡Ay, ojos claros, / que os adoro y os respeto! / Dido.— . . . (*Aparte.*) ¡Ay, cielos! / que responde con un salto / a cada razón que dice / un corazón lastimado!" (181). The asides continue throughout Eneas's storytelling and demonstrate the conflict building in both of the characters as they become aware of their desire and its implications. Lacking the narrative possibilities of the *Aeneid*, which so carefully portrays Dido's passion as she listens to Aeneas and "volnus alit venis et caeco carpitur igni" 'nurses the wound through her veins and is eaten away by hidden fire' (4.2), Castro manages to portray the same tension through a vivid contrast between the external appearances and the internal feelings of each character.

Dido's conflict between love and honor becomes explicit in a conversation that Castro, following Virgil (*Aen*. 4.9–53), stages between her and her sister Ana. Confessing her attraction to Eneas, Dido explains, "Cuando [Eneas] cuenta el fiero estrago / en Troya del bando griego, / parece que todo el fuego / de Troya trujo a Cartago" (183). The familiar metaphor of love as fire demonstrates the nature of Dido's passion. Moreover, the specific comparison of her desire to the blaze that destroyed Troy is an ominous analogy that anticipates her own destruction and eventually that of Carthage in the Punic wars with Rome. She soon recognizes this possibility, noting that "así, pues luchando voy / con mi honestidad incierta; / será cierto el quedar muerta / si ya agora no lo estoy, / pues por no perder la palma / de honrada, hermana querida, / vendré a pagar con la vida / los sentimientos del alma" (183).

---

17. Cf. Dido's remarks to Anna in Virgil: "Quem sese ore ferens, quam forti pectore et armis!" 'With what composure he carries himself, and how strong he is at heart and in arms!' (*Aen*. 4.11).

The conflict between love and honor thus already points toward violence and death. Ana recognizes the threat and suggests, like her Virgilian namesake, that Dido give in to love (184). Dido's honor is still too strong to allow her to accept such a proposal:

> De mi Siqueo las glorias,
> que adoraré eternamente,
> la castidad permanente
> prometida a sus memorias
> ¿se ha de acabar sin mi vida?
> La ley que a mis gentes di
> tan defendida de mí,
> ¿por mí ha de verse rompida?
> . . . .
> ¿Yo he de pasar al troyano
> las memorias de Siqueo?
> ¿Yo admitir otro deseo
> y yo tocar otra mano?
> ¿Yo no he de ser lo que soy?
> ¿Yo mudable? ¿Yo liviana?
> No, hermana mía; no, hermana.
> Mas ¡ay, cielo, muerta estoy! (185)

Yet in the same conversation, it is clear that her resolve is already breaking down: "¿Qué haré, ¡ay triste!, pues en mí / ¡ay, hermana!, triste yo, / la boca dice que no / y el alma dice que sí?" (185).

In contrast to Dido's resistance to desire during this first stage, Eneas has apparently disregarded his honor and accepted his passion for her. He decides to reveal his desire through the use of allusions to the "inconcessos hymenaeos" 'forbidden vows' (*Aen.* 1.651) of Paris and Helen. Dido provides the ideal opportunity when she mentions in passing the contempt in which she holds the infamous couple. The following dialogue ensues:

> Eneas.—Desculpa les doy bastante,
> viendo con alma piadosa
> que fué Elena muy hermosa
> y fué Paris muy amante.
> Dido.—No los nombres, pues es llano
> que fueron, la razón ciega,
> infiel esposa la griega
> y mal huésped el troyano.

> Eneas.—Cuando vi la perdición
> de una ciudad que adoré,
> con la cólera culpé
> su locura y su traición;
> pero ya viendo el rigor,
> con más flema y más cordura
> tanta fuerza de hermosura,
> disculpo mucho su error;
> y tanto el pecho le apoya,
> que a darme la misma pena,
> la hermosura de otra Elena
> otra vez perdiera a Troya. (188)

Dido's characterization of Elena as an unfaithful wife shows that her sense of honor still dominates. By contrast, in confessing that the beauty of "otra Elena," surely an allusion to Dido, would lead him to permit the destruction of Troy all over again, Eneas is attempting to seduce the queen. His comparison turns out to be prophetic: Dido will become the "infiel esposa" and Eneas the "mal huésped" that she condemns. Accordingly, Walthaus suggests that "no puede ser fortuito que Dido le aplique aquí el mismo calificativo a Paris, que el que la tradición literaria suele asignar a Eneas después de su abandono" (80). Castro fully exploits this analogy that is only briefly mentioned in the *Aeneid*.[18] Doing so allows him to integrate the Latin subtext into the familiar pattern of the *comedia*: erotic desire that inevitably leads to violence.

For the time being, Dido succeeds in foiling Eneas's advances and orders him to leave. But her determination is rapidly deteriorating, as her aside suggests: "Con la boca le despido, / y le sigo con el alma" (188). Castro uses the famous hunting scene of the *Aeneid* (4.129–59) at the end of act 2 to stage the final defeat of her honor. As Walthaus observes: "Derribado el león, vencido bajo el pie triunfador de Eneas, se ha quebrado la resistencia que la reina hasta ese momento había opuesto a sus sentimientos íntimos" (84). Dido's surrender is symbolically confirmed when, to escape the approaching storm, Eneas asks for permission to carry her into a nearby cave, to which she responds: "Toma la que tú quisieres" (192).

Once Dido's resistance is broken, the second stage of her relationship

---

18. In his prayer to Jupiter, Iarbas mentions "ille Paris cum semiviro comitatu" 'that little Paris with his sissy retinue' (*Aen.* 4.215), but there is no discussion of the subject between Dido and Aeneas.

with Eneas develops, characterized by her continued resignation to love at the same time as Eneas experiences an awakening of his scruples of honor. At the beginning of act 3 his sailors begin to feel uneasy at the length of time they have spent in Carthage (apparently several months have passed since the end of act 2). When Acates questions him about his state of mind, Eneas tellingly responds, "Tengo amor, / en cuya gozada gloria / hallo pena y pierdo honor" (192). His answer confirms the play's basic opposition and signals the beginning of his awareness that he will never be able to reconcile its two terms.

The opposition between love and honor reappears in the following scene, a highly suggestive passage that is also Castro's own invention. As Eneas lies next to Dido, a musician enters and sings of the passing delights of love (194). The stage directions then indicate, "Duérmese Eneas y tocan al arma dentro" (194). Eneas awakens and cries out, "¡Guerra, guerra!" but then decides that the sounds were a product of his imagination and falls back asleep (195). The call to arms continues to alternate with the musician's love song, and Eneas finally awakens for good and exclaims: "¡Gran prodigio, bravo estruendo! / Entre amorosas canciones / y bélicos instrumentos / en mi corazón compiten / enojados Marte y Venus" (195).

The explicit contrast between Marte and Venus is significant and represents another subtle but important difference with respect to the *Aeneid*, where control over the hero's actions is disputed by Venus and Juno. The replacement of Juno with Marte better reflects the basic concerns of the *comedia*. As both goddess of love and Eneas's mother, Venus represents the force of desire (*amor*) that influences Eneas to stay with Dido in Carthage. In contrast, Marte, the god of war, represents the fame and reputation (*honra*) that Eneas stands to gain through war against Italy.[19]

The balance between love and honor soon swings in favor of the latter. The ghost of Eneas's father Anquises appears to his son and pronounces the following speech:

> Pío Eneas, no escapaste
> de los troyanos incendios
> para vivir en Cartago

---

19. The opposition between the two deities is not maintained consistently throughout the play. When Venus appears to Eneas in act 1, besides mentioning Carthage she hints that "pasando a Italia, / serás Rey de Italia toda, / por premio de tu valor, / y por dote de tu esposa, / y habrá descendientes tuyos / que añadan valor y honra / a la cabeza del mundo, / que tendrá por nombre Roma" (176). Her suggestion advocates the same *honra* that Marte later represents.

ocupando blandos lechos,
a las ternezas rendido
y a los regalos sujeto;
para provincias mayores
y más dilatados reinos
te preservaron los hados
y te previenen los tiempos.
De los Dioses soberanos
todo el sagrado Colegio
está enojado contigo,
por quien a mandarte vengo
que te vayas; obedece.
Vete hijo; parte luego;
deja los tiernos brazos,
surca los mares soberbios,
viste las templadas armas
y saca el valiente acero.
Italia te está aguardando,
por mí no pierdan mis nietos
y los descendientes suyos
las coronas y los cetros
de la cabeza del mundo.
(195)

A comparison of this speech with the following one from the *Aeneid*, which Mercury makes for the same purpose, reveals the subtly distinct focus of Castro's play:

Tu nunc Karthaginis altae
fundamenta locas pulchramque uxorius urbem
extruis? Heu! Regni rerumque oblite tuarum!
Ipse deum tibi me claro demittit Olympo
regnator, caelum et terras qui numine torquet;
ipse haec ferre iubet celeris mandata per auras.
Quid struis? Aut qua spe Libycis teris otia terris?
Si te nulla movet tantarum gloria rerum
nec super ipse tua moliris laude laborem,
Ascanium surgentem et spes heredis Iuli
respice, cui regnum Italiae Romanaque tellus
debentur. (4.265–76)

> [Are you now laying the foundations of lofty Carthage and building up your wife's fair city? Alas, so forgetful of your own kingdom and affairs! The king of the gods himself, who controls heaven and earth with his divine will, has sent me to you from bright Olympus. He himself has ordered me to convey these words to you over the swift winds. What are you contriving? With what hope do you spend idle hours in Libyan lands? If the glory of future deeds does not move you and you will not take up the task for the sake of your own praise, have some regard for growing Ascanius and the promise of your heir Iulus, to whom the kingdom of Italy and the land of Rome are due.]

Anquises's speech is full of the rhetoric of honor in its invocation of the key concepts of piety, obligation, and fame, a feature that brings it close to Mercury's speech. Even so, the sharp contrast that Castro draws between *honra* ("las coronas y los cetros de la cabeza del mundo") and love (the "blandos lechos" and "tiernos brazos" of Dido) is absent in Virgil and reveals the distinct thematic concerns of the *comedia*.

Anquises's speech marks the turning point of the play in that it represents the passage from the second stage of Dido and Eneas's relationship to the third, characterized by Eneas's decision to leave Carthage for the sake of his *honra* and Dido's firm commitment to love. Eneas's decision does not come easily. He strongly protests against the injustice of the gods, "que no merecen los cielos" (196), a reaction that Craft views as indicative of his firm character in contrast to the "marcada cualidad pasiva" (14) of Virgil's hero. Eneas finally decides to leave Carthage without facing Dido, because, as he puts it, "siento más que el dejalla / el decilla que la dejo" (198). He speaks of the need to "torcer mi voluntad, / a vengar una amistad, / como si fuera un agravio" (198) and clearly recognizes what is at stake for both of them when he declares, "¡Ay, honra; ay, amor! Perdido / estoy; quisiera tener / dos sujetos, para ser / honrado y agradecido" (198).

Dido learns of the Trojans' planned departure, and, when she confronts Eneas about it, the question of honor forms the central issue of their discussion. Eneas recapitulates what Anquises has told him, arguing that although he prefers to stay in Carthage, he is bound by *fama* to depart (200–201). His logic represents an important change with respect to Virgil, whose hero states that if he had his way, he would return to Troy

(*Aen.* 4.340-44). Castro's alteration places greater force behind Eneas's love and thus heightens the conflict with his honor. Eneas clinches his argument with a rhetorical question: "En mis escritas historias / ¿qué dirán si una mujer / ha podido detener / la corriente de mis glorias?" (202). Dido, in contrast, shows that she is willing to trade her honor for love:

> Que el dulce nombre de esposo
> ya no me atrevo a ponerlo
> en mi boca, por temer
> que afrenta debe de ser,
> pues vas huyendo de serlo;
> mas trocaréle, si quieres,
> aunque de mi honor se arguya,
> pues a trueco de ser tuya
> seré lo que tú quisieres. (200)

When she sees that this argument is not persuading him, she tries a new one that goes to the heart of the question of honor: "¿Los dioses han de querer / tu mal trato, tu mal nombre? / ¿Y es honra, adorando un hombre / engañar a una mujer?" (201). This statement shows how smoothly Castro has adapted the ideology of the *Aeneid* to the concerns of the *comedia*. Dido displaces the meaning of *honra* from the principal context that it has occupied in the play up to this point (and in which it is close to the semantic space of Virgil's *pietas* and *fama*) to one that governs sexual relations between men and women in the *comedia*. Eneas cannot hope to achieve *honra*, Dido implies, precisely because he has dishonored her. In the first place, he has led her to betray the fidelity she promised to Siqueo, a betrayal evident in her accusation that "mi honestidad venciste / y mi honor aniquilaste" (200). In the second place, when Eneas abandons her after she has committed herself to loving him, "el honor me lleva" (202), as she comments soberly to her advisors. In Virgil, although Aeneas's actions toward Dido might seem questionable and although he and Dido are described as "oblitos famae melioris" 'disregarding their grander fame' (*Aen.* 4.221), the weight of his achievement in founding the Roman state tilts the scales of opinion in his favor. In the *comedia*'s scheme of values, by contrast, the fame achieved through future generations could never outweigh this double dishonor brought upon a woman.

Eneas realizes his act of dishonor and, in a final and significant twist that Castro adds to the play, returns to Carthage when he learns that Hiarbas and his troops are attacking (because of Dido's rejection of his marriage proposal). His words on arriving perfectly capture the Spanish ideology into which Castro has molded the Latin myth: "Aunque por sólo el amor / que tengo a Dido, volviera, / pero la causa primera, / por quien vuelvo, es por mi honor" (204). Eneas is determined not only to rectify the offenses committed against the queen but also to defend her city from the destruction of Hiarbas, urging that "defendamos a Cartago, / pues que perdimos a Troya" (204). The *comedia*'s typical rivalry of two men over a woman appears imminent.

At this point Castro has all the ingredients necessary to pull off the miraculous happy ending so characteristic of the *comedia*: an option he employs, in fact, in his other mythological play, *Progne y Filomena* (see Friedman). In *Dido y Eneas*, he could simply have Eneas return, defeat Hiarbas, and win Dido's hand. Significantly, he elects not to do so and follows the grisly end of Virgil's Dido. In dramatizing her suicide, Castro risks breaching his thus far seamless integration of myth into the conventions of the *comedia*, in which suicide was generally avoided.[20] He manages to avoid or at least to cover this breach by portraying her death as, more than a suicide, a sacrifice designed to stop the violence, analogous to what occurs beforehand in the *Trajedia de Narciso* and afterward in the wife-murder plays. Dido's sacrifice succeeds in both avenging her dishonor to Siqueo and in mediating the rivalry between Eneas and Hiarbas. All set to draw their swords and fight for the queen, the adversaries turn away in peace at her death: "Hiarbas.—Pues que la causa ha cesado / con tanta desdicha nuestra, / yo voy a llorar su muerte. / Eneas.—Y yo es justo que me vuelva / adonde me trague el mar" (205). Because Castro is able to blend to such an extent the myth of Dido into the *comedia*'s basic ideological conflict of love and honor, her suicide as such passes virtually unnoticed among critics of the play.[21]

As the opposition between love and honor is played out in the three

20. See Green, *Spain* 3:204–24, who concludes, "At no time is [suicide] admitted 'easily'—that is to say, without traces of bad conscience—as a literary theme." An example of such "bad conscience" occurs in Pedro Rosete Niño's curious *Comedia famosa de Píramo y Tisbe* (unmentioned by Green): "Y don Pedro Rosete / fin a la tragedia dura / destos amantes encierne, / cuyas almas importunas, / se fueron de mancomún / a los infiernos sin duda" (196–97n).

21. Green, for example, does not mention Castro's play in his analysis. This glaring omission is compounded by the question with which he opens his discussion: "May an author cause his heroine to sacrifice herself as Dido did on the pyre at Carthage?" (*Spain* 3:204).

stages of desire between Dido and Eneas, it is manifested at the paraverbal level in the most recurrent symbol of the play: the sword. At the literal level, the function of the sword links it to violence, vengeance, and, consequently, honor: "La espada se presenta como atributo de guerra (acto primero) y sobre todo como accesorio visual que salve [sic] el honor. Este significado lo comparte con la daga de las escenas de Celio y Celeusia, episodio que gira en torno al honor agraviado y la venganza del hombre cuya hermana—una viuda—transgrede la ley púnica de la castidad" (Walthaus 81). Walthaus comments on the scene in act 2 in which Dido, after the conversation with Ana discussed earlier, begins to address a portrait of her husband Siqueo and requests that he "aconséjame, señor, / en qué forma, de qué suerte, / sin dar la vida a la muerte / dé la pureza al honor" (185). The stage directions then indicate, "Desaparece el retrato de Siqueo y aparece en su lugar otro de una espada desnuda y sangrienta" (185). Dido interprets the omen in the following way:

> ¡Ay triste, pues de mi afrenta
> huyendo su imagen santa,
> a los cielos se levanta,
> y una espada me presenta
> tan rigurosa y sangrienta,
> que fin fatal y violento
> anuncia mi sentimiento!
> ¡Ay, que aunque más me retiro,
> en sus rigores me miro
> y en mis entrañas la siento! (186)

Her suicide at the end of the play validates her reading of the omen. The sword restores Siqueo's honor through an act of *venganza* that recalls to Dido's mind the Celeusia episode: "Erré, al fin, como mujer; / las maldiciones de aquella / que a las llamas condené / me alcanzan" (204). In both cases Walthaus sees the sword as an arm of justice that executes the punishment (82).

At the figurative level, which Walthaus does not analyze, the sword's ancient function as a phallic symbol links it to erotic desire.[22] It is not

---

22. As Burkert notes, whether "it be a stick or a club, a spear or a sword, a gun or a cannon, as a symbol of masculinity the weapon has been equivalent to and almost interchangeable with the sexual organs from Stone Age drawings to modern advertising" (*Homo Necans* 59). Roman writers, in particular, were acutely conscious of the phallic symbolism of

coincidental that Ana recommends Eneas's potential role as a companion in the same breath as the valor of his sword, suggesting that "estará bien tu persona / de otro esposo acompañada, / con cuyo valor y espada / asegures tu corona" (186). Seen in this light, the bloodstained sword into which Siqueo's portrait is converted acquires a new significance. As the proof of virginity and by extension, fidelity, the blood on the sword declares Siqueo's sexual possession of Dido, which is about to be jeopardized, at the same time that it announces the measures to be taken in order to avenge the offense.

In both the literal and figurative senses, the sword is characterized by a fundamental ambiguity. As a weapon, in addition to restoring honor, it is an instrument of dishonor. The Greeks use swords to kill the Trojans in the war scene of act 1, as Pigmaleón does to murder Siqueo (167). Furthermore, just as the sword in its role as weapon can either honor or dishonor, as phallus it can either love or rape. Dido expresses this ambiguity with ingenious conceit when Eneas plans to abandon her, noting that "todos matan alcanzando, / sólo tú matas huyendo" (200). "Matar alcanzando" refers to the positive force of love conceived of in terms of a gain (thus *alcanzar*) and expressed by the frequent phrase "Muerto/a soy/estoy." "Matar huyendo," by contrast, reveals the negative power of love that kills through rejection and is conceived of as loss, as fraud, as dishonor (hence the frequent conception of love as a loss of virginity).

The ambiguity of the sword at both the literal and metaphorical levels points to the protean nature of desire that serves as such an ideal dramatic device. It is appropriate and consistent with Castro's rewriting of the myth that Dido should kill herself with not just any weapon but *Eneas's* weapon, which as a sword represents both dishonor and vengeance (restoration of honor) and as a phallus, love and rejection: all the manifestations of aggressive and erotic desire that Castro adapts from classical myth to inform his play. Dido's brief peace in Carthage is thus punctuated by two acts of aggression with the sword that demonstrate the fundamental ambiguity of both violence and love in the *comedia*, as both ensurers and disrupters of social stability.

It is important to note, in conclusion, that in staging the conflict between love and honor, Castro disengages desire from the mechanism of

---

the sword. An example is Ovid's story of Cinyras and Mirrha in *Met.* 10, in which sword and phallus are virtually indistinguishable (see esp. v. 475). See also Phaedra's response to Hippolytus's threats to kill her with his sword in Seneca, *Phaedra* 710–12.

fate that hangs over the *Aeneid* and that is evident in Aeneas's terse "Italiam non sponte sequor" 'Not of my own will do I seek Italy' (4.361). Jean Escribano points to the importance of free will in the last two acts of the play but argues as follows with regard to the first: "Both Dido and Eneas find themselves in a situation over which they have no control, for it was pre-ordained by fate and all their actions have been guided by supernatural elements such as ghosts and the sudden appearance of gods" (149).[23] Such statements are inaccurate. Throughout the play, every decision the protagonists take is their own, and at every juncture in the *Aeneid* in which the gods determine human action, Castro either eliminates or alters the narrative to make mortals responsible for their decisions. The only deity that Castro keeps in the play, in fact, is Venus, whose appearance at the end of act 1 serves mainly to inform Eneas of his surroundings.

More significant are those gods whose intervention Castro eliminates. Juno, for example, does not create the storm that in the *Aeneid* propels Aeneas and his crew to Carthage (1.81–123), nor does Venus send Cupid in the form of Ascanius to force Dido to fall in love (*Aen.* 1.657–94). Finally, Mercury is not the figure who persuades Eneas to leave Carthage (*Aen.* 4.222–76). His replacement by Anquises is significant because, although a representative of the gods, Anquises is human and does not have the power to force Eneas's will. The same situation pertains to the other ghosts that appear in the play: they can inform the characters of their responsibilities but cannot make them comply. In addition, while the use of the omen might seem to indicate the presence of fate, Castro makes heavy use of this device in at least nineteen of his plays, as L. L. Barrett has shown. Since seventeen such works are nonmythological, overtly Christian pieces, the use of the omen cannot be indicative of a distinct ontological order.

Castro's displacement of desire from the realm of divine meddling to that of individual choice may well obey an intention to Christianize ancient myth, as Escribano argues in her article. Regardless of his intentions, the effect produced by this rechanneling of desire is to foreground human passion at the expense of an abstract conception of fate. In doing so Castro vindicates both the effectiveness of mythological desire as a dramatic motive and the viability of dramatic fiction as a form of entertain-

---

23. The quotation appears in Escribano's short article "The Function." Chapter 3 of her doctoral dissertation of the same title gives a fuller but essentially identical account of this view. For similar judgments, see Powers 336 and García Lorenzo, *El teatro de Guillén* 190.

ment, as García Lorenzo suggests: "La ficción dramática siguiendo el relato de Virgilio ha triunfado, artísticamente, sobre la verdad histórica en que se asienta la promesa de la mujer enamorada" (*El teatro de Guillén* 186). Castro's own vindication came in the great success that *Dido y Eneas* enjoyed with the public, in marked contrast to the nearly forgotten works of Virués and Lobo Lasso de la Vega.

This is not to suggest that Castro successfully killed the defense of Dido as a topic in Spanish theater. In 1654 Álvaro Cubillo de Aragón's *La honestidad defendida de Elisa Dido, reina y fundadora de Cartago* reinitiated the virulent attacks against the Virgilian tradition: "No importa que fabuloso / finja y mienta ese escritor [Virgilio], / que no faltará otro autor / más auténtico y piadoso / que castiga y reprehenda / sus torpes adulaciones" (qtd. in Lida de Malkiel 123–24). Cubillo's piece is at least the sixth to dramatize the myth of Dido and Aeneas in the early Spanish theater (along with the plays of Cirne, Virués, Lobo Lasso de la Vega, Cuevas [lost], and Castro), making the tale one of the most popular classical sources in the peninsular tradition. Nevertheless, none of these adaptations so successfully integrates mythological material into the framework of the *comedia* as Castro's *Dido y Eneas*, and his achievement stands as a yardstick with which to measure similar attempts by Lope and Calderón.

The Theatricality of Desire: Lope de Vega's *El laberinto de Creta*

Eight of Lope de Vega's mythological plays have survived to the present day. At least half of them proceed from an attempt to reinscribe desire into the context of the Spanish honor code. In *Las mujeres sin hombres*, which McGaha calls the most original of Lope's mythological plays ("Las comedias" 78), the Greek heroes Hércules, Jasón, and Teseo besiege the famous city of the Amazons in Temiscira.[24] Teseo enters the city as ambassador but is quickly smitten by desire for the queen, Antiopía, who returns his feelings. The two characters' initial choice of love for each other over honor toward their respective causes forms the basic conflict of the play, as Jasón observes: "Teseo no ha de dejar / La gloria de su deseo / Por cuantos tiene la fama" (60). Honor eventually wins and conflict seems

24. For the sources of this peculiar play, see McGaha's "The Sources."

imminent, much to Antiopía's chagrin: "¡Oh, cuánto puedes, honor! / Aunque á las almas cruel, / Tus sienes son de laurel, / Pues que vences tanto amor" (66). War is averted through a last-minute compromise of the kind so typical in Lope's drama, in which each of the heroes picks the Amazon of his choice to take back to Greece. Love, although secondary to honor, serves to effect a happy solution to the conflict.

Two other mythological plays pose similar problems. Jasón's robbery of Medea along with the Golden Fleece in *El vellocino de oro* leaves the king and Fineo (Medea's cousin and suitor) clamoring for revenge: "¡Armas, vasallos, al arma! / Vamos por tierra tras ellos; / Que bien sabemos adónde / Tomarán sus naves puerto. / Toca trompetas y caja, / Formen escuadrones luego: / ¡Vamos contra Grecia, amigos!" (171). The play ends somewhat abruptly at this point without resolving the impending crisis. Its brevity suggests that it may have been part of a trilogy that Lope never finished. Or perhaps he considered *La fábula de Perseo* as a resolution of *El vellocino*.[25] It, too, presents a typical triangle in which Perseo's liberation of Andrómeda from the sea monster compromises the honor of Fineo. Andrómeda's suitor before the arrival of Perseo, Fineo finds himself forced to challenge Perseo to a duel: "Baja, y haremos los dos / batalla, y si yo te venzo, será solamente mía" (2821-23). Unlike his namesake of *El vellocino*, the Fineo of *El Perseo* is allowed to save face by marrying Laura.

An interesting feature of both plays is what McGaha calls their "antiheroic bias":

> In *El Perseo* Lope took the minor character Phineus—in fact a villain in Ovid's version—and made him the real hero of the play. In *El vellocino de oro* the character Fineo, who didn't even exist in earlier versions of the myth, not only steals the show from Jason but actually has over 140 more lines than Jason. In both plays the supposed hero is portrayed as a rather crass interloper. Though both heroes presumably are rewarded by the gods for their virtue, we see little evidence of that virtue in action. ("Lope's *El vellocino*")

25. McGaha suggests that Lope "seems to have written *El vellocino de oro* immediately after *El Perseo* or perhaps to have worked on both simultaneously" ("Lope's *El vellocino*"). This opinion represents a revision of his previous statement that Lope's *Adonis y Venus* was "la única comedia mitológica de Lope anterior al *Perseo*" (Vega, *La fábula* 26). He places the composition of the latter "en los últimos meses de 1611 o en 1612" (ibid. 3). In any case, *El vellocino* and *El Perseo* were written closely enough in time to be considered a unit.

Because *El laberinto de Creta* was in all likelihood the mythological play that followed *El Perseo* and *El vellocino*, it will be useful to read it in light of the alleged antiheroism of the latter two works.

Based on the myth of Theseus narrated in *Met.* 8.1–182, *El laberinto de Creta* is one of the most interesting and, at the same time, least studied of Lope's mythological plays.[26] Whereas Castro demonstrates the adaptability of myth to the stage through the dramatization of desire, Lope goes a step further and lays bare the self-consciously theatrical nature of desire in order to force the myth into the framework of the *comedia*. In doing so, however, he also exposes the artificiality of the structures of love and honor insofar as those structures are based on desire, so that the adaptation of myth ends up bringing the *comedia*'s conventions into full scrutiny within the boundaries of the play.

Lope uses the principal incidents of Ovid's narrative to generate a chain of dishonor and vengeance typical of the *comedia*.[27] The opening lines of the play, spoken by King Minos of Crete, immediately announce the subject matter: "En cuanto la humana gloria / Deleites, Feniso, alcanza, / El primero es la venganza, / Y el segundo es la victoria. / Hoy entrambos los poseo, / Pues he tenido, Feniso, / Con la victoria de Niso / La venganza de Androgeo" (113). According to Ovid, Androgeos, the son of Minos, was murdered in Athens, for which his father sought revenge

---

26. The prologue to Lope's *Decimosexta parte*, in the form of a dialogue between a "Forastero" and "Teatro," praises *El laberinto de Creta* and a handful of other works (two of them also mythological pieces: *El Perseo* and *Adonis y Venus*), as "de suerte escritas, que parece que se detuvo en ellas" (Vega, Prólogo xxvi). Nevertheless, the play has received almost no critical attention apart from Menéndez Pelayo's introduction (Vega, *Comedias mitológicas* xlvi–li), which concentrates mainly on sources. McGaha's comments are limited to a plot summary ("Las comedias" 78), and Demetrius's brief treatment of the play (605) is riddled with inaccuracies.

27. Whether Lope read Ovid in Latin is a vexing issue that has been the subject of much scholarly debate. For a brief review of the arguments, see McGaha, "*El marido más firme*" 391–92, who makes a convincing case for Lope's use of translated material in his composition of *La bella Aurora*; elsewhere he makes the same argument with regard to the *Perseo* (Vega, *La fábula* 12–13). Even so, McGaha's conclusions do not nullify the possibility of Lope's having read the *Metamorphoses* in Bustamante's Spanish translation *in addition to* the Latin text. It seems unlikely that someone of Lope's intellectual curiosity and voracious reading habits would have been satisfied with a translation of the principal source of classical myth in the Renaissance. Lope may have relied on Bustamante to guide him through the Latin and probably used some of the variations found in his translation, but he almost certainly recognized them as variations and used them consciously as such. Even if he did not read the original Latin, he could have read more reliable translations of Ovid, such as that of Sánchez de Viana (Beardsley, item 112), which Neumeister calls one of the "most important texts [i.e., sources of mythology], especially so for the drama of the *siglo de oro*" (95). He was probably also familiar with the account provided in Pérez de Moya 482–86; 4.26.

with "iustis armis" 'lawful arms' (*Met.* 7.458) against King Nisus of Megara (see also *Aen.* 6.20). Minos was able to win the war only through the treachery of Scylla, Nisus's daughter, who fell in love with Minos and cut off the purple lock of her father's hair on which his life and the city's defense depended, in the hope that her betrayal would win the Cretan's love (*Met.* 8.81–94). Minos was horrified by the act and, cursing Scylla as a "nostri infamia saecli" 'disgrace to our time,' refused to take her back with him to Crete (8.94–100).

Lope modifies this initial episode in a significant way. Minos explains that he agreed before the murder to take Cila back to Crete, presumably as his bride, if she could help him win victory: "Mató Cila, patricida, / Al Rey, su padre, por mí, / Á quien la palabra di / Indigna de ser cumplida. / Entregarme la ciudad / Lo prometió, y lo cumplió; / Pero no pensaba yo / Que fuera con tal crueldad" (113). He then uses a suspiciously sophistic argument to disengage himself from the debt that he owes Cila: "La ciudad entrado habemos, / Y aunque la puerta me ha dado, / Yo quedo desobligado, / Porque los reyes queremos / De la victoria, el valor, / Por traidor ó por leal, / Pero es cosa natural / Aborrecer al traidor" (113).

Feniso's reaction is indicative of the way in which Minos's actions would be judged according to the contemporary Spanish honor code: "Ella, con la confianza / De que tu mujer sería, / Te dió, Minos, en un día / Ciudad, victoria y venganza. / Agora no sé si es bien / Que la dejes de este modo" (114). Unlike Ovid's Minos, who is justifiably outraged by Scylla's actions, Lope's Minos is indebted (*obligado*) to Cila, first, because of the "amor tan grande" (114), as she puts it, that her act of betrayal reveals but, more important, because of the promise that he made to her. For a gentleman to break his word, especially regarding marriage to a woman, was considered an act of great dishonor, as Don Juan's actions in *El burlador de Sevilla* demonstrate. Significantly, Feniso alludes to Minos's capacity as a *burlador*: "Bien dejarás su deseo / Bastantemente burlado" (114). The dishonor that the king commits in deserting Cila is the first in a long chain that forms the core of action in the play.

The second comes from the king's wife, Pasife. Lope has the messenger Polineces relate to Minos the bizarre story of the queen's passion for a bull, which has produced the Minotaur as offspring. Again there is a significant alteration of the Ovidian version:

> Enamoróse Pasife
> De este animal, dando asombro

> Á Creta, aunque hay opiniones
> Que es Júpiter poderoso,
> Que como á la bella Europa,
> De quien tomó el nombre heroico
> La tercer parte del mundo,
> Enamoró cauteloso
> En forma de toro blanco:
> Tienen por cierto que él sólo
> Pudo hallar en sus deseos
> De la ejecución el modo. (116)

Pasife's passion has resulted in an outrageous dishonor to Minos, as he states on his return home: "Vencido vengo yo, mi honor perdido" (119). While there is no mention of vengeance in Ovid, it is the only possible option in the Spanish context, as Minos tells his daughters: "Dejadme aquí mientras venganza emprendo" (119). Yet because of the possibility that the offender may be Júpiter, he cannot follow the normal path to vengeance (murder): "Matara el Minotauro; pero temo / La ira del gran Júpiter si es suyo" (120). Instead, he asks his architect Dédalo to construct "una fábrica / Donde pueda encerrar aquesta fiera, / De tan sutil ingenio y artificio, / Que el que entrare una vez salir no pueda" (120). On the surface, Minos's labyrinth is similar to one described by Ovid (*Met.* 8.159–68), but the reasoning behind its construction betrays a heavy dependence on the Spanish honor code.

The first purpose of the labyrinth is to "encerrar aquesta fiera," which was Minos's initial concern on hearing of the Minotaur's existence: "Apáguese la lámpara Febea, / Porque no pueda ver la mortal gente / Tal monstruo de mi honor eternamente" (116). Because *honra* equals reputation, *deshonra* is harmful only if publicized: "No hay cosa como callar," as a popular proverb of the period and the title of a play by Calderón illustrate. In this case, however, visual identification ("Porque no pueda *ver* la mortal gente . . .") rather than mere rumor seems to be the crucial issue, perhaps related to the monstrous appearance of the beast. Minos cannot kill the Minotaur; hiding it from public view is his next best option. In addition, the labyrinth must assure that "el que entrare una vez salir no pueda," so that anyone who sees the king's dishonor can never escape. Finally, the labyrinth will serve as a gruesome way for the king to vent his vengeance. When he demands to the defeated Athenians that "me deis cada año / Diez hombres de vosotros, que devore / Y coma aqueste monstruo de Pasife" (117), Albante comments somberly, "Querrá / Vengarse," and Teseo replies, "Vengarse puede" (118). With this vengeance-based emphasis that he places on the Greek concept of sacrifice, Lope has managed, up to this point in the play, to adapt the myth quite proficiently to suit the peculiar demands of the Spanish honor code.

Teseo is the first victim to arrive in Crete, having been chosen by a common lottery of Athenian citizens. Unfortunately for all involved, Minos's two daughters, Ariadna and Fedra, become interested in him when they catch sight of him at the end of act 1. Ariadna sympathizes with him on account of "su edad, / Su hermosura y gentileza" and wishes out loud to Fedra, "¡Ay, hermana, quién pudiera / Dar vida á aqueste mancebo!" (122). The two sisters consult on the best way to free Teseo from the labyrinth and finally meet with him to discuss their idea. Their plan follows Ovid's account as far as the thread that will lead Teseo out of the labyrinth is concerned (*Met.* 8.172–73) but introduces a new element: three loaves of venom-soaked bread that Teseo will use to poison the Minotaur before killing it.[28] The most important variation from Ovid comes in the following statement made by Ariadna to Teseo:

> Pero porque el padre mío
> Ha de saber quién te ha dado
> La industria, y vengar airado
> En mi amor su desvarío,
>   Palabra nos has de dar
> De llevarnos á tu tierra,
> Adonde se intenta guerra,
> Y si quisiere vengar,[29]
>   Tú nos podrás defender. (124)

Teseo responds: "Palabra á los cielos doy / Que serás, y lo eres hoy, / Mi bien, mi reina y mujer" (124). Just as Minos gave his word to take the princess Cila with him as his bride, Teseo promises to take Ariadna as his wife if he escapes. Lope establishes a perfect parallel between the two cases, not only geographically (Athens to Crete in the first instance and

---

28. Lope may have borrowed this element from Bustamante's translation, which mentions "tres pelotas confacionadas de çerote y otras cosas" that Teseo hurls into the mouth of the Minotaur (fol. 127r). Bustamante also says that the thread was made of gold, a detail included in Lope's account that does not come from Ovid or Pérez de Moya.

29. These two verses should probably read, "Adonde si intenta guerra / Y se quisiere vengar," although I have not had access to the first edition manuscript for verification.

Crete to Athens in the second), but also morally. As Minos was obligated to Cila for the victory over Athens, Teseo is obligated to Ariadna for his life.

Ariadna's offer to help Teseo escape from the labyrinth, in the context of the Spanish honor code, can lead only to disaster, as it does in the Greek tradition. In the first place, his escape will break the terms of the agreement between Athens and Crete and overturn the newly established balance of power. More important, it will upset the sacrificial mechanism that Minos has used to restore his own honor, for if Teseo enters and then leaves the labyrinth, he will carry with him a visual record of the king's dishonor. Finally, once he has escaped, his promise to Ariadna places before him the horns of a serious dilemma. If he takes her with him, he offends both her father and her *novio*, Oranteo, and risks another war between Athens and Crete; if he abandons her, he dishonors her and leaves her at the mercy of her male guardians. The only peaceful and honorable solution is to remain in the labyrinth and accept his fate, an alternative not found in any ancient author.

Significantly, Lope follows Ovid and has Teseo kill the Minotaur and escape from the labyrinth in act 2. Fulfilling his promise to Ariadna for the time being, he quickly leaves Crete with her, Fedra, and his servant Fineo. When Polineces, whose role in the play seems limited to that of a messenger of doom, announces that the king's daughters have disappeared and hints that they have escaped with Teseo, Minos warns: "Advierte bien, Polineces / Que es mi muerte lo que dices" (129). His response illustrates the familiar equivalency of dishonor with death (given that honor equals life).

Minos decides to pursue his offender, but his action proves unnecessary, because Oranteo, who has just won the official bid to marry Ariadna, decides to avenge the dishonor by declaring war on Athens (129). It is noteworthy that in no ancient source does Minos pursue Theseus for robbing him of his daughters, although he pursues Daedalus for different motives (see Plutarch 37–41; 1.19). In order to follow the demands of the Spanish honor code to their logical conclusion, Lope is obliged to reconstruct the desires of the myth in a way that moves his adaptation further and further from the original context. The resistance of the Ovidian myth to the conventions of the *comedia* and the resulting distance between Lope's adaptation and its source grow ever more prominent as the play progresses.

At the end of act 2 the scene switches to the island of Lesbos, where

Teseo has come ashore ostensibly because Ariadna and Fedra are seasick (129). But one soon learns that he has other intentions: "Que adoro en Fedra, Fineo, / Y que de un justo deseo / No es bien que te escandalices. / En el camino del mar, / De Fedra me enamoré" (130). Because of his sudden desire for Fedra, he decides to abandon Ariadna on Lesbos. On the same grounds that Feniso objected to Minos's desertion of Cila, Fineo now protests against Teseo's plan:

>Si justo ó si injusto fué,
>Yo no quiero disputar;
> Pero dejar á Ariadna,
>Esa es bajeza, señor,
>Indigna de tu valor,
>Y una ingratitud villana;
> Que Ariadna te dió á ti
>La vida en una ocasión
>Tan notable, y no es razón
>Que se lo pagues así. (130)

When Fineo continues to protest, Teseo threatens to kill him (130). Fineo manages to escape while Teseo schemes to have music played so that "duerma Ariadna, / Pues la trata el mar tan mal" (130). When she falls asleep, he leaves both her and Fineo on the island, carrying Fedra off by force.

Lope probably borrowed from Bustamante (fol. 127v) the idea of having Teseo fall in love with Fedra at sea, since in Ovid's version Theseus does not take Phaedra with him when he escapes from Crete. Bustamante's account is more appealing because, in the first place, it explains why Teseo abandons Ariadna (which Ovid does not do) and, in the second, provides the material for another conflict between love (Teseo's desire for Fedra) and honor (his obligation toward Ariadna, stressed by Fineo). As Teseo continues to disregard honor, a process that began with his decision to flee the labyrinth, Lope portrays him as increasingly villainous and unsympathetic in a way that recalls the antiheroic bias of *El vellocino* and *El Perseo*.

Yet, to the extent that ancient writers themselves portrayed Theseus in an ambiguous fashion (as Seneca does, for example, in his *Phaedra*), Teseo's antiheroism also demonstrates a case of the resistance of myth to complete inscription in the norms of honor and heroism dominant in the *comedia.* Up to this point, Lope has been able to exploit the negative qualities of the mythological Theseus in order to generate an exciting plot, but the classical prototype simply cannot be made to share fully, no matter how much it is forced, the ideology of a Spanish nobleman. As it becomes progressively more difficult to smooth over the differences between the ideologies of desire in myth and the *comedia,* Teseo serves increasingly to dramatize the limitations of the latter, and Lope will be forced to resolve the conflict through an act of theatrical wizardry that seeks to neutralize the resistance of myth to the *comedia*'s rules of desire.

Lesbos turns out to be the home of Oranteo, Ariadna's spurned *novio.* He now returns home in order to make the preparations for challenging Teseo to a duel:

> La venganza me abrasa é inquieta:
> Parte, Luscindo, á Atenas; parte luego,
> Y al bárbaro Teseo desafía,
> Paris troyano de la prenda mía;
>   Dile que de sus armas ofendido
> El Príncipe de Lesbos, Oranteo,
> Le reta de traidor y mal nacido,
> Y que serlo de Júpiter no creo;
> Dile que fué cobarde y atrevido,
> No vencedor del Minotauro feo,
> Sino engañoso Ulises, que importuno
> Quitó la vida al hijo de Neptuno. (132)

In the meantime, Ariadna has discovered Oranteo's presence on the island and begins to regret having left him for Teseo (135). She decides to remain in disguise until the opportunity for reconciliation presents itself.

Teseo arrives on Lesbos in response to Oranteo's challenge at the same time that Minos comes ashore apparently blown off course by a storm. Minos praises Oranteo's impending duel with Teseo as a noble defense of his honor (141) and sets the stage for the challenge. At the climactic moment, Ariadna, whom everyone had presumed dead, reveals herself, and Minos tells her, "Dale la mano á Oranteo, / Y en paz haremos las fiestas" (143). Ariadna is able to marry Oranteo because, even though Teseo abandoned her, he did not rape her, as evidenced by her statement at the end of act 2: "Doylas [gracias] en desdichas tantas, / Pues [Teseo] deja con honra [i.e., virginity] un cuerpo / De donde se eleva el alma" (132).

As Alexander Parker notes, "It is an essential convention of the Spanish drama that marriage symbolizes the stability of the social order under the sanction of divine law. . . . the marriages at the end of so many Spanish plays—marriages which from the realistic point of view appear hasty and unconvincing—signify that chaos gives way to order" (695). The sacrament of marriage with which *El laberinto de Creta* ends restores order and rechannels the desires that had briefly careened out of control.

Lope, the consummate crowd pleaser and avowed defender of tragicomedy, opts for the happy ending that Castro rejects in *Dido y Eneas*.[30] He achieves this effect by transforming Ovid's Liber (Bacchus), who rescues Ariadne from her plight (*Met.* 8.177), into the human Oranteo, a substitution that works rather well. This move, however, leaves him with the awkward question of what to do with Teseo, the principal subject of acts 1 and 2. To allow Teseo to continue in the path of dishonorable desire that has generated the plot and that befits the classical Theseus would considerably mitigate the happy ending. Lope's resolution of this problem is simply to have Teseo declare tersely, "Aquí cesa / la enemistad" (143). An examination of the ludic framework in which Lope has portrayed the conflict between love and honor will demonstrate how he manages to deliver this contrived solution and brazenly push Teseo offstage when his mythological persona begins to get in the way.

Many of the incidents that either offend or restore honor throughout the play are represented as conventions of drama. Lope's selection of the island of Lesbos for the site of Ariadna's abandonment, for example, is an intriguing one that contradicts both Ovid (*Met.* 8:174) and Bustamante (fol. 127v). Its location in the eastern Aegean near the Phrygian coast certainly makes it an improbable stopover point between Crete and Athens. Lope's choice has much more to do with theatrics than with geography. A dishonored woman such as Ariadna faced few options in seventeenth-century Spanish drama. If she were not killed by the avenging husband, father, or brother and could not marry the offender, her only alternative was to escape from men by entering the sisterhood. Since Lesbos had been famous since antiquity for being home to female homo-

30. In his *Arte nuevo*, Lope defends the subgenre of "tragicomedy," a term originally coined by Plautus (*Amphitryon* 50–63), as the preferred mode of representation because the mix of tragic and comic elements "deleita mucho" (178) and imitates nature, "que por tal variedad tiene belleza" (180).

sexuals, Lope chooses it, in a playful parody, as the ideal spot for Ariadna to be abandoned by the man she loves.

The parody reaches buffoonish proportions when Ariadna disguises herself as a shepherd, Montano, and is immediately pursued by the over-eager shepherdess Diana, who complains of Ariadna's lack of interest (133). The *comedia*'s frequent convention in which a woman disguises herself as a man for the purpose of restoring her honor (one need only think of Rosaura in *La vida es sueño*) takes on a whole new dimension in the quasi-pastoral setting of Lope's Lesbos. Furthermore, Oranteo sees Ariadna disguised as Montano and begins to fall in love with the semblance of his former *novia*: "Lauro, yo estoy sin mí, pues he llegado / Á imaginar que este pastor parece / En todo á la bellísima Ariadna" (135). A locus of ambivalent gender relations, the island serves as a minitheater on which the conventions of honor are played out in highly stylized form.

Additionally, the bull with which Pasife dishonors Minos is, according to rumor, not really a bull but Júpiter in disguise. The king of the gods descends from heaven, in other words, to perform a role as an actor on stage. The people, however, have trouble in distinguishing acting from reality, as Minos laments:

> Que de imaginación de un blanco toro,
> En que Júpiter vino transformado,
> Pasife, indigna del real decoro,
> Haya el monstruo que dices engendrado,
> No fuera tanta ofensa del tesoro
> Que en el honor divino está guardado;
> Mas nunca el vulgo juzga bien; que en todo
> Elige siempre el más indigno modo. (116)

The complaint is tellingly similar to the observation, made by Lope himself in the *Arte nuevo*, that

> si acaso un recitante
> hace un traidor, es tan odioso a todos,
> que lo que va a comprar no se le vende,
> y huye el vulgo de él cuando le encuentra;
> y si es leal le prestan y convidan,
> y hasta los principales le honran y aman,
> le buscan, le regalan y le aclaman. (331–37)

Minos's dishonor would not be so great, in other words, if the *vulgo* could see through the theatrical garb in which it is disguised.

As the offspring of Júpiter in disguise, the Minotaur is in a sense the fruit of performance. It is thus appropriate that the labyrinth, constructed to both hide and house the beastly dishonor, should function within the play as a miniature stage on which Teseo and the monster perform. Oranteo's comments to Lauro as Teseo enters the labyrinth cannot but suggest the audience of a public theater: "De aquesta parte, en rejas y balcones / La gente mira un hombre de buen talle / Que ha entrado en él"; he then decides to watch the performance for himself (125). When Oranteo asks, "¿Entró el ateniense?" Lauro replies, "Entró / Dándole aplauso la gente" (126), suggesting the response of an audience to the movements of an actor. Fedra and Ariadna, moreover, arrive on the scene "en hábito de hombres con capas y espadas," according to the stage directions (127). Their disguises will allow them to observe the happenings unharassed: "Con este disfraz, seguras / Á la puerta aguardaremos / Del Laberinto, hasta ver / La disposición del cielo" (127). The multidimensional spectacle that results—real-world actresses who play Fedra and Ariadna, who play male characters who watch Teseo perform—creates a theatrical *mise en abyme* that calls attention to the conventions of drama within the play itself, recalling something of the self-conscious nature of Senecan tragedy.

The duel that Oranteo seeks with Teseo in order to avenge the kidnapping of Ariadna is also portrayed as theatrical. Oranteo orders Lucindo to tell Teseo that their confrontation should take place at sea: "Porque el teatro que estas islas cierra / Nos servirá de plaza belicosa, / Donde nos puede dar la de un navío / Lugar seguro y libre al desafío" (132). Albante, a servant of Teseo's, confirms the metaphor when he asks Teseo rhetorically, "¿La mar quieres que sea / Teatro de este campo de batalla?" (137). In describing the dueling arena as a theater, Lope exploits a common metaphor of the period (see Curtius 138–44) in order to lay bare the performative, showy nature of the duel as well as the artificiality of *venganza* as a means of restoring honor. Both are exposed for exactly what they are: theatrical conventions.

Finally, one of the crucial elements that help secure peace and restore honor at the end of the play is the result of pure theatrics. As mentioned, Ariadna disguises herself as a man, the shepherd Montano, in order to restore her honor. This act alone, like her earlier appearance in cloak and dagger at the labyrinth, may be viewed as a performance and as such exposes the conventions of the theater as genre, but a later incident pushes the metaphor even further. The local inhabitants of Lesbos happen to be celebrating their annual festival of Venus. The shepherd Florelo describes one of the principal events of the celebration: a contest in which a statue of the goddess Minerva will handpick "los reyes, y ella / Lo dice al besarle el pie, / Porque pone en la cabeza / De los que han de ser, la mano" (136). Liseno, another shepherd, also alludes to the theatrical nature of the ceremony: "Traiga Florelo las flores, / Corte laurel de las selvas; / Que yo haré un rico teatro / Adonde asentarse pueda / El mismo Rey" (136).

Ariadna wanders unwittingly into this "rico teatro." The shepherdess Doriclea, eager to be crowned queen and believing Ariadna to be the shepherd Montano, requests that she (Ariadna/Montano) disguise herself as the goddess, since "tu hermosura, Montano, / Es mayor que su belleza. / Y así podrás escogerme / Para que yo reina sea" (137). When Ariadna reacts with surprise, Doriclea replies, "¿Qué importa, pues eres hombre, / Que seas mujer por defuera?" (137). Her response describes, of course, precisely the opposite of the true state of affairs. For Ariadna, already disguised as Montano, to "play" a woman actually implies revealing and dis-playing herself as herself. After her performance she is recognized by Oranteo, Teseo, and Minos, an act that ultimately leads to establishing the peace.[31]

Whereas, on the one hand, this peace, like the wedding that follows it, signals a conservative, restorative force at work in the play, on the other hand, the transvestite figure Ariadna/Montano announces what Marjorie Garber calls a "category crisis," that is, the "failure of definitional distinction, a borderline that becomes permeable, that permits of border crossings from one (apparently distinct) category to another: black/white, Jew/Christian, noble/bourgeois, master/servant, master/slave" (16). In the case of *Laberinto*, this permeable borderline exists precisely between the preconceived realms of theater and reality, acting and being, signaling an ontological anxiety that would achieve maximum expression in Calderón's *La vida es sueño*. Curiously, the category crisis of acting/being in Lope's play permits a happy resolution to the problem of what to do with Teseo. Because acting is equated with being and in fact replaces being at so many crucial junctures of the play (Júpiter's disguise, the labyrinth, the

---

31. It is only because Ariadna reappears, alive and well, that the duel is suspended, as Minos's comments illustrate: "Hija, de verte me pesa / En tanto mal; pero hallarte, / Notablemente me alegra. / Dale la mano á Oranteo, / Y en paz haremos las fiestas" (143).

duel, the final peace), Lope is able to neutralize Teseo's menace to love and honor and banish him from the stage when he threatens disaster.

Dishonor and *olvido*, the opposites of honor and love, are the ingredients of disaster and appear in abundance throughout the play. Both are inevitably associated with absence, as the following citations illustrate (interlocutors are indicated in parentheses):

> Y si ausencia suele ser
> Del honor ladrón sutil,
> Seas el hombre más vil
> Que fué jamás por mujer. (Cila to Minos, 115)

> Con esto pienso volver
> Á la patria que mi ausencia
> Siente con tanto rigor. (Minos to Feniso, 115)

> Cuantos males nacieron en el mundo,
> Hijos fueron de la ausencia. (Minos to Athenians, 117)

> Pero para vuestra ausencia
> Corta vida me prometo. (Ariadna to Oranteo, 118)

> Así, donde ausencia alcanza,
> Aunque son sus fuegos hielos,
> Trueca en lo azul de los celos
> Lo verde de la esperanza. (Ariadna to Fedra, 119)

> Pero si la fiera ausencia
> Es del amor resistencia,
> Lo mismo será de ti:
>   Si te olvida, olvidarás. (Fedra to Ariadna, 119)

> Que de ausencia temo olvido. (Oranteo to Lauro, 126)

By extension, love and honor are believed to be rooted in a pure presence that disintegrates when a third party comes between the self and other and creates the typical triangle of the *comedia*, as Teseo does in the case of Ariadna and Oranteo.

Yet the opposition between presence and absence is deconstructed in the play by a middle term: acting. Performance is located somewhere between presence and absence, inasmuch as representation both re-presents (makes present) and calls attention to an absence, the signification of a reality somewhere offstage. Not surprisingly, at those crucial junctures in the piece where honor comes into play and threatens to send the plot toward a disastrous end, performance appears thematized. By consciously invoking the play's "category crisis" emblematized in the transvestite figure Ariadna/Montano, Lope signals the highly theatrical nature of conflicts based on love and honor and directly snubs the convention that says dishonor equals loss equals disaster. The result is the "monstrous" blending of the tragic and the comic—tragicomedy—in which honor and love are disengaged from the rhetoric of presence.

As part of this process, the dishonor and *olvido* of Teseo's character are effectively neutralized, forcing him to declare an end to the hostilities. A sonnet that Ariadna recites at the end of the play bears eloquent testimony to this process of neutralization:

> Arrepentido amor de haber querido
> Bastardo amor contra el amor primero,
> Volvió á querer; que el fuego verdadero
> Estaba en las entrañas escondido.
>   Bien dicen que el ausencia causa olvido,
> Culpa le pongo y disculparme quiero;
> Pero probar que no es olvido espero,
> Amor que vuelve á ser como había sido.
>   Mientras que en la memoria el fuego asista,
> No importa que le falte la presencia
> Para que del olvido se resista.
>   Cubrióle la ceniza de la ausencia,
> Pero como sopló la dulce visa,
> Volvió la llama á su primera esencia. (135)

Love, in the final analysis, is not bound by pure presence, as long as "en la memoria el fuego asista." This crucial statement demonstrates that love is rooted not in presence but in the *fuego* of memory, in desire, which is predicated on absence insofar as the desired object must be absent to be desired. In this rather radical notion, Lope approaches the Lacanian viewpoint that the desired object is always absent, symbolically speaking, in the sense that union with the other can never be fully achieved. The rewriting of desire in this way depolarizes the metaphysical distinction between presence and absence and those oppositions founded upon this distinction (*amor/olvido, honor/deshonor*), so that Oranteo's absence ultimately exercises a stronger control over Ariadna than does Teseo's presence. From this vantage point, it is a simple maneuver to push the offending villain offstage when necessary.

Like Castro, Lope reinscribes the desires of myth within the conflictive ideology of love and honor in the *comedia* but, unlike him, does not blend the two nearly so well. When Teseo's mythological persona begins to interfere too much with the *comedia*'s most cherished conventions, Lope appeals to the ludic space of tragicomedy to force the myth into the framework of the *comedia*. This move, however, comes at the expense of revealing the *comedia*'s underlying oppositions as artificial. In the trade-off that must be made between adherence to the classical model and conformity to the conventions of the genre, *El laberinto* represents a midway point that manages something of both without fully achieving either.

Desire Unleashed: The Crisis of Reciprocal Logic in Pedro Calderón de la Barca's *Los tres mayores prodigios*

Calderón left some eighteen plays based on plots or characters of classical mythology, excluding the ten *autos sacramentales* formed from similar models.[32] Although his voluminous output ranks as "the largest group of mythological plays written by any single non-ancient author" (ter Horst, *Calderón* 7), it is really only in the past two decades that critical interest has come to focus on this significant portion of Calderón's dramaturgy.[33]

---

32. For a discussion of these fascinating mystery plays, see Páramo, Acosta, and Voght.

33. The first article devoted exclusively to the subject is Leopold Schmidt's study from 1856, in which he deals mainly with sources and engages in little literary criticism. Subsequent negative assessments of the plays by authorities such as Menéndez Pelayo, *Calderón* 365 and Paris 557 all but killed interest in the plays until Ángel Valbuena Prat suggested in 1941 that they were "uno de los géneros de nuestra dramática del XVII más próximos a la sensibilidad y gusto actuales" (*Calderón* 169). W. C. Chapman's seminal article followed in 1954, and Ángel Valbuena Briones's *Perspectiva crítica*, of which a large segment was devoted to the mythological plays (325-402), appeared in 1965. Since then at least five dissertations (Mooney, MacKinnon, DiPuccio, Benedetti, Duncan-Irvin), six books (Haverbeck, Neumeister, ter Horst, de Armas, T. O'Connor, Greer), and several important articles (Haverbeck, Aubrun, T. O'Connor) have focused on various aspects of Calderonian myth. For a more detailed historical review of criticism through the late 1970s, see Mooney 5-24; MacKinnon 10-80; and Neumeister 27-45.

One point that recent critics have used to justify studying the plays is that most of them, beginning with *Amado y aborrecido* in 1650, date from the second half of the century and as such represent the mature poet at the peak of his artistic ability.[34] Even so, the later mythological plays coincide with the full decadence of the *comedia* and represent concerns distinct from those dramatized during the genre's peak in the 1630s. Erotic desire, to be sure, continues to be an important motif and Calderón exploits it to the fullest in all his mythological plays, as ter Horst notes (*Calderón* 5), but the emphasis on honor, in particular, wanes after the thirties. Of the ten dramas that Valbuena Briones classifies as "dramas de honor" (Calderón, *Dramas* 33) only two date from after the thirties and none from after the forties.[35]

To examine the prototypical conflict of love and honor in the most prolific representative of the mythological *comedia*, one must turn to Calderón's second such play, *Los tres mayores prodigios*, a piece often dismissed as one of the poorer works of a genre already maligned for its inferiority.[36] Yet more recent approaches to the play, beginning with A. I. Watson's indispensable article, "Hercules and the Tunic of Shame," have begun to grasp its immense scope and intricate complexity.

Los tres mayores prodigios is essentially an honor drama, although Valbuena Briones does not characterize it as such (Calderón, *Dramas* 33–34). Perhaps his failure to capture the importance of honor in the play is related to his deletion of the play's *loa* from the Aguilar edition.[37] In this *loa*, Jasón and Teseo find their friend Hércules in an apparently suicidal state. When they ask him what has happened, he explains that the centaur Neso has just kidnapped his wife Deyanira. Calderón chooses this minor incident from classical myth as the basis for his play.

The story of Nessus's kidnapping of Deianira and Hercules' revenge is

---

34. Valbuena Prat, *Calderón* 169; Chapman 35; ter Horst, *Calderón* 1; Wardropper, "Calderón" 35; T. O'Connor, "On Love" 120–21.

35. Late Calderonian drama may reflect the significant changes that the poet experienced in his personal life. In 1651 he was ordained a priest and ceased to write for the public theaters, serving as the court-appointed playwright from 1656 until his death in 1681. For more details on Calderón's life, see Cotarelo's classic *Ensayo*.

36. Schack 414; Valbuena Briones in Calderón, *Dramas* 1640; Chapman 51; DiPuccio 41.

37. Because of this omission, all references to the *loa* will come from the facsimile edition of Cruickshank and Varey. Elsewhere, Valbuena Briones's edition, unfortunately the only standard edition of Calderón's works to date, will provide the text of the main body of the play, but the many typographical errors will be emended according to the facsimile edition. Where necessary, the two editions will be distinguished by the notations "CV" (Cruickshank and Varey) and "VB" (Valbuena Briones).

related in Ovid's *Metamorphoses* (9.98–272) and Seneca's *Hercules Oetaeus* (491f). Calderón probably used both classical sources as well as Pérez de Moya's *Philosophía secreta* (464–66; 4.15) and Vitoria's *Teatro* (2:174–87; 2.2.23), which give standard accounts of the tale. In addition, Colahan and Rodríguez suggest a contemporaneous Spanish play, Francisco López de Zárate's *Tragedia de Hércules furente y Oeta* (not published until 1651 but probably written between 1619 and 1629), as a possible influence upon Calderón. Like Lope, Calderón reinscribes the desires of his models into the framework of the *comedia*; in contrast to him, he does little to counteract or neutralize their resistance to inscription. The resulting play challenges the viability of the honor code as a judicial system capable of restoring perceived loss. Vengeance is shown to be ultimately impotent to the extent that the desires that foment it are consistently frustrated by what may be termed a pervasive logic of diminishing returns.

The vocabulary that Hércules employs in describing Neso's act (*ofensa, agravio*) leaves no doubt that the playwright has situated the incident within the framework of honor. Hércules explains that seeking vengeance will be difficult,

> porque estos Centauros tienen
> por patria el mar, y la tierra,
> y si con ella trasciende
> los montes, es impossible
> seguirle, si passar quiere
> a essotra parte del mundo
> por essos mares, no puede
> mi furia alcançarle, ved
> si es mi desdicha bien fuerte,
> pues ay mortal que me agravie,
> y no ay Dioses que me venguen. (fol. 252r)

Teseo and Jasón both give their solemn word to help Hércules restore his honor. Jasón agrees to search all of Asia, Teseo will scout throughout Europe, and Hércules will remain in Africa (the setting of the *loa*), where the three will meet again in a year to compare their findings.

The *loa* is essential for grasping the principal unity of the play, which lies in the quest to restore Hércules' honor. Watson was apparently the first to observe this point ("Hercules" 775–76). As evidence for the centrality of Hércules' story, he cites the peculiar, experimental staging of the play, which is described in detail by Shergold (285–87) and which, for a long time, tended to deflect critical attention from the play's content. But the adventures of Jasón and Teseo are more than parenthetical to the question of Hércules' honor, which is not decided until act 3. Because they give their solemn word to Hércules, they place their own reputation at stake; whatever occurs in their adventures impinges on their *honra* as friends and as heroes. The implicit extension of a "caso de la honra" to Jasón and Teseo heightens interest in their own actions and lends a sense of autonomy to their adventures. Each of the first two acts forms a minidrama whose contents, while causally related to Hércules' own situation in the way that Watson has shown, also mirror that situation thematically in dramatizing the pivotal conflict between love and honor.

Act 1 relates the famous tale of Jason's conquest of the Golden Fleece with the aid of Medea.[38] The act opens with the arrival of Friso in Colchis. Bearing the fleece, he recounts a lengthy, fairly traditional version of how he and his sister were forced to flee from their evil stepmother by means of the golden ram, whose hide he now wishes to dedicate to Marte for having helped him reach safety (1641–42). Marte accepts the gift "con gusto tanto, / que guardarle determino; porque de mi templo santo / nunca falte el vellocino" (1643). As in the ancient world, the Golden Fleece in Calderón's play takes on special significance. Juan Pérez de Moya offers the first clue to interpreting this important image: "Y el decir duraría el estado de Colchos mientras el vellocino dorado allí estuviese es porque sin dineros no se pueden [*sic*] sustentar ninguna gente de guerra para defenderse el reino" (561; 4.52). The fleece represents money and, by extension, power to be gained through military ventures. On it the

---

38. The myth of Jason and the Argonauts as explorers of the East must have held a special fascination for the Spaniards as explorers of the West, especially given the historical significance of the Burgundian Order of the Golden Fleece (see Elliott 157; Huizinga 94–96). Of the main classical sources of the tale—Apollonius Rhodius's *Argonautica*, Euripides' *Medea*, Ovid's *Metamorphoses* 7.1–401, Seneca's *Medea*, and Apollodorus's *Library* 1:92–125; 1.9.16–9.28—it is likely that Calderón had direct knowledge only of Ovid and Seneca. Seneca's play, much inspired by Euripides', deals mainly with the events that occurred after Jason and Medea returned to Thessaly and provides only a few elliptical flashbacks of the events at Colchis (for example, vv. 129–36, 465–76, and 911–14). It seems most probable that Ovid was Calderón's principal classical model. The summaries provided in the manuals of Pérez de Moya 559–62; 4.52–53 and Vitoria 1:287–98; 1.3.12–13 do not contradict the Ovidian version of the tale but do fill in several elements of the myth eliminated by Ovid and only alluded to by Seneca, such as Medea's ghastly murder of her brother. In addition, Lope's *El vellocino de oro* cannot be discounted as a possible source. Calderón probably read the contemporary Spanish material along with the classics, supplementing all sources with innovations of his own.

reputation or *honra* of the state depends, recalling the fleece's function as an instrument of royal power in Seneca's *Thyestes* (225–31).

This interpretation of the fleece is supported by certain political implications of the play that Frederick de Armas suggests in a remarkable reading:

> Not only are the astral connotations manifested from the start, but so are the political implications of the action. Philip IV was born under the sign of Aries. By centering the action of the first act of the *comedia* around the Golden Fleece, Calderón seems to be paying homage to the king. The purpose of the summer celebration was to praise the king as a solar hero on the night of the luminary's exaltation, the summer solstice. Indeed, the *loa* that precedes the spectacle play speaks of the king as "Quarto Planeta de España," equating him with the sun. (151)

The equation of the fleece with Aries and by extension with the king of Spain shows to what extent *honra* and power are invested in the animal skin. The fleece is a material object that can be gained or lost in the same way that *honra* was conceived of as an external quality subject to augmentation and diminution. The placement of the fleece in the temple of Marte at Colchis represents an ostensible increase in the prestige of King Aetes, and the villagers celebrate its consecration with jubilant festivities (1644).

But the fleece, like honor itself, is an illusory possession that only bodes misfortune. A mere trace of the now absent animal, the hide without the body emphasizes the superficiality of humanity's strongest desires.[39] In a Girardian context, the fleece functions as a double sacrificial substitute. Friso offers the skin as thanks for his having escaped the violence of his past. But the hide is only a substitute for the animal, which itself serves as a surrogate for the originary human sacrifice, according to Girard (*Violence*, chap. 1). The supplemental logic that underlies these various implicit substitutions emphasizes the diminished potential of the sacrificial act and announces its potentially destabilizing effects or, to put it another way, its ineffective restabilizing effects.[40] The political and historical con-

39. Cf. Seneca's *Thyestes*, in which Thyestes talks of the "fulgore falso" 'deceptive gleam' of royal power (415; see also 446–70).

40. Friso's sacrifice of the fleece to Marte recalls in a curious way Prometheus's sacrifice to Zeus in Hesiod's *Theogony*: "Before the rest he set the flesh and inner parts thick with fat

text of the play again supports this reading, for "el vellocino de oro que Jasón roba del templo de Marte con la ayuda de Medea inevitablemente recuerda a los espectadores la terrible devaluación del vellón en marzo del 36 y el forzoso cambio de plata por vellón a partir del 35" (Hernández Araico 89). Just as the heavily guarded fleece can be robbed with little effort and the seemingly inexhaustible Spanish treasury devalued with the stroke of a pen, a nobleman's *honra* can be crippled with a whisper and a lady's *honor* sabotaged against her will.

The fleece begins to cause trouble almost immediately after its arrival on Colchis. The king's daughter, Medea, who regards herself as a goddess, becomes enraged that someone could offer a sacrifice to a deity other than herself (1647). De Armas views Medea's megalomania as a veiled criticism of the influence that the count duke of Olivares held over Philip (151); her resistance to Friso's sacrifice to Marte and her efforts to acquire the fleece stem from a desire for "complete control of the heavens" (155). Whatever its symbolic significance, Calderón exploits this facet of Medea's character to stimulate a rivalry that will reintegrate the Jasón of the *loa*, who arrives at Colchis in search of Deyanira, into the classical narrative in which Jason journeys to Asia in search of the Golden Fleece. The playwright has Jasón's arrival nearly coincide with Friso's so that both characters are present to compete for Medea's favor, which becomes reified in the fleece.[41]

Medea convenes an *academia de amor* or rhetorical contest on love between Jasón and Friso, ostensibly because she wishes to "dar algo al entendimiento: / no todo ha de ser valor" (1650). Offering a sash to Friso and then requesting one from Jasón, she asks:

> A Friso una banda he dado,
> y de Jasón recibido
> otra: si hubiera querido

---

upon the hide, covering them with an ox paunch; but for Zeus he put the white bones dressed up with cunning art and covered with shining fat" (538–41). Like the fat, whose rich appearance promises inner delicacies but instead offers only bones, the resplendent fleece has been gutted of substance. Similarly, like Prometheus's offering, which unleashes the ire of Zeus, Friso's sacrifice spells ultimate disaster for Colchis. Calderón may have caught on to the potentially negative character of the fleece after reading Lope's *El vellocino de oro*, where it can be seen to represent "the triumph of materialism—and sheer good fortune—over true love" (McGaha, "Lope's *El vellocino*").

41. The overlapping of the story of Friso with that of Jasón again has a precedent in Lope's *El vellocino de oro*. See Martin 143 for more details.

manifestar yo un cuidado,
dentro del alma guardado,
¿cuál de los dos ahora fuera
(responded) el que estuviera
favorecido de mí? (1650)

Friso responds that since giving is a noble action and receiving a vile one, Medea must have favored him, "pues con grandeza / quiso que obligue a su lustre, / yo a hacer una acción ilustre, / y tú [Jasón] a hacer una bajeza" (1650). Jasón easily turns this argument on its head, noting that "al llegar yo a advertir / que he dado, y tú has recibido, / verme a mí airoso ha querido, / y a ti no; luego ya en esto / al que deja más bien puesto, / deja más favorecido" (1651). The sophistry continues in this manner but becomes increasingly threatening as the stage directions indicate that Jasón and Friso stand suddenly to confront each other (1651), suggesting the preliminary stages of a duel.

The two male characters have become involved in a logic of rivalry that so far involves complete reciprocity, symbolized by Medea's giving and receiving of the sash. Their arguments mirror each other while their gestures perfectly parry the opponent's moves, blurring the duelers' identities in a manner that Girard views as typical of rivalry (*Violence*, chap. 6). This carefully staged posturing replicates an assumption of reciprocity at the heart of the concept of *venganza* that motivates the action of the play: Hércules believes that by dueling with his offender he can recover what he has lost with its original purity intact. What happens in this act will serve as an indicator of what can be expected in the play's denouement.

As the act progresses it becomes clear that reciprocity is an illusion and that strategies of offending and restoring honor do not simply cancel one another out but rather have important consequences. Medea feigns annoyance at Jasón's and Friso's increased antagonism and protests: "¿Así ofendéis mi decoro? / Argüir y disputar / no es reñir, ni conquistar / el vellocino de oro" (1651). The sudden introduction of the fleece into a contest supposedly directed toward *entendimiento* as opposed to *valor* shows that *valor* and by extension, *honra*, is precisely what is at stake. The question of the fleece's worth is emblematized in a battle of manliness between rivals who must compete for Medea's favor. Jasón recognizes Medea's veiled suggestion and responds affirmatively that "ya que esto no es conquistar / el dorado vellocino, / lo será ir por él, y verle / hoy a tus plantas rendido" (1651).

This is a crucial moment that lends the act an autonomy of its own. Even as Calderón nudges act 1 back into a recognizably classical outline, he establishes the prototypical Spanish conflict of love and honor. Because the fleece has come to replace Deyanira as the object of Jasón's search, winning Medea's love now outweighs restoring Hércules' honor, and Jasón finds himself forced to apologize to his absent friend (1651).[42] As in the case of Lope's Teseo, the classical hero fails to fit neatly into the conventions of the *comedia*, a failure that will be magnified as the play progresses.

Friso, meanwhile, is automatically eliminated from the competition for the fleece as the reciprocity between him and Jasón breaks down: "Yo a esa empresa no te sigo, / porque se lo di a Marte, / y nunca lo que doy quito" (1651). The comparison of the fleece to honor now becomes particularly relevant: Jasón's proposal to win Medea's love by stealing the fleece not only impinges on his honor toward Hércules (by delaying the search for Deyanira) but also offends Friso. The function of the animal skin as a reification of honor is unmistakable in Friso's warning to Jasón that "si tú le conquistas, / en público desafío / te le quitaré yo a ti" (1651).

With the help of Medea's *hechizos*, Jasón easily kills the bulls and the serpent that guard the fleece, much as the typical *galán* of the *comedia* relies on the spells and charms of a Celestina-like figure to break down his lady's resistance. Because Medea's actions are viewed as treachery, she must flee Colchis with Jasón. Although Calderón avoids the more gruesome details of this stage of the myth, in particular the "parvus comes / divisus ense" 'young companion dismembered by the sword,' as Seneca describes Medea's brother (*Medea* 131–32), Medea leaves her land in obvious disarray, with her father and Friso in hot pursuit. Jasón not only has failed to restore Hércules' honor but also has created a new crisis by robbing both the state's prized possession and the king's daughter. The fleece that arrived at Colchis with the promise of increasing its prestige has left the island with a considerable deficit of *honra*.

A similar situation occurs in act 2, whose plot Alan Soons tellingly characterizes as one of "love, rivalry and ambition" (4). In developing the story of Theseus, Ariadna, and the labyrinth, Calderón confronts a problem with respect to his models similar to the one that he faced in the first

---

42. Jasón's delay in Colchis recalls the way in which the mythical Heracles is sidetracked on Kios by the search for Hylas. See Apollonius 1.1207 and following.

act.[43] Since Teseo arrives on Crete in search of Deyanira, Calderón realigns the plot of the play into the myth's classical mold, in which Theseus arrives as a sacrificial victim of the Minotaur. The act opens as Fedra, Ariadna, and the servant Flora run across the stage crying for help, while Teseo, accompanied by his *gracioso* Pantuflo, follows close behind with his sword unsheathed. The reader learns that Teseo has killed a bear that was chasing the women (1653). After Teseo introduces himself and states his mission, Fedra begins to explain her own situation but is interrupted by the appearance of the character Flavio. Fleeing across the stage with his hands tied, he makes the following impassioned plea to Teseo:

> Merezca
> vuestro amparo; honor y vida
> me importa que no me prendan
> los que me siguen. Si acaso
> por aquesta parte llegan,
> responded que no me visteis,
> mientras yo por la maleza
> deste monte hallo una gruta
> que me sirva de defensa. (1655)

When Lidoro and Libio arrive shortly afterward and ask after Flavio's whereabouts, Teseo respects the latter's wishes and responds, "Por esta parte ninguno / pasó" (1655).

Lidoro then recounts the standard Ovidian version of Pasiphae's passion for the bull and Minos's attempts to construct a "viva / sepultura a una honra muerta" (1656). Although Calderón perhaps follows Lope in having the labyrinth function as a shield for the king's dishonor, the following detail regarding the sacrifice of the victims to the Minotaur is definitely his own: "Es establecida ley / a las guardas, que a cualquiera / que falte, se han de sortear / hasta el número ellas mesmas, / además de la opinión / mía" (1656). Lidoro has Libio seize Teseo and Pantuflo to sub-

---

43. According to Adrienne Schizzano Mandel 86 n. 8, Calderón's principal sources were Ovid's *Metamorphoses* 8.152–82 and Pérez de Moya's *Philosophía* 482–86; 4.26. She omits the play by Lope de Vega studied earlier, to which Calderón might easily have had access, as well as Vitoria's *Teatro* 1:434–37; 2.4.21. Soons's article deals not with possible precursors of Calderón but rather with three later plays based on the same myth: Juan Bautista Diamante's *El labyrinto de Creta* (before 1667), Sor Juana and Juan de Guevara's collaborative effort *Amor es más laberinto* (1689), and António José da Silva's *O labirinto de Creta* (1736).

stitute for Flavio and another victim that escaped with him, "para que así aseguremos / nuestras vidas con las vuestras" (1656).

Like the first act, the second begins with an instance of double sacrificial substitution. Just as the fleece substituted for the ram and ultimately for a human victim, Teseo and Pantuflo are surrogates for Lidoro and Libio, who themselves were to replace the escapees. And just as the sacrificial logic of the fleece led to disaster, the substitution that occurs early in this act is emblematic of a destabilized social order and undermines the principles of reciprocal justice.

The first indication that reciprocity is failing comes when Minos explains that he has imprisoned his daughters (a variation that never occurs in the classical sources): "Hijas, adiós, pues ya de aquesta quinta / que bosqueja el abril y el mayo pinta, / nunca habéis de salir, que mi cuidado, / aunque sea tarde, en mí me ha escarmentado" (1658). The king, whose *honra* has been destroyed by his wife's unnatural desire, claims to have learned his lesson. To prevent similar incidents from occurring, he has chosen to deprive his daughters of their liberty in exchange for safeguarding their *honor* or chastity. This logic, which seeks to erase the past by mortgaging the future of innocent victims, is based on a cruel reciprocity that underpins so much of the *comedia* and that, in this play, fails, along with the prison walls. Fedra and Ariadna's escape from the tower leads to their encounter with Teseo, who ultimately destroys the honor so heavily guarded by Minos.

Because of the perverse logic of reciprocity by which they are imprisoned, when Fedra and Ariadna recognize Teseo and Pantuflo in the procession of prisoners being led to the labyrinth, they are prevented from repaying their debt to Teseo (for saving them from the bear) because doing so would reveal the fact that they had left the tower: "Considera," Fedra warns Ariadna, "que licencia las dos nunca tuvimos / de salir de la torre en que vivimos, / y que será culparnos el libralle" (1658). The sisters' dilemma points to the crisis of a system that mandates contradictory acts of conciliation: gratitude to Teseo on the one hand and obedience to their father on the other. Their inability to comply with both demands indicates that the traditional hierarchy that places honor above all else is breaking down and, with it, the reciprocal logic that the hegemony of honor establishes.

This breakdown manifests itself most obviously in actions centered on the figure of Ariadna. According to Soons, she is "the first to be treasonable with regard to her father" (5) since, following the ancient accounts, she helps Teseo to kill the Minotaur with a poison concocted by Dédalo and then to escape from the labyrinth by means of the golden thread (1661).[44] Ariadna frees Teseo at least partly because she feels indebted to him for saving her from the bear, as Mandel notes (87). Yet the very fact that Teseo had to save Ariadna and Fedra inevitably highlights the failure of the tower to keep Minos's daughters imprisoned and points to the king's inability to make up for the honor destroyed by his wife. Furthermore, Ariadna's assistance in Teseo's escape from the labyrinth foils the system established to cover up Minos's dishonor and expurgate it through sacrifice. Both of Ariadna's actions, her own escape and her aid in Teseo's escape, bear all the traces of the breakdown of reciprocal logic underlying the honor code.

Against this background, what occurs at the end of the act should not surprise, although it may certainly disconcert. In the first place, Lidoro, the king's favorite, fails to repay Minos's goodwill toward him and continues the treachery that led him to send Teseo to the labyrinth. The spectator now witnesses his confession of desire to Ariadna: "Amor es dios, y no teme / que lo sagrado le estorbe. / Dél te he de sacar huyendo / a más remotas regiones, / y hacer que agravios consigan / lo que no pueden favores" (1664). Just as he saved her from the bear, so now Teseo arrives on the scene to save Ariadna from Lidoro's brutish intentions. Significantly, however, Lidoro mentions as he falls to his death that Teseo caught him unarmed (1664): not the most valiant way for a hero to challenge an offender and a small glimpse of the dishonorable conduct that Teseo will soon demonstrate in abundance.

When Flora tells Ariadna and Fedra that their father has learned of their "favor a Teseo, y a entrambas / amenazan sus rigores" (1665), they beg Teseo to take them with him. The problem is that he has room for only one of them on his horse and must choose which to save. His decision implies the familiar choice between love and honor, a quandary that brings the action to bear on the rivalry between Ariadna and Fedra (Mandel 86–87). Whereas Teseo's passion inclines him toward Fedra, he owes his life to Ariadna, who sums up his options in the following manner: "Esse es gusto, y este honor, / y podrá vivir un hombre / bien en el mundo, sin ser / amante; no sin ser noble" (1665; CV 271v).[45] Teseo justifies his final decision in the following speech:

---

44. The poison and the golden thread, as mentioned in the discussion of Lope's play (see n. 28, this chapter), do not come from classical sources. Calderón probably drew them from Bustamante's translation or from Lope's play itself.

45. VB: "Ese gusto, y este honor." "Ese" and "este" carry a neuter force and refer to the choice for Fedra or Ariadna respectively.

> ¿Qué dudo? Que aunque me noten
> de ingrato, he de ser amante.
> Todo el pundonor perdone;
> que las pasiones de amor
> son soberanas pasiones.
> Acúsenme los atentos;
> que a mí me basta que tomen
> mi disculpa los que, amando,
> dejan sus obligaciones. *Vase, y llévase a Fedra.* (1665–66)

Teseo's choice, while conforming to that of the Theseus of myth, is astounding for a nobleman of early modern Spanish drama and once again shows the incompatibility of myth with complete inscription in the *comedia*. Ariadna makes a long, outraged cry against him, in which she clearly invokes the standards of the honor code: "Yo te seguiré, yo misma / vengaré tus sinrazones. / Diréle a mi padre el Rey, / que te siga y que se vengue" (1667; CV 272r).[46] Considering that the fabric of reciprocity is so severely torn, it is unlikely that her curse will carry any more force than the wind to which she pronounces it: "El pianto conmovedor de ésta es la exhortación inútil de una traidora a su vez víctima de la traición" (Hernández Araico 90).

Mandel characterizes Teseo's actions as antiheroic (89). Similarly, Thomas O'Connor explains that Teseo, like Jasón, has failed to avenge Hércules: "As Jasón of Act I was deflected from his goal of seeking Neso in Asia, now Teseo too is deflected from honor's obligation in Europe. Both experience the disruptive influence of passion on their lives, causing them to flee obligation as they pursue their own satisfaction" (*Myth* 143). But the antiheroism of the pair, more than a failure, is, as in Lope's play, an accurate representation of classical heroes, who lacked the scruples of honor of Spanish noblemen. Both Jasón and Teseo, in seeking to restore Hércules' honor, have ended up duplicating his offense, as Hernández Araico notes: "En las primeras dos jornadas el código de honor no opera sino por contradicción total. Pues en ambas el héroe y otros personajes ejemplifican la traición sin escrúpulo alguno. . . . [Jasón y Teseo] se asemejan al centauro Neso por un rapto traicionero" (90). The uniqueness of the play lies in Calderón's association of Hércules, whom he has proficiently transformed into the typical outraged husband of the *comedia*, with

---

46. VB: "que te sigue y que se vengue."

Jasón and Teseo, who resist such transformation. The consequence of this uneven juxtaposition is the catastrophic ending of the play, in which the impotence of the honor code is demonstrated in different ways by all three characters.

Act 3 begins on a promising note. When Neso appears with Deyanira, the reader learns that he has not yet raped her and robbed her of her honor (that is, her fidelity to Hércules), preferring to "robarte también el alma . . . por ver si mi fineza / merecía un favor de tu belleza" (1671). Deyanira makes her position clear:

> ¿Ves el monte que dices, o el Atlante,
> que atalaya del sol, al sol se atreve,
> dando batalla en derretida nieve
> al mar, que espera menos arrogante?
>   Pues ya sobre las nubes se levante,
> y ya se atreva al que sus ondas bebe,
> comparado al honor, que a mí me mueve,
> menos firme será, menos constante. (1671)

Unable to win her favor through seduction after a year of trying, Neso, like Tereo in Timoneda's play (see above, Chapter 2, page 43), finally decides to resort to force (1671). Just at the point when Deyanira determines to kill herself in order to prevent the attainment of his desire, Hércules and his *gracioso* Clarín appear on the scene.

What ensues is a perfect dramatization of the logic of reciprocity that underlies the honor code and informs so many of the wife-murder plays. Neso grabs Deyanira and thrusts her in front of him to shield him from the venomous arrows with which Hércules is armed. Seeing her plight, Deyanira calls out to her husband:

> ¿Qué dudas, esposo mío,
> si ves a quien te ofendió?
> ¿Qué importa que muera yo?
> Tuyo es todo mi albedrío.
> Venga con valiente brío
> tu agravio prudente y sabio.
> El pie, la mano y el labio
> mueve; sé tú mi homicida,
> pues importará mi vida

> mucho menos que tu agravio.
> Si a mí misma me mataba
> yo, porque a ti te adoré,
> ¿qué importa que otro me dé
> la muerte que yo me daba? (1672)

Hércules, like the typical husband confronted with the imperative to murder his wife, anguishes over his responsibility. His self-doubt and vacillation are manifested in the statement "No sé / quién soy, porque en esta hora, / ajeno yo de mi mismo, / aún no sé si soy mi sombra" (1673), a direct contrast to Don Quixote's famous heroic affirmation (Cervantes 1:106; 1.5). Hércules' paralysis suggests that even he may have doubts about the power of reciprocal logic to achieve the expected returns. Even so, when Neso crosses the river and threatens to carry Deyanira away forever, he manages to cast aside his doubts at least temporarily. He shoots an arrow toward the centaur with full knowledge that it will also kill his wife: "Bellísima Deyanira, / aquesta crueldad perdona: / harto dilaté tu muerte: / mas ya tu vida ¿qué importa?" (1673). Hércules' merciless logic provides strong justification for Gwynne Edwards's suggestion that "between *Los tres mayores prodigios* and *El pintor de su deshonra* there are very close parallels" (333) and that "in particular, the vision of the world expressed by Calderón in both the 'ancient' and the 'modern' play is essentially the same" (326; see also Watson, "*El pintor*" 220).

What is different in *Los tres mayores prodigios* from the wife-murder plays, in terms of plot, is that Deyanira miraculously survives. Hércules' initial jubilation on seeing her quickly changes to what Watson describes as a "curious mixture of shame and jealousy" ("Hercules" 778). His is the typical dilemma of the nobleman subjected to the whims of *honra*. Even though Deyanira is above all suspicion and has heroically maintained her fidelity to Hércules, the "malicias ajenas" will not necessarily think in the same way: "En el poder has estado / de una fiera rigurosa; / el mundo sabe mis ansias; / pues hasta en Asia y Europa / mi opinión están perdiendo / los que piensan que la cobran; / y ya espero que vendrán / de publicar mi deshonra" (1675). According to the harsh logic of the honor code, as long as Deyanira lives, Hércules' offense remains unavenged.

By inserting this curious twist (the survival of Deyanira) into the plot of the play, Calderón forces the logic of reciprocity underlying the honor code to the breaking point. The scenario is even more extreme than that of *El pintor*. Not only is Deyanira innocent, like Serafina, but she also survives the attempt to restore honor. Hércules would appear to be in the enviable position of having his cake and eating it too: he has done everything required of the offended nobleman and, by a remarkable stroke of luck, has seen his wife returned to him alive and well. Yet he still finds himself in an unacceptable situation. His solution demonstrates exactly what is at stake:

>   Todos piensan
> que moriste entre las ondas,
> y yo sólo sé que vives;
> la voz de tu muerte corra,
> y vive para mí solo;
> con lo cual a un tiempo logra
> mi desengaño tu vida
> y tu muerte mi congoja.
> En todos aquestos montes
> no hay nadie que te conozca:
> y así en ellos estarás
> en traje de labradora.
> Vive, mas yo no te vea;
> vive, mas yo no te oiga. (1675–76)

Hércules' love for Deyanira keeps him from killing her, but his honor demands that the love remain unfulfilled. Like Minos in act 2, he attempts to hide his dishonor, for as long as no one knows about it there can be no shame.

In an eloquent response, Deyanira marshals every conceivable objection to this logic of concealment:

>   Espera,
> que es necia, es injusta, es loca,
> esta determinación
> que contra ti mismo tomas.
> ¿Por qué has de pensar de ti,
> tan vilmente, que antepongas
> la satisfacción ajena,
> mi bien, a la tuya propia?
> ¿Por qué has de pensar que al verme
> contigo, siendo tu esposa,

te han de murmurar, pues antes
cierras[47] con esto la boca
a la malicia? ¿Tan poco
fías tú de ti, que pongas
duda en tu honor, fomentando
malicias escrupulosas?
¿Por qué has de pensar de ti
que habrá en el mundo persona
que piense de ti, que has dado
ensanchas a tu deshonra?
Ten de ti satisfacción,
tendránla las gentes todas;
porque si tú tu honra dudas,
¿quién ha de creer tu honra?
O me imaginas culpada
o inocente (aquesto nota):
si culpada, aquese acero
mi pecho infelice rompa;
si inocente, aquesos brazos
mansamente me recojan;
que esto no tiene más medio
que el castigo[48] o la lisonja. (1676; CV 279r)

Deyanira's logic is compelling to the modern reader; indeed, her arguments are based on assumptions that many critics have made regarding Hércules. Watson, for example, describes the hero's sense of shame as "totally irrational since no one at any time blames Hercules in any way for having spared Deianira" ("Hercules" 781). Similarly, Thomas O'Connor refers to Hércules' "warped mind" (*Myth* 147), and Cascardi suggests that the hero's unstable reasoning gives "cause to question any wholesale trust in the powers of the mind" (95). These statements are misleading. Hércules' reasoning is perfectly sound within the logic of honor that declares public opinion to be the utmost necessity. Deyanira's predication of his options upon the two possibilities of whether he imagines her innocent or guilty is based upon an opposition that is irrelevant in terms of the honor code. What is important is not his opinion but that of others, and he recognizes that "no seré yo el primero, / Deyanira, que conozca / que no

47. VB: "cierran."
48. VB: "camino."

esté agraviado, y tome / satisfacción; porque importa / la satisfacción ajena / a veces, más que la propia" (1676).

The problem is one of two mutually exclusive worldviews, each with its own standards and laws: one based on *honra* and the other on *honor*. Hércules' reply to Deyanira's protest, which critics of the play have overlooked, is crucial to understanding the work's basic conflict: "Bien dices; mas yo también / digo bien; que, en fin, hay cosas / donde a todos la razón / falta porque a todos sobra" (1676). His statement accurately defines the impasse of the situation in terms of a crisis of reason. Paradoxically, logic or truth is lacking because there is a critical surplus of logic. The logic of reciprocity that underlies *honra*, which now demands that Hércules abandon his wife, stands in direct conflict with the obligations of *honor*, or his personal duty to care for her. The result is what Thomas O'Connor has defined in another context as "reason's impasse" ("Calderón").

The failure of reciprocal logic is heightened when Floro, Licas, and others arrive on the scene before Hércules can carry out his plan of abandoning Deyanira. As soon as they see her, his plan becomes invalid, since his *deshonra* is now public: "Vergüenza tengo de que / me vean. ¡Qué escrupulosa / la conciencia es del honor!" (1676). The return of Jasón and Teseo only compounds the problem. As Hércules' two friends tell how their adventures ended after the termination of acts 1 and 2, it becomes apparent that the failure of reciprocity is complete. Jasón explains how Friso and Absinto followed him in search of Medea, "y vinieron donde pudo / sujetarlos mi arrogancia" (1679). Teseo, for his part, states that at Fedra's request he decided not to abandon Ariadna but instead brought her along, "porque / siguiéndome su venganza, / con Minos, en Calidonia / fué mi triunfo: que estas armas / me dió su rey" (1679).

Although both Jasón and Teseo have committed what could only be considered the gravest of offenses, they have managed to defy the logic of reciprocity that demanded vengeance on the part of the offended parties (Friso and Absinto in Jasón's case; Ariadna and Minos in Teseo's). Ariadna's description of herself and of the failure of her efforts at vengeance are a strong indictment of the honor code: "Es la que ahora veis esclava / suya, porque son las penas / cobardes, que siempre andan / de cuadrilla, y nunca vino / una sola a la desgracia" (1679). It is apparent that far from ever being able to help Hércules restore his honor, Jasón and Teseo have contributed to a breakdown of the system.

The solution to the play's crisis is, as in so many of the other works studied, a sacrificial one. Before dying, in an attempt to seek a posthumous revenge on Hércules, Neso had suggested to Deyanira that

>si Hércules, considerando
>que en mi poder tan a costa
>de sus celos has vivido,
>te desdeña o te baldona,
>o te quisiera dar muerte,
>haz que aquesta piel se ponga;
>que la que no me sirvió
>a mí de defensa ahora,
>te servirá de defensa
>a ti; pues en ella sola
>está el hechizo con que
>te adoré. (1674)

Because of Hércules' reluctance to accept Deyanira again as his wife and because of the failure of his own plan to abandon her, she decides to use the blood-soaked tunic to reawaken his desire. With this detail Calderón adapts the classical narrative, in which Deianira uses the tunic out of jealousy of Hercules' relationship with Iole, to the context of Spanish honor. This adaptation is fitting, since, just as honor was the motive that precipitated the action of the play, Hércules' scruples of honor now become the cause both of his death and of the end of the play.

When Hércules puts on the tunic, its poison, which Watson perceives as a symbolic manifestation of the inner poison of *celos* gnawing at his soul (782), dissolves his flesh and brings about an agonizing death. A sacrifice that he had been planning to Júpiter, to take place on the day that he defeated Neso, would have celebrated the triumph of vengeance and reciprocal logic (1676). Instead, the occasion becomes a monument to the failure of reciprocity and the bankruptcy of the honor code as Hércules, unable to bear his agony any longer, hurls himself onto the pyre that was to serve for a sacrificial animal:

>¿Mas para qué pido a nadie
>mi muerte? Esa viva llama,
>esa hoguera, que encendida
>para el sacrificio estaba,
>será mi pira. Recibe,
>sagrado fuego, en tus aras,

ardiendo en fuego mayor,
aquesta víctima humana
que a Júpiter le dedico. (1680)

Deyanira, crushed by the guilt of having killed her own husband, quickly follows his fate. Appropriately, the play in which the chaos of the first two acts had been emblematized by sacrificial substitutions of diminished potential brings the disorder of the third act under control with a double human sacrifice that represents a substitution of increased potential.

In this way Calderón ties together all the threads of the vast amalgam of myths on which *Los tres mayores prodigios* is based. Valbuena Briones notes that Calderón's splicing together of the stories of Hércules, Jasón, and Teseo is not totally unprecedented in antiquity: "Herakles fue amigo de Theseus y éste le dio asilo cuando aquél mató a Megara y a sus hijos en un rapto de furia. También se suele dar el nombre del esforzado campeón de los doce trabajos como uno de los héroes que acompañó a Iason en la famosa expedición de los argonautas" (*Perspectiva* 334). Thomas O'Connor suggests further connections between the three mythical figures (*Myth* 136–37) that are certainly interesting and could even be expanded.[49] Nevertheless, no link between the three characters is necessary other than that offered by the title of the play. Jasón, Teseo, and Hércules are cast as the three greatest "prodigies" of classical myth, and their status as such is essential in understanding Calderón's use of his sources.

The term *prodigio* is ambiguous. On the one hand, it has a positive application that associates it with the miraculous; on the other, it is a "sucesso extraño que excede à los límites regulares de la naturaleza" (Real Academia), a definition that draws the term close to the monstrous. The dragon and serpents that Jasón kills as well as the Minotaur that Teseo slays are referred to as *prodigios* (1643, 1662). The ambiguity of *prodigios* also accurately describes the heroes of classical antiquity, who, as pointed out, were not always characterized by the qualities now associated with the term *heroism*. In this sense it is not totally accurate to regard Calderón's treatment of his heroes as demythifying or antiheroic.[50] It is true that by the time of the Renaissance the heroes had been adapted into a new interpretative scheme, but there still remained ineluctable

---

49. A contemporary source for the association of the three characters might be Lope's own *Las mujeres sin hombres*. Although rich in potential, as suggested in the few points mentioned in this analysis, the role of Lope's mythological plays in Calderón has been seriously neglected.

50. As do Benedetti 53–61, 101–26; de Armas 162; T. O'Connor, *Myth* 152; Mandel 89; and Hernández Araico 90.

traces of their classical ambiguity that kept them from fitting squarely into the mold of the *comedia*. This inherent resistance of myth to complete adaptation reveals the ideological rift underlying so many of the *comedias mitológicas*, which Castro manages to patch over completely and Lope only partially, while Calderón fully allows it to cast many of the *comedia*'s conventions in an ironic light.

In the latter case, the failure of the heroes to "fit" into the honor code—the impunity with which Teseo and Jasón commit their offenses, together with Hércules' inability to avenge his own—spotlights the logic that "a todos falta porque a todos sobra." In permitting the desires of classical mythology to inflect his own rewriting of them, Calderón points to the honor code's inability to cope with the expression of desire along anything other than orthodox channels.

More than a hundred years ago Menéndez Pelayo observed that the heroes of the mythological plays, especially those of Calderón, are "caballeros galantes y cortesanos, lo mismo que los héroes de las comedias de capa y espada" (*Calderón* 365). Similarly, Antonio Rubió y Lluch declared that "los héroes de la antigüedad griega, ya se llamaran Hércules ó Teseo, Minos ó Ariadna, Neso ó Deyanira . . . aparecían siempre como españoles, ó cortados á la medida y gusto de sus espectadores españoles" (41). In this chapter's examination of the plays by Castro, Lope, and Calderón, I have sought to define the formula that facilitated this hispanization of myth, showing that the playwrights adapt myth to the generic rules of the *comedia* by using the desires of classical mythology as variables for insertion into the overarching framework of Spanish honor. The adaptability of desire and its inherent stage appeal account for a large part of the formula's success.

At the same time, Rubió y Lluch's and Menéndez Pelayo's statements are too sweeping, for the themes and structures of mythology do not always fit squarely into the norms of the *comedia* and often end up inflecting its monolithic ideology as much as they are adapted to it. Of the three authors studied, Castro was the best at smoothing over this inevitable conflict between the two sets of conventions, as evidenced in his skillful transformation of Dido's suicide into an act of vengeance. Calderón, in contrast, brings out the distinctly non-Spanish aspects of the classical heroes in a way that problematizes the rigid logic of honor. *El laberinto de Creta* represents a midpoint between the other two not only chronologically but also ideologically and artistically. Lope allows the manifestation of Teseo's more-negative mythological associations in order to create the beginnings of an exciting plot, but, at the same time, he is forced to reveal the artificiality of the plot in order to harness the unruly desires of Teseo's mythological inheritance.

The flexibility of the formula that the playwrights used in their adaptations and the great variety of results that it produced seriously challenge those who would impose an a priori moral-allegorical reading on any mythological work of the early modern period. My intention in the present study is not to deny the existence of the allegorical tradition but, in contrast to Green's static view of three centuries ("Fingen los poetas"), to support as salutary statements such as the following: "La interpretación del tema mitológico va evolucionando desde el Renacimiento al Barroco. La mitología es vista, primero, con respeto, como un paradigma en el cual deben mirarse los hombres. Después—con Trento y la Contrarreforma—surgen las interpretaciones alegóricas, las versiones 'a lo divino.' Finalmente, la crisis del mundo renacentista hace que se desarrolle la parodia burlesca" (Haverbeck, *El tema* 172). Because of this more fluid situation, F. Schalk is correct in observing that "in the mythological theater we may well detect the sound of a contrary note, one that reflects a world of plurality and change and that eludes doctrinaire treatment" (264). This state of affairs is especially true in the first half of the *comedia*, when myth reacted with the *comedia*'s rules of desire to produce a hybrid genre of plays noteworthy for its dynamic diversity.

This is not to claim that the immensely popular manuals of mythology, such as Pérez de Moya's *Philosophía*, which the proponents of the allegorical interpretation are quick to cite, had no influence upon the composition of the secular mythological plays, and in this analysis I have pointed out the occasions in which these works may have influenced the playwrights. Yet more than forcing the myths into a moral framework, the manuals offered the dramatists a gold mine of information from which to draw minutiae of characterization as they re-created the desires of the protagonists. Generally arranged in convenient, encyclopedic form with headings by character rather than by incident, the manuals broke down the narrative unity of the ancient stories and reintegrated it into a Who's Who of classical mythology. They represent an important bridge between myth as plot, the overriding concern of the sixteenth-century dramatists studied above in Chapter 2, and myth as character, a meaning that those of the twentieth century would exploit.

Thus, while Alexander Parker's premise of the "primacy of action over character drawing" (706) may be the general rule, the three plays, written at the height of the influence of "manual mythology," provide ample space for the development of character. Castro's characterization of Dido's anguish, for example, is well done, as is Calderón's portrayal of Hércules' suspicion and self-doubt. Benedetti suggests, in fact, that "Calderón's mythological characters are imbued with a psychological complexity that makes their characterizations more significant than the total action of the play" (80). And even though Lope's play is the most action packed of the three, it still makes room for Cila's lyrical complaint to Minos at the beginning of act 1 as well as Ariadna's realization that she has been abandoned at the end of act 2.

Historical Postscript

The mythological play continued to survive and even flourish in the second half of the seventeenth century, as plays by authors as diverse as Rojas Zorrilla, Juana Inés de la Cruz, Juan Bautista Diamante, Antonio de Zamora, Agustín de Salazar y Torres, and José de Cañizares demonstrate. However, the increasing penchant for abstraction and philosophical speculation, which turned the theater into a haven for those seeking refuge from the unpleasant reality of contemporary Spain, brought deep-seated changes to both the *comedia* and its use of myth. It is in this context, which witnessed the explosion of the *auto sacramental*, that the allegorical interpretation of myth is most valid and such phrases as the following are safest: "Es propio de la comedia mitológica el que se sitúa fuera del tiempo y del espacio humanos, es decir en ningún momento histórico preciso y en ningún lugar geográfico comprobado" (Aubrun, "Estructura" 148). The contrast with the worldly concerns of the earlier plays is striking.

As the seventeenth century came to a close and the eighteenth approached, mythological plays were more and more likely to betray an enthusiasm for the superficial and lavish that some critics have sought to read back into all of them. The Calderonian *zarzuela*, something like a one-act opera, survived into the eighteenth century, as did rehashings of the most successful mythological *comedias*. Soon, however, the entrenchment of the Bourbon monarchy and the subsequent gallicizing of Spanish literature imposed a new set of tastes and standards upon playwrights.

The literary honor code that had reigned with such success in the previous century lost its vitality, and the mythological play, except for a few rare exceptions (such as Martínez de la Rosa's Romantically inspired *Edipo*), lay dormant until the twentieth century.

For Art's Sake

From Conventional to Radical Desire in the Early Twentieth-Century Theater

One word surfaces again and again in descriptions of late nineteenth-century Spanish theater: *decadence.* Despite attempts at reform by such pioneers of the *alta comedia* as Adelardo López de Ayala (1828–72) and Manuel Tamayo y Baus (1829–98), by the end of the century the national drama had become mired in a set of conventions that allowed artistic expression only through "a thick protective screen of morality and conformism," to use Donald Shaw's description (*A Literary History* 78). In G. G. Brown's words, "What good taste would not admit [in the theater] was any attempt to puzzle or worry the audience, or to reflect any moral or social values other than those of the bejewelled matrons of the orchestra stalls" (111).

The undisputed master of the stage during this period was José de Echegaray (1832–1916), an engineer turned dramatist whose prolific output and remarkable sense of stagecraft have earned him a permanent, if unfavorable, place in Spanish literary history. One of his harshest critics is Francisco Ruiz Ramón, who characterizes his entire output as *drama-ripio,* asserting that "el teatro de Echegaray es, por excelencia, teatro fantasmagórico, puro *flatus voci* [sic], en el que cada personaje, sin distinción de sexo, es, en su sustancia y en sus accidentes, una pasión inútil, hueca de toda verdad" (*Historia . . . desde* 350–51). Although Gonzalo Sobejano reprimands Ruiz Ramón for the severity and sweeping nature of his judgments, he too must admit that there is "en la mayoría de los dramas de Echegaray una gratuidad argumental y un recargamiento patético que parecen colocarlos al margen de la realidad humana compatible o convivible" ("Echegaray" 95).

No less harsh with Echegaray was a prestigious group of contemporary intellectuals who, galvanized by Spain's humiliating defeat in the War of 1898, had coalesced around the goal of guiding their country into the modern world. When the Spanish press organized a tribute to Echegaray after he won the Nobel Prize in literature in 1904, several writers whom critics would later group together in the so-called Generation of 1898, along with others, composed a formal letter of protest (Brown 111). Azorín offered a penetrating and virulent assessment of Echegaray's drama in viewing its ideology as complicitous with the nefarious values of the restored Bourbon monarchy:

> Y este lirismo, esta exaltación, esta inconsciencia (que envía millares y millares de hombres a la muerte en las colonias, o que sobre las tablas escénicas produce bárbaros y absurdos asesinatos), todo esto es lo que encontramos en la obra del señor Echegaray. Y precisamente esta exaltación y este lirismo es lo que se pretende conmemorar ahora, cuando ha pasado el desastre, cuando vamos abriendo los ojos a la experiencia dolorosa, cuando vamos conviniendo todos en que no es la exaltación loca, audaz y grandilocuente de nuestra persona lo que nos ha de salvar, sino la reflexión fría, sencilla, la renuncia a todo lirismo, la observación minuciosa, exacta, prosaica de la realidad cotidiana. (qtd. in Sobejano, "Razón" 46–47)

The strong condemnation of Echegaray by Hispanic intellectuals at the turn of the century responds to the political component of his theater that such a forward-thinking group could never find acceptable.

The dramatic output of the authors to be studied in this chapter must be considered against the fin-de-siècle theater's double axes of artistic bankruptcy and political reaction as epitomized in Echegaray's work. Two of these authors, Miguel de Unamuno (1864–1936) and Jacinto Grau

(1877–1958), signed the document mentioned above and are usually associated with an experimental theater of the early twentieth century in Spain whose output, because it strained against the forces of convention, was rarely successful economically, if it ever reached the stage. The trend toward experimentation and renovation was, moreover, part of a European-wide concern of which Ortega y Gasset's famous essay on "dehumanized" art proposed to cite the salient characteristics: the turn away from realism (21–22), the tendency toward deformation and abstraction (34–36), and the importance of metaphor (43–45) and irony (56–58). While Grau's work may in retrospect be comfortably read within Ortega's parameters, Unamuno's theater, even though it shares some of the same elements, is a much more individual "teatro de conciencia," to use the title of Zavala's book on the subject. Still, both coincide fully in the trend toward experimentation and dissent, for which reason Ruiz Ramón places them in his chapter on "Innovadores y disidentes" (*Historia . . . siglo XX* 77–169).

Arturo del Hoyo further confirms the association between the two dramatists by placing them, along with Azorín, Gómez de la Serna, García Lorca, and Max Aub in the volume titled *Teatro inquieto español*. In the prologue to this collection, Antonio Espina justifies the choice of the authors included in the following way: "Hay obras dramáticas que son ensayos y tanteos por conseguir lo casi imposible de manifestar escénicamente. Obras que, por lo pronto, muestran el anhelo, la inquietud del autor y su afán de salirse de lo vulgar. El autor se entrega al azar experimental, al ejercicio osado y difícil. Esto es ya, por sí mismo, un mérito" (15–16). Most important for the purposes of this study, Unamuno and Grau both turned, within the space of ten years, to classical myth in order to achieve the renovation of drama that they desired.

Before examining their plays, however, one must consider the work of an earlier writer, Benito Pérez Galdós (1843–1920), who, although not generally associated with the full-blown experimentalism of the "autores inquietos," nevertheless took the first really positive (in the sense of irreversible) steps toward renovating the decadent theater of the time. Insofar as he laid the framework upon which the later innovators would build, Galdós's relationship to the Spanish avant-garde is somewhat analogous to Ibsen's place in the Scandinavian and German traditions.[1] Tell-

---

1. Ibsen and Galdós have been the subject of frequent, if somewhat controversial, com-

ingly, on several occasions Galdós used classical myth to accomplish his objectives.

Nearly every critic to have written on Galdós's theater as a whole has recognized the enormous advance that it represents in the history of contemporary Spanish drama.[2] Nothing better than the playwright's own words demonstrates how keenly he was aware of the causes of the late nineteenth-century theater's decadence and of the steps that should be taken in order to revitalize its former prestige. Two remarkable passages illustrate these points. In the first, Galdós manifests his disgust with contemporary theater:

> El público burgués y casero dominante en la generación última, no ha tenido poca parte en la decadencia del teatro. A él se debe el predominio de esa moral escénica, que informa las obras contemporáneas, una moral exclusivamente destinada a aderezar la literatura dramática, moral, enteramente artificiosa y circunstancial, como de una sociedad que vive de ficciones y convencionalismos. La restricción que esta moral impone al desarrollo de la idea dramática, es causa de que los caracteres se hayan reducido a una tanda de tres o cuatro figuras que se repiten siempre. Su acción es también muy restringida, y analizando bien todo el teatro contemporáneo, se verá que en todo él no hay más que media docena de asuntos, repetidos hasta la saciedad y aderezados con distinta salsa. El lenguaje, por influencia de esa moral postiza, también se ha restringido, y el vocabulario de teatro es de los más pobres. (*Nuestro teatro* 154–55)

---

parisons. See, for example, Sobejano, "Razón y suceso," Rubio's reply in "Ibsen y Galdós," Sobejano's rebuttal in "Echegaray," and Rubio's follow-up in "Galdós." I do not wish to share in these polemical exchanges but rather to make a simple comparison based on the general place of each playwright in his respective dramatic tradition.

2. Wallace 362; Starkie 117; Pérez Minik, *Debates* 101; Carney 332–33; González López 459; Guerrero Zamora 232; Goenaga and Maguna 440; Ruiz Ramón, *Historia . . . desde* 365; Sobejano, "Razón" 39, 52; Casalduero, "El teatro" 519; Sackett, "Galdós dramaturgo"; D. Lida 279; Berenguer 328; Menéndez Onrubia, "El olvidado" 246. The secondary literature on Galdós is vast, but it would be irresponsible to follow Hinterhäuser's advice and simply "push it aside" (284). The above references and the ones that follow, by no means exhaustive, are those that have had the greatest bearing on the present study. For further references on Galdosian theater, see Sackett's indispensable *Galdós y las máscaras*, an exhaustive (except for unpublished Ph.D. theses), annotated bibliography complete through 1979.

In the second, he takes aim at a single culprit:

> Para que el teatro entre con pie derecho en la escuela de la naturalidad, es preciso que un autor de grandes alientos rompa la marcha y acometa con recursos de primer orden esta gran reforma. Echegaray, que posee la capacidad más vasta que es posible imaginar, es el llamado a marcar este camino. No le faltarían recursos para ello. Necesitaría únicamente cortarse un poco las alas, abatir el vuelo, atender más a la verdadera expresión de los sentimientos humanos que a los efectos obtenidos por conflictos excepcionales y por combinaciones de parentescos y lugares. (*Nuestro teatro* 141–42)

With characteristic perspicacity and foresight, Galdós captures perfectly in these passages the two-horned predicament (political and artistic) of contemporary theater that Hispanic intellectuals would lament some twenty years later.

One of the elements that Galdós apparently objected to most in Echegaray's theater was the subjection of human passion to what Ruiz Ramón calls "un sistemático proceso de falseamiento, de medular vaciamiento de su verdad humana" (*Historia . . . desde* 351–52). The character Tarsis of *El caballero encantado* (1912) might well be speaking for Galdós when he states: "Toda nuestra literatura dramática es esencialmente *latosa*, toda convencional, encogida, sin médula pasional, cuando no es grosera y desquiciada" (232). Written in 1885, the second passage cited above may be read as a plea to Echegaray to free desire from the conventional constraints that deform it and drain its dramatic force. When, by the end of the century, this plea had not been answered, Galdós decided to take matters into his own hands.

Drama was actually Galdós's earliest literary venture, although none of the pieces that he wrote in his youth was ever produced. By the 1890s, with his fame as a novelist preceding him, he again started writing for the stage and achieved moderate success throughout the decade.[3] Encouraged by these events, he began preparing a work that was destined to

---

3. Of the eight plays from the 1890s, Sackett qualifies three (*Realidad*, 1892; *La de San Quintín*, 1894; and *Doña Perfecta*, 1896) as outright successes based on contemporary critical response. Two others (*Voluntad*, 1895 and *La fiera*, 1896) he calls "éxitos dudosos"; the remaining three (*La loca de la casa*, 1893; *Gerona*, 1893; and *Los condenados*, 1894) receive the label of failures (*Galdós y las máscaras* xiv).

scandalize the country but that, despite its title, has never been studied for its ingenious adaptation of Greek myth and bold reinscription of desire.

Playing with Fire: The Conflict of Truth and Desire in Benito Pérez Galdós's *Electra*

Much of what has been written about *Electra* is devoted to the extraordinary contemporary circumstances that accompanied its performance, an event that Inman Fox calls "one of the most important happenings in the intellectual history of Spain at the turn of the century" (131). The attention paid to this aspect of the play is certainly understandable, for the staging of *Electra* was believed to have contributed to the fall of the conservative government in power at the time as well as to have led to the verdict handed down in a contemporary lawsuit. In addition, the debut caused riots in the streets of Madrid and prompted several provincial churches to declare attendance at its performance a mortal sin.[4] Unfortunately, the sensational nature of these events has tended to distract attention from the content of the play, and most of the critics who bother to engage the piece as dramatic literature find it mediocre at best: flawed, they feel, by inexplicable and superfluous elements and by Galdós's supposed inability to distinguish the narrative from the theatrical genre. Nevertheless, many of the features that critics have read as forced or contrived make perfect sense when read in the context of the myth of Electra.[5]

---

4. On the contemporary circumstances and repercussions of *Electra*, Fox (who reprints an important article of Maeztu's first published by Beser) is indispensable. In addition, see Berkowitz, "Apotheosis"; Blanquat; Regalado García 340–44; Elizalde, "Azorín" (which relies heavily on Fox); Litvak; and Catena. Contemporary reviews in the Spanish press are summarized by Sackett, *Galdós y las máscaras* 136–202. Two interesting foreign perspectives from the period are those offered by Mérimée ("A propos" 195–96) and Ellis. Finally, Díez-Canedo 1:87–89 provides a fascinating view of one of the many remakes of *Electra*.

5. There are five tragedies of classical antiquity in which the heroine Electra plays a prominent role: Aeschylus's *Libation-Bearers* (the second play in the *Oresteia* trilogy), Sophocles' *Electra*, Euripides' *Electra* and *Orestes*, and Seneca's *Agamemnon*. For a concise summary of the bloody myth of the house of Pelops and its dramatic manifestations, see Rose 247; Graves 25–84 provides a much more extensive account. Berkowitz's inventory of Galdós's library lists French translations of Aeschylus and of Sophocles' *Electra* (*La biblioteca* 186–87),

The classical model suggests itself at once in the title of the play. Even so, most readers who discuss the title either express mystification or categorically deny that Galdós's *Electra* has anything to do with the ancient plays.[6] Some of these critics explain the title as a pun on *electricidad*, which at the time symbolized progress and the triumph of science over stagnation and superstition. Others more willing to concede a classical precedent do so only briefly or in the vaguest of terms.[7] Despite the critical reticence, it is possible from today's vantage point to find in 1901 a Galdós who was already beginning to manifest in his theater, as he had long done in his novels, a love and knowledge of Greek myth and literature that would culminate in the composition of *Alceste* (1914), a skillful and undeniable adaptation of Euripides' play of the same title.[8]

Galdós specifies that the action of *Electra* is set in contemporary Madrid, and the only explicit reference to the classical Electra within the play comes in the following exchange between Don Urbano and the marquis of Ronda:

---

as well as a Spanish edition of Seneca's tragedies in Latin (195). Nothing by Euripides is cataloged, but, as Berkowitz notes, the inventory might well be incomplete (11–12). Even if Galdós never owned copies of Euripides' works, he could have borrowed copies or read them elsewhere. He himself reveals an intimate knowledge of Euripides' *Alcestis* (see n. 8, this chapter), and, based on the analysis that follows, it seems highly probable that he also knew *Electra* and *Orestes*.

6. Carney 310; Goenaga and Maguna 423; Catena 95–96; Gountiñas 470; Menéndez Onrubia, *Introducción* 187; Hinterhäuser 280.

7. Morley xxxv; Guerrero Zamora 237; Casalduero, *Vida* 148; Rubio, "Galdós" 63. A notable exception is Finkenthal, who devotes several pages (136–38) to the issue. Even so, he limits his observations to surface similarities between Galdós's play and Euripides' *Electra*, such as the critique of contemporary events and the relation between justice and religion. He either does not notice or prefers not to discuss the fundamental similarities of plot and character that in the following analysis I propose between Galdós's work and the quintet of ancient tragedies on the subject. Similarly, while Sackett's archetypal approach might promise to reveal just such similarities, it yields only one parallel between the classical and Spanish heroines, namely that "por primera y única vez en el drama, Electra presenta características de su arquetipo griego, la Electra indignada por las calumnias, al protestar de los ataques de Pantoja contra la reputación de su madre" ("*Electra*" 480).

8. In the prologue to this often overlooked play, Galdós confesses that for some time he felt "cautivado por la tradición de Alceste, reina de Tesalia, ejemplo y cifra de abnegación sublime, alma candorosa y poética que ilumina las edades remotas en que la Historia se confunde con la Mitología" (*Alceste* 1248), and he goes on to demonstrate an intimate acquaintance with the trajectory of the myth. For critical commentary, see Caballero 207; Morley xli–xlii; Díaz-Regañón 279–82; Bourne, chap. 4; Casalduero, "*Alceste*"; and Gountiñas. *Casandra* (1910, adapted from the novel of the same title) also has definite mythological associations, as the protagonist is recognized within the play as possessing a "nombre de profetisa" (1166). Like those of *Electra*, these associations have passed largely unnoticed.

Urbano.—Esta niña, cuyo padre se ignora, se crió junto a su madre hasta los cinco años. Después la llevaron a las Ursulinas de Bayona. Allí, ya fuese por abreviar, ya por embellecer el nombre, dieron en llamarla Electra, que es de grande novedad.

Marqués.—Perdone usted, novedad no es; a su desdichada madre, Eleuteria Díaz, los íntimos la llamábamos también "Electra", no sólo por abreviar, sino porque a su padre, militar muy valiente, desgraciadísimo en su vida conyugal, le pusieron Agamenón. (850; 1.2)

Ronda's explanation, which denies the "grande novedad" of Electra's name, has seemed to satisfy most readers of the play.[9] By locating the origin of the name in Eleuteria's nickname—a nickname, furthermore, itself apparently related to Electra's grandfather—Galdós toys with his readers as he does so often in his narrative works, feeding them information that serves to placate their curiosity and distract them from crucial interpretative clues. The fact is that Electra's relationship with her mother and father in the play duplicates rather closely the basic structure of the myth.

In the first place, Eleuteria's name, as Sobejano has recognized ("Echegaray" 115), denotes freedom in Greek (*eleutheria*). Sobejano interprets this choice as symbolic of Electra's quest for freedom, but the name is also indicative of the promiscuity or sexual freedom of Eleuteria, whose escapades scandalized Madrid from 1880 to 1885, according to Urbano (850; 1.2). Finkenthal is the only critic to have pointed out the evident connection between these events and those of Clytemnestra in his observation that "el escandaloso comportamiento de [Eleuteria] durante cinco años recuerda el comportamiento adúltero de la Clitemnestra griega durante la ausencia de su esposo" (137). By giving a sexually promiscuous character a name with positive connotations such as "freedom," Galdós rejects the bourgeois values of the contemporary theater and overturns the double standard that glorified male sexual exploits while condemning those of women.[10] In this way he emphasizes the "praiseworthy" qualities of Clytemnestra: her strong-willed feminine independence and insistence

---

9. In order to avoid confusion, in this analysis I will refer to Electra's mother (whom the marquis calls Electra I) as Eleuteria, reserving "Electra" for the protagonist of the play.

10. For a more extended discussion of the nascent feminism of this play, see Catena, who views Galdós as a mouthpiece for "las nuevas e incipientes ideas sobre la mujer" (107).

on defending the rights of the dead, characteristics that bring her close to Electra herself.[11]

Eleuteria's independence does not lead her to murder Electra's father (at least so far as the readers are told) as Clytemnestra does in the different versions of the myth. Yet her promiscuity and her use of men for her own pleasure end up producing what amounts to a similar result from Electra's perspective: the absence of a father. Into this void enters a gallery of male figures who will actively compete for paternity rights, so to speak, to Electra: Urbano García Yuste, Leonardo Cuesta, Salvador Pantoja, and finally, Máximo Yuste. Through their characters more clues turn up that reveal the classical outlines of the play.

Urbano is the husband of Evarista, the first cousin of the deceased Eleuteria. Together they have assumed responsibility for Electra, since they have no children of their own and seem to be constantly in search of new ways to put their considerable wealth, gained through stocks and other investments, to charitable use (hence the etymology of Evarista's name: "most noble or virtuous one"). Their role as Electra's foster parents is close to that of the mythical Electra's real parents. It soon becomes clear that Evarista is the dominant figure in the marriage and that she is responsible for the decisions regarding Electra. As Urbano tells the marquis later in the play: "Querido marqués, pídame usted que altere, que trastorne todo el sistema planetario, que quite los astros de aquí para ponerlos allá; pero no me pida cosa contraria a los pareceres de mi mujer" (884; 4.4). Urbano's compliance with his wife's every demand recalls the husband-wife relationship of Aeschylus's *Agamemnon* (an important precursor of the Electra plays), particularly the scene in which the king, on returning home from the war, finds himself unable to refuse his wife's wishes and enters his palace by walking on a purple carpet, a deeply symbolic act that seals his doom (914–57).

Despite her name, Evarista reveals a streak of antimaternalism when she tells Máximo not to bring his children into their house: "No me los traigas, no. Adoro a las criaturas; pero a mi lado no las quiero. Todo me

---

11. Clytemnestra's name in Greek, although obscure, may suggest "praiseworthy wooing" (Graves 2:386). One of the justifications that she frequently invokes for murdering her husband is that in doing so she sought revenge on him for the sacrifice of Iphigeneia. See Aeschylus, *Agamemnon* 1431–32; Sophocles, *Electra* 528–33; Euripides, *Electra* 1011–29 and *Iphigeneia at Aulis* 1180–90; Seneca, *Agamemnon* 192–202. In Aeschylus, Euripides (*Electra*), and Seneca, she goes on to admit jealousy over Cassandra as well.

lo revuelven, todo me lo ensucian. El alboroto de sus pataditas, de sus risotadas, de sus berrinches, me enloquece" (861; 2.2). Her ambivalent attitude toward children suggests that of Clytemnestra, who murders her husband to avenge the death of one daughter, Iphigeneia, but treats the other, Electra, with contempt. Sophocles' Clytemnestra describes this ambivalence with characteristic brevity: "Strange [*deinon*: also 'wondrous,' 'terrible,' 'formidable'] is the force of motherhood [*tiktein*]" (770).

Leonardo Cuesta is an ailing accountant responsible for the financial success of Urbano and Evarista. Early in the play one learns, in addition, that he feels a paternal obligation toward Electra, which he hints is a biological one. He reveals that he knew Eleuteria when Electra was still a baby and that when he saw her after she arrived in Madrid he felt "un dulce afecto, el más puro de los afectos, mezclado con alaridos de mi conciencia" (857; 1.9). Confessing a desire to address the consequences of his "errores graves," he explains that he plans to leave Electra a generous inheritance, "lo suficiente para vivir con independencia decorosa" (857; 1.9). When he dies a few days later, Electra loses another father figure.

Salvador Pantoja is the most controversial character of the play. A spiritual advisor of sorts to Evarista, he, like Cuesta, reveals to Electra a dubious past corresponding to the period before she was born: "Cuando yo me envilecí, cuando me encenagué en el pecado, no había usted nacido" (859; 1.11). Also like Cuesta, he tells Electra of an obligation he feels toward her that grows from "mi cariño intensísimo, como la fuerza nace del calor. Y mi protección obra es de mi conciencia" (859; 1.11). Unlike Cuesta, instead of giving her the means with which to become free and independent, he wants to constrict her liberty so that she will not follow in the footsteps of her mother. Scandalized by the young woman's boundless energy and thinly veiled sexuality, he convinces Evarista that the only option is to place Electra somewhere "donde no vea ejemplos de liviandad, ni oiga ninguna palabra con dejos maliciosos. . . . Donde no la trastorne el zumbido de los venenosos pretendientes sin pudor" (868; 2.12). The place he has in mind is the convent San José de la Penitencia, where Eleuteria herself died while repenting the error of her ways.

Although Pantoja is not a priest, his capacity as spiritual advisor to Evarista, his philanthropy toward the church and the convents, his frequent use of religious metaphor, his tendency to dress all in black, and, whether or not Galdós intended it, the striking similarity of his influence in Electra's life to that of the real-life Father Cermeño in the notorious Ubao case, all lead one to identify in him an "authoritarian-clerical principle," as Hinterhäuser describes it (276; see also Catena 93). Even if he is not the biological father of Electra, a possibility that he hints at but never explicitly claims, his spiritual influence over her converts him into another undeniable father figure that calls attention to the absence of her real father.

Pantoja's principal adversary in the struggle over Electra's will is Máximo Yuste (along with Maximo's ally, the marquis of Ronda), the nephew of Evarista and Urbano and who lives and works in an apartment on their estate. A scientist specializing in electrical conduction, Máximo is a widower with two small children. The closest in age to eighteen-year-old Electra of all the paternal figures mentioned thus far (Urbano is fifty-five; Cuesta and Pantoja, both fifty), at thirty-five Máximo is still old enough to be her father, and this fact is emphasized in the romantic relationship in which they become involved. In the middle of the play, Electra briefly escapes from the tyranny of Pantoja and Evarista and seeks shelter in Máximo's apartment. When she complains to him of the oppression that she feels in the García Yuste household, he responds: "No temas. Confía en mí. Yo te reclamaré como protector tuyo, como maestro" (877; 3.8).

Electra accepts and even encourages this father-daughter hierarchy in their relationship, as her astonishing reply demonstrates: "Pero no tardes. Por la salud de tus hijos, Máximo, no tardes. Oye lo que se me ocurre: ¿por qué no me tomas como a uno de tus niños, y me tienes como ellos y con ellos?" (877; 3.8); later she addresses him as "maestro" (882; 4.2). In the absence of a real father, she has apparently settled on Máximo as a convenient substitute. The love she invests in this relationship is similar to the feelings of the Greek Electra, as Euripides has Clytemnestra explain: "Child, still thy nature bids thee love thy sire. / 'Tis ever thus: some cleave unto their father, / Some more the mothers than the father love" (*Electra* 1102–4).[12]

At the end of act 3, Máximo and Electra declare their intentions to get married. Although Urbano and Evarista are quite satisfied with this classic solution to Electra's scandalous behavior, Pantoja is furious, and when he is unsuccessful at convincing Evarista to change her mind (4.6), he decides to take matters into his own hands. Two scenes later, he confronts Electra and tells her that he cannot avoid causing her "una penita, un

---

12. Cf. *Iphigeneia at Aulis* 638–39, where Clytemnestra speaks similarly of Iphigencia.

sinsabor ..." (887; 4.8). The dialogue that ensues is crucial to the outcome of the play:

Electra.—Ya sé que el padre de Máximo y usted fueron terribles enemigos ... También me han dicho que aquel buen señor, honradísimo en los negocios, fue un poquito calavera ..., ya usted me entiende ... Pero eso a mí nada me afecta.
Pantoja.—Inocentísima criatura, no sabes lo que dices.
Electra.—Digo que ... aquel excelente hombre ...
Pantoja.—Lázaro Yuste, sí ... Al nombrarle, tengo que asociar su triste memoria a la de una persona que no existe ... muy querida para ti ...
. . . .
Electra.—(*Con terror, en voz apenas perceptible.*) ¡Mi madre! (*Pantoja hace signos afirmativos con la cabeza.*) ¡Mi madre! (*Atónita, deseando y temiendo la explicación.*) (887–88; 4.8)

Pantoja is implying, of course, that Lázaro Yuste, Máximo's father, is also Electra's father. In the same scene, he goes on to suggest that Lázaro fathered Máximo by Eleuteria and then took him away to France, where he was raised by a French woman, Josefina Perret, whom everyone believed to be his real mother. Pantoja expects that the horror of incest resulting from this scenario will be sufficient to destroy any hopes Electra has of marrying Máximo.

This is precisely her reaction. Maddened by the possibility that the man she loves is her brother, she breaks off the engagement and secludes herself from the world in San José de la Penitencia, where she repeatedly reports hearing voices, especially that of her mother (5.6–8). Meanwhile, Máximo and the marquis, with the will of the recently deceased Cuesta to bolster their efforts, have been making plans to rescue her from the convent. Then, in a highly controversial scene, what seems to be the ghost of Electra's mother appears before her and tells her that Máximo is not her brother and that she should follow her heart: "Si el amor conyugal y los goces de la familia solicitan tu alma, déjate llevar de esa dulce atracción, y no pretendas aquí una santidad que no alcanzarías" (897; 5.9). In the last scene, Máximo and Ronda arrive, and Electra makes a motion to run toward them. When Pantoja asks her if she is fleeing from him, Máximo utters the famous last lines of the play, which evoked deafening applause from the Madrid audiences of 1901: "No huye, no ... Resucita."

Many critics, especially the anonymous contemporary reviewers of the piece, interpret the confrontation between the scientist Máximo and the zealot Pantoja as a symbolic, even allegorical dramatization of the contemporary fight between progressive and conservative forces over the soul of Spain, which they see embodied in the young Electra.[13] The circumstances of the Ubao case, which was under consideration exactly at the time of the play's debut, certainly seemed to invite such a view. "Electra" suddenly became a household word synonymous with progress and left-wing politics, and a contemporary journal established to promote such views was named after the enormously successful play (see Litvak). Perhaps because of such contemporary repercussions, later criticism on *Electra* has fallen into a rigid set of a priori assumptions. Everyone who has discussed the play, for example, takes for granted that Pantoja is categorically lying when he tells Electra that Máximo is her brother. Yet there is a strong possibility that he may be, willingly or not, speaking at least a half-truth, and this possibility is crucial to determining the significance of *Electra.*

There are three major pieces of evidence that seem to support the assumption that Pantoja has fabricated the story about Electra's relation to Máximo. First among them is the possibility that he may himself be her father. In addition to the scene (11) in act 1 in which he tells Electra of his interest in her, the following passage from a conversation with Evarista is noteworthy: "Amo a Electra con amor tan intenso, que no acierten a declararlo todas las sutilezas de la palabra humana. Desde que la vieron mis ojos, la voz de la sangre clamó dentro de mí diciéndome que esa criatura me pertenece ... Quiero y debo tenerla bajo mi dominio santamente, paternalmente ..." (885; 4.6). Later in the same conversation, he refers to Electra as "mi hija" (885; 4.6). These statements, combined with his declaration to Máximo that he strives toward his ends "por los caminos posibles" (890; 4.10), may lead one to conclude that his actions are those of an overpossessive father fighting by any means necessary for control of his daughter. This is certainly a possibility, but there is no conclusive proof offered anywhere in the play that Pantoja is Electra's father, nor does it

---

13. One of the best-known manifestations of this reading is the lavishly enthusiastic review of Andrés Ovejero, while a notable exception is to be found in Lace 65–66. Later readers often follow the Manichean view of Ovejero. Starkie, for example, declares that *Electra* "evidently symbolizes the triumph of science and liberal ideas in Máximo and Electra and the defeat of the old superstitions of Spain in Pantoja. The dramas of Galdós often recall the ancient Morality plays with their allegorical representation of virtues and vices" (115). As recently as 1981, Rubio suggests the same stereotypical division, which he then condemns as "un procedimiento típicamente melodramático" ("Galdós" 64).

seem that there could be, given Eleuteria's much commented-on promiscuity. In fact, the figure of Leonardo Cuesta functions precisely to question Pantoja's claim, as Salvador Canals noted long ago (215). In either case, Máximo and Electra could still share the same mother, in which case they would be half-siblings.

The second piece of evidence is presented by the marquis to Evarista: "Para que usted acabe de formar juicio, óigame lo que voy a decirle. Virginia [Ronda's wife] me asegura que de Josefina Perret, sin que en ello pueda haber mistificación ni engaño ..., nació el hombre que ve usted ahí [Máximo] ... Y lo prueba, lo demuestra como el problema más claro y sencillo. Además, yo he podido comprobar que Lázaro Yuste faltó de Madrid desde el sesenta y tres al sesenta y seis" (893; 5.3). Whereas the first piece of evidence cited above raises the question of Electra's father, this one brings up that of Máximo's mother. Yet this scenario, too, leaves open the possibility that Máximo and Electra might be half-siblings. Even if Josefina Perret is Máximo's mother, if Lázaro Yuste was the "calavera" that Electra mentions, he could still be the father of both (given, of course, that neither Pantoja nor Cuesta is the father). The dates of Lázaro's purported absence from Madrid only confirm this possibility. Galdós specifies that the action of his play is "rigurosamente contemporánea" (that is, close to 1901) and that Máximo is thirty-five at the time that it takes place, suggesting that he must have been born around the year 1865 or 1866, precisely the period of Lázaro's absence. In this chronology, Lázaro could have fathered Máximo in France by Josefina Perret and returned to Madrid to father Electra, who, if she is eighteen at the time the play takes place, would have been born around the year 1882 or 1883, during the "scandalous" period (1880–85) of Eleuteria's life. Ronda's "evidence," instead of resolving the issue, only opens up further possibilities.[14]

What seems to be the most weighty piece of evidence against Pantoja's story is at the same time the most controversial element of the play: the apparition of Eleuteria at the end of act 5. Critic after critic has expressed puzzlement, dissatisfaction, even anger over the fact that Galdós would resort to an apparently supernatural resolution to a play that he defines as strictly contemporary.[15] These reactions all beg the same question: that

---

14. The accumulation of specious evidence in this way recalls the scene in Sophocles' *Oedipus* between Oedipus, the messenger, and the herdsman. See verses 924–1181 and the corresponding discussion in Ahl, *Sophocles' Oedipus*, chaps. 6 and 7.

15. Mérimée, "A propos" 199; Valverde López 21; González Serrano 116; Gómez de Baquero 195; Martinenche 835; "Benito Pérez Galdós" (anonymous) 10–11; Morley xxxv; Starkie 115; Carney 243–44; Cardona and Sobejano 63–64.

the appearance of Eleuteria *is* a supernatural occurrence. There are, in fact, two equally valid alternative explanations.

The first was offered some time ago by Mérimée, who notes that "l'auteur s'efforce à rendre le miracle vraisemblable, et même à le réduire à un phénomène subjectif, extériorisé pour les nécessités de la représentation" ("A propos" 199). More recently, Finkenthal (146) and Sobejano ("Echegaray" 114) have repeated the same idea. Finkenthal is particularly provocative with his suggestion that Electra's desire to see her mother, which is manifested throughout the play, stems from "la tensión nerviosa que empieza a sentir cuando Pantoja le insinúa que él puede ser su padre" (146). Yet none of these readers confronts the consequences of their quite valid suggestions: if the ghost is really a manifestation of Electra's unstable mind, how can one possibly impute to the "evidence" that it reveals an unquestionable truth value? It seems more likely, psychologically speaking, that Electra, in the throes of delirium, would displace Pantoja's unsettling disclosure with a more sanguine account of her own, bolstered by the perceived authority of the supernatural. To accept the shade's words as incontrovertible amounts, in this scenario, to a complicity with the rhetoric of infantile fantasy.

There is another scenario that is equally probable but that has gone completely unperceived: that the apparition is the result of neither supernatural nor psychological forces but rather of a quite mundane collaboration between Máximo, the marquis, and Sor Dorotea, one of the nuns of the convent. In the first half of act 5, Máximo and Ronda discuss their options for winning back Electra. When asked by the marquis what he plans to do, Máximo replies: "Llevármela de grado o por fuerza. Si no tengo poder bastante, buscarlo, adquirirlo, comprarlo; traer amigos, cómplices, un escuadrón, un ejército ... (*Con creciente calor y brío.*) Renacen en mí los tiempos románticos y las ferocidades del feudalismo" (894; 5.5). Máximo's suggestion of buying power and accomplices is not lost on Ronda, who assures him, "Ya tengo las llaves para entrar por la calle Nueva. La Hermana Dorotea nos pertenece" (894; 5.5).

These comments are extremely significant in interpreting the ending of the play and should be read in conjunction with the following dialogue between Electra and Dorotea, which occurs just before the appearance of the "ghost":

Dorotea.—Ven ... A la iglesia, no.
Electra.—Aquí ... Quiero respirar ... Quiero vivir.
Dorotea.—(*Aparte, inquieta.*) Ya es la hora fijada por el marqués ...

> Aprovechemos los minutos, los segundos, o todo se perderá. (*Mirando a la izquierda.*) Voy a franquearles el paso a este patio ... (*Alto.*) Hermana, espérame aquí.
> Electra.—(*Asustada.*) ¿Adónde vas? (*La coge del brazo.*)
> Dorotea.—(*Con decisión, defendiéndose.*) A mirar por ti, a devolverte la salud, la vida ... Disponte a salir de esta sepultura, y llévame contigo.
> Electra.—(*Trémula.*) Hermana ..., no te alejes de mí.
> Dorotea.—Este instante decide de tu suerte. Volverás al mundo ..., verás a Máximo.
> Electra.—¿Cuándo?
> Dorotea.—Ahora ... le verás entrar por allí ... (*Señala a la izquierda.*) ¡Silencio ..., valor! No me detengas ... No te muevas de aquí. (*Vase corriendo por la izquierda.*) (896; 5.8)

Immediately after Dorotea's departure, the ghost appears.

Dorotea's behavior in this scene is odd, to say the least. Her eagerness to leave the room but to have Electra remain rooted to the spot is suspicious. Her own explanation, that Máximo and the marquis are waiting outside, is unconvincing. Why should she have to "franquearles el paso" for two grown men? Why could not Electra simply leave the room with her and meet them outside? What is to happen at the "hora fijada por el marqués," and why is it a question of minutes, even seconds?

All these problems are explained if one imagines a scenario in which the apparition, which materializes, according to the stage directions, "vestida de monja" (896; 5.8) and which only "vagamente se destaca en la oscuridad del fondo" (896; 5.9), is simply Dorotea posing as Eleuteria and reading a speech invented by Máximo and the marquis. It certainly would not be difficult to deceive Electra in her crazed state of mind, and the Greek etymology of Dorotea's name ("gift of god") implicates the nun in an all-too-human version of a supposed *dea ex machina*. Etymologies aside, the episode also has a powerful literary precedent in an author for whom Galdós's admiration is well known: Cervantes. In chapters 29 and 30 of part 1 of the *Quixote*, the character Dorotea, instructed by the priest and the barber, disguises herself as the fictional princess Micomicona in order to lead the deluded knight back home and back to his sanity. This is precisely what Galdós's Dorotea aims at with her promise to "mirar por ti, a devolverte la salud, la vida."[16]

16. The ghost scene, when interpreted in this way, has an ancient parallel in Sophocles'

Even if, as a final possibility, the ending of the play is interpreted as a bona fide supernatural occurrence or *dea ex machina*—the "sombra," after all, figures in the cast of characters and was played in the debut by a different actress from the one who played Dorotea—there is no guarantee that it speaks the truth. If Galdós really aimed to rid the contemporary theater of conventional ways of thinking, he would have found a compelling method for achieving his goal by dramatizing a deity or similar figure that blatantly and consciously distorted the truth. This technique recalls somewhat that of Euripides' *Orestes*, at the end of which Apollo suddenly appears to announce an impossible and unbelievable resolution to the crisis of the play. William Arrowsmith's provocative commentary on this play is revealing and equally applicable to the case of Galdós's *Electra:* "What we have here, I think, is a transparent tour de force, an apparent resolution which in fact resolves nothing, the illusion of a *deus ex machina* intervening to stop the terrible momentum of the play by means of a solution so inadequate and so unreal by contrast with the created reality of the play that it is doomed into insignificance" (Arrowsmith 110). If, as Finkenthal suggests (146), the appearance of the ghost is a typical Euripidean technique, then it remains possible, despite all the evidence to the contrary that is presented in the play, that Máximo is Electra's brother or, at least, half-brother. The radical textual ambiguity permits a multitude of scenarios, including three possible fathers to Electra (Cuesta, Pantoja, Lázaro Yuste) and two possible mothers to Máximo (Eleuteria, Josefina Perret), thus precluding a definitive conclusion to the issue. Pantoja, willingly or not, may be telling the truth.

This scenario casts Máximo in the role of Orestes, brother of the mythical Electra, an association supported by several other elements of the play. First, Máximo's name, which might seem to confirm the nobility and lofty goals of one dedicated to the pursuit of science and truth, also suggests the high altitude at which a mountaineer (the meaning of *orestes* in Greek) would typically be found. Second, Máximo's intentions are not always so pure as one would expect, as becomes abundantly clear in the last act of the play: "¡A la violencia!" he gleefully chants to Ronda (894; 5.5). According to Finkenthal, Máximo is Galdós's "primer protagonista con un temperamento científico contrarrestado por el deseo de actuar de forma violenta si es necesario" (148).

Philoctetes, at the end of which Heracles' sudden appearance, crucial in convincing Philoctetes to leave for Troy, may simply be Odysseus (who has just departed the stage) in disguise. See verses 1293–471.

This puzzling component of Máximo's character has a striking precedent in the Greek Orestes, especially as portrayed in the play that bears his name. Euripides goes to great lengths to demythify the hero vindicated in Aeschylus and Sophocles by presenting a completely unsympathetic figure: deranged, bloodthirsty, unable to comprehend the gravity of his crimes and willing to add to them the murder of Helen and Hermione. "To Helen's death: the watchword [*sumbolon*] know I well" (1130), he declares cheerfully and, in a frenzied act of gratuitous destruction, sets fire to the house of Menelaus. Suddenly Máximo's alarming cries of "hay que matarlo [a Pantoja]" and "[hay que] pegar fuego a esta casa" (894; 5.5) take on a new dimension.

The Orestian ambivalence (hero/villain) of Máximo finds perfect expression, furthermore, in the epithet that is constantly applied to him: "el mágico prodigioso." This description refers in part to the curious way that in Spain, science was always confused with magic, a tradition that Cervantes ridicules mercilessly in *La cueva de Salamanca*. Yet it also recalls Calderón's *El mágico prodigioso*, a play whose ambiguous title applies equally well to the hero, Cipriano, and to the villain, the Devil himself.

If Lázaro Yuste is taken to be the father of Electra, as Pantoja suggests, then the context of the myth helps to clarify the latter's role in the play as well. Pantoja tells Máximo that "tu padre, Lázaro Yuste, y yo, ¡ay dolor!, tuvimos desavenencias profundas, de las que más vale no hablar ahora" (880; 3.10); later Electra, in the scene mentioned earlier, recalls how Pantoja and Lázaro were "terrible enemies." It seems probable, as Canals suggests (215), that Eleuteria was the cause of these conflicts: in other words, that Pantoja and Lázaro were antagonistic rivals over Electra's mother. If Lázaro was the actual father, corresponding to the Agamemnon of mythology, Pantoja's actions as guilty lover of Eleuteria and vicious enemy of the father of her child place him squarely in the role of Aegisthus, Clytemnestra's lover and accomplice to murder. Galdós never reveals how Máximo's father died, but if one supposes that he was roughly the same age as Pantoja when they were rivals for Eleuteria, then he must have died an early death, for Pantoja is fifty when the play takes place. Pantoja refers constantly to the sins of his past. Could one of them have been foul play involving the death of Lázaro?

It is important to note, nonetheless, that Pantoja is not fundamentally evil, and several critics have even credited him with a certain sincerity and humanity.[17] This circumstance, too, has a possible precedent in the myth.

---

17. González Serrano 115; Gómez de Baquero 202–3; Martinenche 835; anonymous ("Be-

Even though Aegisthus has received little sympathetic treatment in ancient literature, it is worth pointing out that his treacherous behavior toward Agamemnon is not gratuitous but rather is an effort to redress a long history of family violence, as recounted in Seneca's *Thyestes*, for example. Similarly, Pantoja believes that his actions toward Electra are ultimately justified by his honorable ends. Thus he declares to Máximo, with all the ring of Greek tragedy, that "el monstruo no soy yo. Es un monstruo terrible, que se alimenta de los hechos humanos. Se llama la Historia" (889; 4.10).

This reading of *Electra* shows how Galdós delicately and ambiguously superimposes the plot of his play upon the basic structure of the myth of Electra—the underlying family relations, alliances, and antagonisms—teasing out of the fraternal bond that united Electra and Orestes desires of an entirely different nature. His rewriting of the tale in this way is not unprecedented; a Freudian perspective suggests that he simply substitutes the brother for the father as the object of Electra's incestuous longing.[18] Máximo, in fact, plays both father and brother to Electra: father in the psychological hierarchy of their courtship noted earlier, and brother in the strict biological sense. Thus the "modelo argumental [of *Electra*] no está muy lejos del mito," as Rubio notes. Given this context, however, it is inconceivable that the play should be taken as "una apología de la familia burguesa, en la que el marido y la mujer tienen ya reservadas sus funciones respectivas," as Rubio goes on to suggest ("Galdós" 63).

Electra is a far more radical project than Rubio allows himself to admit. Although the piece may possess some of the ingredients traditionally associated with melodrama, Sobejano is correct in noting that "el uso que hace Galdós de estos ingredientes todos, atenúa considerablemente o llega a anular su condición melodramática" ("Echegaray" 113). This statement is key to interpreting Galdós's use of myth in *Electra* within the context of his agenda for renovating contemporary theater.

Throughout the play, false clues appear that function as bait for those readers or spectators willing to accept facile solutions to the problems raised in the work. The composite picture suggested by these clues indeed

---

nito Pérez Galdós" 1911) 10. Recent critics have tended to be the harshest in their judgments of Pantoja.

18. It should be noted that Freud never endorsed the term "Electra complex" (which was apparently coined by Jung), not because he disagreed with the theories espoused in it but because he believed that female desire for the father was adequately described by his own designation, the "Oedipus complex." See his "Female Sexuality" 229; "Outline" 194; and "Psychogenesis" 155 n. 1.

carries melodramatic tones: a clear-cut division between science and liberalism on the one hand (Máximo) and superstition and reaction on the other (Pantoja). In particular, the issue of truth posed so often in the play seems to signal Máximo as its prime standard-bearer. Over and over again the young scientist declares himself a seeker and defender of truth and righteousness, as at the end of act 4: "Devolvedme a la verdad, devolvedme a la ciencia. Este mundo incierto, mentiroso, no es para mí" (891; 4.12). Pantoja, by contrast, when one fails to examine his supposed manipulation of evidence, is forced into a metaphysical space opposite that of Máximo. It is understandable how such a reading could lead one to conclude that "la verdad para Galdós es absoluta" (Rubio, "Ibsen" 220).

Yet the subtle outlines of the myth of Electra radically disrupt all these assumptions. Máximo's tendency toward the violence and extortion of Orestes shows that he holds no monopoly on truth or justice, a fact that Pantoja recognizes early in the play: "No me fío de la expresión de tus ojos. Penetro en el doble fondo de tu mente: allí veo lo que piensas ... No te interrogué por saber tu intención, que ya sabía, sino por oírte las bonitas promesas con que la encubres ... En ti no mora la verdad; en ti no mora el bien, no, no ..., no ..." (880; 3.10). For his part, Pantoja, although he may strike some as an unsympathetic character, believes that his actions are fully justified, as could be argued for his mythical counterpart Aegisthus. Throughout the play he speaks with conviction and sincerity and carries himself with calm dignity.

What, then, does Galdós's play demonstrate in dramatizing Pantoja's clash with Máximo over Electra, if not a titanic battle of opposites? Among other things, it shows that truth is not a metaphysical quantity that can be "fought for," as Máximo believes (893; 5.3). It suggests, instead, a pervasive circularity of human action and cognition: "Los extremos se tocan" (894; 5.5), as Máximo himself is forced to admit to the marquis when questioned about his alarming trend toward violence. Finally, it points to the disconcerting fact that truth does not always form an alliance with science, liberalism, justice, or even the supernatural, but rather may adhere to the most unpalatable of scenarios: incest, for example.

In dramatizing these ideas, Galdós uses all the elements of melodrama to deconstruct (although he obviously could not have chosen this word to describe his project) the fundamental philosophical assumptions of melodrama, handing his audience a feast à la Echegaray while all along poisoning its ingredients and forcing his unsuspecting readers or spectators into complicity with the fictional characters that wander before them on the page or stage. In this way he follows the bold Euripidean tradition of baiting audiences with conventional assumptions about myth while debunking those assumptions under their noses.[19] If, he may have mused wryly to himself, he could not force a change in the bourgeois tastes that he believed were destroying the contemporary theater, at least he could have a good laugh at those who were to greet with wild enthusiasm a play that, on one level at least, stages the triumph of incestuous desire.

This is not to deny that, politically speaking, Galdós's play represents a progressive vision of the future. Yet the political implications of *Electra* form only one side of the author's response to the double predicament of late nineteenth-century theater. To emphasize them to the point of obscuring the outlines of the myth of Electra is to disregard the serious artistic renovation implied in the play's dramatization of conflicting truths and uncomfortable desires.

Naked Drama and Christian Desire: Miguel de Unamuno's *Fedra*

While Galdós's attempt at renovating the theater through the use of classical myth was ignored by those who allowed themselves to be seduced by *Electra*'s contemporaneity, it was not lost on a young writer who, from the safe distance of his quiet office in Salamanca, could observe with bemused detachment the frenzied response of the Madrid audiences. The day after *Electra*'s debut, Unamuno wrote a letter to Galdós to congratulate him on his success, promising to write back once he had read the play (Nuez and Schraibman 57). Unfortunately there is no record of such a letter, which might have offered crucial insights into Unamuno's interpretation of *Electra*. In its place, a close reading of *Fedra* will confirm the kinship between the two authors' respective works.[20]

Like Galdós, Unamuno was keenly aware of the causes of the late nineteenth-century theater's decline, as he makes clear in an article first pub-

---

19. The difference is that Euripides—and Sophocles, too, as discussed above (see n. 14, this chapter)—used skillful dramatic technique to undermine myth, whereas Galdós uses the myth of Electra to subvert theatrical convention.

20. What does exist is a letter from 1912 in which Unamuno, again writing to Galdós, explains that he is enclosing a copy of his recently composed *Fedra* for the perusal of his "querido amigo y maestro" (Nuez and Schraibman 70).

lished in 1896: "Éste y no otro es hoy en España el mal mayor del teatro, el convencionalismo del cromo teatral" ("La regeneración" 14).[21] Two years later he began writing his own plays, and, although he enjoyed little success as a dramatist, he dedicated himself to the activity, on and off, throughout the remainder of his life.[22]

Although in that early article Unamuno calls for a return to the popular traditions of the classical Spanish stage, by 1910 he felt compelled to turn to classical Athenian theater to achieve the renovation that he desired. As professor of Greek at the University of Salamanca, he possessed both the knowledge and the resources to do so, as García Blanco's indispensable survey makes clear. Curiously, Unamuno never devoted a page of criticism to his academic specialty, nor had he, before this moment (1910), felt inclined to incorporate Greek themes or characters into his vast literary output. Yet now he suddenly saw the need for using Greek myth to dramatize the sort of raging, authentic desire—"pasión rugiente," he called it (*Teatro completo* 87)—that was in severe shortage on the contemporary stage. In a letter from 1911, Unamuno's judgment of Jacinto Benavente (1866–1954), who by that time had replaced Echegaray as master of the theatrical scene, is indicative of his attitude toward the current theater: "Nuestro supremo dramaturgo de hoy, Benavente, es muy ingenioso y fino, pero *apatético*. Resulta frío e incisivo" (*Teatro completo* 85).

Unamuno's solution to Benavente's "apathetic" theater is what he calls naked tragedy or, alternatively, poetic theater. A few passages from the prologue to *Fedra* help to clarify these concepts:

> Llamo desnudo en la tragedia o desnudez trágica al efecto que se obtiene presentando la tragedia en toda su augusta y solemne majestad.
> Libre primero de todos los perifollos de la ornamentación escénica. (*Fedra* 186)

---

21. This negative opinion was generally shared by his contemporaries, as Monleón notes ("Unamuno" 22). However, it is worth repeating that, contrary to Aszyk's suggestion that Unamuno was perhaps "el primero que a finales del siglo XIX planteó el problema de los males del teatro en España y de la urgente necesidad de regeneración" (30), Galdós's successors simply reiterate what he had expressed at least a decade earlier.

22. As in the case of Galdós's theater, Unamuno's dramatic output has suffered from neglect in favor of his prose writings. Recent years, however, have seen a notable increase in interest, first kindled by Lázaro's still indispensable article and by the publication of the volume *Teatro completo*, edited by Garcia Blanco. See, in addition, Ayllón; Zavala; Monleón, "Unamuno"; Garasa; Tornos; Torre; Anderson; Franco; Macrí; Gullón; García Lorenzo, *El teatro español* 49–53; Shaw, "Sobre algunos" and "Three Plays"; Ruiz Ramón, *Historia . . . siglo XX* 77–93; Robertson; Aszyk; and Elizalde, "Características."

[T]eatro poético será el que cree caracteres, ponga en pie almas agitadas por las pasiones eternas y nos las meta al alma, purificándonosla, sin necesidad de ayuda, sino la precisa, de las artes auxiliares. (*Fedra* 187)

The first passage shows that Unamuno sought to reduce theater to its barest dialogic core, eliminating all paraverbal elements that had no direct bearing on the action of the play, a technique that parallels that of his novel *Abel Sánchez* and prompts Guillermo de Torre's comment that Unamuno "fundió y confundió" all genres (14). While this may be true, Unamuno's concept of *desnudez*, when applied specifically to his theater, has the effect of placing his plays in a technical proximity to classical drama that few other contemporary pieces based on ancient myth can claim. Thus Adriano Tilgher characterizes *Fedra* as "un dramma di semplicità veramente greca ridotto alle linee essenziali e nude della tragedia classica" (165; see Bourne 153–54 for a similar view).

Unamuno never defines more precisely what he means by "tragedy" in relation to *Fedra*, and his alternation of the term with "teatro poético" suggests a loosely defined, generic term that is equivalent to something like "serious drama." The second passage above demonstrates that, with respect to content, what interested Unamuno in Greek tragedy was its dramatization of true passion—desire—which could be used to restore to theater the serious, reflective tone lacking in the superficial spectacles of Echegaray and Benavente. It is no surprise, then, that his "professional familiarity" with the Greek tragedians, as he describes his academic training (*Fedra* 187), would lead him to choose as the inspiration for his most "naked" play precisely that Greek text—Euripides' *Hippolytus*—that dramatizes sexual passion to the fullest.[23] He also made use of Racine's *Phèdre*, whose influence he acknowledges, and it seems probable that he was inspired by Seneca's *Phaedra* as well, although he maintains a curious silence on this issue.[24] Nevertheless, inasmuch as the central, overwhelming desire of the Greek heroine for her stepson remains a constant in both the French and Latin texts, Euripides' *Hippolytus* may rightly be considered Unamuno's principal source of inspiration. He himself states that

---

23. Violence is the primary manifestation of desire in the ancient Greek theater, which, as noted in Chapter 1 (see page 12), generally represents erotic desire in strikingly subdued form—a noteworthy contrast to Ovidian narrative and Senecan drama.

24. On the possible influence of Seneca in *Fedra*, see Fernández Almagro; Lasso, "*Fedra*" 239–43; García Viñó 444; and Valbuena Briones, "La *Fedra*" 4–5. Valbuena suggests, quite plausibly, that Unamuno's silence regarding the Senecan model may have been due to the harsh judgment in which writers of his time tended to hold the Neronian poet.

"mi *Fedra* . . . no es sino una modernización de la de Eurípides, o mejor dicho, el mismo argumento de ella, sólo con personajes de hoy en día, y cristianos por tanto—lo que la hace muy otra" (*Fedra* 186).

These statements suggest that Unamuno is not as liberal with the content of the myth as was his predecessor Galdós. Most of the incidents of the plot either remain identical to those of Euripides or come from Seneca or Racine.[25] Instead of radically altering the plot of the traditional tale, Unamuno modifies character through an emphasis on Christian ideology. As in the other plays studied, desire is a key element with which he inflects the myth with his particular concerns. By way of comparison, the following passage on desire from a long choral recitation in Euripides' *Hippolytus* is significant:

> O Eros, O Eros, how melts love's yearning
> From thine eyes, when thy sweet spell witcheth the heart
> Of them against whom thou hast marched in thy might! (525–28)

Seneca's chorus addresses desire in the following way:

> Diva non miti generata ponto,
> quam vocat matrem geminus Cupido,
> impotens flammis simul et sagittis,
> iste lascivus puer et renidens
> tela quam certo moderatur arcu!
> Labitur totas furor in medullas
> igne furtivo populante venas. (274–80)

> [Goddess born of the fierce sea, whom the two faces of Cupid call mother, how that lustful, shining boy of yours, unrestrained with his shafts of fire and iron, guides the missiles of his unfailing bow! His madness creeps into the marrow of the bones and ravages the veins with its hidden fire.]

---

25. Whether Unamuno had access to Gabriele D'Annunzio's *Fedra* (1909) before composing his own version of the myth is uncertain; he himself makes no mention of the Italian play in any of his published letters from the period. What remains clear is that, as Lasso de la Vega explains, "la vena de sensualidad que rompe en la *Fedra* del italiano no ha inspirado al vasco" ("*Fedra*" 221). For a useful summary of the myth of Phaedra in European literature and film, see López Caballero.

Finally, Racine's Phèdre cries in agony toward the end of a long soliloquy:

> Ce n'est plus une ardeur dans mes veines cachée:
> C'est Vénus toute entière à sa proie attachée. (1.3.305–6)

These passages, when compared to Unamuno's *Fedra*, reveal the most apparent way in which the expression of desire is reoriented in the Spanish text. Whereas in Euripides, Seneca, and, to a lesser degree, Racine, human passion is often a highly lyrical manifestation of either choral monologues or character soliloquies, in Unamuno's *Fedra*, because of the piece's *desnudez*, desire is almost entirely revealed through dialogue, creating what Iris Zavala calls a representation of the "ser interior que pugna contra la *palabra ajena*" ("La dialogía" 17). Highly charged dialogue runs throughout the play, whereas narration is kept to an absolute minimum. The long-winded messenger speeches of Greek tragedy, for example, are nonexistent, and the chorus, as several critics have noted, has been incorporated dialogically into the text.[26]

The content of the play reveals a parallel reworking that reveals Unamuno's effort to Christianize desire. He replaces allusions to the pagan divinities of the classical and Renaissance texts with references to Christian deities. Artemis, who appears only in Euripides' play, is transformed into a human Diana whom Hipólito mentions as the only woman he would consider marrying (200; 1.4). Fedra also makes reference to Jesús (225; 3.1), the Devil (194; 1.1), and, most important, the Virgen de los Dolores. Given the traditional associations of Mary with Venus (see above, Chapter 2, page 37), it is not difficult to read the Virgin's role in Unamuno as a structural replacement of the classical goddess of love. Fedra's comment to Eustaquia in the first scene of the play reinforces this role: "He querido resistir ..., ¡imposible! Pido consuelo y luces a la Virgen de los Dolores, y parece me empuja" (194). Like Aphrodite/Venus in Euripides and Seneca, who maliciously causes Phaedra to fall in love as an instrument of revenge, the Virgen de los Dolores, true to her name, appears to be pushing Fedra toward catastrophe even as Fedra prays to her for help.

Several other reconfigurations of desire on the human plane are important in Unamuno's adaptation of the myth. The playwright transforms the Theseus of legend into the bourgeois, aged Pedro, whose name (*piedra* < *petra*) suggests, as Valbuena Briones notes ("La *Fedra*" 6), a coldness that

---

26. Díez-Canedo 1:12; Mesa 244–45; Bourne 169–71; Lasso, *"Fedra"* 215; Franco 151.

contrasts vividly with the passion of his young wife. Furthermore, as Donald Shaw keenly observes, Pedro's presence throughout the play "upsets Fedra's moral position," since she cannot claim that her desire for Hipólito stems from loneliness ("Three Plays" 257). This circumstance serves to emphasize the uncontrollable and reckless nature of Fedra's passion, but it also allows for more development of Pedro's character, which Carlos Feal Deibe (20) views as the most original element of the play.

In effect, Unamuno capitalizes on Pedro's difficult position, caught as he is between the desires of son and wife, in order to dramatize the conflict of "un ser desgarrado por la duda" (Feal Deibe 21), a characterization that leads Zavala to interpret his character as inconsistent (*Unamuno* 58). Finally, Pedro's atavistic conception of honor—"¡El honor ante todo!" he cries after Fedra tells him that Hipólito desires her (220; 2.10)—reveals a "preoccupation with the external self" (Anderson 56) that informs the text with the aggressive desires underlying the traditional honor code (see above, Chapter 3, pages 64–67). Yet Unamuno softens the rigidity of desire displayed in the typical husband of the *comedia* by endowing Pedro with the capacity of forgiveness, as Franco notes (151). This recourse, while not exceptional or unique, is noteworthy as another means by which the author relocates the myth within a Christian context.

The accusations of critics that Hipólito's character lacks stature (Zavala, *Unamuno* 57) and represents a type of asexual individual (Franco 148) overlook subtle but important clues that reveal the sexual desires, perhaps suppressed, of this central figure. In the culminating scene of act 1, in which Fedra confesses her desires to her stepson, Hipólito replies: "Estás loca, madre, loca perdida, y tu locura es contagiosa ..." (202; 1.4). Fedra attempts to capitalize on this small chink in Hipólito's armor of chastity: "Pues ven, ven que te la pegue, y locos los dos, Hipólito, los dos locos ..." (203), but Hipólito immediately realizes the implications of his desires and resolutely determines that he and Fedra must no longer see each other alone. Luis González del Valle uses these statements, along with others from the same scene, to suggest that Hipólito may be flirting with his stepmother (46) and goes on to ask rhetorically whether Hipólito "teme corresponder a su madrastra" (47).

González del Valle fails to mention a comment made several scenes later that could serve to reinforce his argument. When Fedra tells her husband that Hipólito is harboring erotic feelings toward her and that she has fought to resist him, Pedro responds: "¡Oh, mi hijo, mi propio hijo! Pero él también ha luchado ... lucha ... sí, sí, ¿qué es si no esa manía de la caza? Busca en ella el olvido de su pasión ... ¡pobrecillo!" (213; 2.4). His comment, although it may appear misplaced if Fedra's accusation is assumed to be apocryphal, accurately describes the tension of Hipólito's desires, if González del Valle's interpretation is valid. Pedro's statement also reveals another possible debt to Seneca. Whereas Euripides' Hippolytus actively cultivates chastity and other virtues associated with it at the expense of eros (hence the opposition of Artemis and Aphrodite in the play), and there is never any indication of his sexual desires, the Senecan hero reveals a curious ambivalence toward women. Although he claims that "dux malorum femina [est]" 'woman is the director of evil' (559) and that a stepmother "mitior nil est feris" 'is no more compassionate than the beasts' (558), when Phaedra appears he treats her gently and tells her to entrust her cares to his ears (608). Commenting on this scene, Frederick Ahl asks whether Hippolytus might be feeling a repressed desire for Phaedra and suggests that Phaedra's "hunger for death by [Hippolytus's] sword endows the act of killing with a sense of sexual consummation" (Seneca, *Three Tragedies* 177).

Unamuno does not go this far, for his Fedra kills herself by poison rather than by the sword. Yet the playwright exploits the vague undertones of the Senecan Hippolytus's desire in order to create a more engaging and believable figure, since the extreme chastity of Euripides' protagonist would be difficult to accept in a contemporary, secular setting (given the absence of modern cults of Artemis). Racine dealt with the same problem by abolishing it altogether and giving Hippolyte a lover in the figure of Aricie; Unamuno, by contrast, preserves more faithfully the structure of the ancient story while still allowing its Christianization. The possibility that Hipólito desires his stepmother and engages in hunting to liberate the sexual tension he feels toward her is fitting in this Christian context. Unamuno's solution rationalizes the thematic opposition of Aphrodite and Artemis found in Euripides into a plausible relation of cause and effect: Hipólito devotes himself to hunting and chastity (Artemis) *because of* (in order to release), rather than in the absence of, his erotic desire (Aphrodite).

Another important character, although she never appears onstage, is Fedra's mother. An analysis of Fedra herself would be incomplete without a look at this controversial figure, to the extent that the mother-daughter relationship informs a major part of the text and is of primary importance in Unamuno's revision of desire in the myth. Fedra makes frequent allusions to her unfortunate mother, always mentioning a vague but enduring and endearing memory of her, as in the following dialogue with Eustaquia:

Fedra.—Y ahora es cuando más me acuerdo de mi madre ...
Eustaquia.—¿Acordarte? No puede ser ...
Fedra.—Sí, aunque te parezca mentira me acuerdo de esa madre de la que perdí toda memoria ... ¿toda? de esa madre a la que apenas conocí. Paréceme sentir sobre mis labios su beso, un beso de fuego en lágrimas, cuando tenía yo ... no sé ... dos años, uno y medio, uno, acaso menos ... Como algo vislumbrado entre brumas.
Eustaquia.—Sueños. (191; 1.1)

These comments point to the prominent role of determinism in the play and to the heroine's fight to escape the destiny of her mother, another theme that closely parallels Galdós's *Electra*. Like Galdós, Unamuno finds it necessary to elide the most shocking features of the myth, in this case the Cretan queen's unnatural passion for the bull. Interestingly, however, instead of directly contradicting this detail, Unamuno simply omits any reference to it, and Fedra's mother goes unnamed throughout the play. Yet the ancestral presence of the mythic Pasiphae ominously haunts the stage, as García Viñó notes (446), and continuously threatens Fedra's well-being.

Fedra, of course, knows nothing of the past (Eustaquia refuses to reveal anything of it to her), and, like Galdós's heroine, she looks to her mother for inspiration: "Ahora, en estos días de lucha, es cuando más necesito de su memoria," she tells Eustaquia (192; 1.1). Yet the ghost of Fedra's mother, rather than appearing onstage to urge her daughter to follow her heart, drives her passion from within. In this way Unamuno, just as he displaces Artemis's influence over Hipólito, transposes the origin of Fedra's desire from the ethereal realm of Olympus to the more plausible world of biology and genetics.[27]

The one memory that Fedra has of her mother, "un beso de fuego en lágrimas," is crucial to interpreting their relationship. In this extraordinary metaphor Unamuno encapsulates the tension that both propels the protagonist toward disaster and underlies the Christianization of desire. Insofar as the kiss is conceived of as a commodity that can be exchanged,

---

27. According to Dolores de Asís Garrote 349, D'Annunzio is the first playwright to introduce the element of heredity into the myth of Phaedra. Again, however, it is impossible to know whether Unamuno had access to this play before composing his own.

it represents the transmission of both heredity and the propensity for disaster from mother to daughter, as Eustaquia suggests later in the play: "Parece que con aquel beso, lo único que de ella recuerda ésta, le transmitió su alma y su sino" (226; 3.3). The ambivalence of the kiss is especially significant, as it represents sexual feeling toward an alien object of desire as well as maternal love toward the daughter. There is something unsettling in the image of a mother giving her daughter "fiery" kisses, an uncanniness that stems from a confusion of maternal and erotic sentiments. The tears that accompany the kiss might well point to the mother's pain over this realization. The entire metaphor, then, conveys a confusion of desire underlying Fedra's actions.

Fedra, in fact, has been characterized by precisely the same confusion of erotic and maternal sentiments (Sedwick 310; Barbieri 43). Her desire for children, exacerbated by her apparent infertility—a distinctly Unamunesque detail not encountered in other versions of the myth—is partially satisfied when her marriage to Pedro brings with it the responsibility of motherhood toward Hipólito. As she tells Eustaquia: "Y vino mi matrimonio con Pedro, tú sabes mejor que nadie cómo. Fui vencida por su generosidad y entré en esta casa, la de Hipólito ... Empezó llamándome 'madre.' ¡Madre! ¡Qué nombre tan sabroso! ¡Cómo remeje las entrañas!" (192–93; 1.1). But Hipólito was apparently too advanced in age and too sexually appealing to be considered her son, and soon her erotic desire overtook her maternal instincts: "Y era él, su padre, mi marido, el que al principio, viéndole tan encogido y tímido, le decía para animarle: 'anda, hijo, da un beso a tu nueva madre ... ¡a tu madre!' ¡Aquellos besos ...!" (193; 1.1).

The kiss thus reappears as a symbol of confused desire. Fedra later uses the same metaphor of the "beso de fuego en lágrimas" (203; 1.5), but the new context—the statement comes just after her declaration of passion to Hipólito—now suggests that the kiss refers to those exchanged between her and her son. In the following act, Fedra confesses that she is dying from "la sed de tus besos. . . . ¿Por qué no me besas como antes, Hipólito?" (210; 2.3).

The mixture of pleasure, love, and pain implied in the "kiss of tearful fire" suggests, finally, another subtext crucial to Unamuno's revision of desire in the play and consistent with the "tragic sense of life" proposed in his nonfiction prose: the life of Christ. As discussed above in Chapter 2 (see page 40), the history of the word *passión* evolved from a fusion of the active sense of desiring and the passive one of suffering. In reference to

Christ, the word normally conveys the passive sense related to his crucifixion. Yet it is also possible to find active desire in several erotically charged scenes of the Bible, for example, those in which a woman of ill repute kisses and anoints Christ's feet, as in Luke 7.36–50.[28] The theme also has a long history in Spanish literature. The *autos sacramentales* based on pagan mythology frequently draw parallels between Christ's love for humanity and erotic desire, as in Sor Juana's *El divino Narciso*. Similarly, the mystical poetry of San Juan de la Cruz (one of Unamuno's preferred authors) often portrays the union of Christ the lover and the human soul, conveniently feminine in gender, as in the "Cántico espiritual," the "Noche oscura," and, especially, in the following passage from the "Llama de amor viva":

> ¡O llama de amor viva,
> que tiernamente hyeres
> de mi alma en el más profundo centro!
> pues ya no eres esquiva,
> acava ya, si quieres;
> rompe la tela de este dulce encuentro. (Juan de la Cruz 337)

In this stanza the poet refers on one level, of course, to the *tela* of human flesh, broken only by death, that keeps the soul from its union with God. On another level, however, the breach of the *tela* symbolizes the rupture of the hymen associated with the act of sexual consummation, as José Nieto (108 n. 56) and Willis Barnstone (185) have suggested.[29]

It is difficult to imagine that Unamuno could have written the following lines of his *Cristo de Velázquez* (1920) without the imagery of San Juan's "Llama de amor viva":

> ¡Blanca llama de fuego que devora,
> hoguera del amor: como a la enjuta
> yesca mi corazón entero abrasa;
> mi carne de pecado se consuma,
> y hágale pavesas tu restregón! (828–32)

---

28. Also Matt. 26.6–13; Mark 14.3–9; and John 12.1–8.
29. For a rebuttal of this reading, still controversial among traditional critics, see Ynduráin 211–12.

Later in the same poem, in a section devoted to the power of Christ's "verija," Unamuno allegorizes, based on the relationship of Jesus and Mary, an Adam-and-Eve scenario:

> De la Eva de la gracia, Madre Virgen,
> en las entrañas Tú, Adán de gracia,
> carne de padre pecador, tomando
> virgen la diste de la cruz al lecho.
> Y engendraste al morir. Cristo, tu muerte
> fué lo que te hizo padre de la vida
> de la gracia, tu muerte la primicia
> de tu virilidad; con ella al cabo
> la Humanidad esposa conociste
> y su esposo de sangre te obligaste. (2163–68)

Thus the idea of Jesus' passion, both in the Bible and in more secular literary texts, including Unamuno's own poetry, inevitably suggests the element of erotic desire. In this sense Fedra's "pasión desnuda," epitomized in the highly ambiguous "beso de fuego en lágrimas," casts her in the role of a modern Christ figure, tempted by the sins of the flesh in the figure of Hipólito.

These associations are confirmed in the last act of the play. After Fedra repents of having accused Hipólito, whom Pedro promptly banished from the house, she decides to give her life to restore the truth and repair the relationship between father and son: "Quiero que se abracen padre e hijo sobre mi recuerdo" (224; 3.1). María Dolores de Asís Garrote points to Unamuno's attempt to "poner en correlación frases del Evangelio claramente referidas a la redención que realiza Jesús, con la situación de la protagonista: La muerte voluntaria de Fedra con la muerte de Jesús" (361). In effect, Fedra emphasizes the pain associated with her sacrifice, comparing it to Jesus': "Jesús mío, maestro del dolor, tú con el dolor me has dado la fe salvadora. Nunca hubiese creído que en vaso tan frágil como cuerpo de mujer cabría tanto dolor sin hacerle pedazos" (225; 3.1). The pain comes from the desire that she feels toward Hipólito, but it is a pain that, like Jesus' suffering, carries with it the power of redemption. In this way Unamuno rechannels the purely destructive power of Phaedra's desire in Euripides, Seneca, and Racine into a constructive, Christian model.

Even so, there is something not quite right, in strictly Christian terms, about the last act of the play. Fedra makes an issue out of dying in pureness and truth but does so in a passage that again evokes her mother's kisses: "Sí, murió pura, besándome. Y yo moriré pura también. Sólo la verdad purifica. Todo lo verdadero y lo verdadero solo es limpio. Si no me presento con la verdad, ¿cómo me admitirán en el cielo y me perdonarán lo mucho que he pecado en gracia a lo mucho que he amado?" (224; 3.1; cf. Luke 7.47). Given the ambivalence of the "beso de fuego en lágrimas," Fedra's association of this gesture with pureness and truth is highly problematic. Similarly so is her insistence that Hipólito come one last time to see her on her deathbed. She seems to have planned the whole scene, in fact, to lure him back: "¡Vendrá, sí, vendrá!" she exults to Eustaquia after revealing her plan (225; 3.1). Hipólito arrives as summoned and enters Fedra's bedroom (231; 3.10), but Unamuno ends the scene at this point and deprives the spectators of the content of their visit. One is left only to conjecture whether she managed to coax out of him the final kiss that she had been dying for. André Rombout chastises her for this behavior and questions her sincerity: "Le spectateur est en droit de se demander si le véritable sacrifice n'aurait pas été, après avoir écrit la lettre d'aveu et pris le poison, de se priver justement de la vue et du baiser d'Hipólito et de prier non pas pour que vienne celui-ci mais pour obtenir, par un repentir sincère, le pardon du péché" (55). Significantly, when Pedro comes out of Fedra's room, he reports that she is delirious and that "ni pudo siquiera darme el beso de despedida" (233; 3.14), as if she had exerted her last forces on Hipólito. Rombout concludes: "Que Fedra soit devenue chez Miguel de Unamuno une héroïne espagnole, il serait difficile de ne pas en convenir. Que sa conduite soit celle que commande une foi profonde et une juste valorisation des conditions du Pardon à une croyante, rien, à la réflexion, ne semble moins sûr après l'analyse du personnage de Fedra et de la phase finale du mythe dans l'interprétation unamunienne" (56). The problem is compounded by the fact that Fedra reveals the truth only after she dies, in a letter composed to Pedro. This rather cowardly act attenuates the nobility of her sacrifice, as Eustaquia points out: "El sacrificio habría sido decir la verdad, toda la verdad" (225; 3.1).

Eustaquia's statement poses a final disconcerting question that must be addressed regarding the ending of the play: What exactly is the "truth" that Fedra seeks to restore and is willing to die for? If Hipólito's innocence is indeed called into question in González del Valle's analysis, with which I concur in the present reading, then the truth for which the protagonist gives her life is suspect at best. Unamuno's technique once again seems to coincide with that of Galdós's *Electra*, this time in the dramatization of a radical epistemology that disrupts the play's sense of perfect closure ostensibly achieved through the pardon of Fedra and the reunion of Pedro and Hipólito, who, unlike his classical predecessors, survives his father's wrath.

This contradictory and unsettling ending may be explained in several ways. In the first place, contradiction is the defining feature of Unamuno's thought and personality, as he himself explains in his well-known *Del sentimiento trágico de la vida* (1913):

> Alguien podrá ver un fondo de contradicción en todo cuanto voy diciendo, anhelando unas veces la vida inatacable, y diciendo otras que esta vida no tiene el valor que se le da. ¿Contradicción? ¡Ya lo creo! ¡La de mi corazón, que dice sí, y mi cabeza, que dice no! Contradicción, naturalmente. ¿Quién no recuerda aquellas palabras del Evangelio: "¡Señor, creo; ayuda a mi incredulidad!"? ¡Contradicción!, ¡naturalmente! Como que sólo vivimos de contradicciones, y por ellas; como que la vida es tragedia, y la tragedia es perpetua lucha, sin victoria ni esperanza de ella; es contradicción. (31)

Here, as elsewhere, the central problem in Unamuno's work is the perennial conflict of reason ("la cabeza") and faith ("el corazón"), a conflict that produces the enigma of existence as he defines it. This contradiction is similar to the one that Fedra experiences: her reason and virtue tell her that her desires toward Hipólito are improper, but her instincts only confirm those desires, in which her entire being is invested. Several critics have seen the piece as emblematic of the "sentimiento trágico de la vida."[30] It should not be surprising, then, that a play founded upon the contradiction of human existence should leave its spectators with a sense of unease even as it appears to tie together all the loose ends.

In the second place, the unsettling ending of the play analyzed in this reading works to upset the bourgeois values of the contemporary theatergoers whose influence Unamuno considered so baneful. Nothing more effective than the theme of incest to achieve this goal. Barbieri believes that Unamuno minimizes the element of incest found in the myth in favor of the theme of unrequited love (43), but a close reading of the text demonstrates that, on the contrary, the incest theme is significant

---

30. Lázaro 19–20; Zavala, *Unamuno* 53; Anderson 54; Franco 156; Dolores de Asís 343.

throughout, embodied in the suggestive image of the kiss. Although Fedra and Hipólito are not actually related by blood, the symbolic value of their relationship is undeniable, as demonstrated by Pedro's shocked reaction to Fedra's revelation: "Pero hijo, Hipólito, ¿cómo te has atrevido a poner ojos ... ojos, y labios en tu *madre*?" (215; 2.6; my emphasis). Furthermore, the fact that Unamuno sets his play in "un ambiente burgués de comienzo del siglo," as Dolores de Asís describes it (353), forces the spectators to contemplate the violation of a tremendous taboo by characters who clearly represent their peers.

Shaw suggests that Unamuno, like Ibsen, uses the incest theme "to shock audiences into reconsidering their moral presuppositions" ("Three Plays" 258). Additionally, the incest theme seems to be a point of departure for a probing inquiry into the meaning of existence. Thus, although he reorients the desires of the classical model into a supposedly Christian framework of redemption, the result is highly unorthodox, perhaps even heretical, and probably not comforting to attentive Christian readers. Rather than feed the spectators an opium in the guise of accepted truths, the play's ambiguity presents them with an element of radical doubt that forces them to confront issues that they might prefer to ignore. This philosophy lies at the core of Unamuno's personal brand of Christianity, founded not on the premise of belief but on the paradox of doubt (cf. *Del sentimiento* 122).

J. I. Ciruelo observes that Fedra incarnates "las virtudes cristianas en lucha con los instintos" (65), and, similarly, several other critics have suggested that she is caught between the forces of biological predetermination and Catholic free will.[31] The present analysis would suggest that the epistemological division of the play is not so simplistic. Quite to the contrary, like the confusion of maternal and erotic sentiments problematized in the image of the kiss, the lines between choice and destiny, between innocence and guilt, between truth and falsehood, are far from fixed.

It would thus seem plausible that Unamuno not only read Galdós's *Electra* but was inspired by its revision of desire as a means of questioning bourgeois ideology and reviving the languishing theater of the time. In *Fedra*, as elsewhere, the Salamancan lacks true originality but proves himself to be ingenious in the art of literary borrowing.[32] Yet, despite the

---

31. Mesa 244; López Caballero 432–33; Lasso, *"Fedra"* 237; García Viñó 447–48; Dolores de Asís 353.

32. For example, Unamuno's celebrated novel *Niebla* bears an undeniable resemblance to Galdós's *El amigo Manso*. His chief work of nonfiction prose, *Del sentimiento trágico de la vida*,

play's lack of complete originality, the preeminent position of its author in twentieth-century Spanish letters makes it an important chapter in the use of classical myth in the prewar period.

From Object to Subject: Fetishism and Autonomy in Jacinto Grau's *El señor de Pigmalión*

Jacinto Grau represents a much more original, although lesser-known, chapter in this time period. The Barcelona-born playwright is noteworthy, like Galdós and Unamuno before him, for his unflinching condemnation of mediocrity on the Spanish stage, which he considered to be a result of the priority given to economic rather than artistic concerns: "Pero el teatro simulador de arte, con pseudo literatura y trucos y frases hechas y viejas recetas torpemente renovadas, de manida cocina escénica, es un agobio, porque es siempre un reflejo espiritual de lo más opuesto al espíritu, a la curiosidad y a la inquietud, o sea del vulgarísimo empresario, un buen señor que lo desconoce todo, incluso la mercancía con que trafica y cuyos asesores suelen ser profesionales de bajo teatro, periodistas sin letras, currinches de bastidores y todo lo más negado y vulgar que pueda temerse" (8). Unfortunately, although Grau, unlike Galdós and Unamuno, devoted his entire career to the theater, his many plays brought him little more success in his native country than Unamuno enjoyed as a dramatist. Instead, his uncompromising view of dramatic art led him to resign himself to the page rather than the stage, as his bitter words demonstrate: "A nosotros nos parece que esta viciosísima y estúpida constitución teatral que padecemos, lleva consigo su penitencia y que todo teatro digno de vivir se perpetúa en el libro, del que pasa fatalmente al teatro, cuando el teatro existe. Mientras no exista, basta el libro para conservarlo. Y cuando es auténtico ese teatro, como el vino, crece en fuerza con los años" (10).

The stubborn self-confidence that these sentences reveal, driven by an

---

owes a substantial debt to Kierkegaardian thought, as the copious references to the Danish philosopher within the text demonstrate. Any claim of originality for the character San Manuel Bueno in the novella that bears his name is undermined by a consideration of Dostoevsky's Grand Inquisitor figure in *The Brothers Karamazov*. Finally, much of Unamuno's finest lyric poetry is heavily inspired by the works of Juan de la Cruz and Luis de León, as the earlier discussion has indicated.

ego that apparently prompted Grau to dub himself Shakespeare's only peer (García Lorenzo, Introducción 14), placed him in virtual oblivion as a dramatist during his lifetime. Posthumously, however, Grau's reputation, as does the wine he so prophetically mentions, has grown in force with the years, and academic critics have recently begun to recognize him as one of the major figures of the Spanish avant-garde theater.[33]

Like Galdós, Grau turned, in his most widely read play, to classical mythology to realize his artistic goals.[34] *El señor de Pigmalión: farsa tragicómica de hombres y muñecos en tres actos y un prólogo* is a lengthy work in which a group of lifelike stage puppets rebels against and ultimately kills its puppeteer, the protagonist of the play, who calls himself Pigmalión.[35] The name is apparently an alias that the protagonist has assumed in conscious acknowledgment of his mythic prototype, "el famoso rey de Chipre, cuyo nombre he tomado ..." (174; J1.10).[36] Thus the title of the play cannot but point to one of the work's principal classical referents: *Metamorphoses* 10.243–97. Even so, those critics who mention the Ovidian source do so only superficially or clumsily. Some abandon the subject completely after an obligatory first reference to the "myth of Pygmalion and Galatea," as if the tale were standardized, while in fact Pygmalion's statue remains unnamed in the Ovidian narrative and throughout the ancient tradition; still others doubt the importance of classical sources in

---

33. For synthesizing views of Grau's theater, see Estévez Ortega; M. J. González; Giuliano, "The Life and Works" and Introduction; O. Fernández; Pérez Minik, *Debates* 141–59; León; Schwartz; Rodríguez Salcedo; Valbuena Prat, "El teatro"; Kronik; Simches; Ezell; Winecoff Díaz; García Lorenzo, *El teatro español* 58–60 and Introducción; Navascués; Ruiz Ramón, *Historia . . . siglo XX* 140–55. Sources that focus on *El señor de Pigmalión* will be cited as necessary.

34. It is worth noting that Grau expressed "in an otherwise undistinguished lecture . . . wholehearted admiration for the plays of Galdós—their style, their characters, their power and depth, their spirit of protest" (Kronik, "Art" 264n).

35. The text was first published in 1921 (Madrid, Yagües) and revised in 1928 for the journal *La Farsa*. The third Losada edition used for the basis of this study is "presumably the last one authorized by Grau before he died in 1958" (Dougherty 356 n. 4). The play was not performed in Spain until its debut in the Teatro Cómico of Madrid in 1928 (for a review, see Díez-Canedo 2:177–82). In the meantime, its translations enjoyed great success on the European stage, including the Théâtre de l'Atelier of Paris in 1923 (dir. Dullin), the National Theater of Prague in 1925 (dir. Čapek), and the Teatro d'Arte of Rome (dir. Pirandello, date uncertain). It was also well received in Germany, Holland, Poland, and Scandinavia (Simches 149).

36. The notation "J1" refers to the "Jornada Primera" in order to distinguish it from the main acts of the play, which will be cited, as usual, with arabic numerals only.

the play, preferring to emphasize Grau's kinship to such contemporary authors as Unamuno, Pirandello, and Čapek.[37]

A careful reading of *El señor de Pigmalión* reveals a different state of affairs. Not only does the narrative of Pygmalion play a major role in the work, but it is also complemented by the classical tale of Prometheus. Together, the two mythical subtexts create an intricate play-universe in which desire is dramatized in a way that problematizes subjectivity and the distinctions between fantasy and reality and that ultimately critiques the profit-driven valorization of popular over intrinsically meaningful art.

The tale of Prometheus is referred to directly in the play but is ignored, except in passing, by all critics except Navascués (*El teatro* 104–5). The first reference comes in act 1, in an exchange between Pigmalión and the duke of Alducara, owner of the theater in which the puppets are to perform: "Duque.—Es usted un nuevo Prometeo. Pigmalión.—Exactamente. Y quizás me castiguen un día los dioses, como al propio Prometeo" (185; 1.2). Grau's allusion to the story of Prometheus is as problematic as it is significant. Because the few critics of the play who mention the Prometheus myth have given incomplete or misleading accounts (Navascués, *El teatro* 105; Giuliano, Introduction 57 n. 4), a brief review of the tale in the classical period will prove useful.

The ancient accounts of the tale clash on Prometheus's mortal status and his relationship to humanity. The oldest written versions, Hesiod's *Theogony* 521–602 and *Works and Days* 47–104, portray Prometheus, son of the Titan Iapetus, as a trickster figure who attempts to dupe Zeus into accepting an unfair apportionment of a sacrificial meal (see above, Chapter 3, n. 40). In retaliation, Zeus withholds fire from mortals, only to have it stolen back by Prometheus. As an even greater punishment, the king of the gods binds Prometheus to a pillar where an eagle makes daily visits to feed off the hero's liver until he is finally freed by Heracles. In the mean-

---

37. References to Galatea are made by Díez-Canedo 2:179; M. J. Gónzalez 27; Giuliano, "Life and Works" 143; Navascués, *El teatro* 96; Kaiser-Lenoir 15; and Segel 137. Winecoff Díaz believes that Grau subordinates the Pygmalion story to "other elements of the play" (216), while Navascués denies the myth's importance altogether (*El teatro* 96 and "Fantasy" 268). For discussions of Grau's similarities to Unamuno, Pirandello, and Čapek, see Monner Sans 73–76; Giuliano, "Life and Works" 143–46; León; García Lorenzo, Introducción 93–96; Standish; and Segel 137. Any arguments for the influence of these contemporary authors on Grau should be read alongside Rodríguez Salcedo's caveat: "Estas relaciones, a mi juicio, aunque justificadas, no deben hacer olvidar que gran parte del teatro de aquella época se preocupaba por la independencia de la criatura artística" (36).

time, Zeus devises a bane for Prometheus's beloved race of mortals: he fashions the temptress Pandora out of clay and introduces the scourge of woman into the heretofore exclusively male race.

In these accounts, although Prometheus is clearly immortal (since he is able to endure his horrific torture without dying), he nevertheless appears as a quasi-human figure because of his sympathy for and frequent association with the human race. In the fifth-century *Prometheus Bound* attributed to Aeschylus (there are those who dispute its authorship: see Howatson and Chilvers 451), the protagonist is portrayed even more sympathetically. The sacrificial hoax and the Pandora incident go unmentioned; instead, Prometheus states that he is being punished for attempting to save the human race from destruction and for improving its quality of life, not only through fire, which has been interpreted as the "material basis of civilisation" in the myth (Thomson 297–98), but also through the development of skills or crafts (*technai*, v. 506). In later authors, Prometheus's identification with humanity becomes so complete that he is sometimes credited with being the actual creator of the human race, as in Hyginus (125; *fabula* 142) and Apollodorus (1:50–51; 1.7.1). The latter claims, in addition, that the hero was mortal until Zeus permitted him to acquire the immortality of Chiron (1:192–93; 2.5.4).[38]

The constant in all these variations is Prometheus's acting in alliance with mortals—whether or not he counts himself as one of them—against a cruel and dangerous god in a young, rapidly changing universe. This conception lies at the heart of the comparison made between Pigmalión and Prometeo in *El señor de Pigmalión*. As Navascués notes, "Pigmalión comparte la actitud rebelde de Prometeo y su deseo de mejorar la raza humana" (105). Furthermore, the variant of the Prometheus myth in which the hero creates human beings emphasizes even more his similarity to the renowned sculptor of Ovidian fame.

Rodríguez Salcedo characterizes *El señor de Pigmalión* as a drama based on interpersonal relations (20). The two myths, when read together in the way Grau juxtaposes them, indeed illuminate several complementary sets of relations, although "interpersonal" is perhaps not the most precise term to refer to them. Just as the story of Prometheus illustrates the relationship between a god and his creation, humanity, the tale of Pygmalion describes that existing between a specific human and his own creation,

---

38. On the issue of Prometheus as creator of humanity, Ovid prefers to let the reader decide. See *Met.* 1.78–83.

which is multiplied, in Grau's version of the tale, into seventeen separate creations. Masquerading as both a Prometeo and a Pigmalión, the protagonist of the play—whose real name is unknown, it must be remembered—forms the nexus of a mini-universe in which desire is played out along four separate sets of axes.[39] The first two—puppet-puppet and puppet-human—are implied in the Pygmalion story and simultaneously mirrored in the second two sets—human-human and human-god—which are encoded in the narrative of Prometheus.

The relations among the puppets occur at the deepest level of the fictional universe created by the play. Designed by Pigmalión to imitate and eventually to supplant stage actors, the marionettes are perpetual role-players whose "true" identities are defined by their stage identities, in much the same way that their master's true identity remains suppressed in favor of the mythic selves that he has assumed. The puppets' personalities are, according to Pigmalión himself, grotesque and represent various Spanish folkloric figures (175; J1.10). As such, they incarnate humankind's basest and weakest of instincts (Navascués, *El teatro* 107) and create an arena for the manifestation of strongly conflicting sexual and aggressive desires.

These desires are dramatized to the fullest in the first scene of act 2, when the human characters have departed and the stage remains bare except for the seventeen cream-colored boxes that house the puppets. The action begins when the puppet Juan, nicknamed "el tonto," opens his box and looks out with curiosity (209). The most "primitive" of the dolls, Juan is capable of uttering only one syllable, "cu," which, as Pigmalión explains earlier in the play, imitates the simple mechanism of a cuckoo clock (187; 1.3). It is the role of the cuckoo bird that Juan assumes in this scene, as he peers out of his box and announces with his "cu, cu" the passage of time that has cleared the stage for his companions. Since Juan is the first puppet that the audience sees acting autonomously, and since the others respond to his announcement, he functions, in a way, as their leader.

One by one, the other marionettes begin to emerge from their boxes and to act out their minidrama. The first to appear is Mingo Revulgo, "el

---

39. Although the protagonist is referred to as Pigmalión or "el señor Pigmalión" within the play, the title of the work inserts a prepositional *de* between the title and name. The preposition functions as a subtle distancing effect that betrays the character's play-status: he is not really Pigmalión but "of Pigmalión" or "Pigmalión-like." Pigmalión, in effect, is a fictional entity whose "real" identity is forever hidden by various masks of theatricality.

más rudo y soez de los muñecos," according to Claudina Kaiser-Lenoir (15). Mingo's comic-sounding name evokes the satirical "Coplas de Mingo Revulgo" that lampooned the government of Enrique IV of Castile (1454–74), and his "cara gorda y vulgarísima" and "panza pronunciada" (191; 1.3) cannot but recall the typical Spanish folkloric character best embodied in the figure of Sancho Panza. In addition, the name alludes to the phrase "más galán que Mingo," current in Cervantes's time and used, for example, in *Quijote* 2.73 (qtd. in Montoto 2:203), and it thus announces the puppet's role as one of the suitors or *galanes* of the beautiful Pomponina.

This role is confirmed when Mingo runs to Pomponina's box and, shaking a bag of coins to entice her, announces, "¡Te espero en mi caja!" (210). Unable to resist the lure of money and the power that it represents, Pomponina creeps out of her box and rushes to Mingo's, into which he abruptly pulls her and slams the cover shut. Grau playfully leaves the readers to their imagination to surmise what the resulting "vibraciones como de reloj de cuerda, que se descompusiese al dar la hora" (210, stage directions) might signify in puppet etiquette. The ever vigilant Juan's "cu, cu" provides the only commentary on the flurry of activity.

The main segment of the puppets' play-within-the-play begins when Pomponina's handsome page, Don Lindo, emerges from his box to find, in his mistress's absence, the taunting insinuations of Juan, who "con su eterno aire de cretino malicioso, llevándose ante él ambas manos a la cabeza e imitando con el índice los cuernos," utters his perennial "cu, cu" (213, stage directions). Furious at the suggestion of infidelity, Don Lindo runs to Pomponina's crate only to find it empty. Finally accepting the dreaded truth, he goes to Mingo's box, where he tearfully pleads for Pomponina to open and rejoin him.

Unfortunately for Don Lindo, another incident occurs that brings him even greater ridicule. The pockmarked, one-eyed Lucas Gómez emerges from his crate to smoke a cigar. Don Lindo, wanting privacy with which to woo back Pomponina, demands that he leave. When Lucas refuses, the page threatens him with a sword. Unwilling to submit to the threats, Lucas, having learned from Pedro de Urdemalas, the cleverest of the puppets, that Lindo's lovely blond hair is a wig, quickly snatches it off to reveal a bare head, "completamente mocha y lisa como una bola de billar" (215, stage directions). Lucas then darts back to his box and seals himself inside, taunting Lindo all the way and calling for Pomponina to come out and contemplate the humiliated page.

Lindo decides to avenge himself on Urdemalas, "que tiene la culpa de todo, por decir al esperpento de Lucas Gómez, si llevo o no postizo el cabello ... ¡Venganza, venganza! ¡Con Urdemalas empezaré a ajustar mis cuentas!" (217). Urdemalas quickly invents a chain of events to exonerate himself: "Ha sido Pero Grullo, que se enteró ayer también, casualmente, como yo, y le fué con el cuento a Periquito entre ellas, que a su vez se lo ha contado a Lucas Gómez" (218). Before Lindo can track down the offenders, Pomponina appears and forces him back to his crate out of fear that she might see him without his hairpiece, even though several other of the puppets have already shared in the spectacle. Pomponina and Urdemalas end the scene by commenting wryly on Lindo's jealousy: "Pomponina.—Yo lo calmo en seguida con una carantoña. Urdemalas.—Qué duda cabe. Lo tienes aquí (*Alzando y moviendo el índice*), enligado completamente" (219). In a later scene, Lindo is subjected to more public humiliation as Pomponina's four maidens corner and taunt him: "Motilón, motilón, motilón" (226; 2.4).

Grau's handling of the puppets in these scenes serves various ends. As Harold Segel has shown, the sudden interest in puppet literature and theater in the early twentieth century attests to attempts by progressive artists to unite several tendencies in opposition to bourgeois tastes: a spurning of traditional genres, a concentration on popular culture, and a predilection for the youthful and prerational perspective of children, all of which are anticipated in Collodi's novel *Pinocchio* (Segel 36–43). Sharing the avant-garde's contempt for bourgeois culture, Grau was naturally led to embrace the puppet figure as a means of subverting the conventional stage he deplored. In one sense, then, the marionettes' characterizations in these scenes, together with Pigmalión's various references to them as "polichinelas," indicate a return to the stock characters of the commedia dell'arte. Pigmalión states, in fact, that in creating his puppets he was inspired by the "máscaras de la comedia italiana, unas de cera pintada, otras de seda, y algunas de gasa extendida sobre hilos de alambre" (177; J1.10).

Yet it should be apparent in the context of this study that the episode just described is also a farcical rendition of the typical *comedia de honor* of the classical Spanish theater. All the ingredients—infidelity, jealousy, public dishonor, and the quest for vengeance—are present in highly stylized form. Pomponina's brazenness, for example, caricatures the unsatisfied wife of the *comedia* who can only dream of extramarital encounters, as in Calderón's *El médico de su honra*. In addition, Juan's capacity as public sentinel casts him squarely in the role of the collective consciousness of the *comedia* that shapes and defines a man's reputation or *honra*. His initial accusation of "cu, cu," which in this context recalls the cuckoo bird's more notorious traditional characteristic, begins the process of dishonor.[40] Lindo's dishonor is compounded by the public revelation that his hair, a mark of his *hombría* (like the traditional nobleman's beard or moustache), is false. Urdemalas's account of how the knowledge is spread, whether genuine or apocryphal, provides a condensed example of the way in which rumor can so quickly destroy a man's *honra*. Finally, the female puppets' chants of "motilón" represent the anonymous chorus of seventeenth-century society that ostracized anyone who did not conform to its standards of conduct and appearance.

Through the puppets' relations among themselves Grau thus revives the vivid desires of Spanish legend and folklore, whose dramatization in stylized form calls attention to the absence of authentic desire on the contemporary stage. It is important to note that the puppets, who are designed to be actors, are themselves played by the real-world actors of the play *El señor de Pigmalión*. This curious situation produces an effect similar to that which Kaiser-Lenoir (15), referring to a different aspect of the play, identifies as an inversion of Platonic mimesis, that is, life (the real-world actors) imitating art (the puppets) rather than the reverse. The implication becomes clear: the current stage is so devoid of authentic emotion that only by making the theater its own referent, in the passion-driven plots of the *comedia*, can desire be restored to its rightful place. As Pérez Minik observes, a jump toward "un nuevo teatro nunca podía reducirse a representar una situación similar a la del teatro griego o a la del renacentista. Es decir, a escenificar unos mitos de procedencia legendaria o política, desprendidos de una naturaleza histórica nacional. El único mito accesible a la conciencia actual era el del teatro mismo" (*Debates* 149). Grau's dramatization of the classical, non-Hispanic myth of Pygmalion is thus ultimately aimed at restoring the vitality of the native Spanish theatrical tradition.

The second set of relations implied in the Pygmalion myth, that which is developed between puppets and humans, is initially manifested as a typical relationship between artist and work of art. Pigmalión explains how, "entre anhelos y fiebres" (173; J1.10), he first conceived of his idea

---

40. The cuckoo bird is known for its habit of laying its eggs in another bird's nest; hence the English *cuckold*, derived from the Old French *cucuault*.

of creating the puppets: "Viendo todo eso, nació en mí la idea de crear artificialmente el actor ideal, mecánico, sin vanidad, sin rebeldías, sumiso al poeta creador, como la masa en los dedos de los escultores. . . . Luego, leyendo en la Enciclopedia de Edimburgo, fuí más lejos en mi propósito, y me tentó el deseo de sobrepujar a la mecánica, y producir muñecos-criaturas, de un barro sensible y complicado como el humano" (177; J1.10). Pigmalión's description reveals the creative imagination of the artist as it transforms, in Jungian fashion, its libidinal energies—"anhelos y fiebres"—into the desired product (see Jung 142–70). The abundance of tactile imagery, which goes on to describe in detail the physical composition of the puppets, both alludes to the central image of the artist as sculptor and anticipates the manifestation of Pigmalión's desires in a decidedly erotic form.

It comes as no surprise, then, when Pigmalión confesses that he is "locamente enamorado de una muñeca, como tantos hombres, sólo que ellos no saben que adoran una muñeca, y yo sí lo sé" (176; J1.10). This comment, which at first glance appears somewhat enigmatic, is significant for several reasons. In the first place, it clearly confirms the Ovidian subtext, in which the sculptor "miratur et haurit / pectore . . . simulati corporis ignes" 'looks on in astonishment as his chest fills with passion for the graven image' (*Met.* 10.252–53). In this context, Pigmalión's comment may be interpreted as a recognition on the part of the protagonist that all sexual desire is ultimately objectifying or destructive, confirming Kessel Schwartz's judgment of Grau's work as a dramatization of the "annihilating quality of sexual desire" (35). In Lacanian terms, one might say that the object of desire, no matter how beloved, can never transcend the subjectivity of an inanimate *muñeca/o* insofar as it can never be fully attained. This extreme view of love, with its subtle suggestions of fetishism, is Grau's contribution to the radicalization of desire that in Galdós and Unamuno takes the form of incest and that in all three authors is clearly aimed at overturning the conventions of the entrenched bourgeois theater.

The relations that the other human characters maintain with the puppets are equally important. When the duke of Alducara, for example, first sees Pomponina, he is instantly overpowered by the same desire that Pigmalión feels toward her. From this moment on his motives change from those of the curious art aficionado to those of the serious collector, so to speak. He bribes the porter into helping him secure time alone with Pomponina (206; 1.7) and then bribes Pomponina into escaping from the theater with him: "Te compraré las piedras preciosas mejores de la tierra; te haré fabricar carrozas de oro y plata, y *autos* eléctricos y silenciosos, con camarines de ébano y palo de rosa, y tendrás mil criados, y serás libre y reina en el mundo" (223–24; 2.3). Unable to resist the promise of riches, which earlier had lured her into the box of Mingo Revulgo, Pomponina escapes with Alducara through the stage window to the outside world, where she is soon followed by the other puppets.

The puppets' interaction with the human duke thus brings about their escape from the stage, an act that is analogous in several ways to Venus's animation of the Ovidian Pygmalion's statue. In the first place, the stage perimeter serves as a kind of ontological prison wall for the puppets. Once they cross it, they take the first step toward gaining the humanity granted to the statue. In the second place, desire is the motivating force behind the puppets' liberation. Just as the Latin Pygmalion's passion for the statue moved Venus, goddess of desire, to animate it with life, Alducara's desire for Pomponina achieves the goal of freedom and humanity for the puppets.

The more time the puppets spend away from the stage and in the presence of humans, the more autonomy they gain and the more humanlike they become. Their transition to human consciousness is exquisitely emblematized at the beginning of act 3, in a scene in which the duke and Pomponina have hidden themselves away in a shack at the side of the highway. The contrast between the two characters is telling. While Alducara fights to contain his erotic desire for his new companion and, finally losing control, attempts to embrace her in a fit of passion (235; 3.1), Pomponina displays an innocence that befits her fledgling humanity. Expressing puzzlement about why she should not be allowed to be seen naked in public, she loses herself in the contemplation of her own image and is unable to stop gazing at herself in a small hand mirror. Although Pomponina's vanity is evident from the beginning of the play and this occasion is not the first in which she observes herself in a mirror, it is certainly the most salient instance and, as such, deserves explanation.

Pomponina's behavior in this scene corresponds to the primary narcissism of the small child, described fifteen years after the first publication of Grau's play, in Jacques Lacan's now classic essay on the "mirror stage": "We have only to understand the mirror stage *as an identification*, in the full sense that analysis gives to that term: namely, the transformation that takes place in the [infantile] subject when he assumes an image.... The *mirror stage* is a drama whose internal thrust is precipitated from insufficiency to anticipation . . . and, lastly, to the assumption of the armour of an alienating identity, which will mark with its rigid structure the subject's entire mental development" (2, 4). The mirror stage is a necessary and inevitable step toward the Lacanian order of the Symbolic (see above, Chapter 1, pages 16–17) and thus toward the acquisition of selfhood, and Pomponina's actions in this scene indicate that she is well on her way to that end.

The full maturation of the puppets occurs in the final scenes, when they are reunited with their creator. The sobering proof that they have become human is found in their acquisition of violent desires. In this sentiment the puppets are led by Pedro de Urdemalas, the remarkably shrewd character ("tan inteligente como yo," Pigmalión affirms [193; 1.3]) of Cervantine lineage whom one critic describes as a "personification of Satan" (Ezell 185). This characterization is something of an exaggeration, however, since Urdemalas has learned everything he knows from Pigmalión. Indeed, in addition to his amorous desires toward Pomponina, Pigmalión displays toward the other puppets nothing short of tyrannical behavior, exemplified in brutish and unnecessary acts of aggression. This conduct becomes evident as he gives the managers their first glimpse of the puppets. When Juan refuses to be silent, for example, he pulls him roughly by the ears (187–88; 1.3), and, later, when the puppets escape, he comes after them with a whip that he does not hesitate to use.

It is appropriate, then, that the puppets' rebellion should turn increasingly violent. Their trend toward aggression builds steadily throughout act 3. First they overpower Julia, the duke's scorned paramour, and shove her into a back room of the cabin where she has locked up Alducara (242–43; 3.5). In all their actions they are led by Urdemalas, who now assumes the role of Pigmalión. "¡Idiotas!" he shouts at the others. "¡Mereceríais que os abandonase a vuestra esclava suerte! ¡Callad y obedecedme!" which leads to the Enano's disconcerted reply, "¡Qué déspota! ¡Habla ya lo mismo que Pigmalión!" (246–47; 3.6). Urdemalas explains his transformation to Don Lindo when asked what the puppets must do: "El mal ... Hagamos el mal, purificador mal, justo mal. ¿Qué ha hecho Pigmalión con nosotros? Hacernos muy mal, de puro querer hacernos muy bien. La prueba, que prepara otros muñecos mejores, que, cuando estén acabados nos sustituirán y nos destruirán. Al mal, pues mayor mal. Destruyamos a Pigmalión aquí mismo, antes que un día nos destruyan a nosotros" (245; 3.6). The puppets' steady progression from the play antics performed in their farces to their arguably justified actions toward Julia (she was threatening Pomponina) to the calculated contemplation of murder is vividly emblematized in the shotgun that Urdemalas finds on the wall of the shack. Realizing its potential, he comments slyly to his companion Ambrosio: "Esta cosa me parece un poco mejor que tu carabina de las farsas, Ambrosio. Está cargada, y no es fácil que esté llena de pólvora sola, como las que empleamos en el teatro" (245; 3.6). Play violence is soon to turn real as the puppets prepare to commit their first irreversible act of aggression since gaining autonomy.

When Pigmalión arrives to round up the puppets, he shows that he has vastly underestimated what their escape from the stage implies. He apparently believes that the autonomy and humanity they have achieved are measurable quantities that can simply be reversed by returning them to the theater. His statements to Urdemalas reveal an ignorance that will prove to be his downfall:

> Pues creí que te habría dado más listeza. Rebelaros contra mí es tan inútil como escaparos. Yo soy el hombre, el fuerte, el amo, el creador. Vosotros sois mis juguetes, mis peleles, mis bufones ... ¡Nada! ¡Tan míos sois como esta fusta con que os azoto! (*Dales otro latigazo. Menos Urdemalas, quéjanse todos, doloridos, arrimándose más a la pared.*) Yo haré muy en breve algo mejor que el hombre; pero vosotros no sois todavía más que polichinelas de mi teatro, capricho ingenioso de mi fantasía y habilidad de mecánico, esclavos míos, en fin. ¡Sois un prodigio, y no sois nada!

Urdemalas's reply aptly demonstrates his confident knowledge that he is now his creator's equal: "Como tú. Tanto orgullo y eres un efímero, y acabarás también en nada, como todos los hombres" (251; 3.9). When Pigmalión orders the puppets into the car, Urdemalas fires the shotgun at him from close range.

Urdemalas is not the only one to seize the day with his newly acquired autonomy. After he orders the puppets into the car and the sound of the motor fades into the distance, Juan emerges from a hiding place in the cabin. As Pigmalión, who is gravely injured but not yet dead, lies on the floor grasping for life and lamenting his attempt to "superar al ser humano," Juan approaches and announces himself with his previously benign "cu, cu" (254; 3.10). Yet instead of complying when Pigmalión asks him for help, he calmly lifts the shotgun and finishes off his former master with a swift blow to the head. With this act Juan not only definitively liberates himself and the other puppets from the tyranny of their creator but also shows that even he, supposedly the most primitive of Pigmalión's creations, has been invested with the will necessary to carry out the acts of aggression that are a defining characteristic of humanity. In contrast to the stupidity that Ruiz Ramón identifies with him (*Historia . . . siglo XX* 148), Juan, in the best Shakespearian tradition, shows that his foolishness runs only skin deep and that he is in fact indispensable not only to his community of peers but also, literally, to the inner rhythm of the play itself, measured by the beat of his "cu"s.

The basic thematic similarity between Grau's version of the Pygmalion myth and the Ovidian narrative should be apparent: the creation and adoration of an artistic masterpiece. In addition, the self-conscious nature of Grau's work, best represented in the play-within-the-play performed by the puppets, has a clear precedent in the Ovidian myth, which comprises part of the song of Orpheus and thus constitutes a subnarration within the larger frame of books 10–11 of the *Metamorphoses*.

The most important differences between Grau's version of the Pygmalion myth and the Ovidian narrative are either necessitated by the great disparity in length between the two works or result from the reconfiguration of desire that informs all the adaptations studied in this analysis. In the first place, Grau multiplies Pygmalion's single statue into seventeen puppets. This change is a practical one, since seventeen characters can generate a much more detailed story line than one. It also permits a greater focus on the object of creation in the play, that is, on the desires of the puppets themselves. Finally, in having the puppets rebel against and kill their creator, Grau reverses the desire of the Ovidian narrative, in which the statue, by all appearances, returns Pygmalion's love.[41] The reasons for this reversal of desire, from love to aggression, become clear when Grau's handling of the Pygmalion story is compared to the way in which he integrates the myth of Prometheus into the play.

The relations between the puppets on the one hand and between the puppets and the humans on the other are mirrored on a smaller scale in the subtext of Prometheus and the relations implied in that narrative. The interaction among the human characters begins in the Jornada Primera. Several critics have complained that this section of the play is either

---

41. The case is somewhat problematic because the statue never speaks, but, considering that it is given life by Venus (goddess of love) and bears a child (Paphos) by Pygmalion, one can only assume that it reciprocates its creator's affections.

tiresome or irrelevant.[42] In contrast, Peter Standish observes that the prologue is important because it "brings together people who are later to be drawn into the fiction of the play-within-the-play" (331). Furthermore, since all the characters in the prologue are human, this section of the play provides an important space for the examination of interhuman relations prior to the introduction of the puppets.

As Segel notes (141), Grau uses the Jornada Primera to ridicule the motives of the contemporary theater, characterized by its scorn for meaningful art because it is not profitable. The words of Don Javier, one of the managers who have hired Pigmalión to perform in their theater, are indicative of this lack of aesthetic appreciation:

> Un artista es siempre un loco o un chiflado, que cree que todo el mundo es imbécil menos él. Y si ese artista tiene fama mundial, como Pigmalión, se convierte en un ser intratable. La primera vez que se presenta al público, todos los literatos, pintores, músicos y demás gentecilla sin un real, que son el tifus y el engorro de los teatros, la nube de langosta del negocio, todos esos señores se apoderan del escenario y rodean al debutante, y chillan y alejan a todo el mundo con sus voces. Y a los tres días no viene nadie al teatro, ni ellos mismos, aunque no les cueste nada el espectáculo. Se contentan con chillar en los cafés, hablando de lo que han visto, y nosotros los empresarios, pagamos muy caro, carísimo, al artista y a su arte. (166–67; J1.8)

Don Javier's words demonstrate that in the contemporary theater in Spain individuals are appreciated not for their artistic worth but for their monetary value, a priority that establishes an economic imperative in human relations that degrades and objectifies humans to the level of Pigmalión's puppets. Thus the managers state their preference for the second-rate comedian Ponzano over the tragic actor Miranda because comedy is a much more lucrative venture in Spain than is tragedy (161; J1.6).

Equally noteworthy are the relations between the duke of Alducara and Pigmalión. The duke initially takes a genuine interest in the artistic dimension of the puppeteer's project, much to the chagrin of the managers, who complain that "nos dé la lata con el buen nombre del teatro y

---

42. O. Fernández 65; Valbuena Prat, "El teatro" 169; Navascués, *El teatro* 99.

el arte dramático y demás zarandajas por el estilo" (163; J1.7). Yet his sudden desire for Pomponina places him in an antagonistic relation with Pigmalión, which the latter had predicted with serene resignation: "Pronto la verá, desgraciadamente para usted, y en cuanto la vea, la simpatía que me tiene se trocará en odio" (176; J1.10).

The new relationship between Pigmalión and Alducara creates an atmosphere of rivalry parallel to the love triangle encompassing Pomponina, Mingo Revulgo, and Don Lindo that was dramatized in the puppets' farce. The parallel is enhanced by the duke's wooing of Pomponina with riches, the same tactic that Mingo had used to lure her into his crate, as Kaiser-Lenoir notes (15 n. 4). Furthermore, the appearance of Julia in act 3 creates another triangle of desire implicating her, the duke, and Pomponina. Not only does Alducara show an appalling lack of respect for Julia by ignoring her in favor of a puppet, but she lowers herself to his level by displaying jealousy over Pomponina and threatening to "dividirla en pedazos" (239; 3.2), a threat that is diverted only when the other puppets arrive and lock her in the back room with the duke. The signs of physical abuse that the two display when they are finally released from the room (248–49; 3.6–7) are a half-comic reminder of the violence underlying their desires.

Human affairs in the play, as dramatized in the managers' treatment of actors in the Jornada Primera and in the relations between Alducara, Pigmalión, and Julia throughout the three main acts, are nothing short of despicable, ruled by aggressive and erotic desires manifested in a lust for sex and power (money). It is no wonder, with models like these, that the puppets turn out the way they do, and with so many parallels between the two classes of beings, it is often difficult to distinguish between them based on behavior alone.

The final tier of relationships implied in the juxtaposition of the two mythic subtexts is that which exists between humans and gods. In the absence of stage divinities, these relations are alluded to in the dialogues between Pigmalión and his puppets. In act 1, when Pigmalión orders Don Lindo back to his box before Pomponina appears, the puppet complains: "¿Por qué me has dado vida, Pigmalión, para hacerme tan desgraciado?" Pigmalión's reply—"Por la misma razón que Dios me dió vida a mí y al mundo, sin consultárnoslo" (197–98; 1.3)—reveals an existential anguish over the uncertainty of the reasons for being at the same time that it establishes a perfect symmetry between his own and his puppets' predicaments. This symmetry is reinforced in a dialogue with Pomponina that takes place shortly afterward:

> Pigmalión.—¿A quién debes agradecer tu hermosura? ¿Quién te ha hecho así?
> Pomponina.—Dios.
> Pigmalión.—He sido yo. No ha sido Dios.
> Pomponina.—¿No dices que a ti te ha hecho Dios?
> Pigmalión.—Sí.
> Pomponina.—Pues si a ti no te hubiera hecho Dios, tú no me hubieses podido hacer a mí. (201; 1.4)

The parallels between creator and creation are reinforced at the end of the play. When Urdemalas tells Pigmalión that he will end up as nothing, like all men, the latter responds with condescension, "¿Qué sabes tú, monigote, qué hay después de la vida?" and the following exchange ensues: "Urdemalas.—Y tú, ¿lo sabes acaso? Pigmalión.—Te atreves a replicarme, estúpido. Yo solo me basto para reducirte a ti, a los demás y a un pueblo entero de polichinelas como vosotros" (251; 3.9).

The scene has undeniable resonances with chapter 31 of Unamuno's *Niebla*, as several critics have documented (see n. 37, this chapter). In particular, it calls attention to the fact that Pigmalión's real creator is Jacinto Grau, although the playwright, possessing the restraint that Unamuno lacked, keeps himself out of his cast of characters. Even so, the implication of the author in his own play as an unseen but powerful god subtly announces that Grau's esthetic and ideological preferences are the laws that will eventually prove triumphant in the play's dramatic universe.

The fundamental difference between *Niebla* and *El señor de Pigmalión* is that, in Grau, the artistic creation ends up destroying the creator. Yet this destruction on the puppet-human plane is counterbalanced by the relations between humans and gods. Pigmalión's last words as he lies dying capture perfectly this sense of balance: "Los dioses vencen eternamente, aniquilando al que quiere robarles su secreto ... Iba a superar al ser humano, y mis primeros autómatas de ensayo me matan alevosamente ... ¡Triste sino el del hombre héroe, humillado continuamente hasta ahora, en su soberbia, por los propios fantoches de su fantasía!" (254; 3.10). While on one level the creator (Pigmalión) is destroyed by the desires of his creation (the puppets), on the other the opposite circumstance is suggested, since God punishes Pigmalión just as Zeus castiga Prometheus for his haughtiness.⁴³ Thus one effect achieved by the reversal of desire in the Pygmalion myth is a sense of structural balance at the end of the play.

Yet there are other more important reasons for this reversal, which, when studied together with the reasons for the juxtaposition of the Pygmalion and Prometheus narratives, offer a key to interpreting the author's adaptation of classical myth. As Dru Dougherty argues in a penetrating study, the rebellion of the puppets may be read as a metaphor for the liberation of the contemporary Spanish theater from the conventions that were sapping its vitality: "The issue of the puppets' freedom is thus joined to the question of the theater's essence. In seeking to escape from their manager, the marionettes initiate a rebellion that will return the theater, in the concluding scene of the play, to its vital tradition" (354). At the metaphorical level of interpretation suggested by Dougherty, the puppets represent the new, exciting experiments in theater that were taking place all over Europe in the 1920s and that received such poor reception in Spain. It is fitting, for example, that Pigmalión's puppets, described as having been enormously successful all over the world, have never debuted in Spain and do so now only because of their demonstrated economic viability (161; J1.6). Although Pigmalión himself reports that he was born in Spain (186; 1.2), the stage directions indicate that he speaks with a "ligerísimo acento exótico" (169; J1.10), in other words, symbolically tinged with the cosmopolitanism of his project. When the puppets rebel against him, they are also rebelling against being forced to perform in a country whose standards of theater are contrary to those with which they were created. Again, Dougherty's words are elucidating: "From a semiotic viewpoint, the last Act dramatizes the displacement of one stage—of one theatrical code—by the other. When the marionettes leap through the windows onto the main stage and eliminate the 'human' characters from the theater, they do more than avenge the oppression they have known. In their aggressive behavior is inscribed the theater's liberation from its commercial constraints. By achieving their freedom, the puppets restore to the theater its primitive discourse" (355). It is significant, in this sense, that there is no Jornada Segunda to complement the play's Jornada Primera.⁴⁴ Because it is the latter section of the play that establishes the dis-

---

43. In the first edition of the play, the connection with Prometheus is made explicit: "Acaba derrumbándome estúpidamente, como una babel, como un nuevo Prometeo" (qtd. in Rodríguez Salcedo 35).
44. The Jornada Primera was called the Prólogo in the first edition of the play (Kronik,

course of mediocrity that pervades the Spanish theater, its failure to complete itself, to frame the play in perfect closure, may be read symbolically as a subtle trace of the disruption of theatrical norms dramatized in the puppets' escape.

The puppets' desires, along with Pigmalión's in his role as Prometheus, raise the essential question of autonomy that lies at the heart of discussions about the value of art. Even before they leave the stage, the puppets show sparks of individuality that lead one to believe they are not totally under their master's control. Juan, for example, when Pigmalión turns his back while showing him to the managers, sticks out his tongue and makes faces at him (187; 1.3). Later, when the puppets have the stage to themselves for their farce, it appears that they exercise complete control over their actions. Kaiser-Lenoir comments on this scene: "Ahora los vemos actuar *no* las farsas para las cuales han sido creados por Pigmalión, sino *su* propia obra" (15). This assertion is debatable, however, since the roles that the puppets play in their "own" farce in 2.1 conform perfectly to the descriptions that Pigmalión gives of each marionette in 1.3. Dougherty has captured best the sense of the play-within-the-play: "It is important to note that this interlude is a spontaneous event. The marionettes are unaware of its art—its pretense—for they merely act in character, living the roles signaled by their traditional histrionic costumes" (354).

Dougherty's observation is valid with regard not only to the interpuppet relations in the farce but also to the puppets' relations with the humans. "Estoy deseando que se me lleven," Pomponina tells the duke (223; 2.3), confirming her genetic relationship to woman's role in the *comedia* as the typical object of male desire. This role leads directly to Pomponina's escape from the stage (with the aid of the duke) and, indirectly, to the liberation of her fellow puppets (who follow her example) and the eventual overthrow of Pigmalión. Similarly, Urdemalas observes regarding the evil that he advocates: "Dejádmelo hacer a mí, que es mi oficio y para eso me hicieron" (245; 3.6). Ironically, because the puppets perform so well the roles of erotic and aggressive desire assigned to them by their creator, they end up transcending those roles and rebelling against him.

It is now possible to grasp a wider meaning behind Grau's inversion of desire in the Pygmalion myth and his juxtaposition of that tale to the Prometheus story. The rebellion of the puppets against their creator not

---

"Vanguardia" 86 n. 29). No one has yet offered an explanation for the change of nomenclature or for the perplexing lack of a Jornada Segunda.

only parallels perfectly Pigmalión-Prometeo's rebellion against the gods, but the problematization of their autonomy also reflects an age-old philosophical dilemma that has successively opposed to human free will various categories such as fate, predetermination, genetics, the environment, and so on. In an era in which both determinism and puppet literature were in vogue, Grau settles on an ingenious solution that deflects the question of autonomy from the human subject to the artistic object. Thus, although the protagonist ends up losing his life in supposed punishment for his presumptuousness, his death also signals an aesthetic victory of sorts, for it calls attention to the transcendent viability of the creation that survives him at the same time that it marks an ideological victory for the experimentalist precepts that the puppets represent, in contrast to the moldering conventions of the mainstream stage.

The three plays studied in this chapter, conveniently spaced ten years apart from one another, provide an excellent opportunity to observe the steady growth of Spanish experimental drama in the first two decades of the twentieth century. A central concern of that drama was to represent desire in a way that challenged the audience's assumptions and upset their tastes and expectations, and the stories of classical mythology, filled with tales of violence and sexual deviance, offered an abundance of potential starting points. Galdós, as he did so often in the narrative genre, provided the impetus for a significant aesthetic and ideological revision in the theater, which eventually developed into the mature avant-garde drama of Valle-Inclán and García Lorca. In his most controversial play, *Electra*, Galdós rechannels the undercurrents of incestuous desire in the myth of Electra into a framework that enables a deconstruction of the principles of melodrama. Perhaps hungering for the enormous success of *Electra* that had always been denied him in the theater, Unamuno followed Galdós's example closely in dramatizing the overpowering desire of the classical Phaedra for her stepson in a way that parallels Christ's passion and upsets traditional notions of Christian sacrifice. Finally, Jacinto Grau, also an admirer of Galdós, juxtaposes the classical narratives of Pygmalion and Prometheus to create an ingenious work that vindicates individual freedom and artistic experimentation through a focus on fetishism and rebellion. All three plays participate in what may be described as a radicalization of desire aimed at no less than the destruction of the bourgeois theater dominated by Echegaray and Benavente.

The three plays also demonstrate the nascent tendency of twentieth-century drama away from the use of myth to achieve plot complexity and toward a reinscription of desire that permits penetrating character portrayal. *Electra* represents a transitional moment in this tendency. Although it depends significantly on action for its development, its length also allows for considerable character development that surpasses anything achieved in the most introspective moments of the seventeenth-century plays studied. In particular, the interaction between Máximo and Electra in act 3 is well crafted, as is Electra's emotional instability climaxing in her nervous breakdown in act 5. Unamuno's *Fedra*, because of the radical streamlining of plot related to the author's concept of the *teatro desnudo*, focuses little on incident and foregrounds instead the heroine's morbid desire for Hipólito, creating the best instance among the three plays of truly psychological drama. Especially noteworthy for its finely developed dramatic tension is Fedra's confession of her desire to Hipólito in act 2. Finally, because Grau's play depends so heavily on the blending of two mythical narratives, it relies more on plot construction than do the other two plays. Even so, the relations developed among the three classes of beings—puppets, humans, and gods—provide for considerable psychological insight and conflict.

Historical Postscript

The use of classical myth did not end with Grau but continued to fuel a steady, if minor, trend in the theater of the 1920s. In 1922, a year after the first publication of *El señor de Pigmalión*, a little-known dramatist, Halma Angélico, published the first edition of a play titled *La nieta de Fedra*, in which the protagonist Berta and her daughter Ángela both fall in love with Lorenzo, stepson and stepbrother to both. Thus Angélico ties to the theme of incestuous desire that of rivalry between mother and daughter.[45] Several years later, around 1925, García Lorca is thought to have begun work on a piece titled *El sacrificio de Ifigenia*, which he referred to as his "alegoría al Mediterráneo" and which, in a letter to Ana María Dalí, he claimed to have completed (Josephs and Caballero 24–25). Unfortunately, the manuscript has not survived. Finally, in 1927, the young Max Aub published his first play in Spain, *Narciso*—a most advanced expres-

---

45. For an excellent analysis of this rather obscure play, see Nieva de la Paz.

sion of the Spanish avant-garde's re-creations of classical myth. In this highly lyrical work, Aub transforms the story of Narcissus into a sensuous spectacle of colors, lights, music, and dance designed to convey the self-absorption of the protagonist and the impossibility of genuine communication: "¡El ser de cada uno es incomprensible hasta para uno mismo!" the Corifeo chants prophetically (129).[46]

Given the trajectory outlined in this chapter together with the generous support extended to the theater by the Second Republic (1931–36), it is reasonable to expect that, if the momentous civil war of 1936–39 had not paralyzed the nascent *teatro inquieto*, classical mythology would have continued to find original and eloquent expression in the hands of Spain's prewar dramatists.[47] Instead, it had to wait until the period following the war, when a new set of social conditions called for its return to the stage.

---

46. For discussions of this play, see Chabás 656–57; Doménech, "Introducción" 27–29; Monleón, *El teatro* 41–42; Kemp 43–51; E. López 55–58; Soldevila-Durante 158–61; Monti, esp. 276–77; and Ruiz Ramón, *Historia . . . siglo XX* 249.

47. A glance at McGaha's checklist of performances during the Second Republic (*The Theatre in Madrid*) reveals a continuing interest in myth. In the first place, there are reproductions of Aeschylus (*Los siete contra Tebas*, item 459), Sophocles (*Electra*, 44), Seneca (*Medea* [trans. Unamuno], 530), and Shaw (*Pigmalión*, 1224). In the second, several original titles suggest a possible mythological inspiration: *La casa de Troya* (119, 1021), *La maravilla de Éfeso* (475), and *Orestes, no te molestes* (781).

5

Postwar, Postmodern, and Beyond

Liberating Desire in the Theater of Dictatorship and Democracy

The civil war of 1936–39 devastated not only the infrastructure, economy, and population of Spain but also its theatrical tradition. Domingo Pérez Minik explains: "Cuando terminó nuestra guerra, y ante un nuevo cuerpo de España dolorido y constristado, lleno de susto y con voluntad de paz, se puede afirmar que no existía un espectador teatral ni una sociedad estructurada para recibir ningún modo de ser de este viejo arte colectivo. Los dramaturgos y el espectador estaban por hacer. Tenían que pasar muchos años para que este país crucificado en dos se rehiciera y estuviera en disposición de asistir al sacrificio o al juego de la escena" (*Teatro* 247–48). Marion Holt notes that theaters in Madrid reopened within days after the Nationalist capture of the city, but he goes on to observe that most of the plays produced in the period immediately following the war "were the products of established playwrights of the older generation or of a few younger writers whose efforts did not offend the regime either because they gave ideological support to traditional values . . . or because they represented an aesthetic concept removed from political or religious considerations" (15). The remarks of Pérez Minik and Holt serve to emphasize two monumental problems that faced any serious playwright in the

1940s. First, the public was so traumatized by the war and its aftermath that it was unlikely to find appeal in the kind of probing *teatro inquieto* produced by the experimental drama earlier in the century. Second, even if audiences were prepared to deal with their psychological demons and to confront them on stage, the aggressive censorship pursued by the Franco regime created a strong impediment to the development of any intellectually responsible or thought-provoking theater.[1]

The radically different historical circumstances of the 1940s thus ended up fostering essentially the same type of mainstream theater that dominated the early part of the century: "todo el quehacer de nuestra nación se mantenía dentro de una línea caduca y convencional. Nos referimos especialmente al género dramático" (Pérez Minik, *Teatro* 383). The term "teatro de evasión" has been developed by historians such as Torrente Ballester to refer to this type of theater (*Teatro* 337–54). Not unlike the increasingly allegorical and philosophical drama of the late seventeenth century, the theater during this period served to provide escape from the painful realities beyond its walls.

In this delicate environment classical myth once again proved to be an effective dramatic device, and the theater's frequent use of it in the postwar and democratic periods surpasses that of any other genre (Lasso de la Vega, *Helenismo* 43; Díez del Corral 191). To explain this phenomenon, one could cite, in addition to the traditional appeal of the classics, both the ability of theater to reach a large segment of the population and the capacity of myth to "infundir en un público demasiado adormecido un mensaje de carácter ideológico, capaz de suscitar la reflexión y el planteamiento de una nueva visión sobre los hechos culturales y, en última instancia, sobre los políticos y sociales" (Vilches 184). In the various conflicts of desire that it presented, myth offered a way of indirectly addressing the issues that spectators desperately needed to confront in order to come to grips with their traumatic past. Additionally, myth served as a veil for disguising protest and dissent and thus offered an effective means of evading the often doltish censors. After the death of Franco and the establishment of democracy, this necessity obviously faded, but, significantly, myth itself did not. If anything, the use of myth in the post-Franco theater has gained momentum as artists employ it for a wider cultural critique of traditional values and morality. The appropriation of the classics in this

---

1. For detailed accounts of censorship in the postwar period, see the two articles by Patricia O'Connor.

way does not imply, however, that myth was harnessed solely in the service of political expediency, for the mythological plays staged both in the Franco dictatorship and in the young democratic Spain have maintained the generally high artistic standards of their predecessors.

Representative of the tendencies of the two periods are Antonio Buero Vallejo (b. 1916) and Luis Riaza (b. 1925). Buero's *Historia de una escalera* (1949) is widely regarded as a watershed in the Franco period because its author dared to dramatize serious issues; he has continued to produce works of equal quality up to the present day. For his part, although lesser known than Buero, Riaza nevertheless represents "uno de los más originales y serios intentos de poner en cuestión, desde el teatro mismo, la autenticidad y la eficacia de las nuevas formas del teatro" (Ruiz Ramón, *Teatro . . . siglo XX* 553). This chapter will be principally devoted to Buero's *La tejedora de sueños* (1952), once called "una de las mejores muestras de la renovación de un tema mítico en nuestro tiempo, aunque pensemos en Giraudoux y en Anouilh," (Valbuena Prat, *Historia del teatro* 662), and to Riaza's *Medea es un buen chico* (1980), which, perhaps because of its author's relative obscurity, has received less attention than it deserves. In addition to these two works, other plays that follow the trends exemplified by Buero and Riaza will receive some discussion.

The Seeds of Dissent

Only five years after the end of the war, Gonzalo Torrente Ballester (1910–99) completed a little-studied work, *El retorno de Ulises*, which was published two years later. The first of a surprising number of plays based on the Ulysses theme in the postwar period (see Paulino), Torrente's piece is also the first dramatic work to engage in a rigorous process of demythification of a famous warrior figure. The playwright goes to great lengths to contrast the "myth," or official version, of Ulises' story with his lesser, but more human, reality. In his absence, Penélope presumes that he has died but covers up her doubts by sending her son on missions to look for him, "aun sabiendo que no ha de devolvérmelo" (130). In addition, she perpetuates and glorifies Ulises' memory by weaving a tapestry that portrays her husband in superhuman form and by encouraging poets to sing his praises. When Ulises finally returns, the difference between his real and mythical personae is emphasized in the contrast between the man and the tapestry that looms behind him larger than life (185). So great is the disparity between the two images that Telémaco refuses to believe that it is his father standing before him. Seeking proof, he requests that Ulises use his bow and arrow to shoot down an apple placed on the top of Penélope's head, a test that the suitors have just failed and that, according to Penélope, Ulises used to perform regularly.[2] Forced to confront his larger-than-life reputation, Ulises is unable to bear the possibility of failure and withdraws from the contest, declaring bitterly, "¡Soy un impostor!" (188).

The myth of Ulysses permits Torrente Ballester to engage a series of volatile contemporary issues that would otherwise be difficult to address for the reasons described above. It is significant in this respect that the title of the play mentions the *return* of Ulysses rather than simply the figure of Ulysses himself. This title as well as the exposition of the play invoke not only the Trojan War, from which the hero is returning, but also his reintegration into a changed society. In relation to contemporary events, these circumstances allude to the Spanish Civil War and its aftermath, including the problem of exile. Elizabeth Rogers, for example, notes that the figure of Ulises in Torrente's play "comes to represent the prototype of the contemporary exile" ("Myth" 118).

The question of desire is foregrounded in the plot of *El retorno de Ulises* but not substantially altered with respect to its Homeric configuration. Penélope is besieged daily by the desires of the suitors, creating an atmosphere of urgency and desperation that hangs constantly over the characters and impinges on their actions. Most important, when Ulises returns and does not measure up to his mythic image, it is love that saves his marriage from disaster. When he announces that he is leaving Ithaca again to begin new journeys "sin nombre y sin esperanza" (188), Penélope states her intention to accompany him because, as she puts it, he is "el único hombre a quien amé en la vida" (189). Desire works to complement or counterbalance the effects of demythification. That is, while the play takes the necessary but painful step of confronting the war and can-

---

2. In this peculiar account of the contest of the suitors, Torrente has evidently fused, on the one hand, the Homeric version in which Penelope proposes that the competitors string Odysseus's bow and shoot the arrows through the eyes of twelve axes (*Od.* 19.572–81), and, on the other, the legend of William Tell, who used a bow and arrow to shoot an apple off the top of his son's head (see Rogers, "Myth" 129 n. 6). Torrente's Penélope explicitly states that Ulises used to shoot the apple off Telémaco's head (182).

didly assessing its impact, it offers love and compassion as an answer to the suffering caused by violence.

José María Pemán (1898–1981), who began his dramatic career before the outbreak of the civil war with *El divino impaciente* (1933), continued a steady production of plays until his death in the early 1980s. In the 1940s he began using themes of Greco-Roman mythology to write a series of works that varied from free translations to artistically inspired re-creations of classical drama. In a lengthy scholarly introduction to his *Antígona*, which appeared the same year as *El retorno de Ulises* (1945), Pemán argues for the contemporary viability of Greek tragedy and explains his approach to reproducing Sophocles' play for the Spanish public:

> La *Antígona* que yo he escrito ha sido inspirada por la persuasión de que la sustancia estética y emocional de la tragedia griega se podría hacer llegar al público—al "gran público," como se dice en lenguaje teatral—tanto más intacta cuanto con más desenvoltura y libertad se manipularan su mecanismo teatral y sus instrumentos de expresión. Creí que ante un público de España—tierra también de sol y de olivos—la línea argumental, el movimiento pasional y el fondo ideológico de la gran tragedia griega podían conservar toda su validez de un modo absoluto y directo, sin más que reformar la manera de transmitir todo ello. (1239)

The kinds of changes that Pemán makes to Sophocles' play, such as "la abreviación de parlamentos y la mayor movilidad de diálogos; la sustitución de los muchos fragmentos argumentales que en Sófocles se cuentan o narran por episodios de acción escritos y dialogados de nuevo; y el tratamiento del 'coro' como personaje teatral" (1241), are aimed at integrating some of the more opaque formal features of classical theater into a context that allows for greater comprehension by a contemporary audience of the play's basic thematic structure, which Pemán leaves intact and describes as "la de la niña que desobedece al tirano porque la ley natural y divina de honrar a Polineces la siente por encima de las leyes positivas del otro, sentimiento puro y bello que la arrastra a su perdición" (1239).

In his next classical endeavor, *Electra* (1949), Pemán takes much greater liberty with myth, as he explains in his "Autocrítica" preceding the play: "Porque el propósito de esta *Electra* no tiene nada que ver con el que inspiró mi *Antígona*. En aquélla intenté una 'versión muy libre'—así la llamé—de la obra de Sófocles. En ésta, la libertad es mayor. Ésta no es 'versión' de ninguna *Electra* determinada del teatro griego. Ésta es una comedia original, cuya fábula es el mito o leyenda de Electra" (*Teatro* 1856). Pemán loosely models his play on the story of Aeschylus's *Oresteia* while emphasizing Electra's desire for Agamenón, present only in subdued form in the Greek plays. In Pemán's version, Clitemnestra and Egisto have sent Orestes out of the country and have refused to educate seventeen-year-old Electra in sexual matters. Their neglect is aimed at keeping her in a sort of libidinal innocence that will prevent her from understanding the significance of the kisses and embraces that she inevitably catches the queen and her lover exchanging. When Agamenón returns home unexpectedly and proceeds to hug and kiss his daughter, he unknowingly sparks a retroactive sexual blossoming in her: "En un instante, en sus brazos, he aprendido más que en diez años ... Oh, besar. . . . ¡Eso que yo sentía y no sabía ponerle nombre! Papá le ha quitado el tapón al chorro de la fuente ..., y ella verá por donde corre" (1880).

Electra's affection for her father, rather than Orestes' sense of duty, becomes the principal force that drives the vengeance taken against Clitemnestra when she and Egisto conspire to murder Agamenón. Orestes, in contrast, maintains the same relationship toward his mother that Electra has with her father. He refuses to believe her capable of crime and prefers the idealized memory of her that he has preserved from childhood: "¡Creo en ella!" he tells Electra (1905). Clitemnestra ends up dying by her own hands after Orestes kills Egisto to atone for Agamenón's murder. By rechanneling desire in these mother-son and father-daughter alliances, Pemán adds a new complexity and dramatic interest to the blood feuds of the *Oresteia*. Moreover, his development of Clitemnestra's character before the return of Agamenón is a significant addition that will reappear in later playwrights.

Both of Pemán's mythological plays from the forties possess sparks of protest and dissent against war, tyranny, and official propaganda. It is difficult to disassociate the composition of his *Antígona*, even though it adheres rather closely to its classical model, from the contemporary circumstances of dictatorship in which it was written, especially given Pemán's own interpretation of the myth noted above.[3] In addition, in his *Electra*, comments made about the Trojan War and its aftermath assume wider meaning in the context of contemporary Spain. When Orestes returns

    3. The use of the Antigone myth as a protest against dictatorship is especially noteworthy in contemporary Spanish American theater. See, for example, Luis Rafael Sánchez's *La pasión según Antígona Pérez*.

from abroad, he tells Electra: "Te advierto que por el mundo se ríen un poco de vuestra guerra de Troya. Aquí es un poema épico ... Pero por ahí es un poco un epigrama. ¡Una guerra por una coqueta!" (1895). As in Torrente's play, there is a sharp contrast drawn between official myth as propagated by poets and a much bleaker reality. This disparity is emphasized further along in the play when Egisto tells Orestes: "Bueno, entre nosotros ... En eso [the story of Troy] se ha exagerado mucho ... Los poetas complican el asunto. En el fondo, fué un poco atropellado aquello. La agricultura sufrió mucho con la ausencia de los muchachos. Desde aquello de Troya, tenemos escasez" (1901). Unlike Torrente, Pemán offers little hope for redemption or personal reconciliation. At the end of the play, Orestes, maddened by the Furies, leaves the country, and Electra, now queen, begins a campaign of misinformation to cover up the disaster.

If one were to demand a biographical justification for this admittedly controversial reading of a playwright who continues to be an obvious "representante para la mayoría de los críticos del teatro más tradicional" (García Lorenzo, *El teatro español* 88), one could reply that Pemán was not an outspoken supporter of Franco and that it was mainly his monarchist sympathies and strict Catholicism that earned him the good graces of the regime (Holt 21). Furthermore, whatever his sympathies, he was undoubtedly a serious, dedicated playwright who began his career, it should be emphasized, in the freedom of the Second Republic. If it seems reasonable that any principled artist, regardless of his or her politics, is liable to feel threatened or at least offended by an authoritarian regime that aggressively censors its best creative talents, then it becomes easier to accept the dissident tones of Pemán's mythological plays as well as those of Torrente, whose *falangista* affiliations, especially just after the war, are well known. Frederick Ahl makes just such a case for a number of Augustan-age Roman poets traditionally considered to be complicitous with royal power (see "The Rider and the Horse"), and in Chapter 2 of this analysis I propose a similar reading of Timoneda (see pages 48–49).

In any case, the most important basis for interpretation—the text itself—supports the readings rendered of Pemán and Torrente. However they intended their texts to be understood, their plays can be legitimately seen, in the context of the postwar period, as suggestive, subtly critical uses of mythology. As such, they set important examples for subsequent playwrights and, together with the other mythological adaptations from the forties, anticipate Buero's *La tejedora de sueños*, which deploys the techniques of demythification and dissent in a way that maximizes the reinscription of desire.

A Loom of Her Own: Feminine Desire and Masculine Discourse in Antonio Buero Vallejo's *La tejedora de sueños*

La tejedora de sueños has elicited a wide range of critical appraisals. Once ruled "experimental" (Ruple 24) or marginal to the author's most "representative" works (Iglesias Feijoo, Introducción 39), it has recently been considered by one critic as fundamental to understanding Buero Vallejo's dramatic production as a whole (Salvat i Ferré 83). In this provocative play, begun in 1949 but temporarily postponed because of its similarities with Torrente's *El retorno de Ulises*, Buero follows with surprising fidelity the incidents of the *Odyssey* to produce a work that differs radically from its Homeric counterpart in tone and character portrayal.[4] A close examination of the playwright's method with respect to the *Odyssey* will explain this seeming paradox as well as, perhaps, the mixed critical reaction.

Buero's adaptation of Homer may be accurately described as a "careful teasing out of warring forces of signification *within the text itself*," to use Barbara Johnson's condensed definition of deconstruction (xiv). In this particular case, Buero mines the excesses of meaning in the Greek epic in order to bring into relief the various conflicting layers of signification. Most of the diverse theories on the composition of the *Iliad* and the *Odyssey* share one thesis: that "Homer's unique style does show clearly that he was heir to a long tradition of oral poetry" (Knox 19). It is logical to suppose that, whoever Homer was, in order to achieve an illusion of wholeness in his poetry, he would have had to smooth over inevitably conflicting accounts of myths and legends of considerable antiquity. In his "Comentario," Buero himself states that reading the *Odyssey* "causa la impresión de que allí se silencian hechos. Y si los protagonistas existieron alguna vez, nada tendría de inverosímil la hipótesis de que su realidad

---

4. On the similarities with Torrente's play, see Buero's own remarks in his fascinating "Comentario" 90. In this document, unfortunately suppressed after the first edition of the play, the author also alludes to what appears to be Pemán's *Electra* as the impetus for his decision to finish his play: "Mucho más tarde volvióme a inquietar el tema y lo acometí de nuevo, estimulado por la idea de que, si cualquier dramaturgo podía escribir su 'Electra,' todos podíamos escribir también nuestra 'Penélope'" (91). See also Buero's "Autocrítica."

histórica hubiese sido sublimada por la vena poética del autor o autores de los cantos odiseos" (94). Buero exploits the poem's lacunae in order to reorient the desires of the protagonists in a powerfully sustained demythification of the virtues traditionally associated with war and heroism, producing a version of the Odysseus myth that, while scrupulously faithful to the Homeric plot, creates such a seemingly contradictory account.

Predicated more on changes of character than of plot, Buero's rewriting of Homer is nowhere more pronounced than in Penélope, the most strongly developed figure of the play.[5] The work as a whole may be read as a vehicle for recovering the inner voice—hopes, fears, dreams, desires—of the heroine, who has seen the finest years of her youth destroyed by the terrible anguish of waiting for her husband to return. The illusion of immediacy created by the theater, as opposed to the distance implied in epic poetry, is especially appropriate for this mission of recovery and restoration of voice. As Pemán does with Clitemnestra's character in the first act of *Electra*, Buero focuses on the untold half of a well-known myth—that corresponding to the hero's wife—and creates Penélope's character not by contradicting Homer but by filling in the empty spaces he leaves or, in Rogers's words, the "neglected inner component of the stories" ("Role Constraints" 310).[6]

Whereas the *Odyssey* presents the hero's wife as faithful, loving, and ever expectant of her husband's return, in *La tejedora de sueños* she appears as a sad and disillusioned character who, in her long wait for Ulises, has fallen in love with one of her suitors, Anfino. Although she never consummates her desire for him, the suggestion that she loves someone other than her famous husband is the first step in Buero's critique of a conception of war and heroism that glorifies the manifestation of sexual and aggressive desire in warriors while taking for granted the repression of those desires in their wives.

---

5. This judgment of Penélope is shared by Müller 57 and Iglesias Feijoo, *La trayectoria* 102. In an article from 1980, John Moore goes so far as to call Penélope "probably Buero Vallejo's best female character so far" (13).

6. In another article Rogers suggests that Buero foregrounds Ulises' absence ("The Humanization" 339), while Guillermo Díaz-Plaja (276) goes so far as to state that this absence is the real protagonist of the play. Buero's own statements concur with the essence of these comments, revealing how "atrevíme . . . al intento de escribir . . . [u]na obra en que lo más grave y horrible ocurriese secretamente en los corazones de los protagonistas. . . . Ningún personaje parecióme más apto para ello que el de la desventurada reina de Itaca" ("Comentario" 92). For an outstanding, point-by-point comparison of *La tejedora de sueños* with its Homeric model, see Iglesias Feijoo, Introducción.

Indispensable to furthering this critique are several mythical figures who, although they never appear on stage, project a perpetual shadow over the action, as Iglesias Feijoo notes (*La trayectoria* 100). These characters include Helena, Agamenón, Clitemnestra, and Orestes, all of whom constantly plague Penélope's thoughts and recall the function of Fedra's mother in Unamuno's play (see above, Chapter 4, pages 151–52). At the beginning of the play the stranger (who, as anyone familiar with Homer can guess, is Ulises in disguise) tells Penélope that he saw Helena during his travels and that she appeared happy. The queen responds: "No es extraño. Una mujer capaz de suscitar tal guerra, no puede ser reflexiva. Ni soñadora. Alegre, alegre como un animalillo satisfecho, ¿no es eso?" (122; act 1). The stranger also relates the story of Agamenón's murder at the hands of Clitemnestra and her lover (119–20; act 1). Later, in a conversation with her nurse Euriclea, Penélope vents her rage at Helena and reveals her opinion of Agamenón's murder:

Penélope.—Si perdemos a nuestros esposos en plena juventud y nos vemos forzadas a quedar al frente de los hogares (*Con odio infinito.*), tan sólo porque un tonto le robó a otro tonto una cualquiera, ¿a quién hay que inculpar de todas las miserias? ¡Responde!
Euriclea.—Le obligaron a partir ... No culpes a Ulises.
Penélope.—¡Qué, a Ulises! ¡A Helena! ¡A esa mujerzuela, a esa perdida! Hace veinte años que se le ocurrió sonreír a otro que no era su esposo ... ¡Allá fueron los jefes de Grecia entera! ¡Nosotras no éramos nada para ellos!
Euriclea.—Agamenón los amenazó y tuvieron que ir ...
Penélope.—Y a su vuelta, su propia mujer lo mató. ¡Ella nos vengó a todas! (140–41; act 1)

The elements that Penélope objects to in Helena are precisely those associated with stereotypical feminine desire. Her whimsical flirtatiousness ("se le ocurrió sonreír a otro") converts her into a passive object of male desire that lacks autonomy ("como un animalillo satisfecho") and, like a precious commodity, is traded, robbed, and fought over. Helena and the many women like her—she is only "una cualquiera"—perpetuate a system that forces Ulises' wife and others in her situation into lives of anonymity and oblivion "al frente de los hogares," while their husbands gain public honor and glory. Penélope's views of Helena recall those that Eneas elicits from Dido on the same subject in Castro's *Dido y Eneas* (see above, Chapter 3, page 76).

Agamenón, in Penélope's account, is the male counterpart of Helena in this system, one of the *tontos* who goes to Troy to recover her. Like his brother, Menelao (husband of Helena), and like Ulises himself, he validates through his aggressive behavior the passive role of women that incites such behavior, thus perpetuating a vicious circle of lust and violence. The allusions to Orestes in the play confirm this spiral of uncontrolled desires: Penélope tells Ulises that by abandoning their wives, he and the other soldiers at Troy have turned their sons into their mothers' assassins (197; act 3). By simply changing the narrative perspective of these myths, that is, by retelling them through the eyes of Penélope, Buero turns Helen and the Trojan War into symbols of male lust and greed, as Joelyn Ruple notes (92).

Similarly, in rewriting the story of Agamemnon, Buero alters the motivations underlying the myth without distorting its principal incidents. While Clytemnestra is generally portrayed negatively in Homer (see, for example, *Od.* 11.421–34), Penélope's vindication of her in the play reinforces Buero's critique of traditional libido types. In contrast to the usual reasons that Clytemnestra gives for the murder of her husband (see above, Chapter 4 n. 11), in *La tejedora de sueños* Penélope insinuates that Clitemnestra punished him for having abandoned her for the sake of "una cualquiera." Her motivations go beyond petty jealousy into a vindication of women's rights that corresponds to Magda Ruggeri Marchetti's view of Penélope as a "prefemminista" (*Il teatro* 116).[7] Even though Penélope assures Euriclea, "Yo soy la fiel Penélope. . . . Yo no lo mataría" (141–42), the parallel between her and Clitemnestra remains firmly established, so much so that Buero Vallejo, in his "Comentario" on the play, considers her one of many "Clitemnestras en potencia" (92).

Exploiting the fundamental ambiguity of Homer's Odysseus, Buero brings about a transformation in Ulises that complements his rewriting of Penélope.[8] As in the *Odyssey*, Ulises returns home in disguise; reveals himself to his son Telémaco, to the swineherd Eumeo, and to the oxherd

---

7. Ruggeri repeats this idea in "La mujer" 38. Similar views are found in Maxwell 17 and Harris, "La desmitificación" 89.

8. The ambiguity of Odysseus in Homer is manifested in his many epithets, including *poluainos* 'of many stories,' *polukēdēs* 'of many cares,' *polukerdēs* 'of many crafts,' *polumēchanos* 'of many devices,' *polumētis* 'of many wiles,' *poluphrōn* 'much wise,' *polutlas* 'much suffering,' *polutlēmōn* 'much enduring,' and *polutropos* 'of many turns' (see Stanford). For an ingenious reading of these epithets, see Pucci 51.

Filetio; discovers where loyalties lie; and proceeds to slaughter the suitors.[9] Like Homer's hero, he carefully plans their destruction in a way that provides him with a maximum of personal safety: he hides the suitors' arms and locks the doors to the patio in which they have participated in the contest of the bow (182–83; act 3).[10] Buero accentuates even more the cowardly side of the hero, which first manifests itself in the contest of the bow.[11] As in Homer, Ulises plans to string the bow himself and fire the arrow through the targets after the suitors have failed. Yet, unlike his counterpart, he evidently does not have enough faith in his abilities to leave things to chance. With the aid of his son, he cheats and tests his strength before the fact: "En empresas como ésta no conviene arriesgarse, hijo mío. Este arco tiene su secreto, pero también es fuerte. Antes podía con él, mas ya soy viejo, y ..." (177; act 2). Ulises' actions in this scene not only reveal his self-doubt and lack of sportsmanship but also recall the way in which, according to Penélope, he won her for his bride: "Este arco se tiende de un modo especial. . . . ¡Oh, no lo recuerdo! Yo misma se lo dije a Ulises para que me ganase con él, y lo he olvidado" (175–76; act 2). By revealing this seemingly trivial point, Buero manages to extend his revision of Ulises' character twenty years into the past, where he shows him to be as cowardly and unscrupulous as he is in the present time of the play.

A small change in the spatial layout of the *Odyssey* contributes powerfully to the demythification of Ulises: Buero has his protagonist kill the suitors (with the exception of Anfino) from the safety of the balcony overlooking the patio. The devastating effect of this scene is magnified by the fact that the suitors, because of the stage configuration, remain invisible to the audience and die like the anonymous victims of a firing squad. The voice of Antinoo, heard just before his death, speaks for the victims and

---

9. One minor difference lies in the number of suitors. More than a hundred in the *Odyssey*, they are reduced, for obvious practical concerns, to five: Antinoo, Eurímaco, Pisandro, Leócrito, and Anfino. Penélope states, however, that there were originally thirty, twenty-five of whom—"los más impacientes"—soon abandoned their quest (157–58; act 2). For a detailed comparison of Buero's suitors with their Homeric counterparts, see Alvar 60–64.

10. Cf. *Od.* 16.284–86, 19.4–5, 21.240–41.

11. The cowardly potential of Homer's Odysseus shows up, for example, when the traitor Melanthios returns the suitors' arms to them and "luto gounata kai philon ētor" 'the knees of Odysseus were loosened and his heart melted' (22.147), precisely the same phrase used to describe the suitors themselves in 22.68.

foregrounds Ulises' lack of courage: "¡Baja aquí, a luchar como un hombre!" (191; act 3).[12]

Penélope completes the attack on Ulises' character in her confrontation with him at the end of the play. Her accusation that his famous prudence is actually cowardice (201; act 3) confirms the negative angle that Buero has chosen to develop in the classical Odysseus's multivalent personality. She continues her onslaught: "¡Te disfrazaste porque te sabías viejo; porque desconfiabas de poder agradarme con tus canas y tus arrugas!" (202). Penélope's harsh words underscore an inevitable fact of life that, in the *Odyssey*, Athena remedies with a wave of the hand: age and the diminished sexual capacity that it implies. The scrutinizing light in which Buero presents Ulises not only calls into question his wartime virtues but also undermines his sexual persona traditionally manifested in the relationships he maintains with the women he encounters in his wanderings (Calypso, Nausicaa, and Circe, for example). Accordingly, Penélope tells him that "tú no habrás tenido en tu camino ninguna mujer que te recuerde joven, porque tú naciste viejo" (203; act 3).

In contrast to the old and weary Ulises stands Anfino, the young suitor with whom Penélope has fallen in love.[13] Many critics have compared the two characters by invoking the opposition of *activo* and *contemplativo*.[14] Indeed, Ulises' role as soldier directly opposes him to that of Anfino as poet, a role that becomes clear at the end of act 1 when he tells Penélope: "Prefiero intentar todas las noches, pensando en ti, el bajo oficio de poeta" (139). This comment comes, furthermore, directly after he has refused an offer to spend the night with one of Penélope's slave women. His

---

12. Given this context, it is difficult to agree with Jean-Paul Borel's judgment: "Nous nous laissons un moment éblouir par le personnage légendaire d'Ulysse, nous admirons le sage, le rusé e prudent roi d'Ithaque qui vient remettre de l'ordre dans son pays, rétablir son autorité, reprendre brillamment son poste après vingt ans d'absence" (168). Carolyn Harris expresses a similar view ("La mujer" 250).

13. Anfino corresponds rather precisely to Homer's Amphinomus. Buero ingeniously exploits the barest suggestion in the *Odyssey* that "above all the others he [Amphinomus] pleased Penelope with his words, for he had an understanding heart" (16.397–98). There is, furthermore, a long counter-Homeric tradition in antiquity regarding the unfaithfulness of Penelope (e.g., Apollodorus 2:305–7; Epitome 7.38–40), although Buero denies prior knowledge of it in his "Comentario" 94.

14. Doménech, *El teatro* 248; González-Cobos 185–87; Podol, "The Theme" 43; Rogers, "The Humanization" 344; Franco Durán, "Interpretación" 318 and "Anfino" 68. See Bourne 70; Halsey, *Antonio* 48; Nonoyama 78; Verdú 38; Iglesias Feijoo, *La trayectoria* 105–7; and Diego 357 for similar contrasts between the two characters.

rejection of her sets him in direct contrast not only to the other four suitors, who entertain themselves nightly with the slaves, but also to Ulises, who went to war over a woman and who, as Penélope suggests, became involved with the women he met during his journeys. Anfino's capacity to restrain his sexual desires inscribes him in a discourse that runs counter to the one traditionally associated with masculinity and that is embodied by the other suitors and Ulises. In addition, even though he possesses physical capabilities apparently superior to those of the other suitors, he declines to use force on them except in cases of self-defense, as demonstrated in his scuffle with Antinoo (130; act 1).

In keeping with this characterization, later in the play Penélope describes one of Anfino's remarks as "almost feminine":

Anfino.—Penélope: yo querré siempre lo que tú quieras.
Penélope.—¡Qué hermosa frase! ...
Anfino.—(*Molesto.*) Sincera.
Penélope.—Y casi femenina ... Una frase que me gustaría decir a mí.
   (155; act 2)

Penélope's comment, while it might easily pass as trivial, accurately accounts for Anfino's role in the context of Buero's transformation of traditional desire. Rather than imposing his desires on Penélope, as in traditional conceptions of male-female relationships, Anfino states that he subordinates his own wishes to Penélope's. This balance of power makes sense, of course, considering that Penélope is queen and, as the suitor Antinoo exclaims, "¡Y sus deseos son ley!" (126; act 1). Yet it becomes clear from the suitors' reckless behavior that none of them but Anfino lives up to their empty phrases.

Other qualities in Anfino further distinguish him from his peers and from Ulises. Unlike the other suitors, he is a poor orphan and has no supporters to cheer him on in the contest of the bow in act 3: "La orfandad y la pobreza me han forjado," he tells Ulises (193; act 3). His father, Niso Aretíada of Duliquio (cf. *Od.* 16.395) was "un fiel vasallo de Ulises y su mejor amigo" (132; act 1), and Anfino appears to have inherited this loyalty. His first words in the play are "Pero no somos reyes. Sólo Ulises era nuestro rey," whereas Pisandro scoffs, "¿Quién se acuerda de Ulises?" (128; act 1). At the end, when Ulises procede to slaughter the suitors, Anfino is the only one to accept death with dignity. "¡Es justo, Ulises!" he exclaims valiantly, forming a vivid contrast to the cowardice of Ulises. Iglesias Feijoo notes further nonverbal characteristics in act 1 of the play that set Anfino apart from the other suitors: "La separación de Anfino del resto del grupo es un signo escénico que hace visual su diferencia de los demás pretendientes, confirmada por otros hechos: entra detrás, no está ebrio, se opondrá a sus pretensiones de forzar el templete, rehusará unirse con ninguna esclava ..." (Buero Vallejo, *Tejedora* 126 n. 18).

In addition to rewriting these three main characters, Buero, like Guillén de Castro in *Dido y Eneas*, eliminates from the play the concept of fate and divine intervention (see above, Chapter 3, pages 84–85). When Ulises tells Penélope at the end of the play, "Así quieren los dioses labrar nuestra desgracia," she quickly retorts: "No culpes a los dioses. Somos nosotros quienes la labramos" (203; act 3).[15] The mention of deities always occurs in a context that permits them to be considered metaphorically. The blind Euriclea, for example, makes several references to the Furies, as when she tells Penélope in act 2: "Las Furias suben ... y la Venganza sube con ellas. ¿No las oyes?" (117). The sounds that Euriclea has heard, however, turn out to be Telémaco approaching with the disguised Ulises. Symbolically, of course, as Doménech points out, Euriclea is correct: "*en* Ulises vienen las Furias, la venganza" (*El teatro* 249–50). Iglesias Feijoo offers a similar interpretation in reading Ulises and Penélope as "Furias de sí mismos, porque éstas no son sino el castigo que se inflinge [*sic*] el hombre a sí y a sus semejantes" (*La trayectoria* 107). A metaphorical context is equally appropriate for interpreting Penélope's call for sacrifices to the gods of love and war (176; act 2). As in Castro's play, where Venus and Marte represent the incarnation of the lust and violence that govern the plot, the unnamed gods of love and war in Buero are mere abstract manifestations of the characters' erotic and aggressive impulses.

By eliminating the role of fate in his play, Buero, like Castro, makes the protagonists responsible for their desires, as Ruple notes (91). More important, the removal of the cumbersome mechanism of divine intervention and coercion allows Buero to revise Homer's characters along broader psychological and symbolic lines, and an interpretation of their characters must take this new context into account.

The Ulises-Penélope-Anfino triangle reveals a masculine-feminine hierarchy that Penélope and Anfino, even though they fight against it, do not manage to overturn completely. In the context of this hierarchy, Ulises

---

15. Buero cites a passage spoken by Zeus in *Od.* 1.32–34 that may have served as a precedent for Penélope's statement in this scene (see "Comentario" 96).

and the other Greeks who went to Troy represent a rational principle that appropriates logic in the service of violence and vengeance, leading Penélope to declare that "razonaron que había que verter sangre, en una guerra de diez años, para vengar el honor de un pobre idiota llamado Menelao" (157; act 2). Ulises' use of reason for violent ends has a long history in Greek mythology and might be said to represent the governing principle of the universe since the time of Zeus's overthrow of Cronos with the aid of cleverness or *mētis* (personified in some authors by Prometheus). When Ulises returns, he confirms this aggressive deployment of reason through his schemes to kill the suitors. Penélope censures him for being a "mezquino razonador" who is afraid to feel (202; act 3), and, because of this lack, she rejects him forever: "Y si tú me hubieses ofrecido con sencillez y valor tus canas ennoblecidas por la guerra y los azares, ¡tal vez! yo habría reaccionado a tiempo. Hubieras sido, a pesar de todo, el hombre de corazón con quien toda mujer sueña ... El Ulises con quien yo soñé, ahí, los primeros años ... ¡Y no este astuto patán, hipócrita y temeroso, que se me presenta como un viejo ruin para acabar de destruirme toda ilusión posible!" (202; act 3). Penélope's condemnation of Ulises demonstrates one of the constants in Buero Vallejo's early theater, what Martha Halsey calls "the insufficiency or the limits of reason alone" ("The Dreamer" 283).

In contrast to Ulises, as Halsey affirms elsewhere (*Antonio* 46), Penélope and Anfino represent dreaming, the theme from which the play takes its title. To be more explicit, they embody a counterrational or intuitive principle based on emotion and traditionally identified with feminine mentality. Although Anfino insists, "Yo soy hombre y sé razonar" (155), it becomes clear in the subsequent dialogue that he is not guided by this principle. When Penélope tells him that she unravels her tapestry by night, he "deduces" that she must be doing so in order to buy time for Ulises to return (the motive behind the Homeric Penelope's scheme). The following exchange takes place:

Penélope.—¡Ah, qué bien pensáis los hombres! No hay duda. El razonamiento es perfecto. ¡Me admiras!
Anfino.—No quise disgustarte.
Penélope.—(*Violenta.*) Te marcharás mañana, ¿no?
Anfino.—(*Asustado.*) ¿Por qué?
Penélope.—Para seguir tu razonamiento. Sabes que destejo para engañaros. Terminaron tus esperanzas. Amo a Ulises y tú eres de-

masiado bueno para tomarme a la fuerza. Tu razón debe aconsejarte que abandones el campo.
Anfino.—¡No me iré!
Penélope.—(*Irónica.*) ¿Por qué no?
Anfino.—Porque ... Porque ... ¡Oh, basta! (*Se vuelve para marcharse.*)
Penélope. ¡Espera! (*Él se detiene y la mira, subyugado por el calor de su voz.*) Aún no. (*Dulce.*) Te llevo diez años y me pareces como un niño a quien hubieran roto el juguete precioso de su ... razonamiento. Las mujeres no sabemos razonar, pero soñamos. (156–57; act 2)

Anfino's inability to follow the dictates of reason shows that he is guided by a different principle, one based on the love and hope that govern his relationship with Penélope. Significantly, his last words in the play are "La muerte es nuestro gran sueño liberador ... (*Breve pausa.*) Gracias por tus sueños, Penélope" (194), a statement that unmistakably identifies him with the principle of dreaming that Penélope associates with women.

This counterrational principle is manifested most clearly in two of the central images of the play: Penélope's *templete*, or sewing room, and the shroud that she weaves for Ulises' father while inside. The contents of the sewing room remain largely out of sight of the audience, and the only character allowed inside besides Penélope is the nurse Euriclea, whom Buero, in contrast to Homer, has made blind. In the uninvaded solitude of this room, in contrast to the public space of the balcony—the space that Ulises uses to murder the suitors—Penélope is forced to confront her situation and to design her response to it. Several critics have followed Buero's own remarks in the "Comentario" (91) to the effect that the *templete* is symbolic of Penélope's soul.[16] Minako Nonoyama proposes, furthermore, that the room may be viewed as a space in which Penélope's real self is freed from the restrictions imposed by her social self (75), and Fernando de Diego interprets it as a symbol of Penélope's ideal world (358). These observations, when added to the fact that the room is off limits to men and functions as a sanctuary for a traditionally feminine occupation—weaving—suggest a reading of the *templete* as an idealized version of the exclusively feminine space called for by Virginia Woolf at the beginning of the twentieth century. As such, it becomes a matrix of feminine desire that stands in opposition to the masculine discourse of Ulises.

16. Halsey, "The Dreamer" 267, *Antonio* 46; Ruiz Ramón, *Historia . . . siglo XX* 348; Iglesias Feijoo, *La trayectoria* 105.

This opposition becomes evident in the mise-en-scène described in the opening stage directions: "En la pared del templete y a la derecha de la puerta están colgados, bien visibles, la aljaba y el enorme y grueso arco de Ulises" (107). The bow and quiver of Ulises, symbols of his aggression, tellingly stand outside the perimeter of the sewing room and directly above his own space, the balcony. When, at the end of the play, Ulises returns and threatens to break down the door to the room by force (200; act 3), Penélope resists his attempts. Similarly, in act 2, she resists the suitors' attempts to force their way into the room (166). In both cases she successfully preserves the integrity of the interior against masculine incursion.

While inside the room, Penélope weaves a shroud into which she embroiders images that she calls her "dreams," as she explains to Anfino: "A todos les extraña que no quiera enseñar los bordados del sudario. Yo pretexto que sólo la muerte puede verlos. ¡Sin embargo, no son nada terribles, ni siquiera claros de entender! Pero son demasiado íntimos. Tanto que, sólo alguien ..., muy allegado a mí ..., encontraría en ellos significados y parecidos. Porque, hechos al calor de mi angustia de tejedora, son como yo misma. Son ... ¡mis sueños!" (160; act 2). Penélope's dreams represent the subconscious manifestations of her desires or, in Freudian terms, of her wish-fulfillment fantasies (Freud, *Interpretation*, chap. 3). In accordance with Buero's rewriting of her character, these dreams embody her erotic desire for Anfino, and she not too subtly hints to him, in a continuation of the passage cited above, that "me avergüenza enseñarlos. Sería como mostrarme desnuda ... (*Baja la vista.*) Si tú quieres, yo ... te los enseñaré" (160).

Penélope's desires and their oneiric manifestations are related to her essence as a woman. William Giuliano states that the "desire to love and be loved is the greatest motivating force in the behavior of the women in Buero's dramas" ("The Role" 25; see also his *Buero Vallejo* 147). While rather sweeping in its implications, his statement is justifiable in the case of Penélope, who tells Anfino: "Yo no sé razonar y las ideas se me escapan. Nosotras pensamos de cualquier manera, mientras tejemos o cosemos. Y, a lo sumo, ponemos en el bordado, inhábiles y conmovidas, algunas de las cosas que soñamos" (159; act 2). This statement, when compared to the one cited earlier ("razonaron que había que verter sangre"), underscores the opposition between masculine reason and feminine desire. Dreaming is associated with the creative act of weaving or sewing—domestic, traditionally feminine activities—whereas reason is used for the destructive deeds of war and violence—social, traditionally masculine exercises.

Gabriela Chambardón notes that Ulises is the "prototipo del hombre bien integrado en la sociedad" and that to maintain his social integrity he sacrifices his individuality and the deepest values of justice, love, and truth (76). This comment suggests a scenario in which the personal and the domestic are destroyed by the social and the political, a destruction most evident in the murder of Anfino (an orphan disconnected from society) by Ulises (Greece's most famous public figure). In this worldview, dreams become a way of opposing or even subverting reason, insofar as they imply a nonrational, analogical mode of consciousness: "Esperar ... Esperar el día en que los hombres sean como tú [Anfino] ... y no como ése. Que tengan corazón para nosotras y bondad para todos: que no guerreen ni nos abandonen" (206; act 3). Hoping, which is analogous to dreaming or desiring and predicated on feminine consciousness, offers the seed for beginning anew after the disaster brought about by the crisis of reason.

The other characters and their subplots in the play bring into greater relief Penélope's quiet subversion of reason and underscore the necessity of her efforts. One such subplot is the triangle involving Anfino, the slave woman Dione, and Telémaco. Iglesias Feijoo notes that Dione is the only character of Buero's play not taken directly from the *Odyssey*.[17] He believes, in addition, that her role in the play is dramatically unjustified and that the queen's rivalry with her slave over Anfino trivializes Penélope's character (Introducción 50–51; see also *La trayectoria* 99). Nevertheless, a comparison of the two principal triangles of desire in the play, Telémaco-Dione-Anfino and Ulises-Penélope-Anfino, will reveal the importance of Dione's role in the play.

In the first place, as Carmen González-Cobos points out (189), Dione is the antithesis of Penélope insofar as she is characterized by realism and pragmatism. In contrast to the introspection that marks Penélope's character, the aggressive pursuit of desire defines Dione's. Her plan is for Anfino, the object of her desires, to marry Penélope so that then, as king, he can make Dione his mistress and grant her power to govern: "Esta casa también necesita una mujer que sepa dirigirla. . . . Y nadie, sino yo, puede

---

17. Other critics (Bourne 72, Alvar 55) have pointed out that she bears some resemblance to Homer's Melantho (*Od.* 18.321, 19.65). In the *Iliad* (5.370–71) Dione is the mother of Aphrodite, while Hesiod claims that she is a nymph born to Oceanus and Tethys (*Theogony* 353).

ser la verdadera mujer de esta casa ... cuando tú seas el hombre" (152; act 2). Dione's aggressiveness represents an alternative to the passivity of Helena that nevertheless contrasts with Penélope's chosen path of resistance: dreaming. Yet, rather than subverting masculine authority and escaping feminine stereotypes, as Penélope does, Dione becomes an accomplice to authority and ultimately falls victim to it. Her execution at the end of the play suggests the inadequacy of her approach and a parallel vindication of Penélope's.

Furthermore, Dione's rejection of the persistent Telémaco for Anfino parallels Penélope's rejection of Ulises (also for Anfino) and casts Telémaco as a mirror image of his father, a resemblance noted by Ruple (89) and Iglesias Feijoo (*La trayectoria* 108). Ulises and Telémaco use exactly the same phrase—"Tonterías de mujeres"—to describe Penélope's dreams (144, 148; act 2). The parallel between them even extends to Telémaco's rivalry with Anfino, so that both father and son ally against the hapless suitor at the end of the play, recalling the scene of Amphinomus's death in the *Odyssey* (22.89–94).

Borel (169) notes that the final world order in the play ostensibly vindicates the aggressors Ulises and Telémaco, but it is also true that the failure of the two traditionally masculine figures in the play to win the object of their desires (Dione is executed and Penélope remains faithful in spirit to Anfino) signals a critical failure of reason, as Penélope indicates to Ulises: "Y eres tú, tú solamente, quien ha perdido la partida. ¡Yo la he ganado! . . . Y ahora te queda tu mujer, sí, a los ojos de todos; pero teniéndome no tienes ya nada, ¿me oyes? ¡Nada! Porque él [Anfino] se lo ha llevado todo para siempre. Una apariencia; una risible ... cáscara de matrimonio te queda" (203; act 3). Penélope's proposition, "teniéndome no tienes ya nada," logically impossible but nonetheless true, ingeniously employs a type of nonrational *écriture féminine* to allude to a tentative victory of feminine desire. Ulises is left with a "cáscara de matrimonio," a superficial, mendacious relationship that passes into the official version of history by means of the chant that he orders the chorus to invent:

> Penélope fue sola, y circundada
> estuvo de peligros y deseos.
> Mas sólo para Ulises vive ella.
> Y no caerá cual otra Clitemnestra.
> Tejía y destejía durante años
> para burlar así a los pretendientes.

> Ella bordó sus sueños en la tela.
> Sus deseos y sueños son: ¡Ulises! (205; act 3)

The absurdly apocryphal chant, tellingly identical to the Homeric version of the story, presents a dramatic contrast to the actual state of affairs that inevitably calls attention to Penélope's "inner" victory: her vindication of truth in the face of official lies, of feminine desire in the face of masculine discourse.

Even so, Buero's play is not nearly so black and white as it might first appear, and Penélope does not fit squarely into the mold of a modern feminist. Several features of her personality place her in a more dubious position. Her view of the suitors, for example, reveals a petty jealousy of Helena:

> Treinta jóvenes jefes, hoy viejos o muertos, conducían nuestros ejércitos en Troya por causa de Helena. ¡Y treinta jóvenes jefes, hijos de los anteriores muchos de ellos, venían a rivalizar por mí! ¡No por Helena, no! Sino por Penélope. (*Pausa.*) *Era mi pequeño desquite* ... Mi pequeña guerra de Troya. Me sentía vivir. Había que hacer durar, como fuese, esta lucha vuestra, que alimentaba mi amor propio herido, que me daba la seguridad de mi propia existencia, como no la había vuelto a sentir desde ... Ulises me ganó a otros diecinueve príncipes, hace muchos años. (157; act 2)

Later, she shouts to the suitors, "¡Reñid por mí, si sois hombres!" (170; act 2), confirming a rather traditional relationship between men and women. In addition, she refers to herself as "una débil mujer" (115; act 1), a characterization that Harris ("La mujer" 250–51) reads in light of Judith Fetterley's feminist theory and that Lamartina-Lens (32) interprets as a major "flaw" in the play. Flawed or not, even though Penélope struggles against masculine discourse and authority, her character remains undeniably ambiguous, tainted by the traces of a masculine-feminine dialectic that has not yet been transcended.

This ambiguity is densely encoded in the image of the shroud that Penélope weaves. A product of the feminine space of the *templete*, the shroud signifies, in one sense, a resistance to masculine power. It is, after all, designed to be placed over—to erase—Ulises' father, who, in his son's absence, represents the center of the patriarchal norms that Penélope fights against. Moreover, the weavings on the shroud, besides embodying

Penélope's dreams, can, in the context of the preliterate society in which they are produced ("anterior a los días de Homero" [105]), be interpreted as a type of *archi-écriture* that records and preserves feminine voice and situates it in an always-already relationship with respect to masculine discourse.

In contrast, Penélope's ruse of unraveling the shroud becomes, in the new context created by Buero, a destruction of her dreams and a frustration of her desires, literally woven as they are into its fabric. This destruction is only appropriate, however, since the very possibility of the ruse is a product of Penélope's own *mētis* and logic, traits that befit Ulises himself: "Pensando en la necesaria prudencia, en la astucia conveniente para que no le matasen [a Anfino] ..." (159; act 2). It is no coincidence that Euriclea compares Penélope to Ulises: "Sé que eres fuerte y astuta, como tu esposo Ulises" (116; act 1). By once again delicately altering the motivations of his classical source, Buero converts Penelope's loyalty to Odysseus, manifested in her famous stratagem of weaving and unraveling, into precisely the opposite scenario, in which her stratagem is designed to buy time not for her husband but for the new object of her desire.

Yet, precisely because Penélope appropriates cleverness to combat cleverness, she finds herself in an impossible situation, compromised both by the threat of male oppression and by her very resistance to it. Completing the shroud would symbolically anticipate the effacement of patriarchy in the interment of Ulises' father, but it would also force her to choose from among the four despicable male suitors, since she cannot choose Anfino because he lacks an army to protect him, and she is afraid that the other four would kill him out of jealousy (139; act 2). In contrast, by unraveling the shroud as she does, she not only buys time for Anfino but also unknowingly aligns herself with Homer's Penelope and allows time for Ulises to return. It is indicative of Penélope's double bind that the shroud intended for Ulises' father ends up, by Ulises' orders, covering Anfino himself (205; act 3).

The explanation of Penélope's ambiguous character and predicament lies in the complexity of Buero's project with respect to his Homeric sources. The feminine space of the *templete* and that which is associated with it mark the first step in a deconstruction of the cultural opposition of male and female. This step is characterized by the reversal of a binary epistemology that privileges men over women and that in the play is manifested in the series of oppositions mapped out in this study: war/love, fighting/weaving, destruction/creation, public/private, political/personal, outer/inner, balcony/*templete*, reason/dreams, myth/truth. The overturning of these oppositions achieves an effective demythification of Ulises' character by revealing an alternative, darker side to his traditional virtues. Yet overturning hierarchies does not eliminate the mental categories that make their oppositions possible; it merely changes their component terms. As long as the terms are permitted to exist in a conceptually contiguous relation to one another, it is impossible for one to appear without the other. In practical terms, it is impossible for Penélope to disassociate herself completely from traditionally feminine desire (Helena) or to liberate herself from traditionally masculine discourse (Ulises), an impossibility that shows up in the ambiguity of her character.

The second step of the deconstructive process is the crucial one: "Deconstruction . . . must, by means of a double gesture, a double science, a double writing, practice an *overturning* of the classical opposition *and* a general *displacement* of the system" (Derrida 329). Although this secondary gesture does not occur in the play, it is enabled by the demythification of Ulises and anticipated when Penélope imagines a day in which "no haya más Helenas ... ni Ulises en el mundo!" (206; act 3): the two most obvious representatives of the masculine-feminine binary. The play thus ends on a note of hope, a key ingredient in Buero's theater (Pérez Minik, *Teatro* 388).

Considered in the wider context of postwar Spain and of the life of Buero Vallejo, who was imprisoned and sentenced to death for his efforts on behalf of the Republican side of the war (a sentence later commuted to life in prison and then to probational release), the critique of patriarchy in *La tejedora de sueños* becomes a rather bold attack on the civil war and the subsequent repression of the Franco regime: "Esta obra fue la que más mella hizo, a nuestro entender, en el alto aparato oficial del franquismo. Estrenada, como las anteriores, en un teatro nacional, tenía todo el valor de un desafío y de un valeroso reto. Quien quiso entender la reflexión sobre la reciente guerra civil y sus terribles consecuencias, pudo entenderlo. El atreverse a 'leer' la fiel Penélope como una arriesgada y valiente Clitemnestra, cambiaba todos los esquemas de la aparentemente tranquila y satisfecha conciencia cultural del franquismo" (Salvat i Ferré 84).[18] In addition, Ulises' role of silencing truth and disseminating in its

---

18. This reading is the boldest in a series of overtly political interpretations of the play that have appeared in recent years with increasing frequency. See Giuliano, *Buero* 94; Ruple 36–37; Holt 114; González-Cobos 183; Podol, "The Theme" 45; Iglesias Feijoo, *La trayectoria* 109; Rogers, "Role Constraints" 319 n. 22; Cazorla, "El retorno" 43–44; Lamartina-Lens 34; Diego 358; and Ragué Arias, *Lo que fue Troya* 35.

place the sugar-coated lies of the chorus parallels the official propaganda machine of the Franco regime.

Thus, apart from the remarkable balance that it strikes between fidelity to tradition and artistic originality, Buero's play is noteworthy for its veiled political critique. This use of myth, which has already been noted in the plays of Torrente and Pemán from the 1940s, reappears with increasing frequency and urgency in the Franco period.

From the Political to the Cultural

José María Pemán returned to the theatrical scene in the 1950s with two more mythological plays: *Tyestes* (1952) and *Edipo* (1953). *Edipo* is similar to Pemán's *Antígona* in that the author "tampers as little as possible with the basic material" (Bourne 182). Pemán explains: "El *Edipo* que he escrito con fervor y humildad tiene por principal objeto intentar traer al espectador actual, con la menor pérdida posible, toda la validez dramática de la más grande tragedia de la Humanidad" (*Edipo* 7). Even so, to dramatize the expulsion of a guilty king in the midst of a right-wing dictatorship is laden with symbolic potential.[19]

Debuting the same year as *La tejedora de sueños*, Pemán's *Tyestes*, like his *Electra*, represents an authentic re-creation of classical myth. In his "Autocrítica" the author reveals his intention to dramatize the conflict of two psychologies: Atreo's reflective rancor and Tyestes' blind optimism (qtd. in Bourne 278). Subtitled *La tragedia de la venganza*, the play reveals, more than anything, the conflict of two brothers' passion for the same woman and the violence that results. In Seneca's *Thyestes*, the explicit model of the play, one of the motives that compels Atreus to seek revenge on Thyestes is the latter's seduction of his brother's wife (220–44). Pemán foregrounds this rivalry over the "corrupta coniunx" 'unfaithful wife' to the exclusion of the other factors motivating the revenge, most important, the "imperi quassa fides" 'violation of the governing agreement' (239). In the Spanish version of the play, Tyestes rules Micenas while his brother is off at war. When Atreo returns, he banishes Tyestes because he has become too popular as a ruler: "temí que su gobierno / benigno—¡todos le querían!— / persiguiera como una sombra mala / de recuerdo y contraste

---

19. In contrast to the questions that Ahl raises about Sophocles' *Oedipus*, there is no room left to doubt Edipo's guilt in Pemán's play.

mi mando riguroso" (41). With the passage of time he comes genuinely to regret his decision and, since his late wife Érope left no heirs, invites Tyestes and his two children back to the palace to share rule with him. By chance, Atreo discovers that his wife was unfaithful to him with Tyestes while he was away at war. Consumed with rage, he avenges himself by killing Tyestes' children, the product of the illicit love affair, and serving them to his brother for dinner.

Pemán's principal departures from the Senecan model reveal the new emphasis he gives to his play. As the product of his affair with Érope, Tyestes' children become both the result of the offense and the instrument of revenge; as such, they serve as a symbolic matrix of the erotic, aggressive, and nutritive desires used for revising the myth.[20] Furthermore, it is noteworthy that Atreo banishes Tyestes after the conclusion of the war that separates them and that his exile was not limited to "sólo el destierro ... El Rey borró su nombre / de piedras y columnas ... El Rey dijo: / ¡No ha existido Tyestes!" (31). It is tempting to read in these passages a critique of the censorship and propaganda of the Franco regime. Finally, the dramatization of a myth of such horrific fraternal strife, in which innocent children become the victims of violence between adults, would be an appropriate choice for someone seeking to criticize the internecine strife of the country's recent civil war. As in his other mythological plays, Pemán's subtle use of myth authorizes such interpretations.[21]

Two other plays from the 1950s, based on the myth of Medea, proceed along similar lines. Alfonso Sastre's *Medea* (1958) is not so significant for its rewriting of Euripides, which amounts to little more than a loose translation, as for the reflections it provoked in its author some thirty years later: "Hablando de las virtualidades actuales de esta tragedia, no es posible olvidar una obvia lectura feminista y, en estos años, el problema creciente de los extranjeros en Europa. Oyendo a Medea, se eschucha una voz, también, contra la xenofobia y el racismo" (6). These sentiments are given new meaning in José Bergamín's one-act *Medea la encantadora* (1954),

---

20. There is no suggestion in Seneca that the murdered children were born to Aerope; Atreus does, however, state that Thyestes would have killed Atreus's children had Thyestes not thought himself their father (1104–10).

21. For excellent analyses of all Pemán's mythological plays, including detailed comparisons with their classical sources, see Bourne. Torrente Ballester provides a short analysis of *Tyestes* (*Teatro* 539–40). Ragué Arias's claim that Pemán's plays "utilizaban pomposamente el mito para vanagloria del régimen establecido" (*Los personajes* 114; see also *Lo que fue Troya* 55–63) seems to be based more on the author's biography than on a careful reading of his plays.

which sets the myth of Medea in modern Córdoba. Written mainly in verse, this brief work makes exceptional use of metaphor through frequent images of blood, fire, heart, and soul. Bergamín creates a highly lyrical dramatization of Medea's uncontrollable hatred, which, in a peculiarly Senecan twist, he links to her equally profound love. The heroine tells Creusa in an extraordinary passage:

> ¿Puede haber odio sin amor? Yo enmascaré con mi alma, por amor, los crímenes que Jasón cometía por este amor mío. Yo puse mi alma en su camino para que esos monstruos del amor, ocultándoselos, le dieran fuerzas a su brazo y pureza a su sangre. Y nombre a su virtud: gloria, fama. Yo puse mis manos de sueño entre las suyas para empapar con ellas, con mi alma, la sangre de los hombres que morían por culpa nuestra, por culpa de nuestro único y divino amor. Yo tomé sus crímenes en mis manos para que no lo fuesen. Sólo el amor podía hacer por mis manos ese prodigio. Yo alimenté, de la más secreta angustia inmortal de mi ser, la ilusión de nuestra ventura: el fantasma de un amor eterno. (36)

The paradoxical association between love and hatred that underpins Bergamín's rewriting of the myth might be read as a poetic extension of an isolated phrase spoken by Seneca's heroine, namely that "nullum scelus / irata feci; movit infelix amor" 'I committed no crime out of rage; unhappy love was what moved me' (*Medea* 135–36). Besides calling one's attention to the emotional ambivalence of its protagonist's desires, *Medea la encantadora* is noteworthy for its casting of Medea as an Andalusian gypsy and Jasón as a Spaniard. The racism implicit in the Euripidean Jason's condemnation of Medea's "barbarism" (*Medea* 1330–32, 1339–40) assumes new meaning in this contemporary context.[22]

These examples demonstrate that while the mythological plays of the forties and fifties often proffered veiled political statements against war and the official propaganda of the Franco regime—statements that continued to be made in plays based on the Ulysses theme, for example (see Paulino)—they also planted the seeds of a wider cultural critique that intensified after the death of Franco (1975) and the subsequent restora-

---

22. In another mythological work, *La sangre de Antígona*, Bergamín uses the potentially explosive myth of Antigone to dramatize the struggle of the heroine who "eleva hasta los cielos su grito, como una interrogación acusadora, entre los vivos y los muertos" (48). The date of composition of this play is uncertain, as it was published posthumously. For an analysis of Bergamín's rarely studied theater, see Penalva.

tion of democracy and artistic freedom.[23] Feminism, one of the strongest flowerings of this seed, assumed a definitive presence in Spanish theater in the 1980s. Concha Romero's *Así aman los dioses*, written in 1982, skillfully laces together various mythological narratives—Cupid and Psyche, Mars and Venus, Venus and Adonis, the Judgment of Paris—around the question of desire, as Carlos García Gual notes in the prologue: "Concha Romero ha entresacado los motivos eróticos de la mitología clásica y los ha zurcido, con sutil habilidad y un gran sentido teatral, en esta original farsa celeste" (xii). Significantly, most of the women, whether human or divine, who become involved with men in the play end up either victimized by male deception (as Júpiter and Cupido deceive Juno and Alma) or objectified by male desire (as in Venus's relations with Marte, Vulcano, and Adonis). In contrast to these female figures the virgin goddess Minerva reveals a total repudiation of desire: "El amor te hace esclava. Te somete al varón y vives celosa, celada o engañada. . . . He vencido el deseo y me he ganado a mí" (25–26). Romero's play offers no suggestions on striking a balance between the extremes of subjugation and isolation, and the comic undertones of the play prevent it from attaining a level of moral indignation. Rather than presenting the work as a feminist manifesto, the author exploits the conflicts of desire for their dramatic effectiveness, both serious and comic.

In *Lagartijas, gaviotas y mariposas* María José Ragué Arias goes a step further and turns her academic study of Greek tragedy into a creative reproduction of the myth of Phaedra.[24] Following Unamuno's *Fedra*, her play is set in a contemporary bourgeois environment. Unlike Unamuno's protagonist, Ragué Arias's Teresa—the counterpart of Phaedra—rejects her husband Pedro explicitly because "al principio me gustaba, pero yo no tenía placer, me lo inventaba, me sentía feliz cuando le veía satisfecho, me gustaba entregarme a él, pero placer no, yo no tenía placer" (45).

---

23. Four plays from the fifties by Juan Germán Schroeder would be interesting to read in this context: *La esfinge furiosa* (1951), *Medea* (1954), *Hécuba* (1955), and *Hipólito coronado* (1959). See Ragué Arias, *Els personatges* 125. Unfortunately, I have been unable to acquire any of these plays. In addition, Domingo Miras wrote a fascinating trio of mythological plays between 1970 and 1972 that exemplify the pattern of political and cultural critique mentioned above: *Egisto*, *Penélope*, and *Fedra* have recently been published in the volume *Teatro mitológico*, accompanied by an excellent introduction and bibliography. See also the analysis in Ragué Arias, *Lo que fue Troya* 89–104.

24. The play was first composed in Catalán with the title *La llibertat de Fedra* (1986), subsequently revised to *Crits de gavina* (1990), and finally rewritten in Castilian with the present title.

Teresa's attraction to her stepson Juan becomes a function of her frustration of desire that in the classical models was due to Theseus's frequent absence from home. In his introduction to the play, Alberto Miralles writes: "[Teresa] es un personaje que necesita ser contemplado desde la óptica de la liberación femenina, donde conceptos como fidelidad y matrimonio cobran una nueva dimensión, quizá la de no ser ya el cauce por el que obligatoriamente debe discurrir una mujer" (14–15). In this light, Ragué Arias's revision of the myth fully vindicates women's rights to sexual pleasure; accordingly, Teresa consummates her desire for Juan in act 1 and leaves Pedro at the end of the play.

"Queer" interpretations inform one of the more recent trends in the rewriting of classical mythology in the postwar theater. In the same way that Spanish feminists have sought to revise the ancient tales from a perspective that gives voice to women and their particular concerns, gay and lesbian writers and those sympathetic to their interests have enriched twentieth-century Spain's growing body of mythological plays with works that dramatize the oppression of the homosexual community and its struggle for equality. A postal worker whose father was imprisoned by the Franco regime, Luis Riaza is one such playwright. Despite his inability to devote himself fully to his adopted profession, he has proved to be an outstanding talent among the experimental playwrights of the postwar period, and his *Medea es un buen chico* offers an extraordinarily original, often outrageous, interpretation of the story of Medea.[25]

Queer Myth and the Fallacy of Heterosexual Desire: Luis Riaza's *Medea es un buen chico*

Riaza's reconstruction of classical mythology might strike one as bizarre in comparison with the others studied in this analysis. Insofar as its treat-

---

25. Another queer rewriting of mythology apparently occurs in Lourdes Ortiz's unpublished *Penteo*, which I have not been able to acquire. See the analysis in Ragué Arias, "Penélope, Agave y Fedra" and *Lo que fue Troya* 127–29. Written in 1980, *Medea es un buen chico* was first performed in 1985 in a coproducción of the Círculo de Bellas Artes and the Centro Nacional de Nuevas Tendencias Estéticas, directed by Luis Vera. Riaza is also author of the brief, one-act *Antígona ... ¡cerda!*, which employs the explosive myth of Antigone to demonstrate the corruptibility of political power and the inherent desire to resist its influence. For an analysis, see Cazorla, "La indestructibilidad" and "The Duality of Power"; and Ragué Arias, *Lo que fue Troya* 114–18. On Riaza's life and career, see the interesting interview conducted by Alicia Ramos.

ment of its sources is based on allusion, role-playing, infinite substitution, and the fragmentation of plot and character, it may be classified as a postmodern rewriting of the myth of Medea.[26] To comprehend the play's full significance, it will be helpful to read it in the context of the author's other works.

Riaza's dramaturgy represents an effort to depict human reality and perception as unstable and potentially indistinguishable from fiction. As Pedro Ruiz Pérez argues, the theater provides Riaza with the ideal format for dramatizing these ideas: "En el teatro la ficción se superpone a la realidad, la anula y la despoja de sus características, adoptándolas para su propio disfraz. En todas y cada una de las obras de Riaza toma cuerpo la conciencia que el autor tiene del teatro como mecanismo de alienación, que funciona sirviéndose de procedimientos de fingimiento y simulación" (479). One feature of Riaza's work that prominently reflects these characteristics is his constant recourse to ludic ritual. Through a thematization of role-playing in which the true identity of the role-player is lost among the masks of theater, Riaza calls into question the stability of human identity and perception. What Peter Podol claims for *El desván de los machos y el sótano de las hembras* is equally valid with respect to *Medea* and other works: "Echoes of Calderón, Goya, Valle-Inclán, Artaud, Arrabal and others notwithstanding, it [*El desván*] constitutes a unique and original utilization of ritual, the very basis of theater, to project a grotesque and disturbing vision of the human condition in today's world" ("Ritual" 17).

In this theater in which nothing is what it appears to be and permanence is an illusion, it is not surprising that ambivalent sexuality and transvestism become privileged topics for dramatization. The core of Euripides' and Seneca's plays—Jason's rejection of Medea and her subsequent revenge—is transposed to a queer context that critiques heterosexual notions of power and desire. Like feminine desire in Buero's *Tejedora*, queer desire—sexual attraction that upsets traditional conceptions of gender pairing—provides the vital link between the classical representations of Medea and Riaza's rewriting. In particular, Riaza concentrates on the predicament of gay men in a sexually polarized world.

The lonely isolation and ostracism that a heterosexually dominant soci-

---

26. I do not propose, in invoking the term *postmodernism*, to take part in the highly charged and wide-ranging debate that surrounds the subject. I use the word merely as a convenient marker for a generally agreed-upon set of aesthetic and epistemological principles that, insofar as they are present in Riaza's work, clearly differentiate it from the other plays considered in this context. For extended discussions of the question of postmodernism, the reader should begin with the crucial works of Habermas, Jameson, Lyotard, and Hassan.

ety imposes on its nonconformist members is conveyed at once in the setting of the play. The stage directions indicate, "Todo el espacio dará la impresión de enclaustramiento y de falta de comunicación con el mundo exterior" (31). The door to the outside world, for example, is not a real door but merely an image drawn "con simples trazos negros fácilmente borrables" onto a white background. The interior of the room in which the entire performance takes place seems to be hermetically sealed from the outside, creating an atmosphere of suffocation and stagnation. The faded nineteenth-century decor of the set contributes to this atmosphere, giving the impression that time itself has come to a halt or lost its meaning. When Medea asks Nodriza what day it is, she replies, "Pongamos que viernes" (40), and, throughout the play, the passage of time is represented only by erasable hands drawn on a clock that is, like the door, imaginary.

In this claustrophobic setting, the entire play consists of a dialogue between two characters, Medea and Nodriza. Nodriza recalls the nurse of Euripides' and Seneca's plays; in Riaza's version, however, both she and Medea are transvestite figures, biologically male but androgynous in appearance and manner.[27] The "action" of the play, if it can be called that, is predicated on Medea's anticipation of the arrival of her lover Jasón. In part 1, as Medea waits, Nodriza bathes her, adorns her in black feminine underwear, and narrates a series of fragmented episodes that center on Medea's relationship with an unnamed man, presumably Jasón, who was apparently stolen from Medea by an anonymous "hija de un Rey." Constructed from elements of memory and fantasy, these episodes serve as a type of psychotherapy through which Medea attempts to come to terms with her fragmented identity.

In the first story, Jasón meets Medea's rival at a racetrack. He tells Medea that he is betting on a wine-and-cinnamon-colored horse because it matches the color of the black hat that he gave her as a gift. But when the horse wins, Jasón approaches it to "acariciar el belfo todavía palpitante de aquella bestia triunfadora" (45), and, as Nodriza recounts: "Junto al 'tres años' ganador estaba su propietaria que no era otra que la hija de un Rey ... Y madame, siempre según la versión que contó a su actriz y nodriza, pudo contemplar, a través de los prismáticos, la sonrisa incitadora de aquella muñeca de sangre real, bajo su chistera de amazona color canela y envuelta en tules color vino" (46). When Medea observes

---

27. Medea and Nodriza are both described with grammatical forms that vary between the masculine and feminine. At the risk of neutralizing the playful ambiguity that this vacillation achieves, I will, for the sake of clarity, refer to both characters in the feminine.

them together, she feels betrayed by Jasón because she realizes that he may have staked his bet on the color of the princess's clothes rather than on the blackness of her own hat.

In the next flashback-fantasy, Medea and Jasón are traveling alone on the Orient Express. At one of the stops, a woman with "cuatrocientos baules [*sic*] y ocho mil sombrereras" (47) climbs on board. The train moves on and Medea falls asleep. She awakens to find herself on the Titanic, where she observes Jasón and the same woman engaged in lively conversation. Nodriza narrates what occurred next:

Nodriza.—Y la desconocida posó sobre la mano de monsieur ...
Medea.—Cubierta de vello, como la garra de un león ...
Nodriza.— ... su propia manita, blanca como una de aquellas gaviotas que sobrevolaban la estela del buque ... Y en uno de los dedos de aquella manita lucía un anillo con una corona principesca tallada en el verde rubí ...
Medea.—(*Ronca.*) ¡Sí! ¡Era ella: la hija de un Rey! (48)

The third story takes place in a casino in which Jasón loses all his money in a roulette game:

Medea.—Y cuando todo lo hubo perdido y sólo le restaba mi amor y mi fortuna que el orgulloso tendría, entonces, que aceptar ...
Nodriza.—Aparece ella, con su tocado de plumas tropicales y se coloca tras la silla de monsieur. Y pone un billete de un millón de francos sobre la negada casilla. Y suena, rompiendo el trágico silencio, la voz del "croupier": faites votres jeux, madames et monsieurs; faites votres jeux. Y sale el trece, par y negro [the combination that Jasón had been betting on] ...
Medea.—¡La magia blanca de aquella maldita hija de un Rey! (48)

In all three of these stories, the princess is identified metonymically with animals: she matches the colors of the horse in the first; she possesses a hand like a lion's in the second; and she wears a headdress with tropical-bird feathers in the third. The animal qualities explain her predatory function that is common to each of the narratives: stealing Jasón away from Medea. This incident is, of course, the basis for the plays by Eurípides and Seneca, and the similarities are reinforced by several other details. The first story, for example, vaguely replicates the outlines of the classical myth, in which Medea, through her black magic (the black hat in Riaza), helps Jason conquer the beasts (the "bestia triunfadora") that guard the Golden Fleece (the money won from the bet) and is then betrayed by him for the daughter of Creon (the Hija de un Rey). In the second story, the setting of Jasón's encounter with the anonymous woman—two historically famous, tourist-oriented vehicles that crossed international boundaries—evokes the motif of exploration in the classical myth of Jason. The Titanic is a particularly appropriate choice, for it recalls the seafaring Argo of the myth and, because of its notorious end, hints at the destruction that eventually befell both the princess of Corinth and, in some accounts, Jason himself.[28] In the context of Riaza's play, the Titanic hints at the disaster likely to spring from Medea's tortured identity. Finally, in the third story, Jasón is again saved by the princess's wealth, confirming the symbolic function of her royalty in the classical myth.

By this relatively early point in the play, it is already clear that Riaza is using the basic contours and imagery of the myth to portray the rejection of gay men (Medea) by a heterosexual world (Jasón and the Hija). How much of the flashbacks is fantasy and how much is memory is irrelevant and indeed impossible to determine given the play's lack of any firm point of reference. What is important is that the flashback-fantasies give narrative form to the psychological problems forced on gay and lesbian members of an intolerant society. In a recent lecture Juliet Mitchell described psychoanalysis as an art of storytelling in which the truth content of the stories is "irrelevant." In much the same way that the patient undergoing analysis narrativizes his or her psychosis, Medea uses these stories to reconstruct in fictional form the source of her problem: her rejection by Jasón and what he represents, that is, mainstream society.

As part 1 of the play progresses, it becomes clear that the stories, in addition to the narrative therapy they offer, serve as potential scripts for the actual reenactment of Medea's abandonment; hence Nodriza's reference to herself as Medea's "actriz." Through the compulsive repetition of these dramas, Medea perhaps seeks both to anesthetize herself to the pain inflicted by the traumatic event and to exact a revenge on Jasón for having caused that pain.

The "script" that Medea and Nodriza choose for performance is, in this

---

28. In some versions of the myth of Jason, the hero was killed by a rotting timber that fell from the hull of the Argo, as Euripides' Medea predicts (*Medea* 1386–88).

case, none of the stories already mentioned but the classical myth itself: "A no ser que madame prefiera los padres de las antiguas letras y fuera aquella vez en que madame y monsieur llegaron, fugitivos de Cadmos, a Corinto, a bordo de una nave que era llamada Argos. Y, en el muelle, los cabellos desnudos y rubios, estaba ella, la hija de un Rey" (48–49). Playing the figure of the Hija de un Rey, Nodriza confronts Medea to tell her of the anticipated wedding with Jasón and to understand the "oscura maraña" in which her future husband has lived up to the present moment (51). Medea recounts her litany of crimes to shock the Hija—the murder of her younger brother, the desecration of the temple in which the fleece was guarded, the surrender of her virginity to Jasón, the recourse to witchcraft (51–53)—and part 1 of the play ends with the Hija's disgusted departure.

In part 2, Medea acts out a revenge on the Hija that roughly parallels the gruesome vengeance exacted in the classical models. She sends her a wedding dress soaked in a poison that bursts into flames at the altar: "Una rueda de llamas surge del vestido y la piel de la nívea princesa se convierte en una costra requemada y negruzca. Del vestido preparado para el himeneo no quda [sic] pronto sino un montón de polvo y cenicillas" (62). Nodriza then plays the part of Creón, who arrives to expel Medea from Corinth and to ask her to leave her children behind:

Nodriza.— ... el principal motivo es el de pedirte que tus hijos, el mayor rastro que una mujer puede dejar de su paso por la tierra, en esta tierra queden. Vine a rogarte, ¡sí, a rogarte!, que tus hijos no partan contigo ...
Medea.—¿De modo y manera que eran ellos, los niños, los que pendían al extremo de los hilos? ¡Eran ellos los manipulados por el gran titiritero, el Rey Creón ...!
Nodriza.—No. Por el Rey no ... Fue la propia princesa, mi hija, la que pidió quedarse con los hijos de Jasón ... (64)

By revealing his interest in the children, the king dooms them to be the instrument of Medea's revenge, in much the same way that Jason's affection for his children plays into Medea's hands in Seneca's play (549–50).

The remainder of the play consists primarily of Medea's revenge on Jasón. The radical difference with respect to both classical models lies in the children themselves, who, instead of being portrayed as human babies, are represented by two small stuffed dogs. Medea takes one of them and slices it open with a scalpel, scattering the sand that filled the dog's insides. In the final moments, as the doorbell begins to ring loudly and incessantly, Medea imagines that Jasón has come to claim his children: "¡Abre, ahora al señor! ¡Viene a recoger a los hijos que en Medea engendró" (70). From this point on, the miniperformance that she and Nodriza act out, reconstructed from traces of memory and desire, fuses into the present time of the play, in which Medea also awaits the arrival of her lover Jasón. As she waits, she takes the second stuffed dog, submerges it in the bathtub, and throws it, soaking wet, against the door. Her wait, however, proves to be a waiting for Godot, and Nodriza finally informs her that it is not Jasón at the door but "el hombre que trae la leche de los perros de la señora. Como todas las mañanas" (71). She then erases the door completely from the white background, heightening the sense of claustrophobia and isolation.

Several points of comparison with the classical models serve to guide a queer reading of Riaza's play. Central to such an interpretation is the issue of Medea's rejection. In transposing the myth into a gender-ambivalent context, Riaza converts the issues of class and race raised by earlier playwrights into one of sexual preference. Significantly, the Glauce/Creusa figure remains nameless and is referred to only by the title Hija de un Rey, which highlights two important characteristics: that she is both a woman and a princess. While in the classical works one of the operative factors in Jason's rejection of Medea is the princess's royalty or what might be termed her *de un Rey*-ness, in Riaza's version it is her gender—the fact that she is an hij*a* and not an hij*o*—that favors her over Medea. Near the end of part 1, when she poses as the Hija who comes to visit Medea, Nodriza observes, "El crimen, el sacrilegio, la droga y el sexo sucio rodeaban a Jasón," identifying all these elements with Medea. Medea replies: "¿Y sabes qué más? . . . ¡Esto! (*Se baja las bragas negras y queda con su masculinidad al aire. Nodriza grita.*)" (53). The sudden revelation of the phallus as one of the defining features of Medea's and Jasón's relationship unquestionably foregrounds the issue of homophobia in the termination of that relationship.

Traditionally associated with power and control, the phallus, when linked to a gay male subject, becomes a marker of rejection and impotence and accounts for the abandonment of Medea. This mechanism is reinforced at the end of the play when Medea tells the absent Jasón: "Ya regresas de tu vivir en el ajeno afuera, tú, Jasón ... Ya regresas con los ojos huidizos y los testículos hueros, después de haberlos vaciado en ese limo femenino repleto de gusanillos oscilantes que un día serán como tú, todos seducción y engaño. . . . Ya regresas después de haber esparcido tu esperma de la perpetuación ... Después de haber traicionado al pobre y estéril invertido, al triste marica que Medea es ..." (69–70). Although the female genitalia are portrayed in a grotesque and alien fashion, they are nevertheless privileged over the phallus as the object of male (Jasón's) desire. Riaza cleverly spotlights an insidious logic of exclusion that leaves no place for gay male identity in a heterosexual world: men, traditionally the dominant term of the male/female binary, are rendered inferior to women in the eyes of other, heterosexual males when they reveal themselves as gay.

This symbolic reversal is emphasized in other paraverbal ways as well. The dogs, for example, that are used to substitute for Medea's children, call attention to the fact that Medea is prohibited biologically from having children. The issue becomes one not of infanticide or even of killing, for the dogs themselves are but substitutes of real dogs. Instead, the stuffed animals signal in grotesque terms the impossibility of Medea's bearing children. Similar to the way in which the very name of García Lorca's Yerma prevents her from fulfilling her maternal role, Riaza's Medea is excluded a priori from producing heirs for Jasón. As in the case of the exposed phallus that repulses male heterosexual desire, biology becomes a criterion for the ostracism and exclusion of gay men.

The role of bodily fluids in the play further reflects this logic of exclusion. In the first scene of the play, as Medea cradles and sings to one of the dogs, Nodriza prepares its "food": her own urine, which she warms over the stove and serves in a baby's bottle. The noxious properties of urine contrast vividly with the nourishing properties of milk, which, since it must be brought from outside the insular setting of the play (as demonstrated by the arrival of the milkman at the end), underscores the absence of female anatomy in the protagonists. In addition, the normally life-giving properties of semen are rendered useless in this context. In the same scene in which Medea reveals her masculinity, the princess notes that her bed reeks "a semen inútil" (53). The mixing of semen with more semen, the implicit result of gay sex, is regarded as "useless" because it has no more power to generate life than urine does to sustain it. The small flasks filled with a "líquido lechoso" (31) seem to advertise the sterility of uncoupled semen and further call attention to the sexual difference that results in Medea's marginalization.

Colors work toward a similar mechanism of exclusion in the play. Medea is consistently identified with dark colors, as in the black hat and underclothes that she wears throughout most of the piece. In contrast, the Hija de un Rey is associated with colors that gradually become lighter as the play progresses. In the skit in which she appears at the racetrack, she is dressed in shades of cinnamon and wine (46); on the Orient Express–Titanic she wears a "velo malva" (47) and the whiteness of her hand is compared to the color of seagulls (48); in the casino she wears tropical plumes in her hair and is identified with white magic (48).

In the reenactment of the story of Jason and Medea, whiteness, both real and metaphorical, comes to contrast most clearly with Medea's black clothes. The Hija de un Rey is initially described as blond, in direct contrast to the black hat Medea wears throughout the play. When she visits Medea, she wears "ropa interior femenina de encaje blanco, idéntico en el estilo y la forma al que lleva, en negro, Medea" (50, stage directions). In part 2, when the wedding with Jasón is to be celebrated, Medea prepares Nodriza by painting her body entirely white (59) to match the lethal wedding dress that she will give her. Medea constantly alludes to this whiteness, as when she imagines the wedding of Jasón and the princess: "Y las voces blancas del coro angelical elevará [sic] su cantora plata hacia las blancas crucerías de la bóvedas blancas. Y Jasón y la hija de un Rey quedarán formando una compacta bola de blancura sacramentada" (54).

In all these instances, outer whiteness is given its traditional association of inner purity and goodness, so that Medea addresses the Hija as "manzanita del bien," invoking an explicit contrast with a Garden-of-Eden scenario in which she and Jasón partake of the apple proffered by "cierta serpiente maligna" and pared with the same knife that Medea used to kill her brother (51). In addition to recalling the implicit racism of the classical plays, black identifies Medea in this colored morality scheme with the witchcraft and sorcery for which the mythical Medea became notorious. Additionally, it associates her with the black leather that in the twentieth century has become a trademark of nontraditional sexual behavior such as sadomasochism and homosexuality. Along with the exposed phallus and the flasks of bodily fluids, the consistent color scheme of the play functions as an arbitrary marker of difference that permits Medea's exclusion from society and that recalls the legacy of institutionalized homophobia, not to mention racism and sexism, left in Spain after Franco's death.

The pernicious effects of isolation on the gay community are most vividly revealed in Medea's uneasy relationship with Nodriza, fittingly characterized by Medea's outburst in part 1: "¡Aparta tus hocicos de mí! ¡Me llenas de ambigüedades!" (46). Such glimpses of their relationship, offered in the lapses between the performances that they act out, allow one to begin to define their problematic existence. Initially, it appears that Nodriza, as her name indicates, is simply Medea's servant, akin to the nurse in the classical plays. She is appropriately described in the stage directions as wearing an "uniforme de un mayordomo ... con los típicos chaleco, pantalón y mandil de rayas verdinegras" (31), and, at the beginning of the play she proclaims, "En esta casa he dado de mi leche a cuatrocientas Medeas, por lo menos. A la propia señora se puede decir que yo la eché al mundo" (36). At times, however, Medea shares an intimacy with Nodriza that leads one to believe that they may be sexual partners. In part 1, for example, as she dresses Medea, the stage directions indicate that Nodriza disappears "dentro de la toalla que envuelve a ambos. Sólo queda visible la cabeza de Medea. Ésta habla dulcemente." When the towel falls to the ground, Nodriza is observed "de rodillas abrazada a la cintura de Medea" (43). Yet such intimacy is frequently followed by outbursts of rage in which Medea seems to reaffirm the superiority of a "señora," as in the continuation of the above scene: "¡Suelta, sierva! ¿O prefieres que me libre de ti arrancándote el pellejo a tiras? ¡Yo también tengo uñas!"

The problematic relationship is amplified by an apparent conflict over the objects of their desire. In part 1, after Nodriza prepares the urine for Medea's "children," she returns to her quarters, which are represented by a scenic space distinct from Medea's boudoir. She proceeds to warm up a bottle of real milk and removes another stuffed dog from a trunk, telling it: "¡Para ti será la leche verdadera ...! ¡Para ti, la única criatura que él puso, a través de mi vientre, en este mundo!" (38). Similarly, at the end of the play, as Medea awaits Jasón's arrival, Nodriza returns to her quarters, which, as the audience is now permitted to see, are identical to Medea's. In Nodriza's bathtub lies a life-size doll of a naked, bearded man, presumably Jasón. Nodriza tells it: "Ya sé lo mucho que se impacienta mi marinero cuando me demoro en ponerme linda para él ... pero puedes fumarte uno de esos cigarrillos orientales, tan tuyos" (67). Nodriza's words and actions reveal a hidden rivalry with Medea over Jasón and the stuffed animals that represent the product of her relationship with him. Medea herself is aware of this rivalry and distrusts Nodriza enough to use their games as an excuse to blindfold her so that she can then search through the servant's quarters, prompting Nodriza's ominous reply, "En cada teatro hay un camerino secreto en el que la dueña del castillo no debe entrar. Si lo hace, la dueña del teatro morirá" (61).

The rivalry between Medea and Nodriza can be profitably interpreted as a product of mimetic desire. Ruiz Pérez, in citing Riaza's explicit admiration for the work of Girard, notes that the loneliness characteristic of Riaza's theater is related to an "enajenante sentido de la emulación competitiva que impide una comunicación efectiva entre los miembros de una colectividad, tal como el propio Riaza formula, siguiendo el pensamiento del pensador francés René Girard" (483–84). Mimetic desire is a particularly appropriate basis for the relationship between Nodriza and Medea, since so much of their existence is imitative; indeed, the whole of their interaction can be reduced to nothing other than performance in the strict sense of the term. Even in the apparent gaps between their playacting, their behavior is irreducibly theatrical. Medea waits for the return of Jasón in the present time of the play even as she reveals his fictionality through the flashbacks, while Nodriza interacts with the life-size doll of Jasón in Medea's absence. The theatricality of the characters' existence is plainly illustrated when Nodriza, looking for the appropriate mask to play the Hija de un Rey, chooses one that, according to the stage directions, is a "reproducción exacta del rostro de Nodriza" (60).

In such a scenario, the possibility of human love and solidarity becomes remote, as evidenced in the following passage:

Medea.—¿Me amas, nodriza?
Nodriza.—Es parte del servicio amar a la señora del amor. (*Una pausa.*)
Medea.—Y yo, nodriza, ¿te amo?
Nodriza.—La niña sólo se ama a sí misma, pero no es correspondida debidamente ... (43)

The suggestion that Medea does not reciprocate her own self-love calls to mind the image of a shattered identity whose constituent parts are at odds with one another. Nodriza's love for Medea, furthermore, is described as the product of an idiotic sense of duty. The dysfunctionality of this relationship is reiterated in part 2:

Medea.—¿Me amas, nodriza?
Nodriza.—Esa es una pregunta que la señora ya me hizo.
Medea.—Respóndeme otra vez. El mundo es una rueda giradora.

Nodriza.—La nodriza ama lo que le dicta su modelo en el arte de amar ...
   La nodriza desea el deseo de Medea. (*Una pausa.*)
Medea.—Y yo, nodriza, ¿te amo?
Nodriza.—También dí [*sic*] cumplida respuesta a esa pregunta: la señora
   tan sólo ama el agujero negro que la señora es ...
Medea.—Entonces tú amas también mi propio vacío ...
Nodriza.—Así debe de ser ... (68)

Like the metaphor of the turning wheel that Medea invokes, the relationship portrayed in this conversation is irreducibly circular and, furthermore, self-devouring. Nodriza can only desire what Medea desires, while Medea loves only the "black hole" of her own self.

If there is ultimately no verifiable difference between the characters' real and stage identities within the play itself, there can be none between the two characters, either. Nodriza, it would seem, is the incarnation of Medea's fantasy as much as is Jasón. This suspicion is confirmed in the devastating last lines of the play:

Medea.—¡Me confundes! ¡Me engañas! ¡Abre la puerta! ¡Haz de Jasón!
Nodriza.—No hay puerta. Sólo existe el interior y en él, también solamente, Medea y su doble ... (*Medea golpea en la espalda de Nodriza con ambos puños mientras ésta continúa borrando la puerta.*)
Medea.—Si al menos me existieras tú, Jasón ...

Even Medea, it appears, is the alter ego of a self that is only alluded to, for Nodriza describes her at one point as behaving as if she "temiera quedarse a solas con Medea" (69). The lack of any stable identity or subjectivity in the characters results in the play's free fall into mindless mimicry.

In this bleak human landscape, the problem of gay identity becomes fused with the mechanics of theater itself, in much the same way that the puppets' freedom is thematized in *El señor de Pigmalión* (see above, Chapter 4, pages 175–76). Toward the end of the play, as Nodriza sorts through a stack of phonograph records, she comes across a title that reads "Los maricas también se aman." Medea's immediate reply is revealing: "No. Esa música es incierta. Los maricas se inventan y huyen de su invención" (68). Role-playing and mimesis become a metaphor for the double life that homosexuals are forced to live in a heterosexual society, confining their authentic desires to closed, suffocating spaces and inventing play identities devoid of meaning.

In many ways, Riaza's heroine suffers a much worse fate than her Greek and Roman prototypes, for she is not allowed to escape to the heavens on a dragon-drawn cart after exacting her revenge on Jasón but instead remains trapped in a lonely, claustrophobic environment or, in popular terms, "in the closet." Even so, several factors attenuate the bitter ending. First, when Medea rejects the record "Los maricas también se aman," Nodriza continues searching through the pile and finally comes across one called "Medea es una buena chica." Medea responds: "Sí. Medea es un buen chico. Elijo esa música" (69). Her reply, which so guilelessly changes the gender of the song's subject, demonstrates the creative power of an isolated community to appropriate popular culture and inflect it with its own concerns. Furthermore, in naming the very play in which she appears as a character, Medea unknowingly establishes a liberating link from her stifling environment to the outside world that watches her perform as a stage character. Even as the multiple layers of fiction work within the play to partition her identity into an infinite series of hollow selves, they provide her with the prize of immortality outside its boundaries, in the play that she has just brought into existence.

Finally, although Jasón almost certainly is a product of Medea's imagination, he encapsulates, in his ultimate rejection of her, the typical response of the heterosexual community to exclude what is supposedly different from itself, to cast it out of its borders. Yet his initial attraction to her exposes the sophistry of this exclusionary move, a move meant to partition artificially what Eve Kosofsky Sedgwick has perceptively identified as a continuum of homosocial desire among males (1–5). As Medea describes, Jasón wildly embraced the pleasures of gay sex: "Jasón me buscaba los agujeros más prohibidos y, en el más allá del placer, oprimido por mis escamas de culebra primigenia, Jasón me gritaba llamándole [*sic*] su pantano y su pitón y su puta" (53). The centrality of the male organ (*pitón*, conveniently identical to the word for "python") as the object of Jasón's desire in this passage, together with its direct exposure only a few lines later, reveals what may be termed the "phallacy" of male heterosexuality: a simultaneous aversion and attraction to the phallus. In revealing queer desire in the heart of Jasón, the representative of social power and authority, Riaza deconstructs the straight-gay opposition and aligns his hero with the nonpolar sexuality of some of the most famous figures of Greek mythology.

Medea es un buen chico exemplifies the process of scapegoating in its most insidious manifestation, in which members of a dominant community, in banishing the victim from among their numbers, seek to exteriorize what they most despise in themselves. Riaza's postmodern heroine thus shares with her classical predecessors the curse of loneliness brought about by institutionalized discrimination and hatred, as Ragué Arias comments in her brief treatment of the play: "Del mito clásico sólo ha quedado la soledad de Medea como exilio, la frustración como sustitución a su maternidad y la imposible muerte de unos que sólo existen en el deseo de Medea, perros de trapo llenos de arena, vacíos de vida y de existencia" (*Los personajes* 112). Yet, even when Medea is exiled to the loneliness of fictional repetition, her image and her desires are reprojected, through the prism house of theater, into the heart of society.

From the Pyrenees to the Peloponnese

The adaptation of desires from classical mythology to the postwar and democratic theaters in Spain follows two fundamental tendencies: on the one hand, a political critique of war and the totalitarian control exercised by the victorious Franco regime and, on the other, a cultural critique of the patriarchal legacy of discrimination that remained after its dissolution. Buero Vallejo's *La tejedora de sueños* in many ways anticipates both these trends. The questioning of the masculine values embodied in Ulises and in his rule of Ithaca makes the piece, which enjoyed greater visibility than did the earlier plays of Torrente and Pemán, an important precedent for political dissent in the postwar period. At the same time, the restoration of Penélope's voice and the vindication of her desire feeds a wider cultural critique that finds parallels in the work of Sastre and Bergamín and that in the post-Franco era develops into the feminist and queer revisions of Romero, Ragué Arias, and Riaza.

A remarkable characteristic shared by many of the plays studied in this chapter is the prominence given to women characters, whether the creation of male or female authors. The myths of Antigone, Clytemnestra, Electra, Medea, Penelope, and Phaedra all attest to this prominence. María José Ragué Arias offers a provocative explanation of this phenomenon: "En nuestro tiempo los personajes femeninos griegos son prototipo también del modelo femenino cultural y se asocian en algunas ocasiones a una actitud positiva en relación al progreso sociocultural. Es en este caso, sobre todo, que son utilizados como prototipo de progreso en épocas de crisis" (*Lo que fue Troya* 149).[29] Even those characters most negatively conceived in their classical models—Clytemnestra, Medea, Phaedra—are rewritten precisely to show that their crimes were a function of the unbearable circumstances in which they found themselves: hence the suggestion of Clitemnestra's loneliness in Buero, Medea's victimization by racist or homophobic standards in Bergamín and Riaza, and Phaedra's sexual frustration in Ragué Arias's own play. The disenfranchised position of women becomes a focal point for the dramatization of dissent and resistance to established norms of discourse and power, converting them into "portadores de valores alternativos al orden patriarcal" (Ragué Arias, *Lo que fue Troya* 149).

The prominence given to these issues allows for a wide development of character through a process of filling in the gaps in the plots of the classical models with psychological details reconstructed from the classical heroines' desires. Much of the force and originality of these reinvented women of mythology come not from what they do, although that factor certainly plays a part, but from what they think and how they conceptualize the world from their own perspective. Their introspection and insights lend to the mythological plays of the postwar period the most definitively psychological, as well as ideological, character of all the periods studied in this analysis.

The contrast between works that emphasize plot and those that concentrate on character portrayal serves as a convenient point of reflection from which to review and synthesize the conclusions of this study as a whole. The proposed hermeneutical model has emphasized the pivotal role in adaptation played by the concept of desire—manifested in the categories of aggression, sexuality, and hunger—whether it functions as a structural tool in the mechanics of plot creation or as a point of departure for penetrating character development. The earlier playwrights, especially in the sixteenth century, were particularly concerned with myth as an "arrangement of incidents." Modifying the structure of desire in the classical models offered them a way of rearranging or expanding the incidents of the model, which in turn allowed them to produce works of artistic originality or *emulatio* in the Erasmian sense. Often this modification involved destabilizing the traditional relationship between two characters, as Encina does in throwing the "cierta discordia" between the mu-

---

29. See the same author's *Els personatges* 110 for a parallel phenomenon in the contemporary Catalonian theater.

tually affectionate Pyramus and Thisbe, prototypes for his Vitoriano and Plácida; as Timoneda does in hinting at Progne's sexual frustration and placing her in charge of Thrace in Tereo's absence; and as Cueva y Silva does in creating a rival to Eco in her pursuit of the effeminate Narcissus. This gesture of destabilization with respect to the model accounts for the structures of irony and inversion frequently noted in the incident-laden plays of the sixteenth century. Significantly, what stands out in one's mind after reading these works is not character portrayal but the density and rapidity of action.

In the seventeenth century, the increasing popularity and availability of manuals led playwrights, still interested primarily in myth as plot, to begin to recognize it also as an "arrangement of characters" subject to potentially infinite development through a remodeling of underlying motivations and desires. Thus, although the primacy of plot remained sacred and the pace of its unfolding was often dizzying, one still recalls vividly Castro's exquisite portrayal of Dido, Lope's plaintive Ariadna and villainous Teseo, and Calderón's doubt-ridden, scruple-bound Hércules. These plays suggest the beginning of a shift in a general poetics of imitation that from the seventeenth century on demands less and less adherence to actual incidents of the model and allows a more allusive, character-based use of myth, a practice that reaches fruition in the twentieth century, particularly in the representation of the desires of feminine protagonists as seen in Galdós, Unamuno, Buero Vallejo, and Riaza.

Keeping these different approaches to imitation in mind, one may detect a parallel movement in the two principal historical periods studied that helps to explain, from a bird's-eye view, the use of myth as political or cultural critique that this analysis has frequently noted. The wide variety of plots developed by the sixteenth-century playwrights, who had no medieval tradition to work with, indicates an atmosphere of artistic experimentation that anticipates the twentieth-century *teatro inquieto*'s struggle to escape from the near wasteland of nineteenth-century drama. In contrast, the seventeenth century, resting solidly on the shoulders of a now firmly established dramatic tradition, began to look to the ideological as well as the artistic component of theater, as demonstrated in the veiled critiques of honor and power expressed in Calderón and, to a lesser extent, Lope. Similarly, the postwar twentieth century, with artistic models such as Galdós, Grau, Valle-Inclán, and García Lorca to build on, began to use theater to express dissent with the Franco regime. In all cases, the flexibility of desire substantiated the viability of myth in the dramatic medium.

Another consequence of focusing on desire in their adaptations is related to the specifically theatrical mode of presentation into which the playwrights situate it, regardless of the genre of its source. The intensity and all-too-human quality of the desires charted in the three categories contributes to the strong "dramatic potentiality" that Kirk sees in the myths and explains their "deep personal interest" (*Myth* 193) or what Burkert would call their "collective importance" (*Structure* 23). Theater, in other words, provides a uniquely appropriate context for the manifestation of myth above and beyond the mode of representation inherited by nondramatic literature. It is altogether fitting that Encina, writing at the height of the Italian Renaissance, chose the fledgling theatrical medium as a means of giving expression to the strong desires of the Pyramus and Thisbe narrative and that, more than four centuries later, his heirs continue to find in the theater an ideal forum for confronting the reckless passions of classical mythology.

Finally, the analogous use of desire by the playwrights studied suggests a pragmatic approach to defining Greek myth, a task that has dogged philologists and historians for centuries. In contrast to examining the topic from the inside, from a structural or typological vantage point, for example, it is not unwarranted to address it from the outside, through the eyes of other creative artists. It is certainly significant that so many Spanish dramatists of diverse backgrounds, literary movements, and historical periods focus on the concept of desire in adapting Greco-Roman myth to a wide variety of scenarios. This fact suggests that the three categories that constitute the theoretical framework of this analysis not only inform a widespread, postclassical strategy of dramatic adaptation but may also represent an inherent, defining feature of the ancient mythological tradition itself.

Epilogue

Future Desires

This study has left many questions unanswered and many stones unturned. For example, the lengthy interval that runs between *Los tres mayores prodigios*, the last play examined in Chapter 3, and the end of the *comedia nueva* (traditionally associated with the death of Calderón in 1681) is full of mythological works, only a few of which were alluded to at the end of Chapter 3. Particularly interesting is the use of myth in the religious mystery play or *auto sacramental*. A study of desire in the *auto sacramental* from the Freudian perspective that views religion and love of God as a sublimated form of human sexuality would have fascinating implications.

In the principal period ignored in this analysis, the eighteenth and nineteenth centuries, there is at least one significant work that deserves mention and that might, for someone so inclined, form the basis of a separate study. Martínez de la Rosa's *Edipo* (1832), briefly alluded to in Chapter 1 (page 2), is a brilliant rewriting of that most uncanny of myths, complete with an elegant language and a coherent symbolism all its own. Apparently the only Spanish dramatization of the Oedipus story up to that point, as the author affirms in his introduction, this sublime revision of Sophocles makes one wonder if other less prominent, but equally noteworthy, mythological adaptations lie forgotten or undiscovered in dusty archives of the neoclassical, Romantic, and post-Romantic periods.

The use of mythology in Spanish American theater could form the subject of a truly fascinating study. It would be especially profitable to compare the function of indigenous mythologies, as evidenced in the anonymous, fifteenth-century *Rabinal Achí* of Guatemala, for example, with that of the Greco-Roman corpus. In the twentieth century, a thorough study of myth as political critique, as in Luis Rafael Sánchez's *La pasión según Antígona Pérez*, begs to be written.

In both Spain and Spanish America, the handling of myth by women playwrights is a topic of great interest. A particularly rewarding investigation might begin with Sor Juana and end with the twentieth-century *dramaturgas* briefly mentioned in Chapters 4 and 5. Whether women writers on the whole treat desire in the same way as do their male counterparts would form an inviting point of departure.

Finally, it would be intriguing to compare the conclusions reached in this study about myth in the dramatic medium to those of a related work that addressed the question of desire from a different generic perspective. Could the qualities of desire that account for myth's appeal in the theater be used to explain its presence in lyric poetry, for example? The early modern period is rich in the *materia prima* of such an undertaking and, along with the other topics discussed here, beckons sirenlike to wayfaring explorers.

Appendix 1: Summary of Principal Plays Studied

Title	Author	Dates*	Myths Dramatized	Prob. Ancient Sources
Chapter 2				
1. *Égloga de Plácida y Vitoriano*	Juan del Encina	1513	Pyramus and Thisbe	Ovid: *Met.* 4.55–166
2. *Tragicomedia llamada Filomena*	Juan Timoneda	1564 (ɸ)	Procne, Tereus, and Philomela	Ovid: *Met.* 6.401–674
3. *Trajedia de Narciso*	Francisco de la Cueva y Silva	c. 1580 (ɸ)	Narcissus and Echo	Ovid: *Met.* 3.339–510
Chapter 3				
1. *Dido y Eneas*	Guillén de Castro	1599?	Dido and Aeneas	Virgil: *Aeneid* 1–4; Justin: *Epitoma* 18.4–6
2. *El laberinto de Creta*	Lope de Vega	1610–15? (ɸ)	Theseus and the Minotaur	Ovid: *Met.* 8.1–182
3. *Los tres mayores prodigios*	Pedro Calderón de la Barca	1636	Jason and Medea; Theseus and Ariadne; Hercules, Nessus, and Deianira	Ovid: *Met.* 7.1–401, 8.152–82, 9.98–272; Seneca: *Medea*, *Hercules Oetaeus*

Appendix 1

Title	Author	Dates*	Myths Dramatized	Prob. Ancient Sources
Chapter 4				
1. *Electra*	Benito Pérez Galdós	1901	Electra and Orestes	Aeschylus: *Oresteia*; Sophocles: *Electra*; Euripides: *Electra, Orestes*; Seneca: *Agamemnon*
2. *Fedra*	Miguel de Unamuno	1910–11 (1918)	Phaedra, Theseus, and Hippolytus	Euripides: *Phaedra*; Seneca: *Phaedra*
3. *El señor de Pigmalión*	Jacinto Grau	1921 (1928)	Pygmalion; Prometheus	Ovid: *Met.* 10.243–97; Hesiod: *Theog.* 521–602, *Works* 47–104; Aeschylus: *Prometheus*
Chapter 5				
1. *La tejedora de sueños*	Antonio Buero Vallejo	1949–50 (1952)	Penelope and Ulysses	Homer: *Odyssey*
2. *Medea es un buen chico*	Luis Riaza	1980 (1985)	Medea and Jason	Euripides: *Medea*; Seneca: *Medea*

*Dates of first performances are indicated in parentheses when they are known to differ from those of composition. A lowercase phi (ɸ) denotes plays with no record of performance.

Appendix 2: Spanish and English Equivalents of Mythological Figures

This list is intended as an aid to those unfamiliar with the Spanish versions of the mythological figures cited in the analysis. Parentheses indicate standard hispanized versions other than those used by the playwright. English spellings are the standard Latinate versions rather than Greek transliterations.

Most of the differences between English and Spanish result from Spanish modifications to Latin spellings that English preserves. In general, Spanish compresses Latin double consonants into single letters and eliminates *h* from *ch* and *th* compounds (*ch* becomes *qu* before *e* and *i*, however). Normally, it also converts Latin *ae* and *oe* to *e*, *ph* to *f*, final *us* to *o*, and *y* to *i*, while *j* (consonantal *i*) often becomes *y*.

For the best manual of mythology in Spanish, see Grimal.

Spanish	English
Acates	Achates
Adonis	Adonis
Aetes (Eetes)	Aeetes
Agamenón	Agamemnon
Androgeo	Androgeos
Andrómeda	Andromeda
Anfino (Anfínomo)	Amphinomus
Anquises	Anchises
Antígona	Antigone
Antinoo (Antínoo)	Antinous
Antiopía (Antíope)	Antiope
Aquiles	Achilles
Ariadna	Ariadne
Atreo	Atreus
Ayax	Ajax
Casandra	Cassandra
Centauro	Centaur
Cila (Escila)	Scylla
Clitemnestra (Clitemestra)	Clytemnestra

Creón	Creon
Creusa (Creúsa)	Creusa
Cupido	Cupid
Dédalo	Daedalus
Deyanira	Deianira
Dido	Dido
Eco	Echo
Edipo	Oedipus
Egisto	Aegisthus
Electra	Electra
Eneas	Aeneas
Érope (Aérope)	Aerope
Esfinge	Sphinx
Eumeo	Eumaeus
Euriclea	Euryclea
Eurímaco	Eurymachus
Europa	Europa
Fedra	Phaedra
Filetio (Filecio)	Philoetius
Filomena (Filomela)	Philomela
Fineo	Phineus
Friso (Frixo)	Phrixus
Hécuba	Hecuba
Helena	Helen
Hércules	Hercules
Hiarbas (Yarbas)	Iarbas
Hipólito	Hippolytus
Hithis (Itis)	Itys
Ifigenia	Iphigeneia
Jasón	Jason
Juno	Juno
Júpiter	Jupiter
Leócrito	Leocritus
Liriope (Liríope)	Liriope
Marte	Mars
Medea	Medea
Menelao	Menelaus
Mercurio	Mercury
Minerva	Minerva
Minos	Minos
Minotauro	Minotaur
Mirrha (Mirra)	Myrrha
Narciso	Narcissus
Neso	Nessus

Equivalents of Mythological Figures

Niso	Nisus
Orestes	Orestes
Pandión	Pandion
Paris	Paris
Pasife (Pasífae)	Pasiphae
Penélope	Penelope
Penteo	Pentheus
Perseo	Perseus
Pigmalión	Pygmalion
Píramo	Pyramus
Pisandro	Peisander
Progne (Procne)	Procne
Prometeo	Prometheus
Siqueo	Sychaeus
Telémaco	Telemachus
Tereo	Tereus
Teseo	Theseus
Tisbe	Thisbe
Tyestes (Tiestes)	Thyestes
Ulises	Ulysses
Venus	Venus
Vulcano	Vulcan
Zeus	Zeus

References

Abel, Lionel. *Metatheatre: A New View of Dramatic Form.* New York: Hill and Wang, 1963.
Acosta, María I. M. "The Mythological *Autos* of Calderón de la Barca." Diss. Columbia University, 1970.
Aeschylus. *Aeschylus.* Trans. Herbert Weir Smith. 2 vols. Loeb Classical Library 145–46. Cambridge: Harvard University Press, 1922–26.
———. *Agamemnon. Aeschylus* 2:1–151.
———. *Prometheus Bound. Aeschylus* 1:209–315.
Ahl, Frederick [M.]. *Lucan: An Introduction.* Cornell Studies in Classical Philology 39. Ithaca: Cornell University Press, 1976.
———. *Metaformations: Soundplay and Wordplay in Ovid and Other Classical Poets.* Ithaca: Cornell University Press, 1985.
———. "The Rider and the Horse: Politics and Power in Roman Poetry from Horace to Statius." *Aufstieg und Niedergang der römischen Welt* 32.1 (1984): 40–110.
———. *Sophocles' Oedipus: Evidence and Self-Conviction.* Ithaca: Cornell University Press, 1991.
Alfonso X (el Sabio). *Estoria de Espanna. Prosa histórica.* Ed. Benito Brancaforte. Letras Hispánicas 194. Madrid: Cátedra, 1984. 43–100.
———. *General Estoria.* Ed. Antonio G. Solalinde et al. Vol. 2.1. Madrid: CSIC, 1957. 2 vols. 1930–57.
Allen, Don Cameron. *Mysteriously Meant: The Rediscovery of Pagan Symbolism and Allegorical Interpretation in the Renaissance.* Baltimore: Johns Hopkins University Press, 1970.
Alvar, Manuel. "Presencia del mito: *La tejedora de sueños.*" *Bulletin Hispanique* 78 (1976): 34–73.
Álvarez de la Villa, Alfredo, ed. *El aucto del repelón.* By Juan del Encina. Paris: Paul Ollendorff, 1910.
Anderson, Robert Floyd. "A Study of Themes in the Theater of Unamuno." Diss. Case Western Reserve University, 1969.
Andrist, Debra D. *Deceit Plus Desire Equals Violence: A Girardian Study of the Spanish "Comedia."* New York: Peter Lang, 1989.
Angélico, Halma. *La nieta de Fedra.* Madrid: Velasco, 1929.
Apollodorus. *The Library.* Trans. James George Frazer. 2 vols. Loeb Classical Library 121–22. London: William Heinemann, 1921.
Apollonius Rhodius. *The Argonautica.* Trans. R. C. Seaton. Loeb Classical Library 1. London: William Heinemann, 1912.

Arco y Garay, Ricardo del. *La sociedad española en las obras dramáticas de Lope de Vega.* Madrid: Real Academia Española, 1941.
Aristotle. *The Poetics.* Trans. W. Hamilton Fyfe. *The Poetics. On the Sublime. On Style.* Trans. W. Hamilton Fyfe and W. Rhys Roberts. Loeb Classical Library 199. Cambridge: Harvard University Press, 1927. 1–118.
Aróstegui, María del Pilar. "La dramaturgia de Juan Timoneda: Estado actual de la cuestión." *Boletín de la Biblioteca de Menéndez Pelayo* 48 (1972): 201–30.
Arrowsmith, William. "Introduction to *Orestes.*" *Euripides IV.* By Euripides. Ed. David Grene and Richmond Lattimore. Chicago: University of Chicago Press, 1958. 106–11.
Artiles, Jenaro. "Bibliografía sobre el problema del honor y la honra en el drama español." *Filología y crítica hispánica: Homenaje al prof. Federico Sánchez Escribano.* Ed. Alberto Porqueras Mayo and Carlos Rojas. Madrid: Alacalá, 1969. 235–41.
———. "La idea de venganza en el drama español del siglo XVII." *Segismundo* 3 (1967): 9–38.
Aszyk, Urszula. "Miguel de Unamuno teórico del teatro." Lasagabaster 27–45.
Aub, Max. *Narciso. Teatro completo.* Madrid: Aguilar, 1968. 127–66.
Aubrun, Charles V. *La comedia española: 1600–1680.* Trans. Julio Lago Alonso. Madrid: Taurus, 1968.
———. "Estructura y significación de las comedias mitológicas de Calderón." *Hacia Calderón: Tercer Congreso Anglogermano.* Ed. Hans Flasche. Berlin: Walter de Gruyter, 1976. 148–55.
Austin, Brother. "Juan del Encina." *Hispania* 39 (1956): 161–74.
Ayala, Francisco. "Sobre el punto de honor castellano." *Revista de Occidente* 2d ser. 2 (1963): 151–74.
Ayllón, Cándido. "Experiments in the Theatre of Unamuno, Valle-Inclán, and Azorín." *Hispania* 46 (1963): 49–56.
Bandera, Cesáreo. *Mimesis conflictiva: ficción literaria y violencia en Cervantes y Calderón.* Madrid: Gredos, 1975.
Barbieri, Marie E. "La 'tragedia desnuda' en *Fedra* y *Yerma.*" *Explicación de Textos Literarios* 19.1 (1990–91): 38–47.
Barnard, Mary E. *The Myth of Apollo and Daphne from Ovid to Quevedo: Love, Agon, and the Grotesque.* Durham: Duke University Press, 1987.
Barnstone, Willis. "Saint John of the Cross: Mystico-Erotic Love in 'O Living Flame of Love.'" *The Poetics of Ecstasy: Varieties of Ekstasis from Sappho to Borges.* New York: Holmes and Meier, 1983. 180–90.
Barrett, L. L. "The Omen in Guillén de Castro's Drama." *Hispania* 22 (1939): 73–78.
Bataillon, Marcel. *Erasmo y España.* Trans. Antonio Alatorre. 2d ed. México: Fondo de Cultura Económica, 1966.
Beardsley, Theodore S. *Hispano-Classical Translations Printed Between 1482 and 1699.* Pittsburgh: Duquesne University Press, 1970.
Benedetti, Thomas. "The Dramatic Components of Calderón's *Comedias Mitológicas.*" Diss. Temple University, 1983.
"Benito Pérez Galdós." *The Drama* 2 (1911): 3–11. (An English translation of *Electra* follows, 12–138.)
Berenguer, Ángel. "Galdós y el teatro." *Madrid en Galdós: Galdós en Madrid.* Madrid: Consejería de Cultura, 1988. 327–45.

Bergamín, José. *Medea la encantadora: explosión trágica en un acto. Entregas de la Licorne* 4 (1954): 15–48.

———. *La sangre de Antígona: Misterio en tres actos. Primer Acto* 198 (1983): 48–69.

Berkowitz, H. Chonon. "Apotheosis." *Benito Pérez Galdós: Spanish Liberal Crusader.* Madison: University of Wisconsin Press, 1948. 346–82.

———. *La biblioteca de Benito Pérez Galdós.* Las Palmas: Museo Canario, 1951.

Beser, Sergio. "Un artículo de Maeztu contra Azorín." *Bulletin Hispanique* 65 (1963): 329–32.

Biedermann, Hans. *Dictionary of Symbolism: Cultural Icons and the Meanings Behind Them.* Trans. James Hulbert. New York: Penguin-Meridian, 1994.

Blanquat, Josette. "Au temps d'*Electra.*" *Bulletin Hispanique* 68 (1966): 253–308.

Boccaccio, Giovanni. *Elegia di madonna Fiammetta da lei alle innamorate donne mandato. L'Elegia di madonna Fiametta con le chiose inedite.* Ed. Vincenzo Pernicone. Scrittori d'Italia 171. Bari: Gius, Laterza e Figli, 1939. 1–169.

Bömer, Franz. *P. Ovidius Naso.* Metamorphosen. *Kommentar.* Vol. 1. Heidelberg: Carl Winter, 1969. 7 vols. 1969–86.

Bonilla y San Martín, Adolfo. *Las bacantes, o del origen del teatro.* Madrid: Rivadeneyra, 1921.

Borel, Jean-Paul. *Théâtre de l'impossible: Essai sur une des dimensions fondamentales du théâtre espagnol au XX siècle.* Neuchâtel (Switzerland): Baconnière, 1963.

Bourne, Marjorie Adele. "Classic Themes in Contemporary Spanish Drama." Diss. Indiana University, 1961.

Brown, G. G. *A Literary History of Spain: The Twentieth Century.* London: Ernest Benn, 1972.

Bruerton, Courtney. "The Chronology of the *Comedias* of Guillén de Castro." *Hispanic Review* 12 (1944): 89–151.

Buero Vallejo, Antonio. "Autocrítica." *Teatro español 1951–1952.* Ed. Carlos Sainz de Robles. Madrid: Aguilar, 1953. 283.

———. "Comentario." *La tejedora de sueños.* Madrid: Alfil, 1952. 89–100.

———. *La tejedora de sueños: Drama en tres actos. La tejedora de sueños. Llegada de los dioses.* Ed. Luis Iglesias Feijoo. 6th ed. Letras Hispánicas 45. Madrid: Cátedra, 1983. 101–208.

Burkert, Walter. *Homo Necans: The Anthropology of Ancient Greek Sacrificial Ritual and Myth.* Trans. Peter Bing. Berkeley and Los Angeles: University of California Press, 1983.

———. *Structure and History in Greek Mythology and Ritual.* Sather Classical Lectures 47. Berkeley and Los Angeles: University of California Press, 1979.

Bustamante, Jorge de. *Las metamorphoses, o transformaciones del muy excelente poeta Ouidio, repartidas en quinze libros y traduzidas en castellano.* Anvers [Antwerp], 1561.

Caballero, P. *Diez años de crítica teatral, 1907–1916.* Madrid: Administración del Apostolado de la Prensa, 1916.

Cabañas, Pablo. *El mito de Orfeo en la literatura española.* Madrid: CSIC, 1948.

Calderón de la Barca, Pedro. "Loa para la comedia de *Los tres mayores prodigios.*" *Comedias.* Ed. D. W. Cruickshank and J. E. Varey. Vol. 5. London: Tamesis, 1973. Folios 249r-253r. 19 vols.

———. *Los tres mayores prodigios. Dramas.* Ed. Ángel Valbuena Briones. 4th ed. Madrid: Aguilar, 1959. Vol. 1 of *Obras completas.* 1635–81. 3 vols.

Canals, Salvador. "Crónica de teatros: *Electra.*" *Nuestro Tiempo* 1 (1901): 210–18.
Cardona, Rodolfo, and Gonzalo Sobejano. "Nuestro teatro selecto." *Teatro selecto de Benito Pérez Galdós.* Ed. Cardona and Sobejano. Madrid: Escelicer, 1972. 60–72.
Carney, Hal. "The Dramatic Technique of Benito Pérez Galdós." Diss. University of Nebraska, 1956.
Caro Baroja, Julio. "Honour and Shame: A Historical Account of Several Conflicts." Trans. R. Johnson. *Honour and Shame: The Values of Mediterranean Society.* Ed. J. G. Peristiany. Chicago: University of Chicago Press, 1966. 79–137.
Casalduero, Joaquín. "*Alceste*: Volver a la vida." *Estudios Escénicos* 18 (1974): 113–29.
———. "El teatro español en el siglo XIX." *Historia de la literatura española.* Ed. José María Díez Borque. Vol. 3. Madrid: Taurus, 1980. 487–527. 4 vols.
———. *Vida y obra de Galdós (1843–1920).* Madrid: Gredos, 1974.
Cascardi, Anthony J. *The Limits of Illusion: A Critical Study of Calderón.* Cambridge: Cambridge University Press, 1984.
Castro, Américo. "Algunas observaciones acerca del concepto del honor en los siglos XVI y XVII." *Revista de Filología Española* 3 (1916): 1–50, 357–85.
———. *De la edad conflictiva: El drama de la honra en España y en su literatura.* Madrid: Taurus, 1961.
———. "Lo hispánico y el erasmismo." *Revista de Filología Hispánica* 2 (1940): 1–34; 4 (1942): 1–66.
Castro y Bellvis, Guillén de. *Dido y Eneas. Obras de don Guillén de Castro y Bellvis.* Ed. Real Academia Española. Vol. 1. Madrid: Revista de Archivos, Bibliotecas y Museos, 1925. 165–205. 3 vols. 1925–27.
Catalán Menéndez Pidal, Diego. "Don Francisco de la Cueva y Silva y los orígenes del teatro nacional." *Nueva Revista de Filología Hispánica* 3 (1949): 130–40.
Catena, Elena. "Circunstancias temporales de la *Electra* de Galdós." *Estudios Escénicos* 18 (1974): 79–112.
Cazorla, Hazel. "The Duality of Power in the Theater of Luis Riaza." *Modern Drama* 24 (1981): 36–43.
———. "La indestructibilidad de Antígona en una obra de Luis Riaza: Antígona ... ¡cerda!" *Estreno* 8.1 (1982): 9–10.
———. "El retorno de Ulises: Dos enfoques contemporáneos del mito en el teatro de Buero Vallejo y Antonio Gala." *Hispanófila* 87 (1986): 43–51.
Cervantes Saavedra, Miguel de. *El ingenioso hidalgo don Quijote de la Mancha.* Ed. Luis Andrés Murillo. 5th ed. 2 vols. Madrid: Castalia, 1987.
Chabás, Juan. "Los dramaturgos jóvenes." *Literatura española contemporánea.* Havana: Cultural, 1952. 652–64.
Chambardón, Gabriela. "El conocimiento poético en el teatro de Antonio Buero Vallejo." *Cuadernos Hispanoamericanos* 253–54 (1971): 52–98.
Chapman, W. C. "Las comedias mitológicas de Calderón." *Revista de Literatura* 5 (1954): 35–67.
Chinchilla, Rosa Helena. "The Evolution of Classical Myth in Spain's Golden Age (1500–1680)." Diss. SUNY Stony Brook, 1989.
Cirne, Juan. *Tragedia de los amores de Eneas y de la reyna Dido.* Ed. Joseph E. Gillet and Edwin B. Williams. *PMLA* 46 (1931): 353–431.
Ciruelo, J. I. "Unamuno frente a los personajes de Medea y Fedra." *Tradición clásica y siglo XX.* Ed. I. Rodríguez Alfageme and A. Bravo García. Madrid: Coloquio, 1986. 56–66.

Colahan, Clark, and Alfred Rodríguez. "*El Hércules* de López de Zárate: Una posible fuente de *Los tres mayores prodigios* de Calderón." García Lorenzo, *Calderón* 3:1271–76.
Cook, John A. *Neo-classic Drama in Spain: Theory and Practice.* Dallas: Southern Methodist University Press, 1959.
Correa, Gustavo. "El doble aspecto de la honra en el teatro del siglo XVII." *Hispanic Review* 26 (1958): 99–107.
Cossío, José María de. *Fábulas mitológicas en España.* Madrid: Espasa-Calpe, 1952.
Cotarelo y Mori, Emilio. *Bibliografía de las controversias sobre la licitud del teatro en España.* Madrid: Revista de Archivos, Bibliotecas y Museos, 1904.
———. *Ensayo sobre la vida y obras de D. Pedro Calderón de la Barca.* Madrid: Revista de Archivos, Bibliotecas y Museos, 1924.
———. "Juan del Encina y los orígenes del teatro español." *Estudios de historia literaria de España.* Vol. 1. Madrid: La Revista Española, 1901. 103–81. (Further volumes were not published.)
Craft, Sandra M. "El destino como fuerza trágica en *Los amores de Dido y Eneas* de Guillén de Castro." Master's thesis. Emory University, 1969.
Crawford, J. P. Wickersham. *Spanish Drama before Lope de Vega.* Rev. ed. Philadelphia: University of Pennsylvania Press, 1967.
———. *The Spanish Pastoral Drama.* Extra Ser. 4. Philadelphia: University of Pennsylvania Dept. of Romanic Languages and Literatures, 1915.
Cruz, Juan de la. *Cántico espiritual. Poesías.* Ed. Cristóbal Cuevas García. Madrid: Alhambra, 1979.
Cruz, Juana Inés de la. *Auto sacramental de* El divino Narciso. *Obra selecta.* Ed. Margo Glantz. Vol. 1. Caracas: Ayacucho, 1994. 330–99. 2 vols.
———. "Loa para el auto sacramental de *El divino Narciso.*" *Obra selecta.* Ed. Margo Glantz. Vol. 1. Caracas: Ayacucho, 1994. 313–29. 2 vols.
Cueva, Juan de la. *Tragedia de la muerte de Ayax Telamón, sobre las armas de Aquiles. Comedias y tragedias de Juan de la Cueva.* Ed. Francisco A. de Icaza. Vol. 1. Madrid: Sociedad de Bibliófilos Españoles, 1917. 278–315. 2 vols.
Cueva y Silva, Francisco de la. *Trajedia de Narciso.* Ed. J. P. Wickersham Crawford. University of Pennsylvania Series in Romanic Languages and Literatures 3. Philadelphia: University of Pennsylvania, 1909.
Cuevas García, Cristóbal, and Enrique Baena, eds. *El teatro de Buero Vallejo: Texto y espectáculo.* Barcelona: Anthropos, 1990.
Curtius, Ernst Robert. *European Literature and the Latin Middle Ages.* Trans. Willard R. Trask. Bollingen Ser. 36. Princeton: Princeton University Press, 1990.
de Armas, Frederick A. *The Return of Astraea: An Astral-Imperial Myth in Calderón.* Lexington: University Press of Kentucky, 1986.
de Man, Paul. *Blindness and Insight: Essays in the Rhetoric of Contemporary Criticism.* 2d rev. ed. Theory and History of Literature 7. Minneapolis: University of Minnesota Press, 1983.
Demetrius, James Kleon. "Elementos griegos y latinos en las obras de Lope de Vega." *Folia Humanística* 14 (1976): 603–5.
Denomy, Alexander J. *The Heresy of Courtly Love.* Boston College Candlemas Lectures on Christian Literature. Gloucester, Mass.: Peter Smith, 1965.
Derrida, Jacques. *Margins of Philosophy.* Trans. Alan Bass. Chicago: University of Chicago Press, 1982.

Díaz-Plaja, Guillermo. "Sobre *La tejedora de sueños*, de Buero Vallejo." *La voz iluminada: Notas sobre el teatro a través de un cuarto de siglo.* Barcelona: Instituto del Teatro, 1952. 273–76.
Díaz-Regañón López, José María. *Los trágicos griegos en España. Anales de la Universidad de Valencia* 29.3 (1955–56): 1–374.
Diego, Fernando de. "Espacio dramático e ideología en *La tejedora de sueños* de A. Buero Vallejo." Cuevas García 351–59.
Díez Borque, José María. *Los géneros dramáticos en el siglo XVI: El teatro hasta Lope de Vega.* Madrid: Taurus, 1987.
———. *Sociología de la comedia española del siglo XVII.* Madrid: Cátedra, 1976.
Díez-Canedo, Enrique. *Artículos de crítica teatral: el teatro español de 1914 a 1936.* 4 vols. México: Joaquín Mortiz, 1968.
Díez del Corral, Luis. *La función del mito clásico en la literatura contemporánea.* 2d ed. Madrid: Gredos, 1974.
DiPuccio, Denise M. "Communicative Structures in Calderón de la Barca's Mythological *Comedias.*" Diss. University of Kansas, 1982.
Dolores de Asís Garrote, María. "Recreación del mito de Fedra en la *Fedra* de Unamuno." Gómez Molleda 341–61.
Doménech, Ricardo. "Introducción al teatro de Max Aub." *Morir por cerrar los ojos.* By Max Aub. Barcelona: Aymá, 1967. 20–64.
———. *El teatro de Buero Vallejo.* Madrid: Gredos, 1973.
Dougherty, Dru. "The Semiosis of Stage Decor in Jacinto Grau's *El señor de Pigmalión.*" *Hispania* 67 (1984): 351–57.
Dumas, Claude, ed. *Les Mythes et leur expression au XIXe siècle dans le monde hispanique et ibéro-américain.* Lille: Presses Universitaires de Lille, 1988.
Duncan-Irvin, Hayden Donelan. "The 'Beast/Monster' and Desire in Three of Calderón de la Barca's Mythological Plays: *Eco y Narciso, El monstruo de los jardines,* and *El mayor encanto, amor.*" Diss. University of Wisconsin, 1991.
Edwards, Gwynne. "Calderón's *Los tres mayores prodigios* and *El pintor de su deshonra*: The Modernization of Ancient Myth." *Bulletin of Hispanic Studies* 61 (1984): 326–34.
Elizalde, Ignacio. "Azorín y el estreno de *Electra* de Pérez Galdós." *Letras de Deusto* 3.6 (1973): 67–79.
———. "Características del teatro de Unamuno." Lasagabaster 47–65.
Elliott, J. H. *Imperial Spain: 1469–1716.* New York: Mentor-New American Library, 1963.
Ellis, Havelock. "*Electra* and the Progressive Movement in Spain." *Critic* 39 (1901): 213–17.
Encina, Juan del. *Égloga de Plácida y Vitoriano. Teatro.* Ed. Ana María Rambaldo. Clásicos Castellanos 227. Madrid: Espasa-Calpe, 1983. 184–274. Vol. 4 of *Obras completas.* 4 vols. 1978–83.
Erasmus, Desiderius. *Ciceronianus or A Dialogue on the Best Style of Speaking.* Trans. Izora Scott. New York: AMS, 1972.
Escribano, Jean [Schneider]. "The Function of Classical Myth in the Theater of Guillén de Castro." Diss. Emory University, 1971.
———. "The Function of Classical Myth in the Theater of Guillén de Castro." *Studies in Language and Literature: The Proceedings of the 23rd Mountain Interstate Foreign Language Conference.* Ed. Charles Nelson. Richmond: Eastern Kentucky University Dept. of Foreign Languages, 1976. 147–51.

References

Estévez-Ortega, E. "El teatro moderno de Jacinto Grau." *Nuevo escenario.* Barcelona: Lux, 1928. 42–49.
Eurípides. *Electra. Eurípides* 2:1–119.
———. *Eurípides.* Trans. Arthur S. Way. 4 vols. Loeb Classical Library 9–12. London: William Heinemann, 1912.
———. *Hippolytus. Eurípides* 4:157–277.
———. *Iphigeneia at Aulis. Eurípides* 1:1–151.
———. *Medea. Eurípides* 4:279–397.
———. *Orestes. Eurípides* 2:121–277.
Ezell, Richard Lee. "The Theater of Jacinto Grau: A Depiction of Man." Diss. University of Oklahoma, 1971.
Feal Deibe, Carlos. "*Fedra* en la obra de Unamuno." *Revue de Littérature Comparée* 49 (1975): 19–27.
Fernández, Óscar. "Jacinto Grau's Dramatic Technique." Diss. University of Wisconsin, 1953.
Fernández, Sebastián. *Tragedia Policiana.* Menéndez Pelayo, *Orígenes* 3:1–59.
Fernández Almagro, M. "*Fedra,* tragedia desnuda." *La Gaceta Literaria* 78 (15 March 1930): 14.
Fichter, William L. *Lope de Vega's* El castigo del discreto *together with a Study of Conjugal Honor in his Theater.* Diss. Columbia University, 1925. New York: Instituto de las Españas, 1925.
Finkenthal, Stanley. *El teatro de Galdós.* Trans. Bruno de Jesús. Madrid: Fundamentos, 1980.
Fox, E. Inman. "Galdós' *Electra*: A Detailed Study of Its Historical Significance and the Polemic between Martínez Ruiz and Maeztu." *Anales Galdosianos* 1 (1966): 131–41.
Franco, Andrés. *El teatro de Unamuno.* Madrid: Ínsula, 1971.
Franco Durán, María Jesús. "Anfino, el elogio del humilde: Alrededor de *La tejedora de sueños* de Buero Vallejo." *Verba Hispanica* 3 (1993): 63–70.
———. "Interpretación del mito clásico en *La tejedora de sueños.*" Cuevas García 313–21.
Frazer, J. G. *The Golden Bough: A Study in Comparative Religion.* 3d ed. 12 vols. London: Macmillan, 1911.
Freud, Sigmund. *Beyond the Pleasure Principle.* Trans. and ed. James Strachey. New York: Norton, 1961.
———. *Civilization and Its Discontents.* Trans. and ed. James Strachey. New York: Norton, 1961.
———. *The Ego and the Id.* Trans. and ed. James Strachey. New York: Norton, 1960.
———. "Female Sexuality." *Standard Edition* 21:221–43.
———. *General Psychological Theory.* Ed. Philip Rieff. New York: Collier-Macmillan, 1969.
———. *Group Psychology and the Analysis of the Ego.* Trans. and ed. James Strachey. New York: Norton, 1959.
———. "Instincts and Their Vicissitudes." Trans. Cecil M. Baines. *General Psychological Theory* 83–103.
———. *The Interpretation of Dreams. The Basic Writings of Sigmund Freud.* Trans. and ed. A. A. Brill. New York: Modern Library, 1938. 179–549.

———. "On Narcissism: An Introduction." Trans. Cecil M. Baines. *General Psychological Theory* 56–82.
———. "An Outline of Psychoanalysis." *Standard Edition* 23:139–207.
———. "The Psychogenesis of a Case of Homosexuality in a Woman." *Standard Edition* 18:145–72.
———. "Psychogenic Visual Disturbance According to Psychoanalytical Conceptions." Trans. E. Colburn Mayne. *Character and Culture.* Ed. Philip Rieff. New York: Collier-Macmillan, 1963. 51–58.
———. *The Standard Edition of the Complete Psychological Works of Sigmund Freud.* Trans. and ed. James Strachey in collaboration with Anna Freud. 24 vols. London: Hogarth, 1953–74.
———. *Three Essays on the Theory of Sexuality.* Trans. and ed. James Strachey. N.p.: HarperCollins, 1962.
———. *Totem and Taboo: Some Points of Agreement between the Mental Lives of Savages and Neurotics.* Trans. James Strachey. New York: Norton, 1950.
———. "Twentieth Lecture: The Sexual Life of Man." *A General Introduction to Psychoanalysis.* Trans. Joan Riviere. New York: Pocket, 1924. 312–28.
Friedman, Edward H. "Guillén de Castro's *Progne y Filomena*: Between the Classic and the Comedia." *Neophilologus* 72 (1988): 213–17.
Froldi, Rinaldo. *Lope de Vega y la formación de la comedia: En torno a la tradición dramática valenciana y al primero teatro de Lope.* Trans. Franco Gabriele and Sra. de Gabriele. 2d ed. Salamanca: Anaya, 1973.
Frye, Northrop. *Anatomy of Criticism: Four Essays.* Princeton: Princeton University Press, 1957.
Gallego Morell, Antonio. *El mito de Faetón en la literatura española.* Madrid: CSIC, 1961.
Garasa, Delfín Leocadio. "Los empeños teatrales de Unamuno." *Ínsula* 216–17 (1964): 23.
Garber, Marjorie. *Vested Interests: Cross-Dressing and Cultural Anxiety.* New York: HarperCollins, 1993.
García Blanco, Manuel. "El mundo clásico de Miguel de Unamuno." *En torno a Unamuno.* Madrid: Taurus, 1965. 79–130.
García de la Huerta, Vicente. *Agamenón vengado.* Raquel y Agamenón vengado. Ed. Augusto Cortina. Buenos Aires: Espasa-Calpe, 1947. 95–164.
García Lorenzo, Luciano. Introducción. *Teatro selecto de Jacinto Grau.* Ed. García Lorenzo. Madrid: Escelicer, 1971. 7–96.
———. *El teatro de Guillén de Castro.* Barcelona: Planeta, 1976.
———. *El teatro español hoy.* Barcelona: Planeta, 1975.
———, ed. *Calderón: Actas del Congreso Internacional sobre Calderón y el Teatro Español del Siglo de Oro.* 3 vols. Madrid: CSIC, 1983.
García Valdecasas, Alfonso. *El hidalgo y el honor.* 2d ed. Madrid: Revista de Occidente, 1958.
García Viñó, M. "La *Fedra* de Unamuno." *Arbor* 85 (1973): 443–51.
Gillet, Joseph E. *Torres Naharro and the Drama of the Renaissance.* Transcribed, edited, and completed by Otis H. Green. Philadelphia: University of Pennsylvania Press, 1961. Vol. 4 of Propalladia *and Other Works of Bartolomé de Torres Naharro.* 4 vols. 1943–61.
Gimeno, Rosalie, ed. *Teatro: Segunda producción dramática.* By Juan del Encina. Madrid: Alhambra, 1977.

Girard, René. *Deceit, Desire, and the Novel.* Trans. Yvonne Freccero. Baltimore: Johns Hopkins University Press, 1965.
———. *Violence and the Sacred.* Trans. Patrick Gregory. Baltimore: Johns Hopkins University Press, 1977.
Giuliano, William P. *Buero Vallejo, Sastre y el teatro de su tiempo.* New York: Las Américas, 1971.
———. Introduction. *El señor de Pigmalión.* By Jacinto Grau. New York: Las Américas, 1952. 1-16.
———. "The Life and Works of Jacinto Grau." Diss. University of Michigan, 1950.
———. "The Role of Man and of Woman in Buero Vallejo's Plays." *Hispanófila* 39 (1970): 21-28.
Glaser, Edward. "Quevedo versus Pérez de Montalbán: The *Auto del Polifemo* and the Odyssean Tradition in Golden Age Spain." *Hispanic Review* 28 (1960): 103-20.
Goenaga, Ángel, and Juan P. Maguna. "Pérez Galdós: *Electra y El abuelo.*" *Teatro español del siglo XIX: Análisis de obras.* New York: Las Américas, 1971. 409-42.
Gómez de Baquero, E. "El teatro de Galdós." *Letras é ideas.* Barcelona: Henrich, 1905. 192-203.
Gómez Molleda, D., ed. *Volumen-homenaje a Miguel de Unamuno.* Salamanca: Casa-Museo Unamuno, 1986.
González, Marie Jacqueline. "The Dramatic Works of Jacinto Grau." Master's thesis. Washington University, 1943.
González-Cobos Dávila, Carmen. *Antonio Buero Vallejo: El hombre y su obra.* Salamanca: Universidad de Salamanca, 1979.
González del Valle, Luis. *La tragedia en el teatro de Unamuno, Valle-Inclán y García Lorca.* New York: Torres and Sons, 1975.
González López, Emilio. "El drama galdosiano." *Historia de la literatura española: La edad moderna (siglos XVIII y XIX).* New York: Las Américas, 1965. 459-66.
González Serrano, U. "*Electra* de Galdós." *La literatura del día: 1900 á 1903.* Barcelona: Henrich, 1903. 111-16.
Gountiñas Tuñón, Orlando. "Notas al *Alceste.*" *Actas del Primer Congreso Internacional de Estudios Galdosianos.* Ed. Alfonso Armas. Madrid: Nacional, 1977. 470-78.
Grau, Jacinto. *El hijo pródigo. El señor de Pigmalión.* 3d ed. Buenos Aires: Losada, 1956.
Graves, Robert. *The Greek Myths.* 2 vols. Baltimore: Penguin, 1955.
Green, Otis H. "'Fingen los poetas': Notes on the Spanish Attitude Toward Pagan Mythology." *Estudios dedicados a Menéndez Pidal.* Vol. 1. Madrid: CSIC, 1950. 275-88. 7 vols. 1950-62.
———. *Spain and the Western Tradition: The Castilian Mind in Literature from* El Cid *to* Calderón. 4 vols. Madison: University of Wisconsin Press, 1963-66.
Greer, Margaret Rich. *The Play of Power: Mythological Court Dramas of Calderón de la Barca.* Princeton: Princeton University Press, 1991.
Grimal, Pierre. *Diccionario de mitología griega y romana.* Trans. Francisco Payarols. Barcelona: Paidós, 1981.
Grismer, Raymond Leonard. *The Influence of Plautus in Spain before Lope de Vega.* New York: Hispanic Institute, 1944.
Guerrero Zamora, Juan. "Benito Pérez Galdós (1843-1920)." *Historia del teatro contemporáneo.* Vol. 4. Barcelona: Juan Flors, 1967. 232-40. 4 vols. 1961-67.

Gullón, Ricardo. "Teatro del alma." Sánchez-Barbudo 385–99. Rptd. from *Revista de la Universidad de Madrid* 13 (1965).
———. "Unamuno en su teatro." Lasagabaster 227–41.
Gutiérrez Nieto, Juan Ignacio. "Honra y utilidad social: En torno a los conceptos de honor y honra." García Lorenzo, *Calderón* 2:881–95.
Habermas, Jürgen. "Modernity versus Postmodernity." Trans. Seyla Ben-Habib. *New German Critique* 22 (1981): 3–14.
Halsey, Martha T. *Antonio Buero Vallejo*. New York: Twayne, 1973.
———. "The Dreamer in the Tragic Theater of Buero Vallejo." *Revista de Estudios Hispánicos* 2 (1968): 265–85.
Hamerton-Kelly, Robert G., ed. *Violent Origins: Walter Burkert, René Girard, and Jonathan Z. Smith on Ritual Killing and Cultural Formation*. Stanford: Stanford University Press, 1987.
Harris, Carolyn J. "La desmitificación de Penélope en *La tejedora de sueños, ¿Por qué corres, Ulises?* y *Ulises no vuelve*." *Pennsylvania Foreign Language Conference Selected Proceedings*. Pittsburgh: Duquesne University, 1988. 81–91.
——— "La mujer en el teatro de Buero Vallejo: Una lectura femenina." *Letras Peninsulares* 3 (1990): 247–57.
Hart, Georg. *Die Pyramus- und Thisbe-Sage in Holland, England, Italien und Spanien*. Passau, 1891.
———. *Ursprung und Verbreitung der Pyramus- und Thisbe-Sage*. Passau, 1889.
Hassan, Ihab. *The Postmodern Turn: Essays in Postmodern Theory and Culture*. Columbus: Ohio State University Press, 1987.
Hathaway, Robert L. *Love in the Early Spanish Theatre*. Madrid: Playor, 1975.
Haverbeck O[jeda], [N.] Erwin. "La comedia mitológica calderoniana: Soberbia y castigo." *Revista de Filología Española* 56 (1973): 67–93.
———. *El tema mitológico en el teatro de Calderón*. Valdivia: Universidad Austral de Chile, 1975.
Hermenegildo, Alfredo. *La tragedia en el renacimiento español*. Barcelona: Planeta, 1973.
Hernández Araico, Susana. "Política imperial en *Los tres mayores prodigios*." *Homenaje a Hans Flasche: Festschrift zum 80 Geburtstag am 25 November 1991*. Ed. Karl-Hermann Körner and Günther Zimmermann. Stuttgart: Franz Steiner, 1991. 83–94.
Hesiod. *Hesiod, the Homeric Hymns, and Homerica*. Trans. Hugh G. Evelyn-White. Loeb Classical Library 57. London: William Heinemann, 1914.
———. *Theogony*. Hesiod 78–154.
———. *Works and Days*. Hesiod 2–65.
Highet, Gilbert. *The Classical Tradition: Greek and Roman Influences on Western Literature*. New York: Oxford University Press, 1949.
Hilborn, Harry W. *A Chronology of the Plays of Don Pedro Calderón de la Barca*. Toronto: University of Toronto Press, 1938.
Hinterhäuser, Hans. "Benito Pérez Galdós: *Electra*." *Das spanische Theater vom Mittelalter bis zur Gegenwart*. Ed. Volker Roloff and Harald Wentzlaff-Eggebert. Düsseldorf: Bagel, 1988. 274–86.
Holt, Marion P. *The Contemporary Spanish Theater (1949–1972)*. Boston: Twayne, 1975.
Homer. *The Iliad*. Trans. A. T. Murray. 2 vols. Loeb Classical Library 170–71. London: William Heinemann, 1924.

———. *The Odyssey*. Trans. A. T. Murray. 2 vols. Loeb Classical Library 104–5. London: William Heinemann, 1919.
Honig, Edwin. *Calderón and the Seizures of Honor*. Cambridge: Harvard University Press, 1972.
Horace [Quintus Horatius Flaccus]. *Ars Poetica. Satires, Epistles, and Ars Poetica.* Trans. H. Rushton Fairclough. Loeb Classical Library 194. Cambridge: Harvard University Press, 1929. 450–89.
Howatson, M. C., and Ian Chilvers, eds. *The Concise Oxford Companion to Classical Literature*. Oxford: Oxford University Press, 1993.
Hoyo, Arturo del, ed. *Teatro inquieto español*. Madrid: Aguilar, 1967.
Huizinga, Johan. *The Autumn of the Middle Ages*. Trans. Rodney J. Payton and Ulrich Mammitzsch. Chicago: University of Chicago Press, 1996.
Hyginus. *Fabulae*. Ed. Peter K. Marshall. Lepzig: Teubner, 1993.
Iglesias Feijoo, Luis. Introducción. Buero Vallejo, *La tejedora de sueños* 9–82.
———. *La trayectoria dramática de Antonio Buero Vallejo*. Santiago de Compostela: Universidad de Santiago, 1982.
Jameson, Fredric. "Postmodernism, or the Cultural Logic of Late Capitalism." *New Left Review* 146 (1984): 53–92.
Johnson, Barbara. Translator's Introduction. *Dissemination*. By Jacques Derrida. Trans. Johnson. Chicago: University of Chicago Press, 1981. vii-xxxiii.
Jones, C. A. "*Honor* in Spanish Golden-Age Drama: Its Relation to Real Life and to Morals." *Bulletin of Hispanic Studies* 35 (1958): 199–210.
Josephs, Allen, and Juan Caballero. Introducción. *Bodas de sangre*. By Federico García Lorca. Ed. Josephs and Caballero. 2d ed. Letras Hispánicas 231. Madrid: Cátedra, 1986. 9–80.
Juliá Martínez, Eduardo. "Originalidad de Timoneda." *Revista Valenciana de Filología* 5 (1955–58): 91–151.
Jung, C. G. *Symbols of Transformation: An Analysis of the Prelude to a Case of Schizophrenia*. Trans. R. F. C. Hull. 2d ed. Bollingen Ser. 20. Princeton: Princeton University Press, 1967.
Justin [Marcus Junianus Justinus]. *Epitoma historiarum philippicarum Pompei Trogi*. Ed. Alfredo de Gutschmid. Leipzig, 1886.
Kaiser-Lenoir, Claudina. "*El señor de Pigmalión*, de Jacinto Grau: Una subversión doble." *Ínsula* 432 (1982): 15–16.
Kemp, Lois Anne. "The Plays of Max Aub: A Kaleidoscopic Approach to Theater." Diss. University of Wisconsin, 1972.
Kirk, G. S. *Myth: Its Meaning and Functions in Ancient and Other Cultures*. Sather Classical Lectures 40. Berkeley and Los Angeles: University of California Press, 1970.
———. *The Nature of Greek Myths*. London: Penguin, 1974.
Knoespel, Kenneth J. *Narcissus and the Invention of Personal History*. New York: Garland, 1985.
Knox, Bernard. Introduction. *The Iliad*. By Homer. Trans. Robert Fagles. New York: Viking-Penguin, 1990. 3–64.
Kohler, Eugen, ed. *Representaciones de Juan del Encina*. Bibliotheca Románica 208–10. Strasbourg: n. p., [1914?].
———, ed. *Sieben spanische dramatische Eklogen*. Gesellschaft für romanische Literatur 27. Dresden: Gesellschaft für romanische Literatur, 1911.

Kronik, John W. "Art and Ideology in the Theater of Jacinto Grau." *Kentucky Romance Quarterly* 16 (1969): 261–76.

———. "Vanguardia y tradición en el teatro de Jacinto Grau." *El teatro en España: Entre la tradición y la vanguardia, 1918–1939.* Ed. Dru Dougherty and María Francisca Vilches de Frutos. Madrid: CSIC, 1992. 79–87.

Lacan, Jacques. *Écrits: A Selection.* Trans. Alan Sheridan. London: Tavistock, 1977.

Lace, José de. *Balance teatral de 1900–1901.* Madrid: Hijos de Hernández, 1901.

La Du, Robert Richard. "Honor in the Theater of Guillén de Castro." Diss. University of Washington, 1960.

Lamartina-Lens, Iride. "Myth of Penelope and Ulysses in *La tejedora de sueños, ¿Por qué corres, Ulises?,* and *Ulises no vuelve.*" *Estreno* 12.2 (1986): 31–34.

Larson, Donald R. *The Honor Plays of Lope de Vega.* Cambridge: Harvard University Press, 1977.

Lasagabaster, Jesús María, ed. *El teatro de Miguel de Unamuno.* San Sebastián: Universidad de Deusto, 1987.

Lasso de la Vega, José S. "*Fedra* de Unamuno." *De Sófocles a Brecht.* Barcelona: Planeta, 1970. 205–48.

———. *Helenismo y literatura contemporánea.* Madrid: Prensa Española, 1967.

Lázaro, Fernando. "El teatro de Unamuno." *Cuadernos de la Cátedra Miguel de Unamuno* 7 (1956): 5–29.

León, J. Chicharro de. "Pirandelismo en la literatura española." *Quaderni Ibero-Americani* 15 (1954): 406–14.

Levan, John Richard. "From Tradition to Masterpiece: Circe and Calderón." Diss. University of Texas, 1981.

Lévi-Strauss, Claude. *Structural Anthropology.* Trans. Claire Jacobson and Brooke Grundfest Schoepf. New York: Basic Books, 1963.

Lewis, Christopher Ian. "A Study of the Relationship between the Themes of Love, Honour, and Jealousy in Calderón's *comedias de capa y espada.*" Diss. Cambridge University, 1982.

Lida, Denah. "Galdós y el teatro: Teoría y práctica." *Homenaje a Ana María Barrenechea.* Ed. Lía Schwartz and Isaías Lerner. Madrid: Castalia, 1984. 271–79.

Lida de Malkiel, María Rosa. *Dido en la literatura española: Su retrato y defensa.* London: Tamesis, 1974.

Litvak, Lily. "'Los Tres' y *Electra*: La creación de un grupo generacional bajo el magisterio de Galdós." *Anales Galdosianos* 8 (1973): 89–94.

Lobo Lasso de la Vega, Gabriel. *Tragedia de la honra de Dido restaurada.* Ed. Alfredo Hermenegildo. Kassel: Reichenberger, 1986.

López, Estela R. *El teatro de Max Aub.* Río Piedras: Universidad de Puerto Rico, 1976.

López Caballero, Alberto. "El tema de Fedra en la literatura." *Razón y Fe* 170 (1964): 425–38.

López Morales, Humberto. "Celestina y Eritrea: La huella de la tragicomedia en el teatro de Encina." *La Celestina y su contorno social: Actas del I Congreso Internacional sobre* La Celestina. Ed. Manuel Criado de Val. Barcelona: Hispam, 1977. 315–23.

———. *Tradición y creación en los orígenes del teatro castellano.* Madrid: Alcalá, 1968.

López Pinciano, Alonso. *Philosophía antigua poética.* Vol. 3. Madrid: CSIC, 1953. 3 vols.

Lucan [Marcus Annaeus Lucanus]. *The Civil War (Pharsalia)*. Trans. J. D. Duff. Loeb Classical Library 220. Cambridge: Harvard University Press, 1928.
Lyotard, Jean-François. *The Postmodern Condition: A Report on Knowledge*. Trans. Geoff Bennington and Brian Massumi. Minneapolis: University of Minnesota Press, 1984.
McClelland, I. L. *Spanish Drama of Pathos, 1750–1808*. Vol. 1. Liverpool: Liverpool University Press, 1970. 2 vols.
McGaha, Michael D. "Las comedias mitológicas de Lope de Vega." *Estudios sobre el Siglo de Oro en homenaje a Raymond R. MacCurdy*. Ed. Ángel González et al. Madrid: Cátedra, 1983. 67–82.
———. "From Mantua to Madrid: The Origins of the Mythological Play in Spain." Paper presented at the American Association of University Professors of Italian Convention. University of California at Los Angeles, Nov. 1981.
———. "Lope's *El vellocino de oro* and His *Perseo*: Two Variations on a Single Theme." Paper presented at the Sixth Annual Golden Age Theatre Symposium. University of Texas at El Paso, March 1988.
———. "*El marido más firme* y *La bella Aurora*: Variaciones sobre un tema." *Lope de Vega y los orígenes del teatro español*. Ed. Manuel Criado de Val. Madrid: Edi-6, 1981. 389–97. Trans. and rptd. from "New Myths from Old: Lope Metamorphosizes Ovid," *Mester* 9.1 (1980): 57–66.
———. "The Sources and Feminism of Lope's *Las mujeres sin hombres*." *The Perception of Women in the Spanish Theater of the Golden Age*. Ed. Anita Stoll and Dawn Smith. Lewisburg: Bucknell University Press, 1990. 157–69.
———. *The Theatre in Madrid during the Second Republic: A Checklist*. Research Bibliographies and Checklists 29. London: Grant and Cutler, 1979.
McGrady, Donald. "An Unperceived Popular Story in Encina's *Plácida y Vitoriano*." *Bulletin of the Comediantes* 32 (1980): 139–41.
McKendrick, Melveena. *Theatre in Spain: 1490–1700*. Cambridge: Cambridge University Press, 1989.
MacKinnon, David Norris. "The Mythological Dramas of Pedro Calderón de la Barca." Diss. University of Kentucky, 1977.
Macrí, Oreste. "Ejemplaridad en el teatro de Unamuno." Sánchez-Barbudo 377–84.
Malinowski, Bronislaw. *Myth in Primitive Psychology*. Westport, Conn.: Negro University Press, 1971.
Mancini, Guido. "Una veglia funebre profana: La 'Vigilia de la enamorada muerta' di Juan del Encina." *Studi dell'Istituto Linguistico* 14 (1981): 187–202.
Mandel, Adrienne Schizzano. "Elaboración de un mito: Ariadna en Hardy, Calderón y Corneille." *Varia hispánica: Homenaje a Alberto Porqueras Mayo*. Ed. Joseph L. Laurenti and Vern G. Williamsen. Kassel: Reichenberger, 1989. 81–94.
Marshall, Donald G. *Contemporary Critical Theory: A Selective Bibliography*. New York: Modern Language Association, 1993.
Martin, Henry M. "Lope de Vega's *El vellocino de oro* in Relation to Its Sources." *MLN* 39 (1924): 142–49.
Martinenche, Ernest. "Littérature espagnole: Le théâtre de M. Pérez Galdós." *Revue des Deux Mondes* 32 (1906): 815–50.
Martínez de la Rosa, Francisco. *Edipo. Obras dramáticas*. Paris, 1845. 225–88. Vol. 2 of *Obras completas*.

Maxwell Dial, Eleanore. *Circe y los cerdos.* México: Costa-Amic, 1976. Bilingual transcription of a paper presented at the Congress of Inter-American Women Writers (April 1976).
Mazzei, Pilade. *Contributo allo studio delle fonti, specialmente italiane del teatro di Juan del Enzina e Torres Naharro.* Lucca: Amadei, 1922.
Menéndez Onrubia, Carmen. *Introducción al teatro de Benito Pérez Galdós.* Anejos de la Revista *Segismundo* 7. Madrid: CSIC, 1983.
———. "El olvidado teatro de Benito Pérez Galdós." *Ínsula* 561 (1993): 23–25.
Menéndez Pelayo, Marcelino. *Calderón y su teatro.* 3d. ed. Madrid, 1884.
———. *Orígenes de la novela.* 4 vols. Madrid: Bailly/Bailliere, 1905–15.
———. Prólogo. Antología de poetas líricos castellanos desde la formación del idioma hasta nuestros días. Vol. 7. Madrid, 1898. i-cclxxx. 14 vols. 1890–1916.
Menéndez Pidal, Ramón. "Del honor en el teatro español." *De Cervantes y Lope de Vega.* Buenos Aires: Espasa-Calpe, 1940. 153–84.
Meredith, Joseph A. *Introito and Loa in the Spanish Drama of the Sixteenth Century.* Diss. University of Pennsylvania, 1928. Romanic Languages and Literature 16. Philadelphia: University of Pennsylvania, 1928.
Mérimée, Henri. "A propos de *l'Electra* de M. Pérez Galdós." *Bulletin Hispanique* 3 (1901): 195–202.
———. *L'Art dramatique à Valencia depuis les origines jusqu'au commencement du XVIIe siècle.* Toulouse: Édouard Privat, 1913.
Mesa, Enrique de. "*Fedra* y el drama pseudohistórico." *Apostillas a la escena.* Madrid: Renacimiento, 1929. 240–48.
Miras, Domingo. *Teatro mitológico.* Ed. Virtudes Serrano. Ciudad Real: Biblioteca de Autores y Temas Manchegos, 1995.
Mitchell, Juliet. "Trauma, Abuse, Hysteria ... Sigmund Freud, Frederick Crews, etcetera." Paper presented at the Psychoanalytic Forum. Cornell University, April 1995.
Monleón, José. *El teatro de Max Aub.* Madrid: Taurus, 1971.
———. "Unamuno y el teatro de su tiempo." *Primer Acto* 58 (1964): 22–32.
Monner Sans, José María. *Panorama del nuevo teatro.* Buenos Aires: Losada, 1942.
Montesinos, José F. "La paradoja del 'Arte Nuevo.'" *Estudios sobre Lope de Vega.* Nueva ed. Salamanca: Anaya, 1967. 1–20.
Monti, Silvia. "La comunicazione come problema nel primo teatro di Max Aub." *Quaderni di Lingue e Letterature* 3–4 (1978–79): 267–83.
Montoto y Rautenstrauch, Luis. *Personajes, personas y personillas que corren por las tierras de ambas Castillas.* 2d ed. 2 vols. Seville: Gironés, 1921.
Mooney, Paul Arthur. "A Reevaluation of Past and Current Critical Opinion on the *Comedias Mitológicas* of Pedro Calderón de la Barca." Diss. Pennsylvania State University, 1973.
Moore, John A. "Buero Vallejo—Good Mistresses and Bad Wives." *Romance Notes* 21 (1980): 10–15.
Morley, S. Griswold. Introduction. *Mariucha: Comedia en cinco actos.* By Benito Pérez Galdós. Ed. Morley. Boston: Heath, 1921. vii-xliv.
Morley, S. Griswold, and Courtney Bruerton. *Cronología de las comedias de Lope de Vega.* Trans. María Rosa Cartes. Rev. ed. Madrid: Gredos, 1968.
Morón Arroyo, Ciriaco. *Nuevas meditaciones del* Quijote. Madrid: Gredos, 1976.
Moya del Baño, Francisca. *El tema de Hero y Leandro en la literatura española.* Murcia: Publicaciones de la Universidad de Murcia, 1966.

Müller, Rainer. "Antonio Buero Vallejo: Studien zum Spanischen Nachkriegstheater." Diss. Universität zu Köln, 1970.
Navascués, Michael [Miguel]. "Fantasy and the View of Destiny in the Theater of Jacinto Grau." *Revista de Estudios Hispánicos* 11 (1977): 265–85.
———. *El teatro de Jacinto Grau: Estudio de sus obras principales.* Madrid: Playor, 1975.
Neumeister, Sebastian. *Mythos und Repräsentation: Die mythologischen Festspiele Calderóns.* Munich: Wilhelm Fink, 1978.
Nieto, José C. *Místico, poeta, rebelde, santo: En torno a San Juan de la Cruz.* México: Fondo de Cultura Económica, 1982.
Nieva de la Paz, Pilar. "Recreación y transformación de un mito: *La nieta de Fedra*, drama de Halma Angélico." *Estreno* 20.2 (1994): 18–22, 44.
Nonoyama, Minako. "La personalidad en los dramas de Buero Vallejo y de Unamuno." *Hispanófila* 49 (1973): 69–78.
Nuez, Sebastián de la, and José Schraibman, eds. *Cartas del archivo de Galdós.* Madrid: Taurus, 1967.
O'Connor, Patricia W. "Censorship in the Contemporary Spanish Theater and Antonio Buero Vallejo." *Hispania* 52 (1969): 282–88.
———. "Government Censorship in the Contemporary Spanish Theater." *Educational Theater Journal* 18 (1966): 443–49.
O'Connor, Thomas Austin. "Calderón and Reason's Impasse: The Case of *La estatua de Prometeo*." *La Chispa '81: Selected Proceedings.* Ed. Gilbert Paolini. New Orleans: Tulane University, 1981. 229–37.
———. *Myth and Mythology in the Theater of Pedro Calderón de la Barca.* [San Antonio]: Trinity University Press, 1988.
———. "On Love and the Human Condition: A Prolegomenon to Calderón's Mythological Plays." *Calderón de la Barca at the Tercentenary: Comparative Views.* Ed. Wendell M. Aycock and Sydney P. Cravens. Lubbock: Texas Tech University Press, 1982. 119–34.
Ortega y Gasset, José. *La deshumanización del arte.* 11th ed. Madrid: Revista de Occidente, 1976.
Ovejero, Andrés. "Galdós en el teatro." *El Globo* [Madrid] (Jan. 31, 1901): 1–2.
Ovid [Publius Ovidius Naso]. *Ars amatoria. Art of Love* 11–175.
———. *The Art of Love and Other Poems.* Trans. J. H. Mozley. 2d ed. Loeb Classical Library 232. Cambridge: Harvard University Press, 1979.
———. *Metamorphoses.* Trans. Frank Justus Miller. 3d ed. 2 vols. Loeb Classical Library 42–43. Cambridge: Harvard University Press, 1977.
———. *Remedia amoris. Art of Love* 177–233.
Palli Bonet, Julio. *Homero en España.* Barcelona: Universidad de Barcelona, 1953.
Páramo Pomareda, Jorge. "Consideraciones sobre los 'autos mitológicos' de Calderón de la Barca." *Thesaurus* 12 (1957): 51–80.
Paris, Pierre. "La Mythologie de Calderón: *Apolo y Climene, El hijo del sol, Faetón.*" *Homenaje ofrecido a Menéndez Pidal.* Vol. 1. Madrid: Hernando, 1925. 557–70. 3 vols.
Parker, Alexander A. "The Spanish Drama of the Golden Age: A Method of Analysis and Interpretation." *The Great Playwrights: Twenty-Five Plays with Commentaries by Critics and Scholars.* Ed. Eric Russell Bentley. Vol. 1. Garden City, NY: Doubleday, 1970. 679–707. 2 vols. Reprinted from the edition of the Hispanic and Luso-Brazilian Councils (London, 1957).

Paulino, José C. "Ulises en el teatro español contempóraneo: Una revisión panorámica." *Anales de la Literatura Española Contemporánea* 19 (1994): 327–42.
Pemán, José María. *Antígona: Adaptación muy libre de la tragedia de Sófocles. Teatro* 1231–312.
———. *Edipo: Versión nueva y libre de un mito antiguo.* Madrid: Escelicer, 1953.
———. *Electra: Tragicomedia en dos partes (visión libre y moderna de un mito clásico). Teatro* 1853–906.
———. *Teatro.* Madrid: Escelicer, 1950. Vol. 4 of *Obras completas.*
———. *Tyestes: La tragedia de la venganza.* Madrid: Alfil, 1952.
Penalva, Gonzalo. "José Bergamín y el lenguaje de la máscara." *Primer Acto* 183 (1983): 33–39.
Pérez, Eliza. "La influencia del romancero en Guillén de Castro." Diss. University of Wisconsin, 1932.
Pérez de Moya, Juan. *Philosophía secreta.* Ed. Carlos Clavería. Letras Hispánicas 404. Madrid: Cátedra, 1995.
Pérez Galdós, Benito. *Alceste. Novelas* 1248–77.
———. *El caballero encantado. Novelas* 223–343.
———. *Casandra. Novelas* 1156–93.
———. *Electra. Novelas* 848–98.
———. *Novelas. Teatro. Miscelánea.* Ed. Federico Carlos Sainz de Robles. Madrid: Aguilar, 1961. Vol. 6 of *Obras completas.* 6 vols.
———. *Nuestro teatro.* Madrid: Renacimiento, 1923.
Pérez Minik, Domingo. *Debates sobre el teatro español contemporáneo.* Santa Cruz de Tenerife: Goya, 1953.
———. *Teatro europeo contemporáneo: Su libertad y compromisos.* Madrid: Guadarrama, 1961.
Pérez Pastor, Cristóbal. *Nuevos datos acerca del histrionismo español en los siglos XVI y XVII.* Madrid: La Revista Española, 1901.
Pérez Priego, Miguel Ángel. Introducción. *Teatro completo.* By Juan del Encina. Ed. Pérez Priego. Letras Hispánicas 339. Madrid: Cátedra, 1991. 9–94.
Pigman, G. W. "Versions of Imitation in the Renaissance." *Renaissance Quarterly* 33 (1980): 1–32.
Plato. *Phaedo. Euthyphro. Apology. Crito. Phaedo. Phaedrus.* Trans. Harold North Fowler. Loeb Classical Library 36. Cambridge: Harvard University Press, 1914. 193–403.
———. *Protagoras. Laches. Protagoras. Meno. Euthydemus.* Trans. W. R. M. Lamb. Loeb Classical Library 165. Cambridge: Harvard University Press, 1924. 85–257.
———. *Republic.* Trans. Paul Shorey. 2 vols. Loeb Classical Library 237, 276. Cambridge: Harvard University Press, 1930–35.
Plautus, Titus Maccius. *Amphitryon. Plautus.* Trans. Paul Nixon. Vol. 1. Loeb Classical Library 60. Cambridge: Harvard University Press, 1916. 1–121. 5 vols.
Plutarch [Ploutarchos]. *Plutarch's Lives.* Trans. Bernadotte Perrin. Vol. 1. Loeb Classical Library 46. London: William Heinemann, 1914. 11 vols. 1914–26.
Podol, Peter L. "Ritual and Ceremony in Luis Riaza's Theater of the Grotesque." *Estreno* 8.1 (1982): 7–8, 17.
———. "The Theme of Honor in Two Plays of Buero Vallejo: *Las palabras en la arena* and *La tejedora de sueños.*" *Hispanófila* 68 (1980): 39–46.

Poesse, Walter. "Utilización de las palabras 'honor' y 'honra' en la comedia española." *Homenaje a Don Agapito Rey.* Ed. Josep Roca-Pons. Bloomington: Indiana University Dept. of Spanish and Portuguese, 1980. 289–303.
Powers, Dorothea Thompson. "The Dramatic Art of Guillén de Castro." Diss. University of New Mexico, 1958.
Pucci, Pietro. "The Proem of the *Odyssey*." *Arethusa* 15 (1982): 39–62.
Quintilian [Marcus Fabius Quintilianus]. *Institutio oratoria.* Books 10–12. Trans. H. E. Butler. Vol. 4. Loeb Classical Library 127. London: William Heinemann, 1922. 4 vols. 1920–22.
Rabinal Achí. Los clásicos del teatro hispanoamericano. Ed. Gerardo Luzuriaga and Richard Reeve. 2d ed. Vol. 1. México: Fondo de Cultura Económica, 1994. 15–53. 2 vols.
Racine, Jean. *Phèdre.* Ed. Jean Salles. Paris: Bordas, 1963.
Ragué Arias, María José [Maria-Josep Ragúe i Àrias]. *Lagartijas, gaviotas y mariposas (lectura moderna del mito de Fedra).* Murcia: Universidad de Murcia, 1991.
———. *Lo que fue Troya: Los mitos griegos en el teatro español actual.* Madrid: Asociación de Autores de Teatro, 1993.
———. "Penélope, Agave y Fedra, personajes femeninos griegos, en el teatro de Carmen Resino y de Lourdes Ortiz." *Estreno* 15.1 (1989): 23–24.
———. "Los personajes femeninos de la tragedia griega en el teatro del siglo XX en España." Diss. Universidad de Barcelona, 1986.
———. *Los personajes y temas de la tragedia griega en el teatro gallego contemporáneo.* La Coruña: Do Castro, 1991.
———. *Els personatges femenins de la tragèdia grega en el teatre català del segle XX.* Sabadell: Ausa, [1990].
Ramos, Alicia. "Luis Riaza: El dramaturgo y su obra." *Estreno* 8.1 (1982): 18–21. (Interview.)
Real Academia Española. *Diccionario de Autoridades.* Ed. facsímil. 3 vols. Madrid: Gredos, 1964.
Regalado García, Antonio. *Benito Pérez Galdós y la novela histórica española: 1868–1912.* Madrid: Ínsula, 1966.
Regueiro, José Miguel. "Juan Timoneda y la tradición dramática española." Diss. University of Pennsylvania, 1972.
Reichenberger, Arnold G. "The Uniqueness of the *Comedia*." *Hispanic Review* 27 (1959): 303–16; 38 (1970): 163–73.
Reynolds, John J. *Juan Timoneda.* Boston: Twayne, 1975.
Riaza, Luis. *Antígona . . . ¡cerda! Estreno* 8.1 (1982): 11–16.
———. *Medea es un buen chico. Pipirijaina. Textos* 18 (1981): 29–71.
Robertson, David. "Unas notas sobre el teatro de Unamuno." *Cuadernos de la Cátedra Miguel de Unamuno* 27–28 (1983): 175–79.
Rodríguez Salcedo, Gerardo. "Introducción al teatro de Jacinto Grau." *Papeles de Son Armadans* 42 (1966): 13–42.
Rogers, Elizabeth. "The Humanization of Archetypes in Buero Vallejo's *La tejedora de sueños*." *Revista de Estudios Hispánicos* 15 (1981): 339–48.
———. "Myth, Man, and Exile in *El retorno de Ulises* and *¿Por qué corres, Ulises?*" *Anales de la Literatura Española Contemporánea* 9.1–3 (1984): 117–30.
———. "Role Constraints versus Self-Identity in *La tejedora de sueños* and *Anillos para una dama*." *Modern Dramas* 26 (1983): 310–19.

Rojas, Fernando de. *La Celestina.* Ed. Dorothy S. Severin. Letras Hispánicas 4. Madrid: Cátedra, 1990.
Rombout, André. "Unamuno et le catholicisme de Fedra." *España, teatro y mujeres: Estudios dedicados a Henk Oostendorp.* Ed. Martin Gosman and Hub. Hermans. Amsterdam: Rodopi, 1989. 49–56.
Romero, Concha. *Así aman los dioses.* Madrid: Ediciones Clásicas, 1991.
Rose, H. J. *A Handbook of Greek Mythology.* New York: Penguin, 1991.
Rosete Niño, Pedro. *Comedia famosa de Píramo y Tisbe.* Ed. Pedro Correa Rodríguez. Pamplona: Universidad de Navarra, 1977.
Rubio, Isaac. "Galdós y el melodrama." *Anales Galdosianos* 16 (1981): 57–67.
———. "Ibsen y Galdós." *Letras de Deusto* 4.8 (1974): 207–24.
Rubió y Lluch, Antonio. *El sentimiento del honor en el teatro de Calderón.* Barcelona, 1882.
Ruggeri Marchetti, Magda. "La mujer en el teatro de Antonio Buero Vallejo." *Anthropos* 79 (1987): 37–42.
———. *Il teatro de Antonio Buero Vallejo o il processo verso la verità.* Rome: Bulzoni, 1981.
Ruiz Pérez, Pedro. "Teatro y metateatro en la dramaturgia de Luis Riaza." *Anales de Literatura Española* 5 (1986–87): 479–94.
Ruiz Ramón, Francisco. *Historia del teatro español (desde sus orígenes hasta mil novecientos).* 8th ed. Madrid: Cátedra, 1992.
———. *Historia del teatro espanol: Siglo XX.* 9th ed. Madrid: Cátedra, 1992.
Ruiz Ramón, Francisco, and César Oliva, eds. *El mito en el teatro clásico español: Ponencias y debates de las VII jornadas de teatro clásico español.* Madrid: Taurus, 1988.
Ruple, Joelyn. *Antonio Buero Vallejo (The First Fifteen Years).* New York: Torres and Sons, 1971.
Sackett, Theodore Alan. "*Electra* desde la perspectiva de la crítica semiológica y arquetípica." *Revista de Literatura* 51 (1989): 463–82.
———. "Galdós dramaturgo, reformador del teatro de su tiempo." *Estreno* 7.1 (1981): 6–10.
———. *Galdós y las máscaras: Historia teatral y bibliografía anotada.* Verona: Università di Padova, 1982.
Salvat i Ferré, Ricard. "El más fascinador de los juegos (el teatro de Buero Vallejo y su incidencia social)." *Antonio Buero Vallejo: Premio de Literatura en Lengua Castellana "Miguel de Cervantes" 1986.* Ed. Ministerio de Cultura. Barcelona: Anthropos, 1987. 75–99.
Sánchez, Luis Rafael. *La pasión según Antígona Pérez.* Río Piedras: Cultural, 1968.
Sánchez-Barbudo, A., ed. *Miguel de Unamuno.* Madrid: Taurus, 1974.
Sastre, Alfonso. *Medea: Versión para un teatro popular.* 1958. Hondarribia: Argitaletxe, n. d. [1992?].
Schack, A. F. *Historia de la literatura y del arte dramático en España.* Trans. Eduardo de Mier. Vol. 4. Madrid, 1887. 5 vols. 1885–87.
Schalk, F. "Zur Rolle der Mythologie in der Literatur des Siglo de Oro." *Classical Influences on European Culture A. D. 1500–1700.* Ed. R. R. Bolgar. Cambridge: Cambridge University Press, 1976. 259–70.
Schevill, Rudolph. *Ovid and the Renascence in Spain.* University of California Publications in Modern Philology 4.1. Berkeley and Los Angeles: University of California Press, 1913.

Schmidt, Leopold. "Ueber Calderon's Behandlung antiker Mythen: Ein Beitrag zur Geschichte der Mythologie." *Rheinisches Museum für Philologie* 10 (1856): 313–57.
Schmitt-Von Mühlenfels, Franz. *Pyramus und Thisbe: Rezeptionstypen eines Ovidischen Stoffes in Literatur, Kunst und Musik.* Heidelberg: Carl Winter, 1972.
Schrader, Ludwig. "Odysseus im Siglo de Oro: Zur mythologischen Allegorie im Theater Calderóns und seiner Zeitgenossen." *Spanische Literatur im Goldenen Zeitalter.* Ed. Fritz Schalk. Frankfurt: Vittorio Klostermann, 1973. 401–39.
Schwartz, Kessel. "Jacinto Grau and the Meaning of Existence." *Hispania* 44 (1961): 34–41.
Sedgwick, Eve Kosofsky. *Between Men: English Literature and Male Homosocial Desire.* New York: Columbia University Press, 1985.
Sedwick, Frank. "Unamuno and Womanhood: His Theater." *Hispania* 43 (1960): 309–13.
Segel, Harold B. *Pinocchio's Progeny: Puppets, Marionettes, Automatons, and Robots in Modernist and Avant-Garde Drama.* Baltimore: Johns Hopkins University Press, 1995.
Seneca, Lucius Annaeus. *Agamemnon. Tragedies* 2:1–87.
———. *Hercules Oetaeus. Tragedies* 2:183–341.
———. *Medea. Tragedies* 1:225–315.
———. *Phaedra. Tragedies* 1:317–423.
———. *Three Tragedies.* Trans. Frederick Ahl. Ithaca: Cornell University Press, 1986.
———. *Thyestes. Tragedies* 2:89–181.
———. *Tragedies.* Trans. Frank Justus Miller. 2 vols. Loeb Classical Library 62, 78. Cambridge: Harvard University Press, 1979–87.
Serrano Martínez, Encarnación Irene. *"Honneur" y "Honor": Su significación a través de las literaturas francesa y española, desde los orígenes hasta el siglo XVI.* Murcia: Universidad de Murcia, 1956.
Seznec, Jean. *The Survival of the Pagan Gods: The Mythological Tradition and Its Place in Renaissance Humanism and Art.* Trans. Barbara F. Sessions. Bollingen Ser. 38. Princeton: Princeton University Press, 1953.
Shaw, Donald L. *A Literary History of Spain: The Nineteenth Century.* London: Ernest Benn, 1972.
———. "Sobre algunos aspectos técnicos del teatro de Unamuno." Gómez Molleda 501–13.
———. "Three Plays of Unamuno: A Survey of His Dramatic Technique." *Forum for Modern Language Studies* 13 (1977): 253–64.
Shepard, Sanford. *El Pinciano y las teorías literarias del siglo de oro.* 2d ed. Madrid: Gredos, 1970.
Shergold, N. D. *A History of the Spanish Stage from Medieval Times until the End of the Seventeenth Century.* Oxford: Oxford University Press, 1967.
Silverman, Kaja. *The Subject of Semiotics.* New York: Oxford University Press, 1983.
Simches, Seymour O. "The Theater of Jacinto Grau." *Studies in Honor of Samuel Montefiore Waxman.* Ed. Herbert H. Golden. Boston: Boston University Press, 1969. 141–57.
Simpson, Michael. Introduction. *Gods and Heroes of the Greeks: The Library of Apollodorus.* By Apollodorus. Trans. Michael Simpson. Amherst: University of Massachusetts Press, 1976. 1–9.

Sobejano, Gonzalo. "Echegaray, Galdós y el melodrama." *Anales Galdosianos* (anejo, 1976): 91–117.

———. "Razón y suceso de la dramática galdosiana." *Anales Galdosianos* 5 (1970): 39–54.

Soldevila-Durante, Ignacio. "Max Aub, dramaturgo." *Segismundo* 10 (1977): 139–92.

Soons, Alan. "Four Transpositions of the Theseus Legend in the Hispanic Theater." *Cithara* 24.2 (1985): 3–21.

Sophocles. *Electra*. Sophocles 2:121–251.

———. *Oedipus the King*. Sophocles 1:1–139.

———. *Philoctetes*. Sophocles 2:361–493.

———. *Sophocles*. Trans. F. Storr. 2 vols. Loeb Classical Library 20–21. London: William Heinemann, 1912–13.

Standish, Peter. "Pirandello, Pygmalion, and Spain." *Revue de Littérature Comparée* 47 (1973): 327–37.

Stanford, W. B. "Homer's Use of Personal πολυ-Compounds." *Classical Philology* 45 (1950): 108–10.

Starkie, Walter. "Galdós and Modern Spanish Drama." *Bulletin of Spanish Studies* 3 (1925–26): 111–17.

Steiner, George. *The Death of Tragedy*. New York: Oxford University Press, 1961.

Stuart, Donald Clive. "Honor in the Spanish Drama." *Romanic Review* 1 (1910): 247–58.

Sullivan, Henry W. *Juan del Encina*. Boston: Twayne, 1976.

Surtz, Ronald E. *The Birth of a Theater: Dramatic Convention in the Spanish Theater from Juan del Encina to Lope de Vega*. Madrid: Castalia, 1979.

ter Horst, Robert. *Calderón: The Secular Plays*. Lexington: University Press of Kentucky, 1982.

———. "The Duke and Duchess of Alba and Juan del Enzina: Courtly Sponsors of an Uncourtly Genius." *Studies in Honor of William C. McCrary*. Ed. Robert Fiore et al. Lincoln: Society of Spanish and Spanish-American Studies, 1986. 215–20.

———. "*Ut Pictura Poesis:* Self-Portrayal in the Plays of Juan del Enzina." *Brave New Worlds: Studies in Spanish Golden Age Literature*. Ed. Edward H. Friedman and Catherine Larson. New Orleans: University Press of the South, 1996. 1–18.

Testa, Daniel Philip. "The Pyramus and Thisbe Theme in 16th and 17th Century Spanish Poetry." Diss. University of Michigan, 1962.

Thompson, Stith. "Myths and Folktales." *Myth: A Symposium*. Ed. Thomas A. Sebeok. Bloomington: Indiana University Press, 1971. 169–80.

Thomson, George. *Aeschylus and Athens: A Study in the Social Origins of Drama*. New York: Grosset and Dunlap, 1968.

Tilgher, Adriano. "Michele de Unamuno." *La scena e la vita*. Rome: Libreria di Scienze e Lettere, 1925. 158–67.

Timoneda, Juan. *Obras de Juan de Timoneda*. Ed. Eduardo Juliá Martínez. 3 vols. Madrid: Sociedad de Bibliófilos Españoles, 1947–48.

———. *Tragicomedia llamada Filomena. Obras completas*. Ed. Sociedad de Bibliófilos Valencianos. Vol. 1. Valencia: Doménech, 1911. 207–62. (Vols. 2 and 3 were planned but never published.)

Tornos, Andrés M. "Temas y problemas del teatro de Unamuno." *Reseña de Literatura, Artes y Espectáculos* 2 (1965): 65–70.

Toro, Alfonso de. "Die Ehrbegriffe 'Honor/Honra' im Spanien des 16. und 17. Jahrhunderts." *Homenaje a Hans Flasche: Festschrift zum 80. Geburtstag am 25 November 1991*. Ed. Karl-Hermann Körner and Günther Zimmermann. Stuttgart: Franz Steiner, 1991. 674–95.

———. "Sistema semiótico-estructural del drama de honor en Lope de Vega y Calderón de la Barca." *Revista Canadiense de Estudios Hispánicos* 9 (1985): 181–202.

Torre, Guillermo de. "Unamuno y su teatro." *Papeles de Son Armadans* 36 (1965): 13–44.

Torrente Ballester, G[onzalo]. *El retorno de Ulises. Teatro II*. Barcelona: Destino, 1981. 115–89.

———. *Teatro español contemporáneo*. 2d ed. Madrid: Guadarrama, 1968.

Turk, Laurel Herbert. "Juan del Encina and the Spanish Renaissance." Diss. Stanford University, 1933.

Turner, John H. *The Myth of Icarus in Spanish Renaissance Poetry*. London: Tamesis, 1976.

Unamuno, Miguel de. *El Cristo de Velázquez. Obras completas*. Vol. 13. Ed. Manuel García Blanco. Madrid: Afrodisio Aguado, 1958. 647–801.

———. *Del sentimiento trágico de la vida en los hombres y en los pueblos*. Madrid: Alianza, 1986.

———. *Fedra: Tragedia en tres actos. La esfinge. La venda. Fedra*. Ed. José Paulino. Madrid: Castalia, 1987. 183–234.

———. "La regeneración del teatro español." *La España Moderna* 91 (1896): 5–36. Rptd. in *Teatro completo* 1129–58.

———. *Teatro completo*. Ed. Manuel García Blanco. Madrid: Aguilar, 1959.

Valbuena Briones, Ángel. "La *Fedra* de Unamuno a través de la tradición literaria." *Estreno* 13.2 (1987): 4–8.

———. *Perspectiva crítica de los dramas de Calderón*. Madrid: Rialp, 1965.

———. Prólogo. *Dramas de honor*. By Calderón de la Barca. Ed. Valbuena Briones. 2d ed. Vol. 1. Clásicos Castellanos 141. Madrid: Espasa-Calpe, 1967. xi–civ. 2 vols.

Valbuena [Prat], Ángel. *Calderón: Su personalidad, su arte dramático, su estilo y sus obras*. Barcelona: Juventud, 1941.

———. *Historia de la literatura española*. 7th ed. Barcelona: Gustavo Gili, 1963. 3 vols.

———. *Historia del teatro español*. Barcelona: Noguer, 1956.

———. *Literatura dramática española*. Barcelona: Labor, 1930.

———. "El teatro de Jacinto Grau y su situación especial." *Historia general de las literaturas hispánicas*. Ed. Guillermo Díaz-Plaja. Vol. 6. Barcelona: Vergara, 1967. 165–69. 6 vols. 1949–67.

Valverde López, Carlos. *Electromanía: Juicio crítico de* Electra. Málaga: Unión Mercantil, 1901.

Van Beysterveldt, Antony. *La poesía amatoria del siglo XV y el teatro profano de Juan del Encina*. Madrid: Ínsula, 1972.

———. *Répercussions du souci de la pureté de sang sur la conception de l'honneur dans la "comedia nueva" espagnole*. Leiden: E. J. Brill, 1966.

Vega Carpio, Lope Félix de. *Arte nuevo de hacer comedias en este tiempo, dirigido a la Academia de Madrid. Antología del teatro del siglo de oro*. Ed. Eugenio Suárez-Galbán Guerra. Madrid: Orígenes, 1989. 779–89.

———. *Comedias mitológicas. Comedias históricas de asunto extranjero.* Ed. Real Academia Española. Madrid, 1896. Vol. 6 of *Obras de Lope de Vega.*
———. *La fábula de Perseo o la bella Andrómeda.* Ed. Michael D. McGaha. Kassel: Reichenberger, 1985.
———. *El laberinto de Creta. Comedias mitológicas* 109–43.
———. *Las mujeres sin hombres. Comedias mitológicas* 35–69.
———. "Prólogo dialogístico a *La Parte XVI.*" *Comedias escogidas de Frey Lope Félix de Vega Carpio.* Ed. Juan Eugenio Hartzenbusch. Vol. 4. Biblioteca de Autores Españoles 52. Madrid, 1860. xxv-xxvi. 4 vols. 1855–60.
———. *El vellocino de oro. Comedias mitológicas* 145–71.
Verdú de Gregorio, Joaquín. *La luz y la oscuridad en el teatro de Buero Vallejo.* Barcelona: Ariel, 1977.
Vernant, Jean-Pierre. *Myth and Society in Ancient Greece.* Trans. Janet Lloyd. New York: Zone, 1990.
Viel-Castel, Louis de. "Le Théâtre espagnol: De l'honneur comme ressort dramatique." *Revue des Deux Mondes* 25 (1841): 397–421.
Vilches de Frutos, María Francisca. "Introducción al estudio de la recreación de los mitos literarios en el teatro de la postguerra española." *Segismundo* 17 (1983): 183–209.
Villalón, Cristóbal de. *Tragedia de Mirrha. Revue Hispanique* 19 (1908): 159–83.
Vinge, Louise. *The Narcissus Theme in Western European Literature up to the Early Nineteenth Century.* Trans. Robert Dewsnap et al. Lund (Sweden): Gleerups, 1967.
Virgil [Publius Vergilius Maro]. *Aeneid.* Books 1–6. *Eclogues. Georgics. Aeneid.* Trans. H. Rushton Fairclough. Vol. 1. Loeb Classical Library 63. Cambridge: Harvard University Press, 1986. 239–571. 2 vols.
Virués, Cristóbal de. *Elisa Dido. Poetas dramáticos valencianos.* Ed. Real Academia Española. Vol. 2. Madrid: Revista de Archivos, 1929. 146–78. 2 vols.
Vitoria, Baltasar de. *Teatro de los dioses de la gentilidad.* 2 vols. Madrid, 1676.
Voght, Geoffrey M. "The Mythological *Autos* of Calderón de la Barca." Diss. University of Michigan, 1974.
Wallace, Elizabeth. "The Spanish Drama of To-day." *Atlantic Monthly* 102 (1908): 357–66.
Walthaus, Rina. "Imágenes y simbolismo en *Dido y Eneas* de Guillén de Castro." *Neophilologus* 69 (1985): 75–89.
Wardropper, Bruce W. "Calderón de la Barca and Late Seventeenth-Century Theater." *Record of the Art Museum. Princeton University* 41.2 (1982): 35–41.
———. "Metamorphosis in the Theatre of Juan del Encina." *Studies in Philology* 59 (1962): 41–51.
———, ed. *Spanish Poetry of the Golden Age.* New York: Appleton-Century-Crofts, 1971.
Watson, A. I[rvine]. "Hercules and the Tunic of Shame: Calderón's *Los tres mayores prodigios.*" *Homenaje a William L. Fichter: Estudios sobre el teatro antiguo hispánico y otros ensayos.* Ed. A. David Kossoff and José Amor y Vázquez. Madrid: Castalia, 1971. 773–83.
———. "*El pintor de su deshonra* and the Neo-Aristotelian Theory of Tragedy." *Critical Essays on the Theatre of Calderón.* Ed. Bruce W. Wardropper. New York: New York University Press, 1965. 203–23. Rptd. from *Bulletin of Hispanic Studies* 40 (1963): 17–34.

Weiger, John G. "Sobre la originalidad e independencia de Guillén de Castro." *Hispanófila* 31 (1958): 1–15.
Wilson, Margaret. *Spanish Drama of the Golden Age.* Oxford: Pergamon, 1969.
Wilson, William E. *Guillén de Castro.* New York: Twayne, 1973.
Wiltrout, Ann E. "Quien espera desespera: El suicidio en el teatro de Juan del Encina." *Hispanófila* 72 (1981): 1–11.
Wind, Edgar. *Pagan Mysteries in the Renaissance.* Rev. ed. New York: Norton, 1968.
Winecoff Díaz, Janet. "Jacinto Grau and His Concept of the Theater." *Revista de Estudios Hispánicos* 5 (1971): 203–21.
Ynduráin, Domingo. Introducción. *Poesía.* By San Juan de la Cruz. Letras Hispánicas 178. Madrid: Cátedra, 1983. 11–236.
Zavala, Iris M. "La dialogía del teatro unamuniano: Género interno." Lasagabaster 13–26.
———. *Unamuno y su teatro de conciencia.* Salamanca: Universidad de Salamanca, 1963.
Zimic, Stanislav, ed. *Teatro y poesía.* By Juan del Encina. Madrid: Taurus, 1986.
Zuckerman-Ingber, Alix. *El Bien Más Alto: A Reconsideration of Lope de Vega's Honor Plays.* Gainesville: University of Florida Press, 1984.

Index

Note: For references to the principal myths and mythological figures studied in this book, please consult Appendix 1.

Abel, Lionel, 4
Aeschylus
 Agamemnon, 133, 133 n. 11
 Libation-Bearers, 130 n. 5
 Oresteia, 15, 130 n. 5, 186
 portrayal of Orestes by, 142
 Prometheus Bound, 162
 Seven against Thebes (Spanish translation of), 179 n. 47
aggression, aggressive desire (including violence)
 basic definitions of, 11–14, 16, 222
 in Buero Vallejo, 189, 191, 195–96, 198–200
 in Calderón, 105
 in Castro, 72, 76–77, 82–84, 195
 in *comedia nueva*, 66
 in Cueva y Silva, 51–53, 58–59
 in Freud, 11, 11 n. 10
 in Grau, 163, 169–71, 173, 175–77
 in Greek myth and literature, 15, 143, 147 n. 23
 in Jung, 11
 in Ovid, 11–12
 in Pemán, 204–5
 in Pérez Galdós, 141, 144
 in Plato, 10, 10 n. 9
 in Timoneda, 39, 42–47
 in Torrente Ballester, 185
 in Unamuno, 150
Ahl, Frederick, 7, 151, 187, 204 n. 19
Alfonso X el Sabio, 15, 28 n. 14
allegory
 in *comedia nueva*, 63, 121–22, 182
 in Encina, 36–38
 in Pérez Galdós, 137
 in Unamuno, 155
Allen, Don Cameron, 63 n. 1
Álvarez de la Villa, Alfredo, 33
Anderson, Robert Floyd, 150
Andrist, Debra, 14
Angélico, Halma, 178
antiheroism, 87–88, 93, 112, 119
Aphrodite. *See* Venus
Apollodorus, 43 n. 28, 104 n. 38, 162
Apollonius, 104 n. 38
Aristophanes, 15
Aristotle, 5–7, 54
Aróstegui, María del Pilar, 46
Arrowsmith, William, 141
Artiles, Jenaro, 66
Aszyk, Urszula, 146 n. 21
Aub, Max, 127, 178–79
Aubrun, Charles, 64 n. 2, 68, 122
auto sacramental, 101, 122, 154
avant-garde. *See* theater
Ayala, Francisco, 66
Azorín (Leopoldo Alas), 126–27

Bandera, Cesáreo, 14
Barbieri, Marie E., 153, 157
Barnstone, Willis, 154
Barrett, L. L., 85
Bataillon, Marcel, 21
Benavente, Jacinto, 146–47, 177
Benedetti, Thomas, 122
Berceo, Gonzalo de, 37
Bergamín, José, 205–6, 221–22

258   Index

Berkowitz, H. Chonon, 130-31 n. 5
Beser, Sergio, 130 n. 4
Boccaccio, Giovanni, 23-25
Bonilla y San Martín, Adolfo, 49 n. 32
Borel, Jean-Paul, 193 n. 12, 200
Bourbon monarchy, 122, 126
Bourne, Marjorie Adele, 204
Bretón de los Herreros, Manuel, 2
Brown, G. G., 125-26
Bruerton, Courtney, 68 n. 8
Buero Vallejo, Antonio
　compared with Castro, 195
　compared with Unamuno, 190
　Historia de una escalera, 183
　political inclinations of, 203
　La tejedora de sueños, 183, 187-204, 209, 221, 223
　treatment of myth by, 188-89, 191-93, 195, 202-4
Burkert, Walter, 11, 14 n. 11, 16, 83 n. 22, 224
Bustamante, Jorge de, 39 n. 26, 42-43, 88 n. 27, 91 n. 28, 93, 95, 111 n. 44

Calderón de la Barca, Pedro
　A secreto agravio, secreta venganza, 74 n. 16
　allegory in, 64 n. 1
　Amado y aborrecido, 102
　chronology of plays by, 68, 68 n. 8
　compared with Castro, 20, 69, 74 n. 16
　compared with Lope de Vega, 103, 108-9, 112, 120
　important changes in personal life of, 102 n. 35
　El mágico prodigioso, 142
　El médico de su honra, 74 n. 16, 165
　No hay cosa como callar, 90
　El pintor de su deshonra, 74 n. 16, 114
　sources of myth in, 102-3, 104 n. 38, 106 n. 40, 109 n. 43, 111 n. 44, 119 n. 49
　treatment of myth by, 103, 108-9, 118-19
　Los tres mayores prodigios, 68, 102-20, 122, 223
　La vida es sueño, 98
Canals, Salvador, 138, 142
Carvajal, Miguel de, 40
Cascardi, Anthony, 116
Castiglione, Baldassare, 38
Castro, Américo, 25, 64 n. 3, 65

Castro, Guillén de
　chronology of plays by, 68
　compared with Buero Vallejo, 195
　compared with Calderón, 69, 74 n. 16, 120
　compared with Lope de Vega, 69, 74 n. 16, 86, 88, 95, 101, 120
　Dido y Eneas, 69-86, 120, 122, 191, 195, 223
　Progne y Filomena, 82
　sources of myth in, 70-71
　treatment of myth by, 81-82, 84-86
　Virgilian tradition considered by, 70-71
Catalán Menéndez Pidal, Diego, 50 n. 32, 60
Catena, Elena, 132 n. 10
censorship, 8, 182, 205
Cervantes, Miguel de, 60, 114, 140, 142, 164, 169
Chambardón, Gabriela, 199
Chapman, W. C., 101 n. 33
character. *See* myth, character vs. plot; women characters.
Chinchilla, Rosa Helena, 3 n. 2
Cirne, Juan, 19, 70, 86
Ciruelo, J. I., 158
Colahan, Clark (and Alfred Rodríguez), 103
Collodi, Carlo, *Pinocchio*, 165
comedia nueva
　anticipated by Cueva y Silva, 46, 52, 59-60
　conventions of, 63-68, 82, 84, 88, 99, 108, 110, 150, 165-66
commedia dell'arte, 165
Cook, John, 2
Correa, Gustavo, 65-66
Cossío, José María de, 3, 5
courtly love, 25, 30-31, 36
Craft, Sandra, 71, 80
Crawford, J. P. Wickersham, 19, 29, 37 n. 23, 49-50 n. 32
Cruickshank, D. W. (and J. E. Varey), 102 n. 37
Cruz, Juan de la, 154-55, 159 n. 32
Cruz, Juana Inés de la, 54 n. 34, 154
Cubillo de Aragón, Álvaro, 86
Cueva, Juan de la, 20, 22
Cueva y Silva, Francisco de la, 22
　anticipation of *comedia nueva* by, 46, 52, 59-60

compared with Encina, 49
compared with Timoneda, 49
sources of myth in, 53 n. 33
Trajedia de Narciso, 19, 49–61, 223
treatment of myth by, 59
Cuevas, Alonso de las, 71 n. 11, 86
Curtius, Ernst Robert, 27, 97

D'Annunzio, Gabriele, 148 n. 25, 152 n. 27
de Armas, Frederick, 105–6
de Man, Paul, 6
Demetrius, James Kleon, 88 n. 26
demythification, 183–84, 188–89, 192, 203
Denomy, Alexander, 25 n. 6
Derrida, Jacques, 203
desire, general
  basic categories and definitions of, 8–17
  in Buero Vallejo, 189, 194
  in Calderón, 103, 120
  in Castro, 71, 84–85, 88
  in Cueva y Silva, 57–58, 60–61
  in Echegaray, 129
  in Encina, 22, 34–35, 38, 49
  feminine, 58, 143 n. 18, 190, 197–98, 200–201, 203, 209
  in Grau, 161, 163, 166–68, 171, 176
  heterosexual, 215
  homosocial, 220
  in Lope de Vega, 86, 88, 92, 94, 100–101
  male, 176, 190, 207
  mimetic. *See* desire, triangular
  in Pemán, 186
  in Pérez Galdós, 143
  in Plato, 10 n. 9
  in postwar twentieth century, 182, 221–22
  in prewar twentieth century, 177–78
  queer, 209, 220
  in Riaza, 209
  in Romero, 207
  in seventeenth-century *comedia nueva*, 64, 120–22
  in sixteenth century, 21, 60–61
  in Timoneda, 39, 46–49
  in Torrente Ballester, 184
  triangular (including mimetic), 13–14, 50–54, 58–61, 87, 99, 173, 195, 199, 218
  in Unamuno, 146–49, 153–54
  See also aggression; erotic desire; nutritive desire.

determinism, predetermination, 152, 158, 177
deus/dea ex machina, 35–36, 140–41
Díaz-Plaja, Guillermo, 189 n. 6
Diego, Fernando de, 197
Díez Borque, José María, 19, 50 n. 32, 67 n. 6
Díez-Canedo, Enrique, 130 n. 4
Díez del Corral, Luis, 182
DiPuccio, Denise, 64 n. 1
Dolores de Asís Garrote, María, 152 n. 27, 155, 158
Doménech, Ricardo, 195
Dostoevsky, Fyodor, 159 n. 32
Don Juan (character), 4, 89
Dougherty, Dru, 160 n. 35, 175–76
drama. *See* theater
dreams, 9–10, 57, 189, 196–200, 202
Dumas, Claude, 4 n. 4

Echegaray, José de, 125–26, 129, 144, 146–47, 177
Edwards, Gwynne, 114
Elliott, J. H., 48
Ellis, Havelock, 130 n. 4
Encina, Juan del
  compared with Cueva y Silva, 49
  compared with Timoneda, 38–39, 42, 44, 49
  Égloga de Plácida y Vitoriano, 21–38, 60–61, 222–24
  influenced by Italian Renaissance, 37, 224
  place of in Spanish theater, 21
  sources of myth in, 28 n. 14
  treatment of myth by, 36–38
Erasmus, 21, 43, 222
erotic desire (including libido, love, lust, passion, sexual desire, sexuality)
  basic definitions of, 12–13, 222
  in Bergamín, 206
  in Buero Vallejo, 191, 194–95, 197–99
  in Calderón, 102, 104, 106, 108, 111, 115
  in Castro, 71–78, 80–85
  in *comedia nueva*, 67, 67 n. 6, 101, 166
  in Cueva y Silva, 51–52, 55–59
  in Echegaray, 129
  in Encina, 22, 25, 29–30, 32–33, 35–37, 39, 60
  in Freud, 10–11, 13–14, 16, 58

in Grau, 167–68, 173
in Greek myth and literature, 10, 12, 15, 67, 147 n. 23, 220, 224
in Jung, 10, 15
in Latin literature, 12
in Lope de Vega, 86–90, 93–95, 99–100
in Ovid, 89, 168, 171
in Pemán, 186, 204
in Pérez Galdós, 134–35
in Plato, 8, 10 n. 9
in Riaza, 209, 218–19
in scriptures (passion of Christ), 153–55, 177
in Seneca, 151
in Timoneda, 39–45, 47–48
in Torrente Ballester, 184–85
in Unamuno, 147, 149, 150–53
Escribano, Jean, 85
Espina, Antonio, 127
Euripides
   Alcestis, 131
   Electra, 130–31 n. 5, 131 n. 7, 133 n. 11, 135
   Hippolytus, 12, 147–49, 151, 155
   Medea, 104 n. 38, 205–6, 209–11, 212 n. 28
   Orestes, 130–31 n. 5, 141–42
   treatment of myth by, 145, 145 n. 19
Ezell, Richard, 169

fate, 66, 84–85, 177, 195
Feal Deibe, Carlos, 150
feminism. *See* myth, feminist approaches to
fetishism, 167, 177
Fernández, Sebastián, 20
Fetterley, Judith, 201
Finkenthal, Stanley, 131 n. 7, 132, 139, 141
fire, symbolism of, 37–38, 76, 153–54, 162
Fox, Inman, 130
Franco, Andrés, 150
Franco regime, 182–83, 187, 203–6, 208, 216, 221, 223
Frazer, James, 4
Freud, Sigmund
   aim-inhibited desire explained by, 12–13, 40
   hunger explained by, 14
   narcissism explained by, 8, 58–59
   Oedipus myth in, 7
   relation between sexual desire and violence explained by, 13
   taboo explained by, 15
   theory of instincts explained by, 10–11, 15–16
   used to interpret Pérez Galdós, 143
   view of Electra complex in, 143 n. 18
   wish fulfillment in, 198
Friedman, Edward, 71
Froldi, Rinaldo, 45, 48
Frye, Northrup, 4, 8

Garber, Marjorie, 98
García Blanco, Manuel, 146, 146 n. 22
García de la Huerta, Vicente, 2
García Gual, Carlos, 207
García Lorca, Federico, 127, 177–78, 215, 223
García Lorenzo, Luciano, 86, 160, 187
García Valdecasas, Alfonso, 66–67
García Viñó, M., 152
gender issues
   in Buero Vallejo, 190–91, 195–96
   in Castro, 81
   in Cueva y Silva, 52, 58–59
   in Encina, 30–32, 36
   in Lope de Vega, 96
   in Riaza, 209, 212, 214–20
   in Timoneda, 40–42
Generation of 1898, 126
Gillet, Joseph, 25–26, 30, 37, 40
Gimeno, Rosalie, 23 n. 3, 26, 26 n. 8, 29–30, 32 n. 18, 34 n. 20, 35
Girard, René
   mimetic desire explained by, 13–14
   used to interpret Calderón, 105, 107
   used to interpret Castro, 72
   used to interpret Cueva y Silva, 50–54
   used to interpret Riaza, 218
Giuliano, William, 161, 198
gods, representation of, 8, 37–38, 173–75, 195
Golden Fleece (military order), 104 n. 38
Golden Fleece (myth), 104–08, 110
Gómez de la Serna, Ramón, 127
González-Cobos, Carmen, 199
González del Valle, Luis, 150–51, 156
Grau, Jacinto
   compared with Pérez Galdós, 159, 160 n. 34, 167

compared with Riaza, 219
compared with Unamuno, 159, 167
experimentalism of, 126–27, 223
place of in Spanish theater, 159, 223
El señor de Pigmalión, 159–78, 219
sources of myth in, 160–61
treatment of myth by, 171, 175–77
Graves, Robert, 133 n. 11
Green, Otis, 25, 30, 36–38, 82 nn. 20–21, 121
Grismer, Raymond, 24 n. 5

Halsey, Martha, 196
Harris, Carolyn J., 201
Hart, Georg, 23 n. 3
Hathaway, Robert, 25, 26 n. 7, 29, 31 n. 17
Haverbeck, O. N, 121
heresy, 30, 36, 42 n. 7, 158
Hermenegildo, Alfredo, 50 n. 32
Hernández Araico, Susana, 106, 112
Hesiod, 6, 15, 105–6 n. 40, 161, 199 n. 17
Highet, Gilbert, 2
Hilborn, Harry W., 68 n. 8
Hinterhäuser, Hans, 128 n. 2, 135
Holt, Marion, 181, 187
Homer
  Iliad, 6, 188, 199 n. 17
  Odyssey, 184, 188–89, 191–93, 193 n. 13, 199, 199 n. 17, 200
honor
  in Calderón, 102–8, 110–18, 120, 223
  in Castro, 71–72, 74–78, 80–84
  conventions of, 64–68
  general observations on, 8, 59–61, 120, 123
  in Grau, 165–66
  in Lope de Vega, 86–97, 99–101, 223
  in Unamuno, 150
Horace, 20–21, 45, 60
Hoyo, Arturo del, 127
hunger. *See* nutritive desire
Hyginus, 162

Ibsen, Henrik, 127, 127–28 n. 1, 158
iconography, 23–25, 34, 37
Iglesias Feijoo, Luis, 188, 190, 195, 199, 200
incest
  in Angélico, 178
  contemporary interest in, 8

in Pérez Galdós, 136, 143–45, 167, 177
in Unamuno, 157–58, 167

jealousy, suspicion
  in Buero Vallejo, 191, 201–2
  in Calderón, 114, 118, 122
  in Castro, 74
  in *comedia nueva*, 67
  in Cueva y Silva, 51, 52, 59
  in Grau, 165, 173
  in Greek myth and literature, 8, 38–39, 133 n. 11
Johnson, Barbara, 188
Jones, C. A., 64–65
Josephs, Allen (and Juan Caballero), 178
Juliá Martínez, Eduardo, 39 n. 25
Jung, C. G., 4, 10–11, 14–16, 143 n. 18, 167
Justin, 69–70

Kaiser-Lenoir, Claudina, 164, 166, 173, 176
Kierkegaard, Søren, 159 n. 32
Kirk, G. S., 7 n. 8, 224
kisses, kissing, 48, 152–56, 158, 186
Knoespel, Kenneth J., 33, 49, 52, 54, 59
Knox, Bernard, 188
Kronik, John, 160 n. 34

Lacan, Jacques, 16–17, 57, 100, 167–69
Lace, José de, 137 n. 13
Lamartina-Lens, Iride, 201
Larson, Donald, 66
Lasso de la Vega, José S., 148 n. 25, 182
Lázaro, Fernando, 146 n. 22
León, Luis de, 159 n. 32
Lesbos, symbolism of, 95–96
Lévi-Strauss, Claude, 4
libido. *See* erotic desire
Lida de Malkiel, María Rosa, 21–22, 69–71, 74
Lobo Lasso de la Vega, Gabriel, 20–22, 70, 86
López de Ayala, Adelardo, 125
López de Zárate, Francisco, 103
López Morales, Humberto, 29–31
López Pinciano, Alonso, 60 n. 35
love, lust. *See* erotic desire

McClelland, Ivy, 2
McGaha, Michael, 19, 86–87, 88 nn. 26–27, 106 n. 40, 179 n. 47

McGrady, Donald, 23, 26, 31 n. 17, 33 n. 19
Malinowski, Bronislaw, 4
Maeztu, Ricardo de, 130 n. 4
Mancini, Guido, 36 n. 22
Mandel, Adrienne Schizzano, 109 n. 43, 111–12
marriage, weddings, significance of, 89, 95, 98
Martínez de la Rosa, Francisco, 2, 123
melodrama, 143–44, 177
Menéndez Pelayo, Marcelino, 33, 39 n. 25, 68 n. 8, 88 n. 26, 101 n. 33, 120
Menéndez Pidal, Ramón, 65–67
Meredith, Joseph, 23 n. 4
Mérimée, Henri, 68 n. 8, 70, 130 n. 4, 139
metamorphosis, symbolism of, 45, 54
Miralles, Alberto, 208
Miras, Domingo, 207 n. 23
Mitchell, Juliet, 212
Monleón, José, 146 n. 21
Montesinos, José, 64
Moore, John, 189 n. 5
Morley, S. Griswold, 68 n. 8
myth, mythology
  basic categories and definitions of, 5–7
  character vs. plot in, 5–7, 121–22, 177–78, 189, 222–23
  Christian elements in and Christianization of, 36–38, 85, 148–51, 155, 158
  critical approaches to Spanish adaptations of, 2–4
  decline of critical interest in, 4
  in eighteenth and nineteenth centuries in Spain, 2, 4
  feminist approaches to, 207–08, 221
  general sources of in Spanish theater, 7
  manuals of, 121
  political uses of, 48–49, 182–83, 186–88, 203–4, 221, 223
  postmodern approaches to, 209
  pragmatic approach to, 224
  queer approaches to, 208, 208 n. 25, 221
  rationalization of, 25, 59, 151–52
  in seventeenth-century *comedia nueva*, 69, 78, 80–82, 86, 88, 92–94, 101, 103, 108, 112–13, 119–21
  in Spanish avant garde, 178–79
  in Spanish postwar period, 182–83
  in Spanish Renaissance, 19–22
  survey of in Spanish theater, 1–2

See also demythification, women characters, individual authors

narcissism, 8, 11 n. 10, 58–59, 168
Navascués, Michael, 161–63
Nebrija, Antonio de, 25
Neoplatonism, 25, 26 n. 7, 27, 36, 38
Neumeister, Sebastian, 88 n. 27
Nieto, José, 154
Nietzsche, Friedrich, 7
Nonoyama, Minako, 197
Nuez, Sebastián de la (and José Schraibman), 145, 145 n. 20
nutritive desire (including hunger, thirst)
  basic definitions of, 14–15, 222
  in Freud, 11, 11 n. 10
  in Greek myth and literature, 15
  in Jung, 10–11
  in Pemán, 205
  in Plato, 9–10
  in Timoneda, 45–48

O'Connor, Thomas, 112, 116–17, 119
Oliva, César, 3 n. 2
Orestes, myth of, 141–44
Ortega y Gasset, José de, 127
Ortiz, Lourdes, 208 n. 25
Ovejero, Andrés, 137 n. 13
Ovid
  Ars amatoria, 31, 31 n. 17
  erotic desire in, 30, 42, 147 n. 23
  fire symbolism in, 38
  Metamorphoses: in Calderón, 103, 104 n. 38, 109, 109 n. 43; in Cueva y Silva, 49–50, 52–56, 53 n. 33, 58–59; in Encina, 23–24, 26–29, 32–35; in Grau, 160, 162 n. 38, 167–68, 171; in Lope de Vega, 88–93, 91 n. 28, 95; in Timoneda, 39–41, 42 n. 27, 44–45
  phallic symbolism in, 84 n. 22
  Remedia amoris, 28, 31, 31 n. 17
  violence in, 11–12
  wordplay in, 74 n. 15

Paris, Pierre, 101 n. 33
Parker, Alexander A., 24 n. 5, 95, 121–22
parody, 38, 96
passion of Christ. *See* erotic desire, in scriptures
Pemán, José María

Index

Antígona, 185–86, 204
El divino impaciente, 185
Edipo, 204, 204 n. 19
Electra, 185–86, 188 n. 4, 189
  political inclinations of, 187
  treatment of myth by, 185–87
Tyestes, 204–05
Pérez, Eliza, 71 n. 13
Pérez de Moya, Juan, 63, 88 n. 27, 91 n. 28, 103–4, 109 n. 43, 121
Pérez de Oliva, Fernán, 2
Pérez Galdós, Benito
  Alceste, 131, 131 n. 8
  El amigo manso, 158 n. 32
  El caballero encantado, 129
  Casandra, 131 n. 8
  compared with Grau, 159, 160 n. 34, 167
  compared with Echegaray, 144
  compared with Ibsen, 127–28 n. 1
  compared with Unamuno, 148, 152, 157–58
  correspondence of with Unamuno, 145, 145 n. 20
  Electra, 130–45, 152, 157–58, 177–78, 223
  feminism in, 132
  objections of to Echegaray, 129
  place of in Spanish theater, 127–29, 145, 146 n. 21, 223
  sources of myth in, 130–31 n. 5
  treatment of myth by, 141–45
  vocation of for theater, 129
Pérez Minik, Domingo, 166, 181–82, 203
performance, 96–98, 100, 212–14, 217–18
phallic symbolism, 83–84, 214–16, 220
Plato, 8–11, 10 n. 9, 16
Plautus, 95 n. 30
plot construction
  in Calderón, 109, 114
  in *comedia nueva*, 63, 67, 121
  in Cueva y Silva, 49
  in early Spanish theater, 20, 60–61
  in Encina, 24 n. 5, 38–39
  in Lope de Vega, 94–95
  in Pérez Galdós, 143
  in Timoneda, 39, 48
  in Torrente Ballester, 184
  in Unamuno, 148
  See also myth, character vs. plot in
Plutarch, 92
Podol, Peter, 209

Poesse, Walter, 65
Powers, Dorothea, 71 n. 13
presence/absence, 99–101
puppets
  autonomy of, 168–71, 176, 219
  in avant-garde literature, 165, 177
  symbolism of in Grau, 163–66, 175

queer issues. *See* desire, queer; gender issues, in Riaza; myth, queer approaches to

Racine, Jean, 147–49, 151, 155
Ragué Arias, María Jose, 3–4, 205 n. 21, 207–8, 221–22
Rambaldo, Ana María, 23 n. 3, 33 n. 19
rape, 13, 42–44, 84, 94, 113
reason, 9–10, 117, 157, 196–200, 202
Regueiro, José Miguel, 41
Reichenberger, Arnold, 67
revenge, vengeance
  in Buero Vallejo, 196
  in Calderón, 103, 107, 112, 114, 117–18, 120
  in Castro, 74, 82–84
  in *comedia nueva*, 66, 95
  in Cueva y Silva, 51–53, 55, 59, 61
  in Grau, 165
  in Greek myth and literature, 8, 38–39, 133 n. 11, 134, 149, 209
  in Lope de Vega, 87–88, 90–92, 97
  in Pemán, 186, 204–5
  in Riaza, 212–13, 220
  in Timoneda, 44, 47
Riaza, Luis
  Antígona ... ¡cerda!, 208 n. 25
  biographical details of, 208
  compared with Grau, 219
  Medea es un buen chico, 183, 208–21, 223
  sources of myth in, 209
  treatment of myth by, 208–09
rivalry
  in Angélico, 178
  in Buero Vallejo, 199–200
  in Calderón, 106–8, 111
  in Castro, 72, 82
  in Cueva y Silva, 52–53, 59, 223
  in Grau, 173
  in myth, 8
  in Pemán, 204

in Pérez Galdós, 142
in Riaza, 217–18
Rodríguez Salcedo, Gerardo, 161 n. 37, 162
Rogers, Elizabeth, 184, 189, 189 n. 6
Rojas, Fernando de, 27, 30
Rombout, André, 156
Romero, Concha, 207, 221
Rosete Niño, Pedro, 82 n. 20
Rubio, Isaac, 137 n. 13, 143–44
Rubió y Lluch, Antonio, 120
Ruggeri Marchetti, Magda, 191
Ruiz Pérez, Pedro, 209, 218
Ruiz Ramón, Francisco
  on avant-garde playwrights, 127
  on Cueva y Silva, 50 n. 32
  on Echegaray, 125–26, 129
  on Encina, 36
  on Grau, 171
  on honor, 65
  on myth, 3 n. 2
  on Riaza, 183
  on Timoneda, 46
Ruple, Joelyn, 188, 191, 195, 200

Sackett, Theodore, 129 n. 3, 130 n. 4, 131 n. 7
sacrifice
  in Buero Vallejo, 195
  in Burkert, 16
  in Calderón, 105–6, 109–11, 118–19
  in Castro, 82, 82 n. 21
  in Clytemnestra myth, 133 n. 11
  in Cueva y Silva, 52–54, 60
  in Encina, 27
  in Girard, 13
  in Hesiod, 15, 105–6 n. 40, 161–62
  in Lope de Vega, 91–92
  in Sor Juana, 54 n. 34
  in Unamuno, 155–56, 177
Salvat i Ferré, Ricard, 188, 203
Sánchez de Viana, Pedro, 88 n. 27
Sancho Panza (character), 164
Sastre, Alfonso, 205, 221
Saussure, Ferdinand de, 16
scapegoating, 53–54, 220–21
Schalk, F., 121
Schevill, Rudolph, 38
Schmidt, Leopold, 101 n. 33
Schmitt-Von Mühlenfels, Franz, 24–25
Schroeder, Juan Germán, 207 n. 23

Schwartz, Kessel, 167
Sedgwick, Eve Kosofsky, 220
Sedwick, Frank, 153
Segel, Harold, 165, 172
Seneca
  Agamemnon, 130 n. 5, 133 n. 11
  erotic desire in, 147 n. 23
  Hercules Oetaeus, 103
  Medea, 104 n. 38, 108, 179 n. 47, 206, 209–11, 213
  Phaedra, 84 n. 22, 93, 147–49, 151, 155
  self-conscious nature of tragedy in, 97
  special relationship of with Spain, 7
  Thyestes, 105, 105 n. 39, 143, 204–05
  violence in, 11
sensory ambiguity, 54–58
Serrano Martínez, Encarnación Irene, 65
sexual desire, sexuality. *See* erotic desire
Seznec, Jean, 36–37, 63 n. 1
Shakespeare, William, 160, 171
Shaw, Donald, 125, 150, 158
Shaw, George Bernard, 179 n. 47
Shergold, N. D., 104
Silverman, Kaja, 17
Simpson, Michael, 6 n. 6
Sobejano, Gonzalo, 126, 132, 139, 143
Soons, Alan, 108, 109 n. 43, 110
Sophocles
  Antigone, 185
  Electra, 130 n. 5, 134, 179 n. 47
  Oedipus, 138 n. 14, 204 n. 19
  Philoctetes, 140–41 n. 16
  portrayal of Orestes by, 142
  treatment of myth by, 145 n. 19
Spanish Civil War, 8, 179, 181–82, 184–85, 203, 205
Spanish Second Republic, 179, 179 n. 47, 187
Standish, Peter, 172
Starkie, Walter, 137 n. 13
Steiner, George, 4
Stuart, Donald Clive, 66
suicide
  in Castro, 82, 82 n. 20, 120
  in Encina, 23–24, 26, 28, 32–35
  in Virgil, 69, 73
Sullivan, Henry, 22 n. 2, 31 n. 17, 32, 32 n. 19
Surtz, Ronald, 24 n. 5
suspicion. *See* jealousy

Index 265

Tamayo y Baus, Manuel, 125
Tell, William, 184 n. 2
ter Horst, Robert, 21, 26 n. 8, 35–36, 101–2
Testa, Daniel Philip, 23 n. 3
theater
  avant-garde, 127, 165, 175, 177, 182
  bourgeois, 132, 145, 157–58, 165, 167, 177
  illusion of immediacy in, 189
  metaphor of, 97
  psychological, 178, 222
  relation of to myth, 5–7, 224
  ritual in, 209
  of Spanish formative period, 20–22
  of Spanish postwar period, 181–82
  of Spanish Second Republic, 179, 179 n. 47
  of Spanish nineteenth century, 125
  See also *auto sacramental, comedia nueva, deus/dea ex machina,* performance, tragedy, tragicomedy, wife-murder plays
thirst. *See* nutritive desire
Thomson, George, 162
Tilgher, Adriano, 147
time, representation of, 24 n. 5, 31, 210
Timoneda, Juan, 22
  authorship questions in, 39 n. 25
  compared with Cueva y Silva, 49
  compared with Encina, 38–39, 42, 44, 49
  economic motives in theater of, 39
  knowledge of Latin in, 39 n. 26, 47 n. 31
  reaction of to Counter-Reformation, 48–49
  sources of myth in, 39 n. 26, 43 n. 28
  Tragicomedia llamada Filomena, 19, 38–49, 60–61, 113, 223
  treatment of myth by, 39, 48–49, 187
Toro, Alfonso de, 65–66
Torre, Guillermo de, 147
Torrente Ballester, Gonzalo
  on contemporary Spanish theater, 182
  political inclinations of, 187
  El retorno de Ulises, 183–85, 187–88, 221
  sources of myth in, 184 n. 2
  treatment of myth by, 184–85, 204
Torres Naharro, Bartolomé de, 26, 74 n. 16
tragedy
  in Cueva y Silva, 60
  Greek, 12, 143, 149, 185
  relation of to myth, 5–6

  in Rojas, 30
  in Seneca, 97
  in Unamuno, 146–47
  vogue of in Spain, 22, 49, 60 n. 35, 61
tragicomedy, 95, 95 n. 30, 100–101
transvestism, 98, 100, 209–10
Trojan War, 72, 184, 186, 191
truth
  in Buero Vallejo, 201–3
  in Calderón, 117
  in Cueva y Silva, 56–58
  in Encina, 36
  in Pérez Galdós, 139, 141, 144
  in Plato, 5 n. 5
  in Riaza, 212
  in Unamuno, 155–58

Unamuno, Miguel de
  Ábel Sánchez, 147
  attitude of toward Greek myth and literature, 146
  compared with Buero Vallejo, 190
  compared with Grau, 159, 167
  compared with Pérez Galdós, 148, 152, 157–58
  correspondence of with Pérez Galdeos, 145, 145 n. 20
  Cristo de Velázquez, 154–55
  Del sentimiento trágico de la vida, 157–58, 158–59 n. 32
  experimentalism of, 126–27
  Fedra, 145–59, 177–78, 190, 207, 223
  idea of "naked theater" in, 146–47, 178
  importance of dialogue in, 149
  lyric poetry of, 159 n. 32
  Niebla, 158 n. 32, 174
  response of to contemporary theater, 145–47
  San Manuel Bueno, mártir, 159 n. 32
  sources of myth in, 147–48
  treatment of myth by, 147–52, 158
  unorthodoxy of, 158

Valbuena Briones, Angel, 64 n. 3, 101 n. 33, 102, 102 n. 37, 119, 147 n. 24, 149
Valbuena Prat, Angel, 46, 50 n. 32, 101 n. 33, 183
Valle-Inclán, Ramón, 177, 209, 223
Van Beysterveldt, Antony, 28, 34, 37, 37–38 n. 24, 39, 61, 65 n. 5

Vega, Lope de
  Adonis y Venus, 88 n. 26
  Arte nuevo de escribir comedias, 60, 95 n. 30
  La bella Aurora, 88 n. 27
  El castigo sin venganza, 60, 74 n. 16
  chronology of plays by, 68, 68 n. 8
  compared with Calderón, 103, 108–09, 112, 120
  compared with Castro, 69, 74 n. 16, 86, 88, 95, 101, 120
  Decimosexta parte, 68 n. 8, 88 n. 26
  defender of tragicomedy, 95, 95 n. 30
  estimation by of Cueva y Silva, 60
  La fabula de Perseo (El Perseo), 87–88, 93
  founder of *comedia nueva*, 63–64
  El laberinto de Creta, 88–101, 120, 122, 223
  Las mujeres sin hombres, 86–87, 119 n. 49
  sources of myth in, 88 n. 27, 91 n. 28, 93
  treatment of myth by, 86–88, 92–94, 101, 120–21
  El vellocino de oro, 87–88, 93, 104 n. 38, 106 nn. 40–41
vengeance. *See* revenge
Venus (Aphrodite)
  in ancient Rome, 12
  in Castro, 78, 85, 195
  in Encina, 35–36
  in Grau, 168
  in Unamuno, 149, 151
Viel-Castel, Louis de, 66
Vilches de Frutos, María Francisca, 184
Villalón, Cristóbal de, 20
Vinge, Louise, 50 n. 32
violence. *See* aggression
Virgil
  Aeneid, 32–33, 69–71, 72 n. 14, 74–82, 85
  distaste for in Spain, 69–70, 86
Virués, Cristóbal de, 20–22, 70, 70 n. 10, 86
Vitoria, Baltasar de, 103, 104 n. 38, 109 n. 43

Walthaus, Rina, 73, 77, 83
Wardropper, Bruce, 30, 34–36
Watson, I. A., 102–4, 114, 116, 118
weaving, 197–98, 201–2
Weiger, John, 69
wife-murder plays, 60, 74, 82, 113–14
Wilson, Margaret, 67 n. 6
Wilson, William, 71 n. 13
Wiltrout, Ann, 25, 27
Wind, Edgar, 37
Winecoff Díaz, Janet, 161 n. 37
women characters, 221–23

Zavala, Iris, 127, 149–50
Zimic, Stanislav, 23 n. 3

www.ingramcontent.com/pod-product-compliance
Lightning Source LLC
Chambersburg PA
CBHW031547300426
44111CB00006BA/208